For Reference

Do Not Take From the Library

STUDENT'S GUIDE TO
Elections

Student's Guides to U.S. Government

STUDENT'S GUIDE TO

Elections

ADVISORY Editor
Bruce J. Schulman, Ph.D.
Boston University

CQ PRESS

A Division of Congressional Quarterly Inc.
Washington, D.C.

Developed, Designed, and Produced by

DWJ BOOKS LLC

CQ Press
2300 N Street, NW, Suite 800
Washington, DC 20037

Phone: 202-729-1900; toll-free, 1-866-4CQ-PRESS (1-866-427-7737)

Web: www.cqpress.com

Cover design: Matthew Simmons/www.MyselfIncluded.com

Photo acknowledgments for the Primary Source Library: Courtesy of Darrell J. Kozlowski: p. 341; Library of Congress: pp. 325, 326, 327; National Museum of American History, Smithsonian Institute: p. 334; St. Louis Mercantile Library Association: p. 338.

∞ The paper used in this publication exceeds the requirements of the American National Standard for Information Sciences—Permanence of Paper for Printed Library Materials, ANSI Z39.48-1992.

Printed and bound in the United States of America

12 11 10 09 08   1 2 3 4 5

Library of Congress Cataloging-in-Publication Data

Student's guide to elections /
    p. cm.—(Student's guides to U.S. government; v. 1)
    Includes bibliographical references and index.
    ISBN 978-0-87289-552-2 (hardcover: alk. paper)   1. Elections—United States—History.   2. Elections—United States.
I. Schulman, Bruce J.
II. Title.   III. Series.

JK1965.S78 2008
324.973—dc22   2008013032

CONTENTS

LIST OF ILLUSTRATIONS

Reader's Guide

The list that follows is provided as an aid to readers in locating articles on related topics. The Reader's Guide arranges all of the A-Z entries in the Guide according to these 11 key concepts of the curriculum in American Government: Amendments, Elections and Election Campaigns, Electoral Process, Federalism and Politics, National and State Powers, Political Parties, Principles of Government, Public Policies, The Constitution, Three Branches of Government, and Voters and Voting Rights. Some articles appear in more than one category.

Amendments

Fifteenth Amendment
Nineteenth Amendment
Seventeenth Amendment
Twelfth Amendment
Twentieth Amendment
Twenty-fifth Amendment
Twenty-fourth Amendment
Twenty-second Amendment
Twenty-sixth Amendment

Elections and Election Campaigns

Buckley v. Valeo
Campaign Finance
Democratic Party
Election of 1789: George Washington
Election of 1792: George Washington
Election of 1796: John Adams
Election of 1800: Thomas Jefferson
Election of 1804: Thomas Jefferson
Election of 1808: James Madison
Election of 1812: James Madison
Election of 1816: James Monroe
Election of 1820: James Monroe
Election of 1824: John Quincy Adams
Election of 1828: Andrew Jackson
Election of 1832: Andrew Jackson
Election of 1836: Martin Van Buren
Election of 1840: William Henry Harrison
Election of 1844: James Knox Polk
Election of 1848: Zachary Taylor
Election of 1852: Franklin Pierce
Election of 1856: James Buchanan
Election of 1860: Abraham Lincoln
Election of 1864: Abraham Lincoln
Election of 1868: Ulysses S. Grant
Election of 1872: Ulysses S. Grant
Election of 1876: Rutherford Birchard Hayes

Election of 1880: James Abram Garfield
Election of 1884: Grover Cleveland
Election of 1888: Benjamin Harrison
Election of 1892: Grover Cleveland
Election of 1896: William McKinley
Election of 1900: William McKinley
Election of 1904: Theodore Roosevelt
Election of 1908: William Howard Taft
Election of 1912: Woodrow Wilson
Election of 1916: Woodrow Wilson
Election of 1920: Warren Gamaliel Harding
Election of 1924: Calvin Coolidge
Election of 1928: Herbert Hoover
Election of 1932: Franklin Delano Roosevelt
Election of 1936: Franklin Delano Roosevelt
Election of 1940: Franklin Delano Roosevelt
Election of 1944: Franklin Delano Roosevelt
Election of 1948: Harry S. Truman
Election of 1952: Dwight David Eisenhower
Election of 1956: Dwight David Eisenhower
Election of 1960: John Fitzgerald Kennedy
Election of 1964: Lyndon Baines Johnson
Election of 1968: Richard Milhous Nixon
Election of 1972: Richard Milhous Nixon
Election of 1976: James Carter
Election of 1980: Ronald Reagan
Election of 1984: Ronald Reagan
Election of 1988: George Herbert Walker Bush
Election of 1992: William Jefferson Clinton
Election of 1996: William Jefferson Clinton
Election of 2000: George Walker Bush
Election of 2004: George Walker Bush
Election of 2008: Campaigns
Elections, Congressional
Elections, Gubernatorial
Elections, House of Representatives
Elections, Presidential
Elections, Senate

Bruce J. Schulman is The William E. Huntington professor of History at Boston University, a position he has held since 1994. Dr. Schulman has also served as the Director of the American and New England Studies Program at Boston University. Prior to moving to Boston University, he was associate professor of history at the University of California, Los Angeles. Dr. Schulman received his Ph.D. and M.A. from Stanford University; he received his B.A., Summa Cum Laude with Distinction in history, from Yale University.

Since the 1980s, Dr. Schulman has been teaching and writing about the political face of the United States. He has taken an active role in education at the high school level as well as serving as the principal investigator for the Teaching American History Grant program with the Boston Public Schools. He also worked with the History Alive program, a curriculum-based interactive instructional program. In addition, Dr. Schulman served as director of The History Project in California, a joint effort of the University of California and the California State Department of Education to improve history education in the public primary and secondary schools.

Dr. Schulman is the author of several award-winning and notable books that combine his interest in history and politics. Among them are: *From Cotton Belt to Sunbelt: Federal Policy, Economic Development, and the Transformation of the South, 1938–1980; Lyndon B. Johnson and American Liberalism; The Seventies: The Great Shift in American Culture, Politics, and Society;* and *Rightward Bound: Making America Conservative in the 1970s* (co-edited with Julian Zelizer). Dr. Schulman's published books and numerous essays have examined and scrutinized the fabric of America's political and socioeconomic life and its direct impact on today's citizens.

PREFACE

As British Prime Minister Winston Churchill once remarked, "It has been said that democracy is the worst form of government except for all those others that have been tried." In CQ Press's new series, Student's Guides to U.S. Government, librarians, educators, students, and other researchers will find essential resources for understanding the strange wonder, alternately inspiring and frustrating, that is American democracy.

In the *Student's Guide to Elections*, the first volume in the Student's Guides series, young and experienced researchers, especially students and teachers, will find information on all aspects of how Americans choose their leaders: the constitutional provisions and legal procedures, the pivotal campaigns, the parties, the tactics and strategies, the controversies and key issues—the pure pageantry of American politics. The *Student's Guide to Elections* provides insight into the historical development of American elections—the ways they have changed over the past two-and-a-half centuries as well as their current status—unlocking the mysteries surrounding such contemporary issues as delegate selection for presidential nominees, campaign finance, and electoral college reform.

Each of the three parts of the *Student's Guide to Elections* takes a unique approach to enhancing users' understanding of elections. Part One features three essays, each of which addresses a provocative question about American elections: "Could a Candidate Win the Most Votes and Still Lose the Election?"; "What Is the Role of Political Parties? Are They Even Necessary?"; and "Majority Rule vs. Minority Rights: What Makes America Democratic?"

Part Two features 153 A to Z entries covering everything from "Absentee Voting" to "ZZZ," which discusses voter apathy about elections and government. Entries address presidential elec-

tions from 1789–2004, the presidential campaigns of 2008 and numerous aspects of the electoral process, including major and third parties, the Electoral College, and the evolution of the franchise. Special features within Part Two abound: "Point/Counterpoint" highlights opposing views on the same issue, using primary evidence, and concludes with a thought-provoking "Document-Based Question." "Spotlight" focuses on unique situations and events. "Decision Makers" takes a closer look at notable individuals, and "Justice for All" examines important moments in the long journey to obtain the vote for all Americans.

Part Three contains a "Primary Source Library" of key documents, photos, and political cartoons that are essential to understanding the history of American elections. These documents complement the information conveyed in the essays in Part One and the A to Z entries in Part Two. Part Three also provides guidelines for using the Primary Source Library and for general research. The guidelines provide direction on Researching with Primary and Secondary Sources, Developing Research Questions, Identifying Sources of Information, Planning and Organizing research for use in a paper or report, Documenting Sources for the Bibliography, and Citing Sources.

Other helpful tools include a List of Illustrations, a Reader's Guide that arranges material thematically in accord with the key concepts of the American Government curriculum, and a timeline of Historical Milestones in U.S. Elections. The *Guide* concludes with a Glossary of political and elections terminology, a Selected Bibliography, and an Index.

An eye-catching, user-friendly design enhances the text. Throughout, numerous charts, graphs, tables, maps, cross-references, sources for further reading, cartoons, and photos illustrate concepts.

The *Student's Guides to U.S. Government* Series

Additional titles in the Student's Guides to U.S. Government series will include the *Student's Guide to Congress,* the *Student's Guide to the Presidency,* and the *Student's Guide to the Supreme Court.* Collectively, these titles will offer indispensable data drawn from CQ Press's deep archive of content and presented in a manner accessible to secondary level students of American history and government. The volumes will place at the reader's fingertips essential information about the evolution of American politics, from the struggles to create the United States government in the late eighteenth century through the ongoing controversies and dramatic strides of the early twenty-first century.

For study in American history, the Student's Guides to U.S. Government collect a treasury of useful, often hard-to-find facts and present them in the context of the political environment for researching topics, answering document-based questions, and writing essays or reports.

The Student's Guides offer valuable tools for civics education and for the study of American politics and government. They introduce young people to the institutions, procedures, and rules that form the foundations of American government. They assemble for students and teachers the essential material for understanding the workings of American politics and the nature of political participation in the United States. The Guides explain the roots and development of representative democracy, the system of federalism, the separation of powers, and the specific roles of legislators, executives, and judges in the American system of governance. The Guides provide immediate access to the details about the changing nature of political participation by ordinary Americans and the essential role of citizens in a representative democracy.

At the heart of the Student's Guides to U.S. Government is the conviction that the continued success of the American experiment in self-government and the survival of democratic ideals depend on a knowledgeable and engaged citizenry—on educating the next generation of American citizens. Understanding American government and history is essential to that education; indeed freedom stems from the knowledge of knowing how our system of governance evolved, and how we are governed.

By learning the rudiments of American government—the policies, procedures, and processes that built the modern United States—young people can fulfill the promise of American life. By placing at hand—in comprehensive essays, in easily recovered alphabetical format, and in pivotal primary source documents—the essential information needed by student researchers and all educators, the Student's Guides to U.S. Government offer valuable, authoritative resources for civics and history education.

Bruce J. Schulman, Ph.D., Advisory Editor
The William E. Huntington Professor
of History, Boston University

1787 The "Great Compromise" is reached.

1789: George Washington wins the first presidential election on February 4.

1800: Thomas Jefferson and Aaron Burr tie in the election for president.

1804: The Twelfth Amendment is ratified requiring that electors vote separately for president and vice president.

1807: Jefferson continues Washington's two-term precedent for presidents.

1824: Andrew Jackson wins the popular vote but does not get an electoral vote majority. The election must be decided by the House of Representatives, which elects John Quincy Adams.

1828: Andrew Jackson is elected president.

1831: The first national party conventions are held in Baltimore.

1832: Andrew Jackson is reelected.

1837: For the first and only time, the Senate decides the vice-presidential election of Richard M. Johnson.

1840: Van Buren loses to Whig William Henry Harrison.

1841: William Henry Harrison dies after one month in office; John Tyler becomes president.

1844: The Democrats nominate the first "dark-horse" presidential candidate, James K. Polk, who wins the election.

1854: Anti-slavery supporters gather at Ripon, Wisconsin, and form the Republican Party.

1856: Democrat Franklin Pierce becomes the only elected president denied renomination by his party. James Buchanan wins the presidency.

1860: The new Republican Party elects its first president, Abraham Lincoln.

1865: President Lincoln is assassinated six weeks after the start of his second term. Vice President Andrew Johnson becomes president and comes into conflict with the Radical Republicans.

1870: The Fifteenth Amendment, enfranchising newly freed slaves, is ratified on February 3.

1874: Mississippi Republican Blanche K. Bruce is elected to the Senate and becomes the first black senator to serve a full term.

1876: Democrat Samuel J. Tilden wins the popular vote against Republican Rutherford B. Hayes, but electoral vote hangs on one vote and three states dispute the results.

1881: President James A. Garfield is shot by Charles J. Guiteau in Washington, D.C.

1887: Congress passes the Electoral Count Act.

1888: Benjamin Harrison becomes the third president elected without winning the popular vote.

1892: First mechanical voting machine is used in Lockport, New York.

1901: President William McKinley is shot in Buffalo, New York.

1904: Theodore Roosevelt is elected president.

1912: Roosevelt leaves the Republican Party and forms the "Bull Moose" Party.

1913: Seventeenth Amendment is ratified, requiring senators to be elected by popular vote.

1916: Jeannette Rankin becomes the first woman elected to the U.S. House.

1920: The Nineteenth Amendment is ratified, giving women the right to vote.

1923: President Harding dies in office. Calvin Coolidge becomes president.

1924: Miriam Ferguson of Texas and Nellie Tayloe Ross of Wyoming become the first women elected governors of their respective states.

1928: Republican Herbert Hoover is elected president over Democratic liberal Alfred E. Smith.

1932: Democrat Franklin D. Roosevelt promises a "new deal" for the American people and wins an election landslide.

1934: Seventy-third Congress meets on January 3 according to the Twentieth Amendment (1933).

1940: President Roosevelt breaks the two-term precedent and is elected to a third term.

1944: The Supreme Court decides that political parties cannot exclude blacks.

1945: Roosevelt dies in office on April 12 and Harry S. Truman becomes president.

1948: President Truman defeats Thomas E. Dewey.

1951: The Twenty-second Amendment, setting a two-term limit, is passed.

1952: Richard Nixon delivers his "Checkers speech."

1954: Strom Thurmond becomes the only senator elected by write-in vote.

1958: Hiram L. Fong of Hawaii becomes the first Asian American member of Congress.

1960: The first debate between John F. Kennedy and Richard M. Nixon is televised from Chicago.

1961: The Twenty-third Amendment is passed, giving residents of Washington, D.C., the right to vote in presidential elections.

1962: The Supreme Court rules in favor of "one person, one vote."

1963: President Kennedy is assassinated in Dallas, Texas.

1964: The Twenty-fourth Amendment is ratified, abolishing the poll tax. President Johnson wins the presidency by the largest landslide in history.

1965: The Voting Rights Act, protecting African Americans' right to vote, is passed.

1967: The Twenty-fifth Amendment is passed providing procedures in case the president is ill.

1968: Civil rights leader Martin Luther King, Jr., is assassinated.

1971: The Twenty-sixth Amendment is passed, lowering the national voting age to eighteen.

1972: Richard Nixon wins reelection.

1973: Vice President Spiro T. Agnew resigns because of corruption and Nixon nominates Gerald Ford to replace him.

1974: President Nixon resigns because of the Watergate scandal.

1976: The first debate between vice-presidential candidates, Walter F. Mondale and Bob Dole, is televised from Houston, Texas.

1981: Ronald Reagan becomes president and is wounded in an assassination attempt.

1984: Geraldine Ferraro becomes the first woman on a major party presidential ticket.

1988: Republican George Bush becomes the first sitting vice president to be elected president since 1836.

1989: Virginia elects the first African American governor, L. Douglas Wilder.

1990: Kansas elects Joan Finney governor, making it the first state to have a woman governor, senator, and House member at the same time.

1992: Bush loses reelection thanks to H. Ross Perot, a billionaire who mounted the strongest ever individual campaign, which split the Republican vote.

1994: The Republican Party wins control of Congress, despite Democrat Bill Clinton being president.

1995: The Supreme Court rules that only a constitutional amendment could impose term limits on House and Senate members.

1996: President Clinton is elected to a second term. The country becomes strongly politically divided by region.

1998: A sex scandal threatens the Clinton presidency and the House votes for impeachment.

1999: The Senate acquits Clinton of the charges, having failed to get a two-thirds majority vote.

2000: The Supreme Court settles a disputed presidential election between Al Gore and George W. Bush, giving the election to Bush.

2001: The Senate is split 50–50, although the GOP retains power because Vice President Cheney casts a vote in the case of a tie.

2002: Congress passes the McCain-Feingold campaign finance reform law.

2004: President George W. Bush wins reelection by a 51–48 split in the popular vote.

2006: Spurred by dissatisfaction with the Bush presidency, voters elect Democrats as the majority in Congress.

2007: Louisiana voters elect Piyush "Bobby" Jindal as governor, making him the first Indian American governor in history.

2008: Senator Hillary Clinton—the first serious female U.S. presidential contender—and senator Barack Obama—the first African American contender since Jesse Jackson in 1988—campaign for the Democratic nomination.

PART ONE

Essays

Could a Candidate Win the Most Votes and Still Lose the Election?

Yes! Four times in U.S. history the winner of the popular vote has lost the White House! How can this be? For more than two centuries, Americans have been electing their presidents through the Electoral College—instead of voting directly for the candidate of their choice.

Created by the framers of the Constitution as a compromise between selection by Congress and election by direct popular vote, the electoral college system has remained in place even though the United States has grown from a small nation of thirteen states to a world power. Since the founding of our nation, however, people have criticized the electoral college. Thomas Jefferson called it "the most dangerous blot on our Constitution." People have been calling for its elimination or reform ever since.

The term *electoral college* itself does not appear in the Constitution. It was first used unofficially in the early 1800s and became the official designation for the electoral body in 1845.

How Does the Electoral College Work?

Under the electoral college system, each state is entitled to electoral votes equal in number to its congressional delegation—

Both Republican and Democratic voters felt strongly about the results of the 2000 presidential election–one of the closest in history. Democratic candidate Al Gore won the national popular vote yet lost the presidency because Republican George W. Bush won all 25 of Florida's electoral votes–by a statewide margin of 537 votes. (Scott J. Ferrell/CQ)

that is, the number of representatives from the state, plus two for the state's two senators. (The District of Columbia has three electoral votes, the number it would have if it were a state, making the total electoral college membership 538.)

As it works today, the electoral college is a "winner-take-all" system. The candidate who receives a plurality—the largest number—of a state's popular vote is almost certain to receive all of that state's electoral votes. (Exceptions are Maine and Nebraska, where two electoral votes are awarded to the statewide winner and the others are allocated by election districts that match the states' congressional districts—two in Maine and three in Nebraska). There also have been cases of a so-called faithless elector, who cast his or her electoral vote for a candidate other than the one who won the popular vote in the elector's state.

Critics call the electoral college dated and antidemocratic. Many believe that direct election is fairer and more likely to express the will of the people. Public opinion polls consistently show that most Americans favor switching to direct popular vote, especially after the hard-fought election of 2000.

Supporters, however, view the electoral college as a safeguard of federalism and the two-party system. They note that most of the time it works flawlessly. They maintain that the system forces a winning candidate to build a national coalition covering many states, which usually enables the president to govern from a wide base even if the popular vote margin of victory was close.

Constitutional Background

Delegates to the Constitutional Convention were faced with a key question: How do we elect the chief executive—by direct popular election, by Congress, by state legislatures, or by intermediate electors? Most delegates opposed direct election because they believed that the people lacked enough knowledge about the character and qualifications of candidates to make an intelligent choice. Many delegates also feared that the people would be unlikely to agree on a single person, casting their votes for local candidates instead.

The delegates also considered the possibility of giving Congress the power to choose the president. This plan was rejected, however, largely because the delegates feared it would endanger the chief executive's ability to govern. Similarly, a plan to let state legislatures choose the president was turned down. Many delegates thought the president might feel too indebted to the states and possibly allow the states to defy federal authority.

Unable to agree on a plan, the convention appointed a "Committee of Eleven" to solve the problem. After a few days, the committee suggested a compromise. Under this compromise plan, each state would appoint presidential electors equal to the total number of its representatives and senators. The electors, chosen in a manner determined by each state legislature, would meet in their own states and each cast votes for two persons. The votes would be counted in Congress, with the candidate receiving a majority being elected president and the second-highest candidate becoming vice president.

No distinction was made between ballots for president and vice president. Furthermore, the plan did not allow for the development of national political parties. With no distinction between the presidential and vice-presidential nominees, the danger arose of a tie vote between the two.

That actually happened in 1800, leading to a change in the original electoral system with ratification of the Twelfth Amendment in 1804.

The committee's compromise plan was a great concession to the less populous states, because it ensured them a minimum of three votes (two for their two senators and at least one for their representative), however small their populations might be. Even today, the votes of citizens in the least populous states carry more weight. The plan also allowed an important power to remain with the states—allowing state legislatures to determine the method of choosing electors.

Many delegates believed that in most presidential elections no candidate would receive a majority of the electoral votes. Thus, the delegates decided that the House of Representatives would decide the winner from among the top three candidates. Again, the interests of the small states were preserved by giving each state's delegation only one vote in the House on roll call votes to elect a president.

The electoral college system adopted by the Constitutional Convention was a compromise that emerged from several issues and concerns of the time. Among these were the slavery problem, big-state versus small-state rivalries, and the delegates' attempt to balance power among different branches of the government. Moreover, it was probably as close to a direct popular election as the men who wrote the Constitution thought possible and appropriate at the time.

The Big Issue

In four elections, the electoral college has chosen presidents who ran behind their opponents in the popular vote. In two of these instances—those of Republican Rutherford B. Hayes in 1876 and Republican Benjamin Harrison in 1888—the winning candidate carried a number of key states by close margins, while losing other states by wide margins. In the third instance—that of Democratic-Republican John Quincy Adams in 1824—the House chose the new president after no candidate had achieved a majority in the electoral college. In the fourth instance, the 2000 election hinged on Florida's twenty-five contested electoral votes, which went to Republican George W. Bush when the U.S. Supreme Court rejected Democrat Al Gore's challenge of the state's vote count.

Was the will of the people overturned in these four elections? Should the electoral college be replaced? If so, by what?

From the beginning, the electoral college has had few defenders, and many efforts at electoral college reform have been undertaken. Prospects for reform seemed favorable after the close 1968 presidential election, but the Ninety-first Congress (1969–1971) did not take final action on a proposed amendment. Reform legislation was reintroduced in the Senate during the Ninety-fourth Congress (1975–1977) and Ninety-fifth Congress (1977–1979). In the 107th Congress (2001–2003), more talk of reforming or replacing the electoral college system followed the fiercely fought 2000 election. Yet no possible amendments have come up for a vote in Congress.

The Election of 1800 and the Twelfth Amendment

Only once since ratification of the Constitution in 1788 has an amendment been adopted that changed the method of electing the president. The election of 1800 was the first in which the Constitution's election procedures were put to the test and the House elected the president. The Federalists, a declining but still potent political force, nominated John Adams for a second term and chose Charles Cotesworth Pinckney as his running mate. A Democratic-Republican congressional caucus chose Vice President Thomas Jefferson for president and Aaron Burr for vice president.

The electors met in each state on December 4, with the following results: Jefferson and Burr, seventy-three electoral votes each; Adams, sixty-five; Pinckney, sixty-four; and John Jay, one. The Federalists had lost but, because the Democratic-Republicans had neglected to withhold one electoral vote from Burr, their presidential and vice-presidential candidates were tied, and the election was thrown into the House.

The lame-duck Congress, with a Federalist majority, was still in office for the electoral count, and the possibilities for intrigue were great. After toying with and rejecting a proposal to block any election until March 4, when Adams' term expired, the Federalists decided to support Burr and thereby elect a relatively weak politician over a man they considered a "dangerous radical."

" *Alexander Hamilton opposed this move:*

I trust the Federalists will not finally be so mad as to vote for Burr. . . . I speak with intimate and accurate knowledge of his character. His elevation can only promote the purposes of the desperate and the profligate. If there be a man in the world I ought to hate, it is Jefferson. With Burr I have always been personally well. But the public good must be paramount to every private consideration.

On February 11, 1801, Congress met in joint session—with Jefferson, the outgoing vice president, in the chair—to count the electoral vote. This ritual ended, the House retired to its own chamber to elect a president. When the House met, it became apparent that Hamilton's advice had been rejected; a majority of Federalists insisted on backing Burr over Jefferson, the man they despised more. Indeed, if Burr had given clear assurances that he would run the country as a Federalist, he might have been elected. Yet Burr was unwilling to make those assurances, and, as one chronicler put it, "No one knows whether it was honor or a wretched indecision which gagged Burr's lips."

In all, there were 106 members of the House at the time, fifty-eight Federalists and forty-eight Democratic-Republicans. If each member of the House cast his own ballot, Burr would have been elected, but the Constitution provided that each state should cast a single vote and that a majority of states was necessary for election.

★ ★ ★ ★ ★ ★ ★ ★ ★ ★ ★ ★ ★ ★ ★ ★ ★ ★ ★

Essays

On the first ballot Jefferson received the votes of eight states, one short of a majority of the sixteen states then in the Union. Six states backed Burr. The representatives of Vermont and Maryland were equally divided and, therefore, could not cast their states' votes. By midnight of the first day of voting, nineteen ballots had been taken, and the deadlock remained.

In all, thirty-six ballots were taken before the House came to a decision on February 17. Predictably, there were men who sought to exploit the situation for personal gain.

> **M**any attempts have been made to obtain terms and promises from me. I have declared to them unequivocally that I would not receive the Government on capitulation; that I would not go in with my hands tied.

Thomas Jefferson wrote:

The impasse was finally broken when Vermont and Maryland switched to support Jefferson. Delaware and South Carolina also withdrew their support from Burr by casting blank ballots. The final vote: ten states for Jefferson, four (all in New England) for Burr. Jefferson became president, and Burr, under the Constitution as it then stood, automatically became vice president.

The Jefferson-Burr contest clearly illustrated the dangers of the double-balloting system established by the original Constitution, and pressure began to build for an amendment requiring separate votes for president and vice president. Congress approved the Twelfth Amendment in December 1803, and the states—acting with unexpected speed—ratified it in time for the 1804 election.

John Quincy Adams Election

The only other time the House of Representatives elected a president was in 1825. There were many contenders in the 1824 election, but four candidates led: John Quincy Adams, Henry Clay, William H. Crawford, and Andrew Jackson. Crawford, secretary of the Treasury under President James Monroe, was the early front-runner, but his candidacy faltered after he suffered an incapacitating illness in 1823.

When the electoral votes were counted, Jackson had ninety-nine, Adams eighty-four, Crawford forty-one, and Clay thirty-seven. With eighteen of the twenty-four states choosing their electors by popular vote, Jackson also led in the popular voting. Under the Twelfth Amendment, the names of the three top contenders—Jackson, Adams, and the ailing Crawford—were placed before the House. Clay's support was vital to either of the two front-runners.

From the start, Clay apparently intended to support Adams. However, before the House voted, a great scandal erupted. A Philadelphia newspaper published an anonymous letter claiming that Clay had agreed to support Adams in return for being made secretary of state. The letter also noted that Clay would have been willing to make the same deal with Jackson.

Clay immediately denied the charge and pronounced the writer of the letter "a base and infamous character, a dastard and a liar."

When the House met to vote, Adams was supported by the six New England states and New York and, in large part through Clay's backing, by Maryland, Ohio, Kentucky, Illinois, Missouri, and Louisiana. A majority of thirteen delegations voted for him—the bare minimum he needed for election, because there were twenty-four states in the Union at the time. Adams was elected on the first ballot, but he took office under the cloud of the "corrupt bargain."

Jackson had believed the charges and found his suspicions justified when Adams, after the election, did appoint Clay as secretary of state.

❝ *Andrew Jackson wrote:* **W**as there ever witnessed such a bare-faced corruption in any country before?

Jackson's successful 1828 campaign made much of his contention that the House of Representatives had overturned the will of the people by denying him the presidency in 1825, even though he had been the leader in the popular and electoral votes.

Hayes-Tilden Contest

The 1876 campaign pitted Republican Rutherford B. Hayes against Democrat Samuel Tilden. Early returns indicated that Tilden had been elected. He had won the swing states of Indiana, New York, Connecticut, and New Jersey. Those states plus his expected southern support would give Tilden the election. However, by the following morning it became apparent that if the Republicans could hold South Carolina, Florida, and Louisiana, Hayes would be elected with 185 electoral votes to 184 for Tilden. Still, if a single elector in any of these states voted for Tilden, he would throw the election to the Democrats. Tilden led in the popular-vote count by more than a quarter million votes.

Both parties pursued the votes of the three states, and, in the end, double sets of elector returns were sent to Congress from all three. Oregon also sent two sets of returns. Although Hayes carried that state, the Democratic governor discovered that one of the Hayes electors was a postmaster and therefore ineligible under the Constitution, so he certified the election of the top-polling Democratic elector. However, the Republican electors met, received the resignation of their ineligible colleague, then immediately reappointed him to the vacancy because he had in the meantime resigned his postmastership.

Congress created a joint committee to work out a plan, and the resulting Electoral Commission Law was approved by large majorities and signed into law January 29, 1877—only days before the date scheduled for counting the electoral votes.

The law, which applied only to the 1876 electoral vote count, established a fifteen-member commission that was to have final authority over disputed electoral votes, unless both houses of Congress agreed to over-

★ ★ ★ ★ ★ ★ ★ ★ ★ ★ ★ ★ ★ ★ ★ ★ ★

rule it. The commission was to consist of five senators, five representatives, and five Supreme Court justices. Each chamber was to appoint its own members of the commission, with the understanding that the majority party would have three members and the minority two. Four justices, two from each party, were named in the bill, and these four were to select the fifth. It was expected that they would choose Justice David Davis, who was considered a political independent, but he disqualified himself when the Illinois legislature named him to a Senate seat. Justice Joseph P. Bradley, a Republican, was then named to the fifteenth seat. The Democrats supported his selection because they considered him the most independent of the remaining justices, all of whom were Republicans. However, he was to vote with the Republicans on every dispute and thus ultimately ensure the Hayes victory.

The electoral count began in Congress February 1 (moved up from the second Wednesday in February for this one election), and the proceedings continued until March 2. States were called in alphabetical order and, as each disputed state was reached, objections were raised to both the Hayes and Tilden electors. The question was then referred to the electoral commission, which in every case voted 8–7 for Hayes. In each case, the Democratic House rejected the commission's decision, but the Republican Senate upheld it, so the decision stood.

As the count went on, Democrats in the House threatened to launch a filibuster to block resumption of joint sessions so that the count could not be completed before Inauguration Day. The threat was never carried out because of an agreement reached between Hayes' supporters and southern conservatives. The southerners agreed to let the electoral count continue without obstruction. In return Hayes agreed that, as president, he would withdraw federal troops from the South, end Reconstruction, and make other concessions. The southerners, for their part, pledged to respect Negro rights, a pledge they did not honor.

Finally, at 4 A.M., March 2, 1877, the president of the Senate was able to announce that Hayes had been elected president with 185 electoral votes, against 184 votes for Tilden. Later that day Hayes arrived in Washington. The next evening he took the oath of office privately at the White House because March 4 fell on a Sunday. His formal inauguration followed on Monday. The country consented. So ended a crisis that could easily have resulted in civil war.

Not until 1887 did Congress enact permanent legislation on the handling of disputed electoral votes. The Electoral Count Act of that year gave each state final authority in determining the legality of its choice of electors and required a concurrent majority of both the Senate and House to reject any electoral votes. The act also established procedures for counting electoral votes in Congress.

The Election of 2000

On election night in November 2000, the popular vote in several states was so close that no one could quickly determine who would win those states'

electoral votes. At first, the television networks called Florida for the Republican nominee, Texas governor George W. Bush. Later, the networks changed their prediction to Vice President Al Gore, the Democratic nominee. By early morning, it became clear that whoever won Florida's electoral vote would win the presidency.

Because the popular vote in Florida was so close, the votes were counted and recounted—well into December. The Florida Supreme Court had directed the recounts to continue, but the United States Supreme Court overruled the state court by determining that there was no time left to keep recounting. Bush won Florida by 537 popular votes, and thus earned the state's 25 electoral votes. With Florida's votes, Bush had a total of 271 electoral votes, one more than the required 270 needed for victory. Interestingly, more than 105 million votes were cast for president, but the election was decided by a fraction of 1 percent of those votes.

However, in the popular vote, Vice President Gore led by more than a half-million votes. African Americans were particularly dissatisfied with the result. They had overwhelmingly supported Gore nationally, and in Florida their votes made up a disproportionately large share of the ballots not counted because of problems with the obsolete punch-card voting system used in many counties. They and many others felt that the majority had been disenfranchised and that Gore might have won had the Court not stopped the recount.

However, the ruling in *Bush v. Gore* left no recourse through the judicial system. Only one step remained before the 2000 election was officially closed: the formal counting of the 538 electoral votes by both chambers of Congress. When that day came, on January 5, 2001, twenty House members, mostly members of the Congressional Black Caucus, made a last-ditch effort to deny Florida's twenty-five electoral votes to Bush. With Gore presiding, each of the twenty house members submitted a written objection to the counting of Florida's votes. Gore asked each representative if the objection was also signed by a senator, as the 1887 law required. When each responded "no," Gore ruled the objection out of order. (In the 2001 counting, there was one abstention, by a District of Columbia elector for Gore, resulting in a total of 537 electoral votes being cast.) The U.S. Supreme Court's peremptory 5–4 vote ending the recount of Florida's extremely close presidential vote left many Americans angry and embittered.

More Historical Quirks

The nation's complicated and indirect system of electing the president has led to other irregularities and quirks. In 1836, for example, the Whig Party—a major political party in the early part of the nineteenth century—sought to take advantage of the electoral system by running different presidential candidates in different parts of the country. William Henry Harrison ran in most of New England, the mid-Atlantic states, and the Midwest; Daniel Webster ran in Massachusetts; Hugh White of Tennessee ran in the South. The theory was that each candidate could capture electoral votes for the Whig Party in the region where he was strongest. Then

Essays

the Whig electors could combine on one candidate or, alternatively, throw the election into the House, whichever seemed to their advantage. However, the scheme did not work because Martin Van Buren, the Democratic nominee, captured a majority of the electoral vote.

Another quirk in the system surfaced in 1872. The Democratic presidential nominee, Horace Greeley, died between the time of the popular vote and the meeting of the presidential electors. The Democratic electors had no living nominee to vote for, and each was left to his own judgment. Forty-two of the sixty-six Democratic electors chose to vote for the Democratic governor-elect of Indiana, Thomas Hendricks. The rest of the electors split their votes among three other politicians: eighteen for B. Gratz Brown of Missouri, the Democratic vice-presidential nominee; two for Charles J. Jenkins of Georgia; and one for David Davis of Illinois. Three Georgia electors insisted on casting their votes for Greeley, but Congress refused to count them.

The Senate has chosen the vice president only once. That was in 1837, when Van Buren was elected president with 170 of the 294 electoral votes while his vice-presidential running mate, Richard M. Johnson, received only 147 electoral votes—one less than a majority. This discrepancy occurred because Van Buren electors from Virginia boycotted Johnson, reportedly in protest against his social behavior. The Senate elected Johnson, 33–16, over Francis Granger of New York, the runner-up in the electoral vote for vice president.

In 1912, President William Howard Taft's vice president, James S. Sherman, died in October after he and Taft won renomination by the Republican Party. Taft and his substitute running mate, Nicholas Murray Butler, lost the election to Democrats Woodrow Wilson and Thomas R. Marshall. Because it had been too late to change the Republican ballots, Butler won Sherman's eight electoral votes.

Although only two presidential elections actually have been decided by the House, a number of others—including those of 1836, 1856, 1860, 1892, 1948, 1960, and 1968—could have been thrown into the House by only a small shift in the popular vote.

The threat of House election was most evident in 1968, when George C. Wallace of Alabama ran as a strong third-party candidate. Wallace frequently asserted that he could win an outright majority in the electoral college by the addition of key Midwestern and Mountain states to his hoped-for base in the South and Border States. In reality, the Wallace campaign had a narrower goal: to win the balance of power in electoral college voting, thereby keeping either major party from the clear majority required for election. Wallace made it clear that he then would expect one of the major party candidates to make concessions in return for enough votes from Wallace electors to win the election. Wallace indicated that he expected the election to be settled in the electoral college and not in the House of Representatives. At the end of the campaign Wallace noted that he had obtained written affidavits from all of his electors, in which they promised to vote for Wallace "or whomsoever he may direct" in the electoral college.

In response to the Wallace challenge, both major party candidates, Republican Richard Nixon and Democrat Hubert H. Humphrey, maintained that they would refuse to bargain with Wallace for his electoral votes. Nixon asserted that the House, if the decision rested there, should elect the popular-vote winner. Humphrey said the representatives should select "the president they believe would be best for the country." **Bipartisan** efforts to obtain advance agreements from House candidates to vote for the national popular-vote winner if the election should go to the House ended in failure. Neither Nixon nor Humphrey replied to suggestions that they pledge before the election to swing enough electoral votes to the popular-vote winner to ensure his election without help from Wallace.

In the end, Wallace received only 13.5 percent of the popular vote and forty-six electoral votes (including the vote of one Republican defector), all from southern states. He failed to win the balance of power in the electoral college, which he had hoped to use to receive concessions from one of the major party candidates. If Wallace had won a few border states, or if a few thousand more Democratic votes had been cast in northern states barely carried by Nixon, reducing Nixon's electoral vote below 270, Wallace would have been in a position to bargain off his electoral votes or to throw the election into the House for final settlement. Wallace later noted that he would have tried to instruct his electors to vote for Nixon rather than to have the election go to the House.

Reform Proposals

Since January 6, 1797, when Representative William L. Smith, a South Carolina Federalist, introduced in Congress the first proposed constitutional amendment for reform of the electoral college system, hardly a session of Congress has passed without the introduction of one or more resolutions of this nature. In all, more than seven hundred such proposals have been submitted, but only one—the Twelfth Amendment, ratified in 1804—ever has been approved.

In recent years, public interest in a change in the electoral college system was spurred by the close elections of 1960, 1968, 2000, and 2004. Nonetheless, Congress has not passed any reform proposals.

House Approval of a Proposed Amendment

Early in 1969, President Richard Nixon asked Congress to take prompt action on electoral college reform. He said he would support any plan that would eliminate individual electors and distribute among the presidential candidates the electoral vote of every state and the District of Columbia in a manner more closely approximating the popular vote.

Later that year, the House approved, 338–70, a resolution proposing a constitutional amendment to eliminate the electoral college and to provide instead for direct popular election of the president and vice president. The measure set a minimum of 40 percent of the popular vote as sufficient for election and provided for a runoff election between the two top candidates

Essays

for the presidency if no candidate received 40 percent. Under this plan the House of Representatives could no longer be called upon to select a president. The proposed amendment also authorized Congress to provide a method of filling vacancies caused by the death, resignation, or disability of presidential nominees before the election and a method of filling post-election vacancies caused by the death of the president-elect or vice president-elect.

Nixon, who originally had favored a proportional plan of allocating each state's electoral votes, endorsed the House resolution and urged the Senate to adopt it. To become effective, however, the proposed amendment had to be approved by a two-thirds majority in both the Senate and House and be ratified by the legislatures of three-fourths of the states. When the proposal reached the Senate floor in September 1970, senators from small states and the South succeeded in blocking final action. The resolution was eventually put aside.

Carter Endorsement of the Plan

Another major effort to eliminate the electoral college occurred in 1977, when President Jimmy Carter included such a proposal in his election reform package. Carter supported the amendment approved by the House in 1969 to replace the electoral college with direct popular election of the president and vice president, and provide for a runoff if no candidate received at least 40 percent of the vote. Because the Senate again was seen as the major stumbling block, the House waited to see what the Senate would do before beginning any deliberation of its own.

After several months of deadlock, the Senate Judiciary Committee approved the direct presidential election plan by a 9–8 vote. However, Senate opponents threatened a filibuster, and the Senate leadership decided it could not spare the time or effort to try to break it. The measure was never brought to the floor and died when the Ninety-fifth Congress adjourned in 1978.

On January 15, 1979, the opening day of the Ninety-sixth Congress, Senator Birch Bayh, an Indiana Democrat, began another effort to abolish the electoral college through a constitutional amendment. Finally, a proposed constitutional amendment to abolish the electoral college and elect the president by popular vote reached the Senate floor in July 1979. The Senate voted in favor of the measure, 51 to 48, fifteen votes short of the two-thirds majority of those present and voting that was required to approve a constitutional amendment.

Supporters of the resolution blamed defections by several Northern liberals for the margin of defeat. Major Jewish and African American groups extensively lobbied the Northern senators, arguing that the voting strength of African American and Jewish voters is maximized under the Electoral College system because both groups are concentrated in urban areas of the large electoral vote states.

Alternative Plans

Besides direct election of the president and vice president, two other major proposals to replace the electoral college have gained considerable

support. One is the district plan, similar to the Maine and Nebraska systems that would award an electoral vote to the candidate who carried a congressional district and two to the candidate who carried the state as a whole. The other is the proportional plan that would distribute a state's electoral votes on the basis of the proportion of the vote each candidate received.

Had any of the three plans been in effect since 1960, the outcome of several close elections would have been different, according to Stephen J. Wayne, professor of American Government at Georgetown University. In his book *The Road to the White House, 2000,* Wayne calculates that the district plan would have elected Richard Nixon in 1960 over John F. Kennedy, and that in 1976, it would have resulted in an electoral college tie between Gerald R. Ford and Jimmy Carter. The proportional plan would have thrown the 1960, 1968, 1992, and 1996 elections to the House of Representatives, because none of the candidates would have received an electoral vote majority.

Of the presidential elections since 1960, only the 2000 presidential election would have had a different result under direct election. As the popular vote winner, Gore would have been elected over Bush. Although the 1960 popular vote was even closer, Kennedy won *both* the popular and electoral college votes.

Does the electoral college still work? While many people argue that it is undemocratic, others see the system as an example of federalism in action. Still others point out that only three times since its beginnings in 1789—in 1876, 1888, and 2000—has the electoral college system awarded the presidency to the candidate who lost the popular vote. Furthermore, any change to the manner in which the president is elected will require amending the Constitution—a task deliberately made difficult by the nation's Founders.

See also: Democratic-Republican Party; Elections, Presidential; Federalist Party; Twelfth Amendment (1804).

Further Reading

Edwards III, George C. *Why the Electoral College is Bad for America.* New Haven: Yale University Press, 2005.

Gould, Lewis L. *The Modern American Presidency.* Lawrence, Kansas: University Press of Kansas, 2003.

Grant, George. *The Importance of the Electoral College.* San Antonio, Texas: Vision Forum Ministries, 2004.

National Archives and Records Administration (NARA) www.archives.gov/federal-register/electoral-college.

Ross, Tara. *Enlightened Democracy: The Case for the Electoral College.* Dallas, Texas: Colonial Press, 2004.

Schumaker, Paul D. *Choosing a President: The Electoral College and Beyond.* Washington, DC: CQ Press, 2002.

What Is the Role of Political Parties? Are They Even Necessary?

 Political parties have been an essential part of the nation's system of government since the early days of the Republic. Today, although some citizens may question the need for political parties, more voters than ever identify themselves as "independents." Political parties attempt to create loyalty among their members. They strive to ensure that all officials elected under the party banner support the party's program. Party unity remains a key goal of every party.

Political parties have played a key role in government at all levels—federal, state, and local. Yet, despite their importance and influence, political parties are not mentioned in the U.S. Constitution.

Traditionally, political parties have performed the following functions:

- frame party platforms
- nominate candidates
- educate voters through literature and the media
- arouse interest in public issues
- create a spirit of loyalty among legislators and persuade them to support the party's position on legislation
- confront the opposing party and expose its shortcomings
- coordinate the party's agenda among the branches of government.

What Are Political Parties?

Political parties are organizations that seek to gain control of government to further their social, economic, or ideological goals. The United States has usually had a two-party system, dominated since 1860 by the Democratic and Republican Parties. Yet more than eighty political parties have formed since the 1790s, and "third parties" have occasionally had a decisive impact on presidential elections. For example, in 1912, the "Bull Moose Party" of former president Theodore Roosevelt siphoned enough Republican votes from the incumbent, William Howard Taft, to enable the Democrat, Woodrow Wilson, to win the election.

The United States did not start out with a two-party system—or any parties at all. Initially there were no formal parties, and in the early 1820s, the nation had in effect only one party. The Founders did not anticipate parties—which they derisively called factions. As a result, this central aspect of American politics was unplanned and had no formal

★ ★ ★ ★ ★ ★ ★ ★ ★ ★ ★ ★ ★ ★ ★ ★ ★ ★ ★

constitutional or legal status. Indeed, having seen the ill effects of overzealous parties in monarchical England and, beginning in 1789, in revolutionary France, the nation's Founders hoped to avoid similar pitfalls. Thus, in "Federalist 10," James Madison noted that one of the Constitution's great virtues was that it would head off "the mischiefs of faction."

❝ *Thomas Jefferson quipped:*

If I could not go to heaven but with a party, I would not go there at all.

Similarly, in his farewell address in 1796, George Washington warned that, in elective popular governments, the dangers of excess in the "spirit of party" demanded "a uniform vigilance to prevent its bursting into a flame."

By the time Washington issued his warning, he was essentially the head of the Federalist Party, which faded after 1800 and, except for some local officeholders, was dead by 1821. Meanwhile, since 1794, Madison and Jefferson had been the leaders of another party, variously called the Democratic-Republicans, the Jeffersonian Democrats, and the Jeffersonian Republicans. This party eventually became the modern Democratic Party.

Political Issues and the Emergence of Parties

The debate over ratification of the Constitution led to the organization of factions but not parties. Future Democratic-Republicans and Federalists, like Madison and Alexander Hamilton, worked together for ratification, just as future Democratic-Republicans and Federalists, like James Monroe and Samuel Chase, worked against ratification of the Constitution.

Ratification brought about a new national government where parties were unknown. Presidential electors unanimously elected Washington as the first president, and nearly half of them supported Adams, who was easily elected vice president. Washington's cabinet included future leaders of the nation's first two parties: the future Federalist leader Alexander Hamilton and the future leader of the Democratic-Republicans, Thomas Jefferson.

By the end of Washington's administration, two parties were fully engaged in politics. The parties differed over the nature of public policy and the interpretation of the Constitution. The Federalists, led by Hamilton, John Adams, and John Jay, favored a national government vigorously involved in economic development. These elements were key to the Federalist program: the establishment of a national bank, federal funding at face value of all state and national bonds issued during the Revolution, and a flexible interpretation of the Constitution. The Federalists also wanted to strengthen diplomatic and commercial ties with England.

Jefferson's followers, called Democratic-Republicans at this time, opposed funding the war debts at par because many of the original bondhold-

★ ★ ★ ★ ★ ★ ★ ★ ★ ★ ★ ★ ★ ★ ★ ★ ★ ★ ★

What Is the Role of Political Parties? Are They Even Necessary? ★ 15

Essays

ers had sold their bonds at depreciated values to speculators. Their hostility to commerce and business also led them to oppose the establishment of a national bank. Unsuccessful on these issues, the Democratic-Republicans were nonetheless able to thwart Hamilton's plan to use high tariffs to stimulate commerce and manufacturing in the new country. Jefferson and his followers wanted a strict interpretation of the Constitution, favored states' rights over national power, and in foreign policy supported France in its wars with England.

On issues involving race, slavery, and foreign policy, the parties also differed. The Federalists favored giving full diplomatic recognition to Haiti, a black republic in the Caribbean, and refused to seek the return of slaves who had escaped with the British at the end of the Revolution. Jefferson, by contrast, unsuccessfully demanded the return of the slaves, but was successful as president in blocking any diplomatic ties to Haiti.

Presidents, Parties, and Policies, 1800–1860

By the time of Jefferson's election in 1800, ending twelve years of Federalist control, the party concept was entrenched in U.S. politics. Despite his previous denunciation of parties, Jefferson justified his own party leadership as a necessary opposition to the Federalists. Jefferson's election by the House, after a 73–73 tie vote between him and Aaron Burr in the electoral college, the body that elects the president, between him and Aaron Burr, led to adoption of the Twelfth Amendment to the Constitution in 1804. That amendment, which required electors to vote separately for president and vice president, further buried the likelihood of "partyless" U.S. elections.

Federalists nearly won the presidency in 1800 and 1812, but the party quickly withered after the War of 1812, when many party leaders opposed the war and flirted with secession, most notably at the Hartford Convention of 1814–1815. Federalists made a brief comeback in 1819–1820 during the debates over allowing slavery in Missouri on its admission to the Union, but the party was effectively dead by the end of 1820, when James Monroe ran unopposed for reelection.

A system with only one party was less stable than a system with two or more parties. In 1824, four candidates competed for the presidency, with no one getting a majority of the popular or the electoral vote. The House of Representatives chose John Quincy Adams, who ran second in both categories. Andrew Jackson, who had led in popular and electoral votes, immediately began his campaign for the presidency, and he won in 1828. In 1832, the Anti-Masonic Party made its brief appearance, winning seven electoral votes, while Jackson was easily reelected. Jackson inherited the mantle of Jefferson and his party, while his political and personal opponents, such as Daniel Webster, Henry Clay, and John Quincy Adams, moved in the 1830s to the newly formed Whig Party. They adopted the name *Whigs* after a British political party that favored a constitutional monarchy, as opposed to absolute rule. In 1836, four Whigs, representing different regions of the country, competed for the presidency against Jackson's heir, Martin Van Buren.

The Whigs won the presidency in 1840 and 1848; Democrats won in 1836, 1844, 1852, and 1856. The Whigs favored a national bank, federal support for internal improvements, national bankruptcy laws, protective tariffs, and a relatively humane policy toward American Indians. The Democrats disagreed with all these positions. Whigs opposed territorial acquisition, especially by force, whereas Democrats annexed Texas and eventually pushed the United States into a war with Mexico to gain new territory in the Southwest, advocating that it was the **Manifest Destiny** of the United States to control the continent.

While the Jacksonian Democrats pushed for universal adult white male suffrage throughout the country, they also worked to take the vote away from free blacks and to strengthen slavery at the national and local level. Jackson's presidency is most remembered for his veto of the rechartering of the Second Bank of the United States, his successful opposition to internal improvements, and his policy of Indian removal, which pushed almost all Native Americans in the East into the Indian Territory (present-day Oklahoma). On an important issue that seemed to go beyond party politics, Jackson vigorously opposed extreme states' rights ideology when South Carolina attempted to **nullify** a federal tariff. However, following the nullification crisis, the Democrats became increasingly attentive to **states' rights** and Southern demands for protections of slavery. Jackson and his fellow Democrats also accepted the South Carolinians' critique of the tariff, even as they rejected the Carolinians' response— nullification.

The nation had two major parties in the 1840s, but third parties influenced some elections. In 1844, the antislavery Liberty Party won enough votes in New York to cost the Whigs the state and the presidential election, assuming all the Liberty voters would have supported the Whigs. The Whig candidate, Henry Clay, opposed expansion and was more moderate on slavery than his opponent, but it seems unlikely that the committed abolitionists who voted for the Liberty Party would otherwise have voted for the slave-owning Clay as the lesser of two evils. In 1848, however, the Free Soil candidate, former president Martin Van Buren, won more than 290,000 votes, many of which would have otherwise gone to the Democratic candidate, Lewis Cass of Michigan. As a result, the Whig candidate, General Zachary Taylor, won the election. Equally significant, Free Soilers won state and local races, and in Ohio they held the balance of power in the state legislature and were able to elect an antislavery Democrat, Salmon P. Chase, to the U.S. Senate.

Yet the victorious Whigs of 1848 managed to carry only four states in 1852, and the party disappeared two years later. The 1856 election saw two new parties emerge: the Know Nothing (American) Party and the Republican Party.

The Know Nothing, or American, Party was a single-issue party, opposed to immigration in general and Catholic immigration in particular. The Know Nothings won a number of governorships and dominated a few state legislatures, including Massachusetts, in this period. In 1856, the

Speaker of the House of Representatives, Nathaniel Banks, was a Know Nothing.

The Republican Party adopted many Whig policies but opposed the extension of slavery into the western territories. Many Republican leaders were former Whigs, including Abraham Lincoln and his secretary of state, William H. Seward. Others came from the antislavery wing of the Democratic Party, among them Lincoln's vice president, Hannibal Hamlin, and Secretary of the Treasury, Salmon P. Chase. By 1858, many Know Nothings had also joined this party. In 1856, the Republican candidate, John C. Fremont, and the Know Nothing candidate, Millard Fillmore, together won about 400,000 more popular votes than James Buchanan, but Buchanan had the **plurality** of popular votes. More important, Buchanan carried nineteen states to win the election. As fourteen of the states he carried were in the South. Buchanan was the first "sectional" president since 1824. This election underscored the fact that the Democrats had become the party of slavery and the South.

The proslavery southerners who controlled the Democratic Party insisted on loyalty to their program to expand slavery into the territories. This arrangement unraveled in 1860, as the Democrats split into two parties—regular Democrats nominating Stephen A. Douglas of Illinois and southern Democrats nominating John C. Breckinridge of Kentucky. The Republican candidate, Abraham Lincoln, carried every Northern state. Moderates in the North and the South supported the Constitutional Union Party, which hoped to hold the Union together by not discussing any of the key issues. The two Democratic parties and the Constitutional Unionists combined for more popular votes than Lincoln—who was not even on the ballot in many Southern states—but Lincoln carried eighteen states and easily won a majority of the electoral college.

Parties in U.S. Politics since 1860

Lincoln's victory set the stage for Republican dominance in national politics for the next half-century. During this period, the Republicans stood at various times for preservation of the Union, homestead laws to facilitate western settlement, federal support for a transcontinental railroad, protective tariffs, abolition of slavery, guarantees of African American civil rights, and the suppression of Mormon **polygamists** in the West.

Democrats favored lower tariffs; opposed emancipation and civil rights; and championed white immigrants (but not immigrants from Asia), labor unions, and (at the end of the nineteenth century) small farmers in the South and West. In international affairs, the late-nineteenth-century Republicans favored expansion, ultimately leading to war with Spain and the acquisition of an overseas empire, while Democrats opposed these trends, with Grover Cleveland (the only Democratic president in this period) refusing to annex Hawaii.

From 1868 to 1908, various third parties—including the Liberal Republican, Greenback, Prohibitionist, Equal Rights, Anti-Monopoly, Workers, Socialist Labor, Socialist, United Christian, and Populist Parties—ran

candidates. With the exception of the Populists in 1892, however, none ever won any electoral votes. Some of these parties did, however, elect candidates to state and local office and to Congress. James B. Weaver, for example, ran successfully for Congress on the Greenback ticket in 1878, 1884, and 1886; ran for president on the Greenback ticket in 1880; and ran for president on the Populist ticket in 1892.

In 1912, a third party determined the outcome of the presidential race. The Republicans split as former president Theodore Roosevelt tried, and failed, to gain renomination after a term out of the White House. Roosevelt thought that his successor, William Howard Taft, had abandoned the progressive goals of the party. Running on the Progressive, or Bull Moose, ticket, Roosevelt carried six states and won about half a million more popular votes than Taft. Together they outpolled Wilson, but Wilson carried forty states and won the election. The Socialist candidate, Eugene V. Debs, won nearly a million votes in the 1912 election, and, although he carried no states, Socialists won various local elections and sent some party members to Congress. Victor Berger of Milwaukee, for example, served in Congress as a Socialist from 1911 to 1913 and again from 1923 to 1929.

Between the 1910s and the 1940s, Democrats became increasingly **internationalist,** while most Republicans opposed American entrance into the League of Nations after World War I (1917–1918). Most Republicans were increasingly **isolationist** in the 1930s as the world moved toward a second world war. Democratic support came from labor, white southerners, and most northern urban immigrant groups. Also, by the 1930s, African Americans began to leave the Republican Party, and they were welcomed into the Democrats' emerging New Deal coalition. The Republicans by this time had become the party of conservative business interests, white Protestants (outside the South), small town and rural northerners, and owners of small businesses.

Various third parties ran presidential candidates in the 1920s and 1930s, but only Robert M. La Follette, running as the Progressive Party candidate in 1924, won any electoral votes. In 1948, though, southern "Dixiecrats," who abandoned the Democratic Party to protest President Harry S. Truman's support for civil rights and racial equality, took four Deep South states. Some other Democrats supported former vice president Henry A. Wallace, running on the Progressive ticket that year. Despite these defections, Truman won. At the state and local level, third parties were sometimes successful, and various candidates running on socialist, communist, or a number of other tickets sporadically held office. For example, Wisconsin elected Progressives Robert M. La Follette Jr. to the Senate in 1934 and 1940 and Merlin Hull to the House from 1934 to 1944. Benjamin J. Davis, running as a Communist, served on the New York City Council as the "Communist Councilman from Harlem," while Vito Marcantonio, who had served one term in Congress as a Republican (1935–1937), served six terms in Congress (1939–1951) running on the ticket of the American Labor Party, which had Communist Party support. Independents also had some success; Henry F. Reams of Ohio, for example, served two full terms in the House (1951–1955).

By the 1960s, Republicans and Democrats had swapped places on the issue of African American civil rights of a hundred years earlier. In 1964, large numbers of white southerners left the Democratic Party over President Lyndon Johnson's support for civil rights. Since then, the Democratic constituency has been generally comprised of urban, northern, and far western liberals; Catholics and Jews; African Americans, Hispanics, Asian-Americans, and other minorities; blue-collar workers; and the underprivileged. Republicans are viewed as conservatives, and the party is populated by southerners, white Protestants, and business interests.

Third parties continued to run presidential candidates, and in some places candidates for Congress and state and local offices. In the 1960s, John Lindsay, a former Republican congressman, was elected mayor of New York City on the Liberal Party ticket, and in 1970, James L. Buckley won a U.S. Senate seat from New York, running on the Conservative Party line. Third-party candidates have also been spoilers, as in 1980, when

Incumbent president George W. Bush waves to convention delegates as he receives the 2004 Republican presidential nomination. He went on to win the November election with 286 electoral votes and 50.7 percent of the popular vote. (Dennis Brack/Landov)

incumbent Republican senator Jacob Javits of New York lost his party's nomination and ran as a Liberal Party candidate, dividing the votes of moderates, liberals, and Democrats and thus allowing for the election of conservative Republican Alfonse D'Amato.

George C. Wallace, running in 1968 as the presidential candidate of the segregationist American Independent Party, captured five states in the South. In 1980, former U.S. representative John Anderson ran on the National Unity Party ticket and carried more than 5 million popular votes, but he did not affect the election of Ronald Reagan. In 1992, H. Ross Perot ran as an independent and won almost 20 million votes, possibly costing the incumbent, George Herbert Walker Bush, a few states. Perot influenced policy in the 1990s by highlighting the importance of the national debt and thus nudging a change in policy that brought balanced budgets and a declining debt by the end of the decade. When he

Essays

ran again in 1996, however, he had no effect on the election. In 2000, Ralph Nader, running on the Green Party ticket, won enough votes in several states to give their electoral college votes to Governor George W. Bush instead of Vice President Al Gore. Several third-party candidates ran in the 2004 presidential election, but none affected the election outcome.

Party Systems

Historians and political scientists often use the concept "party systems" to refer to eras that more or less hang together in terms of major party alignment:

- 1789 to approximately 1824: Era of the Virginia Dynasty; marked the emergence of a two-party system
- 1828 through 1854: Marked the years from Andrew Jackson's elections through the demise of the Whig Party
- 1856 through 1896: Marked the emergence of the Republican Party and its rise to dominance
- Election of 1896: Marked a transition to a period that featured the Progressive era and persisted through World War I and the 1920s.

The election of Franklin D. Roosevelt in 1932 marked another great electoral realignment, although the Democrats occasionally lost the presidency or one or both chambers of Congress in the years that followed.

In the period from 1933 through 2009, Democrats held the White House for forty years. The exceptions were the eight Eisenhower years (1953–1961), the eight Nixon-Ford years (1969–1977), the twelve Reagan-Bush years (1981–1993), and the eight George W. Bush years (2001–2009).

Internal Party Politics

Although all presidents since 1852 have been either Democrats or Republicans, their parties have sometimes borrowed ideas from third parties that quickly faded from the U.S. political scene. For example, the Democrats under Andrew Jackson in 1832 followed the example of the Anti-Masons in holding a national convention to nominate their presidential candidate. Previously, party caucuses in Congress, called King Caucus, chose their nominees in secret meetings. The 1824 election of John Quincy Adams, nominated by the Massachusetts legislature, spelled the end of King Caucus. The House decided the election when none of the four candidates, all Democratic-Republicans, failed to win the required electoral vote majority. The 1828 election, won by Jackson, marked a transition to the convention system.

National nominating conventions have remained a staple of the political party system, but they have been more show than substance in the age of primaries and television. With the presumptive nominee known well in advance, the convention nomination is a formality, although the convention still has the important duty of writing a party platform.

What Is the Role of Political Parties? Are They Even Necessary? ★ **21**

Essays

The Democratic convention of 1952, which chose Adlai Stevenson to oppose Republican Dwight D. Eisenhower, was the most recent to require more than one ballot to select a nominee. Multiple ballots were common earlier, particularly at Democratic conventions because of the party's **two-thirds nominating rule** requiring a two-thirds majority for nomination. Democrats dropped the rule, never used by Republicans, in 1936.

Political Primaries

The primary system was a creation of the **Progressive era** of the early twentieth century. Progressive governor Robert M. La Follette of Wisconsin pushed through a state primary law in 1905, but few other states followed suit until after 1968. Primary elections and caucuses became the de facto presidential nominating mechanisms after the tumultuous 1968 Democratic convention, won by Hubert H. Humphrey without entering any primaries. As the Democrats strengthened their primary rules in the 1970s and 1980s, primaries proliferated in both parties, and they came earlier and earlier in the election year. In 1996, most states held presidential primaries, most of them before April. In 2004, John Kerry and George W. Bush had locked up their nominations early in the primary season.

Federal and state campaign finance reforms enacted since the 1970s have both helped and hindered political parties. Beginning in 1976 presidential candidates became eligible for public financing of their campaigns, which reduced their reliance on money from party coffers. However, the legislation allowed "soft money," contributions given directly to the parties, ostensibly for party building but often diverted to indirect support for the party's candidate. The reform legislation also permitted interest groups and candidates to form political action committees (PACs) to raise and spend money for campaigns. This further reduced candidates' dependence on the political parties, with the result that more and more campaigns are candidate-centered rather than party-centered.

Third Parties

Although the United States has always had a two-party system, third parties have frequently played a vital role in the political order. No third-party candidate has ever been elected to the presidency, but many have been elected to other federal, state, and local offices. The votes garnered by third parties have also been a crucial factor in the outcome of elections. Moreover, the issues spotlighted by minor parties have often ended up being co-opted into the platforms of the major parties.

Nineteenth-century Third Parties

As the original party system of Hamiltonian Federalists and Jeffersonian Democratic-Republicans broke down, and the National Republican Party developed and transformed itself into the Whig Party, there also arose the Anti-Masonic Party which ran William Wirt for president in 1832, gaining almost 8 percent of the popular vote. Nonetheless, they achieved some state and local offices, particularly in New York State, where the party originated.

In 1844, the Liberty Party, which opposed slavery, won 2.3 percent of the popular vote, which may have affected the outcome of the election. In 1848, however, the less radical Free Soil Party, which was dedicated to stopping the spread of slavery in the territories, played the role of spoiler. Running former president Martin Van Buren, the party won enough votes, mostly from Democrats, to enable the Whig candidate, Zachary Taylor, to defeat the Democrat, Lewis Cass. It ran John P. Hale for president in 1852, obtaining 5 percent of the popular vote. The demise of the Free Soil Party was caused primarily by the rise of the Republican Party, which took up its stance in opposition to slavery in the territories.

In the 1850s, the American Party, otherwise known as the Know Nothing Party, reaped large votes in Pennsylvania and New York and even briefly gained control over the Massachusetts government. The party's main goals were excluding Catholics from public office, enacting restrictive immigration laws, and establishing literacy tests for voting.

Parties such as the Greenback Party (1874–1884) and the Prohibition Party, which started in 1869 and has continued ever since, never attracted many votes on the national level, but their success rested in convincing one of the major parties to take up their cause. Eventually the Republican Party embraced Prohibition, while the Democratic Party espoused the expansion of the money supply, albeit with the free coinage of silver rather than by printing greenbacks.

The Populist (or People's) Party, which represented the interests of farmers and labor, arose in the South and West in the 1880s. Because it spoke for a perennial debtor class, the party tended to favor the free coinage of silver and backed free trade and the regulation of the railroads. The goals of the Populist platform would eventually be adopted by the Democratic Party under its 1896 presidential candidate, William Jennings Bryan.

Third Parties in the Twentieth Century and Today

The Socialist Party came to prominence in the Progressive era, with members winning state and local offices and serving in Congress. In 1904, it ran Eugene V. Debs for president, winning 3 percent of the vote against the Republican incumbent Theodore Roosevelt and Alton B. Parker, the Democrat. Debs would run again in 1908, 1912, and 1920, and in this last election (campaigning from a federal penitentiary, where he was imprisoned for opposition to World War I) he tallied 915,490 votes (3.4 percent). Later, Norman Thomas would serve as the Socialist Party standard-bearer in several elections, with his largest vote in 1932 when he won 884,649 votes (2.2 percent). Before World War I, socialist Victor Berger served as mayor of Milwaukee and served as a member of the House of Representatives from 1911 to 1913 and from 1923 to 1929.

Although they lack the long-term ideological impact of the third parties described above, some minor parties have served as vehicles for the candidacies of certain individuals. The Progressive (or Bull Moose) Party

Essays

became a vehicle for Theodore Roosevelt's attempt to recapture the White House in 1912, running against Democrat Woodrow Wilson and Republican William Howard Taft. In that race, all three candidates were Progressives to an extent. When Taft's people prevented Roosevelt delegates from some states from being seated at the Republican convention, Roosevelt bolted the party and ran as a Progressive. The result was a split of the Republican vote and a victory for Wilson.

In 1924, the Progressive Party ran Robert M. La Follette for president, capturing 16.6 percent of the vote. In 1948, using the Progressive Party label, Henry A. Wallace, Franklin D. Roosevelt's former vice president and secretary of agriculture, scored 2.4 percent of the vote in a four-way race that saw Harry Truman reelected. Wallace ran to the left of Truman on both domestic and foreign affairs, where he pushed for greater cooperation with the Soviet Union. The 1948 election also saw the emergence of another third party, the States' Rights, or Dixiecrat, Party. The Dixiecrats ran J. Strom Thurmond, the governor of South Carolina, for president, opposing the Democratic Party's adoption of a civil rights plank in its 1948 platform. Thurmond won 2.4 percent of the vote.

In the close 1968 presidential race between Republican Richard M. Nixon and Democrat Hubert H. Humphrey, George C. Wallace, the governor of Alabama, captured 13.5 percent of the popular vote and forty-six electoral votes. He ran on the American Independent ticket, pushing a conservative and racist agenda. In 1980, John B. Anderson ran on an independent line against Republican Ronald Reagan and Democrat Jimmy Carter and received 6.6 percent of the popular vote, but no electoral votes. In 1992, H. Ross Perot ran for president as an Independent, receiving 18.9 percent of the vote but no electoral votes. In 1996, he ran again under the Reform Party banner. This party has run candidates for state and local office across the country, and in 1998, Jesse Ventura was elected governor of Minnesota on the Reform Party line. In 2000, the Reform Party seemed destined for oblivion as it split down the middle over the contested nomination of Patrick J. Buchanan for president.

Today, the Libertarian Party and the Green Party offer fairly consistent ideologies through their third-party movements. Because they are primarily ideologically-based, however, they are the more likely to be absorbed eventually by a major party that has co-opted their ideas and won over their constituencies.

Political Parties Today

Today, the Democratic and Republican parties continue to dominate the national political scene. Compared with the mid-1900s, however, they no longer hold as much sway over voters. Today, more voters are likely to identify themselves as independents and more voters are likely to vote a "split-ticket," that is, casting ballots for members of either of the major parties, third parties, or independents.

The major parties today continue to play an important role in our nation's political system. For example, political parties still attempt to

Essays

educate voters and arouse interest in contemporary issues. At their national nominating conventions, parties still write a party platform for their standard-bearer and strive to create a sense of political loyalty among party members that will carry their nominees into office.

See also: Anti-Masonic Party; Constitution of the United States; Democratic Party; Election of 1804; Election of 1824; Election of 1912; Election of 1948; Election of 1968; Election of 1992; Electoral College; Federalist Party; Party Platforms; Republican Party; Third Parties; Twelfth Amendment; Voting, Voting Behavior, and Voter Turnout; Whig Party.

Further Reading

Bauder, Julia (ed.). *Is the Political Divide Harming America?* Farmington Hill, MI: Greenhaven Press, 2006.

Cox, Vicki. *The History of the Third Parties.* New York: Chelsea House, 2007.

Gould, Lewis L. *Grand Old Party: A History of the Republicans.* New York: Random House, 2003.

Kronenwetter, Michael. *Political Parties of the United States.* Berkeley Heights, NJ: Enslow Publishers, 1996.

Schlesinger, Arthur M. *History of U.S. Political Parties.* New York: Chelsea House, 2002.

Witcover, Jules. *Party of the People: A History of the Democrats.* New York: Random House, 2003.

Majority Rule vs. Minority Rights: What Makes America Democratic?

 American political history is a story of eras—and eras within eras. Throughout it all, there have never been more than two major political parties at one time occupying center stage—one in the majority and one in the minority. When the majority is in command, the minority works to regain control of government. This peaceful shifting of power from one party to the other is the essence of democracy.

In the early years of the Republic, the two parties were the Federalists and the Democratic-Republicans; through the mid-1800s, the Democrats and the Whigs; and since the Civil War, the Democrats and the Republicans. External events have played a key role in which party held the majority. The successful prosecution of the Civil War (1861–1865) propelled the Republicans into dominance for nearly three-quarters of a century. During the first half of the twentieth century, the Great Depression helped move the Democrats into control for the generation that followed. The turmoil of the 1960s—from racial rioting in many of the nation's cities to the controversial war in Vietnam—left a political landscape that neither party has been able to control. Interludes have occurred within each era in which the partisan balance has temporarily shifted.

Diversity: Minority Voices

During this history of U.S. elections, the American electorate has steadily grown and become more diverse. Barely 365,000 voters cast ballots in the election of 1824, the first in which there is record of a nationwide popular vote for president. Less than 5 million voters participated in 1860, when Abraham Lincoln (1861–1865) became the nation's first Republican president, beginning an era of GOP domination that lasted almost one-third of the way through the twentieth century. Nearly 40 million voters took part in the Depression-era election of 1932, which conclusively shifted the balance of power to the Democrats, led by Franklin D. Roosevelt (1933–1945), for the next generation.

More than 105 million voters cast ballots in the election of 2000, which—in its historic closeness—confirmed a nation at the dawn of the twenty-first century almost evenly divided between the two major parties. When all the ballots had been counted, Republican George W. Bush (2001–2009) had won a bare majority of electoral votes, even though he was the first presidential winner in more than a century to lose the pop-

ular vote. In 2004, Bush was reelected in another close race, this time winning more than 50 percent of the popular vote.

In 2000, there were roughly 205 million Americans of voting age, almost 160 million of whom had taken the critical first step of registering to vote. Of those who participated in the 2000 election, exit polls showed that almost 20 percent were from minority groups—principally African Americans, Hispanics, and Asians. One-fourth of the voters were Catholic. Fewer than half were white Protestants. Slightly more women than men cast ballots.

That diversity was a far cry from the early years of the Republic, when the franchise was largely limited to a comparative handful of white male landowners. Women were not given the right to vote nationally until 1920; large numbers of African Americans across the South were denied the ballot until the 1960s; and it was not until 1971—in the midst of the Vietnam War—that the voting age was lowered nationally from twenty-one to eighteen.

The steady expansion of the voting pool has been accompanied by demographic changes that have dramatically altered the complexion of the electorate. In its early years the Republic was a rural, agrarian society. It became increasingly urban in the decades of industrialization and immigration that followed the Civil War. As the nation became more mobile over the course of the twentieth century, the population began to move out from central cities into sprawling, fast-growing suburbs.

The Rise of the Suburbs

Gradually, the suburbs have assumed the balance of power in American politics. Tending to have a more mobile, more affluent, and less politically rooted citizenry than the cities or small-town America, the suburbs have been strongholds of political independence. Since the end of World War II (1941–1945), they have often been the decisive voting bloc in state and national elections.

With the rise of the suburbs, and independent voting in general, voters have been increasingly willing to split their ticket between candidates of different parties. The result has been long periods of divided government—primarily a Republican president and a Democratic Congress, but in the last years of the twentieth century, a Democratic president and a Republican Congress.

Challenging the Two Parties

Through it all, third parties have remained part of the supporting cast, though assuming an increasingly critical role in influencing election outcomes in recent years. Throughout American history, third parties have served as a warning to the two major parties of areas of disaffection within the citizenry. Examples of these types of issues include the slavery question prior to the Civil War, trade and currency issues in the late nineteenth century, government and corporate reform in both the early and late twentieth century, and the issues of states' rights and racial poli-

tics in the mid-twentieth century. Traditionally, however, third parties have had neither the money nor the numbers of supporters to compete effectively.

That changed a bit, though, in the volatile political atmosphere of the late twentieth century. Former Alabama Governor George C. Wallace mounted a third-party campaign in 1968 that polled 13.5 percent of the nationwide popular vote, carried five Southern states, and served as an important bridge in the transformation of the South from a cornerstone of the Democratic Party to the prime building block of the Republican Party. Twelve years later Republican Representative John B. Anderson of Illinois drew 7 percent of the vote running as an Independent. In 1992, Texas billionaire H. Ross Perot won 19 percent, also as an Independent, and four years later took 8 percent as the nominee of his newly created Reform Party. In 2004, however, the impact of third parties was negligible.

The Basic Layout

The American electoral process has remained essentially the same since the Republic was launched in 1789. The president serves a term of four years and from the beginning has been formally elected by a majority vote of the electoral college. Each state's electoral vote is equal to its total of senators and House members. If no candidate wins an electoral vote majority, the choice is made by the House of Representatives. That has happened twice, in 1800 and 1824. On three other occasions—1876, 1888, and 2000—the winner of the electoral vote has lost the popular vote.

Election Reforms

Over the course of the nation's history, there have been three periods of great electoral reform. The first, in the 1820s and 1830s, saw several steps taken toward direct democracy—an expansion of the vote among white males as property and taxpaying qualifications began to be relaxed; the institution of popular balloting for presidential electors on a nationwide basis; and the advent of party conventions to nominate presidential candidates. Before conventions, the selection of a party's standard-bearer had been made in most cases by a caucus of the party's members in Congress.

The second great period of electoral reform came in the early 1900s, with the institution of direct election of senators, the creation of the first presidential primaries to give voters an advisory role in the nominating process, and the extension of the vote to women in 1920.

The third period of electoral reform came in the 1960s and 1970s. The voting age was lowered across the country from twenty-one to eighteen. The vote was extended to millions of African Americans across the South. The number of presidential primaries increased, to the point where they replaced conventions as the determining step in the nominating process. Public financing of presidential campaigns was launched. Finally, "one person, one vote" became the law of the land in drawing congressional districts.

Essays

As the size of the electorate has grown over the decades, voter participation—as a percentage of the voting-age population—has tended to decline. In the late 1800s, for instance, around 80 percent of eligible voters often cast ballots in presidential elections. With the waves of foreign immigration around the turn of the century, followed by the expansion of the vote to women, turnout rates plunged to roughly 50 percent in the early 1920s. They moved upward into the 60 percent range in the 1960s, only to begin falling downward again with the lowering of the voting age in the early 1970s. By the beginning of the twenty-first century, the national turnout rate hovered around 50 percent for presidential elections and 35 percent for midterm elections, when the number of ballots cast is always much lower.

Republicans Start Fast

The first period of electoral reform took place under the long shadow of Andrew Jackson, a Democrat with both a large and a small "d." At first, the Democrats' prime competition came from the ill-starred Whig Party, whose only two presidential victories (in 1840 and 1848) were followed by the death in office of the winner.

The Whigs dissolved in the political turmoil that preceded the Civil War, with the newly formed Republican Party filling the void. Rooted solely in the North and with opposition to the expansion of slavery into the territories as their primary cause, the Republicans made headway quickly, winning control of the House of Representatives in 1858, just four years after the party came into existence.

With regional splits within the more broadly based Democratic Party, Republicans captured the presidency and both houses of Congress in 1860. Democrats broke apart that year, with the northern and southern wings of the party each fielding a presidential ticket. The split enabled the GOP standard-bearer, Abraham Lincoln, to win the White House with less than 40 percent of the popular vote, the lowest winning percentage for any presidential candidate with the exception of the election of 1824.

Republicans were to dominate the political scene for the next seventy-two years—controlling the White House for fifty-six of those years, the Senate for sixty, and the House for fifty. As wartime memories faded, the GOP was able to tie together a winning coalition of urban and rural voters above the Mason-Dixon line, while the South remained solidly Democratic.

Democratic problems were compounded by their convention nominating rules. While Republicans nominated their presidential candidate by a simple majority vote, Democrats until 1936 required a two-thirds majority. The result, on occasion, was a long, exhausting convention that ultimately nominated a colorless compromise candidate.

The era of Republican dominance saw only two Democrats advance to the White House—Grover Cleveland, who won two nonconsecutive terms in the late nineteenth century, and Woodrow Wilson, who capitalized on the split within Republican ranks in 1912 between President William Howard Taft and former president Theodore Roosevelt, and won with a modest 42 percent of the popular vote.

Essays

Republicans rebounded strongly from the eight-year "Wilson aberration," dominating both ends of Pennsylvania Avenue in the 1920s. At the beginning of 1929, the party was near its zenith. Herbert Hoover had been elected president the previous November with 58 percent of the vote—the second-highest winning percentage up to that time in the nation's history—and Republicans held roughly 60 percent of the seats in both the Senate and House.

With the stock market crash in October 1929 and the onset of the Great Depression, dramatic changes in the political landscape came quickly. In the midterm election of 1930, Democrats won control of the House and pulled virtually even with the Republicans in the Senate.

Republicans identified as the party of the Depression

Democrats Take Charge

In 1932, Democrats completed their breakthrough, easily capturing the White House and both houses of Congress. Roosevelt led the Democratic sweep, besting Hoover in all but six northeastern states, and his long coattails helped Democrats emerge with more than 70 percent of the seats in the House and more than 60 percent in the Senate.

The next two elections were just as important. They affirmed that 1932 was not a one-time, anti-Republican vote, but the start of a new political era in which the Democrats would dominate. Historically, the party occupying the White House has lost congressional seats in midterm elections, but in 1934 Democrats added to their hefty majorities in both the Senate and the House. In 1936, they gained even more seats, as FDR swept to a landslide reelection victory.

Roosevelt carried all but two states, Maine and Vermont, winning 60.8 percent of the popular vote (second only to Lyndon B. Johnson's 61.1 percent in 1964) and registering a 523–8 victory in the electoral vote, the most lopsided margin in the nation's history. Meanwhile, the Democrats emerged from the 1936 election with 333 seats in the House and 75 seats in the Senate, the most that either party has held in either chamber.

Put another way, the Republicans—who had dominated American politics since the Civil War—were about as close to extinction as any major party has been. They staggered away from the election of 1936 with just 20 percent of the seats in the House of Representatives, 18 percent of those in the Senate, 15 percent of the nation's governorships, and just 2 percent of the electoral vote for president.

Over the next decade, the Republicans would steadily gain ground and the Democrats lose it. The Democrats remained the nation's majority party for the next generation, however, because they were able to maintain the cornerstone of their new coalition, the South and the cities. The South, in particular, had a strong voice in the party's congressional leadership. Alben W. Barkley of Kentucky and Lyndon B. Johnson of Texas held the post of Senate majority leader for much of the 1940s and 1950s, while Sam Rayburn of Texas served as House speaker through much of the same period.

★ ★ ★ ★ ★ ★ ★ ★ ★ ★ ★ ★ ★ ★ ★ ★ ★ ★

To be sure, Democratic dominance during this period was not monolithic. Republicans won both houses of Congress in the midterm election of 1946 and again in 1952, when Republican Dwight D. Eisenhower (1953–1961) won the first of his two terms as president. Congressional Republicans were also able to frustrate more than one Democratic president during this period by joining with conservative Democrats, mainly from the South, to form a "conservative coalition" that prevailed on a number of issues.

Still, the Democrats' control from 1932 to 1968 was about as solid as it had been for the Republicans during the previous era; it was just half as long. The Democrats held the White House for twenty-eight of the thirty-six years, and both the Senate and the House for thirty-two of them.

Unlike the previous GOP era, though, when Republicans were arguably strongest near its close, Democrats were most dominant at the beginning of their era—when Republicans were clearly identified as the "party of the Depression" and Democrats were associated with the activist, optimistic government of FDR's New Deal.

From 1940 through 1956, the Democratic share of the presidential vote declined each election. It was, however, the end of World War II, or maybe more precisely, the death of Roosevelt in April 1945, that marked a transition from a strongly Democratic era to a more tenuous one.

Through the post-Depression years of the 1930s and the war effort in the early 1940s, FDR defined American politics. With his death, and the end of World War II several months later, the political playing field changed. The electorate began to grow more mobile, suburbs began to sprout, and voters began to show an increasing independence from the political machines and their interest group allies that held sway in the past. Neither party had a leader to loom over the political landscape as FDR did through his four presidential election victories.

Both the liberal and conservative wings of the Democratic Party fielded tickets of their own in 1948. On Truman's left was former vice president Henry A. Wallace (during FDR's third term), who led the Progressive Party. On Truman's right, South Carolina governor J. Strom Thurmond headed the States' Rights Party, informally called the Dixiecrats.

The rest is legend. Trailing Republican Thomas E. Dewey in the polls throughout much of the year and looking hopelessly beaten, Truman ran a spirited fall campaign that produced one of the greatest upsets in American political history. Truman carried twenty-eight states, rolling over the New York governor in every region except the Northeast, while the Thurmond and Wallace challenges were held in check. Thurmond carried four southern states, but Truman won the rest of the region. Wallace ended up carrying no states.

However, the Democrats' joy with Truman's comeback victory and the election of a Democratic Congress masked the fact that Truman had won with less than a majority of the popular vote—a poorer showing than FDR in any of his four presidential election victories. The 1948 election was conducted against a backdrop of voter apathy; turnout was just 51 percent of

Majority Rule vs. Minority Rights: What Makes America Democratic? ★ *31*

Essays

the voting-age population, the lowest for any presidential election since the 1920s.

Four years later, Republican Eisenhower won the White House and helped the GOP win both houses of Congress as well. It soon became apparent, however, that Ike's was a personal, not a party, victory. In 1954, Democrats regained Congress, and two years later they added seats to their congressional majorities, even as Eisenhower was coasting to a landslide reelection victory.

Postwar Politics: Kennedy and Nixon

It was not Eisenhower—who had led the Allied troops during World War II—who defined American politics in the immediate postwar period, but two junior officers in the Navy, John F. Kennedy and Richard M. Nixon. They proved to be among the most ambitious and successful politicians of their generation.

Both won House seats in 1946: Democrat Kennedy in the Boston area, Republican Nixon in the fast-growing suburbs of southern California. Both won Senate seats in the early 1950s. Although Nixon was elected vice president in 1952, Kennedy also vaulted onto the national stage in 1956 with a nearly successful bid for the Democratic vice-presidential nomination.

The two faced each other in the presidential election of 1960 in a race that was close from beginning to end. Throughout, it had a special drama to it, particularly surrounding Kennedy. As vice president, Nixon had the air of a semi-incumbent and ran unopposed for the Republican nomination. Kennedy did not have that luxury and, as a Catholic, felt he had to demonstrate his electability in the scattered array of presidential primaries. He succeeded, culminating with a legendary victory over Senator Hubert H. Humphrey of Minnesota in heavily Protestant West Virginia, which put Kennedy within range of the nomination.

Voter interest in the race, already high, was heightened that fall by a series of televised debates—the first ever between presidential nominees. On election day, 63 percent of the voting-age population turned out, the highest percentage in any presidential contest since World War I (1917–1918). The result was one of the closest presidential elections ever, with Kennedy winning by barely 100,000 votes out of nearly 70 million cast.

Critical to Kennedy's victory was the Democrats' urban base. His winning margins in New York City (New York), Philadelphia (Pennsylvania), Baltimore (Maryland), Detroit (Michigan), Chicago (Illinois), and St. Louis (Missouri), were larger than his victory margins in each of those states. Like Truman twelve years earlier, Kennedy was able to win a large portion of the South.

The political environment of the 1960s, though, was buffeted by trauma and tragedy, starting with Kennedy's assassination in November 1963. The event shocked Americans and created a sympathy vote of sorts for Kennedy's successor, Lyndon B. Johnson, who led a Democratic landslide the following year almost equal in scope to the party's titanic win in 1936.

Johnson defeated Republican Senator Barry M. Goldwater of Arizona with a record 61.1 percent of the popular vote, and the Democrats emerged with 295 seats in the House and 68 in the Senate, their highest totals since the 1930s.

Instead of reviving the Democratic era, the election of 1964 proved to be the era's "last hurrah." Against the backdrop of an increasingly unpopular war in Southeast Asia and racial rioting in many of the nation's cities, Johnson launched a series of liberal "Great Society" programs that quickly proved controversial. In 1966, Republicans gained forty-seven seats in the House and three in the Senate. Two years later, they won the presidency.

Split-Level Realignment

The election of 1968 proved to be one of those rare realigning elections, like 1860 and 1932, that define American politics for a generation to come. However, instead of producing a top-down realignment felt at all levels of government, the 1968 election brought about a split-level realignment: Republicans dominated presidential contests for the next two decades, but Democrats retained the upper hand in Congress and the states.

The political environment in 1968 was highly volatile. Not only was there war abroad and racial rioting at home, but violence impacted the presidential campaign as well. Civil rights leader Martin Luther King, Jr., was assassinated in April 1968. Senator Robert F. Kennedy of New York, a brother of the late president and a leading candidate for the Democratic presidential nomination, was killed two months later, after winning the California primary.

That August, Vice President Humphrey was nominated by the Democratic convention in Chicago, as thousands of demonstrators took to the streets to oppose both the war and the lack of openness in the party's nominating process. Humphrey had not competed that spring in a single primary state, but, backed by the party establishment, he was nominated on the first ballot. Down in the polls and with the Democrats divided, Humphrey rallied in the fall but still fell roughly 500,000 votes short of Republican Richard Nixon (1969–1974), with nearly ten million votes going to third-party candidate George Wallace. Nixon and Wallace emphasized law and order, though, with Wallace also touting states' rights.

Nixon won only 43 percent of the popular vote yet carried thirty-two states. The focus of political transition was in the South, where Nixon won seven states, Wallace carried five, and Humphrey just one (LBJ's home state of Texas). It was by far the fewest number of southern states that any Democratic presidential nominee had carried since the Civil War.

For the rest of the century, the South was to be the cornerstone of the Republican presidential coalition. Through the 1970s and 1980s, the GOP also dominated presidential voting in the growing suburbs and much of rural America, which helped give the party five victories in a twenty-year span. The lone Democratic winner in this period was Jimmy Carter who, in the wake of the Watergate scandal that forced Nixon's resignation from office in 1974, won by a margin of only 2 percentage points two years later.

The rest of the time Republican presidential candidates won by huge margins. Nixon in 1972, Ronald Reagan in 1980 and 1984, and George Bush in 1988 each carried at least forty states, with Nixon and Reagan sweeping forty-nine in their landslide reelection victories. So dominant had the GOP become at the presidential level that by the late 1980s there was talk of a Republican "lock" on the electoral college.

Yet Democrats continued to control Congress as well as most of the nation's statehouses. With an assist from Reagan's coattails, Republicans would win the Senate in 1980 for a six-year span, but would not take both houses of Congress until 1994, by which time Democrat Bill Clinton would be in the White House.

Altogether, from 1968 to the end of the century, one party controlled both ends of Pennsylvania Avenue for just six of the thirty-two years—the four years of the Carter administration in the late 1970s, and the first two years of the Clinton administration in the early 1990s. For fourteen years, there was a Republican president and a Democratic Congress and for six years, a Democratic president and a Republican Congress. The other six years, there was a Republican president and Senate, but a Democratic House.

"Divided government" became the catchword to describe the unique new political arrangement. It was due, in part, to changes in the country—namely, an increasingly independent electorate of voters who were willing to split their tickets.

Through the 1970s and 1980s, the basic tendency was for the Democrats to nominate candidates on the left side of the political spectrum, and Republicans to nominate candidates on the right. Barry M. Goldwater in 1964 had set the tone for the rightward movement of the GOP with a campaign that stressed limited government and strident anticommunism. The conservative movement, however, did not come to full flower until the election of Reagan in 1980.

It was a rare example of presidential coattails in the era of divided government. With Reagan soundly defeating President Carter by 10 percentage points, Republicans picked up a dozen Senate seats to win control of the upper chamber and approached parity in the governorships. The GOP remained a minority in the House, but with the addition of thirty-three House seats they were able to rejuvenate the "conservative coalition"—the decades-old alliance of Republicans and conservative Democrats on Capitol Hill—to give Reagan a number of legislative victories.

The Era of Closeness

For nearly a quarter century after 1968, the basic norm had been a Republican president and a Democratic Congress. In the early 1990s, however, the political equation reversed.

Since Kennedy, every Democrat who won the presidency has been from the South. In 1992 Democrats captured the White House with an all-southern ticket led by Arkansas Governor Bill Clinton. With Senator

Al Gore of Tennessee as Clinton's running mate, the Democratic ticket consciously positioned itself near the political center.

Meanwhile, President Bush was bedeviled on several fronts. His success a year earlier in the Persian Gulf War—where the United States led a coalition of twenty-eight nations in turning back an Iraqi invasion of neighboring Kuwait—was overshadowed by the widespread perception of recession in 1992. Conservative Republicans were restive, upset by a tax hike in the middle of his administration. Texas billionaire H. Ross Perot also mounted a well-financed independent candidacy that aimed much of its fire at Bush and the Republicans.

Clinton won with just 43 percent of the popular vote, but still scored the most sweeping Democratic presidential victory since 1964. He carried thirty-two states, making deep inroads into the suburbs and even rural America. In addition, Democratic majorities in both the Senate and the House accompanied him to Washington.

The first two years of the Clinton administration, cul-minating with an ill-

After the passage of the Nineteenth Amendment, women voters cast their first ballots for United States president in the election of 1920. Republican senator Warren G. Harding won a landside victory over Democratic governor James M. Cox. Only about one-third of the eligible women voters went to the polls that year. (Library of Congress)

starred attempt to overhaul the national health care system, left the Democrats even more vulnerable. Republicans in 1994 took advantage of that vulnerability with their promises for government reform encapsu-lated in a document called the "Contract with America." Republicans gained fifty-two seats in the House and eight in the Senate, to win both houses of Congress for the first time since 1952. The GOP posted gains in all parts of the country in 1994, gaining six House seats in Washington state alone, where one of the Democratic casualties was House Speaker Thomas S. Foley. In addition, the number of Republican governors jumped to thirty, the party's highest total in a quarter century.

Yet it was the South, already the cornerstone of the Republican presi-dential coalition, which was the centerpiece of the party's landslide in

Majority Rule vs. Minority Rights: What Makes America Democratic? ★ 35

Essays

1994. The combination of anti-Clinton sentiment, a plethora of Democratic retirements, and favorable congressional redistricting that eliminated a number of racially marginal Democratic districts finally enabled the Republicans to capture dozens of districts across the South that had been voting Republican for president for decades.

American politics has grown closer and closer at all levels, culminating in the election of 2000, which became an instant classic because of its almost-impossible-to-resolve closeness. For the first time since 1888, there were different winners in the electoral vote (Republican George W. Bush) and the popular vote (Democrat Al Gore). Bush's margin of five in the electoral vote was the closest since 1876; Gore's margin of barely 500,000 votes in the popular vote was the closest since 1968.

The closeness of the election led to a historic intervention by the U.S. Supreme Court, which by a 5–4 margin halted the recount in Florida, where the national electoral college outcome hung in the balance. The Court's ruling that the manual recount violated voters' civil rights left an uncertain legacy for the U.S. electoral process.

Exit polls showed some of the same partisan divisions within the electorate that had existed for decades. Men favored Bush, women favored Gore (the so-called "gender gap"); whites preferred Bush, nonwhites backed Gore; the more affluent voted strongly for Bush, the less affluent heavily favored Gore; rural and small-town America went for Bush, urban America for Gore.

Several other groups that had broken sharply for one party or the other over much of the previous generation were "swing voters" in the election of 2000. Suburban voters and independents, both Republican-leaning groups in presidential voting in the 1970s and 1980s, split almost evenly between Bush and Gore in 2000. So did Catholics, a cornerstone of the Democratic coalition from 1932 to 1968. In 2004, although incumbent president George W. Bush won the electoral college vote, he won the popular vote by a very narrow margin. Bush's narrow victory, however, is proof that the election was competitive.

Democracy: Alive and Well

The highly competitive nature of the 2004 presidential election is a necessary condition of democratic elections. The election demonstrates several examples of a healthy democracy. First, the governmental authority of the majority Republicans did not silence or limit the minority Democrats in any way. Indeed, in the subsequent 2006 mid-term elections, the Democrats won control of both houses of Congress for the first time since 1992. Secondly, the election contrasts favorably with elections in many other countries. For example, in the last Russian presidential election, Vladimir Putin claimed victory with 71 percent of the vote. In other nations, where free elections are a sham, the winning candidate often receives 99 percent of the vote—thus demonstrating the absence of a competitive democracy and a situation where the majority ignores minority rights.

See also: Constitution of the United States; Democratic Party; Election of 2000; One Person, One Vote; Republican Party; Whig Party.

Further Reading

Binder, Sarah A. *Minority Rights, Majority Rule: Partisanship and the Development of Congress.* London: Cambridge University Press, 1997.

Cox, Gary W., and Matthew D. McCubbins. *Setting the Agenda: Responsible Party Government in the U.S. House of Representatives.* London: Cambridge University Press, 2005.

Gould, Lewis L. *Grand Old Party: A History of the Republicans.* New York: Random House, 2003.

Witcover, Jules. *Party of the People: A History of the Democrats.* New York: Random House, 2003.

PART TWO

Elections A to Z

Absentee Voting

The ability to cast a ballot before election day or to cast a ballot away from one's home voting district. Absentee voting began during the Civil War when Union soldiers were caught up in the politics of the time and, with Abraham Lincoln's encouragement, wanted to participate in the elections back home. Since then, the absentee ballot has become widely used in American elections, especially in today's busy world, when voters may not have the time or ability to travel to the polls on election day.

About half the states now have an "early voting" option, including "no-fault" absentee voting open to all voters who want to vote before election day. Moreover, the number of early voters has grown so large that candidates are increasingly adapting their campaign strategies to them. In Florida in the elections of 2000, for example, the Republican Party mailed applications for absentee ballots to about two million registered party members. The Democrats also used this strategy, mailing roughly 150,000 absentee ballots. In 2000, about 15 percent of voters nationwide cast absentee ballots; in California, however, the figure was 25 percent.

To receive an absentee ballot, the voter must apply for a ballot, which must then be returned within a designated period set by law. For the vote to be certified and counted, the voter must carefully follow the canvassing board's instructions, because in a recount, a flawed ballot will

be challenged and might be thrown out. Absentee votes often decide close elections. Many of the lawsuits that occurred in Florida after the 2000 presidential election revolved around absentee ballots that lacked the proper postmarks and requests for absentee ballots that lacked voter identification numbers.

Absentee Fraud

Absentee ballots are easily subject to fraud. Thus, election workers devote large amounts of time to ensuring that they are legitimate. When the ballot is received, a worker usually checks the name on the envelope to verify that the person is a qualified absentee voter and that the signatures match. The worker also verifies that the person has not already voted.

In many states, the absentee ballot may then be entered into a computer that counts it, but by law, the ballot cannot actually be added to the tally until after the polls close on election day. In contrast, the ballots marked in a voting booth are presumed to be authentic and are counted at the polling place or a central election station when the polls close. Mechanical or computerized voting machines provide an immediate tally at each polling place.

Because many absentee voters mail or drop off their ballots at the last minute, election workers already may be swamped with regular returns when the last batches of time-consuming absentee ballots come in. The absentee ballots are usually set aside, sometimes by law, to be dealt with the day after the election—or as long as it takes to verify that they are not fraudulent.

A-B

A – Z

ABSENTEE VOTING

In recent years, many states have made absentee voting easier than it ever was in the past. For the most part, voters simply request an absentee ballot—whether they are away from their home on Election Day or not. The *Cincinnati Enquirer* believes that absentee voting increases voter participation. Professor Dan Tokaji of Moritz College at The Ohio State University, however, opposes easy access to absentee ballots.

The Cincinnati Enquirer

[The Tuesday election] marks the second general election since absentee voting was opened to everyone, regardless whether they are going to be absent or not. Elections officials say more and more people are discovering how easy it is and are taking advantage of the option. Absentee ballots are counted first and are expected to make up between 9.5 and 11 percent of the total ballots cast in the [Cincinnati] region.

Elections officials expect roughly 51,000 absentee ballots by Tuesday evening. That would represent between 10 and 13 percent of estimated votes cast.

November 5, 2007

Professor Dan Tokaji

. . . [T]he provision [of a proposed Ohio law] would allow "no fault" absentee voting by mail. That means that voters could receive and send in an

---

If the election is close, it may be days, weeks, or even months before the winner is known.

During the 2000 elections, the absentee count in California took several days because of the great volume—more than two million absentee ballots. Moreover, California counties had twenty-eight days from the date of the election to forward absentee ballots to the state capital. In other states, including Florida, the process also took more than a week because election workers had to wait for all ballots postmarked on election day to arrive. In Washington state officials count qualified absentee ballots received as many as fifteen days after the election, provided the ballot was postmarked on or before election day. California and Oregon count only ballots received before the polls close at 8:00 P.M. on election day.

Overseas and Military Absentee Voting

In 1976, President Gerald R. Ford signed the Overseas Citizens Voting Rights Act (OCVRA) establishing absentee voting procedures for American citizens who lived overseas. OCVRA gives Americans living abroad the right to vote by absentee ballot. Before going overseas, they must have voted in the state where they last lived. Most states limit this group to absentee balloting in federal elections. Both major political parties currently have overseas organizations of absentee voters, Democrats Abroad and Republicans Abroad.

Men and women in military service make up one of the biggest blocs of absentee voters. Their right to vote, as well as that of other Americans living abroad, is protected by the

absentee ballot, without any excuse. I'm opposed to such a requirement, because I think that mail-in absentee voting is the one area within our system that is genuinely subject to fraud and coercion. In addition, voters tend to make more mistakes when they vote by mail-in absentee ballot, since they don't have the benefit of error correction technology that's available with in precinct voting.

Others support no fault absentee voting on the ground that it will expand access and include more people in the voting process. While this is an important objective, in-person early voting is a better way of accomplishing it. In contrast to absentee voting, in-person early voting takes place in the privacy of the voting booth, set up at central location such as a county registrar's office or public library. It thereby preserves the secret and anonymous ballot that is a critical ingredient of system integrity. Of course, mail-in absentee voting will remain essential for elderly and disabled people who aren't able to go to a polling place. But for others, early voting is a better way to go.

May 4, 2007

DOCUMENT-BASED QUESTION:
For what reasons does the Cincinnati Enquirer *support absentee voting? Why does Professor Tokaji oppose most absentee ballots?*

Federal Voting Assistance Act of 1955 (FVAA) and OCVRA. FVAA applies to military and merchant marine personnel temporarily stationed outside the United States, as well as to their spouses and dependents.

Under both FVAA and OCVRA, application for an absentee ballot is made on a federal postcard application, a postage-free U.S. government form that also serves as a voter registration form. Most states accept the postcard as a registration or waive their own registration requirement when the postcard is submitted. A few send out their own registration form along with the absentee ballot.

Beginning with the 1996 elections, the Federal Voting Assistance Program (FVAP) implemented a program—in cooperation with state and county election bodies—that allowed military personnel to register by fax and in some cases vote by fax as well. Enactment of the 1975 OCVRA changed the meaning of the term *voting residence* for U.S. citizens living outside the country. Under the act, their state of residence became the last one they voted in, even if they had no home there and no intention to return there.

Previously, under the Constitution, states determined eligibility for voting, usually defining residence as the place where the voter or a candidate actually lived. Gradually, over the years after OCVRA, the Supreme Court struck down the strictest residency requirements, giving more weight to the national right to vote and holding, in effect, that the voter or candidate is the one who decides what to call home for voting purposes.

A-B

A – Z

Voting by Mail

Given the success of absentee voting and the dependability of the postal service, various groups have advocated vote-by-mail plans to encourage wider participation in the electoral process. In the United States, voter turnout is generally much lower than in other industrialized countries. Proponents argue that the benefits of voting by mail—including convenience, speed, and lower costs—outweigh the disadvantages, including the possible abuse of the system.

In 1995 and 1996, the vote-by-mail concept was tested in two states, Nevada and Oregon. In Nevada, the 1996 Republican presidential primary was held entirely by mail-in vote. Oregon in 1995 conducted the larger test, using mail-in votes for a special election to fill a vacant Senate seat. The winner was Democrat Ron Wyden, the first senator elected by mail. Both the Senate primaries in 1995 and the general election in early 1996 were conducted by mail. Oregon officials were pleased with the turnout—about 57 percent of the eligible 1.8 million voters. More than three-quarters of those Oregonians polled said they preferred voting by mail over going to the polling places. Women and older voters were strongest in favor of mail voting.

Oregon subsequently became the first state to decide to hold all elections by mail, approving a ballot measure in 1998 requiring voters to vote by mail in biennial primary and general elections. The measure eliminated polling places, but it did not affect existing laws allowing absentee ballots or voting at local election offices. Oregon conducted all of its 2000 balloting by mail. The rate of voter participation in Oregon in 2000 was reported to be about 80 percent, significantly higher than the national average.

A possible abuse of the vote-by-mail system surfaced in Oregon when candidates were able to obtain from election officials the names of voters who had not yet returned their ballots. Critics said this information left voters open to harassment by candidates.

An argument against use of the mail to provide a longer voting period is that it could invite fraud. Indeed, there have been instances where the number of votes cast in an election, including absentee ballots, exceeded the number of people living in the community. Another problem with mail-in votes is that duplicate or undelivered ballots can be cast by the wrong persons. However, the chances of this particular fraud being successful are reduced by the standard requirement that the voter's signature be on the envelope.

Mail elections are estimated to cost one-third to one-half less than conventional elections. The U.S. Postal Service has estimated that the cost of postal voting can be as much as $1 million lower, because there are no polling personnel to pay, no space to rent, and no polling equipment to transport and set up.

Postal voting is part of a larger trend since the 1980s toward easier voting. A few states such as Colorado, Texas, and Tennessee have experimented with opening voting-style booths before election day in stores or other public places. Most states, however, have simply made absentee ballots available to all, creating a mixed system that proponents of postal mail note is the worst of both worlds—combining the labor-intensive costs of absentee voting with the equipment and location costs of voting booth elections.

More than twenty states have early voting options, with polling stations open as many as twenty-one days before the election. Citizens can use them to vote early without giving a reason, and their votes are counted on election day like regular ballots, causing no delays. Because of their growing numbers, early voters are being increasingly courted by candidates.

Voting by Internet

Voting by telephone or on the Internet has been suggested as another way to make voting more convenient. Computerized voting machines can report their totals through modems, and with passwords and other security precautions, they could receive the voters' choices just as easily.

In 1996, the Reform Party sent 1.3 million primary ballots to Reform Party members across the country in conducting their one-week-long "national primary." Party members could choose to vote via mail, phone, or electronic mail. Ross Perot won his party's nomination by these methods.

Between 1996 and 2000, the Defense Department began to develop an Internet-based system for military voters. By the 2000 elections, the Federal Voting Assistance Program had in place a demonstration project that allowed a small sample of test voters from the armed services to cast their ballots over the Internet. The goal was to prove that the concept met the basic goals of an Internet-based voting system: secrecy of the ballot, security of the ballot from tampering, and consistency with all requirements of a paper ballot, including a (digital) signature.

After the controversial presidential election of 2000, which revealed an array of problems with old-fashioned voting machinery, Congress and voting organizations began to look more closely at Internet voting in the drive to modernize voting systems. As with the military test program in 2000, once Internet ballot security and secrecy can be guaranteed, Internet voting may become widespread in the near future.

See also: Motor-Voter Registration; Voters, Voting Behavior, and Voter Turnout; Voting Systems; Women Voters.

Further Reading

Abramowitz, Alan. *Voice of the People: Elections and Voting in the United States.* New York: The McGraw-Hill Companies, 2003.

Crigler, Anne N., ed., et al. *Rethinking the Vote: The Politics and Prospects of American Election Reform.* New York: Oxford University Press, 2003.

Fortier, John C. *Absentee and Early Voting.* Washington, D.C.: AEI Press, 2006.

Adams, Abigail

See Election of 1796; Election of 1824.

Advertising

See Campaign Finance.

African American Voters

A-B

African Americans have long struggled for equal voting rights. In no period of U.S. history, however, were all African Americans excluded from the polls. At the time of the 1787 Constitutional Convention, free African Americans had the right of suffrage in all the original states except Georgia, South Carolina, and Virginia. Their right to vote stemmed from the fact that the first Africans were brought to America not as slaves but as indentured servants who could expect freedom after a fixed number of years' service to a master. As slavery spread, so did disenfranchisement. At the outbreak of the Civil War (1861–1865), black Americans were disfranchised in all but six of the thirty-three states solely on the basis of their race.

The Thirteenth Amendment (1865) freed the slaves but did not accord them voting rights. To ease the impact of change on the South, Lincoln preferred to move cautiously in expanding the black electorate. After the Civil War, several Southern states promptly enacted "Black Codes" barring the newly liberated slaves from voting or holding office. Radical Republicans in Congress responded by passing the Reconstruction Act of 1867 that established provisional military governments in the Southern states. The return of civilian control was conditioned on their ratification of the Fourteenth Amendment, which buttressed individual liberty with "due process" and "equal protection" under the law. The amendment's second section threatened to reduce any state's representation in Congress for denying the vote to any male citizen twenty-one years of age or older.

The Reconstruction Act further stated that a secessionist state could not be readmitted to the Union unless it extended the vote to all adult males, white and African American. Congress followed in February 1869 by submitting the Fifteenth Amendment, prohibiting racial discrimination in voting, to the states. It was ratified twelve months later. The Radical Republican majority in Congress feared that unless African

A – Z

A-B

A - Z

The number of registered African American voters increased significantly after the passage of the Voting Rights Act of 1965. (AP Photo/Dozier Mobley)

Americans were allowed to vote, Democrats and ex-rebels would quickly regain control of the national government.

After Reconstruction

In 1870 Congress passed an enforcement act to protect African American voting rights in the South, but in 1876 the Supreme Court ruled that Congress had exceeded its authority. In the case *United States v. Reese,* the Court held that the Fifteenth Amendment did not give anyone the right to vote; it simply guaranteed the right to be free from racial discrimination in exercising that right. The extension of the right to vote itself, the Court said, was up to the states, not the federal government.

At the same time, the North was growing weary of the crusade for betterment of the condition of African Americans. When the federal troops were withdrawn from the South in April 1877, the remaining Radical Reconstruction governments in the South quickly disintegrated. Mississippi led the way in prohibiting African

Americans' political activity. A new state constitution drawn up in 1890 required voters to pay a poll tax of two dollars and to demonstrate their ability to read any section of the state constitution or to interpret it when it was read to them.

Literacy Tests for Voters

In Mississippi and other Southern states that adopted voter literacy tests, care was taken not to disfranchise illiterate whites. Five states exempted white voters from literacy and other requirements by grandfather clauses—regulations allowing prospective voters, if not otherwise qualified, to register if they were descended from persons who had voted, or served in the state's military forces, before 1867. Other provisions allowed illiterates to register if they owned a certain amount of property or could show themselves to be of good moral character—requirements easily twisted to exclude only blacks.

Reports of extreme voter discrimination in the South gradually moved Congress to search for remedial legislation. In 1965, it passed a

Registered African American Voters, by Age and Sex, 2004

| | | Total population | | | |
| | | Reported registered | | Not registered | |
	Total*	Number	Percent	Number	Percent
BOTH SEXES					
Total 18 years and over	24,910	16,035	64.4	8,875	35.6
18 to 24 years	3,942	2,094	53.1	1,848	46.9
25 to 44 years	10,366	6,446	62.2	3,922	37.8
45 to 64 years	7,690	5,350	69.6	2,341	30.4
65 to 74 years	1,725	1,263	73.2	462	26.8
75 years and over	1,185	883	74.5	303	25.5
MALE					
Total 18 years and over	11,072	6,644	60.0	4,428	40.0
18 to 24 years	1,867	870	46.6	997	53.4
25 to 44 years	4,634	2,663	57.5	1,971	42.5
45 to 64 years	3,452	2,277	66.0	1,175	34.0
65 to 74 years	731	542	74.1	190	25.9
75 years and over	388	292	75.3	96	24.7
FEMALE					
Total 18 years and over	13,838	9,391	67.9	4,447	32.1
18 to 24 years	2,075	1,224	59.0	851	41.0
25 to 44 years	5,734	3,783	66.0	1,951	34.0
45 to 64 years	4,239	3,073	72.5	1,166	27.5
65 to 74 years	993	721	72.6	272	27.4
75 years and over	797	590	74.1	207	25.9

Source: U.S. Census Bureau, Current Population Survey
*in thousands

The number of registered African American voters has increased greatly since the civil rights movement of the 1960s. Among several age groups, the percentage of registered voters exceeds 70 percent.

A-B

A – Z

sweeping Voting Rights Act that suspended literacy tests in seven Southern states and parts of another. Five years later Congress expanded the law to bar all voter-literacy tests.

Poll-Tax Barrier to Voting

The first poll taxes in the United States were an alternative to property ownership and were intended to enlarge the number of voters. Only a few states retained them at the time of the Civil War. After the war, they were revived for a far different purpose—to restrict who could vote in all eleven states of the old Confederacy: Florida (1889), Mississippi and Tennessee (1890), Arkansas (1892), South Carolina (1895), Louisiana (1898), North Carolina (1900), Alabama (1901), Virginia and Texas (1902), and Georgia (1908).

After the Populist Era (1880–1900) many states voluntarily dropped the poll tax. Proposals to abolish the poll tax were introduced in every Congress from 1939 to 1962. By 1960, only four states still required payment by voters. In August 1962, the House approved a constitutional amendment—already accepted by the Senate—that outlawed poll taxes in federal elections, and that amendment, the Twenty-fourth, was ratified in January 1964. In 1966, the Supreme Court held that the poll tax was an

A-B

A – Z

unconstitutional requirement for voting in state and local elections as well. Wrote Justice William O. Douglas (1939–1975) in *Harper v. Virginia Board of Elections,*

> **V**oter qualifications have no relation to wealth nor to paying or not paying this or any other tax. Wealth, like race, creed, or color, is not germane to one's ability to participate intelligently in the electoral process, . . .

White Primaries

Even more than literacy tests or poll taxes, perhaps the most effective disfranchisement of Southern African Americans was their exclusion from the Democratic Party's primary elections. In the solidly Democratic South of the post-Reconstruction era, winning the party's nomination virtually assured election. Being excluded from voting in the primary was equivalent to being excluded from voting altogether.

Finally, in 1944, after a series of cases, the Court held that the all-white primary was unconstitutional. This case, *Smith v. Allwright,* arose out of the refusal of S.S. Allwright, a county election official, to permit Lonnie E. Smith, an African American man, to vote in the 1940 Texas Democratic primary. Smith sued, saying Allwright had deprived him of his civil rights. Smith was represented by two attorneys for the National Association for the Advancement of Colored People (NAACP), William H. Hastie and Thurgood Marshall. Both were later made judges, with Marshall becoming the first African American justice on the Supreme Court.

The efforts of Texas Democrats to maintain the white primary at last ended in 1953 with another Supreme Court decision. In one county, an all-white Democratic organization conducted all-white primary elections under the name of Jaybird Club, a self-declared private club. In *Terry v. Adams* the Court declared this a ploy in violation of the Fifteenth Amendment.

Physical and Psychic Threats

Throughout this period, legal devices to limit black political activity were reinforced by physical, as well as economic, intimidation. African Americans who summoned up the courage to try to register often encountered delays and verbal

harassment sufficient to send them away. If applicants persisted, **registrars** were likely to ignore them, tell them that there were no more registration forms, or direct them to another place of registration, which, if it existed, was usually closed. Sometimes, registrars implied that African Americans could lose their jobs if they tried to register. Southern registrars also displayed a tendency to lose registration forms filled out by African American applicants.

More subtle practices limited African American political participation in the North as well. With the exception of Chicago, white-controlled city machines excluded African American people from any significant role in politics for the first half of the twentieth century. During that time, Congress did virtually nothing to encourage African American voting.

Civil Rights Legislation

Not until the 1950s, when the civil rights movement began to gather force, did Congress, at the urging of the executive branch, begin to reassert federal power to ensure the right of African American citizens to vote. Congress's first action was passage of the Civil Rights Act of 1957, which was intended to enforce the voting guarantee set out in the Fifteenth Amendment. This act, however, was generally ineffective.

The 1957 act authorized the attorney general to bring lawsuits to halt public and private interference with the right of people to vote and expanded federal jurisdiction over such suits. The law also created the Civil Rights Commission to investigate and publicly disclose problems of racial discrimination, including voting problems. The investigatory procedures of the commission and the authorization of the federal lawsuits were upheld by the Supreme Court in 1960, in *United States v. Raines.*

Responding to reports that progress in securing voting rights for African Americans still was slow even under the provisions of the 1957 act, Congress in 1960 passed a measure that permitted the U.S. attorney general to sue a state for deprivation of voting rights even if the individuals named initially as defendants— usually voting registrars—had left office. This provision remedied a situation that had arisen in a suit brought by the United States against

Alabama voting officials. In addition, Title VI of the 1960 law authorized the appointment of special federal "voting referees" to oversee voter registration in counties where a federal court detected a pattern of voter discrimination.

The Civil Rights Act of 1964 mandated state adoption of standard procedures and requirements for all persons seeking to register to vote. The law also required local officials to justify rejecting an applicant who had completed the sixth grade or had equivalent evidence of intellectual competence. Other provisions of the 1964 law expedited the movement of voting rights cases to the Supreme Court.

In two cases brought under the 1964 act, *United States v. Louisiana* and *United States v. Mississippi,* the Supreme Court in 1965 supported the government's efforts to break the pattern of case-by-case legal action to prosecute voting rights violations. The Court upheld federal power to challenge a state's entire constitutional legal framework for voter registration and its conduct of elections.

Progress still was slow. In Dallas County, Alabama, three new federal laws and four years of legal action had produced the registration of only 383 African American voters out of a potential pool of fifteen thousand. On March 8, 1965, the Reverend Martin Luther King, Jr., (b. 1929–d. 1968) led a "Walk for Freedom" to dramatize the need for additional efforts in behalf of registering African American voters in Selma, the county seat, and elsewhere in the South. The violent reaction of local white law enforcement officers and white bystanders to the peaceful demonstration drew nationwide attention to the size of the problem.

A week later, President Lyndon B. Johnson (1963–1969) addressed a joint session of Congress to ask for passage of a new voting rights measure to close legal loopholes that enabled local officials to stall African American voter registration. Within five months, Congress had approved the sweeping Voting Rights Act of 1965.

The law suspended literacy tests and provided for the appointment of federal supervisors of voter registration in all states and counties where literacy tests or similar qualifying devices were in effect on November 1, 1964, and where fewer than 50 percent of the voting-age residents had registered to vote or voted in the 1964 presidential election. The Voting Rights Act of 1965 has been extended by Congress several times, most recently in 2006.

Court Decisions in the 1990s

Entering the 1990s, African Americans as well as Hispanics were still underrepresented in Congress. To remedy this situation, the Justice Department sought to use the "preclearance" provision of the Voting Rights Act to encourage states with histories of minority voting rights violations to create so-called **majority-minority districts**—districts where African American or Hispanic populations were in the majority.

With newly drawn majority-minority districts, the 1992 election produced a large increase in the total of African American and Hispanic House members. The number of African Americans jumped from twenty-six to thirty-nine; the number of Hispanics, from eleven to seventeen. Some of the districts, however, were sharply criticized as a form of racial **gerrymandering** because of their irregular shapes, and the Supreme Court in 1993 demonstrated that these districts would come under tough legal examination.

At issue in 1993 was a district picking up African American neighborhoods in four metropolitan areas as it wound its way in a snakelike fashion through central North Carolina. The district, drawn at the urging of the Justice Department, was challenged by a group of white voters who alleged that North Carolina had set up "a racially discriminatory voting process" and deprived them of the right to vote in "a color-blind" election. Their suit was dismissed by a federal district court but reinstated by the Supreme Court in a 5–4 decision, *Shaw v. Reno* (1993).

Meanwhile, challenges to racially drawn redistricting plans were taking place in other states, which the Supreme Court used to refine its position on racial redistricting. In 1995, the Court struck down a Georgia plan that had created three African-American-majority districts, including one that stretched from the Atlanta suburbs across half the state to the coastal city of Savannah. The 5–4 vote in *Miller v. Johnson* was the same as in the North Carolina case, but the Court made clear that challenges were not limited to plans with irregularly shaped districts.

A-B

A-Z

A-B

A – Z

The decision was widely criticized. President Bill Clinton (1993–2001) called the ruling "a setback in the struggle to ensure that all Americans participate fully in the electoral process." The criticism, however, did not sway the Court's majority. In 1996, the same five-justice majority in *Shaw v. Hunt* rejected the serpentine North Carolina district that it had examined in 1993, noting that the state had ignored traditional districting criteria, such as compactness, while overemphasizing the importance of race.

Civil rights groups complained that these rulings would make it more difficult for minorities to be elected to Congress. Their warnings, however, were tempered by the election results. In 2006, the number of African American representatives elected to the 110th Congress rose to a high of forty-two, including two non-voting delegates.

See also: African Americans in Congress; Fifteenth Amendment; Twenty-fourth Amendment; Voting Rights Act of 1965; 📖 Voting Rights Act of 1965 in the **Primary Source Library.**

Further Reading

Barboza, Steven. *African American Values.* New York: Doubleday, 1998.

Obama, Barack. *Audacity of Hope: Thoughts on Reclaiming the American Dream.* New York: Crown, 2006.

West, Cornel. *Race Matters.* Boston: Beacon Press, 2001.

African Americans in Congress

Since 1870, more than 100 African Americans have served in Congress. John W. Menard holds the distinction of being the first African American elected to Congress. His 1868 election in Louisiana was disputed, however, and the House denied him a seat in Congress. Hiram R. Revels of Mississippi, who filled an unexpired Senate term from February 1870 to March 1871, thus became the first African American actually to serve in Congress. The first African American to serve in the House was Joseph H. Rainey of South Carolina, from December 1870 to March 1879.

Menard, Revels, and Rainey were elected during the post–Civil War Reconstruction era (1865–1877), when many white voters were **disenfranchised** and Confederate veterans were barred from holding office. During that period, sixteen African American men were sent to Congress from Alabama, Georgia, Florida, Louisiana, Mississippi, North Carolina, and South Carolina. From the end of Reconstruction until the end of the nineteenth century, however, only seven African American men were elected to Congress, all from the Carolinas and Virginia. They, like their predecessors, were Republicans.

As federal controls were lifted in the South, literacy and other voter tests, poll taxes, and violence eroded African American voting rights. From the time Blanche K. Bruce of Mississippi left the Senate in 1881, no other African American person served in that body until Edward W. Brooke, a Republican from Massachusetts, from 1967 to 1979. In 1992, Illinois Democrat Carol Moseley-Braun was elected to the Senate, becoming the first African American woman to gain a Senate seat. She served one term, losing her reelection bid in 1998.

The last African American elected to the House in the nineteenth century was Republican George Henry White of North Carolina. He was elected in 1896 and 1898 but did not seek renomination in 1900. For nearly three decades, there were no African American members of Congress—not until Oscar De Priest, Republican from Illinois, entered the House in 1929 and served three terms. During the next quarter-century, only three other African Americans were elected to Congress: Arthur W. Mitchell in 1934, William L. Dawson in 1942, and Adam Clayton Powell, Jr., in 1944. All three represented big-city African American constituencies, in Chicago (Mitchell and Dawson) and New York (Powell).

Moreover, all three were Democrats, reflecting a switch in African American voting habits. President Franklin D. Roosevelt had pulled a majority of African American voters away from the party of Abraham Lincoln into a coalition of Depression-era urban laborers, farmers, and intellectuals. Mitchell, the first African American Democrat elected to the House, was brought in by the Democratic sweep in the 1934 election. That election also removed the Republican,

DECISION MAKERS

Shirley Chisholm

The first African American woman elected to Congress. Born in 1924, Shirley Chisholm attended Brooklyn College. She graduated in 1946 with honors. After teaching, Chisholm entered politics, running for the New York State Assembly in 1964. In 1968, Chisholm ran for U.S. Congress. She served as a member of the House of Representatives from 1969 until 1982. Chisholm championed both civil rights and women's rights, as well as opposed the expanding Vietnam War. Campaigning for equal justice, gun control, prison reform, and an end to the war in Southeast Asia, Chisholm sought the Democratic presidential nomination in 1972. Although she did not win the nomination, she earned about 10 percent of her party's votes. She announced her retirement from Congress in 1982 and then taught politics and women's studies at Mt. Holyoke College in Massachusetts. Chisholm died in 2005.

A-B

A - Z

De Priest, and marked the beginning of a fifty-six-year absence of African American representation among House Republicans. That absence ended in November 1990 when Connecticut elected Gary Franks, an African American Republican real-estate investor from Waterbury who had once captained Yale's basketball team. Franks was defeated for reelection in 1996.

House Democrats, in contrast, steadily gained African American members. Only two were added in the 1950s—Charles C. Diggs, Jr., a Democrat from Michigan, and Robert N.C. Nix, a Democrat from Pennsylvania—but after that the pace quickened. Five more were elected in the 1960s, and fourteen each in the 1970s and 1980s. The number of African Americans elected to Congress more than doubled during the 1990s—thirty-six were elected to the House, all but two Democrats, and one (Mosley-Braun) to the Senate.

The Supreme Court's "one-person, one-vote" rulings in the early 1960s, ratification of the Twenty-fourth Amendment in 1964, and congressional passage of the 1965 Voting Rights Act are credited with opening up the polls to African American voters as never before. The Voting Rights Act provided for federal oversight in jurisdictions where African American registration and voting was exceptionally low; the

Twenty-fourth Amendment outlawed poll taxes and similar restrictions on voting; and the courts eventually ended a Southern practice of diluting African American voting power by gerrymandering voting districts. As African American voter turnouts increased, so did African American representation in Congress.

In 1968, Representative Shirley Chisholm, a Democrat from New York, became the first African American woman to be elected to Congress. She was joined in the House by Yvonne Brathwaite Burke, a Democrat from California, and Barbara C. Jordan, a Democrat from Texas, who both served from 1973 until 1979.

The 103rd Congress (1993–1995) included several firsts for African Americans. In addition to Moseley-Braun becoming the first African American woman ever elected to the Senate, for the first time since the Reconstruction era, the House delegations from Alabama, Florida, North Carolina, South Carolina, and Virginia included African American members. Georgia elected its first African American woman representative, Cynthia McKinney. The dramatic gains for African Americans in the 1992 elections was in large measure a result of redistricting aimed at increasing minority strength in Congress—a legacy of the civil rights era. This effort to draw so-called minority-majority districts, however, came under attack as the decade of the 1990s wore on. By the end of the decade, however, the Supreme Court in several decisions set new standards that limited this method of increasing African American representation in Congress.

Despite the steady gains of African Americans being elected to Congress and the growing power of senior African American members, African Americans remained numerically underrepresented in Congress. In 2008, they made up about 12 percent of the population, but only 9 percent of the House and 1 percent of the Senate.

See also: One Person, One Vote; Voting Rights Act of 1965, The; 📖 The Voting Rights Act of 1965 in the **Primary Source Library.**

Further Reading

Freedman, Eric, and Stephen Jones. *African Americans in Congress: A Documentary History.* Washington, DC: CQ Press, 2007.

Obama, Barack. *Audacity of Hope: Thoughts on Reclaiming the American Dream.* New York: Crown, 2006.

Swain, Carol M. *Black Faces, Black Interests: The Representation of African Americans in Congress.* Lanham, MD: University Press of America, 2006.

Alabama governor George Wallace addresses the 1972 Democratic Convention in July of that year. Wallace had been paralyzed after an assassination attempt in May 1972, while campaigning for the Democratic presidential nomination. (Associated Press)

Age and Voter Turnout

See Voters and Voter Turnout.

American Independent Party (1968–) and American Party (1972–)

In the United States, two related political parties that are rooted in the American Independent Party, the party of George C. Wallace's third-party presidential candidacy in 1968. Wallace

was governor of Alabama from 1963 to 1967 and from 1971 to 1979.

Wallace burst onto the national scene in 1964 as a Democratic presidential candidate opposed to the 1964 Civil Rights Act. Entering three Northern primaries—Wisconsin, Indiana, and Maryland—he surprised political observers by winning between 30 percent and 43 percent of the popular vote in the three states. His strong showing brought the term *white backlash* into the political vocabulary to describe the racial undertone of the Wallace vote.

In 1968, Wallace broke with the Democrats and launched his second presidential campaign as a third-party candidate under the American Independent Party label. His candidacy capitalized on the bitter reactions of millions of voters, especially whites and blue-collar workers. Many of these voters took issue with civil rights activism, urban riots, antiwar demonstrations, and the heavy federal spending of Lyndon Johnson's Great Society programs of the mid-1960s. With the help of his Alabama advisers and volunteer groups, Wallace was able to get his party on the ballot in all fifty states.

The former governor did not hold a convention for his party, but in October he announced his vice-presidential running mate—retired air force general Curtis LeMay—and released a platform. In the November election the Wallace-LeMay ticket received 9,906,473 votes, or 13.5 percent of the popular vote. It carried five Southern states, and won forty-six electoral votes. The party's showing was the best by a third party since 1924, when Robert M. La Follette collected 16.6 percent of the vote on the Progressive Party ticket. After his defeat in that election, Wallace returned to the Democratic Party, competing in Democratic presidential primaries in 1972 and 1976.

Wallace's American Independent Party began to break into factions after the 1968 election, but in 1972 united behind John G. Schmitz, a Republican U.S. representative from southern California (1970–1973), as its presidential nominee. In many states, the party shortened its name to American Party. In the November election, the ticket won 1,099,482 votes, or 1.4 percent of the popular vote, but failed to win any electoral votes. The ticket ran best in the West, taking 9 percent of the vote in Idaho, 7 percent in Alaska, and 6 percent in Utah.

In December 1972, a bitter fight occurred for the leadership of the American Independent Party and the group began to fall apart. By 1976 there were two distinct groups: the American Party and the American Independent Party. Both parties ran candidates for the presidency in 1976, but they each won less than 1 percent of the popular vote.

By 1980, neither party was much of a force in American politics. Both retained the same basic platforms, but each was on the ballot in only a handful of states. The American Independent Party did not field a presidential candidate in 1984, while the American Party placed Delmar Dennis, a book publisher from Pigeon Forge, Tennessee, on the ballot in six states.

In 1988, the American Party won 3,475 votes.

The American Independent Party fared better, receiving 27,818 votes. By 1992, fortunes for both parties had dwindled. The 1992 American Party presidential nominee, Robert J. Smith, was on the ballot only in Utah and received 292 votes. In 1996, the American Party collected 1,847 votes. The American Independent Party did not appear on any presidential ballots in the 1990s.

See also: Election of 1968; Progressive (La Follette) Party; Third Parties

Anthony, Susan B.

See League of Women Voters.

Anti-Federalists (1789–1796)

Patriot Patrick Henry, a fervent Anti-Federalist from Virginia, opposed ratification of the new Constitution. Unlike the Federalists, he believed it would make the central government too powerful. (Library of Congress)

A-B

A–Z

A loosely organized group opposed to the adoption of the United States Constitution. With the ratification of the Constitution in 1788, the Anti-Federalists, never a formal political party, served as the opposition to the Federalists—who favored a strong national government—in the early years of Congress.

Anti-Federalists were primarily rural, agrarian men from inland regions who favored individual freedom and states' rights. They believed that these rights would be jeopardized by the new Constitution. After ratification, the efforts of the Anti-Federalists led to adoption of the first ten amendments, the Bill of Rights, which spelled out the major limitations on federal power.

As the opposition faction in Congress during the early years of the Republic, the Anti-Federalists held to a strict interpretation of the Constitution. Anti-Federalists were especially concerned about the economic proposals of Treasury Secretary Alexander Hamilton (1789–1795), which tended to centralize more power in the federal government.

Although never the majority faction in Congress, the Anti-Federalists were a forerunner of third president Thomas Jefferson's Democratic-Republican Party, which came into existence in the 1790s and dominated American politics for the first quarter of the nineteenth century.

Further Reading

Storing, Herbert J. *What the Anti-Federalists Were For.* Chicago: University of Chicago Press, 1981.

Anti-Masonic Party (1828–1836)

A third party that arose in opposition to a secret fraternal organization: the Masons. The Masons were a secret fraternal organization with membership drawn largely from the upper class. Conversely, the appeal of the Anti-Masonic movement was to the common person—especially poor farmers and laborers—who resented the secrecy and privilege of the Masons.

The spark that created the party came in 1826 when William Morgan, a dissident Mason

from Batavia, New York, allegedly on the verge of exposing the inner workings of the order, mysteriously disappeared and never was seen again. Refusal of Masonic leaders to cooperate in the investigation of Morgan's disappearance led to suspicions that Masons had kidnapped and murdered him and were suppressing the inquiry.

From 1828 through 1831, the new Anti-Masonic Party spread through New England and the Middle Atlantic states, in many places establishing itself as the primary opposition to the Democrats. In addition to its appeal to the working classes, particularly in northern rural areas, and its opposition to Masonry, the Anti-Masons displayed a fervor against immorality—in slavery, intemperance, and urban life.

In September 1831, the party held the first national nominating convention in American history. One hundred and sixteen delegates from thirteen states gathered in Baltimore, Maryland, and nominated former Attorney General William Wirt of Maryland for the presidency. In the 1832 elections, Wirt received only 100,715 votes (7.8 percent of the popular vote) and carried just one state, Vermont, but it was the first third party in U.S. politics to win any electoral college votes. The Anti-Masons did well at other levels, however, winning the Vermont governorship several years and competing in close elections in a few other states. In the U.S. House the Anti-Masons had fifteen members in the Twenty-second Congress (1831–1833) and twenty-four in the Twenty-third Congress (1833–1835).

However, the decline of Masonry, especially in New York, where the number of lodges dropped from 507 in 1826 to forty-eight six years later, robbed the Anti-Masons of an emotional issue and hastened their decline. The 1832 election was the high point for the Anti-Masons as a national party. In the 1836 campaign, the party endorsed Whig candidate William Henry Harrison. Subsequently, most Anti-Masons moved into the Whig Party. In 1836, the major parties also held their own conventions and wrote their own platforms. Despite its short life, the Anti-Masons were one of the most important American third parties, contributing to the openness of the system, and establishing party platforms and conventions as part of modern political practices.

A-B

A–Z

Baker v. Carr (1962)

A landmark Supreme Court decision that required states to redraw representative district boundaries to ensure equal districts. Ultimately, the ruling increased the power of urban areas and decreased the influence of rural areas.

For more than half a century, since 1901, the Tennessee legislature had refused to reapportion itself, even though what is known as a decennial reapportionment, based on population, was specifically required by the state's constitution. In the meantime, Tennessee's population had grown and shifted dramatically to urban areas. By 1960, the House legislative districts ranged from 3,454 to 36,031 in population, while the Senate districts ranged from 39,727 to 108,094. Appeals by urban residents to the rural-controlled Tennessee legislature proved fruitless. A suit brought in the state courts to force reapportionment was rejected on grounds that the courts should stay out of legislative matters.

City dwellers then appealed to the federal courts, stating that they had no redress: the legislature had refused to act for more than half a century, the state courts had refused to intervene, and Tennessee had no referendum or initiative laws. They charged that there was "a debasement of their votes by virtue of the incorrect, obsolete and unconstitutional apportionment" to such an extent that they were being deprived of their right to equal protection of the laws under the Fourteenth Amendment.

The Supreme Court on March 26, 1962, handed down its historic decision in *Baker v. Carr,* ruling 6–2 in favor of the Tennessee city dwellers. In the majority opinion, Justice William J. Brennan, Jr., (served, 1956–1990) emphasized that the federal judiciary had the power to review the apportionment of state legislatures under the Fourteenth Amendment's equal protection clause. "The mere fact that a suit seeks protection as a political right," Brennan wrote, "does not mean that it presents a political question" that the courts should avoid.

In a vigorous dissent, Justice Felix Frankfurter (served, 1939–1962) said the majority decision constituted "a massive repudiation of the experience of our whole past" and was an assertion of "destructively novel judicial power." He contended that the lack of any clear basis for relief "catapults the lower courts" into a "mathematical quagmire." Frankfurter insisted "there is not under our Constitution a judicial remedy for every political mischief." Appeal for relief, Frankfurter maintained, should not be made in the courts, but "to an informed civically militant electorate."

The Court had abandoned the view that malapportionment questions were outside its competence. However, it stopped there and in *Baker v. Carr* did not address the merits of the challenge to the legislative districts, stating only that federal courts had the power to resolve constitutional challenges to maldistribution of voters among districts.

See also: 📖 *Baker v. Carr* (1962) in the **Primary Source Library**; Reapportionment and Redistricting.

Ballots

See Voting Systems.

A-B

A – Z

Bill of Rights

The first ten amendments to the United States Constitution, added in 1791. When the new Constitution was submitted to the states for ratification, it did not include any guarantee of basic rights. The omission of a Bill of Rights became a major issue in seeking the states' approval of the Constitution. Federalists, who supported the new Constitution, met this opposition by pledging early enactment of a Bill of Rights as the first amendments to the Constitution. Both Massachusetts and Virginia were particularly determined that a Bill of Rights should be added.

In 1789, during the first session of Congress, Representative James Madison proposed twelve articles of amendment. Congress approved these and sent them to the states for ratification. Of the twelve, the states approved articles three through twelve, and these ten amendments, now known collectively as the Bill of Rights, were ratified in 1791.

The first of Madison's articles concerned reapportionment of the House of Representatives and never became part of the Constitution. The second article, concerning salary increases for members of Congress, became the Twenty-seventh Amendment in 1992—more than 200 years after it was initially submitted to the states.

The Bill of Rights protects the rights of the people and limits the powers of the federal government:

Amendment I Congress shall make no law respecting an establishment of religion, or prohibiting the free exercise thereof; or abridging the freedom of speech, or of the press; or the right of the people peaceably to assemble, and to petition the government for a redress of grievances.

Amendment II A well regulated militia, being necessary to the security of a free state, the right of the people to keep and bear arms, shall not be infringed.

Amendment III No soldier shall, in time of peace be quartered in any house, without the consent of the owner, nor in time of war, but in a manner to be prescribed by law.

Amendment IV The right of the people to be secure in their persons, houses, papers, and effects, against unreasonable searches and seizures, shall not be violated, and no warrants shall issue, but upon probable cause, supported by oath or affirmation, and particularly describing the place to be searched, and the persons or things to be seized.

Amendment V No person shall be held to answer for a capital, or otherwise infamous crime, unless on a presentment or indictment of a grand jury, except in cases arising in the land or naval forces, or in the militia, when in actual service in time of war or public danger; nor shall any person be subject for the same offense to be twice put in jeopardy of life or limb; nor shall be compelled in any criminal case to be a witness against himself, nor be deprived of life, liberty, or property, without due process of law; nor shall private property be taken for public use, without just compensation.

Amendment VI In all criminal prosecutions, the accused shall enjoy the right to a speedy and public trial, by an impartial jury of the state and district wherein the crime shall have been committed, which district shall have been previously ascertained by law, and to be informed of the nature and cause of the accusation; to be confronted with the witnesses against him; to have compulsory process for obtaining witnesses in his favor, and to have the assistance of counsel for his defense.

Amendment VII In suits at common law, where the value in controversy shall exceed twenty dollars, the right of trial by jury shall be preserved, and no fact tried by a jury, shall be otherwise reexamined in any court of the United States, than according to the rules of the common law.

Amendment VIII Excessive bail shall not be required, nor excessive fines imposed, nor cruel and unusual punishments inflicted.

Amendment IX The enumeration in the Constitution, of certain rights, shall not be construed to deny or disparage others retained by the people.

Amendment X The powers not delegated to the United States by the Constitution, nor prohibited by it to the states, are reserved to the states respectively, or to the people.

Brooke, Edward W.

See Elections, Senate.

Buckley v. Valeo (1976)

A major decision of the United States Supreme Court that directly affected campaign financing. As soon as the Federal Election Campaign Act Amendments of 1974 took effect, the law was challenged in court by several plaintiffs including Senator James L. Buckley, (Conservative from New York); former Senator Eugene J. McCarthy (Democrat from Minnesota); the New York Civil Liberties Union; and *Human Events,* a conservative publication. They filed suit on January 2, 1975.

Their basic arguments were that the law's new limits on campaign contributions and expenditures curbed the freedom of contributors and candidates to express themselves in the political marketplace. The plaintiffs also noted that the public financing provisions discriminated against minor parties and lesser-known candidates in favor of the major parties and better-known candidates.

The U.S. Court of Appeals for the District of Columbia on August 14, 1975, upheld all of the law's major provisions, thus setting the stage for Supreme Court action. The Supreme Court handed down its ruling, *Buckley v. Valeo,* on January 30, 1976, in an unsigned 137-page opinion. In five separate, signed opinions, several justices concurred with and dissented from separate issues in the case.

In its decision, the Court upheld provisions that:

- Set limits on how much individuals and political committees could contribute to candidates;
- Provided for the public financing of presidential primary and general election campaigns;
- Required the disclosure of campaign contributions of more than $100 and campaign expenditures of more than $100.

But the Court overturned other features of the law, ruling that the campaign spending limits were unconstitutional violations of the First Amendment guarantee of free expression. For presidential candidates who accepted federal matching funds, however, the ceiling on the expenditures remained intact. The Court also struck down the method for selecting members of the FEC.

Spending Limits Overturned

The Court stated: "A restriction on the amount of money a person or group can spend on political communication during a campaign necessarily reduces the quantity of expression by restricting the number of issues discussed, the depth of their exploration and the size of the audience reached. This is because virtually every

POINT / COUNTERPOINT

SHOULD THE GOVERNMENT LIMIT CAMPAIGN CONTRIBUTIONS?

The issue of campaign spending continues to be controversial. In 1976, the United States Supreme Court struck down most spending limits as a violation of the First Amendment's guarantee of free speech. Still, many citizens, as well as politicians, believe that campaign spending needs to be controlled.

Brenda Wright of the National Voting Rights Institute

Given the explosion of spending on political campaigns in recent years, everyone knows that the average citizen with average financial resources might as well forget running for elective office. But things have really gotten bad when multimillionaires can no longer keep up with the fund-raising arms race. Senator Mark Dayton, D-Minn., the heir to a department store fortune who spent $12 million of his own funds to win office in 2000, recently announced he is leaving Congress. "I cannot stand to do the fund raising necessary to wage a successful campaign," he said, "and I cannot be an effective senator while also being a nearly full-time candidate." On both counts, of course, Dayton was simply saying out loud what a growing number of politicians already believe: The demands of campaign fund raising are simply incompatible with the practical and ethical demands of the office itself. . . .

A legal battle that started in Vermont could change all this. In *Landell v. Sorrell* (2004), the 2d U.S. Circuit Court of Appeals has ruled that, despite *Buckley*, mandatory spending limits may now be able to pass constitutional muster. Because the 2d Circuit ruling is binding for New York and Connecti-

means of communicating ideas in today's mass society requires the expenditure of money."

Only Justice Byron R. White dissented on this point—he would have upheld the limitations. Rejecting the argument that money is speech, White wrote that there are "many expensive campaign activities that are not themselves communicative or remotely related to speech."

Although the Court acknowledged that contribution and spending limits had First Amendment implications, it distinguished between the two by saying that the act's "expenditure ceilings impose significantly more severe restrictions on protected freedom of political

expression and association than do its limitations on financial contributions."

The Court removed all the limits imposed on political spending and, by so doing, weakened the effect of the contribution ceilings. The law had placed spending limits on House, Senate, and presidential campaigns and on party nominating conventions. To plug a loophole in the contribution limits, the bill also had placed a $1,000 annual limit on how much an individual could spend independently on behalf of a candidate.

The independent expenditure ceiling, the opinion said, was a clear violation of the First Amendment. The Court wrote:

A-B

A - Z

cut as well as Vermont, those states now are free to adopt spending limits as well, so long as the caps are carefully tailored to avoid unduly restricting candidate speech. . . .

Senator Mitch McConnell, Republican of Kentucky

Proponents of campaign-spending limits are stuck between a rock and a hard place: the Constitution and reality.

It is impossible constitutionally to limit all campaign-related spending. The Supreme Court has been quite clear on this matter, most notably in the 1976 *Buckley v. Valeo* decision: "The First Amendment denies government the power to determine that spending to promote one's political views is wasteful, excessive, or unwise. In the free society ordained by our Constitution it is not the government but the people—individually as citizens and candidates and collectively as associations and political committees—who must retain control over the quantity and range of debate on public issues in a political campaign."

For those who do not at first blush see the link between the First Amendment and campaign spending, the Court elaborates: "A restriction on the amount of money a person or group can spend on political communication during a campaign necessarily reduces the quantity of expression by restricting the number of issues discussed, the depth of their exploration, and the size of the audience reached. This is because virtually every means of communicating ideas in today's mass society requires the expenditure of money."

DOCUMENT-BASED QUESTION
What is the major difference between the views of Ms. Wright and Senator McConnell?

While the . . . ceiling thus fails to serve any substantial governmental interest in stemming the reality or appearance of corruption in the electoral process, it heavily burdens core First Amendment expression. . . . Advocacy of the election or defeat of candidates for federal office is no less entitled to protection under the First Amendment than the discussion of political policy generally or advocacy of the passage or defeat of legislation.

The Court also struck down the limits on how much of their own money candidates could spend on their campaigns. The law had set a $25,000 limit on House candidates, $35,000 on Senate candidates, and $50,000 on presidential candidates. "The candidate, no less than any other person, has a First Amendment right to engage in the discussion of public issues and vigorously and tirelessly to advocate his own election and the election of other candidates," the opinion said.

The ruling made it possible for a wealthy candidate to finance his own campaign and thus to avoid the limits on how much others could give him. The Court wrote that "the use of personal funds reduces the candidate's dependence on outside contributions and thereby counteracts the coercive pressures and attendant risks of abuse to which the act's contribution limitations are directed."

Justice Thurgood Marshall rejected the Court's reasoning in striking down the limit on how much candidates may spend on their campaigns. "It would appear to follow," he said, "that the candidate with a substantial personal fortune at his disposal is off to a significant 'head start.'" Moreover, he added, keeping the limitations on contributions but not on spending "put[s] a premium on a candidate's personal wealth."

See also: Bill of Rights; Campaign Finance.

Further Reading

Hasen, Richard. *The Supreme Court and Election Law: Judging Equality From Baker v. Carr to Bush v. Gore.* New York: NYU Press.

Bull Moose Party

See Progressive Party.

Burr, Aaron

See Election of 1800; Twelfth Amendment.

Bush v. Gore (2000)

A controversial Supreme Court decision that ultimately determined the winner of the 2000 presidential election. Until 2000, the Court had never become involved in a presidential election. Although Vice President Al Gore received 539,947 more votes than Texas governor George W. Bush, he lost. Gore received 50,996,116 votes, while Bush received 50,456,169. State electors cast the true votes for president, and in

all but two states—Maine and Nebraska—the state's electors vote as a bloc for one candidate. The winner of the state's popular vote, even if by a mere handful of votes, receives all of the electors' votes.

Moreover, the process of counting votes is not as exact as many people might have assumed. Different states and different counties, even neighboring precincts, use varying means of counting votes, and that difference determines the likelihood that a vote will be counted. In Florida in 2000, some precincts used paper card ballots that were punched out by the voter and counted by a tabulating machine. Others used more modern computer scanning systems. The older punch card system does not count as high a percentage of ballots as more modern systems, and in a close election such a difference alone can be vital.

Election Night

On election night, the television networks first called Gore the winner in Florida, but later changed it to Bush. By early the next morning, the networks gave up and said it was too close to call. That is where things stood for more than a month. Gore had won 267 electoral votes, just short of the 271 needed for victory, and Bush had won 246. Florida's twenty-five electoral votes would determine the winner. On election night, Bush had a lead of 1,784 votes in Florida, but his margin decreased to 327 votes after the mandatory machine recount. Gore and his lawyers, convinced a majority of Floridians had voted Democratic, decided to challenge the outcome in court. Bush's advisers said the Texas governor had won narrowly but fairly, and the election was over.

Gore's legal team faced an uphill fight from the start. Florida's election laws were somewhat confusing and out-of-date. Moreover, they were written to regulate the sixty-seven county election boards, not the state as a whole. Gore could not simply ask for a statewide recount under Florida law. He had to take his fight to the individual counties. Over the next month, petitions were heard by county courts and the Florida Supreme Court.

A-B

A - Z

Recounts

Florida's Secretary of State Katherine Harris, an elected Republican, announced two key interpretations of state law that supported Bush's argument that a recount was not called for. First, she said the "inability of voting systems to read an improperly punched punch card ballot is not 'an error in the vote tabulation' and would not trigger the requirement" for a manual recount. Second, she said her office would enforce a one-week deadline for the counties to submit their election tallies. State law says the county's returns must be submitted "on the 7th day following" the election and that "such returns may be ignored" if they are not filed on time.

Fearing that Harris would ignore the recounts, Gore's lawyers appealed to state circuit court judge Terry Lewis, but lost. "I give great deference to the interpretation by the Secretary of the election laws," he said, in addition to concurring that she "may" ignore the manual recounts if they are filed late. The Florida Supreme Court then stepped in to resolve the legal conflict between the county election boards' duty to manually recount ballots and the secretary of state's refusal to include those votes in the final tally. In the first major ruling of the developing legal dispute, the Florida Supreme Court sided 7-0 with Gore and the county officials, thus contradicting Harris. "[T]he will of the people, not a hyper-technical reliance upon statutory provisions, should be our guiding principle in election cases," the state justices said in *Palm Beach County Canvassing Board v. Harris* (2000). Getting the right result was more important than getting it done on time, they concluded. Their decision, handed down on November 21, extended the time for the counties to recount ballots for five more days, until Sunday, November 26.

The day after the Florida Supreme Court ruled, Washington attorney Theodore B. Olson, representing Bush, asked the U.S. Supreme Court to intervene. While lawyers for Gore and Bush had been fighting in the Florida state courts, Olson had taken a separate track into the federal courts, believing that the ultimate decision may well depend on the Supreme Court.

On November 24, the Court announced that it would hear the Republicans' challenge to the Florida court's decision extending the deadlines. It was not clear what constitutional matters were at issue or whether the extended deadline made much difference. Two days later, on November 26, Harris's office declared Bush the winner of Florida's twenty-five electoral votes. The final tally was 2,912,790 for Bush and 2,912,253 for Gore, a difference of 537 votes.

Then Gore's lawyers challenged the state's decision to certify the winner under a separate provision of state law called a Contest of Election. It states that candidates can contest the result in court if they can point to the "rejection of a number of legal votes sufficient to change or place in doubt the result of the election." A judge who finds merit in the challenge may "provide any relief appropriate under the circumstances." Gore's lawyers noted that more than 9,000 punch card ballots in Miami-Dade alone had gone through the tabulating machines, but were not counted as votes. If these ballots contained legal votes, they would certainly "place in doubt" the outcome of the Florida election, they argued. On Friday, December 8, a divided Florida Supreme Court agreed. "This election should be determined by a careful examination of the votes of Florida's citizens," the state court said. "In close elections the necessity for counting all legal votes becomes critical." In a 4-3 vote, it ordered a hand recount of all the remaining untabulated ballots in Florida by December 12, beginning with the 9,000 ballots in Miami Dade. By some estimates, more than 40,000 ballots statewide needed to be tallied by hand.

The December 12 deadline came from federal law. The disputed presidential election of 1876 between Republican Rutherford B. Hayes and Democrat Samuel Tilden also turned on Florida, which had submitted two slates of electors. In response to this fiasco, Congress passed the Electoral Vote Count Act of 1887 to set rules for resolving such disputes. It says a state's electors "shall meet and give their votes on the first Monday after the second Wednesday in December." In 2000, December 18 was the first Monday after the second Wednesday. Another provision

A-B

A–Z

of the law says the state result "shall be conclusive" if all controversy over the selection of the electors is resolved "at least six days before the time fixed for the meeting of electors." In the fight for Florida, December 12 was therefore the deadline for resolving the controversy.

The Florida Supreme Court, in its concluding sentence, instructed that the recounting teams do their best to determine what the voters intended. The Republicans had complained of the use of a "selective" recount in a few Democratic-leaning counties. Taking that criticism into account, the state judges said that all the counties should tabulate their "undervotes," referring to a punch card ballot that did not register as a vote when it went through the tabulating machine. This occurred mostly when the voter had not punched out the paper hole cleanly and instead left a "hanging chad." Sometimes, the voter put only a dent in the card, failing to punch through it. The Florida court's opinion did not establish a standard for whether an indented ballot should be counted as a legal vote. The court also did not order a count of so-called overvotes—ballots with more than one marking—because Gore had not asked for one. For example, if a voter punched out a chad next to Bush-Cheney, and then wrote below "BUSH," the ballot could not be counted because it had two markings, although the voter's intent was entirely clear. Some of the state justices said they would have voted to tally these overvotes as well when the voter's intent was clear.

Time, however, was short. The hurried recount started again on December 9, but at midday it was halted by a surprise order from the U.S. Supreme Court. In a 5–4 vote, the justices had granted an emergency motion filed by Olson to block the Florida court's ruling from taking effect. To obtain an emergency order that stays a lower court decision the appealing party must show he will suffer "an irreparable harm" unless the court intervenes. Beyond that, he must assert convincingly that five justices—a majority—are likely to rule for him and reverse the lower court. For lawyers, showing an "irreparable harm" to their client is quite difficult.

In Bush's motion, Olson said the Texas governor would suffer an irreparable harm if the Floridians conducted a "standardless" recount. Five members of the Court agreed: Chief Justice Rehnquist, and Justices O'Connor, Scalia, Kennedy, and Thomas. "It suffices to say that . . . a majority of the Court . . . believe that the petitioner [Bush] has a substantial probability of success," Scalia said in a statement defending the stay. "The counting of votes that are of questionable legality does in my view threaten irreparable harm to [Bush] and to the country, by casting a cloud upon what he claims to be the legitimacy of his election."

Justice Stevens spoke for the four dissenters. "Counting every legally cast vote cannot constitute irreparable harm. On the other hand, there is a danger that a stay may cause irreparable harm to the respondents [Gore and Lieberman]—and, more importantly, the public at large. . . . Preventing the recount from being completed will inevitably cast a cloud on the legitimacy of the election."

The stay order signaled the end of the fight for Florida and a final victory for George Bush. Lawyers then hastily filed new briefs on Sunday, and on Monday morning, the Court heard an oral argument that was later broadcast nationwide via audiotape.

The Court's Decision

On December 12, the Court handed out copies of its decision in *Bush v. Gore* (2000). It was an unsigned opinion and labeled a "per curiam," or opinion of the court. This usually refers to a unanimous and uncontroversial ruling, but this decision was anything but. Attached were four separate dissents by Justices Breyer, Ginsburg, Souter, and Stevens. In addition, a concurring opinion written by Chief Rehnquist was joined by Justices Scalia and Thomas. That meant, by a process of deduction, that the authors of the decisive opinion were the two unnamed members of the Court: Justices Kennedy and O'Connor. During the oral argument, Kennedy in particular spoke about the equal protection problem, and he is credited as being the opinion's primary author.

Bush's appeal had raised two questions: whether the Florida courts had violated federal election law by establishing "new standards" for resolving the disputed election and whether the "use of standardless manual recounts violates the Equal Protection and Due Process Clauses" of the Fourteenth Amendment. "[W]e find a violation of the Equal Protection Clause," the Court said. "The individual citizen has no federal constitutional right to vote for electors for the President of the United States," the Court's opinion said, unless and until the state legislature chooses popular election as the means of choosing its electors. Once it has settled on elections, however, the state must give "equal weight . . . to each vote and equal dignity . . . to each voter. . . . The State may not, by later arbitrary and disparate treatment, value one person's vote over that of another." As precedent, the opinion cited the Warren Court rulings that abolished poll taxes and set the "one-person, one-vote" rule for drawing electoral districts.

Of course, both sides claimed they were protecting the right to vote, as the Court noted. The Democrats said the recounts were needed to assure that every voter's ballot was counted. The Republicans said a flawed recount based on hazy and subjective rules was fundamentally unfair and unreliable. The Court adopted the second argument. "The recount mechanisms . . . do not satisfy the minimum requirement for non-arbitrary treatment of voters necessary to secure the fundamental right" to vote, the opinion said. Since the case had developed quickly, the justices had only limited information on how the recounts were being conducted. Republican officials complained that some recount teams were counting ballots that were only dented, while others counted them only when the hole was punched through. This difference did not necessarily amount to discrimination against Bush and in favor of Gore, but the Court concluded it did amount to "unequal evaluation of ballots."

Without question, however, the Court's ruling ensured Bush's victory. It said December 12 was indeed the deadline for recounting votes in Florida, and by handing down the opinion at 10 P.M. on December 12, the possibility for any further action in Florida was foreclosed. "That date is upon us, and there is no recount procedure in place . . . that comports with minimal constitutional standards," the Court concluded.

The Court's ruling succeeded in bringing a swift and decisive end to a seemingly endless election battle. Less than twenty-four hours after the decision, Gore conceded defeat. "While I strongly disagree with the Court's decision, I accept it," he said in a televised address. The Court had never previously decided such an intensely political case. The public's reaction appeared to be muted. Opinion polls taken after *Bush v. Gore* showed the Court retained a high level of public confidence.

See also: 📖 *George W. Bush, et al., petitioners, v. Albert Gore, J., et al., 2000* in the **Primary Source Library;** Election of 1876; Election of 2000; Electoral College; One Person, One Vote.

Further Reading

Hasen, Richard. *The Supreme Court and Election Law: Judging Equality From Baker v. Carr to Bush v. Gore.* New York: NYU Press.

Pyle, Ransford C., Heather Slusher, and Carol M. Bast. *Bush v. Gore: Understanding the American Legal System.* Upper Saddle River, NJ: Prentice Hall, 2001.

Sergis, Diana K. *Bush v. Gore: Controversial Presidential Election Case.* Berkeley Heights, NJ: Enslow Publishers, 2003.

Thompson, Dennis F. *Just Elections: Creating a Fair Electoral Process in the United States.* Chicago: University of Chicago Press, 2004.

A-B

A-Z

Campaign Finance

The various ways in which political campaigns are paid for. Campaign finance has changed dramatically over the past century, going from its early freewheeling days to a heavily regulated system. Campaigns now must disclose where their money comes from and how it is spent. Contributors must adhere to specific limits on how much they can give to federal candidates.

Detailed campaign reports are available for public study, even on the Internet. Most presidential candidates limit their spending in return for public funds. Campaigns hire lawyers and bookkeepers just to comply with federal laws.

The changes have been striking. Yet the similarities have been striking as well. Demands for reform at the beginning of the twenty-first century sound much the same as those voiced at the beginning of the twentieth century. Reformers are still calling for curbs on the ability of special interests and wealthy individuals to dominate campaign money; they still call for disclosure of the sources and uses of money moving outside federal disclosure requirements.

Controversy

Critics of the campaign financing system became increasingly vocal in the closing decades of the twentieth century and the beginning of the twenty-first century. But reaching a consensus on what was wrong with the system—or even whether there was something wrong, let alone what would make it right—seemed almost impossible at times. Some critics expressed dismay at skyrocketing campaign

costs, but others said the costs were small when compared with a major corporation's advertising budget or what Americans spent on cosmetics. Others pointed to the unlimited and basically unregulated soft money from corporations, labor unions, and individuals to the political parties, but others welcomed the resulting resurgence of parties as major players in electoral politics.

Critics wanted to regulate advertising they said crossed the line between advocating issues to advocating particular candidates, but others defended the ads as important tools in educating voters. Some condemned the role special interests, particularly political action committees (PACs), played in American politics, but others defended this role as a manifestation of democracy's pluralism. Some called for limits on congressional campaign spending, but others charged that limits would only further entrench incumbents and put challengers at a disadvantage. Some saw public money as the way to eliminate outside influences in politics, but others scoffed at the use of taxpayer money, even in times of budget surpluses. Some criticized independent expenditures for or against candidates, but others saw such spending as part of their First Amendment right to free speech.

Beyond specific policy disagreements was the less tangible love-hate relationship some politicians had with the system. A presidential candidate might call for a ban on soft money, while at the same time benefiting from an elaborate advertising campaign paid for with party soft money. Members of Congress were being asked to vote to change a system that returned the vast majority of them to the halls of Congress election after election. As Senator Robert

Public Funds in Presidential Campaigns, 1976–2004

	Primary Matching Funds	Convention	General Election Campaign
1976	$24,789,566	$4,149,630	$43,640,000
1980	$31,343,128	$8,832,000	$63,122,304
1984	$36,519,405	$16,160,000	$80,800,000
1988	$67,547,821	$18,440,000	$92,200,000
1992	$42,862,123	$22,096,000	$110,480,000
1996	$58,538,356	$24,728,000	$152,695,400
2000	$62,261,374	$29,546,690	$147,733,452
2004	$28,375,506	$29,848,000	$149,240,000

Source: Federal Election Commission
Overall, spending in presidential election campaigns tends to continue to grow, even as campaign finance reforms are put in place.

C. Byrd, a Democrat from West Virginia, once explained:

> **W**e are afraid to let go of the slick ads and the high-priced consultants, afraid to let go of the PAC money and the polls, unsure that we want to change the rules of the game that we all understand and know so well.

Uncertainties in Change

Campaign finance reformers faced the enormous task of proposing legislation that would bridge the differences between Democrats and Republicans, representatives and senators, incumbents and challengers. Politicians were apprehensive of the unknowns that surrounded change—how each party would adapt to it and whether it might give the opposing party an advantage.

Their caution was well-founded. It was difficult to calculate all the ramifications of the many reform proposals on the table at any one time. As political scientist Frank J. Sorauf described it:

Available money seeks an outlet, and if some outlets are narrowed or closed off, money flows with increased pressure to the outlets still open. It is the law that systems of campaign finance share with hydraulic systems.

There have been many examples of changes with unanticipated results. Congressional attempts to curtail the influence of wealthy donors in the wake of the 1970s Watergate scandal resulted in more stringent limits on individual contributions than on political committees. This made contributions through PACs much more attractive to some givers and in turn became a significant factor in the rise of PACs.

Section 527 of the tax code—written in the wake of the Watergate scandal to set tax rules for political groups—contained a loophole allowing a new breed of political organizations to avoid disclosing their campaign spending, until Congress changed the law in 2000.

The dramatic growth of soft money was another example of a development no one had expected. Soft money was the unlimited, largely unregulated money contributed primarily to political parties for activities and expenses not directly related to specific federal elections. It was called "soft" to distinguish it from the "hard money" that was used for federal election campaigns and regulated by the Federal Election Campaign Act (FECA)—money that was "hard" to raise because of the FECA's limits and restrictions. Corporations and labor unions had been prohibited from participating directly in federal elections for a good part of the twentieth century. Individuals were subject to contribution limits beginning in the 1970s. Soft money, however, opened a whole new outlet for contributing to the parties or spending on nonfederal activities.

In the 1970s, the Federal Election Commission (FEC), the independent agency charged with overseeing the federal election laws, relaxed some of the rules covering the separation of federal campaign funds from state and local parties' nonfederal money. The FEC allowed the state and local parties for the first time to use

C-D

A - Z

nonfederal soft money to pay for a portion of their administrative expenses, as well as voter drives and generic party activities, even if they had an indirect effect on federal campaigns. Congress then passed legislation to encourage greater participation of these parties in presidential election campaigns, allowing them to spend unlimited amounts of hard money on things such as voter drives and campaign materials.

The combination of these actions by the FEC and Congress triggered the surge in soft money. Once the national parties determined that they, too, could use soft money for certain expenses, they began raising millions of dollars for their nonfederal accounts. Soon the money was being spent, not only for get-out-the-vote drives, but also for major advertising campaigns said to promote party issues, not candidates. Being able to use soft money for certain party expenses had the added advantage of freeing up more hard dollars for direct aid to federal candidates, further fueling the upward spiral of campaign spending.

The parties' enthusiasm for soft money in the 1996 election campaign helped produce the most significant campaign finance scandal since the Watergate scandal.

1996 Scandal

Public attention was drawn to the flaws of the campaign finance system by actions taken during the 1996 presidential election campaign. At the root of the scandal were allegations that foreign money—particularly Chinese—had made it into the campaign in violation of federal law and that the parties' pursuit and use of soft money may have crossed the line into illegal activity.

The early focus was on the Democrats. As the scandal unfolded, it was revealed that the Democratic National Committee (DNC) had unwittingly accepted nearly $3 million in illegal or suspect contributions, money the DNC said it would return. The fund-raising tactics of President Bill Clinton and Vice President Al Gore were also questioned. For example, the news media provided accounts of the Clintons entertaining large donors at private White

House coffees and inviting some contributors for overnight stays in the Lincoln bedroom or to go along on government foreign trade missions.

The Republican-led Congress launched investigations in both chambers. However, Senate Governmental Affairs Committee investigators in 1997 came up with no proof of allegations that the Chinese government had conspired to influence U.S. elections through large campaign contributions. They also determined that the White House had not knowingly accepted illegal foreign contributions or that the Clinton administration had ever changed policy in exchange for campaign contributions. Also, Democrats revealed that a Republican National Committee (RNC) think tank, the National Policy Forum, had also accepted foreign money that may have been passed on to the RNC. A parallel campaign finance investigation was conducted by the House Government Reform and Oversight Committee.

Dissatisfaction

The 1996 scandal did little to improve public confidence in the system. Although campaign finance was not high on their list of priorities Washington should attend to, people still registered a deep scorn for the system.

A 1997 public opinion survey found that a majority (57 percent) of Americans were dissatisfied with the state of the political system and that the role of money was one of the main sources of that discontent. About two-thirds of those polled cited as major problems the influence of political contributions on elections and government policy. They also cited the conflict of interest created when elected officials solicited or took contributions while making policy decisions. Majorities also said that elected officials spent too much time fund-raising and that the high cost of campaigns discouraged good people from running for office.

Similarly, a Gallup poll in January 2001 found that 56 percent of Americans were dissatisfied with the country's campaign finance laws and another poll in March 2001 showed that Americans, by a margin of 76 percent to 19 percent, favored new laws limiting contributions by individuals or groups to the political parties.

Reform Efforts

Campaign finance reformers have sought to curb campaign spending by limiting and regulating campaign expenditures and donations made to candidates. They have also sought to inform voters of the amounts and sources of the donations, and the amounts, purposes, and recipients of the expenditures. Disclosure was intended to reveal which candidates, if any, were unduly indebted to interest groups in time to forewarn the voters.

The June 1972 break-in at Democratic national headquarters in Washington's Watergate office building touched off a scandal that became the 1970s code word for governmental corruption. Although the scandal had many aspects, money in politics was at its roots. Included among the Watergate scandal's misdeeds were specific violations of campaign spending laws, violations of other criminal laws because of virtually unlimited campaign contributions, and still other instances where the use of campaign funds suggested influence peddling.

Congress had begun to move on campaign finance even before Watergate. Less than six months before the break-in, Congress had adopted two pieces of legislation containing some of the ground rules under which elections were being conducted. By mid-2001 these ground rules were still operative and highly significant. First, Congress approved legislation allowing a one-dollar tax checkoff to finance presidential campaigns. (The amount was increased to three dollars by 1993 legislation.) Congress also passed the Federal Election Campaign Act (FECA). This law required disclosure of campaign contributions and expenditures by candidates for federal office and placed a limit on the amount of money candidates could spend on media advertising. (The media spending limits were repealed in 1974.) The 1971 FECA, however, ultimately had a limited impact on controlling campaign spending.

The Watergate scandal focused public attention on campaign spending at all levels of government and produced a mood in Congress that even the most reluctant legislators found diffi-

cult to resist. In the aftermath came the most significant overhaul in campaign finance legislation in the nation's history. Major legislation enacted in 1974 and 1976, coming on the heels of the 1971 legislation, radically altered the system of financing federal elections.

The FECA Amendments of 1974 set limits on contributions and expenditures for congressional and presidential elections. It also established the FEC and created the framework for providing presidential candidates with public financing.

Before the sweeping 1974 act received its first real test, it was extensively trimmed by the Supreme Court. The Court in its 1976 decision in *Buckley v. Valeo* upheld the FECA's disclosure requirements, contribution limitations, and public financing of presidential elections. It struck down spending limits for congressional and presidential races, including restraints on the use of a candidate's personal assets, except for presidential candidates who accepted public financing. It also struck down limits on independent expenditures, which were expenditures made in support of or opposition to a candidate but without the knowledge or cooperation of the candidate.

Many later efforts to change the campaign finance system were driven by the desire to find a way to limit congressional campaign spending without violating the mandates of the Court decision. With the ceilings on expenditures removed, campaign costs grew quickly and candidates became increasingly dependent on raising money in what was then the easiest and most cost-effective way—from PACs.

In striking down restraints on independent expenditures, the Supreme Court opened the door for individuals and PACs to spend millions of dollars independently. These campaign contributors were generally derided by candidates and party leaders as unwelcome "loose cannons" in the political process. Sharply negative ads underwritten by **ideological PACs** earned the anger of both parties.

In 1979, Congress amended the FECA, in part to encourage more grassroots and political party activity in federal campaigns. Included in the package of amendments was the section all-

C-D

A–Z

owing state and local parties to underwrite voter drives in behalf of presidential tickets without regard to financial limits.

Throughout the late 1970s reformers sought to extend public financing to congressional races, but their efforts failed. A bill to limit the role of PACs was passed by the House in 1979 but blocked by the threat of a filibuster in the Senate.

Later Scandals

After the 1970s, Congress proved less amenable to further major changes in campaign financing. Proposals were debated, but it would be a decade before either chamber passed a major campaign finance bill. And once again it would be scandals that provided the impetus.

In 1989, claims of ethical violations and questionable financial dealings involving Speaker of the House Jim Wright (1987–1989), a Democrat from Texas, increased pressures on House Democrats to act on campaign finance legislation. Wright, facing charges that would eventually lead to his resignation from Congress, embraced campaign finance reform and created a bipartisan task force to develop a reform plan.

Further pressure for change came the following year after the Keating Five scandal, so named for five senators suspected of doing favors for a wealthy campaign contributor, Charles H. Keating, Jr. At the heart of the scandal was $1.5 million in contributions made or solicited by Keating, the powerful owner of a savings and loan and real estate empire, to support the campaigns or other political causes of the five senators.

Both chambers passed bills in 1990, over Republican objections, but action came late in the session and the bills died when Congress adjourned and went home for the elections. The House and Senate again passed bills in 1991. There were vast differences between the two versions and compromise seemed unlikely. However, this time, scandals at the House bank and post office sent Democratic leaders on a reform mission and reignited the campaign finance issue. Conferees reconciled differences in 1992 by let-

ting each chamber live by its own rules. But President George Bush (1989–1993) objected to that approach, along with the bill's spending limits and public funding provisions, and vetoed the bill.

Reformers' hopes were high when President William Clinton (1993–2001) came into the White House vowing to overhaul the system. Both chambers approved radically different bills in 1993, but the Democrats did not work out a compromise until late the next year.

Many expected that the scandal surrounding the 1996 election would renew fervor for reform. And it did, but not enough to lead to enactment of a new law. The House passed a bill in 1998, but the Senate bill was again blocked by a GOP filibuster. The same thing happened in the next Congress.

After more than twenty years, a new campaign finance-related law was finally enacted in 2000. The statute required a group of political organizations, named "527s" in a section of the tax code, to disclose their previously secret finances. It was a small but highly controversial part of campaign finance.

The passage of the 2002 Bipartisan Campaign Reform Act, also known as the McCain-Feingold Act, prohibited political parties from raising or spending soft money. Before the law's passage, soft money could be used for a variety of activities, including "issue advertising," which included any ad that did not specifically endorse or call for the defeat of a candidate. Because the cost of these ads was not paid for by a candidate, there were no limits. Although the law limits party activities, other organizations may still use soft money.

See also: Buckley v. Valeo (1976); Political Action Committees (PACs); Watergate.

Further Reading

Ackerman, Bruce, and Ian Ayres. *Voting with Dollars.* New Haven, CT: Yale University Press, 2004.

Malbin, Michael. *The Election After Reform: Money, Politics, and the Bipartisan Campaign Reform Act.* Lanham, MD: Rowman and Littlefield Publishing Group, 2006.

Samples, John. *The Fallacy of Campaign Finance Reform.* Chicago: University of Chicago Press, 2006.

Campaigning

See Campaign Finance.

Caucus System

The process by which presidential candidates were selected in the early years of the Republic, especially before the emergence of strong political parties. The Constitution did not provide a

C-D

A-Z

VIEWPOINTS

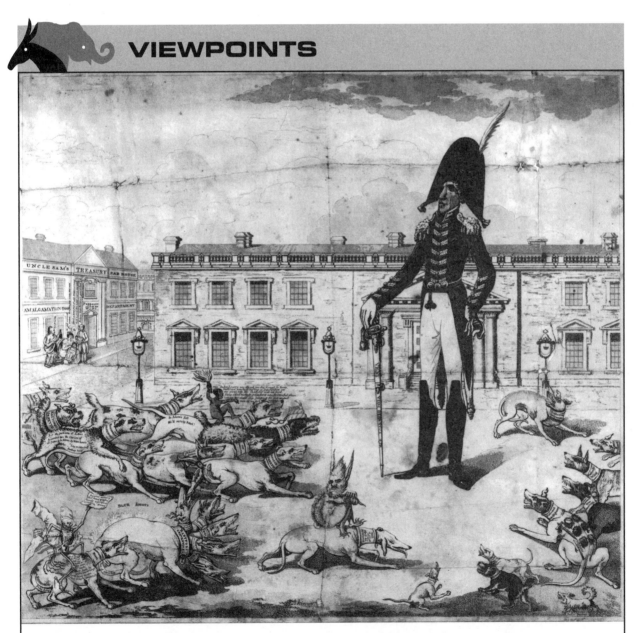

A political cartoon from 1824 criticizes the treatment of presidential candidate Andrew Jackson by the press; the snarling dogs are labeled with the names of hostile newspapers. (Library of Congress)

method of selecting presidential candidates. Thus, few if any rules guided the selections of early nominees. In 1804, the Twelfth Amendment required each elector to vote for a presidential and a vice-presidential candidate. Beginning at about this time, and lasting until about 1829, the congressional leaders of the Federalist and Democratic-Republican parties usually selected the party's nominees. The term *King Caucus* stems from this period of time because of the power of the congressional caucuses.

The dominance of the Democratic-Republican Party and the decline of the Federalists led to factional politics and unsettled rules for selecting candidates. During the 1820s the caucus system came to be viewed as undemocratic. In September 1831, the Anti-Mason Party held the first national nominating convention in Baltimore. In 1832, the Democratic Party held its first nominating convention, also in Baltimore, renominating President Andrew Jackson. The Democrats have held a national convention every four years since that date. Today's Republican Party held its first nominating convention in Philadelphia in 1856, nominating John C. Fremont as its presidential nominee. The Republicans, too, have held a nominating convention every four years since 1856.

See also: Democratic Party (1828–); Nominating Conventions; Republican Party (1854–); 📖 Twelfth Amendment, 1804 in the **Primary Source Library**.

Census

The count of the United States population that takes place every ten years, for the purpose of representation in the House of Representatives. Article 1, Section 2, states:

> **R**epresentatives . . . shall be apportioned among the several States which may be included within this Union, according to their respective Numbers, which shall be determined by adding

to the whole Number of free Persons, including those bound to Service for a Term of Years, and excluding Indians not taxed, three fifths of all other Persons. The actual Enumeration shall be made within three Years after the first Meeting of the Congress of the United States, and within every subsequent Term of ten Years, in such Manner as they shall by Law direct.

Since the first census in 1790, it has served as the basis for reapportioning the seats of the House of Representatives every ten years—except after the 1920 census. For the first time, urban residents outnumbered rural residents. Rural and farm interests, now being a minority, prevented any legislation that would shift power to urban congressional districts.

In 1902, Congress made the Census Bureau a permanent institution with the Department of Commerce.

Illegal Aliens

Members of Congress and other public officials also have taken a strong interest in the traditional inclusion of illegal aliens in the census. Some complain that the Census Bureau's effort to count all people living in the United States has unfair political ramifications.

The Fourteenth Amendment states that

> . . .**r**epresentatives shall be apportioned among the several states according to their respective numbers, counting the whole number of persons in each state, excluding Indians not taxed.

The Census Bureau has never attempted to exclude illegal aliens from the census—a policy troubling to states that fear losing House seats and influence to states with large numbers of illegal aliens.

The Census Bureau does not have a method for excluding illegal aliens, although it has studied some alternatives. Some supporters of the current policy say that any questions used to separate out illegal aliens could discourage others from responding, thus undermining the accuracy of the census.

Overseas Personnel

For the 1990 census the Commerce Department reversed a long-standing policy and counted military personnel and dependents stationed overseas. "Historically we have not included them because the census is based on the concept of usual residence," said Charles Jones, associate director of the Census Bureau. "People overseas have a 'usual residence' overseas." An exception was made once in 1970 during the Vietnam War. This policy was continued in the 2000 census. For the purposes of reapportionment, overseas personnel were assigned to the state each individual considered home.

See also: Reapportionment and Redistricting.

Checks and Balances

See Constitution of the United States; Constitutional Convention.

Chisholm, Shirley

See African Americans in Congress.

Clinton, Hillary Rodham

See Election of 1992; Election of 1996.

Communist Party (1919–)

A far-left political party in the United States formed shortly after the Russian Revolution. In 1919, Soviet communists encouraged American left-wing groups to withdraw from the So-

cialist Party and to form a communist party in the United States. The party arose at that time as part of the social and economic turmoil that followed World War I and the Bolshevik Revolution in Russia. Two organizations emerged from the American Socialist Party: the larger Communist Party of America and the Communist Labor Party. Both were aggressively prosecuted by the U.S. government in the early 1920s, causing a drop in their already small membership and forcing them underground.

By the mid-1920s, the Communist Party of the USA was formed to implant the revolutionary aims of the Soviet Union in America. In 1924, William Z. Foster, a labor organizer, was the party's first presidential candidate. The party ran national presidential tickets through 1940 and from 1968 through 1984, but the party's peak year at the polls was 1932, when Foster received 103,253 votes, or 0.3 percent of the popular vote.

The Communists have a unique place in American political history as the only party to have been part of an international movement. In 1929, the party organized as the Communist Party of the United States, with acknowledged status as a part of the worldwide communist movement.

In 1944, however, the party's leader in the United States, Earl Browder, dissolved the party and committed the movement to operate within the two-party system. In the 1944 campaign the Communists endorsed President Franklin D. Roosevelt, who rejected their support.

However, with the break up of the U.S.-Soviet alliance after World War II, the Communists reorganized themselves as a political party. They supported Henry Wallace's Progressive Party in 1948. During the cold war era of the 1950s, the party was severely restricted by federal and state laws that virtually outlawed it. As restrictions eased, the Communist Party resumed its activities in the late 1960s. In a policy statement written in 1966, the party described itself as "a revolutionary party whose aim is the fundamental transformation of society."

The party's success at the polls, however, continued to be minimal. Its presidential candidates in 1968, 1972, 1976, 1980, and 1984—the

C-D

A–Z

C-D

A-Z

Gus Hall was a leader of the Communist Party and ran as the party's presidential candidate four times–1972, 1976, 1980, and 1984. He failed to win any electoral votes. (Bettmann/Corbis)

last year that they appeared on the ballot—each received less than one-tenth of 1 percent of the vote.

See also: Third Parties.

Conservative Party (1962–)

A political party, based in New York, which considers other parties too liberal. In 1962, the New York State Conservative Party was organized under the direction of J. Daniel Mahoney, a New York attorney, and his brother-in-law, Kieran O'-

Doherty. They were motivated by the belief that real political alternatives were no longer being offered to the state's voters. They saw the three dominant parties in the state—the Liberal Party, the Democratic Party, and the Republican Party under Gov. Nelson A. Rockefeller and Sen. Jacob K. Javits—as offering a liberal agenda.

Political experts predicted the early demise of the party, especially after Barry Goldwater's overwhelming defeat in the 1964 presidential elections. However the party continued to grow. In 1965, the nationally known columnist William F. Buckley ran for mayor of New York City as a Conservative, generating national publicity for the party. One year later, the Conservative candidate for governor, Professor Paul Adams, outpolled Liberal Party candidate Franklin D. Roosevelt Jr. enabling the Conservative Party to obtain Row C of the ballot. This Conservative victory was important because, in New York, a party's position on the ballot is determined by the number of votes cast for its candidate for governor. Thus, appearing in Row C is significant because the higher the row, the more notice voters are likely to take of the party's candidates. In 1970, James Buckley was elected to the U.S. Senate on Row C alone. From the mid-1970s onward, no statewide Republican candidate gained office without the Conservative Party's endorsement.

Although the Conservative Party suffered some setbacks, such as the loss of Row C to the Reform Party in 1996 and the defection of some supporters to the Right to Life Party, it remains a major force in New York State politics. The Conservative Party has opposed abortion since it became a political issue; nonetheless, the party has occasionally backed pro-choice candidates whose conservative credentials were otherwise satisfactory.

Even though some members of the Conservative Party are Protestant fundamentalists, the plurality of its membership and much of its leadership are traditional Roman Catholics. The rise of the party has mirrored the rise of the conservative movement in the United States— from Goldwater's capture of the 1964 Republican nomination to Ronald Reagan's electoral triumphs in 1980 and 1984. In addition, the party has successfully fought the image of extremism while generally remaining true to its core principles: tax limitation, education reform, and tough anticrime policies.

See also: Election of 1964, Election of 1980, Election of 1984.

Constitution of the United States

The governing document of the United States since 1788. Crafted in Philadelphia during the summer of 1787 by fifty-five delegates representing twelve of the thirteen states, the Constitution of the United States created a strong federal government. The convention delegates completed their work on September 17, 1787. The Constitution went into effect on June 21, 1788, after ratification by New Hampshire, the ninth state to do so.

Among the Constitution's key features are three branches of government—legislative, executive, and judicial—each with unique as well as overlapping powers, thus creating a separation of powers as well as a system of checks and balances. The Constitution further divides the legislative branch into two houses: the House of Representatives and the Senate. Both houses of the legislature must pass identical versions of a bill before it can be sent to the president for approval or veto. All appropriations bills, however, must originate in the House.

Electoral Rules for Congress

The new Constitution set forth specific methods for selecting members of the new government. Members of the lower house of Congress, the House of Representatives, were to be elected directly by the people of each state. Senators—two from each state—were to be chosen by the state legislatures. The Framers were concerned about placing too much power in the hands of the common peo-

ple. The Seventeenth Amendment, however, ratified in 1913, provided for direct popular election of senators.

Electoral Rules for the Presidency

After much disagreement, the Framers finally decided that the president would be elected indirectly by an electoral college. In the early years of the Republic, state legislatures often selected the members of the Electoral College who cast two votes. According to the Constitution, the person who received the most votes became president and the runner-up became vice president. Later, as political parties developed and with the ratification of the Twelfth Amendment in 1804, each state would choose electors, who would in turn cast two ballots: one for president and one for vice president. If no candidate received a majority of the electoral vote, the House of Representatives elected the president from the top three vote getters. If no vice-presidential candidate received a majority of the electoral votes, the Senate selected the vice president from the top two candidates.

See also: Bill of Rights; Constitutional Convention; Separation of Powers; Thirteenth Amendment; Twelfth Amendment; 📖 Twelfth Amendment in the **Primary Source Library.**

Constitutional Convention

Held in the summer of 1787, the assembly of delegates from twelve of the thirteen states, which created the present plan of government of the United States. Philadelphia, Pennsylvania, was the site of the Constitutional Convention. Philadelphia was by far the largest American city, with a population of around 45,000. One reason Philadelphia was chosen as the convention's site was its central location.

One of Philadelphia's least-appealing qualities, however, was its notoriously hot, humid,

C-D

A–Z

C-D

A-Z

and insect-ridden summers. The summer of 1787, especially after a heat wave struck on June 11, was no exception. The city sweltered for almost the entire time of the Constitutional Convention. The delegates found that although closed windows made the heat even more stifling, open windows were invitations to Philadelphia's infamous black flies during the day and its mosquitoes at night.

Delegates

About sixty to seventy-five delegates were selected by the various states to represent them at the convention in Philadelphia; of these, fifty-five actually attended. The fifty-five delegates were generally united in their belief that a stronger national government was vital to the new American nation. In part, this was because many of them had shared similar experiences. Forty-two were current or former members of Congress; twenty-one had fought in the Revolutionary War (1775–1783); eight had signed the Declaration of Independence (1776).

Other shared characteristics contributed to the delegates' common outlook on many issues. Almost all were prosperous—around half were lawyers and another quarter owned plantations or large farms. Only two delegates were small farmers, who made up 85 percent of the nation's white population. All had held public office; indeed, more than forty currently occupied positions in their state governments, including ten judges, thirty legislators, and three governors. Several had helped to write their state constitutions. All were well known in their states; about one-fourth had national reputations.

All of the delegates to the convention were white men. All but the two Roman Catholics were Protestant Christians. Twenty-six had attended college, at a time when a college education was rigorous and rare.

Collectively, the convention was young. Later called the "Father of the Constitution," James Madison, at thirty-six, was older than eleven other delegates, including several who were to play significant roles at the convention, such as

Gouverneur Morris of Pennsylvania (thirty-five) and Edmund Randolph of Virginia (thirty-three). The youngest delegate, Jonathan Dayton of New Jersey, was twenty-six. The average age of the delegates—even counting Benjamin Franklin, age eighty-one—was forty-three.

The Virginia Plan

The Virginia Plan, introduced on May 29 by Governor Edmund Randolph but written mainly by Madison, offered a radical departure from the weak, one-branch government of the Articles of Confederation. The plan proposed to create a three-branch national government.

According to the Virginia Plan, the heart of the national government would be a **bicameral** legislature, with the lower house apportioned according to population and its members selected by the people and the upper house elected by the lower house. The legislature's powers would include broad authority to pass laws, to conduct foreign policy, and to appoint most government officials, including judges.

A national judiciary, organized into one or more "supreme tribunals" and various "inferior tribunals" and appointed (with life tenure) by the legislature, would form a second branch.

The government also would have an executive branch, although it was vaguely defined in the Virginia Plan. The "national executive" (the plan left unresolved the question of whether this would be a person or a group) was "to be chosen by the National Legislature for a term of ___ years." The delegates' response to the Virginia Plan was remarkably calm, especially considering the radical departure in the direction of a strong national government that the plan proposed.

New Jersey Plan

One part of the Virginia Plan was especially controversial: the provision that both houses of the national legislature be apportioned according to population. Delegates from the states that thought of themselves as large (specifically, those from Virginia, Massachusetts, Pennsylvania, and the three states whose populations were growing most rapidly—Georgia, North Carolina, and South Carolina) favored the idea. They split sharply with the delegates from the small states who feared that their citizens would be outnumbered in the legislature. Thus, the small states favored the arrangement as in the Articles of Confederation: equal representation in Congress for each state. A compromise plan, proposed by Roger Sherman of Connecticut on June 11, 1787, would have apportioned the lower house of the legislature according to population and the upper house based on one state, one vote, but few delegates were ready yet for compromise. Instead, small states responded to the Virginia Plan with a counterproposal of their own that was introduced on June 15, 1787, by William Paterson of New Jersey.

The New Jersey Plan was essentially a series of amendments to the Articles of Confederation, rather than a new constitution. It proposed to add two new branches to the one-branch national government—a plural, or committee-style, executive, to be elected by Congress for a single term and a supreme court, with its judges appointed by the executive for lifetime terms. The plan also would declare national laws and treaties to be "the supreme law of the respective States" and would authorize the executive to use force if necessary to implement them. In addition, Congress would be empowered to regulate interstate and international commerce and to impose taxes. The main purpose of the New Jersey Plan, however, was an unstated one: to preserve the structure of Congress under the Articles—a single house in which each state, regardless of size, would cast one vote.

Convention Debate

On June 20, 1787, with Virginian George Washington as president of the convention, the delegates began their clause-by-clause evaluation of the plans of government. More than any other issue, legislative apportionment consumed the convention's time and attention during five weeks of debate. Delegates from the small states pressed for equal representation of the

states in Congress. The large state delegates were equally unyielding in their insistence on representation according to population.

A special committee, with members from every state, was appointed on July 2 to propose a compromise. On July 5, after a break to celebrate Independence Day, the committee recommended a compromise plan. The upper house would have equal representation from each state. The lower house would be apportioned according to population (with each slave counted as three-fifths of a person).

For more than a week, the delegates engaged in a complex and sometimes bitter debate over the proposal. On July 16, the convention voted narrowly to approve the main points of the compromise proposal, sometimes called the Connecticut Compromise in honor of its original author, Roger Sherman.

Committee of Detail

On July 24, 1787, the convention voted to appoint a Committee of Detail to review all of its actions and draft a plan of government. The five-member committee included representatives of the three main regions of the country: Nathaniel Gorham of Massachusetts and Oliver Ellsworth of Connecticut from New England, James Wilson of Pennsylvania from the middle states, and Edmund Randolph of Virginia and John Rutledge of South Carolina from the South. The committee worked while the rest of the convention adjourned until August 6.

Most of the memorable terms and phrases in the Constitution were written by the Committee of Detail, including "state of the Union" and "We the People." Institutions were named: the executive became the "president"; the national tribunal, the "Supreme Court"; and the legislature, "Congress," with its upper house called the "Senate" and the lower house the "House of Representatives."

Perhaps the most important decision of the Committee of Detail was to transform general grants of power into specific ones. What had been Congress's broad authority "to legislate in all cases for the general interests of the Union" became instead a list of eighteen enumerated

C-D

A - Z

powers. The powers included the power to "lay and collect taxes," regulate interstate commerce, establish post offices, make war, elect a national treasurer, and set up inferior courts, concluding in a sweeping grant "to make all laws that shall be necessary and proper for carrying into execution" these and "all other powers vested" in the government. The states were forbidden certain powers—notably, to make treaties with other nations, to print money, and to tax imports.

Convention Debate

As they had with the Virginia Plan and the New Jersey Plan, the delegates reviewed the draft constitution that was proposed by the Committee of Detail clause by clause. Much of the draft was approved. Some parts, however, were modified and the delegates tinkered with several provisions of the Committee of Detail's draft.

- Congress's power to "make war" was judged too sweeping to protect the national security during times when Congress was out of session. It was revised to read: "declare war."

- Congress was forbidden to pass **ex post facto laws**—that is, retroactive criminal laws—and **bills of attainder**—laws that declare a person guilty of a crime without a trial.

- Congress was empowered to call forth the militia of any state "to execute the laws of the Union, suppress insurrections, and repel invasions."

- A procedure was created to amend the Constitution: "on the application of the legislatures of two-thirds of the states in the Union for an amendment of this Constitution, the legislature of the United States shall call a convention for that purpose."

- Religious tests were prohibited as a requirement for holding office.

- The Committee of Detail had proposed that the new constitution take effect when ratified by a certain number of state conventions (not state legislatures), but had left the number unspecified. The delegates now voted to set it at nine.

Controversies

Some sections of the Committee of Detail's draft became matters of serious controversy. The draft constitution's stand on slavery came under attack from several northern delegates, both the three-fifths rule for counting slaves as part of the population and the provision against laws banning the importation of new slaves. Much of the North's concern derived from fear of slave rebellions, which might attract foreign invaders and, in any event, probably would require northern arms and money to be subdued. Southern delegates not only defended the provisions protecting slavery, but also insisted that their states would not ratify any constitution that placed slavery in jeopardy.

As it had with the large state–small state controversy, the convention appointed a special committee on August 22, 1787, to seek a compromise solution. Two days later, the committee proposed that Congress be authorized, if it so decided, to end the importation of slaves after 1800. In the meantime, Congress could tax imported slaves at a rate no higher than ten dollars each. (A euphemism—not "slaves" but "such Persons"—was used in the Constitution.) General Charles C. Pinckney persuaded the convention to change 1800 to 1808. The committee's recommendation, as amended, was passed.

Controversies over two other matters caused the convention to bog down: the powers of the Senate (which delegates from the large states wanted to minimize and delegates from the small states wanted to maximize) and a cluster of issues regarding presidential selection. On August 31, nearing the end of its labors, the convention appointed a Committee on Postponed Matters, with a member from each state delegation, to resolve these vexing issues.

Committee on Postponed Matters

Beginning on September 4, 1787, the Committee on Postponed Matters, chaired by David Brearley of New Jersey, made several recommendations concerning the presidency. The committee proposed a term of four years rather than seven, with no restriction on the president's eligibility for reelection. The president was to be chosen by an electoral college, not by Congress. To make up the electoral college, each state would be assigned the right to select, by whatever means it chose, electors equal in number to its representatives and senators in Congress. The candidate who received the greatest number of electoral votes would become president. The candidate who finished second would become vice president. (This was the first mention of the vice presidency at the convention.) If no candidate received a majority, the Senate would select a president and vice president from among the five candidates who had received the greatest number of electoral votes.

In addition to its proposal for an electoral college, the committee recommended that certain responsibilities be assigned to the vice president—namely, to preside over the Senate, with the right to cast tie-breaking votes, and to act as president if the office became vacant before the expiration of the president's term. Finally, the committee recommended that qualifications for president be stated in the Constitution. The president would have to be at least thirty-five years old, a natural born citizen of the United States or a citizen at the time of the Constitution's enactment, and a resident of the United States for at least fourteen years.

For several days, the delegates gave critical scrutiny to the committee's complex proposal for presidential selection. On September 7, they passed it after making only one substantial change: the House of Representatives, rather than the Senate, would choose the president in the event of an electoral college deadlock, with each state delegation casting one vote. The Senate still would choose the vice president if the electoral college failed to produce a winner.

Having approved the electoral college, the convention quickly took other actions. The president was granted the authority to make treaties and to appoint ambassadors, public ministers, consuls, Supreme Court justices, federal judges,

and all other officers whose appointments were not otherwise provided for. Senate confirmation was made a requirement for all of these appointments and a two-thirds vote by the Senate was stipulated to ratify treaties.

On September 8, the convention approved two final proposals of the Committee on Postponed Matters. The president was to be impeached by the House and, on grounds of "treason or bribery or other high crimes and misdemeanors against the United States," removed from office on conviction by the Senate. The delegates added the vice president and other civil officers to the roster of those subject to impeachment but raised the majority needed for Senate conviction from a simple majority to a two-thirds majority. In addition, the House was empowered to originate "all bills for raising revenue."

Having thus completed their work on the Constitution, the delegates ended the day's business on September 8, 1787, by voting to create a five-member Committee of Style to write a polished, final draft for them to sign. Among the committee's members were Gouverneur Morris (who seems to have done most of its work), James Madison, and Alexander Hamilton.

Final Adjustments

Even as the Committee of Style labored, the convention continued to modify its earlier decisions. On September 10, 1787, Madison urged that special constitutional conventions not be a part of the process of amending the Constitution. Instead, he argued, amendments should be initiated by a two-thirds vote of Congress or by two-thirds of the state legislatures, with subsequent approval by three-fourths of the states needed for ratification. The Committee of Style incorporated Madison's idea into its draft.

On September 12, Hugh Williamson of North Carolina successfully moved that the requirement for overriding a president's veto be reduced from a three-fourths vote of each house of Congress to a two-thirds vote. Meanwhile, some delegates expressed fundamental reservations about the Constitution. George Mason of

Virginia joined Elbridge Gerry of Massachusetts in objecting to the absence of a bill of rights.

The committee's draft met with widespread approval from the delegates, but their tinkering continued. A provision was added that the Constitution could not be altered to deprive a state of equal representation in the Senate without the state's consent. At the initiative of Gouverneur Morris and Elbridge Gerry, a compromise procedure for amending the Constitution was created that incorporated both the Committee of Detail's recommendation and Madison's plan. As finally agreed, a constitutional amendment could be proposed by either a two-thirds vote of both houses of Congress or a convention that Congress was required to call if two-thirds of the state legislatures requested one. In either case, three-fourths of the states would have to ratify an amendment for it to become part of the Constitution.

The convention's labors completed, the delegates assembled on September 17, 1787, to sign an **engrossed,** or final, copy of the Constitution. (This is the copy on public display at the National Archives in Washington, D.C.) Forty-one of the original fifty-five delegates still were present at the convention, and all but Edmund Randolph, George Mason, and Elbridge Gerry signed the document.

Later, as the last delegates waited to affix their signatures to the Constitution, Franklin offered an informal benediction. He gestured to Washington's chair and said to those standing nearby:

> **P**ainters have found it difficult to distinguish in their art a rising from a setting sun. I have often in the course of this session . . . looked at that sun behind the President without being able to tell whether it was rising or setting. But now, at length, I have the happiness to know that it is a rising and not a setting sun.

Even later that day, according to an oft-repeated story, someone asked Franklin as he left the hall,

> **W**ell, Doctor, what have we got? A republic or a monarchy? A republic, Franklin replied, if you can keep it.

See also: Constitution of the United States; Bill of Rights; Twelfth Amendment.

Further Reading

Berkin, Carol. *A Brilliant Solution: Inventing the American Constitution.* New York: Harvest Books, 2003.

Bowen, Catherine Drinker. *Miracle at Philadelphia: The Story of the Constitutional Convention.* New York: Back Bay Books, 1986.

Collier, Christopher. *Decision in Philadelphia: The Constitutional Convention of 1787.* New York: Ballantine Books, 2007.

Madison, James, Edward J. Larson, and Michael P. Winship. *The Constitutional Convention: A Narrative from the Notes of James Madison.* New York: Modern Library, 2005.

Constitutional Union Party (1860)

A short-lived political party formed in 1859 to promote national conciliation in the face of sectionalism, or extreme regional interests, and the threat by Southern states to secede from the Union. The Constitutional Union Party appealed to conservative remnants of the American, or Know Nothing, and Whig parties, whose members viewed preservation of the Union as their main goal.

The Constitutional Union Party held its first and only national convention in Baltimore in May 1860. For president, the party nominated John Bell of Tennessee, a former senator and Speaker of the House of Representatives, who previously had been both a Democrat and a Whig. The convention adopted a short platform, which intentionally avoided controversial subjects, most notably the slavery issue. Instead, the platform simply urged sup-

John Bell (b.1797-d.1869), a wealthy Tennessee slaveholder, was the presidential candidate of the Constitutional Union Party in the Election of 1860. The party formed before the outbreak of the Civil War to try to save the Union. Bell won 39 electoral votes. Initially opposing secession, Bell sided with the Confederacy after Fort Sumter, South Carolina, was fired upon on April 12, 1861. (Library of Congress)

port for "the Constitution, the Union and the Laws."

In the 1860 election, Bell received 590,901 votes, or 12.6 percent of the popular vote, and won Kentucky, Tennessee, and Virginia. However, the Bell ticket finished last in the four-way presidential race and, together with the split in the Democratic Party, was a key factor in the victory of Republican Abraham Lincoln.

In the months after the 1860 election, the Constitutional Union Party continued to urge national conciliation, but with the outbreak of the Civil War in 1861, the party disappeared.

See also: Election of 1860; Third Parties.

Conventions

See Nominating Conventions.

Democratic Party (1828–)

The oldest political organization in the United States. Indeed, a history of the Democratic Party is in some ways a political history of the nation. In the first few years of the Republic, political parties did not exist, although factions tied to issues and the ambitions of political leaders influenced elections and policies. The Democratic Party traces its roots to this factionalism, beginning with opposition to the Federalist policies of Alexander Hamilton during George Washington's first term.

Origins of the Democratic Party

Opposition to Federalist policies, organized by Representative James Madison and Secretary of State Thomas Jefferson, first formed around Hamilton's proposal for a national bank, which Congress passed and Washington signed, over the strong objections of Jefferson and Madison. The two Virginians were more successful, however, in preventing the adoption of Hamilton's plan for federal support for the development of American industry. The Federalists, led by Hamilton and John Adams, favored a strong central government and a flexible interpretation of the Constitution. Key to their program was a national bank, which would facilitate economic growth and strengthen national and international commerce.

Jefferson's Democratic-Republicans advocated strict construction of the Constitution and opposed a national bank. Moreover, they favored friendly relations with France, while the Federalists sought to forge friendly diplomatic and commercial relations with Great Britain. Both parties had supporters throughout the country, but the Democratic-Republicans were strongest in the South and among slaveholders, and the Federalists were strongest in New England and among leaders with commercial and manufacturing interests. From the 1790s until the late 1820s various terms—Democratic-Republicans, Jeffersonian Republicans, Jeffersonian Democrats, and National Republicans—were applied to the people and leaders who, opposed to the Federalists, gradually became known as Democrats.

The Democratic-Republicans grew stronger as the Federalists began to fade during the presidency of John Adams. An alliance of southerners and urban northerners helped Jefferson defeat Adams in 1800 and win reelection in 1804. After Jefferson, the presidency went to his friends and allies, James Madison (1809–1817) and James Monroe (1817–1825). By 1820, the Federalist Party had all but disappeared, and James Monroe won reelection with no opposition.

The inherent instability of one-party politics became clear in 1824, as four candidates—Andrew Jackson, John Quincy Adams, William Crawford, and Henry Clay, all claiming to represent the Jeffersonian tradition—ran for president. No candidate received a majority of popular or electoral votes, and the House of Representatives chose John Quincy Adams, although Andrew Jackson had received more popular votes and more electoral votes.

The Jackson Legacy

War of 1812 hero Andrew Jackson defeated John Quincy Adams in 1828 and became the first president to represent the "Democratic Party." The party has maintained that name ever since. Jackson, nominated in 1828 by the Tennessee legislature, led the Democrats into adopting a nominating convention as the method for choosing the party's future candidates. The Democrats held their first national convention in Baltimore, Maryland, in 1832, eight months after the Anti-Masons held the first such convention, also in Baltimore.

From Jackson's election in 1828 through the end of James Buchanan's term in 1861, the Democrats dominated national politics. During this period the Democrats opposed any national bank, high tariffs, and internal improvements. High points of Jackson's presidency included his veto of bills to support internal improvements and to extend the charter of the Second Bank of the United States. Jackson and other Democrats in this period vigorously supported territorial expansion through Indian removal, the annexation of Texas, and, ultimately, the Mexican-American War. Their support for territorial gains followed Jefferson's expansionist policies that led to the purchase of Louisiana from France in 1803. Most Democrats supported the demands of the South between 1828 and 1861 on issues involving slavery. Meanwhile, Jackson's opponents—led by Henry Clay, Daniel Webster, and William Henry Harrison—formed the Whig Party. The Whigs—who favored higher tariffs, a national bank, federally funded internal improvements, and a weak presidency—provided the main opposition to the Democrats until the emergence of the Republican Party in 1854.

Jackson's election ushered in an era known as "Jacksonian Democracy" which stressed political equality—for white men. Jacksonians throughout the country discriminated against free black voters, taking away their voting rights in Pennsylvania, New Jersey, Tennessee, and North Carolina and opposing their voting rights elsewhere. Jackson himself led the movement to force Native Americans out of the states east of the Mississippi River.

Jefferson, already considered the father of the Democratic Party, had been the first president to remove officeholders and replace them with his supporters. Jackson renewed this policy through the **spoils system,** a term that

stemmed from the phrase "to the victors go the spoils." As the party in power during most of the period from 1829 to 1861, the Democrats controlled the growing bureaucracy and rewarded many supporters with patronage jobs.

Jackson's legacy was a Democratic Party that has endured into the twenty-first century. Dominating national politics during the first half of the nineteenth century, the Democrats lost the presidential election only twice—in 1840 and 1848—between 1800 and 1856.

Despite their long-term success, the Democrats barely survived their severest test—over slavery and secession. In 1846, northern Democrats supported the Wilmot Proviso, introduced in the House by Pennsylvania Democrat David Wilmot. The proviso would have prohibited slavery in any territory acquired during the Mexican-American War. Southern Democrats opposed the proviso. In 1848, many antislavery Democrats from New York, Pennsylvania, and New England voted for former president Martin Van Buren who was running on the Free Soil Party ticket. These defections led to the election of the Whig candidate, Zachary Taylor. The Democrats regained the presidency in 1852, but slavery soon splintered the party. In 1856, Democrat Franklin Pierce became the first elected president denied renomination by his own party. He had alienated fellow northerners by signing legislation that allowed slavery into Kansas Territory, which in turn led it to become a battleground between pro- and antislavery forces. Another northerner, James Buchanan, won the nomination but also became a one-term president. By 1860, many northern Democrats, among them Senators Salmon P. Chase of Ohio and Hannibal Hamlin of Maine, had joined the new Republican Party.

At the 1860 convention in Charleston, South Carolina, northern and southern Democrats were divided. Northerners, backing Stephen A. Douglas of Illinois, favored opening all territories to slavery under a system of **popular sovereignty,** in which settlers would decide for themselves whether to permit slavery. Most of the southerners bolted after the convention failed to call for a federal slave code for the territories

C-D

A-Z

C-D

A–Z

and for federal guarantees of slaveholders' rights to take their human property into the territories. The northern delegates nominated Douglas for president and the southern Democrats nominated John C. Breckinridge of Kentucky. Even had the Democrats remained united, it is doubtful they could have prevented the Republican candidate, Abraham Lincoln, from winning an electoral majority, as he swept every free state but New Jersey, which he split with Douglas.

Decline and Resurgence

During the Civil War, northern Democrats remained divided. War Democrats generally supported the war effort and Lincoln's initial goal of bringing the South back into the Union. They objected, however, to Lincoln's emancipation policies, and after 1863 were less enthusiastic about the war or its goals. Throughout the war, by contrast, the Copperhead faction opposed the war effort and sought peace negotiations with the Confederacy.

Democrats came back together after the Civil War, but both their commitment to white supremacy and their image of disloyalty continued. During Reconstruction, Democrats opposed civil rights laws and the Fourteenth and Fifteenth Amendments, which were designed to establish blacks citizenship, recognize blacks' civil rights, and guarantee blacks voting rights. As late as the 1880s, the Democrats were termed the party of "rum, romanism, and rebellion," because of the party's opposition to temperance laws, its support among Irish Catholics, and the fact that much of its support came from former Confederates.

In 1876, the Democratic governor of New York, Samuel J. Tilden, won the popular vote against Republican Rutherford B. Hayes, but Tilden lost the election when a congressional compromise awarded Hayes all the disputed electoral votes of three southern states. Election fraud, intimidation, and outright violence by white southern Democrats prevented thousands of blacks from voting. Had the election been run fairly, it is likely that Hayes would have won outright. As part of the compromise that brought Hayes to the White House, the new

president promised to remove federal troops from the South, ending Reconstruction. The troops' removal led to a gradual loss of African American voting rights in the South, which became solidly Democratic and would remain so until the 1964 presidential election. Despite a virtual lock on all southern electoral votes, the Democrats captured the presidency only twice between 1860 and 1912: Grover Cleveland won in 1884 and 1892.

By the late nineteenth century the Democratic Party's policies had changed somewhat from the antebellum period. Still a "white man's party," it was hostile to African Americans' civil rights and to Chinese immigration. With slavery ended, however, the party no longer favored expansionism. Cleveland refused to annex Hawaii, and some Democrats opposed the Spanish-American War in 1898. Democrats remained hostile to high tariffs, but they split on the issue of an expansive monetary policy; western Democrats favored the free coinage of silver, and eastern Democrats, among them Cleveland, opposed it.

The Republican Party continued to dominate presidential politics for twelve years into the twentieth century. In 1912, the Republicans split when former president Theodore Roosevelt failed in his attempt to gain his party's nomination over the incumbent, William Howard Taft. Roosevelt ran anyway, on the Progressive—or Bull Moose—ticket, winning six states and 4.1 million votes. Roosevelt came in second, and Taft a distant third, but Taft and Roosevelt combined for 1.3 million more popular votes than did the Democrat, Woodrow Wilson. Had the Republicans been united, their candidate—either Roosevelt or Taft—would have won. Divided, they enabled Wilson to carry forty states and the election. Wilson demonstrated the Democrats' hostility to civil rights and racial equality, as he ordered the segregation of all federal facilities in Washington, D.C. He was, however, a progressive reformer on many issues, and favored such innovations as the Federal Reserve System.

Wilson also led the Democrats away from their historic position on foreign policy. In 1917, Wilson, an effort that ultimately failed.

C-D

A - Z

successfully asked Congress for a declaration of war, and he continued his policies after the end of World War I, as he worked to bring the United States into the League of Nations, an effort that ultimately failed. For the next half-century the Democratic Party stood for intervention and international responsibility, while the Republicans retreated into isolationism.

After World War I, the Republicans took back the White House in 1920, kept it in 1924, and won again with Herbert Hoover's 1928 victory over Democrat Alfred E. Smith, the first Roman Catholic presidential nominee. After the stock market crashed in 1929, however, the Great Depression paved the way for a new Democratic dominance in the White House and an even longer one in Congress.

New Deal to Great Society

The 1932 election of Franklin D. Roosevelt made a dramatic and lasting change in American politics. Democrats sang "Happy Days Are Here Again" as they became the majority party and rallied behind FDR's bold New Deal programs. Democrats, long the party of states' rights, became identified with national initiatives on economic and social issues. Once a party opposed to regulation, the Democrats helped create a massive bureaucracy to regulate the economy. Social programs, most notably Social Security, set the stage for the modern nation that provides a social safety net for citizens.

During the Roosevelt years and after, for the first time in its history, the Democratic Party welcomed African American support and even supported some civil rights legislation. President Roosevelt and his successor, Harry S. Truman, issued executive orders to combat some types of racial segregation and discrimination. The New Deal coalition—northern African Americans, southern whites, farmers, labor unionists, intellectuals, and ethnic urban voters—kept Roosevelt and Truman in office for twenty consecutive years, ending in 1953.

As Europe moved toward war in the 1930s, Roosevelt pushed an international agenda, build-

ing on Wilson's legacy. Opposition came from Republican isolationists but, unlike Wilson, FDR was able to bring the nation along with him, and thus the United States took the lead in establishing the United Nations (UN). Truman continued this internationalist policy, first with the Marshall Plan to help Europe recover from World War II and then with the development of NATO and other international defense pacts. In 1950, Truman pushed for UN intervention when North Korea attacked South Korea, and soon the United States was heavily involved in another war in Asia.

In domestic politics, Truman pushed an activist agenda that he called the Fair Deal and called for expanded enforcement of African American civil rights. Running for another term in 1948, he confronted splits within his party from two quarters: the South and the left. Displeased with Truman's civil rights stand, conservative southerners bolted the Democratic Party in 1948 and ran J. Strom Thurmond of South Carolina as the States' Rights Democratic, or Dixiecrat, nominee. Under the Progressive Party banner, Henry A. Wallace also challenged Truman. Thurmond won four states; Wallace took none. Despite the split, Truman defeated Republican Thomas E. Dewey.

After Truman left office in 1953, a Republican, Dwight D. Eisenhower, served the next two terms, but then the Democrats took back the White House in 1960, as John F. Kennedy, the first Roman Catholic president, narrowly defeated Eisenhower's vice president, Richard Nixon. Kennedy's slogan, the New Frontier, mirrored traditional Democratic slogans, such as Wilson's New Freedom, FDR's New Deal, and Truman's Fair Deal. Kennedy continued the Democratic agenda of internationalism, with the Peace Corps and aid to the pro-Western regime in South Vietnam, and of federal support for domestic improvements, with a massive tax cut proposal and federal programs in housing. Kennedy made tentative moves in civil rights, but he went cautiously because of the power of southern whites within his party.

After Kennedy's assassination in 1963, President Lyndon B. Johnson completed much of

Kennedy's New Frontier agenda and called for additional programs in pursuit of the Great Society, including a civil rights program that was termed by some a "Second Reconstruction." Applying all the skills he had learned as Senate majority leader, Johnson pushed through the Civil Rights Act of 1964. Johnson's support for civil rights ended the Solid South as a Democratic stronghold. In 1964, Johnson won in a landslide. Carrying all but five states, he took 61.1 percent of the popular vote, the largest popular victory of any presidential election in U.S. history. The Deep South, however, supported Republican Barry Goldwater, who had opposed the Civil Rights Act of 1964. Johnson's mandate enabled him to win passage of the Voting Rights Act of 1965, further solidifying Democratic support among African Americans while further undermining Democratic power among white southerners.

Johnson expanded U.S. involvement in the unpopular war in Vietnam, thereby splitting the party and prompting his decision not to run for reelection in 1968. Vice President Hubert H. Humphrey, nominated without entering any primaries, faced competition in November from the American Independent candidacy of George C. Wallace, former Democratic governor of Alabama. These divisive factors contributed to Humphrey's narrow defeat by Republican Richard Nixon.

The Democratic Party Since 1968

In the 1970s, the Democrats drastically reformed their delegate-selection and nominating rules, encouraging minority representation, dividing delegations equally between men and women, and awarding delegates to candidates in proportion to their primary votes. The changes enhanced the role of primary elections in the nominating process, leading to more primaries and fewer state caucuses.

The 1972 election was the last privately financed presidential election. Nixon raised $61.4 million versus McGovern's $21.2 million. McGovern, running as a peace candidate with a commitment to massive domestic spending, lost

to Nixon in a landslide. The election-related Watergate scandal, however, drove Nixon from office two years later and brought Vice President Gerald R. Ford to the presidency.

Skillful use of the primaries, as well as Ford's unpopular full pardon of President Nixon for his criminal activities in the Watergate cover-up, helped the relatively unknown Jimmy Carter of Georgia defeat incumbent Ford in 1976. Carter's primary strategy also served him in 1980, surviving a renomination challenge from Senator Edward M. Kennedy, brother of the late president. Nevertheless, Carter's inability to curb inflation or obtain the release of American hostages held in Iran for 444 days doomed him to a one-term presidency and to defeat at the hands of Republican Ronald Reagan.

Although the popular Reagan handily won reelection in 1984, his vice president and successor, George Herbert Walker Bush, fell victim in 1992 to Bill Clinton of Arkansas, as Democrats returned to the White House after twelve Republican years. As a presidential candidate, Clinton addressed economic worries. His advisers reminded campaign workers, "It's the economy, stupid," and the strategy worked. He was the first Democrat to win without taking Texas and, with Al Gore of Tennessee as his running mate, the first president elected on an all-South ticket since 1828. He won 43 percent of the popular vote.

Clinton won as a moderate, declaring, "the era of big government is over." His support came from a modified New Deal coalition that included "Reagan Democrats," union members, women, African Americans, Hispanics, Jews, a majority of Roman Catholics, public sector employees, and intellectuals. Peace and an improved economy soon had the Democratic administration basking in high approval ratings in public opinion polls. Nevertheless, the voters in 1994 broke the Democratic lock on Congress, turning both chambers over to Republican control.

Two years later the electorate opted to continue a divided government, giving Clinton another four-year term in 1996 while leaving

Congress in Republican hands. Although he was the first Democrat elected to a second full term since Franklin Roosevelt, Clinton again won with less than a majority of the popular vote.

Democrats made history several times from 1960 through the end of the century. In 1960, the party ran the nation's first successful Catholic presidential candidate, John F. Kennedy. In 1968, New York voters elected Democrat Shirley Chisholm as the first African American woman member of the House of Representatives, and in 1992 another Democrat, Carol Moseley-Braun of Illinois, became the first African American woman senator. When former vice president Walter F. Mondale chose Geraldine A. Ferraro as his running mate against Reagan in 1984, she became the first woman in American history to run on a major-party ticket. In 1989, L. Douglas Wilder of Virginia became the first African American to be elected state governor. In 2000, the Democratic nominee for president, Vice President Al Gore, chose Senator Joseph Lieberman of Connecticut as his running mate. This was the first time a Jew was on a national ticket. Also in 2000, Hillary Rodham Clinton became the first presidential wife to seek a major elective office, winning a Senate seat from New York.

Nevertheless, the 2000 elections were a major disappointment for Democrats. Gore lost a disputed election to Republican George W. Bush, son of the former president. Moreover, the Republicans retained control of both houses of Congress, although by the narrowest of margins.

The 2000 and 2004 presidential elections reasserted trends of recent years. In the South, the Republicans reasserted their strength. The Democrats' strength was on the west and east coasts, north of Virginia, and in the industrial heartland of the upper Midwest. The Republicans dominated everywhere else—a giant "L"-shaped area from the South through the Plains states and Southwest and into the Mountain states.

See also: Election of 1876; Election of 1972; Election of 1980; Election of 2000; Political

Parties, Development and Role of; Republican Party; Whig Party.

Further Reading

Schislinger, Galbraith. *Of the People: The 200 Year History of the Democratic Party.* North York, ON: Stoddart, 1992.

Political Party Identification: Yearly Averages

	Repub-lican	Demo-crat	Independent/ Other
1987	29	34	37
1989	33	33	34
1990	31	33	36
1991	31	32	37
1992	28	33	39
1993	27	34	39
1994	30	32	38
1995	32	30	38
1996	29	33	38
1997	28	33	39
1998	28	33	39
1999	27	33	40
2000	28	33	39
2001	29	34	37
2002	30	31	39
2003	30	31	39
2004	29	33	38
2005	33	33	34
2006	34	31	35
2007	34	28	38
2008	36	28	36

The strength of the Republican and Democratic parties varies from year to year. Both domestic and foreign policy issues affect voters' preferences.

Wagner, Heather Lehr. *The History of the Demo-cratic Party.* New York: Chelsea House Publications, 2007.

Witcover, Jules. *Party of the People: A History of the Democrats.* New York: Random House, 2003.

C-D

A – Z

Democratic-Republican Party (1792–1828)

A political party that developed in the 1790s in opposition to the Federalists, one of the first political parties, whose leaders wanted to ratify the Constitution. The Democratic-Republican Party emerged from the Anti-Federalists, those leaders who opposed the ratification of the Constitution. The Democratic-Republican Party was organized as the opposition to the Federalist Party and to the policies of the George Washington administration. The Democratic-Republicans feared the concentration of power in the federal government.

Thomas Jefferson was the leader of the new party, whose members as early as 1792 referred to themselves as Republicans. This remained their primary name throughout the party's history, although in some states they became known as Democratic-Republicans, the label used frequently by historians to avoid confusing Jefferson's party with the later Republican Party, which began in 1854. Party members were called Jeffersonian Republicans as well.

The Democratic-Republicans favored states' rights, a strict interpretation of the Constitution, and expanded democracy through extension of suffrage to white males. Rural interests dominated the party. Wealthy plantation owners and farmers were determined to maintain their dominance over the growing commercial and industrial power of the Northeast. The principal strength of the party came from states in the South and Middle Atlantic.

The Democratic-Republicans gained control of the federal government in 1800, when Jefferson was elected president and the party won majorities in both houses of Congress. For the next twenty-four years, the party controlled both the White House and Congress, the last eight years virtually without opposition.

Lacking an opposition party, the Democratic-Republicans in the 1820s became increasingly divided. In 1824, when four party leaders ran for president, John Quincy Adams won the election in the House of Representatives, although Andrew Jackson had received more popular votes.

The deep divisions in the 1824 election doomed the dominant position of the Democratic-Republican Party. The two-party system revived with the emergence of the National Republican Party, an outgrowth of Adams' supporters, and the Democratic-Republican Party, the political organization of the Jackson faction. After 1830, the Jacksonians adopted the name Democratic Party.

See also: Democratic Party; Election of 1824; Election of 1828; Federalist Party; Third Parties.

Dixiecrats (States' Rights Party) (1948)

A conservative splinter party that defected from the Democratic Party in 1948. Popularly known as the Dixiecrats, the States' Rights Democratic Party split from the Democrats because of dissatisfaction with President Harry Truman's civil rights program. The Dixiecrat effort to maintain a segregated way of life was also an attempt to demonstrate the political power of the twentieth-century southern Democrats, as well as to reestablish their importance in the Democratic Party.

The Mississippi Democratic Party's state executive committee met in Jackson in May 1948 to lay the groundwork for the party split. The meeting called on southern delegates to leave if the Democratic National Convention endorsed Truman's civil rights program. When the convention did approve a strong civil rights plank, the entire Mississippi delegation and half the Alabama delegation left the convention. Governor Fielding L. Wright of Mississippi invited all anti-Truman delegates to meet in Birmingham three days after the Democratic convention to select a states' rights ticket.

Most southern Democrats with something at stake—national prominence, seniority in Congress, patronage privileges—shunned the new Dixiecrat Party. The party's leaders came from the ranks of southern governors and other state and local officials. The Birmingham convention chose two governors to lead the party: J. Strom Thurmond of South Carolina for president and Wright of Mississippi for vice president.

Other than the presidential ticket, the Dixiecrats did not run candidates for any office. Rather than try to develop an independent party organization, the Dixiecrats whenever possible used existing Democratic Party apparatus.

The party was on the ballot in only one state outside the South and in the November election received only 1,157,326 votes, or 2.4 percent of the popular vote. The Thurmond ticket carried four Deep South states where it ran under the Democratic Party label, but it failed to prevent the reelection of President Truman.

After the election, the party ceased to exist almost as quickly as it had begun, and most of its members returned to the Democratic Party. In a statement upon rejoining the Democrats, Thurmond characterized the Dixiecrat incident as "a fight within our family." While serving in the U.S. Senate sixteen years later, Thurmond switched to the Republican Party.

During his 1948 presidential campaign as a Dixiecrat, Strom Thurmond (left) attracted the support of many white Southern politicians. Thurmond won 39 electoral votes, all from the Deep South. (Bettmann/Corbis)

See also: Election of 1948, Third Parties.

Further Reading

Frederickson, Kari. *The Dixiecrat Revolt and the End of the Solid South, 1932–1968.* Chapel Hill, NC: The University of North Carolina Press, 2000.

Durr, Virginia Foster

See Poll Tax.

Election Day

Since 1845, election day for national elections has been uniform across the country. In that year, Congress established the first Tuesday after the first Monday in November in even-numbered years for national elections. Many states and localities also hold state-wide or local elections on the same day. However, states and other localities may choose to hold elections on different days or in odd-numbered years, according to state or local law.

In federal elections, all members of the House of Representatives are up for election for two-year terms every two years (in even-numbered years). One-third of the Senate is also up for election every two years for six-year terms.

The president and vice president are elected every four years, in even years that are divisible by four. Each state determines how the members of the electoral college are chosen.

In Oregon, where all elections are **vote-by-mail,** ballots must be received by a set time on election day. In general, **absentee ballots** follow similar regulations.

Election of 1789: George Washington

The first presidential election under the United States Constitution. With the ratification of the United States Constitution in July 1788—nearly nine months after the close of the Constitutional Convention in Philadelphia—the nation's new government went into effect. The Conti-

nental Congress decided that New York City would serve as the temporary capital. There, on September 13, 1788, Congress passed a resolution requiring the states to appoint presidential electors on the first Wednesday in January, the electors to assemble and vote in their respective states on the first Wednesday in February, and the new government to convene on the first Wednesday in March.

Under the U.S. Constitution, the method of choosing electors was left up to the individual state legislatures. The requirement that all electors be chosen on the same day was problematic for the states. Some did not have time to call elections. In New York, for example, where electors were to have been chosen by the legislature, disagreement between the two legislative houses led to a stalemate, preventing the state from participating in the election.

No formal nomination of candidates took place in 1788. Nevertheless, it had been widely anticipated that George Washington of Virginia, the reluctant hero of the Revolutionary War, would be president. The only real question was who would be the vice president. Leaders of the Federalists, a group organized in the fall of 1787 to achieve ratification of the Constitution, ultimately decided to support John Adams of Massachusetts.

The flaws of the electoral system became evident quickly. Under the Constitution, each elector was to cast two votes for president. The two votes had to be for different persons, and the two candidates had to be from different states. The individual receiving the votes of a majority of the electors was to be named president, and the person receiving the second highest total was to be named vice president. Because no distinction was made between balloting for president and vice president, it was possible for more than one candidate to receive an

E

A - Z

President George Washington delivers his first inaugural address in April 1789. Washington was 57 years old. (Library of Congress)

equal number of votes, thereby throwing the election into the House of Representatives. It also was possible that a candidate for vice president—either accidentally or by devious plot—actually could win the most votes and become president.

The Federalist leader Alexander Hamilton recognized the danger, and his personal dislike of Adams caused him concern. In response, he plotted to siphon away votes from Adams. In a letter to James Wilson of Pennsylvania, Hamilton wrote, "Everybody is aware of that defect in the constitution which renders it possible that the man intended for vice president may in fact turn up president." To prevent such a crisis, Hamilton recommended that several votes that would otherwise have gone to Adams be thrown away on other candidates,

have proposed to friends in Connecticut to throw away 2 [votes], to others in New Jersey to throw away an equal number and I submit to you whether it would not be well to lose three or four in Pennsylvania.

Hamilton's efforts were successful. Washington was unanimously elected president with sixty-nine electoral votes. Adams, however, won the vice presidency with only thirty-four electoral votes. Just two states—New Hampshire and his own Massachusetts—voted solidly for him. Because in other states Federalist leaders withheld support from Adams and sometimes worked against him, he did not receive *any* votes from Delaware, Georgia, Maryland, and South Carolina, and he received only one vote from New Jersey. The remaining votes were spread among ten other candidates, including John Jay, John Hancock, Robert Harrison, John Rutledge, and George Clinton.

Although the new government was to officially begin on March 4, 1789, not enough members of Congress had arrived in New York City by that date to achieve a **quorum.** After the Senate finally convened on April 6 and counted the electoral votes, a messenger was sent on horseback to deliver the news to President-elect Washington at his home in Mount Vernon, Virginia. He received the news on April 14. Washington

E

A-Z

Electoral Votes: Election of 1789	
George Washington	69
John Adams	34
John Jay	9
Robert Harrison	6
John Rutledge	6
John Hancock	4
George Clinton	3
Others	7

Receiving one vote from each of the sixty-nine electors, George Washington was unanimously elected as the first president.

then set out for New York, where he was sworn in on April 30.

Before the end of Washington's first term, political divisions developed that would lead to a party system. James Madison emerged as the opposition leader in Congress. Seventeen members of the House of Representatives regularly sided with Madison, and a bloc of fifteen supported the administration. The other dozen or so members of the House switched back and forth between the administration's and Madison's group.

The election of 1789 demonstrated the potential for partisanship and intrigue in presidential contests. It also reminded participants of the danger of the constitutional "defect" in the selection process that made it possible for the person intended to be vice president to become president.

See also: Democratic-Republican Party; Election of 1792; Election of 1800; Electoral College; Federalist Party.

Further Reading

Burns, James MacGregor, and Susan Dunn. *George Washington.* New York: Times Books, Henry Holt and Company, 2004.
Ellis, Joseph, J. *His Excellency: George Washington.* New York: Alfred A. Knopf, 2004.

Election of 1792: George Washington

The second term of President George Washington, which started the two-term tradition that lasted until the election of 1940. George Washington remained first in the hearts of his countrymen when his first term as president

DECISION MAKERS

Martha Washington, The First First Lady

A wealthy widow when she married George Washington on January 6, 1759, Martha Washington has the distinction of being the first First Lady—and the only one who did not live in the White House. Martha was not eager to take on the very public role of First Lady. However, she realized the importance of her actions as the president's wife. Quickly, she assumed the role of hostess for her husband. She hosted weekly formal state dinners designed to emphasize the young nation as an equal to established European governments. Despite the formality of these events, Martha's warm welcomes and charming hospitality put her guests at ease.

ended in 1792. However, national unity was quickly fading as bitterly opposed factions, or groups, began to develop. From these opposing factions arose a system of electoral competition.

Washington won a second unanimous term as president in 1792, but the election produced tough competition for vice president. An openly partisan contest broke out when the Democratic-Republicans, as one faction was now known, decided to challenge the Federalist John Adams. Some of Adams' favorable statements about the British angered his opponents. Adams managed to win reelection, but not before bitter divisions developed.

The 1792 election was different from the 1789 one in another way as well. An act of Congress made the election calendar more flexible, allowing states to choose electors within a thirty-four-day span before the first Wednesday in December when the electors met to vote. This law remained in effect until 1845.

Thomas Jefferson, the leader of the Democratic-Republicans, chose not to run for vice president in 1792, in part because he came from the same state as President Washington, and electors could vote for only one candidate from their own state. Besides, a "balanced ticket" required regional diversity. Instead, Democratic-Republican leaders from New York, Pennsylvania, Virginia, and South Carolina chose New York governor George Clinton as their candidate at a meeting in Philadelphia in October 1792.

Both Washington and Adams were reelected, but Clinton scored well in the electoral college. Adams received seventy-seven electoral votes to Clinton's fifty—with four votes going to Jefferson and one to Senator Aaron Burr of New York. Washington was reelected president by a unanimous electoral vote of 132.

The political tensions brought out by the Adams-Clinton contest became even sharper as policy controversies arose. Thomas Jefferson resigned as Secretary of state in 1793 in protest over Secretary of the Treasury Alexander Hamilton's growing influence in foreign affairs. Jefferson complained,

In place of that noble love of liberty and Republican government which carried us triumphantly through the war, an Anglican, Monarchical, and Aristocratical party has sprung up, whose avowed subject is to draw over us the substance as they have already done the forms of the British government.

Other events further divided the nation's leaders. News of the French Revolution's period of terror divided the nation's political leaders. Federalists were horrified by the violence of the revolution gone awry, while Democratic-Republicans such as Thomas Jefferson expressed sympathy for France's struggle. The federal government's use of troops to suppress the 1794 Whiskey Rebellion, approval of the Jay Treaty of 1794, and maneuvering between the warring French and British also divided the young nation into factions. Beginning at this time, state-level Democratic-Republican societies also formed in opposition to the Federalists.

See also: Democratic-Republican Party; Election of 1789; Election of 1796; Federalist Party.

Election of 1796: John Adams

The third presidential election, which peacefully transferred governmental power from one leader to another. George Washington decided not to run for president again in 1796, even though the Constitution did not bar a third term and the people supported it. With Washington out of the contest, the United States witnessed its first partisan race for president. After Washington's Farewell Address was published in the summer of 1796, the two parties began their competition.

On the Democratic-Republican side, presidential candidate, Thomas Jefferson faced no opposition; a consensus of party leaders selected him to

E

A – Z

Electoral Votes: Election of 1796	
John Adams	71
Thomas Jefferson	68
Thomas Pinckney	59
Aaron Burr	30
Samuel Adams	15
Ellsworth	11
George Clinton	7
John Jay	5
All others	12

John Adams, a Federalist, won the presidency in 1796, but Thomas Jefferson, the leader of the Democratic-Republicans, won the vice presidency.

run in 1796. However, a **caucus** of Democratic-Republican senators was unable to agree on a running mate, producing a tie vote between Senator Aaron Burr of New York and Senator Pierce Butler of South Carolina. That stalemate ended with Butler's supporters walking out of the meeting. As a result, there was no formal Democratic-Republican candidate to run with Jefferson.

The Federalists held a caucus of the party's members of Congress in Philadelphia in May 1796. The gathering chose Vice President Adams and Minister to Great Britain Thomas Pinckney

of South Carolina as the Federalist presidential and vice-presidential candidates. The choice of Adams was not surprising because he was Washington's vice president. Nevertheless, Adams was unpopular in the South, and he continued to be disliked by Hamilton. As a result, Hamilton tried to use the "defect" in the Constitution to make Pinckney president instead of Adams. He urged northern electors to give equal support to Adams and Pinckney in the hopes that the South would not vote for Adams and that Pinckney would therefore win the most votes.

Had the northern electors followed Hamilton's advice, Pinckney might have won the presidency. Instead, eighteen votes were thrown to other Federalists (thereby preventing a Pinckney claim to the presidency), giving Adams the presidency with seventy-one electoral votes. Pinckney—with fifty-nine votes—was not even able to win the vice presidency. Jefferson—the candidate of the opposing Democratic-Republican ticket—came in second with sixty-eight votes and became Adams' vice president.

Although the results again played up the defects in the constitutional procedure for electing presidents, Federalists and Democratic-Republicans did not seem especially concerned that the president and vice president were of opposing parties. Both sides felt that they had prevented the opposition from gaining total victory.

For the first and last time, a foreign figure played an active and public role in the election.

SPOTLIGHT

Abigail Adams and Barbara Bush

Until January 2001, Abigail Adams had the distinction of being the only woman who was both presidential wife and presidential mother. She was the wife of John Adams, the second president, and the mother of John Quincy Adams, the sixth president. Upon the inauguration of President George W. Bush on January 20, 2001, Barbara Bush became the second woman in the nation's history to be both presidential wife and mother. Barbara Bush is the wife of George H.W. Bush, the forty-first president, and the mother of George W. Bush, the forty-third president.

French Ambassador Pierre Adet promoted Jefferson's campaign in appearances and in written statements. Whether the Adet effort helped or hurt Jefferson is uncertain. The effort encouraged supporters of France, but angered others who favored Great Britain or resented outside interference.

See also: Democratic-Republican Party; Election of 1792; Election of 1800; Electoral College; Federalist Party; Twenty-second Amendment.

Further Reading

Diggins, John Patrick. *John Adams.* New York: Times Books, Henry Holt and Company, 2003.

Grant, James. *John Adams: Party of One.* New York: Farrar, Straus and Giroux, 2005.

McCullough, David. *John Adams.* New York: Simon & Schuster, 2001.

Election of 1800: Thomas Jefferson

The first presidential election in which power was peacefully transferred from one political party to another. As a result, the election is often called the "Revolution of 1800." The election of 1800 was the first in which both parties used congressional **caucuses** to nominate candidates for their tickets. Such caucuses were an important innovation in the presidential selection process because they formalized party alignments in Congress and confirmed the appearance of organized political parties.

Federalist members of Congress met in the Senate chamber in Philadelphia on May 3, 1800, to choose their candidates. As in previous presidential elections, Federalists were divided in their support of Adams, yet they felt they had to nominate him because he was the **incumbent** president. Their uncertainty about Adams showed, however, when they nominated both Adams and Major General Charles Cotesworth Pinckney of South Carolina without giving preference to one or the other for president. Charles Pinckney was the older brother of the Federalist vice-presidential candidate in 1796.

Electoral Votes: Election of 1800

Thomas Jefferson	73
Aaron Burr	73
John Adams	65
Charles Pinckney	64
John Jay	1

Before the ratification of the Twelfth Amendment in 1804, electors did not vote for president and vice president on separate ballots. As a result, Jefferson and Burr each received seventy-three electoral votes, causing the election to be decided by the House of Representatives.

The choice of Pinckney was made at Hamilton's insistence. Once again, Hamilton was plotting to use the constitutional "defect" against Adams. In 1796, South Carolina had voted for an all-southern ticket—Jefferson and Thomas Pinckney—even though the two were of opposing parties. Hamilton hoped that South Carolina would vote the same way in 1800, and that all other Federalist electors could be persuaded to vote for Adams and Charles Pinckney. That would give Pinckney more votes than Adams, thus making him president.

Although the deliberations of the Federalist **caucus** were secret, the existence of the meeting was not. It was denounced by the local Democratic-Republican paper, the Philadelphia *Aurora.*

The Democratic-Republicans once again chose Jefferson as the presidential candidate by consensus. On May 11, a caucus of Democratic-Republican members of Congress met at Marache's boarding house in Philadelphia to choose a running mate. Their unanimous choice was Aaron Burr.

Although there was no such thing as a formal **party platform** in 1800, Jefferson wrote detailed statements of principle. Among other things, the Democratic-Republicans believed in states' rights, a small national government, and a relatively weak executive. They opposed standing armies in peacetime, a large naval force, and alliances with other countries. They also denounced the Alien and Sedition Acts, which had

E

A – Z

Democratic-Republican Thomas Jefferson (left) was a political as well as personal opponent of Alexander Hamilton, the Federalist leader. Despite his intense dislike of Jefferson, however, Hamilton helped him gain the necessary House votes to win the presidency in 1800. Hamilton detested Aaron Burr (right), describing him as "a man of irregular and unsatiable ambition . . . who ought not to be trusted with the reins of government." (Library of Congress)

been passed by the Federalists in 1798, allegedly to protect the nation from subversives given the threat of war with France.

The election in 1800 witnessed signs of formal public campaigning. Tickets listing the names of Democratic-Republican electors were printed and distributed in several states, including New York, Massachusetts, Pennsylvania, and Delaware. Speeches on behalf of the candidates were becoming common. Partisan newspapers also helped to spread the party positions—the number of newspapers in the United States had grown dramatically in the 1790s, from ninety-one to 234. Despite attempts by the Federalist Party to silence the opposition press with the passage of the Sedition Act of 1798, partisan newspapers on both sides actively defamed the opposition. Ultimately, the Sedition Act worked against the Federalists by turning the Democratic-Republicans into public champions of a free press.

Increased partisan activity spurred voter participation. Because electors still were chosen indirectly in twelve of the sixteen states, voters often expressed themselves through state legislative elections as a means of influencing future presidential elections.

An indication of future Democratic-Republican success came in May when the New York state party won state legislative elections. Burr managed the state campaign, building a **political machine** with ward and precinct organizations. Burr's efforts showed the importance of large coordinated political efforts—a lesson that would not be lost on the party in future years.

When the electors voted in December, the constitutional defect did not work as Hamilton had hoped. Instead of resulting in a Pinckney victory, the defect produced an unexpected tie vote between the two Democratic-Republican candidates, Jefferson and Burr—each of whom had won seventy-three electoral votes. Adams came in third with sixty-five, and Pinckney followed with sixty-four. Thus, according to the Constitution, the election was thrown into the Federalist-controlled House of Representatives.

Some Federalists felt that Burr was the lesser of the two evils and plotted to elect him president instead of Jefferson, even though Jefferson was clearly the presidential candidate. Hamilton helped to squelch the idea. After thirty-six ballots, Jefferson carried a majority in the House of Representatives. The crisis—which could have fatally wounded the nation by calling into question the legitimacy of the new president—was over. Jefferson was elected president and Burr, vice president.

The near disaster brought about by the constitutional defect led to the passage of the Twelfth Amendment to the Constitution in December 1803. It called for electors to vote for president and vice president on separate ballots, thereby clarifying who was the presidential candidate and eliminating the possibility of a tie between the main candidate and the running mate.

See also: Democratic-Republican Party; Election of 1796; Election of 1804; Electoral College; Federalist Party; Twelfth Amendment; 📖 Twelfth Amendment in the **Primary Source Library.**

Further Reading

Appleby, Joyce. *Thomas Jefferson.* New York: Times Books, Henry Holt and Company, 2003.

Dunn, Susan. *Jefferson's Second Revolution: The Election Crisis of 1800 and the Triumph of Republicanism.* Boston: Houghton Mifflin Company, 2004.

Ferling, John. *Adams vs. Jefferson: The Tumultuous Election of 1800.* New York: Oxford University Press, 2004.

Election of 1804: Thomas Jefferson

The second term of Thomas Jefferson witnessed the inception of electors voting for President and Vice President on separate ballots, as directed by the Twelfth Amendment. By the 1804 election, President Thomas Jefferson had accepted the emergence of a party system. The president wrote, "The party division in this country is certainly not among its pleasant features. To a certain degree it will always exist."

Jefferson's record—lower taxes, a reduced national debt, repeal of the Alien and Sedition Acts, and purchase of the Louisiana Territory from France—assured him of a second term. Particularly important was Jefferson's willingness to expand the nation's reach and power with the Louisiana Purchase, which compromised his committment to strict construction and his opposition to public debt.

The Twelfth Amendment required electors to cast separate votes for president and vice president. This induced parties to specifically designate their presidential and vice-presidential candidates. However, the Democratic-Republicans retained the **caucus system** of nomination, and for the first time they publicly reported their deliberations. When the party caucus met on February 25, 1804, it attracted 108 of the party's senators and representatives. This caucus system remained in place for the next two decades.

President Jefferson was renominated by acclamation, but Vice President Burr, who had fallen out of favor, was not considered for a second term. On the first nominating roll call publicly reported in U.S. political history, New York governor George Clinton was chosen by the caucus to run for vice president. He received sixty-seven votes and easily defeated Senator John Breckinridge of Kentucky, who collected twenty votes. The vote was conducted by secret ballot.

Before adjourning, the caucus appointed a thirteen-member committee to conduct the campaign and promote the success of Democratic-Republican candidates. A forerunner of today's national committees, the new campaign group included members of both the House and Senate, but with no two persons from the same state. Because the Twelfth Amendment had not yet been passed when the caucus met, the committee was designed to "manage" the vote of Democratic-Republican electors to make sure that the events of 1800 were not repeated. In fact, that precaution was not necessary because the Twelfth Amendment was ratified in June—well before the electors voted.

By 1804, the Federalist Party was weakened and disorganized. The new era of dominance by the Virginia-led Democratic-Republicans had begun. The Federalists did not hold a congressional caucus to elect their nominees. Instead, Federalist leaders informally chose Charles Cotesworth Pinckney for president and Rufus King of New York for vice president. How the Federalists formulated this ticket is not clear. There is no record from 1804 of any formal meeting to nominate Federalist candidates.

The Federalists mounted a disorganized and dispirited national campaign. Despite efforts to win at least the votes of New England, the Federalists failed miserably. Pinckney received only fourteen electoral votes—those of Connecticut and Delaware, plus two from Maryland. Jefferson, the Democratic-Republican candidate, was the overwhelming victor with 162 electoral votes.

See also: Election of 1800; Election of 1808; Twelfth Amendment; 📖 Twelfth Amendment in the **Primary Source Library**.

Election of 1808: James Madison

The election of James Madison to his first term. Following George Washington's **precedent,** Thomas Jefferson refused to seek a third term. By the end of Jefferson's second term, the nation was bitterly divided over his policy toward France and Britain. In an attempt to stay out of their war, Jefferson had supported a trade **embargo** so that neither country would seize American ships. Instead, the embargo hurt American business interests. Under attack, Jefferson decided to return to his beloved home of Monticello near Charlottesville, Virginia.

Despite the unpopularity of the administration's European policy, Jefferson's secretary of state and chosen successor, James Madison, easily won the presidency in 1808. Jefferson's retirement provided a serious test to the authority of the Democratic-Republican congressional **caucus** to select presidential candidates. The caucus met on January 23, 1808, after, for the first time, a formal call was issued. Senator Stephen R. Bradley of Vermont, chairman of the 1804 caucus, issued the call to all 146 Democratic-Republicans in Congress and several Federalists sympathetic to the Democratic-Republican cause. A few party leaders questioned Bradley's authority to call the caucus, but various reports indicate that between eighty-nine and ninety-four members of Congress attended.

As in 1804, the balloting took place without names being formally placed in nomination. Madison easily won the presidential nomination with eighty-three votes. Despite earlier support for future Secretary of State James Monroe among Democratic-Republicans in Virginia, and Vice President Clinton's desire to be president, each won only three votes at the caucus. The caucus, however, overwhelmingly renominated Clinton for vice president.

As in the last election, the Democratic-Republican caucus again appointed a committee to conduct the campaign. Formally called the "committee of correspondence and arrangement," the committee was authorized to fill vacancies on the national ticket, should any occur. Before the caucus adjourned, it passed a resolution defending the caucus system as "the most practicable mode of consulting and respecting the interest and wishes of all." Later caucuses adopted similar resolutions.

Still, the Democratic-Republicans suffered divisions. Forty percent of the Democratic-Republican members of Congress had refused to attend the nominating caucus. Monroe refused to withdraw from the presidential race even after his defeat in the caucus. And Clinton, although he was nominated for vice president, was angry at not being nominated for president—so much so that he publicly denounced the caucus, as did Monroe's supporters. Pro-Clinton newspapers in New York launched harsh attacks on Madison and even suggested a Clinton-Monroe ticket. Some Clinton supporters went so far as to hope that Federalists would later nominate Clinton for president. However, the Federalists would not even consider such a plan.

The Federalists chose their ticket at a secret meeting of party leaders in New York City in August 1808. Twenty-five to thirty party leaders from seven states, all north of the Potomac River except South Carolina, attended the meeting. Despite the suggestion from Massachusetts representatives that Clinton be nominated, the gathering decided to run the same ticket they had chosen in 1804: Charles Cotesworth Pinckney and Rufus King.

The Federalists did not actively publicize their ticket. The party itself was divided and devoid of leadership. Indeed, many Virginia Federalists formally endorsed Monroe, even though he was a Democratic-Republican. Others preferred to align themselves with Clinton.

In the end, Madison won a huge victory with 122 electoral votes; Pinckney came in second with forty-seven votes. Monroe received no electoral votes. For the sake of party unity, the Democratic-Republicans had retained Clinton as their vice-presidential nominee even though he had tried to undermine Madison's candidacy. Clinton won the vice presidency, receiving 113 electoral votes.

See also: Democratic-Republican Party; Election of 1804; Election of 1808; Federalist Party.

Further Reading

Wills, Gary. *James Madison.* New York: Times Books, Henry Holt and Company, 2002.

Election of 1812: James Madison

The first presidential election that occurred during wartime. In early 1812, the possibility of war hung over the United States. Great Britain had taken American ships captive for years—boarding the vessels, taking cargo, and intimidating sailors. Anti-British political forces also charged that the British had encouraged Native American attacks against American settlers in the North and West.

The Democratic-Republican Party held its nominating caucus on May 18, 1812. Only eighty-three of the 178 Democratic-Republicans in Congress participated. The New England and New York delegations were poorly represented. Many of the New Yorkers supported the candidacy of their state's lieutenant governor, DeWitt Clinton—George Clinton's nephew—who also was maneuvering for the Federalist nomination. New England representatives were upset with Madison's foreign policy, which was leading to war with England.

Madison won a near-unanimous renomination in the caucus, receiving eighty-two caucus votes. John Langdon of New Hampshire got the vice-presidential nomination by a wide margin, collecting sixty-four votes to sixteen for Governor Elbridge Gerry of Massachusetts. However, Langdon declined the nomination, citing his age, seventy, as the reason. The Democratic-Republicans held a second caucus on June 8 to select another vice-presidential candidate. Gerry was the clear winner with seventy-four caucus votes, and he responded with a formal letter of acceptance.

Democratic-Republicans from New York were unwilling to accept the choice of Madison. They held their own caucus, composed of nearly all party members from the New York state legislature, where they unanimously nominated Clinton, who responded with a written "Address" that was a forerunner to today's party platforms. Clinton later won the endorsement of the Federalists as well.

As they had four years earlier, the Federalists convened a three-day secret meeting in New York City. The September meeting was more than twice the size of the 1808 gathering, with seventy representatives from eleven states attending. Delegates were sent to the conference by Federalist general committees, with all but nine of the delegates coming from the New England and Middle Atlantic states.

Debate centered on whether to run a separate Federalist ticket or to endorse Clinton. After much debate, they decided to endorse Clinton and they nominated Jared Ingersoll of Pennsylvania for vice president. Originally, the caucus's decision was to be secret, but

E

A – Z

E

A-Z

SPOTLIGHT

The President as Commander in Chief

By the third week of August 1814, a British invasion of Washington, D.C., was looming. On August 22, President Madison, as commander in chief, rode on horseback to oversee the troops at Bladensburg, Maryland, who were to help defend the nation's capital. The always-frail Madison was 63 years old. On August 24, fighting began. By two-to-one, the American troops outnumbered the British. The British attacked and, at first, the American defenders held their ground. Then the British soldiers broke through the American lines. Within minutes the American forces, as well as the president, were running in retreat. Madison overruled his generals, ordering sailors from a nearby naval yard to use their cannon and block the British advance. Without Madison's order, the American forces might not have escaped. Later that evening, the British burned government buildings in Washington, D.C., including the White House and the Capitol.

Democratic-Republican newspapers eventually leaked the decision.

On June 1, in response to constant agitation by **war hawks,** the president asked Congress for a declaration of war against Great Britain. Madison, benefiting from the public's willingness to rally in times of national emergency, swept to a second term in November.

The presidential election of 1812 was the first wartime election in the United States. The Federalists, calling Madison a dupe of French emperor Napoleon Bonaparte, positioned themselves as the party of peace and commerce.

Despite all the opposition to President Madison, he beat Clinton by an electoral vote count of 128–89. The vote reflected the growing split between southern agricultural states, which supported Madison, and northern commercial states, which supported Clinton.

The 1812 race was the last real campaign by the Federalists. Disgraced by their obstructionist tactics during the war, isolated by their talk of succession from the Union at the 1815 Hartford Convention, and unable to coordinate a national campaign, the Federalists faded from the party system.

See also: Democratic-Republican Party; Election of 1808; Election of 1816; Federalist Party; Gerrymandering.

Election of 1816: James Monroe

The election of the last president of what was known as "Virginia Dynasty." The inconclusive War of 1812 colored American politics for years. The United States and Great Britain fought to a stalemate. In the end, both parties simply accepted the end of hostilities. Nonetheless, the war sparked a surge of **nationalism.**

Despite his opposition to Madison in 1808, Monroe had been accepted back into the Democratic-Republican Party in the years that followed. In 1811, Madison had named him secretary of state; by 1816, many party members believed he was Madison's logical successor. However, some states were jealous of the "Virginia dynasty," men who had held a grip on the presidency beginning with Jefferson's election in 1800. Democratic-Republicans in such states opposed Monroe—himself a Virginian—and favored Secretary of War William H. Crawford of Georgia.

A Democratic-Republican caucus met in the House chamber on March 12, 1816, but only fifty-eight members of Congress—mostly Crawford supporters—attended. Hoping for better attendance, a second caucus was held on March 16. It drew 119 of the 141 Democratic-Republicans in Congress. There, Monroe narrowly defeated Crawford by a vote of 65–54. Forty of Crawford's votes came from five states: Georgia, Kentucky, New Jersey, New York, and North Carolina. The vice-presidential nomination went to New York governor Daniel D. Tompkins, who won eighty-five caucus votes.

The nominations of Monroe and Tompkins revived a Virginia–New York alliance that extended back to the late eighteenth century. With the lone exception of 1812, every Democratic-Republican ticket from 1800 to 1820 was composed of a presidential candidate from Virginia and a vice-presidential candidate from New York.

Rufus King, the 1804 and 1808 Federalist vice-presidential nominee, revived the Federalist Party in 1816 with his race for the governorship of New York. However, he lost the race and afterward found the job of maintaining the party a "fruitless struggle." Some die-hard Federalists tried to hold another secret meeting in Philadelphia to nominate candidates for president and vice president, but no such meeting occurred.

With the Federalist Party in disarray, the Democratic-Republican ticket won easily. Monroe received 183 electoral votes. The three states—Connecticut, Delaware, and Massachusetts—that had chosen Federalist electors cast their thirty-four electoral votes for Rufus King.

Although the collapse of the Federalists ensured Democratic-Republican rule, it also increased intraparty friction and spurred further attacks on the caucus system. Twenty-two Democratic-Republican members of Congress had not attended the second party caucus, and at least fifteen openly opposed the system. Mass meetings around the country protested the caucus system. Opponents asserted that the writers of the Constitution did not envision the caucus, that presidential nominating should not be a function of Congress, and that the caucus system encouraged candidates to curry the favor of Congress.

See also: Democratic-Republican Party; Election of 1808; Election of 1812; Election of 1820.

Further Reading

Hart, Gary. James Monroe. New York: Times Books, Henry Holt and Company, 2005.

Election of 1820: James Monroe

The only presidential election in which the incumbent, James Monroe, ran unopposed. The 1820 election took place during the "Era of Good Feeling," a phrase coined by a Boston publication, the Columbian Centinel, to describe a brief period of virtual one-party rule in the United States. However, that phrase glosses over serious sectional divisions that were growing during Monroe's presidency. The divisions, however, did not prevent Monroe from winning another term.

Sectional conflict increased during Monroe's first term over the admission of Missouri as a new state. Tensions between northern and southern states had been growing for years. Slavery was the core of the issue.

In the Senate, there was a fragile balance between the two regions—eleven free states and eleven slave states—but the admission of Missouri as a slave state threatened that balance. The two sides finally agreed to a compromise in which both Missouri and Maine (then a part of Massachusetts) would apply for statehood at the same time: Maine as a free state and Missouri as a slave state. Thus, the two regions would continue to be equally represented in the Senate. Monroe remained neutral in the debate leading up to the compromise. Despite a financial panic in 1819, he retained overwhelming popular support, thanks to peace and a wave of nationalistic feeling.

Although several rival Democratic-Republican candidates aspired to win the presidency when Monroe retired in 1824, none wanted to challenge his reelection in 1820. A nominating caucus was called in early March, but fewer than fifty of the Democratic-Republican Party's 191 members of Congress showed up. The caucus voted unanimously to make no nominations and passed a resolution explaining that it did not nominate anyone because so few party members attended. Although Monroe and Tompkins were not formally renominated, electoral slates were filed in their behalf.

Because the Federalist Party was finally dead, Monroe ran unopposed. Even John Adams, the last Federalist president, voted for Monroe as an elector from Massachusetts. Only one elector, a Democratic-Republican from New Hampshire, cast a vote against Monroe, supporting instead John Quincy Adams, son of the former president.

See also: Election of 1816; Election of 1824.

Election of 1824: John Quincy Adams

The first election in which no candidate received an electoral vote majority and was thus decided by the House of Representatives. In 1824, as in 1820, only one working political party existed in the United States: the Democratic-Republican. However, that party had several candidates competing for the presidency: Secretary of State John Quincy Adams of Massachusetts, Senator Andrew Jackson of Tennessee, Secretary of War John C. Calhoun of South Carolina, House Speaker Henry Clay of Kentucky, and Secretary

of the Treasury William H. Crawford. The number of candidates, combined with growing democracy within the American political system, led to the end of the caucus system in 1824.

Early on, Crawford was the leading candidate. He had strong southern support and appeared likely to win the support of New York's Democratic-Republicans. Many party leaders assumed that he would win a caucus if one were held. Not surprisingly, Crawford's opponents quickly joined the growing list of caucus opponents. Crawford's apparent lead suddenly ended in September 1823 when he suffered a severe stroke. Nearly blind and unable even to sign his name, he was disabled and recovered in private for several months.

In early February 1824, eleven Democratic-Republican members of Congress issued a call for a caucus to be held in the middle of the month. Their call was countered by twenty-four other members of Congress from fifteen states who deemed it "inexpedient under existing circumstances" to hold a caucus. They claimed that 181 members of Congress were resolved not to attend if a caucus were held.

The caucus convened in mid-February, but only sixty-six members of Congress showed up. Three-fourths of those attending came from just four states—Georgia, New York, North Carolina, and Virginia. Despite his serious illness, Crawford won the caucus nomination with sixty-four votes. Albert Gallatin of Pennsylvania was selected for vice president with fifty-seven votes. The caucus adopted a resolution defending its actions as "the best means of collecting and concentrating the feelings and wishes of the people of the Union upon this important subject."

However, the caucus's action led to more serious splits within the party. Because so few members of Congress attended the caucus— almost all of them Crawford supporters— opponents argued that the choice was not even representative of the Democratic-Republicans serving in Congress. Crawford's opponents ridiculed his nomination by the caucus, and his

THE ELECTION OF 1824

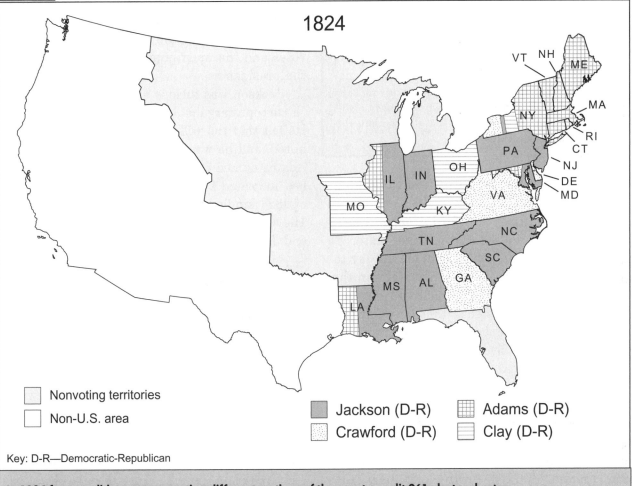

1824

VT NH
ME
MA
NY
RI
CT
PA
NJ
OH
DE
MD
IL IN
VA
MO
KY
NC
TN
SC
MS AL GA
LA

☐ Nonvoting territories
☐ Non-U.S. area

☐ Jackson (D-R)   ☐ Adams (D-R)
☐ Crawford (D-R)   ☐ Clay (D-R)

Key: D-R—Democratic-Republican

In 1824 four candidates, representing different sections of the country, split 261 electoral votes. Ultimately, the House of Representatives chose Adams president from among the top three candidates.

weak physical condition made it even easier for them to reject his nomination. Other candidates simply refused to follow the caucus's decision. Never again were candidates chosen by the caucus system.

With the Democratic-Republican Party lacking unity or leadership, there was no chance of rallying behind a single ticket. In addition, many political issues of the time proved to be divisive. Western expansion and protective tariffs, for example, benefited some parts of the country but hurt others. Thus, the various candidates came to represent the nation's **sectional divisions**.

The candidates themselves recognized that such a crowded field was dangerous. The election would be thrown into the House of Representatives if no candidate received a majority. Therefore, the candidates made efforts to join forces. Adams tried to lure Jackson as his running mate. Adams was a short, stocky, aloof, well-educated New Englander who came from a family of Federalists, while Jackson was a tall, thin, hot-tempered war hero with little formal education who came to symbolize populist democracy. In trying to recruit Jackson onto their team, Adams supporters envisaged a ticket of "the writer

E

A–Z

Electoral Votes: Election of 1824

Andrew Jackson	99
John Quincy Adams	84
William H. Crawford	41
Henry Clay	37

Andrew Jackson led in the popular vote as well as in the electoral votes, but failed to win a majority of the electoral votes, thus throwing the election into the House of Representatives.

and the fighter." Jackson would have nothing of it.

In the meantime, Crawford dropped Gallatin as his vice-presidential running mate. His supporters then tried to persuade Clay to drop his quest for the presidency and join the Crawford team. They hinted that Crawford's physical condition was such that he would probably not finish out a term of office if elected (in fact, he lived ten more years). But Clay was not swayed. Calhoun then dropped his race for the presidency and joined efforts with Jackson.

The four candidates who remained each collected electoral votes. None, however, received a majority. Jackson received the most with ninety-nine, followed by Adams with eighty-four, Crawford with forty-one, and Clay with thirty-seven. Therefore, the election was thrown into the House of Representatives.

In accordance with the Twelfth Amendment, the names of the top three candidates—Jackson, Adams, and Crawford—were placed before the House. Speaker of the House Clay, who had come in fourth, would play a major role in tipping the balance in favor of one of the candidates.

In contrast to Jackson, Adams actively lobbied for support, and the nation's capital was filled with rumors of corruption. Clay informed Adams in January that he would support Adams in the House election—a major blow to Jackson. Shortly thereafter, a letter in a Philadelphia newspaper alleged that Adams had offered Clay the post of secretary of state

in return for his support. Adams went on to win the House election narrowly by carrying thirteen of twenty-four state delegations. Jackson came in second with seven, and Crawford third with the remaining four. Consequently, the candidate who won the most electoral votes and the most popular votes did not win the presidency.

Jackson was furious at what he considered "a corrupt bargain" between Adams and Clay. He felt that the will of the people had been ignored, and he was enraged when President Adams named Clay secretary of state, as rumor had indicated he would. In this way, the events of 1824 kindled the flame of popular democracy. The stage was set for a rematch between Adams and Jackson in 1828.

See also: Democratic Party; Election of 1820; Election of 1828.

Further Reading

Mieczkowski, Yan. *The Routledge Historical Atlas of American Presidential Elections.* London: Routledge, 2001.

Remini, Robert V. *John Quincy Adams.* New York: Times Books, Henry Holt and Company, 2002.

Election of 1828: Andrew Jackson

The first election of Andrew Jackson, often cited as a victory for the "common man." After his bitter defeat to John Quincy Adams in the 1824 election, Jackson and his supporters began to plan for the election of 1828.

While President Adams struggled with competing factions of the Democratic-Republicans, an opposition force was gathering strength. Adams' foes in Congress dealt the president a number of humiliating defeats. Adams' desire for a national program of roads and canals, education, and research in the arts and sciences upset many groups in the country. United States participation in a conference of countries from the Western Hemisphere and the imposition of a **tariff,** a tax on imported goods, also were divisive issues. The opposition was united, however, behind "Old Hickory," as Jackson was called. Jackson's soldiers coined his nickname because they believed he was as tough as hickory wood. Jackson's followers became known as Democrats and formed a new, well-organized political party.

Adams' supporters, now known as the National Republicans, called for the president's re-election. Thus, in the election of 1828, two political parties once again competed for victory.

John C. Calhoun, who had served as Adams' vice president, now fully supported Jackson and became the Democrats choice for vice president. The National Republicans chose Richard Rush, who had served as secretary of state in the Monroe administration (1817–1825), to run as their vice-presidential nominee.

Jackson, hero of the Battle of New Orleans in the War of 1812, had a strong appeal to the "common man," even though he was a wealthy plantation owner. People who met with Jackson talked of his unerring "intuition" about people and politics. Jackson's decision to push for reforms of the punishment of debtors was an important gesture to small business leaders and workers who were held to a kind of **indentured servitude** to their creditors. Senator Martin Van Buren of New York, Jackson's strongest supporter in the Northeast, said the people "were his blood relations—the only blood relations he had."

Andrew Jackson was the first president elected from west of the Appalachian Mountains. (Library of Congress)

Jackson and his running mate, John C. Calhoun, easily beat Adams in their 1828 rematch. Jackson won 178 electoral votes, and Adams won eighty-three. Of the popular vote, Jackson received 643,000 votes—56.0 percent—to Adams' 501,000—43.6 percent. Sectional splits showed in the vote distribution. Adams held all but one of New England's electoral votes, all of Delaware's and New Jersey's, sixteen of New York's thirty-six votes, and six of Maryland's eleven votes. Jackson took all the rest—the South and the West. The newly enfranchised voters in the growing regions of the country, then, decided the election. The electorate, however, was expanding not only in the West, but also in the original states. Between 1824 and 1856, voter participation grew from 3.8 percent to 16.7 percent of the total population.

See also: Democratic Party; Election of 1824; Election of 1832.

Electoral Votes: Election of 1828

Andrew Jackson	178
John Quincy Adams	83

John Quincy Adams' electoral votes all came from the Northeast; Jackson's support was strongest in the South and the West.

Further Reading

Schlesinger, Arthur. M., Jr. *The Age of Jackson.* Old Saybrook, CT: Konecky and Konecky, 1971.

Wilentz, Sean. *Andrew Jackson.* New York: Times Books, Henry Holt and Company, 2005.

Election of 1832: Andrew Jackson

The reelection of Andrew Jackson and the first time that the major political parties—National Republican Party, Democratic Party, and the Anti–Masonic Party— held national conventions. There was never any doubt that Jackson would be renominated in 1832. Indeed, several state legislatures endorsed him even before the convention. Jacksonians from New Hampshire proposed the 1832 Democratic convention, and the president and his advisers jumped at the opportunity. The Anti-Masonic Party had held the only previous national convention in 1831.

Conventions had been the chief way of selecting candidates for local offices since the early part of the century. Compared with the caucus system that preceded it, the convention system was a huge democratic leap forward. The convention system enabled the parties to gather supporters from all geographic areas, and it brought them together as an organized group that ultimately was accountable to the voters. Voters had the opportunity to give approval or disapproval to a party program with one vote. Historian Eugene H. Roseboom has written,

It was representative in character; it divorced nominations from congressional control and added to the independence of the executive; it permitted an authoritative formulation of a party program; and it concentrated the party's strength behind a single ticket, the product of compromise of personal rivalries and group or sectional interests.

Given Jackson's popularity in 1832, the purpose of the convention was to rally behind the president and to select a new vice-presidential candidate. Jackson's adviser and close friend Martin Van Buren got the nomination.

As in 1828, Jackson's political opposition was fragmented. The Whigs—the opposition party that had developed from grassroots protests in the North and West against Jackson's tariff and development policies—held their national convention in Baltimore in December 1831 and unanimously nominated Henry Clay of Kentucky for president. Eighteen states used a variety of selection procedures to determine who would be their convention delegates. The party's platform sharply criticized the Jackson administration's patronage practices, relations with Great Britain, and ill-tempered congressional relations, as well as Supreme Court decisions.

In addition to Henry Clay, Jackson faced two other opponents. The Anti-Masonic Party, a **third party** that formed in 1827 to keep Masons, members of a secret society from holding office. At the 1831 Anti-Masonic convention, they nominated William Wirt as their presidential candidate. Wirt had served as attorney general under Presidents Monroe and John Quincy Adams.

Jackson easily won reelection. The president won 219 electoral votes to Clay's forty-nine, and William Wirt's seven. John Floyd, the former governor of Virginia, received South Carolina's eleven electoral votes. Jackson won all but seven states. Clay won Kentucky, Massachusetts, Rhode Island, Connecticut, and Delaware, plus five electors from Maryland. Wirt won Vermont's seven electoral votes. Jackson won 702,000 popular votes to Clay's 484,000 and Wirt's 101,000.

See also: Anti-Masonic Party; Democratic Party; Election of 1828; Election of 1836; Whig Party.

Election of 1836: Martin Van Buren

Election won by Martin Van Buren, a political follower of Andrew Jackson, and the first in which political organizations played a major role. Van Buren, who had supported Jackson throughout his administration, received the 1836 Democratic nomination at a convention packed with Jackson appointees. The vice-presidential nomination went to Richard M. Johnson of Kentucky. His controversial relationship with a mulatto woman damaged the ticket in the South, but the Democrats won nonetheless.

The Whigs' campaign strategy was to run several favorite sons to prevent any candidate from getting a majority of the electoral votes, thereby throwing the election into the House of Representatives. The Whig expectation was that the House would select either General William Henry Harrison of Ohio or Hugh Lawson White of Tennessee.

Van Buren, however, had Jackson's well-organized political machine, as well as Jackson's personal backing and was able to overcome the Whigs' strategy. Thus, Van Buren took 170 electoral votes—twenty-two more than he needed for election. Of the Whig candidates, Harrison received seventy-three electoral votes; White, twenty-six; and Daniel Webster of Massachusetts, fourteen. Willie Mangum, an Independent Democrat from North Carolina, received eleven electoral votes from the South Carolina legislature, which opposed White because of his role in nullification politics. Van Buren won 764,000 popular votes (50.8 percent); Harrison, 551,000 (36.6 percent); White, 146,000 (9.7 percent); and Webster, 41,000 (2.7 percent).

For the only time in history, the Senate selected the vice president, Richard Johnson, who had fallen one vote shy of election by the electoral college. In the Senate, Johnson defeated Francis Granger by a 33–16 vote.

Van Buren and the Party System

Van Buren helped establish the principle of party government in the United States. That principle, much scorned in the early days of the nation's history, now enjoys widespread allegiance.

Van Buren presented his arguments for a party system in his book, *An Inquiry into the Origin and Course of Political Parties in the United States*. American leaders from George Washington through John Quincy Adams had believed that self-interested factions endangered the functioning and virtue of the Republic. These leaders also had warned against the dangers of democracy, which they often called "mob rule." In the worst possible scenario, permanent parties with strong ideological stances appealed to the mass public for support, undermining the ability of wise national leaders to guide public virtue.

The basic question that Van Buren needed to resolve was the system's need for stability and responsible leadership and the parties' imperative to gain office. How could a party's selfish desire to run the government and award patronage and contracts to political allies benefit the whole system?

Van Buren argued that the absence of parties—that is, collections of people from different backgrounds—resulted in a system of personal politics that fueled demagogy, perpetual campaigns, and a lack of accountability. According to Van Buren, personal presidential politics was more polarizing than the politics of consensus or of coalition building. Mass parties with certain partisan principles would enable presidents to get the backing they needed to do their work.

Significance of the 1836 Election

Many historians consider the election of 1836 to be the most important event in the development of the party system. Van Buren, a Democratic follower of Jackson and a supporter of political parties in a democratic system, easily won the election against an uncoordinated Whig Party. The defeat eventually persuaded Whig leaders

E

A–Z

VIEWPOINTS

A TIPPECANOE PROCESSION.

Supporting candidates William Henry Harrison, known for his victory over the Indians at the Battle of Tippecanoe, and John Tyler, Whig partisans rolled a huge paper ball from city to city, singing, "It is the ball a-rolling on for Tippecanoe and Tyler too." Thus the expression "keep the ball rolling" came into the language. (Library of Congress)

of the need for a permanent organization for political competition. The emergence of two permanent parties finally ended the American suspicion of a party system based on unabashed competition for power.

See also: Democratic Party; Election of 1836; Election of 1840.

Further Reading

Widmer, Ted. *Martin Van Buren.* New York: Times Books, Henry Holt and Company, 2005.

Election of 1840: William Henry Harrison

The first election in which the Whig presidential candidate won and the first in which campaigning by supporters played a major role. The Whigs nominated William Henry Harrison in 1840 after a nomination struggle with Henry Clay. A Clay supporter, John Tyler of Virginia,

was the vice-presidential nominee. Harrison defeated the **incumbent** Martin Van Buren in an electoral vote landslide, receiving 234 of the 294 electoral votes—all the states except Alabama, Arkansas, Illinois, Missouri, New Hampshire, South Carolina, and Virginia. For the popular vote, Harrison won 1.3 million, or 52.9 percent, to Van Buren's 1.1 million, or 46.8 percent.

Harrison's campaign was vague and his government experience was unimpressive. However, after their defeat in 1836, the Whigs were now well organized. The image of Harrison as a sort of frontier everyman—which became popular when a Baltimore newspaper mocked him as a inactive man who would sit in a log cabin and drink cider rather than perform great deeds of leadership—was the theme of numerous parades and mass meetings. On issues from banking and currency to slavery, Harrison spoke in generalities. Harrison's strategist acknowledged that he advised the candidate to "say not a single word about his principles or creed. Let him say nothing—promise nothing."

As it happened, Harrison did not have an opportunity to do much as president besides discipline the aggressive Henry Clay. Clay had assumed that he and the rest of the congressional leadership would play the leading role in the government, but Harrison quickly dispelled that notion in a note scolding him. One month after his inauguration, however, the sixty-eight-year-old Harrison developed pneumonia and died. On April 6, 1841, the burdens of the presidency fell on Vice President John Tyler.

The rift between the White House and Congress widened under Tyler. Clay acted as if he were prime minister during a special session of Congress, pushing through a legislative program that included a recharter of the controversial **Bank of the United States,** higher import taxes, and distribution of proceeds from land sales to the states. Tyler, a lifetime **states' rights** advocate, vetoed two bills for a national bank, and the Whigs in Congress and his cabinet began a bitter feud with the president. In 1842, Clay left the Senate to promote his presidential hopes, and everyone in the cabinet except Secretary of State Daniel Webster quit. Tyler was all alone, but he did manage to defeat the Whig program in his four years as president.

See also: Election of 1836; Election of 1844.

Election of 1844: James K. Polk

The first election in which a **dark-horse candidate** won the presidential contest. James K. Polk of Tennessee defeated the Whig Henry Clay in 1844 by supporting an expansionist program and winning the support of the solid South. One of the key issues in the campaign was whether Texas should be admitted to the Union and, if so, whether it should be slave or free. In 1840, President Van Buren had opposed annexation—opposition that may have cost him the presidency—and the Democrats and Whigs evaded the issue. In 1844, however, Polk endorsed the annexation of Texas as a slave state. Thus, Polk gained the full support of the South.

During the 1844 nominating convention, the Democrats tried to offset the sectional dangers of the Texas issue by combining it with a call for occupying Oregon and eventually bringing that state into the Union. The Democrats also appealed to the Northeast by supporting a high tariff. Both parties spoke out against the growing foreign elements in the cities.

In the election, the Democrat Polk defeated the Whig Clay, winning 1.34 million votes, or 49.5 percent, to Clay's 1.30 million, or 48.1 percent, and 170 electoral votes to Clay's 105. Clay received his strongest support from five northeastern states and five border slave states.

The Liberty Party—an abolitionist party formed out of more than two hundred antislavery societies in time for the 1840 election—may have been the deciding factor in the 1844 race. Although the party received only 2.3 percent of the popular vote and no electoral votes, it was strong enough in New York to prevent the Whigs from winning that state's crucial thirty-six electoral votes. Those votes went to the Democrat Polk rather than to the Whig Clay.

During Polk's term, the deep divisions within the Democratic Party became increasingly evident. For example, President Polk faced the resentment of party factions when he began making appointments after his 1844 win. Westerners were angry when they were shut out of the cabinet and Polk vetoed a rivers and harbors bill. Supporters of both Van Buren and John Calhoun were angry that their faction did not win more prominent positions in the administration. Northeasterners were upset at tariff cuts. In New York, there was a party split

Electoral Votes: Election of 1844	
James K. Polk	170
Henry Clay	105
James G. Birney	0

Democrat James K. Polk won a close contest against Whig Henry Clay.

E

A – Z

E

A–Z

between the reformists and the party-regulars who disagreed on every issue, including banks, currency, internal improvements, and political reforms—and this split also served to disrupt the administration. Creating still more dissension was the war with Mexico (1846–1848), fought because of the dispute over the Texas border and the possible annexation of California. Northerners resented the fact that the country was fighting Mexico over a slave state.

See also: Democratic Party; Election of 1840; Election of 1848; Liberty Party.

Further Reading

Seigenthaler, John. *James K. Polk.* New York: Times Books, Henry Holt and Company, 2004.

James K. Polk was the first dark-horse presidential candidate. He was nominated on the eighth ballot at the Democratic Convention. He was also the first president to retire after one term and not seek reelection. (Library of Congress)

running another military hero, General Zachary Taylor, who was vague on most political issues. A Louisiana slaveholder, Taylor defeated Henry Clay and General Winfield Scott for the nomination on the fourth convention ballot. His running mate was Millard Fillmore of New York.

The Whigs were so determined to avoid sectional party splits that they not only nominated the popular Taylor, but also did not write a platform. Despite such extreme measures to maintain unity, the convention was disturbed by squabbles between pro- and antislavery forces on the question of the Wilmot Proviso which would ban slavery in any territory the United States obtained from Mexico.

At the Democratic national convention, Senator Lewis Cass of Michigan defeated Senator James Buchanan of Pennsylvania and Supreme Court Justice Levi Woodbury for the presidential nomination. General William Butler was picked as his running mate. The Democratic convention experienced splits between two New York fac-

Election of 1848: Zachary Taylor

The second election in which the Whig presidential candidate won the contest. In 1848, the Whigs recaptured the White House by

tions: the Barnburners, who were part of the antislavery movement, and the more conservative Hunkers, who had ties to southerners. The Barnburners finally defected from the Democratic party to become part of the Free Soil Party.

The Democrats supporting Cass praised the administration of President Polk, defended the war with Mexico, and congratulated the French Republic that emerged from the wave of revolution in Europe. They also did everything possible to avoid the slavery issue. The nomination of Cass—a "doughface," or northerner with southern principles—was expected to appeal to both sides of the simmering issue.

Taylor defeated Cass, winning 1.4 million popular votes, or 47.3 percent, to Cass's 1.2 million, or 2.5 percent. New York Democrat Martin Van Buren, the former president, running on the Free Soil ticket, won 291,500 votes, or 10 percent, but no electoral votes. Taylor received 163 electoral votes to Cass's 127, with a strong showing in the North. Taylor won Connecticut, Massachusetts, New Jersey, New York, Pennsylvania, Rhode Island, and Vermont in the North; Delaware, Kentucky, Maryland, North Carolina, and Tennessee in the border states; and Florida, Georgia, and Louisiana in the Deep South. This combination was enough to beat Cass' coalition of seven slave states, six northwestern states, and two New England states.

On July 10, 1850, Fillmore succeeded to the presidency when Taylor died suddenly. After consuming too many refreshments at a Fourth of July celebration, Taylor had developed cramps and then a fatal illness, probably typhoid fever.

See also: Democratic Party; Election of 1844; Election of 1852; Free Soil Party.

Election of 1852: Franklin Pierce

The second election in which a Democratic **dark-horse candidate** won the presidential race. The major issue in the election of 1852

was Henry Clay's compromise on slavery in the territories, known as the Compromise of 1850. The compromise addressed the slavery question in all of the new U.S. territories by making concessions to both sides of the struggle. For the North, California would be admitted as a free state, and the slave trade—but not slavery itself—would be abolished in the District of Columbia. For the South, fugitive slave laws would be strengthened, and the New Mexico territory would be divided into two states where the voters, exercising popular sovereignty, would decide the slave issue.

The compromise was designed to finally settle the issue of slavery in new territories. However, the slavery issue could not be contained by region; it had an increasingly important "spillover" effect. Because of concerns about the congressional balance of power and the difficulties of enforcing slavery provisions such as the fugitive slave law in states that opposed slavery, it was impossible to isolate the slavery question into particular regions as Clay intended.

President Taylor had stalled action on the compromise for months. Nonetheless, his successor, Millard Fillmore, had thrown his support behind the compromise. The Whigs remained divided on the proposal.

General Scott won the Whig nomination in 1852 after platform concessions to the party's southern delegation. Scott's appeal was always limited to the North, while Fillmore appealed to the South and Daniel Webster appealed to New England. Scott won on the fifty-third ballot.

Governor Franklin Pierce of New Hampshire, a dark-horse candidate who gained fame with his Mexican War record, won the Democratic nomination in 1852. His vice-presidential running mate was Senator William Rufus de Vane King of Alabama. The party held together a coalition of groups with contradictory positions on the slavery issue and regional affairs. The convention, meeting in Baltimore, pledged to "abide by, and adhere to" the Compromise of 1850 and to do what it could to smother the slavery issue.

Attempts to introduce other issues into the election, such as economics and foreign affairs,

E

A–Z

failed, and the campaign quickly degenerated into squabbles about personalities. Pierce easily won with 1.6 million popular votes (50.8 percent) to Scott's 1.4 million (43.9 percent.) Pierce carried twenty-seven states and 254 electoral votes to Scott's four states and forty-two electoral votes.

See also: Election of 1848; Election of 1856.

Election of 1856: James Buchanan

By 1856 the North-South split had eliminated the Whigs as a national party and fatally damaged the Democrats' chances for winning national elections in the decades ahead.

Congress opened the slavery issue by passing the Kansas-Nebraska Act of 1854. The act declared "null and void" the Missouri Compromise of 1820 which had prohibited slavery in new territories north of the 36"30' parallel except in Missouri. The 1854 legislation created two territories (Kansas and Nebraska) from the original Nebraska territory and left the slavery issue to be determined by popular sovereignty there and in the Utah and New Mexico territories.

The Kansas-Nebraska Act was a vehicle to spur the development of the West. Such development was part of a long-standing American approach to creating opportunity and freedom via growth. Senator Stephen A. Douglas of Illinois—the promoter of the law and the main advocate of popular sovereignty—held that the law was necessary if the country was to be bound together by rail and telegraph lines and was to drive Great Britain from the continent. The latter goal was based on the widely held suspicion that Britain was exploiting the slavery issue to distract American politics and stunt American growth.

Whatever the economic motives for unification, the Kansas-Nebraska Act was bitterly divisive. Northern state legislatures passed resolutions denouncing the law. The development of sectional parties continued.

A flood of new settlers into Kansas, and the violence that accompanied balloting over whether Kansas was to be a free or a slave state, further inflamed passions. Neighboring Missourians took part in the controversy, arguing that their status as slave owners would be undermined if Kansas voted to be free. Especially in view of the Supreme Court's infamous 1857 *Dred Scott* decision, which denied Congress the power to ban slavery in the territories and barred African Americans from citizenship, and the Lincoln-Douglas debates in Illinois in 1858, the slavery question was becoming decisive in American politics.

The Democrats won the White House in 1856 when the party endorsed the Kansas-Nebraska Act and nominated the pro-South James Buchanan as its presidential candidate. John Breckinridge of Kentucky, who later served as a Confederate general, was Buchanan's running mate. The Democrats, who were becoming mainly a southern party, benefited from close wins in Buchanan's home state of Pennsylvania and in New Jersey, and in western states such as Illinois, Indiana, and California. However, the only strong region for the Democrats was the South. Buchanan won all the slave states except Maryland. Overall, Buchanan won 1.8 million popular votes—45.3 percent—to Fremont's 1.3 million—33.1 percent. The electoral college gave Buchanan a 174–114 victory.

The nativist American Party—or the "Know-Nothings," as they were called—nominated

Electoral Votes: Election of 1856

James Buchanan	174
John C. Fremont	114
Millard Fillmore	8

In the election of 1856, Democrat James Buchanan carried all of the slave-holding states except Maryland. John C. Fremont's support came from northern free states.

former Whig president Millard Fillmore, but the party was never able to move beyond an urban strength based on resistance to immigration and Catholicism. Fillmore won only the state of Maryland; overall, he got 873,000 popular votes—21.5 percent—and eight electoral votes.

Colonel John Charles Fremont was named the Republicans' first presidential candidate. Former Whig senator William Dayton of New Jersey received the vice-presidential nomination. After an 1854 meeting in Ripon, Wisconsin, where a new national party was first proposed, the Republican Party developed quickly. The Republicans had developed a strong grassroots organization in the Northwest after the Kansas-Nebraska Act passed in 1854 and attracted disgruntled abolitionists, Whigs, Know-Nothings, Northern Democrats, and members of the Liberty and Free Soil Parties who were troubled by the possible extension of slavery. Uncertainty about how the extension of slavery would affect laborers who sought opportunity in the territories also helped to unite the new coalition.

The first Republican nominating convention met in Philadelphia in 1856 with delegates from all of the free states, four border states, three territories, and the District of Columbia. The party's opposition to slavery was far from unanimous, but its willingness to address rather than suppress the issue enabled it to redefine the political dialogue. Besides strong antislavery statements, the party platform contained proposals for several internal improvements advantageous to the North. The Republicans did not offer anything to the solidly Democratic South. To win a national election, it would have to sweep the North.

See also: American Party; Democratic Party; Election of 1852; Election of 1860; Republican Party; Whig Party.

Further Reading

Baker, Jean H. *James Buchanan.* New York: Times Books, Henry Holt and Company, 2004.

Election of 1860: Abraham Lincoln

The first presidential contest won by the Republican Party nominee. The main issue was slavery, and it split the nation as never before. Four presidential candidates eventually emerged: Republican, Abraham Lincoln; Northern Democrat, Stephen A. Douglas; Southern Democrat, John C. Breckinridge; and the Constitutional Union Party candidate, John Bell.

In 1860, the Democratic Party held its nominating convention in April in Charleston, South Carolina, where Stephen A. Douglas was the leading candidate. Two **platforms** were presented to the delegates: one calling for Congress to protect slavery and the other favoring **popular sovereignty**—the concept that the states be allowed to decide whether or not to allow slavery. After the convention adopted the popular sovereignty platform, most Southern delegates bolted from the convention. Balloting began for the presidential nominee, but the convention deadlocked. Meeting again in June in Baltimore, the Democrats nominated Douglas on the second ballot. They chose Herschel V. Johnson of Georgia as their vice presidential nominee. Southern Democrats then held their own convention where they nominated Vice President John C. Breckinridge for the presidency and Joseph Lane of Oregon for the vice presidency. The party was hopelessly split.

At a frenzied Republican convention in Chicago, the leading contenders were William H. Seward of New York, Samuel Chase of Ohio, Edward Bates of Missouri, and Abraham Lincoln of Illinois. Lincoln emerged as the consensus compromise choice, receiving the nomination on the third ballot. The fact that Lincoln was known widely throughout Illinois had improved his chances at the Chicago convention. For the vice presidency, the Republicans selected Hannibal Hamlin of Maine, a former Democrat.

E

A - Z

The Constitutional Union Party developed deep divisions. The party nominated John Bell for president and Edward Everett of Massachusetts for vice president.

Because the regional splits that had been tearing the nation apart for decades reached their peak in 1860, none of the four major candidates who were seeking the presidency could compete seriously throughout the nation. Lincoln and Douglas ran in the North, while Breckinridge and Bell competed in the South. In fact, Lincoln was not even on the ballot in most Southern states.

The Democratic Party split enabled Republican Abraham Lincoln to win the 1860 election. Lincoln won easily with a total of 180 electoral votes to Breckinridge's seventy-two, Bell's thirty-nine, and Douglas's twelve. Lincoln's closest competitor in the popular vote was Douglas. Lincoln had 1.9 million northern popular votes (40.0 percent); Douglas had 1.4 million (29.5 percent) spread out geographically. The two other candidates received much less support, which was concentrated in the South: Breckinridge won 848,000 popular votes (18.1 percent); Bell won 591,000 (12.6 percent).

Some southerners had vowed to secede from the Union if Lincoln won the election. In order to address this issue, during the period between the election and Lincoln's inauguration on March 4, 1861, congressional committees sought to put together a compromise that would save the nation from civil war. They failed because of Lincoln's refusal to abandon his policy of containing slavery. He rejected proposals for popular sovereignty or a slave-free geographic division of the western states.

After Lincoln was elected, South Carolina, Louisiana, Mississippi, Alabama, Georgia, Texas, and Florida seceded from the Union. On February 7, 1861, these states adopted a constitution forming the Confederate States of America and elected Jefferson Davis as its president. After a prolonged standoff between the Union soldiers who held Fort Sumter and the Confederate soldiers who controlled South Carolina,

the Confederates fired on the fort. Virginia, Arkansas, North Carolina, and Tennessee then joined the Confederacy, and the Civil War was under way.

The Republicans succeeded in 1860 because they were able to pull together a variety of diverse factions. Above all else, the Republicans stood against the extension of slavery into new territories. By accepting slavery where it already existed, but warning against slavery's spread, the Republicans divided the Democrats and picked up support from an array of factions: radical **abolitionists**, moderate abolitionists, and whites who feared for their position in the economy.

Because of the wide-ranging Republican coalition, Lincoln was able to count on support in the areas that John C. Fremont had won in 1856: New England and the upper Northwest, as well as New York and Ohio. Lincoln's political ties to Illinois, where he practiced law and began his public career, helped carry Illinois and Indiana; and his background as a former Whig gained him support in the Ohio valley. The coal and iron regions of Pennsylvania and Ohio were attracted to the party's high-tariff policy. The vice-presidential selection of Hannibal Hamlin of Maine, a former Democrat, broadened the party's support. Lincoln's often-stated desire not to challenge slavery where it then existed was an appeal to Border States.

See also: Constitutional Union Party; Democratic Party; Election of 1856; Election of 1864; Republican Party; Whig Party.

Further Reading

Carwardine, Richard. *Lincoln.* New York: Alfred A. Knopf, 2006.

Donald, Herbert David. *Lincoln.* New York: Simon & Schuster, 1995.

Harris, William C. *Lincoln's Rise to the Presidency.* Lawrence, KS: University of Kansas Press, 2007.

Election of 1864: Abraham Lincoln

The first presidential election during wartime. Incumbent Abraham Lincoln won renomination and reelection, but his victory was by no means certain. The Union's difficulties in waging the Civil War caused Lincoln to be increasingly unpopular. In addition, splits within the Republican Party jeopardized his chances for renomination and reelection.

As the presidential election approached, frustration over the war caused deep divisions within Lincoln's own cabinet. Treasury Secretary Salmon P. Chase constantly criticized Lincoln's competence to serve as commander in chief. Indeed, the Philadelphia banker Jay Gould briefly led a movement calling for Chase's nomination for president in 1864. Chase withdrew only after the Lincoln forces dealt him a severe blow at the party caucus in his home state of Ohio. Others opposed to the president met in Cleveland in May 1864 and named John C. Fremont, the 1856 Republican nominee, to run against Lincoln in the fall. Fremont withdrew after a series of Union military victories strengthened Lincoln's political standing. In addition to the military problems, the president's announcement in September 1862 of the Emancipation Proclamation, freeing the slaves in rebellious states, created legal and political controversy.

At the Republican convention in Baltimore, however, Lincoln received the party's renomination. The convention chose governor Andrew Johnson of Union-occupied Tennessee—a lifelong Democrat—as the vice-presidential candidate. The Republican convention decided to label this Republican and Democratic team the Union Party in order to attract loyal Democrats and to develop nationwide unity. Yet Lincoln's reelection was so uncertain that he asked his cabinet in August 1864 to sign a statement pledging an orderly transition of power if he lost. The statement read:

This morning, as for some days past, it seems exceedingly probable that this Administration will not be reelected. Then it will be my duty to so cooperate with the President-elect, as to save the Union between the election and the inauguration; as he will have secured his election on such ground that he cannot possibly save it afterwards.

The man for whom Lincoln was planning a wartime transition was Democratic nominee George McClellan, whom Lincoln had fired as general in January 1863. McClellan had won the Democratic nomination with the strong backing of peace Democrats, known as "Copperheads." McClellan's running mate was Representative George Pendleton of Ohio, a leader of the Copperheads.

Although popular with his soldiers, General McClellan had not won a single major battle of the war, despite the addition of extra troops. Yet he blamed Lincoln for the losses. Indeed, he was a vocal critic of Lincoln's administration. McClellan's presidential campaign was built around a call for a cease-fire and a convention to restore the Union. He and his fellow peace Democrats also criticized the administration's violation of civil liberties and other unconstitutional actions.

Lincoln's fortunes greatly improved in the two months before the election. When General William Tecumseh Sherman took Atlanta, the Confederacy was left badly divided geographically. The military victory cut off the Gulf States from the Confederate capital of Richmond. General Philip Sheridan had had important successes in the Shenandoah Valley, and General Ulysses S. Grant had fared well in Virginia. With the Union victories, Lincoln's popularity grew.

Not only did the Democrats face a Republican Party united by recent military victories, but McClellan also had a difficult time developing consistent campaign themes. At times he seemed to be appeasing the Confederacy; on the other hand, he continually expressed his support for the Union soldiers. McClellan also had a

E

A–Z

difficult time selling his peace message to Northern industrialists who were profiting from munitions procurement.

Lincoln overwhelmed McClellan by winning all of the loyal states except Delaware, Kentucky, and New Jersey for a 212–21 electoral vote victory. Lincoln garnered 2.2 million popular votes (55.0 percent) to McClellan's 1.8 million (45.0 percent).

See also: Democratic Party; Election of 1860; Election of 1868; Republican Party.

Further Reading

Waugh, John C. *Reelecting Lincoln: The Battle for the 1864 Presidency.* Cambridge, MA: Da Capo Press, 1997.

Election of 1868: Ulysses S. Grant

The first presidential election after the Civil War. The Republican convention chose the popular Civil War hero General Ulysses S. Grant as its presidential nominee by acclamation: wild shouts and cheers. Several leaders sought the vice presidential nomination, however. Among the chief contenders were Governor Reuben E. Fenton of New York, Senator Henry Wilson of Massachusetts, Senator Benjamin Wade of Ohio, and Speaker of the House Schuyler Colfax. Finally, Colfax won the nomination on the sixth ballot.

The Democrats had a difficult time choosing a nominee. Incumbent President Andrew Johnson sought the Democratic nomination, but his appeal was in the South. Chief Justice Salmon P. Chase, highly regarded for his fairness during Johnson's Senate impeachment trial, was a possible candidate. Senator Thomas A. Hendricks of Indiana was strong in the East, and George Pendleton of Ohio, the party's vice-presidential candidate four years earlier, was strong in the West. General Winfield Scott Hancock of Pennsylvania presented the opportunity of running one military hero against another.

At the Democratic convention in New York City, Horatio Seymour, the national party chair and popular war governor of New York, received the Democratic nomination after twenty-three ballots. He accepted the nomination against his will. General Francis P. Blair, Jr., of Missouri was the vice-presidential nominee. The Democratic platform called for the rapid reentry of Confederate states to the Union with state authority over suffrage questions, as the Fifteenth Amendment, granting the vote to African American men, had not yet been proposed by Congress.

Both sides were well financed in the election, but the Republicans had the edge. The Republican Party's pro-business positions on the tariff, railroad grants, and currency attracted millions of dollars. Newspapers and magazines tended to be pro-Republican because of their urban business orientations. Grant ran his campaign from his home in Galena, Illinois. He did not campaign and was vague about most issues, ranging from currency to voting rights.

On Election Day, Grant defeated Seymour by 3.0 million (52.7 percent) to 2.7 million votes (47.3 percent). The electoral vote tally was 214 for Grant and eighty for Seymour. Grant won all but eight of the thirty-four states taking part in the election. Without the votes of about one-half million recently freed African Americans, Grant probably would have lost the election.

See also: Democratic Party; Election of 1864; Election of 1872; Republican Party.

Further Reading

Bunting, Josiah III. *Ulysses S. Grant.* New York: Times Books, 2004.

Grant, Ulysses S. *Personal Memoirs.* New York: Modern Library, 1999.

Election of 1872: Ulysses S. Grant

The only presidential election in which one of the major candidates died before the electoral votes were counted. The election of 1872 was the only election in which the Democratic Party endorsed the Liberal Republican candidate.

The spoils system was in full swing during the Grant administration. While President Grant himself was not involved in the scramble for booty, many of his aides made money illegally through graft and corruption. Despite the scandals of his administration, Grant again received the Republican convention's nomination by acclamation.

Before the 1872 election, the *New York Sun* exposed the Crédit Mobilier scandal. The newspaper reported that the firm's board of directors had many of the same members as the Union Pacific Railroad Company, which hired it to build a transcontinental route, and that Crédit Mobilier had paid its board exorbitant profits. To avoid a public investigation, Crédit Mobilier offered stock to Vice President Colfax and Representative (later president) James Garfield. Colfax lost his place on the Republican ticket for his role in the scandal; Senator Henry Wilson of New Hampshire took his position as the vice-presidential candidate in 1872.

Liberal Republicans, unhappy with the lack of reform, as well as with protective tariffs and the uneven administration of the southern states, bolted the party in early 1872. The group was interested in policies such as civil service and free trade that would promote individual virtue in a laissez-faire economic system.

Candidates for the nomination from this group of Republicans included former ambassador to Great Britain Charles Francis Adams, son of President John Quincy Adams and grandson of President John Adams; Supreme Court Justice David Davis; Chief Justice Salmon P. Chase; Senator Lyman Trumbull of Illinois; and Horace Greeley, editor of the *New York Tribune*. Greeley won the nomination on the sixth ballot. For vice president, the Liberal Republicans chose the reform-minded governor of Missouri, Benjamin Gratz Brown. The Democrats were in such disarray that they did not field a candidate of their own.

They endorsed the Greeley ticket—so he ran as both a Liberal Republican and as a Democrat.

Since his early days as a newspaper reporter, Greeley had won fame as a sharp social critic. He was a crusading, abolitionist editor and a dedicated reformer, but his rumpled appearance and unpolished speaking style made him appear "unpresidential." Greeley was unable to fashion his campaign promises to various interest groups—African Americans, soldiers, immigrants, and laborers—into a victory over Grant. Groups that Greeley actively courted found him wanting for a variety of reasons. For example, African Americans were suspicious of Greeley because he called for amnesty for Confederate leaders. Immigrants were weary of Greeley because he favored prohibition. Even though Greeley advocated the high tariff favored by the North, he could not cut into Grant's northeastern support.

Beginning in September, Greeley hit the campaign trail and delivered a series of impressive speeches. Greeley, however, could not match the strength of Grant and the regular Republicans. Grant took the entire North and the newly admitted South with 3.6 million popular votes (55.6 percent). Greeley won three Border States, as well as Tennessee, Texas, and Georgia, with 2.8 million popular votes (43.9 percent). Less than a month after the election, Greeley died. Of the electoral votes, which were cast after Greeley's death, Grant received 286; the Democrats' sixty-three electoral votes were scattered among various candidates, and seventeen Democratic electoral votes were not cast.

See also: Democratic Party; Election of 1868; Election of 1876; Republican Party.

Further Reading

Bunting, Josiah III. *Ulysses S. Grant.* New York: Times Books, 2004.

Grant, Ulysses S. *Personal Memoirs.* New York: Modern Library, 1999.

E

A - Z

THE ELECTION OF 1876

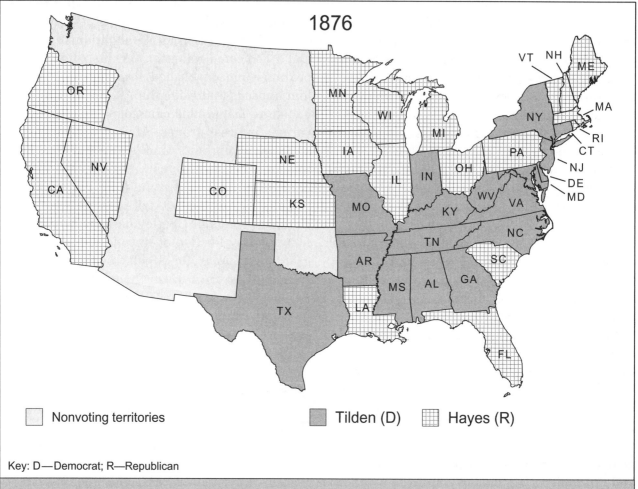

1876

Nonvoting territories   Tilden (D)   Hayes (R)

Key: D—Democrat; R—Republican

In the Election of 1876, the electoral votes of Florida, Louisiana, Oregon, and South Carolina were in dispute. A special committee created by Congress resolved the problem by awarding the disputed votes to Republican Rutherford B. Hayes, who then was declared president by one electoral vote.

Election of 1876: Rutherford B. Hayes

One of the most controversial elections in American history, which many people thought would lead to a second civil war. Republican Rutherford B. Hayes, the three-time governor of Ohio, lost the popular vote and had a questionable hold on the electoral college vote, but he managed to beat Democrat Samuel J. Tilden, the reform-minded governor of New York, for the presidency when the election was settled by a special commission created by Congress. Hayes won 4.0 million votes to Tilden's 4.3 million—48.0 and 51.0 percent of the popular vote, respectively.

The problem arose when the vote tallies in three Southern states—Florida, South Carolina, and Louisiana—were called into question, as well as one of Oregon's electoral votes. Violence had accompanied the voting in all three Southern states, but President Grant had not sent in federal troops to ensure fair balloting. On those states hung the election outcome. There was good reason to be suspicious of any vote count in those and other southern states. While the Republicans had controlled the balloting places and mounted vigorous drives to get African Americans to the polls, the Democrats had used physical intimidation and bribery to keep African Americans away. The bitterness between northern interests and southern whites was apparent in the violence that often took place at polls.

When state election board recounts and investigations did not settle the question of the vote tallies, Congress took up the matter, as the Constitution did not address such disputes. A special electoral commission made up of five senators (three majority-party Republicans, two minority Democrats), five representatives (three majority-party Democrats, two minority Republicans), and five Supreme Court justices (two from each party, one independent) assembled to hear complaints about the disputed states. At the last minute the independent justice disqualified himself, and his place was taken by a Republican. He was accepted by the Democrats because they considered him to be the most independent of the Republican justices. Weeks of bargaining followed, during which the Republican vote totals of the disputed states were confirmed and the southern Democrats extracted promises of financial aid and political independence from the federal government.

When the legality of the Florida vote count for Hayes was challenged, the commission responded that it did not have the capacity to judge the actual conduct of the balloting, only the legality of the certificates presented to Congress. That decision gave the state to Hayes. Challenges to the vote counts of Louisiana, South Carolina, and Oregon were dismissed in a similar way, so Hayes was awarded the presidency by a single electoral vote, 185 to 184.

The compromise settled the dispute between Hayes and Tilden. To reward southern Democrats for throwing the 1876 election to the Republican Hayes, northern politicians agreed to pull federal troops out of the South and to allow southern whites to take over state governments. Thus, the era of **Reconstruction** ended.

See also: Democratic Party; Election of 1872; Election of 1880; Election of 2000; Republican Party.

Further Reading

Trefousse, Hans L. *Rutherford B. Hayes.* New York: Times Books, 2002.

Election of 1880: James A. Garfield

A close presidential election that went to the Republican nominee. President Rutherford B. Hayes honored his pledge to serve only one term, setting off a scramble for both parties' nominations in 1880. Among the Republicans, former President Grant sought the nomination, as did Senator James G. Blaine of Maine, and Treasury Secretary John Sherman of Ohio. When the early momentum for a third term for Grant faltered, the Republican contest became a battle between Grant, Blaine, and Sherman. Grant led the vote on the first-ballot, but could not attract new supporters as the balloting proceeded. A stalemate between Blaine and Sherman ensued.

Representative James Garfield of Ohio, a former preacher and an impressive orator, was the compromise choice for the nomination. He selected as his running mate Chester A. Arthur, the collector of the Port of New York, an important **patronage** job.

The Democrats named General Winfield Hancock of Pennsylvania and former Indiana representative William English to head their ticket. The Democratic platform favored a low tariff to raise revenue, civil service reform, restrictions on Chinese immigration, as well as a late criticism of the 1876 deal that gave the presidency to Hayes. Except for the tariff and 1876 questions, the Democrats' platform was close to the Republicans' statement of principles.

Regionally, the North and West supported Garfield and the South lined up behind Hancock. The popular vote was close—4.45 million (48.27

E

A – Z

percent) to 4.44 million (48.25 percent)—but Garfield won a 214–155 electoral vote victory.

The issue of patronage and civil service came to the forefront soon after Garfield's inauguration. On July 2, 1881, Charles Guiteau, a man described as a "disappointed office-seeker," shot Garfield while he was on his way to Williams College to deliver a commencement address. Garfield died in September, and Chester A. Arthur became president.

The outstanding feature of Arthur's presidency was the easy passage of the Pendleton Act—legislation that set up a commission to regulate the provision of federal jobs and the behavior of civil servants. The number of federal workers removed from the patronage system was at first small, but successive presidents widened the coverage of nonpartisan workers so that today less than 1 percent of all federal workers are appointed by the president.

The tariff question also emerged as crucial during the Arthur presidency. The Republicans championed the Tariff Act of 1883. The Democrats opposed the so-called "Mongrel Tariff" and later worked for the gradual lowering of rates, but they failed. The tariff would be a major issue in later elections.

See also: Democratic Party; Election of 1876; Election of 1884; Republican Party.

Further Reading

Karabell, Zachary. *Chester Alan Arthur.* New York: Times Books, 2004.

Rutkow, Ira. *James A. Garfield.* New York: Times Books, 2006.

Election of 1884: Grover Cleveland

The first Democratic presidential win since before the Civil War. **Incumbent** President Chester A. Arthur wanted the Republican nomination in 1884. His record since assuming the presidency after James A. Garfield's assassination was outstanding. Not only was Arthur an important player in **civil service reform** and

the tariff issue, but he began the modernization of the navy and vetoed the Chinese Exclusion Act of 1882, which prohibited Chinese laborers from entering the United States for ten years. His veto of the $19 million rivers and harbors bill was a model of fiscal honesty.

James Blaine of Maine, secretary of state in Arthur's own administration, stood in Arthur's way. After months of public appeals by old-line Republicans interested in stronger leadership and more generous patronage from their party, Blaine quit his position to oppose Arthur for the nomination.

Blaine was one of the most charming figures of the period. A former teacher, editor, state legislator, and member of Congress, he had made a national name for himself when he opposed an 1876 congressional resolution expressing forgiveness to Civil War rebels including the Confederate president, Jefferson Davis. Col. Robert G. Ingersoll, a rising political figure in the Republican Party, said of Blaine:

> Like an armed warrior, like a plumed knight, James G. Blaine marched down the halls of the American Congress and threw his shining lance full and fair against the brazen forehead of every traitor to his country.

The nickname "Plumed Knight" caught on.

The Republican convention in Chicago praised Arthur's administration. The Republican **platform** promised better protection for raw wool interests, and a protective stance for domestic industry. The platform also called for an international currency conference, railway regulation, a national agency for labor affairs, and further improvements in the navy.

At a frenzied convention, Blaine took the lead over Arthur on the first ballot. Old-line party leaders quickly united behind Blaine. Arthur was unable to unite the support of the reform Republicans. Blaine won the nomination on the fourth ballot. Senator John Logan of Illinois received the vice-presidential nomination.

Among the leading Democrats who sought the presidential nomination were New York Governor Grover Cleveland, Senator Thomas F. Bayard, Jr., of Delaware, and Senator Thomas A. Hendricks of Indiana. Cleveland received the nomination on the second ballot. Hendricks, whose liberal views would balance the more conservative Cleveland, was named the vice-presidential candidate. The Democratic platform promised reform of the tariff laws to make them fairer and promised a more honest and efficient administration.

Cleveland was a former teacher, lawyer, assistant district attorney, and reform mayor of Buffalo who had won the governorship of New York only two years before. Members of both parties underestimated Cleveland's intellect and resolve. As governor, he had made enemies through his vetoes of low public transit fares and aid to sectarian schools. He also had defied Tammany Hall, the Democratic Party organization that dominated New York politics, especially in New York City.

In a move away from the highly partisan and bitter campaigns of the post–Civil War era, Cleveland and his supporters promoted their program through a "literary bureau" that distributed pamphlets describing the party's policy positions. Campaign themes were developed at the national level and distributed through the mails and at meetings with professional and community organizations. This same educational style was adopted by Republican candidate Benjamin Harrison in 1888.

In contrast, Blaine's campaign was one of the dirtiest in U.S. history. He first attempted to spark sectional antagonisms with his "bloody shirt" warnings that the South was trying to reassert its rebel ways through Cleveland. Blaine also tried to rouse the fears of business with claims that Cleveland would institute free-trade policies damaging to domestic industries. That appeal failed, however, because the Democratic platform specifically supported protection of those interests. Finally, Blaine tried to make a scandal of Cleveland's admission that he had fathered a child out of wedlock years before. Cleveland was charged, among other things, with kidnapping both the mother and child to cover up the story.

The campaign eventually turned on Cleveland's victory in New York, which resulted from a number of blunders by Blaine. One blunder had occurred years before, when Blaine mocked New York party boss Roscoe Conkling:

The contempt of that large-minded gentleman is so wilted, his haughty disdain, his grandiloquent swell, his majestic, super eminent, overpowering, turkey-gobbler strut, has been so crushing to myself that I know it was an act of the greatest temerity to venture upon a controversy with him.

Conkling was so irked by the turkey image that he spent his whole career battling Blaine, including during the presidential campaign of 1884. Blaine's own running mate, Logan, sympathized with Conkling in the dispute.

The other Blaine mistake occurred a week before the election when a Protestant minister praised Blaine and proclaimed, "We are Republicans, and do not propose to leave our party and identify ourselves with the party whose antecedents have been rum, Romanism, and rebellion." Blaine did not distance himself from the remark, which angered New York Democrats, as well as ethnic voters everywhere. Ultimately, this anti-Catholic slur cost Blaine many votes. Later the same day, Blaine attended a formal dinner with a number of wealthy supporters that became known as "the millionaires' dinner." Thus, Blaine was portrayed as a friend of the rich, confounding his claim to speak for ordinary people.

Of Irish background, Blaine appealed to Irish immigrants in New York for their votes. Cleveland countered Blaine's Irish tactic by obtaining the last-minute endorsement of the powerful Tammany leader Edward Kelly. On the Saturday before the election, Blaine attended a parade in New York City that attracted forty thousand people chanting: "Blaine, Blaine, James G. Blaine, the Continental Liar from the State of Maine!" With the help of a weak economy and the "Mugwumps"—independents and liberal Republicans offended by Blaine—Cleveland won the presidency.

The race, however, was close. Cleveland received 4.9 million votes (48.5 percent) to Blaine's 4.8 million (48.3 percent). He won the

E

A–Z

solid South, Indiana, Connecticut, New Jersey, and, most important, New York (although by only 1,047 out of 1.13 million votes cast). Still, the election controversy did not end with the balloting. The *New York Tribune* reported that Blaine had won the race, fueling fears about an election deadlock similar to the Hayes-Tilden contest of 1876. But Cleveland received 219 electoral votes to Blaine's 182, making the Democrat the clear winner.

See also: Democratic Party; Election of 1876; Election of 1880; Election of 1888; Republican Party.

Further Reading

Graff, Henry A. *Grover Cleveland.* New York: Times Books, 2002.

Election of 1888: Benjamin Harrison

A close election in which the Republican candidate won the electoral vote but lost the popular vote. At their national convention, the Democrats nominated incumbent President Grover Cleveland by acclamation—wild shouts and cheers—and chose seventy-five-year-old judge Allen G. Thurman of Ohio for the vice presidency. Calling for low tariffs, the Democrats promised that their policies would open world markets to domestic industries. Lower tariffs were said to be necessary for avoiding disastrous federal budget surpluses, preventing the development of monopolies, and ensuring consumers reasonable prices for basic goods.

The 1884 Republican nominee, James G. Blaine, sent word that he would not be a candidate in 1888, leaving the race wide open. Among the leading candidates for the nomination were Senator John Sherman of Ohio, Governor Russell Alger of Michigan, Senator William Allison of Iowa, and Senator Benjamin Harrison of Indiana. At the Republican national convention Sherman led the early balloting, but quickly lost ground to Alger and Harrison. After extensive backroom maneuvering, Harrison, who had the backing of state party bosses, won the nomination on the ninth ballot. Levi Morton, a banker, received the vice-presidential nomination.

Harrison was a former Civil War brigadier general and the grandson of President William Henry Harrison. Characterized by a scandal-free if colorless demeanor, Harrison was a good speaker, but he often appeared aloof. One historian wrote:

> Those who talked with him were met with a frigid look from two expressionless steel grey eyes; and their remarks were sometimes answered in a few chill monosyllables devoid of the slightest note of interest.

Harrison and the Republicans pledged a modernized navy, civil service reforms, and the traditional party policies to promote big business and protect American manufacturing.

The election turned, as in 1884, on New York and Indiana—both states with extensive evidence of voter intimidation and manipulation of vote counts. Harrison won the two states narrowly—New York by only 14,373 votes out of the 1.3 million cast—and captured the White House. Except for Connecticut and New Jersey, Harrison swept the North and West. Cleveland won the South. Overall, Harrison won 5.4 million popular votes (47.8 percent) and 233 electoral votes; Cleveland won 5.5 million popular votes (48.6 percent) and 168 electoral votes.

Cleveland left the White House with an unusual amount of good will among the public because of his honest tariff campaign. His popularity increased during the next four years as the economy hit slumps and as the former president, while practicing law, delivered popular speeches calling for a more democratic brand of politics. Cleveland would be back in 1892 for vindication.

See also: Democratic Party; Election of 1884; Election of 1892; Republican Party.

Further Reading

Calhoun, Charles W. *Benjamin Harrison.* New York: Times Books, 2005.

THE ELECTION OF 1892

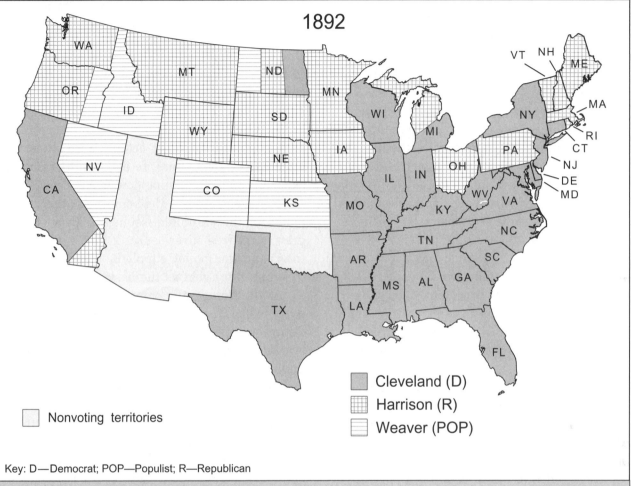

1892

Cleveland (D)

Harrison (R)

Weaver (POP)

Nonvoting territories

Key: D—Democrat; POP—Populist; R—Republican

In the Election of 1892, third-party candidate James B. Weaver won 22 electoral votes–the first third-party candidate to do so since 1860. Winning more than 1 million popular votes, Weaver's strength was centered in the western, rural areas of the country.

E

A-Z

Election of 1892: Grover Cleveland

The only election in which a former president won, resulting in President Grover Cleveland's serving two non-consecutive terms. By 1892, President Benjamin Harrison had lost much of his popularity, both for his aloof manner and his policies. No Republican contender, however, could mount an effective challenge. At the Republican convention, political wizard Mark Hanna, a wealthy coal magnate who had become a powerful behind-the-scenes Republican strategist, promoted Ohio governor William McKinley. Moreover, Secretary of State James G. Blaine became an alternative when he abruptly quit Harrison's administration just before the Republican convention. Nonetheless, Harrison received a first-ballot nomination. Former minister to France Whitelaw Reid of New York received the vice-presidential nomination.

In the battle for the Democratic nomination, former President Grover Cleveland enjoyed widespread backing among rank-and-file voters. New York governor David B. Hill also sought the nomination; he hurriedly called a state convention and won the delegation's support. Democrats across the country, however, rebelled at Hall's move and threw their support to Cleveland.

One problem for Cleveland was the growing support in farming states for free and unlimited coinage of silver—a way to increase sagging farm prices by inducing inflation in the overall economy. Cleveland always had opposed this solution. The former president's consistent, principled stance on the issue enhanced his reputation for integrity, but strongly appealed to the business- and finance-dominated northeastern states. At the convention, Cleveland defeated Hall for the nomination on the first ballot and selected his former first assistant postmaster, Adlai Stevenson of Illinois, as his running mate.

The Populist Party, which was supported in many farm states, nominated James B. Weaver for president. For vice president, they chose James G. Field, a former Confederate general from Virginia. The party favored the free coinage of silver, opposed the gold standard, and fought against national banks.

The fall campaign was uneventful and subdued. Cleveland respected the fact that Harrison's wife Caroline was seriously ill and made few appearances. She died two weeks before the election.

Cleveland won easily, carrying the South and the key northern states of New York, New Jersey, Connecticut, Indiana, Illinois, and Wisconsin. He received 5.6 million popular votes (46.1 percent) to Harrison's 5.2 million (43.0 percent) and 277 electoral votes to Harrison's 145. Populist candidate James B. Weaver won 1.0 million popular votes (8.5 percent) and twenty-two electoral votes—from Idaho, Nevada, Colorado, and Kansas—marking the first time since 1860 that a third-party candidate received any electoral votes.

See also: Democratic Party; Election of 1884; Election of 1888; Election of 1896; Populist Party; Republican Party; Third Parties.

Further Reading
Graff, Henry A. *Grover Cleveland.* New York: Times Books, 2002.

Election of 1896: William McKinley

One of the most dramatic presidential elections in history, which marked the return of Republican dominance. By 1896, a wide variety of issues had led to political unrest in the South and West. A gold crisis, pro-business Supreme Court decisions, and anti-labor actions were all criticized by the Democrats. In addition, the nation experienced an economic downturn, known as the Panic of 1893. At the same time, the demand for the unlimited issuing of silver coins grew, and "free silver" spread; this was a plan to expand the money supply by allowing silver to supplement gold as the basis for currency.

At the Democratic convention in 1896, the party called for the issuance of silver currency. Representative William Jennings Bryan of Nebraska was a fiery speaker who advocated unlimited silver and worked for the plight of farmers. Ultimately, Bryan defeated Richard P. Bland of Missouri for the 1896 Democratic presidential nomination. Arthur Sewall, a wealthy shipbuilder from Maine, was chosen as the vice presidential nominee. A major factor in Bryan's nomination was the strength of his fiery "Cross of Gold" speech.

The speech was one of the most emotional and successful in history. Bryan attacked eastern financial leaders and businessmen who exploited farmers with religious zeal. He sought to expand the traditional Democratic conception of the independent working man to include farmers and factory workers. In his speech, Bryan declared:

> **Y**ou shall not press down upon the brow of labor this crown of thorns, you shall not crucify mankind upon a cross of gold.

In 1896, the Republicans nominated Ohio governor William McKinley. Garret A. Hobart was chosen for the vice-presidential slot.

McKinley had little difficulty defeating Bryan. McKinley outspent Bryan by as much as ten-to-one, and he attracted the pro-gold wing of the Democratic Party. The Republican Party—or Grand Old Party (GOP), as it was called by then—platform called for retention of the gold standard unless international negotiations could produce a bimetallic (silver and gold) currency system. The platform also called for restored tariff protections and an aggressive foreign policy in the Western Hemisphere.

Bryan's campaign was a political hurricane. He spent just $650,000, most of it donated by silver interests, compared with the millions McKinley spent. Bryan traveled eighteen thousand miles and gave some six hundred speeches, and his campaign staffers put out an impressive quantity of literature. Several million copies of *Coin's Financial School,* a pro-silver pamphlet, were distributed during the fall of 1896.

In contrast, McKinley conducted a "front porch" campaign from his home in Canton, Ohio. From his front porch, McKinley would greet the voters and then give a speech. McKinley denounced Bryan's economic ideas as dangerous, noting that they would destroy the nation's economy.

Bryan's appeal to industrial workers to join his partnership of independent businessmen failed, largely because they depended for their livelihoods on the very eastern interests that Bryan attacked. McKinley won not only the East, but also the small cities and towns in Bryan's southern and western belt of support. Bryan, however, was unable to win rural areas in the East. McKinley won the popular vote 7.1 million—51.0 percent—to 6.5 million—46.7 percent—and the electoral vote 271–176.

The effect of the 1896 presidential election was lasting. As historian James Sundquist wrote:

For 20 years the two-party system had been based on dead issues of the past. It had offered the voters no means of expressing a choice on the crucial issues of domestic policy around which the country had been polarizing.... [S]uddenly, with the nomination of Bryan in 1896, the party system took on meaning once again.

As a result of the 1896 election, a strong new Republican coalition emerged. The coalition included residents of cities, where capital and labor were both reasonably content with the economic growth that the GOP tariff policy promoted; farmers in the East and Midwest, who had strong ties to the "party of Lincoln" and who had come to favor high tariffs; Catholic, German Lutheran, and other Christian denominations; and some Border States.

After 1896, the competitive party balance that had prevailed for years began to give way to lopsided party strength according to region-Democrats in the South, Republicans in the North. Strong opposition parties disappeared in all regions of the country, vesting political power in the hands of those already part of the system.

See also: Democratic Party; Election of 1892; Election of 1900; Republican Party.

Further Reading

Phillips, Kevin. *William McKinley.* New York: Times Books, 2003.

Election of 1900: William McKinley

In a rematch of the 1896 election, Republican President William McKinley returned to the White House. As the election of 1900 approached, McKinley's popularity was growing. The nation was prosperous, and the American victory in the Spanish-American War increased national pride. At the Republican convention, McKinley was easily nominated on the first ballot. The convention then focused on the vice-presidential nominee. A new candidate had to be chosen because Vice President Garret A. Hobart had died in 1899. McKinley agreed to accept whomever the delegates selected. Quickly, the progressive governor of New York, Theodore Roosevelt, became the leading contender for the vice-presidential spot. While some Republican delegates were impressed with Roosevelt's successes in the Spanish-American War, others were pleased by the reforms he pushed through in New York. At the same time, some party voices, such as New York's Thomas Platt, were eager to remove the stubborn reformer. The convention nominated Roosevelt. After hearing that Theodore Roosevelt was McKinley's running mate, Mark Hanna, McKinley's campaign manager exclaimed,

> **D**on't any of you realize that there's only one life between that madman and the presidency?

As in 1896, McKinley campaigned from his front porch, greeting voters and giving speeches. Vice-presidential nominee Theodore Roosevelt, however, traveled the country and campaigned vigorously, often giving several speeches a day.

The Democratic Convention chose their 1896 **standard bearer,** William Jennings Bryan. For vice president, they chose former vice president Adlai E. Stevenson, who had served during Cleveland's second term. As in 1896, Bryan campaigned across the country for the free coinage of silver and against the gold standard. He also criticized the **imperialist** polices of the Republicans.

The Populist Party, which had supported Bryan in 1896, nominated its own candidates: Wharton Barkley for president and Ignatius Donnelly for vice president. In addition, the Social Democratic Party, or Socialists, nominated Eugene V. Debs for the presidency.

McKinley's vote totals in 1900 were even greater than in 1896. He won 7.2 million popular votes (51.7 percent) to Bryan's 6.4 million (45.5 percent), and 292 electoral votes to Bryan's 155. McKinley swept to victory with all states except the South and the silver states of the West (Colorado, Montana, Idaho, and Nevada). None of the third party candidates won any electoral votes.

In September 1901, McKinley was attending the Pan-American Conference in Buffalo, New York. While shaking hands with supporters, Leon Czolgosz, an **anarchist,** shot the president with a revolver that had been hidden in his bandaged hand. After emergency surgery, McKinley seemed to improve. Less than a week later, however, the president was dead. At age 42, Theodore Roosevelt became the youngest president to assume office.

See also: Democratic Party; Election of 1896; Election of 1904; Third Parties; Populist Party; Republican Party.

Further Reading

Phillips, Kevin. *William McKinley.* New York: Times Books, 2003.

Election of 1904: Theodore Roosevelt

The election that returned **incumbent** Theodore Roosevelt to the White House, where he continued his progressive policies. Upon assuming the presidency in 1901, Roosevelt continued many conservative Republican policies. At the same time, he also steered the Republicans toward progressive policies. These policies included ideas such as the conservation of natural resources, the enforcement of antitrust laws, the promotion of labor issues, and railroad regulation. The government's lawsuit to dissolve the Northern Securities Company under the Sherman Anti-Trust Act and Roosevelt's intervention in the coal miners' strike, both in 1902, established the activist tone of Roosevelt's presidency. Roosevelt also used his office as a "bully pulpit" to promote his progressive ideology.

Roosevelt had no trouble winning the nomination for election as president in his own right in 1904. The Republican convention, arranged in advance at the White House, unanimously voted for Roosevelt and his platform of tariffs, labor relations, and activist foreign policy. Senator Charles W. Fairbanks of Indiana was the GOP vice-presidential nominee.

To oppose the enthusiastic Roosevelt, the Democrats selected Alton Parker, the somber chief justice of the New York State Court of Appeals. Parker received the backing of the Democratic Party's conservative establishment when former president Grover Cleveland turned down offers to make a fourth presidential run. The Democratic Party leader, William Jennings Bryan, however, forced the party to adopt a liberal platform, as a balance to the conservative presidential nominee. For the vice-presidential candidate, the Democrats chose former senator Henry G. Davis of West Virginia.

The Roosevelt victory was a landslide. He won 7.6 million votes—56.4 percent—to Parker's 5.1 million—37.6 percent—and carried all but the southern states. Roosevelt won 336 electoral votes to Parker's 140. Both houses of Congress were overwhelmingly Republican. President Roosevelt pledged not to seek a second term of his own because he had served most of McKinley's second term. He occupied himself with his progressive agenda and groomed his secretary of war, William Howard Taft, as his successor.

See also: Democratic Party; Election of 1900; Election of 1908; Republican Party.

Further Reading

Auchincloss, Louis. *Theodore Roosevelt*. New York: Times Books, 2001.

Election of 1908: William Howard Taft

An election that sent another progressive Republican to the White House. Soon after his 1904 victory, Roosevelt announced that, because he had served most of McKinley's unfinished term, he would not seek a third term. Nonetheless, he was widely supported by Republicans and many of the party faithful wanted him to run again. Roosevelt, however, threw his support to his friend and secretary of war, William Howard Taft. Even before the

Republican convention, Roosevelt was able to line up state delegations for Taft. Thus, Taft's nomination was never in doubt and he won it on the first ballot. For vice president, the Republicans chose Senator James S. Sherman of New York.

Taft had impressive governmental experience. Before joining Roosevelt's cabinet, he had been a Cincinnati judge, U.S. solicitor general, federal circuit judge, head of the U.S. Commission on the Philippines, and the first civil governor of the Philippines.

At the Democratic convention, the delegates nominated William Jennings Bryan for the third time. After the stinging defeat of Alton Parker in 1904, the Democrats decided the party needed an aggressive challenger to the Republicans. For vice president, the Democrats nominated Representative John W. Kern of Indiana, who was almost unknown outside his home state.

Taft campaigned on the Roosevelt record. He predicted that an economic crisis would hit the nation if Bryan were elected. Bryan called for government ownership of railroads and other liberal measures—such as a lower tariff, campaign finance reform, a graduated income tax, labor reforms, and greater enforcement of antitrust and other business regulations.

With Roosevelt and Taft promoting a progressive agenda, Bryan's message was no longer distinctive, and Taft won easily. He gathered 7.7 million popular votes (51.6 percent) to Bryan's 6.4 million (43.1 percent), and 321 electoral votes to Bryan's 162. The North, most of the West, and the Border States went for the Republicans.

See also: Democratic Party; Election of 1904; Election of 1912; Republican Party.

Further Reading

Mieczkowski, Yan. *The Routledge Historical Atlas of American Presidential Elections*. London: Routledge, 2001.

E

A – Z

Election of 1912: Woodrow Wilson

The first election won by the Democratic nominee since the presidency of Grover Cleveland. As the election of 1912 approached, incumbent President William Howard Taft sought the Republican nomination. He pointed to his success and noted that he was following many of Theodore Roosevelt's policies. Taft, however, was not nearly as popular as was Roosevelt.

Divisions within the Republican Party eventually created rival Taft and Roosevelt factions. Tariffs, Arizona's new state constitution (which included a provision for recall of the governor which Taft opposed), treaties, conservation, the scope of presidential power, and antitrust issues split the former president and the sitting president. In many ways, the dispute was over personalities. Taft carried out Roosevelt's program, but lacked his fervor and decisiveness.

VIEWPOINTS

In this 1912 political cartoon, the Republican elephant and the Democratic donkey express their shock at the appearance of the "Bull Moose" Party, led by former president Theodore Roosevelt. (The Granger Collection, New York)

In a still conservative age, progressives felt they needed more aggressive leadership than Taft would ever give them. They believed he should have been more aggressive in implementing reforms. Thus, the Republican Party was divided.

Even before the Republican convention met, however, Roosevelt announced he wanted the nomination, noting, "My hat is in the ring." When reminded of his earlier statement that he would not seek a third term, he explained that he simply meant he would not seek three consecutive terms. Roosevelt made an all-out effort for the Republican nomination, entering twelve primaries and winning all but three. Three crucial Republican states—Pennsylvania, Illinois, and Ohio—went for Roosevelt. He clearly, then, had great popular appeal and vote-getting ability—perhaps more than ever.

However, Taft won the nomination. The president controlled the Republican Party machinery, and most of the convention's delegates were sent by the state machines.

After the defeat, Roosevelt urged his supporters to continue their fight. They bolted the convention and began to mount a third-party effort, called the Progressive Party. The new party became known as the Bull Moose Party when Roosevelt remarked to a reporter during the GOP convention, "I'm feeling like a bull moose." Of course, Roosevelt won the nomination of the new party.

With the Republicans divided, the Democrats saw their first opportunity to win the presidency since Cleveland in 1892. As the 1912 Democratic convention in Baltimore neared, several national candidates and favorite sons were vying for the nomination. The front-runner was House Speaker James Beauchamp "Champ" Clark of Missouri, a party regular who had party organization support and years of experience to recommend him.

Governor Woodrow Wilson of New Jersey, who held a doctorate in political science and who had moved into politics after a distinguished career as professor and president at Princeton University, was another strong candidate. Wilson's virtues were the opposite of

Clark's. He did not have an extensive political record for opponents to attack, and he was supported enthusiastically because of his dynamic presence and reformist rhetoric. As a newcomer to national politics, Wilson delighted some Democrats, but alienated more traditional party members with his speeches before the convention. He came out strongly for the "radical" platform of referendum, initiative, and recall, prompting a newspaper to report:

> The boldness, the directness, the incisiveness, the fearlessness, and the force of the 'Virginian-Jerseyan's' words crashed at times through the throng like a series of thunderbolt jolts.

Wilson's embrace of the progressive agenda and attacks on business alienated many southerners.

Other Democratic candidates were the conservative representative Oscar Underwood of Alabama, author of a historic tariff act; another conservative, Governor Judson Harmon of Ohio; and four favorite-son governors. Clark appeared to have won the nomination after he won a tenth-ballot majority. The Democrats, however, required that their nominee receive a two-thirds majority. Thus other candidates had time to maneuver behind the scenes. Wilson almost dropped out of the race, but William Jennings Bryan announced his support for Wilson, creating a bandwagon effect for Wilson. On the forty-sixth ballot, Wilson finally won the necessary two-thirds of delegates for the nomination. Governor Thomas Marshall of Indiana, one of the favorite-son candidates, was picked to be the vice-presidential nominee. Underwood, Wilson's choice for vice president, would not accept the nomination.

The Democratic platform was progressive. It called for tariff reduction, utility regulation, banking reforms, legislation to curb monopolies, a national income tax, direct election of senators, campaign finance reforms, and a national presidential primary.

Wilson and Roosevelt quickly became the two main contenders. They both crisscrossed the country giving speeches to enthusiastic crowds. Taft gave few speeches and spent most of the campaign in the White House.

Wilson easily won the election, receiving 435 electoral votes to Roosevelt's eighty-eight and Taft's eight. The Republican split obviously helped Wilson; if Roosevelt and Taft had combined their totals of 4.1 million votes (27.4 percent) and 3.5 million votes (23.2 percent), they would have topped Wilson's 6.3 million (41.8 percent). Yet, it was the worst showing ever for an incumbent president—third place with electoral votes from only two states.

See also: Bull Moose Party; Democratic Party; Election of 1908; Election of 1916; Republican Party.

Further Reading

Auchincloss, Louis. *Theodore Roosevelt.* New York: Times Books, 2001.

Brands, H.W. *Woodrow Wilson.* New York: Times Books, 2003.

Chace, James. *1912: Wilson, Roosevelt, Taft, and Debs—The Election That Changed the Country.* New York: Simon & Schuster, 2004.

Election of 1916: Woodrow Wilson

The very close election that returned Woodrow Wilson to the White House. Despite his strong leadership, highlighted by his stirring oratory, Wilson still faced the prospect in 1916 of a tough reelection. He had won the presidency in 1912 with only 41.8 percent of the popular vote.

Electoral Votes: Election of 1916	
Woodrow Wilson (D)	277
Charles Evans Hughes (R)	254

The election of 1916 was a close contest. The outcome hinged on California's electoral vote, which Wilson won by about 3,000 votes.

E

A–Z

E

A–Z

DECISION MAKERS

Jeannette Rankin

The first woman elected to Congress and a social reformer, suffragist, and peace advocate. Born in 1880 on a Montana ranch, Jeannette Rankin later attended Montana State University and earned a bachelor's degree in biology. She then attended the University of Washington in Seattle and became involved in the women's suffrage movement. Rankin then moved to New York to work for women's rights. As World War I was raging in Europe, she decided to return to Montana and run for Congress as a Republican. Thus, on November 6, 1916, she became the first woman elected to Congress. Rankin made history again when, in 1917, she voted against U.S. entry into World War I. She lost her bid to run for the Senate in 1918 and then returned to Montana to work for peace. Montana sent Rankin to Congress again in 1940. After the Japanese attack on Pearl Harbor, Hawaii, on December 7, 1941, President Franklin D. Roosevelt asked Congress for a declaration of war. Rankin was the only member of Congress to vote against the measure. In 1943, Rankin settled in Montana. Rankin died in 1973.

In addition, World War I in Europe was beginning to disturb American economic growth.

Wilson and Vice President Marshall won renomination without any opposition. The most significant event of the Democratic convention was the passage of the platform, which indicated the party's campaign themes. By calling for national universal suffrage, Wilson helped himself in the eleven western states where women already had won the vote. The platform also praised "the splendid diplomatic victories of our great president, who has preserved the vital interests of our government and its citizens, and kept us out of war." Indeed, "He Kept Us Out Of War" became the Democrats' campaign slogan.

The Republicans gave the presidential nomination to Supreme Court Justice Charles Evans Hughes. Hughes was silent in the months before the convention, but a number of party leaders lined up enough delegates for him to win a third-ballot nomination. Other potential candidates in 1916 included former president Roosevelt, former senator Elihu Root of New York, former vice president Fairbanks, and Senators John Weeks, Albert Cummins, and Lawrence Sherman. Fairbanks won the vice-presidential nomination.

The nation's prosperity limited the campaign themes available to the Republicans. The GOP railed against Wilson's foreign policy, pointing out that it put the United States in danger of entering the war. Hughes also attacked Wilson's military interventions in Mexico, where the United States was supporting various factions in the Mexican civil war. Vigorous campaigning by former President Theodore Roosevelt also helped Hughes.

President Wilson remained in Washington, D.C., throughout the summer of 1916, but he emerged to give a series of speeches in the fall. Meanwhile, Democratic strategists conceived and executed a masterful strategy to return Wilson to the White House. The Democrats concentrated all their resources on "swing states" and ignored states they thought Wilson was sure to lose. Illinois, for example, was ignored since it was a certain Republican state. Furthermore, William Jennings Bryan, the three-time Democratic nominee and now Wilson's secretary of state, toured the West where he was still popular.

Wilson won one of the closest elections in history. California, an uncertain state, ensured Wilson's victory when Wilson's margin of victory was only 3,420 votes in that state because of the urban vote. The president defeated Hughes by a margin of 9.1 million (49.2 percent) to 8.5 million popular votes (46.1 percent). The electoral college gave Wilson 277 votes and Hughes 254.

Even though Wilson's campaign in 1916 was based on his determination to stay out of World War I, the United States was in the war by April 1917. Wilson's conduct of the war made him a war hero, but his diplomatic efforts after the war failed. Wilson was the architect of the Treaty of Versailles, which created a League of Nations to prevent future wars. Wilson, however, was unable to convince the Senate to approve the treaty, and he left office in 1921 a broken and dispirited man.

See also: Democratic Party; Election of 1912; Election of 1920; Republican Party.

Further Reading

Brands, H.W. *Woodrow Wilson.* New York: Times Books, 2003.

Election of 1920: Warren G. Harding

The election that returned the Republican Party to power on the promise of a "return to Normalcy." Senator Warren G. Harding, a product of the GOP machine of Ohio, emerged from a crowded and largely unknown pack to win the Republican nomination in 1920 at a convention dominated by economic interests such as oil, railroads, and steel. The early candidates were General Leonard Wood, an old Roosevelt ally; Governor Frank Lowden of Illinois, who mar-

ried into the Pullman family and therefore had ample financing for a campaign; and Senator Hiram Johnson of California, whose progressive and isolationist stances put him in good stead with voters in many states. A dozen favorite sons hoped that a deadlocked convention might bring the nomination their ways. All of the candidates were on hand in Chicago to maneuver for the nomination.

While Wood, Johnson, and Lowden performed reasonably well in the primaries, Harding won only his home state of Ohio and did not arouse much popular enthusiasm. Under the direction of a shrewd campaign manager, Harry Daugherty, Harding gained the support of the party's bosses. He went on to win the nomination on the tenth ballot, after a brief interview with them in the "smoke-filled room." Governor Calvin Coolidge of Massachusetts, a favorite-son contender for president, became Harding's vice-presidential candidate.

The Democrats selected Governor James Cox, also from Ohio, after lengthy platform battles and balloting for the nomination. Early ballots put former treasury secretary William G. McAdoo and Attorney General Mitchell Palmer in the lead, but Cox gained steadily and had the nomination by the forty-fourth ballot. Franklin D. Roosevelt of New York, the assistant secretary of the navy, was quickly selected to be Cox's running mate.

The image of Woodrow Wilson hung over the convention and would hang over the fall campaign. The Democratic platform praised Wilson's conduct of the war and his domestic reform program. Nevertheless, the results in the November election indicated deep unease over the Democratic administration.

Harding amassed 16.1 million popular votes (60.3 percent) to Cox's 9.1 million (34.2 percent), and 404 electoral votes to Cox's 127. Harding carried the North and West including Oklahoma and all the southern and Border States except Tennessee and Kentucky.

Harding's landslide victory was termed "election by disgust" by political analysts. The wartime sacrifices demanded under Wilson were widely perceived as the cause of Harding's

VIEWPOINTS

Who Says a Watched Pot Never Boils?

Warren G. Harding (1921-1923) won a landslide victory in the Election of 1920, but the Teapot Dome Scandal tarnished his administration. This scandal involved Secretary of the Interior Albert B. Fall's leasing the public oilfields in Teapot Dome, Wyoming without the required competitive bidding. (Library of Congress)

backs and favoritism in the administration began to surface. Several members of the administration quit and two committed suicide. The investigation into the Teapot Dome scandal—so named after the site of naval oil reserves that were transferred to private hands in exchange for bribes—would last five years. The Democrats hoped to make the scandal a major issue in the 1924 election. Democratic complicity in the wrongdoing, however, and the personal integrity of Harding's successor, Calvin Coolidge, defused the issue.

See also: Democratic Party; Election of 1916; Election of 1924; Republican Party.

Further Reading

Dean, John W. *Warren G. Harding.* New York: Times Books, 2004.
Greenberg, David. *Calvin Coolidge.* New York Times Books, 2006.

Election of 1924: Calvin Coolidge

The election of one of the most conservative presidents in American history. Soon after taking office, President Calvin Coolidge fired Attorney General Harry M. Daugherty and other members of Harding's clique. Coolidge, a stern New Englander, projected an image of puritan cleanliness. Coolidge—a taciturn man who had slowly climbed the political ladder in Massachusetts from city council member to city solicitor, mayor, state legislator, lieutenant governor, and governor before he became vice president—expounded a deeply individualistic Yankee philosophy. This, in turn, helped to separate Coolidge from the corrupt men in the Harding White House.

Except for appointing Harlan Fiske Stone, former dean of the Columbia University School of Law, as attorney general, Coolidge allowed others to finish cleaning up the mess left behind by Harding. The new president was concerned about unnecessarily alienating himself from party leaders.

By the time Coolidge sought the presidency

victory, rather than a desire for the ideology or policy proposals that Harding was offering. The *New York Post* editorialized:

> **W**e are in the backwash from the mighty spiritual and physical effort to which America girded herself when she won the war for the Allies. . . . The war has not been repudiated, though the administration that fought it has been overwhelmed. We are now in the chill that comes with the doctor's bills.

President Harding died on August 2, 1923, of a heart attack, just as revelations of kick-in his own right in 1924, the economy had re-bounded. He also skillfully used the radio and the press to increase his popularity. One of the most conservative presidents ever, Coolidge's platform called for additional tax cuts, but said nothing significant about increasingly important agriculture and labor issues. Coolidge also pushed an isolationist foreign policy plank. He won the nomination on the first ballot.

While the Republicans were able to "Keep Cool with Coolidge," the Democrats spent sixteen days in a seemingly endless attempt to pick a nominee in New York's sweltering, unair-conditioned, Madison Square Garden. A fight developed because the party was badly split between its northeastern urban bloc and its more conservative southern and western rural bloc. New York governor Alfred E. Smith and former treasury secretary William McAdoo of California were the key contenders at the convention. After the one-hundredth ballot, party bosses freed the convention delegates to vote as they pleased.

Suspicions between the two regional blocs were intense. A platform plank denouncing the Ku Klux Klan created the most controversy. Northerners wanted to explicitly condemn the society that preached hatred of African Americans, Catholics, and Jews. In the end, however, southerners would settle only for a vaguely worded rebuke. (The Klan had infiltrated the party in many rural areas.) Another divisive issue was **Prohibition,** with northerners attacking the initiative and southerners supporting it.

After the party bosses freed the delegates, a stampede developed for John W. Davis of West Virginia, a former congressional representative and lawyer with Wall Street connections. He finally won the nomination on the 103rd ballot. The ticket was balanced with the vice-presidential selection of Charles W. Bryan of Nebraska, the younger brother of three-time presidential candidate William Jennings Bryan.

Liberal Wisconsin Senator Robert La Follette left the Republican Party and chose to run as a third party candidate. LaFollette and his Progressive followers supported labor unions,

the nationalization of big industries, and increased taxes on the wealthy. Many farmers, union members, and Socialists supported La Follette.

Coolidge won the election easily, with the Democrats polling their smallest percentage ever. Coolidge won 54.1 percent of the vote, Davis won 28.8 percent, and LaFollette won 16.6 percent. Coolidge attracted 15.7 million popular votes and 382 electoral votes. Davis won 8.4 million popular votes and 136 electoral votes. LaFollette won 4.8 million popular votes, but carried only his home state of Wisconsin with thirteen electoral votes.

On August 2, 1927, when Coolidge announced his decision not to seek reelection by passing out a brief note to reporters and then refusing further comment, the Republicans began jockeying for the nomination for the 1928 election.

See also: Democratic Party; Election of 1920; Election of 1928; Progressive Party; Republican Party; Third Parties.

Further Reading

Greenberg, David. *Calvin Coolidge.* New York Times Books, 2006.
Hannaford, Peter, ed. *The Quotable Calvin Coolidge.* Bennington, VT: Images of the Past, Inc., 2001.

Election of 1928: Herbert Hoover

The first modern presidential election—with extensive radio coverage—that sent Republican Herbert Hoover to the White House. Secretary of Commerce Herbert Hoover was the obvious choice to replace Coolidge at the head of the GOP ticket. A native of Iowa who learned mining engineering at Stanford University, Hoover was highly popular with most of the party. Hoover's administration of food distribution programs during World War I (1917–1918) had earned him the status of statesman and humanitarian.

E

A – Z

E

A–Z

Electoral Votes: Election of 1928

Herbert Hoover (R)	444
Al Smith (D)	87

Republican Herbert Hoover won a landslide victory in the election of 1928.

Hoover began working for the nomination soon after Coolidge dropped out, spending $400,000 in the nominating phase of the election. He won the nomination on the first ballot over Governors Frank Lowden of Illinois and Charles Curtis of Kansas. Curtis was named Hoover's running mate.

Hoover was fervent in his zeal for what he called "the American system" of free enterprise and individualism. He did not see any inconsistency in having the government vigorously support businesses with tax breaks, tariffs, public provision of infrastructures, and police protection, while at the same time denying federal aid to people in need. He proposed creation of a special farm board and said he would consider legislation to protect labor unions from abuses in the use of court injunctions.

Al Smith, the governor of New York, was the Democratic nominee. Smith had the support of all the party's northern states, and he won a first-ballot nomination. Senator Joseph T. Robinson of Arkansas was the vice-presidential candidate.

Smith's candidacy divided the electorate, especially in the South. He was the first Roman Catholic to be nominated for president by a major party. He thus endured religious slurs throughout the campaign. Moreover, he favored repeal of **Prohibition**, still a divisive issue. He also was a strong opponent of the Ku Klux Klan, which caused him problems in the South. Finally, he was an unabashed liberal who proposed public works, farm relief programs, stronger protection of workers, and regulation of banking and industry.

During the fall campaign, Hoover acted like the incumbent and Smith barnstormed the country, trying in vain to pick up support in the South and West. The 1928 campaign was the first with extensive radio coverage, and Hoover generally fared better than Smith on the airwaves. Hoover, the "small-town boy" who made good, represented fulfillment of the **American Dream.** Smith, the inner-city boy who made good, also embodied that ideal, but he had too many things working against him.

The November election produced another Republican landslide. Hoover carried forty states with 21.4 million popular votes (58.2 percent) and 444 electoral votes, while Smith carried only eight states with 15.0 million popular votes (40.8 percent) and eighty-seven electoral votes. Smith carried only six southern states.

The national economic boom that had begun at the end of World War I came to an abrupt conclusion on October 29, 1929. After climbing to dizzying new heights for months, the stock market crashed. First described by economists and politicians as a temporary interruption of the good times, the crash quickly led to a wave of business closures, bank failures, mortgage foreclosures, wage cuts, and layoffs. By the end of Hoover's term in 1933, more than twelve million workers had lost their jobs and the unemployment rate was approximately 25 percent. President Hoover, who had celebrated his inauguration with a prediction that poverty and hunger were near an end, did not know how to cope with the crisis. Despite his earnest and tireless efforts, Hoover became a target of widespread hostility. As the election of 1932 approached, the voters looked to new, dynamic leadership.

See also: Democratic Party; Election of 1924; Election of 1932; Republican Party.

Further Reading

Fausold, Martin L. *The Presidency of Herbert Hoover.* Lawrence, KS: University Press of Kansas, 1988.

Mieczkowski, Yan. *The Routledge Historical Atlas of American Presidential Elections.* London: Routledge, 2001.

Election of 1932: Franklin D. Roosevelt

A pivotal election that ended Republican control of the presidency and sent Democrat Franklin D. Roosevelt to the White House. As the election of 1932 approached, incumbent President Herbert Hoover chose to run for reelection. He won the Republican nomination on the first ballot. Charles Curtis was again the vice-presidential nominee. The Republicans stood by their record and insisted that the worst of the Great Depression was over.

The Democrats realized that the nation needed new, dynamic leadership to end the Great Depression. As the Democratic convention began, the field of possible candidates was large. Among them were the 1928 Democratic standard-bearer, Al Smith; John Nance Garner, the Speaker of the House; former Senator James Reed of Missouri; Maryland Governor Albert Ritchie; Ohio Governor George White; Virginia Governor Harry Byrd; and New York Governor Franklin D. Roosevelt, who was considered the front-runner.

The many candidates in the race threatened to deadlock the convention and deny the nomination to the front-runner, as had happened so often in the past. Roosevelt had difficulty with his own region of the country because of his opposition to the Tammany machine in New York. Acquiring the required two-thirds vote of delegates for the nomination was difficult for Roosevelt or any other candidate, but FDR eventually won on the fourth

A *LIFE* magazine cover shows a confident President-elect Franklin D. Roosevelt riding to his inauguration next to a somber, frowning incumbent President Herbert Hoover. (© Bettmann/Corbis)

ballot, after he promised the vice-presidential slot to Garner.

Roosevelt, a fifth cousin to Theodore Roosevelt, had been an activist in state politics, first opposing the state's Tammany machine. As New York governor, he pioneered many relief and reconstruction programs that Hoover refused to expand to the national scale. Roosevelt had been the party's vice-presidential candidate twelve years earlier and he had served as assistant secretary of the navy.

In U.S. political history, Franklin D. Roosevelt was the first candidate to appear before the convention that nominated him. In an acceptance speech to the conventioneers who had staged wild rallies in his support, Roosevelt made passing reference to the "new deal" that his administration would offer Americans. That phrase, picked up in a newspaper cartoon the next day, came to symbolize the renewal for which Americans yearned.

Roosevelt conducted an active campaign, traveling twenty-three thousand miles in forty-one

Electoral Votes: Election of 1932	
Franklin D. Roosevelt (D)	472
Herbert Hoover (R)	59

The election of 1932 brought a sweeping victory to Democrat Franklin D. Roosevelt. Blamed for the Great Depression, incumbent President Herbert Hoover lost the election.

E

A–Z

states to quell any suspicions that his physical handicaps would deter him from performing his job. Besides barnstorming the nation, Roosevelt took to the radio airwaves—he was the first sophisticated electronic media candidate—where he conveyed a sense of warmth and confidence. He also showed an intellectual bent and an open mind when he called on academics and professionals—the famed "brain trust"—for their expert advice on the issues.

Perhaps more important than any of his political accomplishments were FDR's image of strength and optimism. He was also skillful at handling hot issues and the diverse members of the Democratic coalition. Although he was a polio victim, Roosevelt often smiled—a devastating contrast to Hoover. Roosevelt was able to campaign for the presidency without putting forth a comprehensive program. The simple promise of a change in leadership was enough to earn a victory.

Roosevelt won 22.8 million votes (57.4 percent) to Hoover's 15.8 million (39.6 percent). Forty-two of the forty-eight states and 472 of the 531 electoral votes went for Roosevelt.

See also: Democratic Party; Election of 1928; Election of 1936; Republican Party.

Further Reading

Jackson, Robert H. *That Man: An Insider's Portrait of Franklin D. Roosevelt.* New York: Oxford University Press, 2003.

Jenkins, Roy. *Franklin Delano Roosevelt.* New York Times Books, 2003.

Levine, Lawrence W., and Cornelia R. Levine. *The People and the President: America's Conversation with FDR.* Boston: Beacon Press, 2002.

Election of 1936: Franklin D. Roosevelt

The first of Franklin D. Roosevelt's reelection victories that also solidified Democratic control of Congress. At the Democratic convention,

Roosevelt was renominated without opposition. He asked Vice President James N. Garner to run with him a second time. The only important change at the Democratic convention was the repeal of the party's requirement that a candidate receive two-thirds of the delegates to win the nomination. Some southern delegates opposed the change, but later backed it. The governor of Texas wondered aloud if the change was designed for a third Roosevelt run in 1940.

Kansas governor Alfred M. Landon was the early favorite for the 1936 Republican nomination. Senator Charles McNary of Oregon, Senator Arthur Vandenberg of Michigan, and *Chicago Daily News* publisher Frank Knox were also interested in the nomination. Historian James MacGregor Burns observed:

> Landon had just the qualities of common sense, homely competence, cautious liberalism and rocklike 'soundness' that the Republicans hoped would appeal to a people tiring, it was hoped, of the antics and heroics in the White House.

Landon won the nomination on the first ballot. He then selected Frank Knox as his running mate. In 1936, the Republicans could not have stated their opposition to Roosevelt's popular New Deal in any stronger terms. The platform read:

> America is in peril. The welfare of American men and women and the future of our youth are at stake. We dedicate ourselves to the preservation of their political liberty, their individual opportunity, and their character as free citizens, which today for the first time are threatened by government itself.

The Republicans called for ending a wide range of government regulations, returning relief to state and local governments, replacing Social Security, balancing the budget, and changing tariff and currency policies. Landon called for a constitutional amendment allowing the states to regulate the labor of women and children.

At first, Roosevelt had planned a low-key campaign. He crisscrossed the country making "official" inspections of drought states and public works programs and delivering speeches on electrical power, conservation, and social welfare programs, among other topics. At the end of September, Roosevelt assumed the role of partisan leader. The president answered Republican charges point by point, and then lashed out at the Republicans in biting, sarcastic terms. As the campaign progressed and Roosevelt sensed a strong response from the large crowds to his attacks, the attacks became stronger. At the close of the campaign, he said:

> We have not come this far without a struggle and I assure you that we cannot go further without a struggle. For twelve years, our nation was afflicted with a hear-nothing, see-nothing, do-nothing government. The nation looked to the government but the government looked away. Nine mocking years with the golden calf and three long years of the scourge! Nine crazy years at the ticker and three long years at the breadlines! Nine mad years of mirage and three long years of despair! And, my friends, powerful influences strive today to restore that kind of government with its doctrine that that government is best which is most indifferent to mankind. . . . Never before in all of our history have these forces been so united against one candidate as they stand today. They are unanimous in their hate for me—and I welcome their hatred.

The 1936 Literary Digest Poll
Especially to sophisticated campaign technicians of the modern age, a poll that predicted a big Landon victory provides some amusement. The *Literary Digest,* which had predicted past elec-

Electoral Votes: Election of 1936

Franklin D. Roosevelt (D)	523
Alf Landon(R)	8

President Roosevelt's innovative plans to end the Great Depression made him extremely popular. Roosevelt won a sweeping reelection victory in the election of 1936.

tions with accuracy, conducted a postcard poll of its readers that pointed toward a Landon landslide. But the heavy middle- and upper-class bias of the magazine's readership meant that the views of the voters on the lower rungs of the economic ladder were left out of the sample. To this day, the poll is cited as the prime example of bad survey group selection.

The failure of the *Literary Digest*'s survey pointed to the most salient aspect of the election results: the heavy class divisions among the voters. Polls showed that class divisions widened starting around the midpoint of Roosevelt's first term. The broad support Roosevelt had enjoyed because of a common economic disaster had hardened along class lines by the time of the 1936 election.

Election Results
In the 1936 election, Roosevelt won 27.7 million popular votes (60.8 percent) to Landon's 16.7 million (36.5 percent.) Roosevelt carried forty-six of the forty-eight states, and he took 523 of the 531 electoral votes. Landon carried only Maine and Vermont with eight electoral votes. In addition, the Senate's Democratic majority increased to seventy-five of ninety-eight seats, and the House majority increased to 333 of 435 seats.

See also: Democratic Party; Election of 1928; Election of 1932; Election of 1940; Republican Party.

Further Reading
Jackson, Robert H. *That Man: An Insider's Portrait of Franklin D. Roosevelt.* New York: Oxford University Press, 2003.

Jenkins, Roy. *Franklin Delano Roosevelt*. New York Times Books, 2003.

Levine, Lawrence W., and Cornelia R. Levine. *The People and the President: America's Conversation with FDR*. Boston: Beacon Press, 2002.

Election of 1940: Franklin D. Roosevelt

The first election in which a candidate won a third term. As **incumbent** President Franklin D. Roosevelt looked toward the possibility of a third term in 1940, the widening war in Europe posed a difficult problem. Nazi Germany had invaded the Rhineland, Poland, France, Norway, Denmark, Holland, Belgium, and Luxembourg and had made alliances with Italy and the Soviet Union. Japan had invaded China. Adolf Hitler launched the Battle of Britain in the summer of 1940; all-night air raids of London came soon afterward.

Roosevelt publicly maintained that he did not want another term, but he refused to issue a definitive statement begging off the race. Despite the historic precedent against third terms, Roosevelt wanted to remain president. To avoid the appearance of overzealousness, Roosevelt wanted the Democrats to draft him in 1940.

While the nation waited for Roosevelt to act, Vice President Garner announced his candidacy. Postmaster General Farley and Secretary of

Wendell Willkie (standing in car), faced an uphill battle trying to unseat the popular incumbent in the Election of 1940. (The Granger Collection)

Electoral Votes: Election of 1940	
Franklin D. Roosevelt (D)	449
Wendell Willkie(R)	82

Many Americans were opposed to President Roosevelt running for an unprecedented third term in 1940. Yet, Roosevelt won another outstanding electoral victory.

State Cordell Hull also expressed interest in the nomination, and Roosevelt gave both vague assurances of support. Roosevelt, whose relations with Vice President Garner had soured after Roosevelt attempted to increase the number of Supreme Court justices, simply watched the vice president struggle to gain a respectable public profile. Farley and Hull gained little party support.

From a distance, Roosevelt watched state Democratic delegations declare their support. Polls showed Roosevelt's fortunes rising with the deepening European crisis. Roosevelt, however, would not reveal his plans for 1940, even to his closest aides. The president did not forbid aides such as Harry Hopkins to work on a draft, but he did not get involved because he wanted the Democrats to call on him—not the other way around.

At the Democratic convention in Chicago, Senator Alben Barkley told the delegates:

The president has never had, and has not today, any desire or purpose to continue in the office of president. . . . He wishes in all earnestness and sincerity to make it clear that all the delegates of this convention are free to vote for any candidate.

The statement was followed by an hour-long demonstration and Roosevelt's first-ballot nomination. The convention mood turned disagreeable, however, when Roosevelt announced that he wanted the liberal secretary of agriculture, Henry Wallace, as his running mate. The announcement irritated delegates who already had lined up behind other candidates. Nevertheless, Wallace eventually beat Alabama representative

William Bankhead, his strongest opponent for the nomination.

The Republicans mounted their strongest challenge to Roosevelt in 1940, largely based on the charge that Roosevelt was moving the United States toward involvement in the world war. Several moves toward military preparedness had failed at the hands of isolationists in Congress. When Roosevelt asked for increases in defense spending after General Francisco Franco's victory in Spain and Hitler's invasion of Austria in 1938, critics asserted that the president was attempting to cover up domestic failures with foreign adventures. Roosevelt pressed on, however, and Congress passed the Selective Service Act and increases in military spending in 1940.

E

A–Z

A political button expresses the viewpoint of many Democratic voters who supported President Franklin D. Roosevelt's unprecedented third term in 1940. Roosevelt's supporters favored his strong leadership, especially as World War II (1939-1945) loomed in Europe. (Photo by Blank Archives/Getty Images)

The Republican field in 1940 included several fresh faces: Senator Robert A. Taft of Ohio, son of the former president; District Attorney Thomas E. Dewey of New York City; Senator Charles L. McNary of Oregon; and Senator Arthur H. Vandenberg of Michigan, who had been considered long shots for the Republican nomination in 1936. The freshest face of all was Wendell L. Willkie, a utility executive who had never run for political office. A large, pleasant man, former Democrat Willkie had barnstormed the country for seven years speaking in opposition to the New Deal. Hundreds of "Willkie clubs" sprang up in the summer of 1940, and a number of publications, including Henry Luce's *Time* magazine, chronicled Willkie's career and encouraged the Willkie groundswell. Despite concern about Willkie's lack of political experience, which led to a "stop Willkie" movement, the Indianan won a sixth-ballot nomination by acclamation. Senator McNary, the Republicans' Senate floor leader, accepted the vice-presidential nomination.

Traveling thirty thousand miles in thirty-four states, Willkie gave some 540 speeches. By the time his campaign ended, his already husky voice had turned hoarse. The Republicans spent lavishly and organized grassroots clubs for Willkie across the country. Charges against Roosevelt of managerial incompetence, "warmongering," and imperial ambitions punctuated the Willkie effort. The GOP argued that Roosevelt threatened to become a dictator by exceeding the traditional two-term limit established by George Washington. A dramatic moment in the campaign came when Democratic-leaning labor leader John L. Lewis called on workers to back Willkie.

After a period of strictly presidential behavior, Roosevelt took to the campaign trail with partisan vigor, criticizing the Republican's plans. He answered Willkie's warmongering charges with a promise never to involve the United States in "foreign wars," which left Roosevelt free to respond to a direct attack.

Roosevelt won, but by the slimmest popular vote margin of any race since 1912. He received 27.3 million popular votes—54.7 percent—to Willkie's 22.3 million—44.8 percent. The electoral vote tally was 449–82.

See also: Democratic Party; Election of 1936; Election of 1944; Republican Party.

Further Reading

Jackson, Robert H. *That Man: An Insider's Portrait of Franklin D. Roosevelt.* New York: Oxford University Press, 2003.

Jenkins, Roy. *Franklin Delano Roosevelt.* New York Times Books, 2003.

Levine, Lawrence W., and Cornelia R. Levine. *The People and the President: America's Conversation with FDR.* Boston: Beacon Press, 2002.

Election of 1944: Franklin D. Roosevelt

Roosevelt's unprecedented election to a fourth term as president. Roosevelt's third term and fourth election were dominated by World War II. Japan attacked U.S. bases at Pearl Harbor, Hawaii, on December 7, 1941. The president, speaking before Congress, declared the date of the surprise attack "a day that will live in infamy." Congress shook off its isolationist inclinations and declared war. A few days after Pearl Harbor, Germany and Italy declared war on the United States, confronting the nation with a two-front war.

The war did for the economy what the New Deal, by itself, could not: it brought economic prosperity. The number of unemployed workers fell from eight million to one million between 1940 and 1944. The boom brought seven million more people, half of them women, into the job market. Inflation, worker shortages, and occasional shortages in raw materials posed problems for wartime agencies. The number of U.S. families paying taxes quadrupled, and by 1945 tax revenues were twenty times their 1940 level. Budget deficits reached new heights.

The fighting in Europe and Asia was grim during the first two years of the war. Isolationist sentiment again built up in Congress, with the Midwest opposed to Roosevelt's foreign policy.

Criticism of how the Roosevelt administration was managing U.S. participation in the wars on both fronts was rampant. The administration won key congressional votes on the war but faced stubborn resistance on domestic measures.

After initial setbacks, the Allied forces won impressive victories. Allied forces, led by General Dwight D. Eisenhower, routed the Axis powers in North Africa in 1942. The Soviet Union beat back a Nazi assault on Stalingrad in the winter of 1942–1943. The Allies took over Italy in 1943 and struggled with the Nazis in France in 1944. In September 1944, British and American troops entered Germany. In the Pacific war, American offensives protected Australia in 1942 and secured the Philippines in 1944.

Despite the bitter opposition that prevailed through much of his third term, Roosevelt had no trouble winning a fourth term in 1944. The Allies found greater success on the battlefield and on the sea, and the nation did not appear willing to risk untested leadership as the war came to an end. The Republicans turned to the governor of New York, Thomas Dewey. Wendell Willkie wanted another shot at the White House, and his best-selling book *One World* put him in the public eye, but conservatives blamed him for the 1940 election defeat. Governors John Bricker of Ohio and Harold Stassen of Minnesota and General Douglas MacArthur were the other Republican hopefuls.

Dewey's primary victories over Willkie in the Wisconsin, Nebraska, and Oregon primaries ended Willkie's public career. Dewey was too far in front to stop. At the convention, he won a nearly unanimous first-ballot nomination after Bricker and Stassen dropped out. After Governor Earl Warren of California refused the vice-presidential nomination, Bricker accepted it.

The party platform extolled the virtues of free enterprise, but did not criticize the concept of the New Deal and even made bids for the votes of African Americans and women. In his acceptance speech Dewey criticized "stubborn men grown old and tired and quarrelsome in office."

The 1944 election marked the early resistance of the South to the modern Democratic Party. Roosevelt was a shoo-in for the nomination, but southerners wanted a replacement for Wallace as vice president, restoration of the two-thirds nominating rule, and a platform declaration of white supremacy. Some dissatisfied southerners threatened to bolt the party in the November election. After the party adopted only a vague civil rights plank in its platform, however, southern discontent dissipated. The rest of the platform called for an internationalist foreign policy and further New Deal-style reforms domestically.

Roosevelt expressed support for Vice President Wallace but said he would allow the convention to pick his running mate. Wallace gave a stirring convention speech, but disturbed conservatives with his stand against the poll tax and for equal opportunity for all "regardless of race or sex." Senator Harry S. Truman of Missouri, who had won fame as a critic of defense spending, beat Wallace for the vice-presidential nomination on the second ballot.

The Democratic campaign was dominated by references to the need for wartime unity and reminders of the Republican rule under Hoover. One leaflet bore the words "Lest We Forget" and a photograph of an unemployed man selling apples in front of a "Hoover Club"; an inset photograph showed Dewey conferring with former president Hoover.

Roosevelt won with 25.6 million popular votes—53.4 percent—to Dewey's 22.0 million—45.9 percent. The electoral vote was 432 to ninety-nine. President Roosevelt, however, who had reshaped U.S. politics at all levels, did not have the opportunity to see the end of the war or to participate in the making of the postwar

E

A–Z

Electoral Votes: Election of 1944

Franklin D. Roosevelt (D)	432
Thomas E. Dewey(R)	99

President Franklin D. Roosevelt swept to a fourth-term victory in the election of 1944.

world. On April 12, 1945, less than three months after his fourth inauguration, he collapsed while sitting for a portrait in Warm Springs, Georgia, and died a few hours later. Vice President Truman was sworn in as the thirty-third president.

See also: Democratic Party; Election of 1940; Election of 1948; Republican Party.

Further Reading

Jackson, Robert H. *That Man: An Insider's Portrait of Franklin D. Roosevelt.* New York: Oxford University Press, 2003.

Jenkins, Roy. *Franklin Delano Roosevelt.* New York Times Books, 2003.

Levine, Lawrence W., and Cornelia R. Levine. *The People and the President: America's Conversation with FDR.* Boston: Beacon Press, 2002.

Election of 1948: Harry S. Truman

Election that returned President Harry S. Truman to the White House. Truman assumed the presidency in April 1945 after the sudden death of President Franklin D. Roosevelt. During his first term, Truman oversaw the end of World War II overseas, and worked to restore the nation's peacetime economy at home. Truman, a plainspoken Midwesterner, however, was a very different president from Roosevelt. For example, Truman wanted to "keep my feet on the ground" and avoid the "crackpots and lunatic fringe" that had surrounded FDR. Thus, he got rid of Commerce Secretary Henry Wallace and others. The independent journalist I. F. Stone wrote of Truman's personnel moves:

> The little nameplates outside the little doors . . . began to change. In Justice, Treasury, Commerce and elsewhere, the New Dealers began to be replaced by the kind of men one was accustomed to meeting in county court-houses.

The Republican Eightieth Congress, elected in 1946, did not cooperate with Truman. For example, many in Congress worked to dismantle New Deal programs, and they frustrated the president's anti-inflation efforts. Clashing with congress, Truman then vetoed 250 bills (eleven vetoes were overridden). Cautious civil rights initiatives displeased the South and labor unrest was on the rise. Nonetheless, as the election of 1948 approached, Truman sought to win the presidency in his own right.

In August 1948, the Democratic convention appeared to reflect a dangerously polarized nation. Many Democrats did not believe that Truman could win the presidency. Some party leaders worked behind the scenes to keep Truman from winning the nomination. They were unsuccessful—Truman won the nomination on the first ballot. For vice president, the Democrats chose Senator Alben W. Barkley of Kentucky.

Many Democrats—both conservative and liberal—were unhappy with Truman's nomination and the Democrats' platform. After a liberal civil rights platform was adopted by the convention, the "Dixiecrats," under the leadership of South Carolina's Governor J. Strom Thurmond, left the convention to conduct their own fall campaign. Thurmond's candidacy ran under the Democratic Party label in four states (Alabama, Louisiana, Mississippi, and South Carolina) and under the States' Rights Democratic Party elsewhere in the South.

Meanwhile, the party's liberal left wing, behind Henry Wallace, protested Truman's Marshall Plan (a multimillion-dollar program to rebuild the economies of western Europe), military buildup, and confrontational stance toward the Soviet Union. It, too, ran its own fall campaign under the banner of the Progressive Citizens of America, known as the Progressive Party.

Many of FDR's old political allies eventually got behind Truman, but the president's election prospects looked bleak. Some support was grudging—Mrs. Roosevelt offered a straightforward endorsement only to rebut newspaper reports that she favored the Republicans. While the Democratic Party was badly fractured, the Republican Party united behind Thomas E. Dewey.

THE ELECTION OF 1948

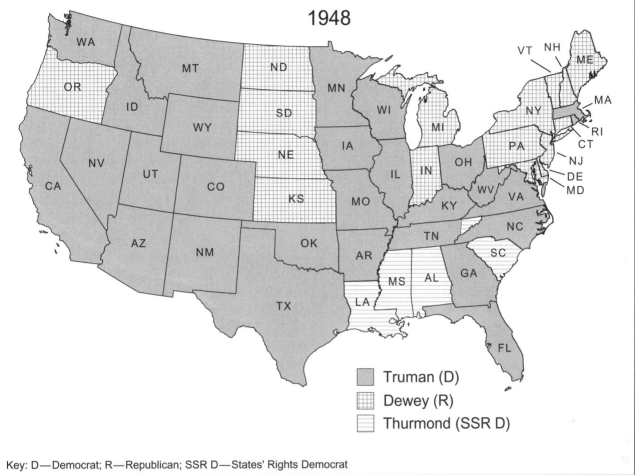

1948

Truman (D)
Dewey (R)
Thurmond (SSR D)

Key: D—Democrat; R—Republican; SSR D—States' Rights Democrat

In the election of 1948, the Democratic Party was split into three: the regular Democrats, the States' Rights Democrats (Dixiecrats), and the Progressives. Republicans were confident of victory. Incumbent President Harry S. Truman ran a strong campaign and swept to victory.

E

A - Z

Dewey, the 1944 GOP candidate, survived a large field of contenders in 1948 to become the nominee once again. Senator Robert A. Taft of Ohio was the main contender, but his isolationism and dull public demeanor were liabilities. The most spirited opposition came from former Governor Harold Stassen of Minnesota, who appealed to the more liberal and internationalist wing of the party. Other candidates or potential convention contenders included Generals Eisenhower and MacArthur, Governor Earl Warren of California, and Senator Arthur H. Vandenberg of Michigan. Polls showed all of the Republicans but Taft beating Truman.

Dewey won an impressive primary victory. Later Dewey was especially tough in a primary debate with Stassen about communism. With these successes, as well as his mastery over convention mechanics, Dewey won the presidential nomination on the third ballot. Earl Warren was selected as the vice-presidential nominee.

From the beginning of the campaign, the media and professional politicians gave Truman little chance of retaining the White House. Early polls showed Dewey with such a strong lead that pollsters simply stopped surveying voters. Nevertheless, the polls failed because of a bias in the way the questions were asked and a presumption that the large undecided vote would cast their ballots in the same way as the rest of the population, when it in fact heavily favored Truman.

Dewey was so certain of victory that he ran as if he were the incumbent. He made a series of bland, almost diplomatic statements rather than energetic campaign speeches. Dewey appeared confident, however, he was careful to avoid the overaggressive posture that he thought had ruined his 1944 campaign against Roosevelt. He even made some initial cabinet and policy decisions.

Truman's strategy from the beginning was to mobilize Roosevelt's New Deal coalition. The biggest danger was apathy, he and campaign aide Clark Clifford reasoned, therefore, the best approach was to give the voters a reason to go to the polling booths. Because the Democrats were the majority party, it was essential that their longtime supporters went to polls and voted.

Truman ran a scrappy and blunt underdog campaign that could have been mistaken for an outsider's effort. Truman was the president, but he ran against the Washington establishment. Crisscrossing the nation on a whistle-stop train tour, Truman traveled about 31,000 miles and spoke before six million people. He turned his record of vetoes into an asset, claiming that the "do-nothing" Republican Eightieth Congress made him do it. He assailed the conservative Republican record on inflation, housing, labor, farm issues, and foreign affairs. The president drew large crowds—sometimes many times the size of Dewey's crowds. Nonetheless, he was virtually the only political professional who believed he would win.

Despite the *Chicago Tribune*'s now-famous headline—"Dewey Defeats Truman"—President Truman prevailed. Early returns put Truman in front, but it was expected that the later-reporting western states would give Dewey the win. When California and Ohio went into the Truman column mid-morning on Wednesday, Dewey conceded defeat.

Considering the Democratic defections, Truman's appeal was widespread. He won twenty-eight states with 24.11 million votes (49.51 percent) and might have won more in the South and North with a united party. As it was, Thurmond won 22 percent of the vote in the South. Dewey won 21.97 million votes (45.12 percent), and Thurmond polled 1.17 million votes (2.40 percent). Henry Wallace won some 1.16 million votes (2.38 percent), but no electoral votes. Wallace's candidacy may have cost Truman New York, Michigan, and Maryland. Yet Wallace may have done Truman a favor by freeing him from the taint of being the most liberal candidate in a time when the electorate was weary of liberalism. Particularly because the Republicans did not have a Midwesterner on their ticket and talked about cutting back agricultural subsidies, farmers felt safer with Truman. In all, Truman won 303 electoral votes, Dewey 189, and Thurmond thirty-nine.

The Democratic defections may have helped Truman by making him the candidate of the center. The Wallace campaign freed the president from suspicions on the right, and the Thurmond defection strengthened Truman's more liberal northern constituency. In addition, the defections may have inspired Democratic voters to turn out in larger numbers than they would have if victory had seemed certain.

See also: Democratic Party; Dixiecrats; Election of 1940; Election of 1948; Progressive Party (Wallace); Republican Party.

Further Reading
Gullen, Harold I. *The Upset that Wasn't: Harry S. Truman and the Election of 1948.* Chicago: Ivan R. Dee Publishers, 1998.

Robbins, Charles. *Last of His Kind: An Informal Portrait of Harry S. Truman.* New York: William Morrow and Company, Inc., 1979.

Schlesinger, Arthur M., Fred L. Israel, and David J. Frent, eds. *The Election of 1948 and the Administration of Harry S. Truman.* Broomall, PA: Mason Crest Publishers, 2003.

Election of 1952: Dwight D. Eisenhower

The election that ended twenty years of Democratic control of the White House. Late in his second term President Truman decided against seeking the Democratic nomination. Thus, in 1952, for the first time in twenty-four years, neither party had an incumbent president as its nominee.

General Dwight D. Eisenhower—who had just left the presidency of Columbia University to take charge of the forces of the North Atlantic Treaty Organization (NATO)—was recruited by Republicans to run when it appeared that other GOP candidates lacked the national appeal to win the White House. Ohio Senator Robert A. Taft was running again, but his isolationism was considered a liability in the postwar age of internationalism.

Eisenhower's popular appeal was revealed when he attracted 50.4 percent of the vote in the New Hampshire primary to Taft's 38.7 percent. Eisenhower performed well in the northeast area primaries, and Taft generally performed well in the Midwest.

When the GOP convention finally met in Chicago, Taft led in convention delegates. In crucial delegate-seating contests, Eisenhower defeated Taft and won the right to seat pro-Eisenhower delegates from the South. Eisenhower had undisputed popular appeal, and he won on the first ballot after his early lead turned into a stampede.

Eisenhower selected Senator Richard Nixon of California as his running mate. The

Electoral Votes: Election of 1952

Dwight D. Eisenhower (R)	442
Adlai E. Stevenson (D)	89

Dwight D. Eisenhower, the popular World War II general, won an easy victory in the election of 1952.

VIEWPOINTS

"I LIKE WHAT I LIKE"

In this political cartoon from the 1950s, the voter (center) indicates his preferences—Republican Dwight D. Eisenhower for president and the policies favored by the Democrats, which are symbolized by the donkey. (Getty Images)

thirty-nine-year-old conservative had won national recognition with his activities on the controversial House Committee on Un-American Activities, which investigated the alleged Soviet ties of Alger Hiss, a former State Department official. Hiss served time for a perjury conviction.

When the Democratic convention met in Chicago, there was no front-runner. Soon, however, three main candidates emerged. Senator Estes Kefauver of Tennessee, who had gained fame with his televised hearings on organized crime, ran an aggressive primary campaign and entered the convention with the lead in delegates. Senator Richard Russell of Georgia was popular among southern delegates. The third contender was Governor Adlai Stevenson of Illinois.

E

A – Z

"I Like Ike" expressed the view of the majority of voters in the 1952 presidential election. (Photo by Julian Wasser/Time Life Pictures/Getty Images)

Stevenson, the grandson of Grover Cleveland's second vice president, had experience in the navy and State Departments before running for governor. President Truman had privately recruited Stevenson for the race—at first unsuccessfully. Then Truman and Illinois backers set up a draft movement for Stevenson. Kefauver was the early leader in convention balloting, but Stevenson, always close, pulled into the lead and won on the third ballot.

The campaign's biggest controversy developed when newspaper reports alleged that Nixon had used a "secret fund" provided by California millionaires to pay for travel and other expenses. To a Democratic Party weary of charges of impropriety, the revelation offered an opportunity to accuse Nixon of being beholden to special interests. Nixon admitted the existence of the fund, but maintained that he used the money solely for travel and that his family did not accept personal gifts.

Nixon originally reacted to the story by asserting that it was a communist smear. When

Eisenhower would not publicly back his running mate, speculation developed that Ike would ask Nixon to leave the ticket—and the Republican *New York Herald Tribune* openly called for him to drop out. When Nixon decided to confront his accusers with a television speech, campaign aides told him he would be dropped if the public reaction was not favorable.

Nixon's speech was remarkable. He denied any wrongdoing and stated that the Stevenson campaign was hypocritical in its criticisms because it had similar funds. More specifically, Nixon denied that he had accepted such gifts as a mink coat for his wife, Pat; he said that his wife wore a "Republican cloth coat." He acknowledged, however, receiving a pet dog named Checkers from a Texas admirer: "And you know, the kids love that dog, and I just want to say this right now, that regardless of what they say about it, we're going to keep it." His folksy message and appeal for telegrams created a wave of sympathy, which Eisenhower rewarded with a pledge of support. The crisis was over.

The candidate crisscrossed the nation as a part of their campaign. Eisenhower campaigned in the South, which no Republican candidate had done in modern times. The Republicans hammered away at the misdeeds of the Democratic administration under Truman. Such issues as the 1949 communist revolution in China ("Who lost China?"), the on-going Korean War, corruption in the Truman administration, and the alleged communist infiltration of the government captured the nation's attention.

In a personal victory—surveys showed that the nation still favored the programs of the New Deal but simply wanted to put the cronyism, sacrifices, and Korean War behind it—Eisenhower swept to the White House. Ike won the entire North and West, parts of the South, and some border states—thirty-nine states to Stevenson's nine. His 442 electoral votes and 33.9 million popular votes (55.1 percent) overwhelmed Stevenson's eighty-nine electoral votes and 27.3 million popular votes (44.4 percent).

See also: Democratic Party; Election of 1948; Election of 1956; Republican Party.

Further Reading
Wicker, Tom. *Dwight D. Eisenhower.* New York Times Books, 2002.

Election of 1956: Dwight D. Eisenhower

A rematch of the 1952 presidential election in which **incumbent** President Dwight D. Eisenhower won an even bigger margin of victory. Despite being sixty-six years old and having had a heart attack in 1955, Eisenhower was the strong favorite to be the GOP nominee for another term. The economy was booming, and Eisenhower had quickly ended the Korean War. His nuclear policy gave the nation a "bigger

bang for the buck" in defense spending and kept the troop requirements low. Federal housing and highway programs gave momentum to **suburbanization,** now considered part of the middle-class **American Dream.** Issues that would in the future become divisive, such as civil rights, were muffled.

In the Democratic camp, Estes Kefauver, the 1952 vice-presidential nominee, challenged Adlai Stevenson for the right to face Eisenhower in the fall. After impressive primary victories in New Hampshire and Minnesota for Kefauver, the Stevenson campaign fought back with a string of primary wins in states as varied as California, Florida, and Oregon.

A variety of other favorite sons also entered the race. Nevertheless, with the help of Eleanor Roosevelt, Stevenson was able to win the nomination for a second time. Stevenson won on the first ballot.

Stevenson left the vice-presidential slot open to the convention delegates. Kefauver, after battling Senators John F. Kennedy of Massachusetts, Albert A. Gore of Tennessee, and Hubert H. Humphrey of Minnesota, and New York mayor Robert Wagner, eventually won. The open contest highlighted the future national political power of Kennedy who, according to later accounts, mainly intended not to win the second spot on the ticket but to gain visibility for a 1960 presidential run.

Few real issues emerged during the campaign. To counter any charges about his health, Eisenhower personally campaigned in thirteen states. He appealed to American values and **bipartisan** consensus. Vice President Nixon attacked the opposition, claiming that Stevenson was inexperienced in foreign affairs. Stevenson traveled more than 37,000 miles during the campaign. He questioned President Eisenhower's health. He called for an end to nuclear testing and for an all-volunteer army.

Eisenhower nailed down another strong victory. He won forty-two states, 457 electoral votes, and 35.6 million popular votes (57.4 percent), compared with Stevenson's six states, seventy-three electoral votes, and 26.0 million popular votes (42.0 percent).

E

A – Z

See also: Democratic Party; Election of 1952; Election of 1960; Republican Party.

Further Reading

Wicker, Tom. *Dwight D. Eisenhower.* New York Times Books, 2002.

Election of 1960: John F. Kennedy

The contest that elected the youngest man ever to the White House. The 1960 Democratic field was dominated by senators: John F. Kennedy of Massachusetts, Lyndon B. Johnson of Texas, Hubert Humphrey of Minnesota, and Stuart Symington of Missouri. Each candidate had important advantages and disadvantages. Kennedy was from a wealthy and politically minded family, but his Roman Catholic faith and unremarkable Senate record were liabilities. Johnson was a masterful majority leader, but no southerner had won the White House since James K. Polk in 1844. Humphrey was popular in the Midwest, but he lacked financial backing and was considered too long-winded and liberal. Symington had a strong Senate record and Harry Truman's backing, but he was considered dull.

Kennedy presented the most intriguing candidacy. He was the son of Joseph P. Kennedy, the millionaire who had been Franklin Roosevelt's ambassador to Britain before their bitter break over U.S. involvement in World War II. John Kennedy also was a graduate of Harvard University, a war hero—described in the book *P.T. 109*—and a Pulitzer Prize winner for *Profiles in Courage* (1957).

Many Democratic leaders, however, doubted whether Kennedy could win the presidential election. No Catholic except Alfred Smith had been a major-party nominee, and Smith's bitter loss and the anti-Catholic sentiments he aroused in 1928 made political professionals wary of naming another Catholic. Some considered Kennedy, at age forty-three, to be too young.

To address the doubts, Kennedy entered primaries that would enable him to demonstrate vote-getting ability and to confront the religion problem. The two key primaries were Wisconsin and West Virginia. In Wisconsin, Kennedy would answer the charge that he was too conservative. In West Virginia, Kennedy would attempt to blunt the religion issue by attracting the votes of an overwhelmingly Protestant electorate.

In the end, Kennedy defeated Humphrey in Wisconsin. Kennedy's impressive campaign treasury enabled him to staff offices in eight of the ten congressional districts in the state; Humphrey had only two offices. Humphrey maintained that the defeat stemmed from crossover Republican Catholic votes and was therefore illegitimate. (Most of the state's Catholics, who made up 31 percent of the population, belonged to the GOP.) Nevertheless, to Kennedy and many political observers, it was still an important victory.

Humphrey wanted to even the score in West Virginia. Kennedy, however, was able to use the primary as a way to deflect the religion issue, as well as the "can't win" problem. Early polls gave Humphrey wide leads, and interviews elicited strong doubts about Kennedy's Catholicism. As the commercials aired and the primary neared, the lead became smaller, and voters privately said they would vote for Kennedy. JFK, as he asked headline writers to call him instead of the youthful-sounding "Jack," easily won the primary, taking 61 percent of the vote to Humphrey's 39 percent.

At the Democratic convention, Kennedy won the nomination on the first ballot. Lyndon B. Johnson was the surprise choice for his running mate. Although some Kennedy supporters had doubts about Johnson, the selection of the southerner was a classic ticket-balancing move.

Incumbent Vice President Richard Nixon was the overwhelming choice for the Republican nomination. Nixon selected United Nations Ambassador Henry Cabot Lodge as his running mate, and the party platform and rhetoric stressed the need for experience in a dangerous

SPOTLIGHT

Election of 1960

The presidential race between Republican Richard M. Nixon and Democrat John F. Kennedy was one of the closest in the nation's history. In the national popular vote, Kennedy beat Nixon by less than one-tenth of 1 percent. In many states, the popular vote was extremely close. Kennedy carried Illinois by 9,000 votes. In California, Kennedy appeared to have carried the state with a margin of 37,000 votes. However, when the absentee ballots were counted, Nixon carried California by 36,000 votes. Ultimately, Kennedy won 303 electoral votes to Nixon's 219 electoral votes.

world. Nixon promised to continue President Dwight Eisenhower's policies. He attempted to portray Kennedy as an inexperienced up-start, even though he was Kennedy's senior by only four years, and the two had entered Congress the same year. Nixon led in the polls at the traditional Labor Day start of the fall campaign.

Kennedy's campaign was based on a promise to "get the nation moving again" after eight years of calm Republican rule. Specifically, he assured voters that he would lead the nation out of the **recession** that had begun in the late 1950s. Kennedy also called for two related changes in national policy: pump up the econ-omy and increase defense spending dramati-cally.

The high point of the campaign came on September 26, 1960, when the candidates de-bated on national television before seventy mil-lion viewers. Kennedy was well rested and tanned; he had spent the week before the de-bate with friends and associates. Nixon was tired from two solid weeks of campaigning; he had spent the preparation period by himself. Their appearances alone greatly influenced the outcome of the debates.

Kennedy's main objective had been simply to look relaxed and "up to" the presidency. He had little to lose. Nixon was always confident of his debating skills, and he performed well in the give-and-take of the debate. Kennedy's managers prepared their candidate better for

the staging of the debate. Nixon's five-o'clock shadow reinforced the cartoon image of him as darkly sinister. As a result of all these fac-tors, polls of radio listeners found that Nixon had "won" the debate, but polls of the more numerous television viewers found that Kennedy had "won." Historian Theodore H. White wrote:

> It was the picture image that had done it—and in 1960 it was television that had won the nation away from sound to images, and that was that.

The candidates held three more debates, addressing issues such as Fidel Castro's Cuba, whether the United States should defend the Chinese offshore islands of Quemoy and Matsu in the event of a military strike by China, and relations with Nikita Khrushchev's Soviet Union. None of the debates had the effect of

Electoral Votes: Election of 1960

John F. Kennedy (D)	303
Richard M. Nixon (R)	219
Harry F. Byrd (D)	15

The election of 1960 was one of the closest in American history. Virginia Senator Harry F. Byrd received the electoral votes of fourteen unpledged Democratic electors and one faithless elector.

E

A – Z

At age 43, John F. Kennedy was the youngest person elected to the presidency. (AP Images)

and 34.1 million for Nixon. The margin was about two-tenths of 1 percent, or 118,574 votes. Moreover, the margins in many states were very close. Kennedy won Illinois by 8,858 votes and Texas by 46,242 votes.

On November 22, 1963, while riding in a motorcade in Dallas, Texas, President Kennedy was assassinated by a gunman named Lee Harvey Oswald. Vice President Johnson assumed the presidency.

See also: Democratic Party; Election of 1956; Election of 1964; Republican Party.

Further Reading

Anthony, Carl Sferrazza. *The Kennedy White House: Family Life and Pictures, 1961–1963.* New York: Simon and Schuster, 2001.
Dallek, Robert. *An Unfinished Life: John F. Kennedy 1917–1963.* New York: Little Brown and Company, 2003.
Salinger, Pierre. *John F. Kennedy: Commander in Chief.* New York: Gramercy Books, 1997.

the first, which neutralized Nixon's advantage as vice president. Nor was Nixon greatly helped by President Eisenhower, who did not campaign for his protégé until late in the campaign.

When the electoral college voted, Kennedy won 303 electoral votes to Nixon's 219. Democratic senator Harry F. Byrd of Virginia attracted fifteen electoral votes. Kennedy won twenty-three states to Nixon's twenty-six. (Six Alabama electors and all eight Mississippi electors, elected as "unpledged Democrats," as well as one Republican elector from Oklahoma, cast their votes for Byrd.) The overall popular vote went 34.2 million for Kennedy

Election of 1964: Lyndon B. Johnson

The election that returned incumbent Lyndon B. Johnson to the White House in his own right. After assuming the presidency in November 1963, Johnson was never in doubt as the Democrats' 1964 nominee. At the convention, he chose liberal Senator Hubert Humphrey of

Minnesota as his running mate. The Democrats were united behind the president. The only Democratic dissent came from Governor George C. Wallace of Alabama, whose segregationist campaign took advantage of a backlash against the civil rights movement. Wallace talked about mounting a third-party bid in the fall, but he backed off.

The Republicans were divided into two bitter camps led by conservative Senator Barry Goldwater of Arizona, the eventual nominee, and by moderate Governor Nelson Rockefeller of New York. The nomination contest was a struggle for the soul of the party. Goldwater lined up strong delegate support to get the nomination before the primary season even began, but he needed to use the primaries to show that he had vote-getting ability. The state organizations that backed him needed evidence that his conservative message would find popular acceptance.

Goldwater won widespread support in the south and had strong primary showings in Illinois and Indiana, but the decisive test came when Goldwater narrowly upset Rockefeller in California.

Goldwater won the nomination on the first ballot. He selected Representative William Miller of New York, another conservative, as his running mate and vowed to purge the party of liberal and moderate elements. In his defiant speech accepting the Republican nomination, Goldwater painted a picture of the United States as inept in international affairs and morally corrupt in domestic pursuits, and he vowed an all-out crusade to change the situation:

Tonight there is violence in our streets, corruption in our highest offices, aimlessness among our youth, anxiety among our elderly, and there's a virtual despair among the many who look beyond the material successes toward the inner meaning of their lives. . . . Extremism in defense of liberty is no vice; moderation in pursuit of justice is no virtue.

President Johnson won the 1964 election in a landslide. He won 486 electoral votes as opposed to Republican Barry Goldwater's fifty-two electoral votes. (Lyndon Baines Johnson Presidential Library and Museum)

The fall campaign was dominated by Goldwater's gaffes, which started long before the campaign began. He said, for example, that troops committed to the North Atlantic Treaty Organization (NATO) in Europe probably could be cut by at least one-third if NATO "commanders" had the authority to use tactical nuclear weapons in an emergency. Goldwater also proposed a number of changes in the Social Security system, called for selling off the Tennessee Valley Authority, criticized the civil rights movement, and denounced the Supreme Court, the National Labor Relations Board, and the federal bureaucracy. Except for the use of nuclear weapons and changes in Social Security, most of Goldwater's proposals when taken alone were not shocking. The sum of his proposals, however, scared many voters.

E

A–Z

President Johnson campaigned very actively to win a mandate for an activist term. He traveled throughout the country making speeches to build a consensus for his domestic programs as well as his reelection. Johnson resisted Goldwater's frequent calls for televised debates.

Johnson desperately wanted a personal mandate to pursue a variety of domestic programs that fell under the phrase the "Great Society"—a term that Johnson used in a 1964 commencement address. The desired landslide—underscored by his campaign slogan, "All the Way with LBJ"—was essential to initiatives in civil rights, health care, community action, education, welfare, housing, and jobs creation. Central to the landslide was not only the nation's economic prosperity, but also peace in the world's trouble spots. Johnson therefore ran as a "peace" candidate.

While he was trying to build a coalition that would sustain his domestic initiatives, Johnson faced an increasingly difficult dilemma about the U.S. role in Vietnam. So while Johnson was campaigning as the peace candidate in 1964, he also was preparing for a major increase in U.S. involvement in Vietnam. In August, Johnson sent to Congress what would be known as the Tonkin Gulf resolution which granted the president broad authority to wage war in Vietnam. The resolution passed quickly and nearly unanimously—after all, the president had instructed congressional leaders to get an overwhelming majority so his policy would be bipartisan.

During the campaign he alluded to some of Goldwater's scarier statements about the war, and he pledged that

We are not about to send American boys nine or ten thousand miles away from home to do what Asian boys ought to be doing for themselves.

A week before the election Johnson said:

The only real issue in this campaign, the only one you ought to get concerned about, is who can best keep the peace.

Johnson's popular vote landslide was the largest in U.S. history. He won 61 percent of the popular vote to Goldwater's 38 percent (or 43.1 million to 27.2 million votes). In the electoral college, Johnson received 486 votes to Goldwater's fifty-two, and he carried forty-four states—all but Goldwater's home state of Arizona and five Deep South states. In addition, the Democratic Party amassed huge majorities in both the Senate (67–33) and the House of Representatives (295–140).

See also: Democratic Party; Election of 1960; Election of 1968; Republican Party; Third Parties.

A still from a 1964 television commercial, which aired only once, made a connection between the atomic bomb and Republican presidential candidate Barry Goldwater. Goldwater lost to incumbent president Lyndon B. Johnson in a historic landslide. (Democratic National Committee)

Further Reading

Caro, Robert A. *The Years of Lyndon Johnson: The Path to Power.* New York: Alfred A. Knopf, Inc., 1982.

Caro, Robert A. *The Years of Lyndon Johnson: Means of Ascent.* New York: Alfred A. Knopf, Inc., 1990.

Caro, Robert A. *The Years of Lyndon Johnson: Master of the Senate.* New York: Alfred A. Knopf, Inc., 2002.

Harwood, Richard, and Haynes Johnson. *Lyndon.* New York: Praeger Publishers, 1973.

Election of 1968: Richard M. Nixon

A close presidential election that sent Richard M. Nixon to the White House. As the 1968 election approached, the nation was divided over the Vietnam War, as well as President Johnson's domestic policy. In December 1967, Senator Eugene McCarthy of Minnesota challenged President Johnson for the Democratic nomination, a move based on McCarthy's antiwar stance. McCarthy did unexpectedly well against Johnson's write-in candidacy in the New Hampshire primary on March 12, 1968, drawing 42.4 percent of the vote to Johnson's 49.5 percent. Anticipating a devastating defeat in the Wisconsin primary on April 2, Johnson dramatically announced his withdrawal from the campaign in a televised address March 31.

After the New Hampshire primary, New York senator Robert F. Kennedy also declared his antiwar candidacy. With the president out of the race, Vice President Humphrey declared his candidacy as well.

McCarthy and Kennedy fought each other in the primaries, and Kennedy appeared to have the upper hand when he closed the primary season with a victory in California on June 5. After making his acceptance speech, however, he was assassinated, and the Democratic Party was in greater turmoil than ever.

At the party convention in Chicago, Humphrey became the Democratic Party's candidate. He had eschewed the primaries; he won the nomination on the strength of endorsements from state party organizations. The vice president took the nomination on the first ballot after Mayor Richard Daley of Chicago committed the Illinois delegation to his effort. Humphrey won with support from the traditional elements of the Democratic coalition—labor, African Americans, urban voters—plus the backers of President Johnson. Humphrey also appealed to many of the party's moderates on the issue of the Vietnam War. Humphrey and his running mate, Senator Edmund S. Muskie of Maine, faced an uphill fight.

Republican Richard M. Nixon won a close victory over Democrat Hubert H. Humphrey and Independent George Wallace in the Election of 1968. The election was expected to be so close that many people thought the House of Representatives would ultimately decide the victor. (The Nixon Library)

The Republicans quickly united behind Richard Nixon, the 1960 nominee, selecting him on the first ballot. For vice president, the Republicans chose Maryland governor Spiro T. Agnew.

During the campaign, Nixon outspent Humphrey two-to-one. He also followed a carefully devised script that avoided the exhausting schedule of his 1960 campaign. He took advantage of the national discontent created by the Vietnam War, urban riots, political assassinations, and general concern about the speed of change brought by the Great Society. Nixon called for the nation to unite and heal its wounds.

As President Johnson resisted calls for a halt in the bombing of North Vietnam, Nixon said he had a "secret plan" to end the war. He appealed to weary Democrats with his pledge of an activist administration and alternative approaches to

THE ELECTION OF 1968

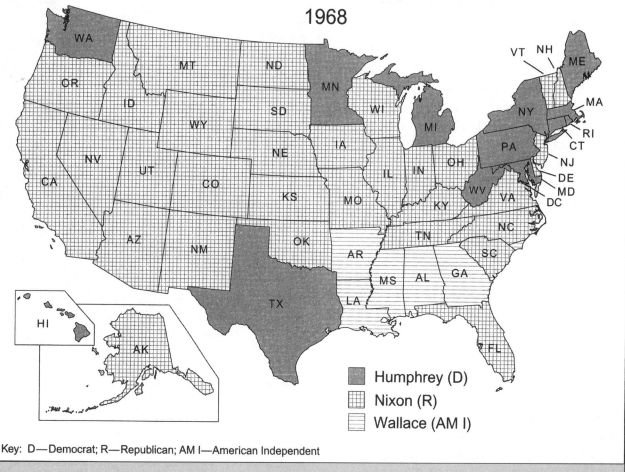

1968

Humphrey (D)
Nixon (R)
Wallace (AM I)

Key: D—Democrat; R—Republican; AM I—American Independent

George C. Wallace made the strongest showing of a third party candidate in the electoral college since Robert M. La Follette in 1924.

dealing with some of the problems the Great Society addressed. Nixon promised to give African Americans, in his words, "a piece of the action with a program to encourage entrepreneurial activity in cities." The "new Nixon" appeared willing to deal with the Soviet Union, which he had scorned earlier in his career. Meanwhile, his vice-presidential nominee, Spiro T. Agnew, offered a slashing critique of the Democrats to middle-class and blue-collar Americans who resented the civil rights laws, government bureaucracy, Vietnam War protesters, and the young protest generation.

A strong third-party candidate also emerged. Governor George C. Wallace of Alabama ran as an antiestablishment conservative, railing away at desegregation, crime, taxes, opponents of the war in Vietnam, social programs, and "pointy-head" bureaucrats and "intellectual morons." Like the earlier third-party campaigns, the Wallace run caused concern about the soundness of the electoral college system. Because the race was so close, it was conceivable that no candidate would win an electoral college victory. Then the House of Representatives would choose the president from among the three candidates with the most electoral votes.

Despite Nixon's early disadvantage, Humphrey made steady inroads into the Republican's support by disassociating himself from Johnson's Vietnam policies. When Johnson on November 1 ordered a halt to all bombing of North Vietnam, Humphrey appeared to be free at last from the stigma of the administration. Nevertheless, this change in policy was not enough to win the election for Humphrey.

The 1968 election was one of the closest in U.S. history. Nixon's victory was not confirmed until the day after the election when California, Ohio, and Illinois—each with very close counts—finally went into the Nixon column. Nixon attracted 31.8 million votes (43.4 percent of all votes cast); Humphrey, 31.3 million votes (42.7 percent); and Wallace, 9.9 million votes (13.5 percent). Nixon won thirty-two states and 301 electoral votes, compared with Humphrey's thirteen states and 191 electoral votes. Nixon won six southern states (Wallace won five others), all of the West except Texas, Washington, and Hawaii, and all the Midwestern states except Michigan and Minnesota. Humphrey won the entire East except New Hampshire, Vermont, New Jersey, and Delaware, plus West Virginia, Maryland, and the District of Columbia.

See also: American Independent Party; Democratic Party; Election of 1960; Election of 1964; Election of 1972; Republican Party; Third Parties.

Further Reading

Drew, Elizabeth. *Richard M. Nixon.* New York Times Books, 2007.

Nixon, Richard. *The Memoirs of Richard Nixon.* New York: Grosset & Dunlap, 1978.

Reeves, Richard. *President Nixon: Alone in the White House.* New York: Simon & Schuster, 2001.

Wicker, Tom. *One of Us: Richard Nixon and the American Dream.* New York: Random House, Inc., 2001.

Election of 1972: Richard M. Nixon

The election that overwhelmingly returned Richard Nixon to the White and that ultimately led to his resignation. At the Republican convention, President Nixon was renominated on the first ballot. Spiro T. Agnew was again chosen for vice president.

Among the Democrats, no fewer than fifteen contenders announced their candidacy. Among the leading contenders were South Dakota senator George McGovern, former vice president Hubert Humphrey, Maine senator Edmund Muskie, and Alabama governor George Wallace. As many as twenty-two primaries to choose 60 percent of the party's delegates—one-third more than in 1968—were to take place over four months.

Muskie won the first-in-the-nation New Hampshire primary, but his 46.4 percent of the vote was considered a "disappointing" showing. Senator McGovern, the antiwar candidate who won 37.1 percent of the vote, was pronounced the real winner by media and pundits. He had attracted a corps of youthful volunteers and his strong showing was a surprise.

After New Hampshire, the Democrats battled through the summer. Wallace turned his antibusing rhetoric into an impressive victory in the Florida primary, winning 41.6 percent. In May 1972, however, Wallace was shot in an assassination attempt. He remained paralyzed for the rest of his life.

McGovern, better organized than the others, won the Wisconsin delegation by winning 29.6 percent of the state vote. McGovern then won an easy Massachusetts victory with 52.7 percent of the vote to Muskie's 21.3 percent. Humphrey edged McGovern in the Ohio primary by 41.2 to 39.6 percent.

The big McGovern-Humphrey showdown was California, which offered 271 delegates to the winner. A spirited campaign, it included a head-to-head debate and strong Humphrey assaults on McGovern's positions on welfare and defense spending. McGovern went on to beat Humphrey by five percentage points in the winner-take-all primary. McGovern also won a majority of the delegates in New Jersey, South Dakota, and New Mexico on the last day of the primary season.

McGovern won the nomination on the first ballot. He then selected Senator Thomas

E

A–Z

E

A–Z

Electoral Votes: Election of 1972

Richard M. Nixon (R)	520
George McGovern (D)	17
John Hospers (Libertarian)	1

Richard M. Nixon swept to a reelection victory in 1972. One Virginia elector cast his ballot for John Hospers, the Libertarian candidate.

Eagleton of Missouri as his running mate after several others declined. McGovern would have been an underdog in the best of circumstances, but his chances were badly damaged by what came to be known as the "Eagleton affair." As the McGovernites celebrated their hard-won nomination, rumors circulated that Eagleton had been hospitalized for exhaustion in the early 1960s. Eagleton finally told McGovern operatives that he had been hospitalized three times for nervous exhaustion and fatigue, and his treatment included electroshock therapy. McGovern stated publicly that he was

...$1,000 percent for Tom Eagleton, and I have no intention of dropping him.

Yet Eagleton left the ticket less than two weeks after his nomination. McGovern eventually replaced Eagleton with his sixth choice, R. Sargent Shriver, former executive of the Peace Corps and Office of Economic Opportunity. Nevertheless, the aura of confusion that surrounded the Eagleton affair and the search for a new vice-presidential candidate hurt the campaign badly.

Nixon was in command of the fall campaign. He boasted of his accomplishments—the Paris peace talks over the Vietnam War, the diplomatic opening to China, the arms limitation treaty with the Soviet Union, and a number of domestic initiatives.

On election day, Nixon won all but Massachusetts and the District of Columbia. His popular vote margin was 47.2 million to McGovern's 29.2 million; the electoral college cast 520 votes for Nixon and only seventeen for McGovern. Nixon's 60.7 percent share of the popular vote stood second only to Johnson's 61.1 percent in 1964.

DECISION MAKERS

Barbara Jordan

Born in Houston, Texas, in 1936, Barbara Jordan was the first African American woman elected to Congress from Texas. Jordan enrolled in Texas Southern University in 1952 and graduated with honors in 1956; she then attended Boston Law School graduating in 1959. After a successful law practice, Jordan ran for the Texas Senate in 1966, where she served for six years. In 1972, Jordan won a seat in the U.S. House of Representatives. As a member of the House Judiciary Committee, she became nationally known during the televised Watergate Hearings, which eventually lead to the resignation of President Richard M. Nixon (1969–1974). In 1976, Jordan was honored as the first African American to be the keynote speaker at the Democratic National Convention, where she nominated Jimmy Carter. She chose not to run for reelection in 1978. Jordan died in Austin, Texas, in 1996.

Soon after his overwhelming victory, rumors emerged about a presidential cover-up of a burglary at the Democratic National Committee headquarters in the Watergate Hotel. At its simplest, the Watergate affair was "a third-rate burglary," followed by a cover-up by President Nixon and his aides. In the summer of 1972, several employees of the Committee to Re-elect the President (dubbed "CREEP") were arrested after they were discovered breaking into and bugging the Democratic National Committee's offices at the Watergate complex in Washington. The break-in was not a major issue in the 1972 election, but the next year a Senate committee began an investigation of the entire affair.

In 1973, before the full impact of the Watergate investigation was known, Nixon's vice president, Spiro Agnew, resigned after pleading "no contest" to charges of taking bribes while he was governor of Maryland. After Agnew's resignation on October 10, 1973, Nixon named House Minority Leader Gerald R. Ford, a longtime GOP stalwart, to become vice president under the Twenty-fifth Amendment.

Throughout 1974, more details concerning the president's involvement in the Watergate affair became known. It was perhaps the greatest political scandal in U.S. history. For the first time, a president was forced to leave office before his term expired. President Nixon resigned on August 9, 1974, when it became apparent that the House of Representatives would impeach him for "high crimes and misdemeanors" and the Senate would convict him. Ford, who had never entered a national election, then became president upon Nixon's resignation and quickly attracted the support of the American public with his modest, earnest disposition.

One month after becoming president, however, Ford ignited a firestorm of criticism with his full pardon of Nixon for all crimes he may have committed while president. Ford testified before Congress that he believed Nixon had suffered enough and that the nation would have been badly torn if a former president were brought to court to face criminal charges. Crit-ics asserted that Ford had made a deal in which Nixon resigned the presidency in exchange for the pardon.

Ford selected former New York governor Nelson Rockefeller to be his vice president. Rockefeller received Senate and House confirmation on December 10 and 19, respectively, after long, difficult hearings that centered on his financial dealings.

See also: Democratic Party; Election of 1968; Election of 1976; Republican Party; Third Parties; Twenty-fifth Amendment; Watergate.

Further Reading

Brinkley, Douglas. *Gerald R. Ford.* New York Times Books, 2007.

Drew, Elizabeth. *Richard M. Nixon.* New York Times Books, 2007.

Ford, Gerald R. *A Time To Heal: The Autobiography of Gerald R. Ford.* New York: Harper & Row Publishers, 1979.

Nixon, Richard. *The Memoirs of Richard Nixon.* New York: Grosset & Dunlap, 1978.

Reeves, Richard. *President Nixon: Alone in the White House.* New York: Simon & Schuster, 2001.

Wicker, Tom. *One of Us: Richard Nixon and the American Dream.* New York: Random House, Inc., 2001.

Election of 1976: Jimmy Carter

A close election that sent Democrat Jimmy Carter to the White House. As the election of 1976 approached, several Democratic contenders sought the presidential nomination. In the aftermath of the Watergate scandal and Ford's pardon of Richard Nixon, the Democrats were confident of victory.

Among the leading candidates were former Alabama governor George Wallace, Arizona representative Morris Udall, Washington senator Henry Jackson, Indiana senator Birch Bayh,

SPOTLIGHT

The Carter Center

In 1981, at the end of his term as president, Jimmy Carter was only 56 years old. He returned to his home in Plains, Georgia, and in 1982, he founded The Carter Center. President Carter and other members of The Carter Center work to resolve conflict, promote democracy, protect human rights, and prevent disease. Since leaving office, President Carter has helped resolve conflicts in Ethiopia and Eritrea (1989), North Korea (1994), Liberia (1994), Haiti (1994), Bosnia (1994), Sudan (1995), Rwanda (1995–1996), Sudan and Uganda (1999), and Venezuela (2002–2003). Under his leadership, The Carter Center has sent forty-five international election monitoring delegations to elections in the Americas, Africa, and Asia. President Carter and his wife, Rosalynn, volunteer one week every year for Habitat for Humanity, an organization that helps people in the United States and in other countries build homes for themselves.

California governor Jerry Brown, and former Georgia governor Jimmy Carter. Carter was a **dark-horse** candidate, little known outside of his home state. At the beginning of the campaign, many people around the country asked "Jimmy Who?"

The Democratic primary elections were hotly contested. Udall performed well in the primaries, but never won a single state; he and other liberals were splitting the liberal vote. Carter ran into strong challenges from Church and Brown in later primaries, but he had the delegates and endorsements by the time of the Democratic convention in New York for a first-ballot nomination. The Democrats quickly united behind Carter and his running mate, Senator Walter F. Mondale of Minnesota.

In the Republican primaries, **incumbent** President Gerald R. Ford faced strong competition from former movie actor and governor of California, Ronald Reagan.

Ford won the early contests, but Reagan, a staunch conservative, scored big wins in the North Carolina and Texas primaries. Reagan was put on the defensive with his proposals for transferring welfare obligations to the states,

but when he focused on foreign policy, he had success. For example, he attacked Ford for his policy of detente with the Soviet Union and his negotiation of a treaty that would turn over U.S. control of the Panama Canal.

In the late summer, Ford and Reagan were locked in a close contest, with an almost even number of convention delegates. Nevertheless, Ford won the nomination on the first ballot. He selected senator Bob Dole of Kansas as his running mate as a consolation prize for disappointed conservatives.

The 1976 campaign was the first governed by campaign finance reform legislation enacted in 1971 and 1974. The Federal Election Campaign Act (FECA) of 1971 limited campaign expenditures and required disclosure of campaign receipts and expenditures. The Revenue Act of 1971 created a tax check-off that enabled taxpayers to allocate $1.00 of their taxes for public financing of elections. The FECA amendments of 1974 limited spending and donations for both primary and general election campaigns, established a system of partial public funding of elections, and created the Federal Election Commission to monitor campaign activities.

Electoral Votes: Election of 1976

States	Electoral Votes	Carter	Ford	Reagan	States	Electoral Votes	Carter	Ford	Reagan
Alabama	(9)	9	-	-	Montana	(4)	-	4	-
Alaska	(3)	-	3	-	Nebraska	(5)	-	5	-
Arizona	(6)	-	6	-	Nevada	(3)	-	3	-
Arkansas	(6)	6	-	-	New Hampshire	(4)	-	4	-
California	(45)	-	45	-	New Jersey	(17)	-	17	-
Colorado	(7)	-	7	-	New Mexico	(4)	-	4	-
Connecticut	(8)	-	8	-	New York	(41)	41	-	-
Delaware	(3)	3	-	-	North Carolina	(13)	13	-	-
District of Columbia	(3)	3	-	-	North Dakota	(3)	-	3	-
Florida	(17)	17	-	-	Ohio	(25)	25	-	-
Georgia	(12)	12	-	-	Oklahoma	(8)	-	8	-
Hawaii	(4)	4	-	-	Oregon	(6)	-	6	-
Idaho	(4)	-	4	-	Pennsylvania	(27)	27	-	-
Illinois	(26)	-	26	-	Rhode Island	(4)	4	-	-
Indiana	(13)	-	13	-	South Carolina	(8)	8	-	-
Iowa	(8)	-	8	-	South Dakota	(4)	-	4	-
Kansas	(7)	-	7	-	Tennessee	(10)	10	-	-
Kentucky	(9)	9	-	-	Texas	(26)	26	-	-
Louisiana	(10)	10	-	-	Utah	(4)	-	4	-
Maine	(4)	-	4	-	Vermont	(3)	-	3	-
Maryland	(10)	10	-	-	Virginia	(12)	-	12	-
Massachusetts	(14)	14	-	-	Washington[2]	(9)	-	8	1
Michigan	(21)	-	21	-	West Virginia	(6)	6	-	-
Minnesota	(10)	10	-	-	Wisconsin	(11)	11	-	-
Mississippi	(7)	7	-	-	Wyoming	(3)	-	3	-
Missouri	(12)	12	-	-	TOTALS	(538)	297	240	1

Democrat Jimmy Carter won a close election over incumbent Republican Gerald R. Ford in the Election of 1976. Ronald Reagan received one electoral vote from a faithless elector from Washington State.

Carter emerged from the Democratic convention with a wide lead over Ford, but the race was too close to call by election day. A number of gaffes—such as Carter's interview with *Playboy* magazine, his ambiguous statements about abortion, and his confused observations on tax reform—hurt the Democratic contender. Ford also gained in the polls when he began to use the patronage powers of the presidency and effectively contrasted his twenty-seven years of Washington experience to Carter's four years as governor of Georgia.

For the first time since 1960, the major candidates took part in televised debates. As the outsider, Carter helped himself by demonstrating a good grasp of national issues and by appealing to Democrats to vote the party line. Ford hurt himself with a claim that Eastern European nations did not consider themselves to be under the control of the Soviet Union. The remark was intended to be testimony to the Europeans' sense of national identity, but it was interpreted as evidence of the president's inexperience.

Carter's main advantage was regional pride. The Democrats had long since lost their hold over the South, but Carter gained widespread support as the first candidate nominated from the region on his own in more than a century. The Democratic Party's many factions—including such big-city mayors as Richard Daley of Chicago and Abraham Beame of New York, civil rights activists, and organized labor—put on a rare display of unity.

Carter defeated Ford by a slim margin, winning 40.8 million votes (50.1 percent) to Ford's 39.1 million (48.0 percent). In the electoral college, 297 votes went to Carter, 240 to Ford. Carter won by pulling together the frazzled New Deal coalition of industrial and urban voters, African Americans, Jews, and southerners. Ford won the West, and Carter won the South, except Virginia. Ford won all the states from the Mississippi River westward except Texas and Hawaii, plus states in his native Midwest such as Iowa, Illinois, Michigan, and Indiana. Ford also won Connecticut and the three northernmost New England states—New Hampshire, Vermont, and Maine.

See also: Democratic Party; Election of 1972; Election of 1980; Republican Party; Watergate.

Further Reading

Brinkley, Douglas. *Gerald R. Ford.* New York: Times Books, 2007.

Carter, Jimmy. *Keeping Faith: Memoirs of a President.* Fayetteville, AR: University of Arkansas Press, 1995.

Election of 1980: Ronald Reagan

The election of Ronald Reagan, which began a new conservative era in the nation's politics. As the election of 1980 approached, incumbent Jimmy Carter sought the nomination, but faced a serious challenge from Massachusetts senator Edward "Ted" Kennedy.

Kennedy was leading Carter in the polls by a two-to-one margin when he announced his challenge to the president in November 1979. Carter overcame that lead by the start of the nominating season when the seizure of American hostages in Iran rallied the nation around the president. Around the same time, Kennedy made a series of political mistakes. Kennedy was unable to develop campaign themes or answer questions about his personal conduct in the 1969 Chappaquiddick incident in which a woman died after a car he was driving went off a bridge. Other "character" issues, such as Kennedy's alleged "womanizing," and more substantive issues, such as his liberal voting record, also hurt him in a year dominated by conservative themes.

In addition, Carter faced competition from liberal Governor Jerry Brown of California. Brown, however, was unable to find much support for his appeal for recognition of economic and environmental limits. He dropped out of the race in April.

Carter won the nomination on the first ballot despite a variety of stop-Carter efforts and Kennedy's attempt to free delegates to vote for any candidate. When Carter won the crucial floor vote on the "open convention" question, Kennedy did not have a chance. Thus, the Carter-Mondale ticket entered the fall campaign as a wounded army unable to generate much enthusiasm from the troops.

The Republicans united early behind former California governor and movie actor Ronald Reagan. By April 22, 1980, less than two months after the New Hampshire primary, six

E

A–Z

Ronald Reagan (1981-1989) was the first president since Dwight D. Eisenhower (1953-1961) to complete two full terms in office. (Ronald Reagan Presidential Library and Foundation)

candidates had dropped out of the race, and George H.W. Bush, Reagan's only surviving competitor, was desperately behind in the delegate count. Reagan's campaign experienced an early scare when Bush beat Reagan in the Iowa caucus, but Reagan rebounded, changed campaign managers and tactics, and won a string of primaries and caucuses. By the time of the convention, Reagan was the consensus candidate, and he won the nomination on the first ballot. He improved party unity by adding Bush to the ticket as the vice-presidential nominee.

Electoral Votes: Election of 1980

Ronald W. Reagan (R)	489
James E. Carter (D)	49

During the 1980 presidential campaign, many political experts thought the election would be close. Instead, Republican Ronald Reagan swept to victory over incumbent President Jimmy Carter.

Reagan called on the electorate to replace politics that he said was marked by "pastels," or compromising and uncertain policies, with "bold colors." Reagan's proposed bold strokes included a 30 percent reduction in marginal income tax rates based on a "supply-side" economic theory—which even Bush had said was a dangerous kind of "voodoo economics"—and massive increases in military expenditures. At the same time, Reagan criticized Carter's alleged indecisiveness and his commitment to liberal policies.

President Carter, who was vulnerable as the hostage crisis neared its first anniversary (on November 4, election day) and high inflation and unemployment rates persisted, attempted to portray Reagan as a dangerous, heartless, and inexperienced amateur. Reagan managed to use Carter's attacks to his own advantage by assuming a posture of hurt feelings at the unfair criticism. When in a televised debate Carter attacked Reagan's previous opposition to social welfare programs, Reagan cut him off with a line, "There you go again," that suggested Carter was unfairly and relentlessly distorting Reagan's record.

Carter strategists also were concerned about the independent candidacy of Rep. John B. Anderson of Illinois, a moderate who dropped out of the Republican race when it became clear that conservatives would dominate that party. After some strong support in the polls, Anderson stood at about 10 percent for the final two months of the campaign. Carter was concerned that Anderson would take more votes from him than from Reagan, even though analysis of Anderson support suggested otherwise.

Polls before election day predicted a close race. Reagan, however, won all but six states and took the White House in an electoral landslide, 489 electoral votes to forty-nine. Reagan won 51 percent of the vote, while Carter managed 41 percent and Anderson 7 percent. Carter ran tight races in ten additional states that could have gone his way with a shift of less than one and one-half percentage points. In twenty-one states, Anderson's vote totals made up most or all of the difference between Reagan and Carter. Despite these factors and polls that regularly showed preference for Carter's policy positions, Reagan's victory was impressive. He beat Carter by a better than two-to-one margin in nine states.

Even more surprising than Reagan's electoral landslide was the Republican takeover of the Senate. The new right's targeting of several Senate liberals—such as George McGovern of South Dakota, Birch Bayh of Indiana, Gaylord Nelson of Wisconsin, and John Culver of Iowa— created the biggest Senate turnover since 1958. The Republicans now held the Senate by a 53–46 margin.

See also: Democratic Party; Election of 1976; Election of 1984; Republican Party; Third Parties; Watergate.

Further Reading

Colacello, Bob. *Ronnie & Nancy: Their Path to the White House–1911–1980.* New York: Warner Books, 2004.

Diggins, John Patrick. *Ronald Reagan: Fate, Freedom, and the Making of History.* New York: W. W. Norton & Co., 2007.

Reagan, Ronald. *An American Life: The Autobiography.* New York: Simon & Schuster, 1990.

Reagan, Ronald. *The Reagan Diaries,* ed. Douglas Brinkley. New York: Harper Collins Publishers, 2007.

Reeves, Richard. *President Reagan: The Triumph of Imagination.* New York: Simon & Schuster, 2005.

Wallison, Peter J. *Ronald Reagan: The Power of Conviction and the Success of His Presidency.* Boulder, CO: Westview Press, 2004.

Election of 1984: Ronald Reagan

The presidential election that sent Ronald Reagan back to the White House. Incumbent Ronald Reagan's popularity dipped to 44 percent in 1983—about the average for modern presidents—but it rebounded when the economy later picked up. As the 1984 election approached, Reagan faced no opposition from Republicans, but a large field of Democrats sought the right to oppose him in the fall.

The Democrats' early front-runner was former vice president Mondale, who had accumulated a wide range of endorsements (AFL-CIO, National Education Association, United Mine Workers, and the National Organization for Women) and an impressive campaign treasury. The more conservative senator John Glenn of Ohio, the first American to orbit the earth, was considered a strong challenger. Other candidates included Senators Gary Hart of Colorado, Alan Cranston of California, and Ernest Hollings of South Carolina, civil rights leader Jesse Jackson, former presidential candidate George McGovern, and former governor Reubin Askew of Florida.

The early primaries eliminated all but Mondale, Hart, and Jackson just sixteen days after the New Hampshire primary. Hart became the serious challenger to Mondale when he finished second in Iowa and first in New Hampshire, creating an explosion of media coverage. After Mondale recovered, the two fought head-to-head until the convention. Jackson, the second African American to run for the presidency, stayed in the race to promote his liberal party agenda.

After interviewing a wide range of candidates, Mondale selected Rep. Geraldine A. Ferraro of New York as his running mate—the first woman ever to receive a major-party nomination for national office. Representative Ferraro's vice-presidential candidacy probably was a drag on the ticket, not because she was a woman, but because of the controversy created by her husband's finances and her stand on the abortion question. The controversies hindered the Democratic campaign's effort to articulate its own vision for the nation.

Ferraro appeared knowledgeable and strong in her debate with Vice President Bush, and she often drew large and enthusiastic crowds. She was stuck, however, in controversy when details of her husband's questionable real estate, trusteeship, and tax practices became public.

Opponents of abortion held prominent and often loud protests at the sites of her speeches, and she got involved in a lengthy public dispute over abortion with Catholic Archbishop John O'Connor. Ferraro also did not help the ticket in regions where the Democrats were weak, such as the South and West.

Mondale ran a generally conservative campaign, concentrating on a proposed tax increase to address the unprecedented budget deficit of more than $200 billion and proposing no new social programs. Mondale criticized Reagan's record on the arms race, but he did not outline basic disagreements on other foreign affairs issues. He charged that Reagan, the oldest president in history, was lazy and out of touch. Only late in the campaign, when his speeches became unabashedly liberal and combative, did Mondale create any excitement.

Just once—in the period after the first presidential debate—did Mondale appear to have a chance to defeat President Reagan. Political pundits had marked Mondale as a poor television performer, but the challenger outfoxed Reagan in the debate and afterward appeared to be gaining ground for a few days. Before the debate, Mondale aides had leaked erroneous information that suggested he would make a slashing attack. Nevertheless, Mondale surprised Reagan by adopting a "gold-watch approach" suitable to a family business retiring an old-timer—"sort of embracing a grandfather, and gently pushing him aside." Mondale gave the president credit for helping to restore national patriotism and beginning a national debate on education reform, but he said it was time for new leadership. Reagan appeared confused and, in the rush to demonstrate statistical knowledge of policies, he failed to outline broad themes.

Although the first debate boosted the Mondale campaign's morale, it never brought Mondale within striking range of Reagan—he never came within ten percentage points of Reagan in the polls. Reagan's campaign was a series of rallies with masses of colorful balloons and confident talk about the United States "standing tall" in domestic and world affairs. Reagan was so sure of victory that he made a last-minute trip to Mondale's home state of Minnesota with the hope of completing a fifty-state sweep of the nation.

As it was, Reagan won forty-nine states, with 2-to-1 margins in eight states. Idaho, Ne-

---

DECISION MAKERS

Geraldine Ferraro

Born in 1935, Geraldine Ferraro attended school in New York, receiving her bachelor's degree from Marymount Manhattan College and her law degree from Fordham College in 1960. After successfully practicing law, in 1974 Ferraro became an assistant district attorney for Queens County in New York. In 1978, she decided to run for Congress, winning the first of three terms. In 1984, Walter Mondale, the Democratic presidential nominee selected Ferraro as his vice-presidential running mate. Ferraro thus became the first woman to run for vice president on a major party ticket.

After losing the 1984 race, Ferraro left Congress. She has written several books and campaigns for other Democratic candidates in New York. She has also appeared as a guest on numerous political talk shows, including *Crossfire.* She continues to support women's issues and social causes.

braska, and Utah each gave Reagan more than 70 percent of the vote. Mondale won only the District of Columbia and his home state of Minnesota, where he beat Reagan by only two-tenths of a percentage point. As for the popular vote, Reagan won 54.5 million votes (58.8 percent) to Mondale's 37.6 million (40.6 percent). In the electoral college, he received 525 votes to Mondale's thirteen votes.

See also: Democratic Party; Election of 1980; Election of 1988; Republican Party.

Further Reading

Colacello, Bob. *Ronnie & Nancy: Their Path to the White House–1911–1980.* New York: Warner Books, 2004.

Diggins, John Patrick. *Ronald Reagan: Fate, Freedom, and the Making of History.* New York: W. W. Norton & Co., 2007.

Reagan, Ronald. *An American Life: The Autobiography.* New York: Simon & Schuster, 1990.

Reagan, Ronald. *The Reagan Diaries,* ed. Douglas Brinkley. New York: Harper Collins Publishers, 2007.

Reeves, Richard. *President Reagan: The Triumph of Imagination.* New York: Simon & Schuster, 2005.

Wallison, Peter J. *Ronald Reagan: The Power of Conviction and the Success of His Presidency.* Boulder, CO: Westview Press, 2004.

Election of 1988: George H.W. Bush

The first election after 1968 in which an **incumbent** president did not run. With no leading figures and no major issues, the campaign was disorderly. As many as fourteen candidates struggled to develop an identity with the voters, and the campaign lurched from one symbolic issue to the next, never developing the overarching themes of previous campaigns.

In the absence of any major new issues, and in a time of general peace and prosperity, Re-

publican vice president George Bush won the presidency. Bush defeated Democratic Massachusetts governor Michael S. Dukakis by a margin of 54 percent to 46 percent—48.9 million votes to 41.8 million votes. Bush's electoral vote margin was more impressive, 426–111. A negative campaign and limited voter registration efforts resulted in the lowest voter turnout rate since the 1920 and 1924 race percentages of 49 percent of all eligible voters. Just a little more than 50 percent of all eligible citizens voted for president in 1988.

Bush, benefiting from the Nixon-Reagan presidential coalition, won all the states of the old Confederacy, the entire West except Oregon and Washington, and several northern industrial states. Dukakis originally had hoped to crack the South by selecting a favorite son, Senator Lloyd M. Bentsen, Jr., of Texas, as his running mate, but that tactic failed. Dukakis lost crucial states, such as California, Pennsylvania, Illinois, Ohio, and Missouri. He won New York, Massachusetts, Wisconsin, Minnesota, Oregon, Washington, West Virginia, Iowa, Rhode Island, Hawaii, and the District of Columbia.

The early Republican front-runners were Bush and Senator Bob Dole of Kansas; former senator Gary Hart of Colorado was considered the early Democratic leader. The campaign got scrambled before it began, however. Hart left the race in 1987 when the Miami *Herald* augmented rumors of Hart's infidelity with a report that he had spent the night with a young model. The newspaper had staked out Hart's Washington townhouse with two reporters, two editors, and a photographer. The investigators sat in a rental car, loitered nearby, and jogged down the street. Hart, considered by many to be the brightest and most issue-oriented candidate, had long faced criticism about his "character."

Senator Joseph R. Biden, Jr., of Delaware was the next casualty of the media's 1987 concern with character issues. Media reports stating that he had committed plagiarism on a law school paper and in campaign speeches led to Biden's early exit from the campaign. Biden had been considered a leading candidate because of his experience and strong speaking style.

With Hart and Biden out of the race, the Democrats were in disarray. The remaining candidates—Reverend Jesse Jackson of Illinois, Governor Michael Dukakis, Representative Richard A. Gephardt of Missouri, Senator Albert A. Gore, Jr., of Tennessee, Senator Paul M. Simon of Illinois, and former Arizona governor Bruce Babbitt—lacked the combination of extensive government experience and strong national bases many observers thought necessary to win the presidency.

The Republicans had problems of their own. Vice President Bush was the early favorite, and he benefited from his association with President Reagan. But Bush's public loyalty to Reagan also created a problem: he was considered a "wimp," unable to stand on his own. Almost every major position Bush had held in his political career was the result of an appointment: ambassador to the United Nations, chair of the Republican National Committee, envoy to China, director of the Central Intelligence Agency, and vice president. Bush had represented Texas for two terms in the House of Representatives, but had lost two Senate races.

At the outset of the race, Dole was considered a strong contender. As Republican leader in the Senate, he had a high profile in national politics and proven fund-raising abilities. His wife, Elizabeth, was prominent as secretary of transportation. Dole also had a biting wit, which gave spark to his campaigning style but irritated some voters. Other GOP candidates were Representative Jack Kemp of New York, former secretary of state Alexander M. Haig, Jr., of Pennsylvania, former Delaware governor Pierre S. "Pete" du Pont IV, and television evangelist Pat Robertson of Virginia.

The Campaign

The marathon campaign for the nomination began with the Iowa caucuses, a significant event only because of intense media attention. Gephardt barely edged Simon in the Democratic contests, and Dole won the Republican race. The big story was how badly Bush performed: he finished third behind Dole and Robertson.

The Iowa loss caused Bush to emerge from his isolation and confront his rivals for the nomination. Bush had been the most restrained and cautious candidate as he tried to benefit from the prestige of the White House. Bush also became more animated on the campaign trail. As a result of these changes—and a series of television advertisements charging that Dole would raise taxes—Bush beat Dole in the New Hampshire primary. Dole had failed to respond quickly to the Bush offensive, and when he snapped on national television about Bush's "lying about my record," he reinforced his image as a mean-spirited candidate.

Among the Democrats, Governor Dukakis easily won the New Hampshire primary, capitalizing on his regional popularity. Most of the Democratic fire in that race took place between the two runners-up, Gephardt and Simon. Dukakis escaped without any major criticism, and his already strong fund-raising machine went into high gear.

The decisive stage of the GOP campaign was Super Tuesday, March 8, when twenty-two states held presidential primaries or caucuses. Benefiting from a well-organized campaign and his new aggressiveness on the campaign trail, Bush won seventeen of the eighteen GOP contests. Dole staked his campaign on the ensuing Illinois primary, but he lost badly, and Bush was virtually ensured the Republican nomination.

On Super Tuesday, Democratic front-runner Dukakis won Texas and Florida and five northern states, thereby confirming his shaky front-runner status. Civil rights leader Jesse Jackson was the big surprise, however, winning five southern states. Gore won seven states. Even though it was designed to help conservative candidates, Super Tuesday fit Jackson's strengths. Six of the nine states in which Jackson had scored best in 1984 held their contests on Super Tuesday in 1988.

The Democratic marathon continued into Illinois, Michigan, and New York. Dukakis took and maintained the lead in delegates with steady wins over Jackson and Gore. Gore finally dropped out after finishing third in a divi-

E

A–Z

sive New York primary, and the rest of the campaign was a one-on-one race between Dukakis and Jackson. Only once—after his victory over Dukakis in the Michigan caucuses—did Jackson appear to have a chance to win the Democratic nomination. But in their next encounter, the Wisconsin primary, Dukakis defeated Jackson.

Jackson was a mixed blessing for the party. An energetic campaigner, he attracted support from African Americans and from farmers and blue-collar workers who were disgruntled by the uneven rewards of economic growth. But Jackson was considerably to the left of the rest of the party and never had held any government office. Race also was a factor: no political professional believed that a liberal African American could be elected president.

The Conventions

As the summer conventions approached, Bush and Dukakis each had the full support of his party. The parties' internal divisions were on display as the prospective nominees considered possible vice-presidential candidates. African Americans lobbied for Jackson's selection by Dukakis, while conservative GOP leaders lobbied against a moderate running mate for Bush.

Dukakis selected conservative senator Lloyd Bentsen of Texas as his running mate before the Atlanta Democratic convention. Jackson complained publicly and privately about the decision, but he eventually embraced Bentsen for the sake of party unity. Dukakis hoped Bentsen would be able to help carry Texas: no Democrat had won the presidency without winning Texas since the state became part of the nation in 1845.

The Republican convention in August did not start out as well. Bush announced his vice-presidential selection, Senator James Danforth "Dan" Quayle of Indiana, when he arrived in New Orleans. After revelations that Quayle had avoided military service in the Vietnam War by enlisting in the Indiana National Guard, many Republicans criticized Bush's choice. Some even said that Quayle might have to be dropped from the ticket. By the end of the convention, however, the Republicans had weathered the storm.

Bush delivered a crisp address, which provided the appealing self-portrait the vice president needed, and moved into the fall campaign for a close battle with Dukakis.

As Dukakis fell behind Bush, his campaign pinned its hopes on two nationally televised debates. Dukakis performed well in the first debate, but Bush appeared to "win" the second debate. Dukakis failed to gain on Bush.

The only major problem for Bush was Quayle. Public polls revealed that most voters thought that Quayle was a bad choice. The Bush campaign tried to minimize the damage by limiting Quayle's public exposure and carefully scripting his statements. Quayle rarely spoke in major media markets; many of his campaign stops were accessible only by bus. While Bush delivered speeches in several states each day, Quayle often made just one speech before schoolchildren or partisan audiences.

After months of inconsistent and confusing strategy, Dukakis finally developed a strong appeal in the last two weeks of the campaign. He told voters he was on their side and portrayed Bush as a toady to the wealthy. Dukakis said the middle class had been "squeezed" by the policies of the Reagan administration and that the Democrats would provide good jobs, affordable housing and health care, and tough enforcement of environmental protection laws.

However, it was not enough. Bush, who had made a fortune in the oil business before entering politics and was the son of a former U.S. senator, persuaded more voters that his experience and values were what they wanted in the very personal choice of a president.

See also: Democratic Party; Election of 1984; Election of 1992; Republican Party.

Further Reading

Greene, John Robert. *The George H.W. Bush Years.* New York: Facts on File, 2005.

Mieczkowski, Yan. *The Routledge Historical Atlas of American Presidential Elections.* London: Routledge, 2001.

Naftali, Timothy. *George H.W. Bush.* New York: Times Books, 2007.

Election of 1992: William Jefferson Clinton

Election in which the Democrats took back the White House—the first Democratic win since the election of 1976. In March 1991, in the aftermath of the U.S.-led victory over Iraq in the Persian Gulf War, **incumbent** President George Bush received the highest approval ratings since opinion polling began: around 90 percent of respondents said they approved of his performance as president. Yet, just a year later, Bush was struggling to keep his job—and he failed.

The Bush Strategy

President Bush began the election cycle looking unbeatable. Coasting on the U.S. victory in the Gulf War, Bush appeared to have the strength to lead the United States into what he called the "new world order." In 1989, the countries of the Soviet bloc—East Germany, Poland, Czechoslovakia, Romania, and Hungary—had broken from communist rule in a series of nonviolent revolutions. In August 1991, an attempted coup in the Soviet Union had failed. Afterward, the Soviet regime—Communist Party and all—had collapsed. The Bush presidency had overseen the most remarkable realignment of world politics since World War II.

Indeed, Bush took credit for presiding over the dramatic changes, but those American "victories" also undermined his position. The Republican Party had dominated recent presidential politics at least partly because of its hawkish policies during the cold war. With the end of the Soviet threat, the GOP no longer had a tough issue to use against the Democrats.

For a while, President Bush looked so strong that many Democrats were reluctant to take him on. The party's leading figures—Governor Mario Cuomo of New York; Senators

Bill Bradley of New Jersey, Al Gore of Tennessee, and Jay Rockefeller of West Virginia; and Representative Richard Gephardt of Missouri—announced they would not run. Only former senator Paul E. Tsongas of Massachusetts, recently recovered from a bout with cancer, announced his candidacy in spring 1991.

By the spring of 1992, however, Bush's support had begun to fade. The president had decided to "sit" on his high popularity ratings and win reelection by avoiding mistakes. Bush's chief of staff, John Sununu, summed up the strategy:

> There's not another single piece of legislation that needs to be passed in the next two years for this president. In fact, if Congress wants to come together, adjourn, and leave, it's all right with us.

The results of this strategy were devastating. In May 1992, a poll found that 76 percent of the public disapproved of the way Bush was handling the economy. His overall approval rating dropped an unprecedented 57 percentage points from the end of the Gulf War to the beginning of the 1992 GOP convention.

The 1992 Primary Season

The Democratic field grew slowly. Besides Tsongas, the field included Arkansas governor William Jefferson (Bill) Clinton and former governor Jerry Brown of California, as well as Senators Thomas Harkin of Iowa and Robert Kerrey of Nebraska.

Clinton won the so-called "invisible primaries" before the formal balloting began; he attracted $3.3 million in contributions by the end of 1991. Harkin was second best with a little more than $2 million. The Clinton campaign then organized supporters in most states holding early contests.

By calling himself a "new Democrat," Clinton hoped to separate himself from some of the rejected Democratic candidates of the past: Jimmy Carter, Walter Mondale, and Michael Dukakis. In keeping with this strategy, Clinton

E

A–Z

DECISION MAKERS

Hillary Rodham Clinton

Born in Illinois in 1947, Hillary Rodham grew up in the suburbs of Chicago. After graduating from Wellesley College in Massachusetts, in 1969 she entered Yale Law School. There she met her husband, Bill Clinton, whom she married in 1975. They moved to Arkansas, where Bill Clinton was elected governor in 1978. Hillary Rodham Clinton served as first lady of Arkansas for twelve years while maintaining a successful law practice.

After Bill Clinton's election to the presidency in 1992, Hillary Rodham Clinton continued her public service. In 1993, at the request of the president, she chaired the Task Force on National Health Care Reform, leading the call for expanded national health care.

In 2000, Hilary Rodham Clinton was elected United States senator from New York, becoming the first First Lady elected to the Senate. In early 2007, she announced her candidacy for the presidency.

promised to move beyond liberal views and "reinvent government." The centerpiece of Clinton's strategy was to appeal to the "forgotten middle class." Suburbanites, the working class, and southerners and westerners had abandoned the Democratic Party since the late 1960s.

As expected, favorite-son Harkin won the Iowa caucuses, winning 76.4 percent of the delegates selected on February 10. Early on, Clinton had led the polling in New Hampshire, but he ran into trouble when the media questioned his character. A woman claimed that she and Clinton had had an affair and that Clinton had helped her to get a state job.

Nevertheless, Clinton hit back. Appearing on the television news show *60 Minutes* after the January 1992 Super Bowl game, Clinton admitted he had "caused pain" in his marriage but said he and his wife had solved their problems. Hillary Clinton's appearance with her husband seemed to close the matter.

Tsongas won the New Hampshire primary on February 18 with 33.2 percent of the vote to Clinton's 24.7 percent. Clinton, who fell some twenty points in the polls in a month, energetically called his second-place finish a victory by

noting Tsongas's ties to the region and declaring himself the "Comeback Kid." His campaign, however, was out of money and had to be rescued by a $3.5 million line of credit from an Arkansas bank.

Tsongas and Brown won a few contests after New Hampshire, but Clinton rolled to the nomination starting with his March 3 victory in the Georgia primary. Kerrey and Harkin dropped out in early March. Clinton's sweep of southern states on "Super Tuesday," March 10, and his decisive wins in Michigan and Illinois on March 17 practically clinched the nomination.

Clinton won thirty-one state primaries with 51.8 percent of the vote; Tsongas, four states with 18.1 percent; and Brown, two states with 20.1 percent. Even as Clinton won state after state and Bush plummeted in the polls, Democratic leaders searched for an alternative; they had grown nervous about Clinton's ability to confront the character issue. In March, almost half the Democratic voters in Connecticut's primary said Clinton lacked the "honesty or integrity" to be president.

President Bush faced an unusual challenge from conservative columnist and former White House aide Patrick J. Buchanan, who charged

The Electoral Votes: Election of 1992

States	Electoral Votes	Clinton	G. Bush	States	Electoral Votes	Clinton	G. Bush
Alabama	(9)	-	9	Montana	(3)	3	-
Alaska	(3)	-	3	Nebraska	(5)	-	5
Arizona	(8)	-	8	Nevada	(4)	4	-
Arkansas	(6)	6	-	New Hampshire	(4)	4	-
California	(54)	54	-	New Jersey	(15)	15	-
Colorado	(8)	8	-	New Mexico	(5)	5	-
Connecticut	(8)	8	-	New York	(33)	33	-
Delaware	(3)	3	-	North Carolina	(14)	-	14
District of Columbia	(3)	3	-	North Dakota	(3)	-	3
Florida	(25)	-	25	Ohio	(21)	21	-
Georgia	(13)	13	-	Oklahoma	(8)	-	8
Hawaii	(4)	4	-	Oregon	(7)	7	-
Idaho	(4)	-	4	Pennsylvania	(23)	23	-
Illinois	(22)	22	-	Rhode Island	(4)	4	-
Indiana	(12)	-	12	South Carolina	(8)	-	8
Iowa	(7)	7	-	South Dakota	(3)	-	3
Kansas	(6)	-	6	Tennessee	(11)	11	-
Kentucky	(8)	8	-	Texas	(32)	-	32
Louisiana	(9)	9	-	Utah	(5)	-	5
Maine	(4)	4	-	Vermont	(3)	3	-
Maryland	(10)	10	-	Virginia	(13)	-	13
Massachusetts	(12)	12	-	Washington	(11)	11	-
Michigan	(18)	18	-	West Virginia	(5)	5	-
Minnesota	(10)	10	-	Wisconsin	(11)	11	-
Mississippi	(7)	-	7	Wyoming	(3)	-	3
Missouri	(11)	11	-	TOTALS	(538)	370	168

In the Election of 1992, although Democrat Bill Clinton won only 43 percent of the popular vote, Clinton won an impressive electoral college victory over incumbent George Bush.

that Bush had betrayed the conservatives. His main point of attack was the 1990 tax increase. He also criticized Bush's activism in world affairs, federal support of arts projects, and the nationwide recession.

Buchanan's campaign in New Hampshire, run by his sister, was simple. He wrote his own speeches, showed roughly designed television ads, and mocked Bush's superior campaign organization and resources. Although in the end Bush won New Hampshire, the media focused on the 37 percent of the vote that the underdog Buchanan received. Buchanan then made a forceful effort to win some of the southern

E

A - Z

Bill Clinton won almost 45 million popular votes in the Election of 1992, compared to George Bush's 39 million votes and H. Ross Perot's almost 20 million. (William J. Clinton Presidential Library and Museum)

contests in early March, but he never matched his New Hampshire numbers. Buchanan continued his campaign until June, assured of media attention by virtue of his unrealistic quest and severe criticism. He did not, however, win any states in the primaries.

A strong independent candidate also ran in the 1992 election: multimillionaire H. Ross Perot. Perot's folksy antigovernment style appealed to voters in the suburbs and high-growth areas of the 1980s. Perot's campaign began where much of the 1992 campaign was waged: on the television talk-show circuit. On the cable TV show *Larry King Live,* Perot said in February that he would run for president if volunteers put him on the ballot in all fifty states. He also said he would spend up to $100 million of his own money to fund a "world-class campaign." At one point, Perot ap-

peared to have a chance to win the presidency. Polls in May showed him in second place nationally behind President Bush and winning some southern and western states outright.

Perot dropped out of the campaign before he had a chance to announce his entry formally. He pointed out that Clinton's selection of Senator Al Gore of Tennessee as his running mate indicated that the Democrats were "getting their act together."

Perot then resumed his campaign in the fall, blaming his temporary exit on a Republican "dirty tricks" effort to smear his family. By then the critical reporting had faded, but it was too late for Perot because his erratic behavior had driven away supporters and curious voters alike. Perot also had difficulty finding a credible running mate. His selection of retired admiral James Stockdale raised more doubts, especially after Stockdale appeared confused during the vice-presidential debates.

Even though Perot had no real chance to win, his campaign was significant. He spent $60 million of his own money, mostly to purchase half-hour television advertisements. Some of the ads, dubbed "infomercials," won critical acclaim for their plain talk about the dangers of the federal budget deficit. Perot's bluntness lent credibility to his relentless attacks on Bush.

The Campaign

The communications revolution changed the way the candidates reached voters. For example, candidates appeared in settings once considered undignified for potential presidents. Television talk shows such as *Larry King Live* and *The Arsenio Hall Show,* as well as radio programs such as *Imus in the Morning,* provided a way for candidates to bypass the establishment media. The blurred lines between news and entertainment were perhaps most evident on cable television in the rock music MTV channel's ongoing coverage of the presidential campaign.

Clinton parroted Perot's rhetoric about the evils of special-interest influence in Washington and promised reforms of the campaign finance system. He also raised money aggressively. The Democrats raised $71 million in 1992, $9 million more than the Republicans. Clinton's selection of moderate senator Gore of Tennessee as a running mate was central to his strategy. Gore's service in Vietnam and military expertise balanced Clinton's lesser status in foreign policy. Moreover, Gore's Washington experience going back to 1976 helped Clinton to compensate for his own lack of experience.

The Republican convention in Houston was a turning point in the campaign. Bush and Vice President Dan Quayle easily won renomination. Strategists decided to shore up Bush's right-wing support and raise doubts about Clinton's character. The party's platform committee was dominated by the right-wing Christian Coalition. Bush's lost convention opportunity was apparent in the meager 3 percentage point "bounce" in poll support, compared with Clinton's 17 to 20 percent increase after the Democratic convention.

Clinton ran a sophisticated general election campaign, coordinated from the "war room" in Little Rock, Arkansas, by strategists, led by James Carville, who choreographed the campaign from television commercials to talk-show appearances to speechwriting to the bus tours of small towns. The campaign professionals were especially adept at answering charges from the opposition. When Bush attacked, Clintonites issued instant, detailed responses. The quick response prevented Bush's charges from dominating the Clinton cycle.

The Bush-Quayle fall campaign was erratic. Early on, it focused on "family values," saying the Democrats were out of touch with ordinary people. Then Bush used the powers of incumbency by announcing billions of dollars in grants to different states. All along, Bush criticized Clinton's character and experience with sharp personal attacks; however, at one point, he said "my dog Millie" would be better at foreign policy than Clinton would.

The Clinton-Gore ticket gave the Democrats a solid base in the Border States to build on.

With Arkansas and Tennessee in the Democratic camp, the Democrats could build outward into the old Confederacy (Georgia, Louisiana, Kentucky), north into the industrial states (Illinois, Michigan, Ohio), and west and north into the farm states (Iowa, Minnesota, Wisconsin). The Democrats had consistently lost those states in presidential elections in the past generation, despite strong support in congressional and statewide races.

The Democrats also built on their core of support in the Northeast (winning all the states from Maine to West Virginia) and capitalized on unhappiness with Bush in the West (California, Colorado, Hawaii, Montana, Nevada, New Mexico, Oregon, and Washington went for Clinton).

Although Clinton took only 43 percent of the popular vote, he won 370 electoral votes. This compared with Bush's 38 percent of the popular vote and 168 electoral votes. Perot's 19 percent share of the vote did not win any states.

See also: Election of 1988; Election of 1996; Primary Elections, Presidential; Super Tuesday.

Further Reading

Clinton, Bill. *My Life*. New York: Vintage Press, 2005.

Mieczkowski, Yan. *The Routledge Historical Atlas of American Presidential Elections*. London: Routledge, 2001.

Stephanopoulos, George. *All Too Human: A Political Education*. Boston: Little, Brown, & Co., 1999.

Election of 1996: William Jefferson Clinton

The reelection of President Clinton was the first reelection of a Democratic president since Franklin D. Roosevelt was reelected in 1936. In

E

A – Z

Hillary Rodham Clinton became the first First Lady to be elected to the United States Senate. In 2006, she announced her intention to seek the Democratic nomination for the presidency. (Michael Jenkins/CQ)

1994, voters had sent a message of disapproval of the president's record by electing a Republican Congress, leading some political analysts to forecast that Clinton would be a one-term president.

While the Republican Congress worked hard for conservative policy change, Clinton adopted moderate positions and portrayed himself as a check against the "extremism" of the GOP. That approach proved successful by the end of 1995. With the president and Republican legislators feuding over spending, Congress failed to pass a budget in time to avoid two temporary government shutdowns. As the deadlock continued, the Republican Congress began to appear difficult to deal with, and the president benefited from the comparison.

The president entered the 1996 election season with high approval ratings. In addition to the political mistakes of the Republicans in Congress, Clinton benefited from a growing economy. A third factor also began to weigh in the president's favor: no Democrat was challenging him for renomination.

From the beginning, Senate Majority Leader Bob Dole of Kansas was the clear front-runner for the Republican Party's nomination. He had the broadest party support of any candidate, the most prominent endorsements, and the best grassroots campaign organization. Although there never was any serious doubt that he would be the Republican nominee, for several months Dole had to fight off a large group of presidential hopefuls including television commentator Pat Buchanan, former Department of Education secretary Lamar Alexander, Texas senator Phil Gramm, Indiana senator Richard Lugar, California representative Robert Dornan, and multimillionaire publisher Malcolm S. "Steve" Forbes Jr.

Even after his nomination was ensured, Dole's campaign failed for weeks to capture the public's attention. As senate majority leader, Dole had found himself in the difficult position of having to manage his official duties while campaigning for president. Dole made a bold strategic gamble when he decided to resign from the Senate to campaign full time for the presidency. His emotional departure from the Senate temporarily energized his campaign.

At his nominating convention in San Diego, Dole performed a tough balancing act in keeping moderates and conservatives from dividing the party. The Republicans struck an awkward compromise: although the party platform was very conservative and kept the antiabortion plank, the convention that the country saw on television was moderate in tone.

Dole surprised many with two bold campaign moves. First, he selected as his running mate former New York representative and secretary of Housing and Urban Development Jack Kemp, who earlier had endorsed Forbes. Second, Dole proposed an across-the-board 15 percent income tax cut.

Clinton's Reelection

Although polls throughout 1996 showed Clinton with a commanding lead against Dole, those same polls pointed to voter uneasiness with the president's apparent character. Because of continued negative media coverage resulting from Whitewater-related charges, the badly handled

White House firing of its travel office staff, and a sexual harassment lawsuit against Clinton, much of the public believed that their president was an individual of low moral character. Yet the polls also indicated that Americans would reelect a flawed president because of their uneasiness with the Republican nominee, their low opinion of the Republican majority in Congress, their general satisfaction with the state of the economy, and the president's famous charisma.

Clinton's strategy was brilliant. He effectively took away from Dole's campaign a number of issues that usually help Republican presidential candidates, such as welfare reform, deficit reduction, and family values. He kept his Democratic base by positioning himself as the only viable check against the "extremism" of the Republican Congress.

In the last weeks of the campaign, when it was clear that Dole had no realistic chance of winning, the Republican candidate made a final gamble: he decided to attack the president's character. Dole's attacks on the president made a difference in the campaign polls when the news media began to report on questionable fund-raising practices by the Democratic National Committee (DNC) and meetings between foreign lobbyists and Clinton. Stories of unethical and possibly illegal Democratic campaign contributions fit with the Dole message that Clinton lacked good character—and that such a fault was unsuitable for the person serving as president.

The Reform Party candidate, H. Ross Perot, also benefited from the negative Clinton press. Although he had never been a serious factor in 1996, as he had been as an independent candidate in 1992, Perot's support increased by several percentage points in the late polls. In the end, Perot had little impact on the elections.

Clinton easily won reelection with 49.2 percent of the popular vote and 379 electoral votes to Dole's 40.7 percent and 159 electoral votes. Reform Party candidate Perot polled 8.4 percent of the vote, less than half of his 1992 total, and received no electoral votes.

See also: Election of 1992.

Further Reading

Cohen, Daniel. *The Impeachment of William J. Clinton.* Minneapolis, MN: Lerner Books, 1999.

Harris, John F. *The Survivor: Bill Clinton in the White House.* New York: Random House, 2005.

Maraniss, David. *First in His Class.* New York: Simon & Schuster, 1996.

Election of 2000: George W. Bush

The last presidential election of the twentieth century, and the closest in forty years, which returned the Republican Party to the White House. The election brought the nation to the brink of a constitutional crisis that was narrowly averted only after an unprecedented thirty-six days of bitter arguing and litigation over who won: Democrat Al Gore or Republican George W. Bush. The eventual outcome, with Texas governor Bush the official winner, did little to unite the electorate, which had split a hundred million votes almost evenly between the two major party candidates.

Although Gore, the departing vice president, clearly won the national popular vote in the 2000 race by more than a half-million votes, Bush claimed the twenty-five electoral votes of Florida, where the election had been extremely close. Ultimately, the state's Republican administration, headed by Governor Jeb Bush, certified his brother as the popular vote winner in Florida, raising the GOP candidate's nationwide electoral vote total to 271: just one more vote than he needed to win. Gore unsuccessfully contested the election on the grounds that the state had stopped the recounts prematurely, leaving thousands of machine-processed ballots not subjected to the scrutiny of human eyes in a hand recount.

In the end, a sharply divided U.S. Supreme Court halted the Florida count, effectively

E

A - Z

In one of the closest elections in the nation's history, Texas governor George W. Bush (left) won the 2000 presidential election after the United States Supreme Court stopped further vote counting in Florida. Vice President Al Gore (right) won more popular votes, but Bush won the electoral college vote, 271 to Gore's 266. (AP Photo/Eric Gay [left], AP Photo/Doug Mills [right])

deciding the election in Bush's favor. It was the first time that the U.S. Supreme Court had taken up a lawsuit, brought by Bush, related to a presidential election. The Court traditionally had left such matters to Congress or to the states.

The Election Campaign

The prolonged dispute over Florida's crucial vote overshadowed all other aspects of the 2000 presidential election, including a lackluster primary season dominated throughout by Vice President Gore on the Democratic side and Governor Bush on the GOP side. Both locked up their nominations early, despite some strong opposition, primarily from Arizona senator John McCain against Bush and former New Jersey senator Bill Bradley against Gore.

Bush entered the race in early 1999 and quickly established himself as the favorite of the Republican establishment and its campaign donors. Without a sitting Democratic president to compete against, the contest attracted a

dozen hopefuls for the GOP nomination. Even before the Iowa caucuses in January 2000, half of the field dropped out, including former vice president Dan Quayle, former Tennessee governor Lamar Alexander, and Elizabeth Dole, head of the Red Cross and wife of 1996 nominee Bob Dole.

By early February, Bush and McCain remained the only serious contenders. McCain upset Bush in the New Hampshire and Michigan primaries, but Bush went on to win a cluster of March 7 primaries and enough convention delegates to clinch the nomination. For Gore, the nomination challenge from Bradley was short-lived. Bradley failed to win a single primary and dropped out of the race in early March.

After the national nominating conventions, Gore, more so than Bush, faced a vote-siphoning threat from the Green Party candidate, consumer advocate Ralph Nader, who received almost 1 percent of the presidential vote in 1996 and was aiming for 5 percent in

2000—a level that would ensure federal campaign funding for the Greens in the 2004 election. Although Republican swing voters were unlikely to switch to corporation-basher Nader, some liberals who supported Bradley found Nader an attractive alternative.

With polls continuing to show the electorate almost evenly divided, the major party race settled down to basically a personality contest between two Ivy Leaguers—Gore (Harvard) and Bush (Yale). The public perceived Bush as personable but perhaps not as intelligent as Gore, despite Bush's master's degree from Harvard's business school. Although known privately as humorous, Gore was seen publicly as somewhat wooden. In the first of their three debates, Gore came off as smart-alecky against Bush, the self-styled "compassionate conservative." The election was expected to be close. Bush and Gore ran neck-and-neck in public opinion polls, right up to election day.

Despite President Bill Clinton's (1993–2001) high job approval ratings, he was perhaps Gore's biggest handicap. Bush and other Republican candidates tried to saddle Gore with the troubles of the Clinton administration, particularly Clinton's December 1998 impeachment for lying under oath about his affair with Monica Lewinsky when she was a White House intern.

Long Election Night

Problems with the crucial Florida vote erupted almost immediately on election day November 7, 2000. Voters in Palm Beach County reported difficulties with an unusual "butterfly" punch-card ballot. Some Democratic voters there thought that they had inadvertently voted for Reform Party nominee Pat Buchanan instead of for Gore. In some of the other twenty-four counties using outmoded punch-card systems, but with regular ballot forms, voters said they were unable to punch out the hole for the candidate of their choice.

Another serious problem emerged shortly after the polls closed, this one having to do with the system—based on exit polling—devised by the news media to project election winners before the votes are counted. The system is usually accurate, but its worst and most embarrassing mistake happened at 7:47 P.M. Eastern Standard Time. At that time, the broadcast networks projected Gore as the winner in Florida. People were still voting in Florida's western panhandle, in the central time zone, when the election was called for Gore. A short time later, the networks retracted and said Florida was too close to call.

In the early hours of November 8, the news reports put Bush ahead. Gore called Bush from Nashville, Tennessee, and told him he was prepared to concede. Later, after being advised that there might be a recount in Florida, Gore called again to Bush in Austin, Texas. "You mean you're retracting your concession?" a surprised Bush reportedly asked. "You don't have to get snippy about it," Gore is said to have replied.

Besides leading nationwide in the popular vote, Gore outside of Florida led in the electoral college vote, 267 to 246 (after the counting of the absentee vote in Oregon and New Mexico concluded several days later). The entire 2000 presidential election therefore hung on the final results of the popular vote in Florida, which would determine the winner of the state's twenty-five electoral votes.

The close election triggered an automatic machine recount, showing Bush ahead by about 300 votes in Florida. But Gore's supporters focused on the thousands of votes that the machines rejected as undervoted, showing no vote for president, or overvoted, showing more than one vote for presidential candidates. Only a manual count of those ballots could discern votes that the machines could not detect, Gore lawyers argued. The Democrats' war cry became, "Every vote counts; count every vote."

The Republicans argued that the votes had been legally counted and recounted, including military and other absentee ballots that favored Bush, and that the canvassers had no uniform standards for gauging the difference between a vote and a nonvote on a punch-card ballot. Allowing more time for recounts, they said, would be changing the rules after the game started.

E

A - Z

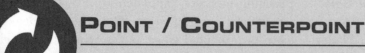

POINT / COUNTERPOINT

The Election of 2000

On November 26, 2000, Katherine Harris, Florida's Secretary of State, certified that Texas Governor George W. Bush, the Republican candidate, won Florida's twenty-five electoral votes. At the time, however, recounts were still underway in some Florida counties. Governor Bush and Vice President Al Gore, the Democratic candidate, responded to Harris's ruling.

George W. Bush, November 26, 2000

The last nineteen days have been extraordinary ones. Our nation watched as we were all reminded on a daily basis of the importance of each and every vote. We were reminded of the strength of our democracy—that while our system is not always perfect, it is fundamentally strong and far better than any other alternative.

The election was close, but tonight, after a count, a recount and yet another manual recount, Secretary Cheney and I are honored and humbled to have won the state of Florida, which gives us the needed electoral votes to win the election. We will therefore undertake the responsibility of preparing to serve as America's next President and Vice President . . .

Two hundred years ago, after a difficult election, President Thomas Jefferson reminded his fellow citizens that "every difference of opinion is not a difference of principle." Vice President Gore and I had our differences of opinion in this election, and so did many candidates for Congress. But there is broad agreement on some important principles: . . . But now that the votes are counted, it is time for the votes to count. The Vice President's lawyers have indicated he will challenge the certified election results. I respectfully ask him to reconsider. Until Florida's votes were certified, the Vice President was working to represent the interests of those who supported him. I didn't agree with his call for additional recounts, but I respected his decision to fight until the votes were finally certified. Now that they are certified, we enter a different phase. If the Vice President chooses to go forward, he is filing a contest to the outcome of the election, and that is not the best route for America.

Al Gore, November 27, 2000

Thank you for taking the time to listen tonight.

Every four years, there is one day when the people have their say. In many ways, the act of voting and having that vote counted is more important than

Katherine Harris, Florida's secretary of state and former cochair of Bush's campaign in the state, announced on November 13 that counties had until the following day, the date set in state law, to submit their returns, without any manual recount figures. Lawsuits prevented

Harris from enforcing the date, however, and the manual counts proceeded by fits and starts until Sunday, November 26, under an extension granted by the seven-member Florida Supreme Court, made up mostly of Democratic appointees. That evening Harris ceremoniously

E

A - Z

who wins the majority of the votes that are cast. Because, whoever wins, the victor will know that the American people have spoken with a voice made mighty by the whole of its integrity. On that one day, every four years, the poor as well as the rich, the weak as well as the strong, women and men alike, citizens of every race, creed and color, or whatever infirmity or political temper, are all equal. They are equal, that is, so long as all of their votes are counted.

A vote is not just a piece of paper. A vote is a human voice; a statement of human principle. And we should not let those voices be silenced. Not for today, not for tomorrow, not for as long as the country's laws and democratic institutions let us stand and fight to let those voices count.

If the people do not in the end choose me, so be it; the outcome will have been fair and the people will have spoken. If they choose me, so be it; I commit to bringing this country together. But whatever the outcome, let the people have their say—and let us listen.

Ignoring votes means ignoring democracy itself. And if we ignore the votes of thousands in Florida in this election, how can you, or any American, have confidence that your vote will not be ignored in a future election?

That is all we have asked since election day: a complete count of all the votes cast in Florida. Not recount after recount, as some have charged—but a single full and accurate count.

We haven't had that yet. Great efforts have been made to prevent the counting of these votes. Lawsuit after lawsuit has been filed to delay the count and to stop the counting for many precious days between election day and the deadline for having the count finished. And this would be over long since, except for these efforts to block the process at every turn . . .

So as provided under Florida law, I have decided to contest this inaccurate and incomplete count—in order to ensure the greatest possible credibility for the outcome.

DOCUMENT-BASED QUESTION
What are the differences between the views of Governor Bush and Vice President Gore?

"certified" Bush as the Florida winner by a mere 537 votes out of six million cast.

Gore scored a short-lived victory on December 8 when the Florida court by a 4–3 vote ordered a resumption of the hand counts, only to have the U.S. Supreme Court quickly halt them the following day, pending its decision in *Bush v. Gore*. In its 5–4 decision, handed down December 12, the Court majority ruled for Bush that the lack of uniform standards for manual recounts denied "equal protection of the laws" to Florida voters. The Court split along ideo-

THE ELECTION OF 2000

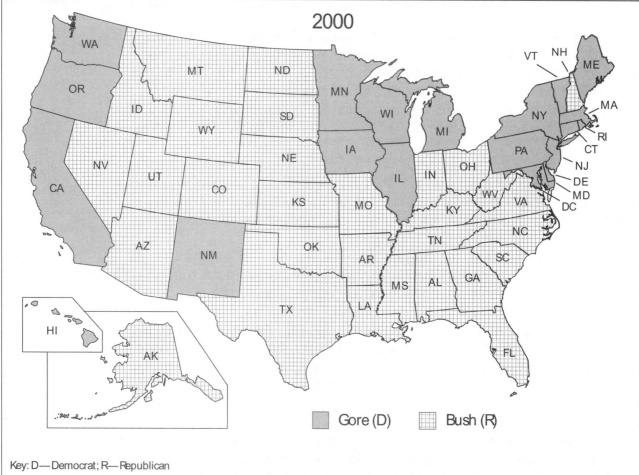

2000

Key: D—Democrat; R—Republican

Gore (D) Bush (R)

In the highly controversial Election of 2000, Texas governor George W. Bush's support was concentrated in the West, the South, and parts of the Midwest. Vice President Al Gore's support came from the Northeast, the upper Midwest, and the far West. After days of uncertainty, Bush was declared the winner by a five-vote electoral margin, 271-266.

logical lines in the unsigned decision. In the majority were conservatives William Rehnquist, Antonin Scalia, Clarence Thomas, Anthony Kennedy, and Sandra Day O'Connor. Dissenting were liberals or moderates Stephen Breyer, Ruth Bader Ginsburg, David Souter, and John Paul Stevens.

The Court action left 42,000 Florida undervotes unexamined, including 35,000 from the punch-card counties, but it effectively resolved the 2000 presidential race and possibly averted a constitutional crisis that might have arisen had the dispute resulted in Florida's sending

two sets of electoral votes to Congress. The state legislature had already designated a slate of electors committed to Bush. Faced with a hopeless situation, Vice President Gore conceded on December 13.

When the presidential electors met in their states December 18 to cast their ballots, one District of Columbia elector, Barbara Lett-Simmons, withheld her vote from Gore in protest of the District's lack of representation in Congress. This reduced Gore's electoral vote total to 266 against 271 for Bush. Gore received 51.0 million votes (48.4 percent) to

50.5 million (47.9 percent) for Bush. Gore's lead in the popular vote was 539,947. Nader's 2.8 million votes amounted to 2.7 percent of the total.

The nation witnessed another peaceful transfer of power with the Bush-Cheney inauguration on January 20, 2001. As historian David McCullough phrased it, the peacefulness was typical of past inaugurations but perhaps for a different reason. "As close as it was, this election was not about visceral issues like slavery or war—things people are really passionate about," McCullough said. "The nation is closely divided, certainly, but we seem to be divided over which party controls the middle of the political spectrum. I'm not sure it's happened quite like that before."

See also: ▢ Al Gore's Concession Speech in the **Primary Source Library;** ▢ *Bush v. Gore* in the **Primary Source Library;** Election of 2004; Electoral College; ▢ George W. Bush's 2000 Acceptance Speech in the **Primary Source Library;** Twenty-second Amendment.

Further Reading

Brady, Henry, Cooper, John Milton, Jr., and Jack N. Rakove, eds. *The Unfinished Election of 2000*. Jackson, TN: Basic Books, 2002.

Dover, E.D. *The Disputed Election of 2000*. Westport, CT: Greenwood Press, 2003.

Toobin, Jeffrey. *Too Close to Call: The Thirty-Six-Day Battle to Decide the 2000 Election*. New York: Random House, 2002.

Election of 2004: George W. Bush

A closely contested election, in which **incumbent** Republican George W. Bush won reelection over his Democratic challenger, Massachusetts Senator John Kerry. Bush was unopposed for the Republican nomination and again chose Richard Cheney as his running mate. Among the Democrats, however, several contenders sought the presidential nomination. Among them were Senators John Kerry of Massachusetts, John Edwards of North Carolina, and Vermont's former governor, Howard Dean.

Early in the campaign, Howard Dean appeared to be the frontrunner, but he lost ground after the Iowa caucuses, in which John Kerry won a surprising victory. Senator John Edwards placed second in Iowa. Kerry again triumphed in the New Hampshire primary, while Edwards won his neighboring state of South Carolina. Kerry went on to win the rest of the Democratic primaries, except Vermont, clinching the presidential nomination. At the Democratic National Convention in July 2004, Kerry chose Edwards as his running mate.

President Bush portrayed himself as a strong leader, able to keep the United States safe in the face of terrorism. Bush had received high poll ratings after the September 11, 2001, terrorist attacks, but his popularity sagged as the War in Iraq dragged on. Kerry campaigned on a theme of "Stronger at home, respected in the world," demonstrating to voters that he would pay more attention to domestic issues and restore America's stature overseas. Overall, the War in Iraq dominated the campaign.

Several third-party candidates also ran in the election. Among them were Ralph Nader (Independent and Reform Parties) Michael Badnarik (Libertarian Party), and David Cobb (Green Party). On election day, however, President Bush won victory: 286 electoral votes to

Electoral Votes: Election of 2004	
George W. Bush (Republican)	286
John Kerry (Democrat)	251

In the election of 2004, one Kerry elector from Minnesota cast his electoral vote for John Edwards. The vote of this faithless elector, however, did not affect the election outcome.

E

A–Z

Kerry's 251. In the popular vote, Bush won 50.7 percent to Kerry's 48.3 percent.

See also: Democratic Party; Faithless Electors; Republican Party; Third Parties.

Further Reading

Campbell, David E., ed. *A Matter of Faith: Religion and the 2004 Presidential Election.* Washington, DC: Brookings Institution Press, 2007.

Freeman, Steven, and Joel Bleifuss. *Was the 2004 Election Stolen?* New York: Seven Stories Press, 2006.

Election of 2008: Campaigns

One of the most closely contested presidential campaigns in recent history. For the first time since 1952, no incumbent president or vice president sought his party's nomination. As early as 2006, several candidates from both parties announced their intention to seek the nomination

Among the Democrats, New York senator Hillary Rodham Clinton—the first serious female presidential contender in U. S. history—was an early favorite, gathering broad support throughout the party. Senator Barack Obama of Illinois–the first African American to seek

the presidency since Jesse Jackson in 1988–and former North Carolina senator and 2004 vice presidential nominee John Edwards were also strong contenders for the nomination. In addition, Connecticut senator Christopher Dodd, Ohio representative Dennis Kucinich, Delaware senator Joe Biden, and former Alaska senator Mike Gravel sought their party's nod.

The Republican contest was equally crowded. Early in the campaign, former New York mayor Rudy Guiliani and former Massachusetts governor Mitt Romney appeared to be the frontrunners, while Arizona senator John McCain's campaign seemed to fade. Other contenders included former Arkansas governor Mike Huckabee, former senator Fred Thompson, and Texas representative Ron Paul.

In late February 2008, consumer activist Ralph Nader announced that he would again seek the presidency as an independent candidate. The effect of his entry on the presidential race was uncertain.

For the first time ever, caucuses and primary elections were held as early as January 2008, and quickly several contenders dropped out after failing to gain the necessary popular support. By February, only Democrats Clinton and Obama remained as serious contenders for the nomination. They fought a neck-and-neck fight that looked as if it needed to be settled at the Democratic Convention in August 2008.

Democratic contenders Hillary Rodham Clinton and Barack Obama waged a series of debates throughout the primary season while Republican John McCain secured his party's nomination by early March 2008. (AP Images/Virginia Sherwood/NBC NewsWire via AP Images [left]; AP Photo/Deborah Cannon, Pool [right])

After a series of Republican primary wins, John McCain surged as the party's frontrunner. By early March, he had won more than the needed 1,191 convention delegates to secure his party's nomination at the Republican Convention in Minneapolis in September 2008.

Elections, Congressional

Americans elect a new Congress the first Tuesday after the first Monday in November of even-numbered years. Early the following January, the elected representatives and senators begin their first session of that Congress. Those elected on November 4, 2008, for instance, were sworn in January 3, 2009, on the opening day of the 111th Congress.

Views of Congress

As an institution, Congress has suffered public criticism almost since the nation's beginnings. Alexis de Tocqueville, the wise French visitor of the late 1820s, observed the "vulgar demeanor" of the House of Representatives, where often he could not detect even one "distinguished man." In contrast, as he wrote in his classic *Democracy in America,* the Senate was

> composed of eloquent advocates, distinguished generals, wise magistrates, and statesmen of note, whose arguments would do honor to the most remarkable parliamentary debates of Europe.

Subsequent views of the entire Congress often have been no more kind than de Tocqueville's opinion of the House. Gallup polls measuring Americans' trust and confidence in governmental institutions show Congress consistently ranking last among the three branches of the federal government. Related Gallup polls, asking whether Americans approve or disapprove of the way Congress is handling its job, have also shown little confidence in the legislative branch. These and other polls suggest that many Americans often view the legislative branch with a skeptical eye. Oddly, however, election results show that voters generally return **incumbents** to office, indicating a more favorable attitude toward their own representatives and senators than the institution as a whole.

In the modern era, the power of incumbency has remained strong with the turnover rate

JUSTICE FOR ALL

Florida's 13th District

The 2006 election of Florida's representative from the Thirteenth District, around Sarasota on the state's west coast, was settled by 373 votes: by less that one-half of 1 percent. As in the 2000 presidential election, the close margin activated an automatic recount of the votes. Republican Vern Buchanan claimed victory, but Democrat Christine Jennings believed there was a serious undervote in the district. Throughout the district, different voting systems were used—including touch screens and optical scanners—and some of the systems do not maintain a "paper trail" that can verify to electronic tallies. Ironically, in the same election, Sarasota County voters passed a referendum requiring a paper-based ballot system in future elections.

E

A – Z

from deaths, resignations, and election defeats averaging about 10 percent or less, historically an exceptionally low level. An incumbent's appeal rests on more than the person's record in Congress and is significantly influenced by the public image projected through television, direct mail, telephone banks, and other means used in election campaigns. Projecting that image, particularly through costly television advertising, is extremely expensive, requiring any candidate to raise substantial campaign funds. Incumbents are particularly well placed to raise money from special interest groups as a result of their service and participation in Congress.

Characteristics of Members

Whether turnover on election day is large or small, a certain uniformity pervades Congress. Congress has been dominated since its beginning by middle-aged white men with backgrounds in law or business. Their levels of income and education have consistently been above the national average. For many of the lawmakers today, however, business occupations are past activities. In recent years, ethics rules have limited the income that can be earned outside of Congress. Moreover, serving in Congress has become a full-time job. Since the 1970s, it has attracted career politicians, whose primary earnings have come from government service.

Ever so slowly, other changes have crept into the makeup of Congress. The numbers of women, African American, and Hispanic American members have increased in recent decades, although still not in proportion to their share of the total population.

Average Age

The average age of members of Congress went up notably between the end of the Civil War (1861–1865) and the 1950s, but remained fairly constant until the mid-1970s. In the Forty-first Congress (1869–1871), the average was 44.6 years; by the Eighty-fifth Congress (1957–1959), it was 53.8. Over the next eighteen years, the average fluctuated only slightly. It dropped again in January 1981, when the House had eight members under 30, the most

since World War II. The younger trend bottomed out in 1983 when the average hit 47 years.

After that came a gradual increase, continuing through the beginning of the 110th Congress in 2007, when the average age climbed to 57. The increasing age of members of Congress was partly attributable to the aging trend of the nation's population, but low turnover in Congress was also a big factor.

Occupations

The legal profession has been the dominant occupational background of members of Congress since its beginning. In the First Congress, more than one-third of the House members had legal training. The proportion of lawyers in Congress peaked at 70 percent in 1840 but remained high. From 1950 to the mid-1970s, it was in the 55–60 percent range.

The first significant decline in members with a law background began with the Ninety-sixth Congress (1979–1981). Although sixty-five of the one hundred senators were lawyers in 1979, for the first time in at least thirty years lawyers made up less than a majority of the House.

After lawyers, members with a business or banking background make up the second largest group in Congress. In the 107th Congress, 159 House members claimed such a background, the same as the 106th Congress but down from 181 in the 105th Congress.

Members of the clergy continue to be underrepresented in Congress. Only a handful of Protestant ministers have served in Congress, and no Catholic priest had done so until 1971, when Representative Robert F. Drinan, a Democrat from Massachusetts and a Jesuit priest, took a House seat. (Father Gabriel Richard was the nonvoting delegate of the Territory of Michigan from 1823 to 1825.) Drinan served five terms but declined to run again in 1980, the year that Pope John Paul II (r. 1978–2005) ordered priests not to hold public office.

A new type of legislator emerged in the 1970s: the career politician whose primary earnings had always come from political office at the local, state, or federal level. This situation became possible because states and localities had begun to think of political positions as full-time jobs and had raised salaries accordingly. In addition, the demands of modern political campaigns left less time to pursue other careers. Members of recent Congresses also tend to lack military experience, continuing a trend prevalent in the 1990s.

Religious Affiliations

Among religious groups, Protestants have comprised nearly three-fourths of the membership of both houses in recent years. However, Roman Catholics form the biggest single religious group—a distinction they have held since taking the lead from Methodists in 1965. Recent Congresses have included Baptists, Methodists, Presbyterians, Episcopalians, and Lutherans, as well as other faiths including Jewish, Mormon, Eastern Christian, Christian Scientist, Unitarian, Pentecostal, Buddhist, and Muslim.

See also: Election Day; Elections, House of Representatives; Elections, Senate; Incumbency.

Further Reading

Davidson, Roger H., Walter J. Oleszek and Frances E. Lee. *Congress and Its Members.* Washington, DC: CQ Press, 2007.

Herrnson, Paul S. *Congressional Elections: Campaigning at Home and in Washington.* Washington, DC: CQ Press, 2007.

Elections, Gubernatorial

Next to the president, governors are the most powerful elected officials in the United States. Some preside over states that are larger than many foreign countries. Every governor but Nebraska's must deal with a legislature that is partisan and bicameral in nature, just like the U.S. Congress.

Over the years, many voters have regarded executive experience as a governor more akin to that of the president than service as a legislator, military commander, or business leader,

which helps to explain why four of the five presidents since 1977 have been governors or former governors. (The exception was George Bush, though his son was governor of Texas when he won the presidency in 2000.)

In all, seventeen of the nation's forty-three presidents (or 40 percent) have first been governors—including Ronald Reagan of California; Calvin Coolidge of Massachusetts; Woodrow Wilson of New Jersey; Grover Cleveland, Theodore Roosevelt, and Franklin D. Roosevelt of New York; and George W. Bush of Texas. More recently, though, it is not only big-state governors who have made the leap to the White House, but executives from smaller states as well, including Jimmy Carter of Georgia and Bill Clinton of Arkansas.

In recent years, many politicians wanting an active role in fashioning policy have found their state capital, and not Washington, D.C., to be the place to be. The downsizing of the federal government in the late twentieth century shifted power to the states, as they became laboratories of government experimentation on issues from education to welfare reform.

For all their power today, though, governors still are on a tighter leash than most other officials elected under our federal system of government. Presidents have been limited to two terms since 1951 by constitutional amendment, but the Supreme Court has nullified state efforts to impose term limits on their members of Congress. By contrast, roughly three-fourths of the states limit their governors to a single term or two consecutive terms, although in many states governors may serve again after a one-term interruption

The election of governors by popular vote goes back to the early years of the Republic in the late eighteenth century. The first female governors, however, were not elected until 1924, four years after the Nineteenth Amendment granted women's suffrage in every state. Elected that year to succeed their husbands were Nellie Tayloe Ross (served, 1925–1927) of Wyoming and Miriam "Ma" Ferguson (served, 1925–1927 and 1933–1935) of Texas, both Democrats.

The first two Hispanic governors were elected in 1974, Democrats Jerry Apodaca in

New Mexico and Raul Castro in neighboring Arizona. The first popularly elected African American governor was Democrat L. Douglas Wilder of Virginia, who was narrowly elected in 1989. Gary Locke, a Democrat of Chinese descent, became the first Asian American governor with his election in Washington in 1996.

Duties and Powers

Gubernatorial duties vary in detail from state to state, but basically they are the same. Most state constitutions today have the "strong governor, weak legislature" system, which is the reverse of the situation that prevailed at the dawn of the American Republic.

The newly freed states looked with suspicion on the office of governor. In the colonial era, the British-appointed governors were the symbols of the mother country's control and, the revolutionaries argued, of tyranny. Colonial assemblies, however, were able to gain control over appropriations and thus became the champions of colonial rights against the governors. After the Revolutionary War, when drawing up their constitutions, states gave most of the power to the legislative bodies and imposed restrictions on governors, including the length of the term of office and the method of election.

Length of Terms

As of 1789 the four New England states—Connecticut, Massachusetts, New Hampshire, and Rhode Island—held gubernatorial elections every year. Some of the Middle Atlantic states favored somewhat longer terms: New York and Pennsylvania had three-year terms for their governors, although New Jersey instituted a one-year term. The border and southern states had a mix: Maryland and North Carolina governors served a one-year term; South Carolina had a two-year term; and Delaware, Virginia, and Georgia had three-year terms. No state had a four-year term.

Over the years, states have changed the length of gubernatorial terms. With some occasional back and forth movement, the general trend has been toward lengthening terms. New York, for example, has changed the term of office of its governor four times. Beginning in 1777 with a three-year term, the state switched to a two-year term in 1820, back to a three-year term in 1876, back to a two-year term in 1894, and to a four-year term beginning in 1938.

The trend toward longer gubernatorial terms shows up clearly by comparing the length of terms in 1900 and 2000. Of the forty-five states in the Union in 1900, twenty-two, almost half, had two-year terms. One, New Jersey, had a three-year term, while Rhode Island and Massachusetts were the only states left with one-year terms. The remaining twenty states had four-year gubernatorial terms.

As of January 2001, forty-three of those same states had four-year terms, and the five states admitted to the Union after 1900—Oklahoma (1907), Arizona and New Mexico (1912), Alaska and Hawaii (1959)—had four-year gubernatorial terms. This left only two states with two-year terms: New Hampshire and Vermont.

Elections in Non-presidential Years

Along with the change to longer terms for governors came another trend—away from holding gubernatorial elections in presidential election years. Except for North Dakota, every state that switched in the twentieth century to four-year gubernatorial terms scheduled its elections in non-presidential years.

These changes left only nine states—Delaware, Indiana, Missouri, Montana, North Carolina, North Dakota, Utah, Washington, and West Virginia—holding quadrennial gubernatorial elections at the same time as the presidential election. New Hampshire and Vermont still had two-year terms, so every other gubernatorial election in these two states occurred in a presidential year. Five states—Kentucky, Louisiana, Mississippi, New Jersey, and Virginia—elect governors in odd-numbered years.

Methods of Election

Yet another way in which Americans of the early federal period restricted their governors was by the method of election. In 1789 only in New York and the four New England states did the people directly choose their governors by popular vote. In the remaining eight states, governors were chosen by the state legislatures, thus enhancing the power of the legislatures in their dealings with the governors. Several factors—including the democratic trend to elect public officials directly, the increasing trust in the office of governor, and the need for a stronger and more independent chief executive—led to the gradual introduction of popular votes in all the states.

By the 1860s, the remaining eight original states had switched to popular ballots. Pennsylvania was first, in 1790, and was followed by Delaware in 1792, Georgia in 1825, North Carolina in 1835, Maryland in 1838, New Jersey in 1844, Virginia in 1851, and South Carolina in 1865, after the Civil War.

All the states admitted to the Union after the original thirteen, with one exception, made provision from the very beginning for popular election of their governors. The exception was Louisiana which, from its admission in 1812 until a change in the state constitution in 1845, had a unique system of gubernatorial elections. The people participated by voting in a first-step popular election. In a second step, the legislature was to select the governor from the two candidates receiving the highest popular vote.

Number of Terms

Another limitation placed on governors is a restriction on the number of terms they are allowed to serve. In the early years at least three states had such limitations. Governors of Maryland were eligible to serve three consecutive one-year terms and then were required to retire for at least one year. Pennsylvania allowed its governors three consecutive three-year terms and then forced retirement for at least one term. In New Jersey, according to the constitution of 1844, a governor could serve only one three-year term before retiring for at least one term.

In the last decades of the twentieth century, increasing voter discontent with government and with politicians stoked a movement to limit the number of years a person could serve in public office. The movement was especially pronounced at the gubernatorial level. By the beginning of the twenty-first century, only eleven states did not impose some term limits on their governors: Connecticut, Illinois, Iowa, Massachu-

setts, Minnesota, New Hampshire, New York, North Dakota, Texas, Vermont, and Wisconsin.

The lack of a term limit has resulted in some long gubernatorial tenures in some of these states. New York's Mario M. Cuomo, a Democrat, was beaten trying for a fourth term as governor in 1994. Wisconsin's Tommy G. Thompson, a Republican, was in the middle of his fourth term when he was tapped to be the secretary of health and human services after the 2000 election. Vermont's Howard B. Dean, a Democrat, was elected to a fifth two-year term in 2000. Most of the other states have placed a limit of two consecutive terms on their governor, which has meant eight years continuously in office. A few states had variations on this theme.

Majority Vote Requirement

A peculiarity of gubernatorial voting that has almost disappeared from the American political scene is the requirement that the winning gubernatorial candidate receive a majority of the popular vote. Otherwise, the choice devolves upon the state legislature or, in some cases, a runoff between the two leading candidates is required. Centered in New England, this practice was used mainly in the nineteenth century. All six present-day New England states, as well as Arizona, Georgia, and Mississippi, had such a provision governing their gubernatorial election at one time or another. New Hampshire, Vermont, Massachusetts, and Connecticut already had the provision when they entered the Union between 1789 and 1791.

Rhode Island required a majority election but did not adopt a provision for legislative election until 1842; Maine adopted a majority provision when it split off from Massachusetts to form a separate state in 1820. Georgia put the majority provision in its constitution when it switched from legislative to popular election of governors in 1825 but, instead of legislative elections, provides for a runoff between the top two contenders three weeks after the general election. Mississippi wrote the majority provision into its constitution in 1890. Arizona adopted a runoff in 1990.

The purpose of the majority provision appears to have been to safeguard against a candidate's

Limitations on Governor Terms

State	Term limit	State	Term limit
Alabama	2	New Jersey[1]	2
Alaska[1]	2	New	
Arizona[1]	2	Mexico[1]	2
Arkansas	2	New York	None
California	2	North	
Colorado	2	Carolina[1]	2
Connecticut	None	North	
Delaware[2]	2	Dakota	None
Florida[3]	2	7	2
Georgia[1]	2	Oklahoma[1]	2
Hawaii	2	Oregon[5]	2
Idaho	None	Pennsyl-	
Illinois	None	vania	2
Indiana[1]	2	Rhode	
Iowa	None	Island	2
Kansas	2	South	
Kentucky	2	Carolina[1]	2
Louisiana[1]	2	South	
Maine[1]	2	Dakota[1]	
Maryland[1]	2	Tennessee[1]	2
Massac-		Texas	None
husetts	None	Utah	None
Michigan	2	Vermont	None
Minnesota	None	Virginia[6]	1
Mississippi[2]	2	Washington	None
Missouri[2]	2	West	
Montana[4]	2	Virginia	2
Nebraska[1]	2	Wisconsin	None
Nevada	2	Wyoming[5]	2
New			
Hampshire	None		

Notes: Gubernatorial term limits as of 2004.

1. After two consecutive terms, must wait four years and/or one full term before being eligible again.

2. Absolute two-term limitation, but not necessarily consecutive.

3. Eligible for eight consecutive years.

4. Eligible for eight years in a sixteen-year period.

5. Eligible for eight out of any period of twelve years.

6. Cannot serve consecutive terms, but after a four-year respite can seek reelection.

Source: Book of the States, 2004–05, vol. 36 (Lexington, Ky.: Council of State Governments, 2004), Table 4.1.

Term limits for the nation's governors vary from no limits in states such as Connecticut and Texas to one non-consecutive term in Virginia.

winning with a small fraction of the popular vote in a multiple field. In most of New England the provision was part of the early state constitutions, formed largely in the 1780s before the development of the two-party system.

The prospect of multiple-candidate fields diminished with the coming of the two-party system. Nevertheless, each of these states had occasion to use the provision at least once. Sometimes, in an extremely close election, minor-party candidates received enough of a vote to keep the winner from getting a majority of the total vote. At other times, strong third-party movements or disintegration of the old party structure resulted in the election's being thrown into the state legislature.

Vermont retains the majority vote provision, and its legislature chose the governor in January 1987, the first time it had done so since 1912. Georgia maintains the requirement for a majority vote for governor but, instead of legislative election, provides for a runoff between the top two contenders three weeks after the general election. Mississippi has a majority vote provision that was not used until 1999, when neither major party candidate received a majority of the vote, throwing the election into the Democratically controlled House of the legislature. On January 4, 2000, as expected, the House elected the Democratic candidate, Lt. Governor Ronnie Musgrove, who had edged Republican Mike Parker in the popular vote, 49.6 percent to 48.5 percent.

See also: Impeachment and Removal, Gubernatorial; Term Limits.

Further Reading

Congressional Quarterly. *Gubernatorial Elections, 1787–1997.* Washington, DC: CQ Press, 1998.

Leal, David L. *Electing America's Governors.* New York: Palgrave Macmillan, 2006.

Elections, House of Representatives

In the United States, elections occur every two years to elect members to the lower house of

Congress. At the Constitutional Convention in 1787, the Framers recognized that the new government needed an executive to carry out the laws and a judiciary to resolve conflicts arising from them. However, it was Congress, the lawmaking body, which the Founders designed to be the heart of the new Republic. There was little question that the new Congress should be **bicameral,** as was the English Parliament. This practice was followed by most of the colonial governments and later, by ten of the thirteen states. As Founder George Mason noted, the minds of Americans were settled on two points: "an attachment to republican government [and] an attachment to more than one branch in the Legislature."

Little agreement existed, however, over how the members of the chambers should be chosen. Some leaders insisted that the new government should be based on the consent of the people, rather than on the state legislatures. Therefore they believed that it was essential that at least "the first branch," or House, be elected popularly. The government "ought to possess . . . the mind or sense of the people at large," said one of the Framers, James Wilson of Pennsylvania. Those

Linda Sanchez (left) and Loretta Sanchez (right) made history when they became the first sisters to serve in the United States House of Representatives. Both sisters represent districts in California. (Reuters/Corbis)

who were suspicious of a national government, fearing it would be too powerful, preferred to have House members elected by the state legislatures. "The people immediately should have as little to do" with electing the government as possible, said Founder Roger Sherman, because "they want [lack] information and are constantly liable to be misled." Election by the legislatures was twice defeated, however, and the Convention agreed to the popular election of House members, with only one state dissenting.

There was little support for the view that the people should also elect the Senate. Nor did the delegates to the Constitutional Convention think that the House should choose members of the Senate from among persons nominated by the state legislatures. Election of the Senate by the state legislatures was agreed to with only two states dissenting. This arrangement persisted until the Seventeenth Amendment was ratified in 1913 requiring that senators be popularly elected.

The Senate is sometimes referred to as the "upper body" of Congress, and the House as the "lower body." Those terms are not used in the Constitution, and in fact, the two chambers are

E

A – Z

equal in stature and legislative power. No bill can become law unless it is passed by both chambers in identical form and signed by the president (or passed over a presidential veto).

Representatives naturally resent having the House called the "lower body." Yet, from the earliest days of the Republic, the House has been generally regarded as less prestigious than the Senate. Indeed, the French scholar Alexis de Tocqueville wrote in the 1830s of "the vulgar demeanor" of the House as compared with the Senate.

The People's Branch

The House of Representatives was to be the branch of government closest to the people. The members would be popularly elected; the terms of office would be two years so that the representatives would remain accountable to their constituents; the House would be the larger branch, with its members having relatively small constituencies.

The lower houses of the state legislatures served as models for the U.S. House. All the states had at least one chamber elected by popular vote. Ten states had two-house legislatures; Georgia, Pennsylvania, and Vermont had popularly elected unicameral, or one-house, legislatures.

Article I, Section 2, of the Constitution set few requirements for election to the House: a representative had to be at least twenty-five years of age, have been a U.S. citizen for seven years, and be an inhabitant of the state from which elected.

The Constitution left the qualification of voters to the states. At first, most states had some kind of property requirement for voting. Five states required ownership of real estate, five mandated either real estate or other property, and three required personal wealth or payment of public taxes. However, the democratic trend of the early nineteenth century swept away most property qualifications, producing almost universal white male suffrage by the 1830s.

Over the years, several changes in the Constitution also broadened the right to vote. The Fifteenth Amendment (1870) extended the vote to formerly enslaved men; the Nineteenth Amendment (1920) granted the right of suffrage to women; the Twenty-third Amendment (1961) extended the presidential vote to the District of Columbia; the Twenty-fourth Amendment (1964) abolished the poll tax; and the Twenty-sixth Amendment (1971) lowered the voting age from twenty-one to eighteen. In 1965, Congress passed the Voting Rights Act to remove barriers several states and localities had erected to keep African Americans and other minorities from voting.

Two-Year Term

Many delegates to the Constitutional Convention preferred annual elections for the House, believing that the body should reflect the wishes of the people as closely as possible. James Madison, however, argued for a three-year term to allow representatives to gain knowledge and experience in national affairs as well as the affairs of their own localities. The delegates compromised on two-year terms.

The two-year term has not always been popular. From time to time, proposals have been made to extend the term to four years. The movement to extend the House term to four years last gained momentum after President Lyndon B. Johnson urged the extension in his 1966 State of the Union address.

However, the proposed amendment never emerged from committee. Opponents criticized the proposal's provision that the four-year term coincide with the presidential term. This would create a House of "coattail riders," critics said, and end the minority party's traditional gains in non-presidential election years. The fear of weakening the independence of the House seemed to be the main factor that killed the proposal.

Size of the House

The size of the original House was written into Article I, Section 2, of the Constitution, along with directions to apportion the House according to population after the first census in 1790. Until the first census and apportionment, the thirteen states were to have the following numbers of representatives: Connecticut, five; Delaware, one; Georgia, three; Maryland, six;

Massachusetts, eight; New Hampshire, three; New Jersey, four; New York, six; North Carolina, five; Pennsylvania, eight; Rhode Island, one; South Carolina, five; Virginia, ten. This apportionment of seats—sixty-five in all—thus mandated by the Constitution remained in effect during the First and Second Congresses (1789–1793). Seats allotted to North Carolina and Rhode Island were not filled until 1790 after those states had ratified the Constitution.

By an act of Congress on April 14, 1792, an apportionment measure provided for a ratio of one member for every 33,000 inhabitants and fixed the exact number of representatives to which each state was entitled. Congress enacted a new apportionment measure, including the mathematical formula to be used, every ten years until a permanent law became effective in 1929.

In 1911, Congress set the maximum size of the House at 435 members where it has remained since the 1912 election—with the exception of a brief period after Alaska and Hawaii became states when the number temporarily increased to 437.

National population figures from the 2000 census showed that, on average, each House member represented about 647,000 persons.

Majority Elections

Five New England states had once required a majority victory in congressional elections. The requirement provided that, to win a seat in the U.S. House, a candidate had to achieve more than 50 percent of the popular vote. If no candidate gained such a majority, new elections were held until one contender succeeded.

The provision was last invoked in Maine in 1844, in New Hampshire in 1845, in Vermont in 1866, in Massachusetts in 1848, and in Rhode Island in 1892. Sometimes multiple elections were necessary because none of the candidates could achieve the required majority. In the Fourth District of Massachusetts in 1848–1849, for example, twelve successive elections were held to try to choose a representative. None of them was successful, and the district remained unrepresented in the House during the Thirty-first Congress (1849–1851).

Multimember Districts

In the early days of the House, several states had districts that elected more than one representative. This situation occurred because states were allowed to determine how representatives would be chosen. For example, in 1824 Maryland's Fifth District chose two representatives, while the remaining seven districts chose one each. In Pennsylvania, two districts elected three representatives each and four districts chose two representatives each.

As late as 1838, New York still had as many as five multimember districts. The practice ended in 1842, however, when Congress enacted a law that "no one district may elect more than one Representative." The provision was a part of the reapportionment legislation following the census of 1840.

Elections in Odd-Numbered Years

Another practice that faded over the years was the holding of House elections in odd-numbered years. Prior to ratification of the Twentieth, or "lame-duck," Amendment in 1933, regular sessions of Congress began in December of odd-numbered years. Because there was a period of several months between elections in November of even-numbered years and the beginning of the congressional session (at that time on March 4 of the year following the election), some states moved congressional elections to odd-numbered years. For example, in 1841 the following states held general elections for representative for the Twenty-seventh Congress convening that year: Alabama, Connecticut, Illinois, Indiana, Kentucky, Maryland, Mississippi, New Hampshire, North Carolina, Rhode Island, Tennessee, and Virginia.

The practice continued until late in the nineteenth century. In 1875, four states still chose their representatives in regular odd-year elections: California, Connecticut, Mississippi, and New Hampshire. By 1880, however, all members of the House were being chosen in even-numbered years (except for special elections to fill vacancies). One major problem encountered by states choosing their representatives in odd-numbered years was the possibility of a special session of the new Congress being called before the states' elections were held. Depending on the date of the election, a state could be unrepresented in the House. For example, California elected its U.S. House delegation to the Fortieth Congress (1867–1869) on September 4, 1867, in plenty of time for the first regular session scheduled for December 2. Yet Congress already had met in two special sessions—March 4 to March 20 and July 3 to July 20—without any representation from California. Over time Congress has passed legislation making the process of electing representatives consistent across the nation. The Twentieth Amendment, ratified in 1933, moved the beginning of congressional sessions to January 3 of the year after the election, thus eliminating the "lame-duck" session of Congress.

Southern Irregularities

Many irregularities in the election of U.S. representatives occurred in the South. That region's experiences with slavery, the Civil War, Reconstruction, and racial issues created special problems for the regular electoral process.

Prior to the Civil War, Article I, Section 2, of the Constitution contained a formula for counting slaves for apportionment purposes: every five slaves would be counted as three persons. Thus, the total population of a state to be used in determining its congressional representation would be the free population plus three-fifths of the slave population.

After the Civil War and the emancipation of the slaves, African Americans were fully counted for the purposes of apportionment. The Fourteenth Amendment required that apportionment be based on "the whole number of persons in each State . . ." On this basis, several Southern states tried to claim immediate additional representation as they were readmitted to the Union. Tennessee, for example, chose an extra U.S. representative, electing him at large in 1868, and claimed that because its slaves were now free the state had added to its apportionment population a sufficient number to give it nine instead of eight representatives. Virginia took similar action in 1869 and 1870; South Carolina did so in 1868 and 1870. The House declined to seat the additional representatives,

however, declaring that states would have to wait for the regular reapportionment following the 1870 census before receiving any change in their representation.

Part of the Fourteenth Amendment affected Southern representation in the House. The second paragraph of the amendment states:

> . . .when the right to vote at any election for the choice of electors for President and Vice President of the United States, Representatives in Congress, the Executive and Judicial officers of a State, or the members of the Legislature thereof, is denied to any of the male inhabitants of such State, being twenty-one years of age, and citizens of the United States, or in any way abridged, except for participation in rebellion, or other crime, the basis of representation [in the U.S. House] shall be reduced in the proportion which the number of such male citizens shall bear to the whole number of male citizens twenty-one years of age in such State.

Designed to force the South to accept African American voting participation, the provision was incorporated in the reapportionment legislation of 1872. According to the legislation, the number of representatives from any state interfering with the exercise of the right to vote was to be reduced in proportion to the number of inhabitants of voting age whose right to go to the polls was denied.

However, the provision was never put into effect because of the difficulty of determining the exact number of persons whose right to vote was being denied and because of the decline of Northern enthusiasm for forcing Reconstruction policies on the South.

As an alternative to invoking the difficult Fourteenth Amendment provision, Congress often considered election challenges filed against members from the South. When Republicans were in control of the House, they often refused to seat Democrats from the former Confederate states on charges that African American voting rights were abused in their districts. For example, during the Forty-seventh Congress (1881–1883) five Democrats from former Confederate states were unseated; in the Fifty-first Congress (1889–1891), six; and in the Fifty-fourth Congress (1895–1897), seven.

Special Elections

When a vacancy occurs in the House, the usual procedure is for the governor of the affected state to call a special election. Such elections may be held at any time throughout the year, and there are usually several during each two-year Congress.

At times there are delays in the calling of special elections. One of the longest periods in modern times when a congressional district went unrepresented occurred after the death of Representative James G. Polk, an Ohio Democrat (1931–1941, 1949–1959), on April 28, 1959. An election to replace him did not take place until November 1960.

Usually states are more prompt in holding special House elections than was Ohio in 1959–1960. One of the most rapid instances of succession occurred in Texas' Tenth District in 1963. Democratic representative Homer Thornberry (1949–1963) submitted his resignation on September 26, 1963, to take effect December 20. A special election was held in his district: the first election was held November 9 and a runoff on December 17. The winner, Democrat J. J. Pickle, was ready to take his seat as soon as Thornberry stepped down. He was sworn in the next day, December 21, 1963.

Disputed House Elections

Occasionally, the full House of Representatives is called upon to settle disputes over the outcome of an election. Among recent examples are:

- "THE MISSISSIPPI FIVE"   One of the most dramatic election disputes settled by the House in modern times was that of the so-called Mississippi Five in 1965. In 1964, Mississippi's governor certified the election to the House of four Democrats and one Republican. Their right to be seated was contested

by the Mississippi Freedom Democratic Party, formed originally to challenge the seating of Mississippi's all-white delegation to the 1964 Democratic National Convention. This group, when unsuccessful in getting its candidates on the 1964 ballot, conducted a rump election in which Annie Devine, Virginia Gray, and Fannie L. Hamer were the winners. The three women, when they sought entrance to the House floor, were barred. In turn, William F. Ryan, a New York Democrat, challenged the regular Mississippi representatives, stating that Mississippi's congressional election was invalid because African Americans had been systematically prevented from voting. On January 4, 1965, however, a resolution to seat the regular Mississippi delegation was adopted by a voice vote.

- MCCLOSKEY-MCINTYRE CONTEST   In 1984, incumbent Frank McCloskey, a Democrat, appeared to have won reelection to his Indiana Eighth District seat by seventy-two votes. However correction of an arithmetical error (ballots in two precincts had been counted twice) gave Republican challenger Richard D. McIntyre an apparent thirty-four-vote victory. On that basis, the Indiana secretary of state certified McIntyre the winner. When Congress convened in January 1985, however, the Democratic-controlled House refused to seat McIntyre, voting instead to declare the seat vacant pending an investigation of alleged irregularities in the election.

Multiple recounts continued to shift the victory between the two candidates. On May 1, 1985, the House approved a resolution to seat McCloskey by a vote of 236–190, with ten Democrats joining the Republicans in voting against it. Republican members walked out of the House chamber in protest, accusing Democrats of stealing the election.

The Supreme Court refused to get involved in the dispute. Without a dissenting vote, it denied Indiana permission to sue the House in the Supreme Court. An Indiana federal district court had dismissed a separate suit filed by

Divided Government, 1860–1998

Election	President	Party winning control House	Senate	Control of presidency and Congress[a]	Election	President	Party winning control House	Senate	Control of presidency and Congress
1860	Lincoln (R)	R	R	All Republican	1930	Hoover (R)	D	R	Congress Split
1862	Lincoln (R)	R	R	All Republican	1932	F. Roosevelt (D)	D	D	All Democrat
1864	Lincoln/ A. Johnson (R)	R	R	All Republican[b]	1934	F. Roosevelt (D)	D	D	All Democrat
1866	A Johnson (R)	R	R	All Republican	1936	F. Roosevelt (D)	D	D	All Democrat
1868	Grant (R)	R	R	All Republican	1938	F. Roosevelt (D)	D	D	All Democrat
1870	Grant (R)	R	R	All Republican	1940	F. Roosevelt (D)	D	D	All Democrat
1872	Grant (R)	R	R	All Republican	1942	F. Roosevelt (D)	D	D	All Democrat
1874	Grant (R)	D	R	Congress Split	1944	F. Roosevelt/ Truman (D)	D	D	All Democrat
1876	Hayes (R)	D	R	Congress Split	1946	Truman (D)	R	R	Divided
1878	Hayes (R)	D	D	Divided	1948	Truman (D)	D	D	All Democrat
1880	Garfield/ Arthur (R)	R	R	All Republican	1950	Truman (D)	D	D	All Democrat
1882	Arthur (R)	D	R	Congress Split	1952	Eisenhower (R)	R	R	All Republican
1884	Cleveland (D)	D	R	Congress Split	1954	Eisenhower (R)	D	D	Divided
1886	Cleveland (D)	D	R	Congress Split	1956	Eisenhower (R)	D	D	Divided
1888	B. Harrison (R)	R	R	All Republican	1958	Eisenhower (R)	D	D	Divided
1890	B. Harrison (R)	D	R	Congress Split	1960	Kennedy (D)	D	D	All Democrat
1892	Cleveland (D)	D	D	All Democrat	1962	Kennedy/ L. Johnson (D)	D	D	All Democrat
1894	Cleveland (D)	R	R	Divided	1964	L. Johnson (D)	D	D	All Democrat
1896	McKinley (R)	R	R	All Republican	1966	L. Johnson (D)	D	D	All Democrat
1898	McKinley (R)	R	R	All Republican	1968	Nixon (R)	D	D	Divided
1900	McKinley/ T. Roosevelt (R)	R	R	All Republican	1970	Nixon (R)	D	D	Divided
1902	T. Roosevelt (R)	R	R	All Republican	1972	Nixon/Ford (R)	D	D	Divided
1904	T. Roosevelt (R)	R	R	All Republican	1974	Ford (R)	D	D	Divided
1906	T. Roosevelt (R)	R	R	All Republican	1976	Carter (D)	D	D	All Democrat
1908	Taft (R)	R	R	All Republican	1978	Carter (D)	D	D	All Democrat
1910	Taft (R)	D	R	Congress Split	1980	Reagan (R)	D	R	Congress Split
1912	Wilson (D)	D	D	All Democrat	1982	Reagan (R)	D	R	Congress Split
1914	Wilson (D)	D	D	All Democrat	1984	Reagan (R)	D	R	Congress Split
1916	Wilson (D)	D	D	All Democrat	1986	Reagan (R)	D	D	Divided
1918	Wilson (D)	R	R	Divided	1988	Bush (R)	D	D	Divided
1920	Harding (R)	R	R	All Republican	1990	Bush (R)	D	D	Divided
1922	Harding/ Coolidge (R)	R	R	All Republican	1992	Clinton (D)	D	D	All Democrat
1924	Coolidge (R)	R	R	All Republican	1994	Clinton (D)	R	R	Divided
1926	Coolidge (R)	R	R	All Republican	1996	Clinton (D)	R	R	Divided
1928	Hoover (R)	R	R	All Republican	1998	Clinton (D)	R	R	Divided

NOTES: Key to abbreviations: D—Democrat; R—Republican. a. "All" indicates that one party controlled the White House and both houses of Congress. "Divided" indicates that one party held the presidency while the other party controlled both houses of Congress. "Congress Split" indicates that control of Congress was split, with one party holding the House and the other the Senate. b. The pro-Republican majority in Congress elected in 1864 was designated Unionist.

During the last half of the twentieth century and the beginning of the twenty-first century, it was not unusual for one party to occupy the White House and the other party to dominate Congress. However, from 1860 to about 1944, it was more common for the same party to control both the White House and Congress.

McIntyre, ruling that the House alone was responsible for determining the validity of contested ballots. In a 1986 rematch, McCloskey handily defeated McIntyre.

- SANCHEZ-DORNAN DISPUTE In early 1998, thirteen months of contentious debate with ethnic overtones ended when the Republican-led House refused to overturn the defeat of California Republican Robert K. Dornan by Democrat Loretta Sanchez, a Hispanic woman. Dornan charged that the 1996 election in California's Forty-sixth District was stolen by the illegal votes of noncitizens, mostly Hispanics. The House rejected his claim by a 378–33 vote on February 12, 1998.

  Dornan's former Orange County district, once a Republican stronghold, had become a swing district through legal and illegal immigration. In the 1998 election, Sanchez kept her seat in a rematch with Dornan.

Party Control Shifts

The Republican Party dominated the House in the first three decades of the twentieth century and the Democratic Party controlled it for much of the balance until the Republicans returned to power late in the century.

The Republicans were the majority party in the House from 1901 to 1911 and 1919 to 1931, but, battered by the Great Depression, they lost the House to the Democrats in the November 1930 elections. Democrats briefly relinquished power in the House after losses in 1946 and again in 1952. After the 1954 election, however, the Democrats held control for the next forty years. In all, they controlled the House for sixty of the seventy years in the period 1931–2001.

Democratic Dominance

In the history of Democratic control of the House, 1956 was the watershed year. In that year, Republican President Dwight D. Eisenhower was reelected in a landslide, but his party failed to recapture the House. It was only the second time that had ever happened—and the first since 1848, when Zachary Taylor was elected president while his Whig Party lost control of the House to the Democrats. Political

writers have noted that the results of the 1848 and 1956 elections were flukes caused by war heroes whose support for president crossed party lines. Yet American voters went on to elect a Republican president and a Democratic House five more times in the twentieth century: in 1968, 1972, 1980, 1984, and 1988.

One theory offered to explain this pattern emphasized the role of the cold war, which seemed a permanent part of life for nearly half a century. During those years the electorate as a whole seemed more comfortable having Republican presidents handle defense and foreign policy issues, while counting on Democrats in Congress to create and sustain popular domestic programs.

Republican Resurgence In Congress

With the end of the cold war in 1991, national security seemed to be a less important issue, as Republican President George Bush learned in 1992. Despite broad foreign policy experience and his triumph in the Persian Gulf War, Bush lost the White House to Arkansas governor Bill Clinton. At the same time, rising resentment of federal tax levels and increasing hostility toward government in general as expensive and inefficient seemed to hurt congressional Democrats.

Republicans were able to capitalize on this in the 1994 election, ending the Democrats' forty-year domination of the House and eight-year tenure in the Senate. The Democrats lost fifty-two House seats, the biggest loss by a president's party in the House since the 1946 midterm election. Other records were shattered as well. The election was the first since the end of Reconstruction in the 1870s in which Republicans won a majority of the congressional districts in the South. Democratic Speaker Thomas S. Foley of Washington State became the first sitting House Speaker to lose reelection since 1862.

The 1996 election, in which Clinton won another term in the White House and the Republicans remained the majority in Congress, was record producing as well. Never before had voters reelected a Democratic president and simultaneously entrusted both chambers of Congress to the Republicans. Moreover, the last time the

Republicans had returned a majority to the House was following the 1928 election.

Republicans held on to Congress in the 1998 and 2000 elections, but just barely. With the economy healthy and the nation at peace, Clinton's popularity remained high through the 1998 midterm election, despite House Republicans' preparations to impeach him on charges that included lying to a federal grand jury about his affair with a White House intern. In what was perceived as a backlash against impeachment, voters sent five more Democrats to the House, making Clinton the first president since Franklin D. Roosevelt in 1934 to gain House seats at midterm. Indeed, it was only the second time since the Civil War that the party not in control of the White House lost seats in a midterm election. The embarrassing setback prompted Newt Gingrich of Georgia, who had led the Republican takeover of the House in 1994, to resign as Speaker and leave the House.

In 2000, the Republicans won a fourth term in the majority for the first time since 1924. However, it was also the third straight election in which the Republicans lost House seats. The election resulted in a 221–212 party split with two independents. It was the closest party split in a House election since 1952.

The Republican Party continued to hold the majority until the 2006 elections, except for the Senate in 2001–2002. In 2001 Vermont Republican Jim Jeffords left the Republican Party declaring himself an independent, and as a result switched the balance of power to the Democrats. In the 2006 elections, the Democrats gained control of the House of Representaives. The Senate split forty-nine Democrats and forty-nine Republicans, but the Democrats still controlled the Senate because two independent senators voted with the Democrats.

See also: African Americans in Congress; Constitutional Convention; Elections, Senate; Hispanics in Congress; Women in Congress.

Further Reading

Koestler-Grack, Rachel A. *The House of Representatives.* New York: Chelsea House Publications, 2007.

Remini, Robert V. *The House: The History of the House of Representatives.* New York: HarperCollins, 2006.

Elections, Presidential

The United States system of selecting a president and vice president through indirect means is perhaps more complicated than it needs to be. It has, however, continued to work with just a few major repairs for more than two hundred years, generally satisfying the citizenry and meeting the nation's changing needs.

The election occurs every four years and permits the peaceful transfer of power or continuation of the status quo for four more years, no matter how bitter or divisive the campaign that preceded it. Indeed, the American electoral system differs from those of other nations and, for all its flaws, is the envy of many other countries. From time to time, however, pressure mounts for abolishing the Electoral College in favor of the direct popular election process used in other major democracies. After each such wave of protest, the demands for reform have gradually faded and the Electoral College has survived into the twenty-first century.

Nevertheless, significant changes have taken place within the system. As the nation and the electorate have grown and technology has evolved, presidential elections have become more expensive, costing more than a billion dollars in 2004. Because of the high costs, money and its abuses account for the biggest continuing blemish on the system, despite the many campaign finance reforms enacted since the 1970s.

On the more positive side, presidential nominations have become more open and representative of the voters at large. Party bosses no longer dictate the choice of nominees. Instead, the nominations are won through a hard-fought series of primary elections and party caucuses, where rank-and-file party members have an opportunity to express their preferences. Once the means for determining who would head the presidential ticket, national party conventions today

Requirements of Office

- A natural-born citizen
- At least 35 years of age
- A resident of the United States for fourteen years

The Constitution places few requirements on presidential candidates. The Twenty-second Amendment, ratified in 1951, limits the president to two terms.

perform different functions, including **ratification** of the nominations won in the primaries.

As televised spectacles, the conventions remain important to the parties' public relations efforts during the weeks before the November election. Although ratings have dropped in recent years, millions of people still watch the conventions on television and major political parties try to capture and hold as much of that audience as possible. With expert advice they have streamlined the proceedings to highlight their nominees in prime time as the countdown begins to election day. In these final campaign stages, today's nominees usually keep intact the organizations they built to help them survive the primaries. These increasingly professional organizations are made up of the candidate, his or her family, a running mate, polling and political consultants, fundraisers, media consultants, issues advisers, schedulers, advance persons, and others. Campaign strategies must be carefully managed if the candidate is to move successfully through the primary season, the nominating conventions, and the general election campaign.

Who Runs for President?

Candidates for president or vice president must meet the same few constitutional requirements. They must be at least thirty-five years old and natural-born citizens who have "been fourteen Years a Resident within the United States."

Another requirement, one that affects very few people, is that the candidate must *not* have been elected president twice before. The Twenty-second Amendment, ratified in 1951, limits presidents to two four-year terms. A vice president

who succeeds to the presidency and serves more than two years may be elected president only once. Franklin D. Roosevelt, whose breaking of the two-term tradition prompted the term limitation, is the only president who served more than eight years. He died in 1945 while in his fourth term.

Even for well-known public figures, the decision to seek the presidency is a difficult one. The prospective candidates must make complicated calculations about financial and time requirements. They must sort out the tangle of party and state rules and the makeup of the electorate in each state. They must assess their own ability to attract endorsements, recruit a competent staff, and develop an "image" suitable for media presentation. They must also consider the effect a campaign will have on their families, the psychological demands of the office, and possible revelations about their personal lives that might hinder a campaign.

The Exploratory Stage

The first stage in a presidential campaign is the exploratory stage when the candidates "test the waters" for a try at the nation's highest office. Before announcing, candidates routinely establish a political action committee (PAC) to raise money. They also set up an exploratory committee to help assess the candidate's chances of challenging the competition. The exploratory advisers identify likely opponents, consider funding prospects and other preliminary factors, and, if conditions appear favorable, the committee may form the nucleus of the candidate's campaign organization.

Since 1976, when Jimmy Carter (1977–1981) won the presidency after a two-year campaign, candidates have tended to announce their intentions well ahead of the election, in part to have time to build a strong public profile and in part because early fund-raising can be crucial to a campaign. In 2000, with Bill Clinton barred from seeking a third term, the looming White House vacancy drew a large field of Republican candidates. Among the first to form an exploratory committee in 1999 was Elizabeth Dole, wife of the 1996 GOP nominee. She decided against running, citing the difficulty of

E

A-Z

competing against George W. Bush's fund-raising powerhouse. Several other prominent Republicans challenged Bush including Arizona senator John McCain who won the primaries in New Hampshire and six other states. Nevertheless, he, like the other contenders, eventually ceded the nomination to Bush.

Dole's decision to pull out of the race one year before the election illustrates a characteristic of U.S. presidential elections: they are endurance contests. From start to finish they are much longer, for example, than the few months typically devoted to parliamentary elections in Great Britain. By Labor Day, a good two months before the November election, many American voters are tired of listening to the candidates and have already made up their minds about whom they will vote for.

The 2004 Democratic candidates, John Kerry and John Edwards, ran a strong campaign against incumbent President George W. Bush. (Scott J. Ferrell/CQ)

The Primary and Caucus Schedule

If a candidate decides to seek a major party nomination, the next step is to enter the primaries and caucuses where Democratic and Republican Party members select delegates to their national conventions. The states and the parties have a wide variety of rules for ballot access qualifications and allocation of delegates. Candidates must follow legal requirements to qualify for state contests, and they also have to adapt their campaign strategies to each state's particular circumstances.

Traditionally, the New Hampshire primary and the Iowa caucus are the first delegate-selection events, a head start that gives the two states extraordinary influence over the selection process. (For forty years, beginning in 1952, no president was elected without first winning the New Hampshire primary. Clinton broke that precedent in 1992 and Bush did likewise in 2000.) Critics have complained that the system is unrepresentative because both states are predominantly rural, with largely white, Anglo-Saxon, Protestant populations. No serious efforts, however, have been made to change the pattern.

Democratic Party rules prevent other states from scheduling their primaries earlier than the New Hampshire and Iowa events. Republican caucuses are permitted earlier in Alaska, Hawaii, Louisiana, and Guam. For other states and territories, the primary and caucus period begins in late February or early March and ends in early June. The early primaries have grown in importance. Especially when the campaign does not have an obvious front-runner, the early contests single out a possible leader. After several early tests, the field of candidates shrinks. In 2000 both Republican Bush and Democrat Al Gore had secured their party's nomination by mid-March, a feat made possible by the "front loading" of primaries earlier and earlier in presidential election years. In 2004, incumbent President Bush faced virtually no competition and swept the Republican primaries. John Kerry, the Democratic candidate, secured the nomination by Super Tuesday on March 2.

The cost of presidential campaigns is offset by grants from the federal income tax checkoff fund. Candidates who accept the grants must abide by limits on campaign spending. In the primary stage, public financing is available to candidates who raise $5,000 in matchable contributions in each of twenty states. PAC contributions are not matchable.

In a typical election year where, unlike 2000 and 2004, the fight for delegates continues after the early primaries, the goal of the remaining candidates is to attract media attention by winning or performing better than expected in the rest of the contests. Candidates who fall behind typically withdraw. The number of delegates at stake, particularly in states that award delegates on the basis of proportional representation, begins to be important. All Democratic primaries use proportional representation. Republican primaries in some states award delegates by the winner-take-all method.

The Presidential Nomination

The primary season culminates in the two national party conventions, usually held in late July or August. At these conventions, where guests and reporters outnumber the thousands of delegates, the presidential and vice-presidential nominees are formally selected and a party **platform**, setting out the party's goals for the next four years, is approved. In recent elections, the convention also has become an important occasion for displaying party unity after the sometimes divisive primary battles.

The first national convention was held in 1831 and for more than a century afterward state party leaders had the ultimate say in deciding who the presidential nominee would be. As direct primaries took hold in the twentieth century, this influence began to decrease. Then in the 1970s and 1980s, the Democrats initiated a series of presidential selection reforms that opened the nominating process. The reforms were expected to result in more open conventions, but instead they led to even more primaries.

Victory in the primaries, however, does not mean the primary leader faces no opposition at the convention. Other candidates may stay in the race because they hope to benefit if the leader falters, or they may use the bloc of delegates committed to them to bargain for specific planks in the platform or to influence the selection of the vice-presidential nominee.

Before the widespread use of primaries, the conventions were more competitive and frenetic than they are today. All the candidates still in the race had substantial campaign operations at the conventions. Campaign managers and strategists kept in close contact with state delegations. Candidates deployed floor leaders and **"whips"** to direct voting on the convention floor and to deal with any problems that arose among state delegations. In addition, **"floaters"** wandered the crowded floor in search of any signs of trouble. Floor leaders, whips, and floaters often wore specially colored clothing or caps so that they could be spotted easily on the convention floor.

At party conventions, nominating speeches mark the beginning of the formal selection process. These remarks are usually followed by a series of short seconding speeches and all of the speeches are accompanied by floor demonstrations staged by delegates supporting the candidate. For many years, a good deal of convention time was taken up by the nomination of **favorite sons,** candidates nominated by their own state's delegation. Such nominations were seldom taken seriously and, since 1972, both parties have instituted rules that have effectively stopped them.

In recent years, the balloting for the presidential nominee has been anticlimactic. More attention focuses on whom the presidential nominee will select as a running mate. Even then, much of the suspense has been removed because the leading presidential candidates may have named their running mates before the convention begins.

With the young, politically moderate, all-southern ticket of Clinton and Gore in 1992 an obvious exception, the choice of the vice-presidential candidate often has been motivated by an effort to balance the ticket geographically. For years, a balanced ticket was one that boasted an easterner and a midwesterner. More recently, the balance has shifted so that the split is more often between a northerner and a southerner, for example: Democrats John F.

E

A – Z

E

A-Z

Kennedy of Massachusetts and Lyndon B. Johnson of Texas in 1960; Johnson and Hubert H. Humphrey of Minnesota in 1964; Jimmy Carter of Georgia and Walter F. Mondale of Minnesota in 1976; Republicans Barry Goldwater of Arizona and William Miller of New York in 1964; and George W. Bush of Texas and Richard Cheney of Wyoming in 2000 and 2004.

Ideology also plays a part in the balance. A liberal presidential candidate may be paired with a more conservative running mate to attract a broader base of votes. The choice of the vice-presidential candidate may also be used to soothe party factions who are unhappy with the presidential candidate. Further, governors generally choose running mates with Washington credentials, such as senators. With the increasing number of vice presidents who go on to be president, more attention is given to the abilities of the person who is chosen, and more prominent figures are willing to accept the nomination.

The method for nominating the vice-presidential candidate mirrors the procedure for presidential nominations. The climax of the convention then occurs with the two nominees' acceptance speeches and their first appearance together, with their families, on the podium.

General Election Campaign

The traditional opening of the presidential election campaign is Labor Day, just two months before the general election on the first Tuesday after the first Monday in November. In recent years, however, candidates have been unwilling to wait until Labor Day to capitalize on their post-convention bounce in the polls. After the 1992 Democratic convention, for example, Clinton and Gore and their wives boarded buses for campaign swings through Pennsylvania and other must-win states. Their opponent, President George W. Bush, went from the GOP convention to Florida, which was recovering from the devastation of Hurricane Andrew. Bush won Florida's twenty-five electoral votes.

The campaign organization for the general election is usually an extension of the nomination organization, and it is separate from the national and state party organizations. Nominees normally have the prerogative of naming their party's national committee chair to help coordinate the campaign.

The national campaign committee, usually based in Washington, D.C., receives its funding from the Federal Election Commission (FEC). In exchange for federal funding, the campaign must agree not to spend more than it receives from the FEC. From 1975, when federal funding of elections began, to 2004 all major party nominees accepted the government funds for their general election campaigns. In 2000, the Bush and Gore organizations each received $75 million for their fall campaigns. Neither campaign, however, lived within that income. Both parties also received so-called hard money, regulated contributions given directly to candidates. Each party's national committee also raised about $243 million in unlimited "soft money" for party activities that indirectly supported their nominees' campaigns.

A president running for reelection has inherent advantages that may tilt the balance in the incumbent's favor. The incumbent already has the stature of the presidency and is able to influence media coverage by using official presidential actions and "pork-barrel politics" to appeal to specific constituencies. The president also benefits from the public's reluctance to reject a tested national leader for an unknown quantity.

In times of economic or foreign policy difficulties, however, the president's prominence can have negative effects on the campaign. Jimmy Carter's bid for a second term was plagued by both a sagging economy and Iran's continued holding of U.S. citizens as hostages. In 1992, after achieving record-high approval ratings for success in the Gulf War, George Bush saw his reelection hopes dashed by an economic recession which he was slow to acknowledge and which the Democrats used to advantage with their emphasis on "it's the economy, stupid."

In 2000, with the economy booming and the Treasury overflowing with surpluses, George W. Bush capitalized on the Clinton administration's successes by campaigning on a platform of tax cuts and more money for popular programs, such as education and national defense. Gore, by contrast, soft-pedaled his close association with Clinton, whose second term was tainted by his impeachment for lying under oath about his

DECISION MAKERS

Harry Reid

Born in 1939, Democrat Harry Reid is the senior senator from Nevada. After attending schools in Nevada, Reid received his bachelor's degree from Utah State University in 1961. He moved to Washington, D.C., where he worked as a Capitol Police Officer while attending George Washington University where he earned his law degree in 1964. After moving back to Nevada in 1967, Reid was elected to several state offices. He went on to win a seat in the House of Representatives in 1982 where he served until 1987. In 1986 Reid was elected senator from Nevada, a position he has held since that date. He became Senate Majority Leader in January 2007 after the Democrats won control of Congress in the 2006 elections.

sexual relationship with White House intern Monica S. Lewinsky. Some strategists felt that Gore missed out by not taking advantage of Clinton's continued popularity and failing to claim his share of the credit for turning the economy around during the eight-year Clinton-Gore administration.

The Popular Vote

The United States' winner-take-all electoral college system gives presidential and vice-presidential nominees an incentive to campaign where the votes are. Because in most states the leading vote-getter wins all that state's electoral votes, the system encourages nominees to win as many populous states as possible. Nominees generally spend most of their time in closely contested states and in "likely win" states they spend just enough time to ensure victory. Appearances in unfavorable states are usually symbolic efforts to show that the candidate is not conceding anything.

In the electoral college states have votes equal to their representation in Congress: two for the senators and at least one for the representatives, for a total of 538 votes. (The District of Columbia has the three votes it would have if it were a state.) Two states, Maine and Nebraska, permit splitting their electoral votes between the statewide winner and the winner in

each of the congressional districts (two in Maine, three in Nebraska), but as of 2004, no such split had occurred.

Congress in the 1950s and 1960s enacted a series of statutes to enforce the Fifteenth Amendment's guarantee against racial discrimination in voting. A law passed in 1970 nullified state residence requirements of longer than thirty days for voting in presidential elections, suspended literacy tests for a five-year period (the suspension was made permanent in 1975), and lowered the minimum voting age to eighteen years from twenty-one, the requirement then in effect in most states. A 1970 Supreme Court ruling upheld the voting-age change for federal elections, but invalidated it for state and local elections. In the same decision, the Court upheld the provision on residence requirements and sustained the suspension of literacy tests with respect to both state and local elections. The Twenty-sixth Amendment was ratified six months after the Court's decision.

The right to vote in presidential elections was extended to citizens of the District of Columbia by the Twenty-third Amendment, ratified in 1961. District residents had been **disenfranchised** from national elections except for a brief period in the 1870s when they elected a nonvoting delegate to the House of Representatives. In

1970, Congress took another step toward full suffrage for District residents by again authorizing the election of a nonvoting delegate to the House.

Electoral College

Even after the winner has declared victory and the loser has conceded defeat, at least two more steps must be taken before a president-elect is officially declared. The first occurs on the first Monday after the second Wednesday in December. On that day electors meet in their respective state capitals to cast their votes for president.

Each state has as many electors as it has members of Congress. Typically, slates of electors are pledged to each of the presidential nominees before the popular election. The presidential nominee who wins the state wins that state's electors. Although the Constitution does not require electors to remain faithful to their pledge of support for a particular candidate, many states have laws to that effect. Such laws, however, are generally regarded as unenforceable and likely unconstitutional. There have been several instances in which "faithless electors" did not vote for their party's nominee.

The second step occurs when the electors' ballots are opened and counted before a joint session of Congress in early January. The candidate who wins a majority of the vote is declared the president-elect and is inaugurated three weeks later on January 20. The counting of electoral votes by a joint session of Congress is normally a routine affair.

In the rare event that no presidential candidate receives a majority of the electoral college vote, the election is thrown into the House of Representatives. If no vice-presidential candidate receives a majority of the electoral college vote, the Senate is called upon to make the selection.

See also: Election Day; Electoral College; Faithless Electors; Fifteenth Amendment; Nominating Conventions; Twelfth Amendment; Twenty-second Amendment; Twenty-sixth Amendment.

Further Reading

Abramowitz, Alan. *Voice of the People: Elections and Voting in the United States.* New York: McGraw-Hill, 2003.

Semiatin, Richard. *Campaigns in the Twenty-First Century.* New York: McGraw-Hill, 2004.

Thurber, James A. *Campaigns and Elections American Style.* Jackson, TN: Westview Press, 2004.

Elections, Senate

The process by which members are elected into the upper house of the United States Congress. The creation of the United States Senate was a result of the so-called "great compromise" at the Constitutional Convention in 1787. The small states wanted equal representation in Congress, fearing domination by the larger states under a population formula. The larger states, however, naturally wished for a legislature based on population, where their strength would prevail.

In compromising this dispute, delegates simply split the basis for representation between the two houses—population for the House of Representatives, equal representation by state for the Senate. By the terms of the compromise, each state was entitled to two senators. In a sense, they were conceived to be ambassadors from the states, representing the sovereign interests of the states to the federal government.

Election by State Legislatures

To elect these "ambassadors," the Founders chose the state legislatures, instead of the people themselves. The argument was that legislatures would be able to give more sober and reflective thought than the people at large to the kind of persons needed to represent the states' interests to the federal government. The delegates also thought the state legislatures, and thus the states, would take a greater interest in the new national government if they were involved in its operations. Furthermore, the state legislatures had chosen the members of the Continental Congress (the Congress under the Articles of Confederation), as well as the members of the Constitutional Convention itself, so the procedure was familiar to the delegates.

In choosing the state legislatures as the instruments of election for senators, the Constitutional Convention considered and abandoned several alternatives. Some delegates had suggested that the senators be elected by the House or appointed by the president from a list of nominees selected by the state legislatures. These ideas were discarded as making the Senate too dependent on another part of the federal government. Also turned down was a scheme for a system of electors, similar to presidential electors, to choose the senators in each state. Popular election was rejected as being too radical.

So deeply entrenched was the ambassadorial aspect of a senator's duty that state legislatures sometimes took it upon themselves to instruct senators on how to vote. This occasionally raised severe problems of conscience among senators and resulted in several resignations. For example, in 1836 future president John Tyler was serving as a U.S. senator from Virginia. That year the Virginia legislature instructed him to vote for a resolution to expunge the Senate censure of President Andrew Jackson for his removal of the federal deposits from the Bank of the United States. Tyler, who had voted for the censure resolution, resigned from the Senate rather than comply.

Another problem for the Founders was the length of the senatorial term. The framers of the Constitution tried to balance two principles: the belief that relatively frequent elections were necessary to promote good behavior and the need for steadiness and continuity in government.

Delegates proposed terms of three, four, five, six, seven, and nine years. They finally settled on six-year staggered terms, with one-third of the members coming up for election every two years.

Barack Obama of Illinois was elected to the Senate in 2004. Obama announced his candidacy for the Democratic presidential nomination in early 2007 and quickly became one of the leading contenders. (Scott J. Ferrell/CQ)

Changing Election Procedures

At first each state made its own arrangements for its state legislature to elect the senators. Many states required an election by the two chambers of the legislature sitting separately. That is, each chamber had to vote for the same candidate for him to be elected. Other states, however, provided for election by a joint ballot of the two chambers sitting together.

However the Constitution specifically authorized Congress to regulate senatorial elections if it so chose. Article I, Section 4, Paragraph 1 states:

The times, places and manner of holding elections for Senators and Representatives shall be prescribed in each state by the legislature thereof; but the Congress may at any time by law make or alter such regulations, except as to the place of chusing Senators.

1866 Act of Congress

In 1866 Congress decided to exercise its authority. Procedures in some states, particularly those requiring concurrent majorities in both

E

A–Z

houses of the state legislature for election to the Senate, had resulted in numerous delays and vacancies.

The new federal law set up the following procedure: the first ballot for senator was to be taken by the two chambers of each state legislature voting separately. If no candidate received a majority of the vote in both houses, then the two chambers were to meet and ballot jointly until a majority choice emerged.

Also included in the 1866 law were provisions for roll-call votes in the state legislatures (secret ballots had been taken in several states) and for a definite timetable. The law directed that the first vote take place on the second Tuesday after the meeting and organization of the legislature, followed by a minimum of a single ballot on every legislative day thereafter until election of a senator resulted.

The new uniform system did not have the desired effect. The requirement for a majority vote continued the frequency of deadlock. In fact one of the worst deadlocks in senatorial election history happened under the 1866 federal law.

The case occurred in Delaware at the end of the nineteenth century. In 1899, with the legislature divided between two factions of the Republican Party and the Democrats in the minority, no majority selection could be made for the senatorial term beginning March 4, 1899. So bitter was the Republican factional dispute that neither side would support a candidate acceptable to the other; nor would the Democrats play kingmaker by siding with one or the other Republican group. The dispute continued throughout the life of the Fifty-sixth Congress (1899–1901) leaving a seat unfilled.

Furthermore, the term of Delaware's other Senate seat ended in 1901 necessitating another election. The same pattern continued, with the legislature unable to fill either seat, leaving Delaware totally unrepresented in the Senate from March 4, 1901, until March 1, 1903, when two senators were finally elected in the closing days of the Fifty-seventh Congress (1901–1903). The deadlock was broken when the two Republican factions split the state's two seats between them.

Abuses of Election by Legislatures

Besides the frequent deadlocks, critics pointed to what they saw as other faults in the system. They charged that the party caucuses in the state legislatures, as well as individual members, were subject to intense and unethical lobbying practices by supporters of various senatorial candidates. The relatively small size of the electing body and the high stakes involved—a seat in the Senate—often tempted the use of questionable methods in conducting the elections.

Allegations that such methods were used involved the Senate itself in election disputes. The Constitution makes Congress the judge of its own members. Article I, Section 5, Paragraph 1 states, "Each House shall be the judge of the elections, returns and qualifications of its own members. . . ."

Critics had still another grievance against the legislative method of choosing senators. They contended that elections to the state legislatures were often overshadowed by senatorial contests. Thus when voters went to the polls to choose their state legislators, they sometimes would be urged to disregard state and local issues and vote for a legislator who promised to support a certain candidate for the U.S. Senate. This, the critics said, led to neglect of state government and issues. Moreover, drawn-out Senate contests tended to hold up the consideration of state business.

Demands for Popular Elections

The main criticism of legislative elections was that they distorted or even blocked the will of the people. Throughout the nineteenth century, the movement toward popular election had taken away from the legislatures the right to elect presidential electors in states that had such provisions. Now attention focused on the Senate.

Five times around the turn of the twentieth century the House passed constitutional amendments to provide for Senate elections by popular vote—in the Fifty-second Congress on January 16, 1893; in the Fifty-third Congress on July 21, 1894; in the Fifty-fifth Congress on May 11, 1898; in the Fifty-sixth Congress on April 13, 1900; and in the Fifty-seventh Con-

E

A – Z

DECISION MAKERS

Edward W. Brooke

Edward W. Brooke was the first popularly elected African American senator. Born in Washington, D.C., in 1919, Brooke received an undergraduate degree from Howard University in 1941. After serving in the United States Army during World War II (1941–1945), he attended Boston University Law School, graduating in 1948.

After serving Massachusetts in several statewide offices, he was elected to the U.S. Senate as a Republican in 1966 where he served until 1979. After leaving the Senate, Brooke served as the head of the Low Income Housing Coalition and went on to other prominent posts. In 2004 he was awarded the Presidential Medal of Freedom.

gress on February 13, 1902. Each time the Senate refused to act.

Frustrated in their desire for direct popular elections, reformers began implementing various formulas for preselecting Senate candidates, attempting to reduce the legislative balloting to something approaching a mere formality. In some cases party conventions endorsed nominees for the Senate, allowing the voters at least to know whom the members of the legislature were likely to support. Southern states early in the century adopted the party primary to choose Senate nominees. However legislators never could be legally bound to support anyone because the Constitution gave them the unfettered power of electing to the Senate whomever they chose.

Oregon took the lead in introducing nonbinding popular elections. Under a 1901 law, voters expressed their choice for senator in popular ballots. While the election results had no legal force, the law required that the popular returns be formally announced to the state legislature before it elected a senator.

At first the law did not work—the winner of the informal popular vote in 1902 was not chosen senator by the legislature. The reformers increased their pressure, however, demanding that candidates for the legislature sign a pledge to vote for the winner of the popular vote. By 1908 the plan was successful. The Republican legisla-

ture elected to the Senate Democrat George Chamberlain, the winner of the popular contest. Several other states—including Colorado, Kansas, Minnesota, Montana, Nevada and Oklahoma—adopted the Oregon method.

The Seventeenth Amendment

Despite these steps, pressures continued to mount for a switch to direct popular elections. Frustrated at the failure of the Senate to act, proponents of change began pushing for a convention to propose this and perhaps other amendments to the Constitution. Conservatives began to fear a convention more than they did popular election of senators. There was no precedent for an amending convention and conservatives worried that it might be dominated by liberals and progressives who would propose numerous amendments and might change the very nature of the government. Consequently, their opposition to popular election of senators diminished.

At the same time, progressives of both parties made strong gains in the midterm elections of 1910. Some successful Senate candidates had made pledges to work for adoption of a constitutional amendment providing for popular election. In this atmosphere the Senate debated and finally passed the amendment on June 12, 1911, by a vote of 64–24. The House concurred in the Senate version on May 13, 1912, by a vote of

E

A–Z

238–39. Ratification of the Seventeenth Amendment was completed by the requisite number of states on April 8, 1913, and was proclaimed a part of the Constitution by Secretary of State William Jennings Bryan on May 31, 1913.

The first popularly elected senator was chosen in a special election in November 1913. He was Senator Blair Lee, a Democrat from Maryland, (1914–1917), elected for the remaining three years of the unexpired term of Democratic Senator Isidor Rayner (1905–1912), who had died in office.

There was no wholesale changeover in membership when the Seventeenth Amendment became effective. In fact, every one of the twenty-three senators elected by state legislatures for their previous terms, and running for reelection to full terms in November 1914, was successful. Seven had retired or died, and two had been defeated for renomination.

The changeover in the method of electing senators ended the frequent legislative stalemates in choosing members of the Senate. Otherwise many things remained the same. There were still election disputes, including charges of corruption, as well as miscounting of votes.

Senate's Three Classes

The Senate is divided into three classes or groups of members. A member's class depends on the year in which he or she is elected. Article I, Section 3, Paragraph 2 of the Constitution, relating to the classification of senators in the first and succeeding Congresses, provides that:

> Immediately after they shall be assembled in consequence of the first election, they shall be divided as equally as may be into three classes. The seats of the Senators of the first class shall be vacated at the expiration of the second year, of the second class at the expiration of the fourth year and of the third class at the expiration of the sixth year, so that one-third may be chosen every second year. . . .

Thus senators belonging to class one began their regular terms in the years 1789, 1791,

1797, 1803, and so on, continuing through the present day to 1989, 1995, 2001, and coming up for reelection in 2012. Senators belonging to class two began their regular terms in 1789, 1793, 1799, 1805, and so on, continuing through to the present day in 1985, 1991, 1997, and coming up for reelection in 2008. Senators belonging to class three began their regular terms in 1789, 1795, 1801, 1807, and so on, continuing through the present day to 1987, 1993, 1999, and coming up for reelection in 2010.

Sessions and Terms

In the fall of 1788, the expiring Continental Congress established a schedule for the incoming government under the new Constitution. The Congress decided that the new government was to commence on the first Wednesday in March 1789: March 4. Even though the House did not achieve a quorum until April 1 and the Senate April 6, and President George Washington was not inaugurated until April 30, Senate, House, and presidential terms were still considered to have begun March 4. The term of the First Congress continued through March 3, 1791. Because congressional and presidential terms were fixed at exactly two, four, and six years, March 4 became the official date of transition from one administration to another every four years and from one Congress to another every two years.

Long and Short Sessions

The Constitution did not mandate a regular congressional session to begin March 4. Instead, Article I, Section 4, Paragraph 2 called for at least one congressional session every year, to convene on the first Monday in December, unless Congress by law set a different day. Consequently, except when called by the president for special session, or when Congress itself set a different day, Congress convened in regular session each December, until the passage of the Twentieth Amendment in 1933.

The December date resulted in a long and short session. The first (long) session would meet in December of an odd-numbered year and continue into the next year, usually adjourning some time the next summer. The second (short) session began in December of an even-numbered year and continued through March 3 of the next year, when its term ran out. It also became customary for the Senate to meet in brief special session on March 4 or March 5, especially in years when a new president was inaugurated, to act on presidential nominations.

The Twentieth Amendment

The political consequence of the short session was to encourage filibusters and other delaying tactics by members determined to block legislation that would die upon the automatic adjournment of Congress on March 3. Moreover, the Congresses that met in short session always included a substantial number of "lame-duck" members who had been defeated at the polls, yet were quite often able to determine the legislative outcome of the session.

Dissatisfaction with the short session began to mount after 1900. During the Wilson administration (1913–1921), each of four such sessions ended with a Senate filibuster and the loss of important bills including several funding bills. Senator George W. Norris, R-Neb. (1913–1943), became the leading advocate of a constitutional amendment to abolish the short session by starting the terms of Congress and the president in January instead of March. The Senate approved the Norris amendment five times during the 1920s, only to see it blocked in the House each time. It was finally approved by both chambers in 1932 and became the Twentieth Amendment upon ratification by the thirty-sixth state in 1933. The amendment provided that the terms of senators and representatives would begin and end at noon on the third day of January of the year following the election.

The Twentieth Amendment also established noon, January 20 as the day on which the president and vice president take office. It provided also that Congress should meet annually on January 3 "unless they shall by law appoint a different day." The second session of the Seventy-third Congress was the first to convene on the new date, January 3, 1934. Franklin D. Roosevelt was the first president and John N. Garner the first vice president to be inaugu-

rated on January 20, at the start of their second terms in 1937. The amendment was intended to permit Congress to extend its first session for as long as necessary and to complete the work of its second session before the next election, thereby ending legislation by a lame-duck body.

The Modern Senate

The Senate is often called the nation's most exclusive club, even though the House of Representatives has equal power. One reason for the Senate's greater prestige is its smaller size. Out of a nation of more than 280 million (as of the 2000 census), only 100 men and women can be senators, compared with 435 representatives. In addition, a state's two senators each represent the entire state, while all but the least populated states are carved into multiple House districts.

Because of the Senate's compact size and an individual's greater opportunity to affect legislation, there is often intense competition and hefty expenditures to capture a seat.

From 1980 into June 2001, partisan control of the Senate changed four times. In 1980 the strong showing of Republican presidential candidate Ronald Reagan helped the GOP pick up a net of twelve Senate seats and wrest control of the upper chamber from the Democrats for the first time in twenty-six years. In the midterm election of 1986, however, without Reagan on the ballot, Democrats regained control, picking up a net of eight seats and ousting many of the Senate freshmen who had been elected with Reagan's help six years earlier.

In 1994, though, the tide turned again in favor of the Republicans as they picked up a net of seven seats. However, unlike the GOP's success in 1980 which was basically nationwide, the party's Senate gains in the 1990s were largely concentrated in the South. By the beginning of the twenty-first century, Republicans in both the Senate and the House held a larger proportion of seats in the once solidly Democratic South than in any other region.

Republicans were able to maintain a clear-cut majority in the Senate from 1994 until the end of

E

A – Z

Article I, Section 3, of the United States Constitution establishes the Senate. Originally, senators were selected by state legislatures; the Seventeenth Amendment, ratified in 1913, provided for senators to be elected directly by the people of each state. (Associated Press)

the century. In the election of 2000, Democrats gained a net of four seats to produce a 50–50 tie. It was the first partisan deadlock in the Senate since the election of 1880—but it lasted only six months until a Republican moderate, Senator James Jeffords of Vermont, decided to leave the Republican Party, become an Independent, and to caucus with the Democrats. Jeffords said he was no longer comfortable with the GOP's increasingly conservative stand on many issues. His decision gave the Democrats a 50–49 margin and allowed them to organize the chamber, including

taking over the chairs of committees and setting the legislative agenda.

The 2000 election also created several other unusual situations. Because the 107th Congress convened on January 3, 2001, when there was still a Democratic vice president (Al Gore) to cast the tie-breaking vote, Democrats were in nominal control of the Senate for the first seventeen days. When the new GOP administration was sworn in January 20, and Republican Vice President Dick Cheney took his seat as the presiding officer (who could cast a tie-breaking vote if necessary), Senate Republicans regained the upper hand. They remained in command until June 5, when Jeffords became an Independent. During those six months, with a shaky advantage, they entered into a unique power-sharing arrangement with the Democrats that resulted in the two parties evenly dividing membership on committees as well as agreeing to committee staffs and budgets of equal size. Republicans, though, chaired the committees.

Throughout its history the Senate has been an almost exclusive preserve of white males. Only four African Americans have served in the Senate since ratification of the Fifteenth Amendment in 1870 gave former slaves the right to vote. The Senate never had more than two female members at the same time until 1993. The number of women senators, though, has grown steadily since then, reaching a total of thirteen as a result of the election of 2000.

Further Reading

Jacobson, Gary C. *The Politics of Congressional Elections.* New York: Longman, 2003.

Lee, Frances E., and Bruce I. Oppenheimer. *Sizing Up the Senate: Unequal Consequences of Equal Representation.* Chicago: University of Chicago Press, 1999.

Mayhew, David R. *Congress: The Electoral Connection.* New Haven, CT: Yale University Press, 2004.

Electoral College

The indirect manner in which U.S. voters elect their president and vice president every four years. At the Constitutional Convention of 1787, there was much disagreement about the new government's chief executive. Several convention delegates supported a plan in which the upper house of Congress would select the president. Other delegates, however, believed that this arrangement would make the chief executive too dependent on the legislature.

Another recommendation was that the president be selected by a "joint ballot" of all the members of the House of Representatives and Senate, following the practice most states used to elect their governors. This decision, by giving the large states a clear majority in the presidential selection process (there would be many more representatives than senators), threatened to reignite the large state–small state controversy that already had split the convention once. To avert this catastrophe, Roger Sherman, the author of the Connecticut Compromise between the large and small states on legislative apportionment, moved on August 31 to refer the whole issue of presidential selection to the Committee on Postponed Matters.

On September 4 the committee proposed the electoral college as a method to elect the president with no restrictions on the president's right to seek reelection. The president would be selected by a majority vote of the electors, who would be chosen by the states using whatever methods they individually adopted. (The delegates expected that most states would entrust the selection of electors to the people.) Each state would receive a number of electoral votes equal to its representation in Congress. If no presidential candidate received votes from a majority of electors, the Senate would elect the president from among the five highest electoral vote recipients. In addition, electors would never meet as a national body—instead, they would vote in their own state capitals and then send the results to the Senate for counting. Finally, to ensure that the electors would not simply support a variety of home-state favorites, each was required to vote for two candidates for president from two different states with the runner-up in the presidential election filling the newly created office of vice president.

Only one aspect of the proposed electoral college was controversial among the delegates— Senate selection of the president in the absence of an electoral college majority. Large-state delegates objected because the Senate underrepresented them in favor of the small states. Moreover, not foreseeing the development of a two-party system, some

E

A–Z

E

A-Z

"Minority" Presidents

Year Elected	Candidate	Percentage of Popular Vote	Candidate	Percentage of Popular Vote	Candidate	Percentage of Popular Vote	Candidate	Percentage of Popular Vote
1824	Jackson	41.34	**Adams**	30.92	Clay	12.99	Crawford	11.17
1844	**Polk**	49.54	Clay	48.08	Birney	2.30		
1848	**Taylor**	47.28	Cass	42.49	Van Buren	10.12		
1856	**Buchanan**	45.28	Fremont	33.11	Fillmore	21.53		
1860	**Lincoln**	39.82	Douglas	29.46	Breckenridge	18.09	Bell	12.61
1876	Tilden	50.97	Hayes	47.95	Cooper	.97		
1880	**Garfield**	48.27	Hancock	48.25	Weaver	3.32	Others	.15
1884	**Cleveland**	48.50	Blaine	48.25	Butler	1.74	St. John	1.47
1888	Cleveland	48.62	**Harrison**	47.82	Fisk	2.19	Streeter	1.29
1892	Cleveland	46.05	Harrison	42.96	Weaver	8.50	Others	2.25
1912	**Wilson**	41.84	T. Roosevelt	27.39	Taft	23.18	Debs	5.99
1916	Wilson	49.24	Hughes	46.11	Benson	3.18	Others	1.46
1948	**Truman**	49.52	Dewey	45.12	Thurmond	2.40	Wallace	2.38
1960	**Kennedy**	49.72	Nixon	49.55	Others	.72		
1968	**Nixon**	43.42	Humphrey	42.72	Wallace	13.53	Others	.33
1992	Clinton	43.01	G. Bush	37.45	Perot	18.91	Others	.64
1996	Clinton	49.24	Dole	40.71	Perot	8.40	Others	1.65
2000	Gore	48.38	**G.W. Bush**	47.87	Nader	2.74	Others	1.01

Source: Guide to U.S. Elections, 5th ed. (Washington, D.C.: CQ Press, 2005), 229.

Under the U.S. electoral system, there have been eighteen presidential elections (decided by either the electoral college itself or by the House of Representatives) where the victor did not receive a majority of the popular votes cast in the election. Four of these presidents—John Quincy Adams in 1824, Rutherford B. Hayes in 1876, Benjamin Harrison in 1888, and George W. Bush in 2000—actually trailed their opponents in the popular vote.

The table above shows the percentage of the popular vote received by candidates in the eighteen elections in which a "minority" president (shown in boldface type) was elected.

delegates believed that after Washington (the obvious choice as the first president) left office, majorities seldom would form in the electoral college and the Senate would choose most presidents.

Once again, Sherman proposed an acceptable compromise: let the House of Representatives elect the president if the electoral college failed to produce a majority, but assign each state delegation a single vote. The Senate still would choose the vice president. Quickly, on September 6, the convention agreed.

See also: Constitutional Convention; Could a Candidate Win the Most Votes and Still Lose the Election? in **Essays**.

Faithless Electors

Members of the electoral college who cast their ballot for someone other than the Presidential candidate to whom they have committed.

Under the Constitution, electors are not bound to vote for any particular candidate; they may cast their ballots any way they wish. By 2000, twenty-nine states and the District of Columbia had laws requiring electors to vote for the state's popular vote winner. These states were Alabama, Alaska, California, Colorado, Connecticut, Delaware, Florida, Hawaii, Maine, Maryland, Massachusetts, Michigan, Mississippi, Montana, Nebraska, Nevada, New Mexico, North Carolina, Ohio, Oklahoma, Oregon, South Carolina, Tennessee, Utah, Vermont, Virginia, Washington, Wisconsin, and Wyoming.

In Michigan, North Carolina, and Utah, a faithless elector was not to be counted, with the remaining electors filling the vacancy. New Mexico, North Carolina, Oklahoma, South Carolina, and Washington provided criminal penalties or fines for violations. However, no faithless elector has ever been punished and experts doubt that it would be constitutionally possible to do so.

In practice, electors are almost always faithful to the candidate of the party with which they are affiliated, law or no law. At times in American political history, however, electors have broken ranks to vote for candidates not supported by their parties. In 1796, a Pennsylvania Federalist elector voted for Democratic-Republican Thomas Jefferson instead of Federalist John Adams. In 1820, a New Hampshire Democratic-Republican elector voted for John Quincy Adams instead of the party nominee, James Monroe.

There was no further instance of faithless electors until 1948, when Preston Parks,

F-G

A - Z

JUSTICE FOR ALL

A Means of Protest

In 2000, rather than voting for Democratic candidate Al Gore, one elector from the District of Columbia cast a blank ballot. Why? Barbara Lett-Simmons, a Democratic elector, did not cast her vote to protest the lack of congressional representation for Washington, D.C. The district, with its African American majority, is only allowed a non-voting representative. Later, Lett-Simmons told *The Washington Post,* "it is an opportunity for us to make blatantly clear our colonial status and the fact that we've been under an oligarchy." Lett-Simmons was the first elector to abstain from voting since 1832, and her blank ballot did not affect the outcome of the election.

a Truman elector in Tennessee, voted for Governor Strom Thurmond of South Carolina, the States Rights Democratic Party, or Dixiecrat, presidential nominee. Since then, there have been the following instances:

- In 1956, W. F. Turner, an Adlai Stevenson elector in Alabama, voted for a local judge, Walter B. Jones.

- In 1960, Henry D. Irwin, a Richard Nixon elector in Oklahoma, voted for Senator Harry F. Byrd, Virginia Democrat.

- In 1968, Dr. Lloyd W. Bailey, a Nixon elector in North Carolina, voted for George C. Wallace, the American Independent Party candidate.

- In 1972, Roger L. MacBride, a Nixon elector in Virginia, voted for John Hospers, the Libertarian Party candidate.

- In 1976, Mike Padden, a Gerald Ford elector in the state of Washington, voted for former governor Ronald Reagan of California.

- In 1988, Margaret Leach, a Dukakis elector in West Virginia, voted for Dukakis' running mate, Senator Lloyd Bentsen of Texas.

- In 2000, Barbara Lett-Simmons, a Gore elector in Washington, D.C., withheld her vote from Gore.

- In 2004, one unidentified Minnesota elector cast his or her ballot for John Kerry's running mate, John Edwards.

See also: Electoral College.

Federalism

A system of government in which power is shared between a national government and state or provincial governments. Power and authority are split between these two levels of government, and citizens have responsibilities to both levels.

The Articles of Confederation, which governed the United States from 1781 until 1789, was a weak federal system. Under the Articles, the central government had little power and was too weak to enforce laws, provide for the common defense. The nation's leaders, concerned about the weaknesses of the Articles, called the Constitutional Convention in 1787. The expressed purpose of this gathering was to revise and strengthen the articles.

Instead, the nation's leaders devised an entirely new form of government which was still based on a federal system. More power was entrusted to the national government, yet the states retained much sovereignty. The Constitution, ratified in 1788, has guided the United States for more than 200 years—with only 27 formal amendments, or changes.

See also: Constitutional Convention.

Federalist Party (1792–1816)

One of the first political parties, the Federalist Party favored a strong federal government and dominated national politics in the 1790s. The Federalist Party emerged from those leaders, also known as Federalists, who favored ratifying the Constitution. Among this group were George Washington, John Adams, Alexander Hamilton, and James Madison.

The men were not identical, however. Madison, after successfully working for the adoption of the new Constitution, led a political opposition that emerged in 1792. He, along with fellow Virginian Thomas Jefferson, argued for strict construction of the Constitution, meaning the powers of the government are spelled out. He also called for limiting the powers of the new national government. They organized a rival political party, the Democratic–(or Jeffersonian) Republicans, which came to power with Jefferson's election in 1800.

The Federalist Party, led by Hamilton as President George Washington's secretary of the Treasury, dominated national politics during the administrations of Washington and John Adams. The Federalists wanted to make the national government stronger by assuming state debts, chartering a national bank, and supporting manufacturing interests. In foreign affairs, they pursued policies that would protect commercial and political friendship with Britain, goals that led to ratification of Jay's Treaty in 1795. Under the treaty, Britain withdrew the last of its troops from American outposts and the United States agreed to honor debts owed to British merchants.

Although committed to a republican form of government, Federalists believed that politics was best left to the "natural aristocracy" of wealthy and talented men. Consequently, Federalists generally sought to limit suffrage, tighten naturalization policy, and silence critics.

Federalists drew their support primarily from the Northeast where their commercial and manufacturing policies attracted merchants and business leaders. Although they had some Southern strongholds in parts of Virginia and the Carolinas, especially Charleston, Federalists had less success in attracting the support of Western farmers and Southern planters because the Federalists were generally opposed to slavery and strongly favored the growing manufacturers of the Northeast.

Several factors contributed to the end of the Federalist Party. Its passage of the highly unpopular Alien and Sedition Acts of 1798 served as a rallying cry for Jeffersonian Republicans. Another factor was the Federalists'

Alexander Hamilton (b.1755-d.1804) was a key leader of the Federalist Party. He favored a strong central government and sought to develop friendly relations with Great Britain. As the first secretary of the treasury, he helped put the young United States on firm financial ground. (Library of Congress)

sharp division in the 1800 elections over Adams' foreign policies. Many Federalists opposed the War of 1812. In 1814, several extreme Federalists convened the Hartford Convention which considered secession from the union. Thus, the Federalist name became associated with disloyalty. Federalists, however, continued to play a limited role in state and local politics into the early 1820s.

Federalist leadership during the nation's critical early years contributed greatly to preserving the American experiment. In large part they were responsible for laying the foundation for a national economy, a national foreign policy agenda, and creating a strong national judicial system. The last of these was perhaps the Federalists' most enduring legacy as John Marshall used his position as chief justice (1801–1835) to incorporate Federalist principles into constitutional law.

See also: Democratic-Republican Party.

Further Reading
Chernow, Ron. *Alexander Hamilton.* New York: The Penguin Press, 2004.

Ferraro, Geraldine

See Election of 1984.

F-G

A-Z

Fifteenth Amendment (1870)

Amendment to the Constitution that granted the right to vote to all African American men over the age of 21, including those newly freed. Before the Union's victory in the Civil War in 1865, only nine states allowed African Americans to vote—the nine northernmost states of New England and the upper Midwest. After the war, the eleven states of the Confederacy were forced by the Reconstruction Act of 1867 to extend suffrage to African Americans as a condition for readmission to the Union.

Congressional Republicans were concerned that Southern African Americans might lose their franchise to white politicians in the South. They were also eager for the support of African Americans who lived in the Northern and border states. Thus, Republicans pushed the Fifteenth Amendment through a lame-duck session of Congress in February 1869. The House of Representatives passed a version of the amendment that forbade states to discriminate against African Americans in matters of suffrage. The Senate, anticipating that "the South could circumvent mere protection of impartial suffrage by imposing race-neutral criteria such as education or property holding," passed a version that would bar discrimination on the basis not just of race and color but also on the basis of property or education. A conference committee voted for the House version, and the amendment as passed provided simply that neither the United States nor any individual state could deprive a citizen of the right to vote "on account of race, color, or previous condition of servitude." The Fifteenth Amendment was ratified on February 3, 1870, by a combination of New England, upper midwestern, and African American–controlled Southern state legislatures.

The amendment secured the Republicans' major short-term political goal by effectively safeguarding the right to vote for Northern African Americans. Southern states, however, which once again came under the control of conservative whites after Union troops left in 1876, found ways to disenfranchise African Americans. These included not just violence and intimidation, but also legal ploys such as literacy tests (illiterate whites were exempted from taking the test if their ancestors had been eligible to vote before 1867—the so-called grandfather clause). Other tactics included the white primaries (political parties, as "private" organizations, were authorized to exclude African Americans from membership and participation).

Although the Supreme Court eventually declared both of these practices to be unconstitutional under the Fifteenth Amendment—the grandfather clause in *Guinn and Beall v. United States* (1915) and the white primary in *Smith v. Allwright* (1944)—voter registration among Southern African Americans remained below 30 percent as late as 1960. Not until the 1965 Voting Rights Act was passed was the Fifteenth Amendment effectively implemented in the South. The act suspended literacy tests (banned permanently in 1970). It also authorized the federal government to take over the registration process in any county in which less than 50 percent of the voting-age population was registered or had voted in the most recent presidential election.

See also: Voting Rights Act of 1965.

Free Soil Party (1848–1852)

A political party that opposed the extension of slavery into the Southwest territories acquired from Mexico as a result of the Treaty of Guadalupe Hidalgo, which ended the Mexican-American War (1846–1848). The Free Soil Party was launched formally at a convention in Buffalo, New York, in August 1848. The Free Soilers were composed of antislavery elements from the Democratic and Whig parties, as well as rem-

Former Democratic president Martin Van Buren (1837-1841) was the presidential nominee of the Free Soil Party in the Election of 1848. Van Buren did not win any electoral votes. (Library of Congress)

Former Democratic president Martin Van Buren (1837–1841) was selected by the convention as the party's presidential candidate and Charles Francis Adams, the son of President John Quincy Adams (1825–1829), was chosen as his running mate.

In the 1848 presidential election, the Free Soil ticket received 291,501 votes, or 10.1 percent of the popular vote, but was unable to carry a single state. The party did better at the congressional level, winning nine House seats and holding the balance of power in the organization of the closely divided new Congress.

The 1848 election marked the peak of the party's influence. With the passage of the Compromise 1850, the Free Soilers lost their basic issue and declined. The party ran its second and last national presidential ticket in 1852, headed by John Hale, who received 155,210 votes, 4.9 percent of the popular vote. As in 1848, the Free Soil ticket failed to carry a single state. Although the party went out of existence soon after the 1852 election, its program and membership joined the Republican Party, founded in 1854.

See also: Democratic Party, Election of 1848, Liberty Party, Republican Party, Whig Party.

nants of the Liberty Party. Representatives from all the Northern states and three border states attended the Buffalo convention, where the slogan "Free Soil, Free Speech, Free Labor and Free Men" was adopted. This slogan expressed the antislavery sentiment of the Free Soilers as well as the desire for cheap Western land.

Gerrymandering

The practice of creating odd-shaped legislative districts, usually with the purpose of benefiting a political party or minority group. Gerrymandering is probably as old as the Republic, but the name originated in 1812. In that year the Massachusetts Legislature carved out of Essex County a district which historian John Fiske said had a "dragonlike contour." When the painter Gilbert Stuart saw the misshapen district, he penciled in a head, wings, and claws and exclaimed, "That will do for a salamander!"—to which editor Benjamin Russell replied, "Better say a Gerrymander"—after Elbridge Gerry, then governor of Massachusetts.

F-G

A-Z

VIEWPOINTS

The gerrymander was created in 1812 and takes its name from Elbridge Gerry, who was the Federalist governor of Massachusetts at the time. (Library of Congress)

By the 1990s, the term had broadened to include the modern-day practice of drawing maps to benefit racial and ethnic groups. In the past, the term was applied largely to districts drawn to benefit incumbents or political parties.

Gerrymandering: The Shape of the House

There are three types of gerrymanders. One is the partisan gerrymander where a single party draws the lines to its advantage. Another is the pro-incumbent—sometimes called the "bi-partisan" or "sweetheart"—gerrymander, where the lines are drawn to protect incumbents, with any gains or losses in the number of seats shared between the two parties. In states where control of the state government is divided, pro-incumbent gerrymanders are common.

A third form of gerrymandering is race-based, where lines are drawn to favor the election of candidates from particular racial or ethnic groups. Initially, racial redistricting referred to the practice of drawing lines to scatter minority voters across several districts, so they would not have a dominant influence in any one district. The impact of the 1965 Voting Rights Act and numerous court rulings, however, has resulted in a new version of racial gerrymandering—designing legislative districts to concentrate minority voters. These majority-minority districts are more likely to elect a minority candidate.

Sweetheart gerrymandering rarely attracts much attention. Nevertheless, this method of mapping has a powerful effect on the House. "Districts get more Democratic for Democrats and more Republican for Republicans. Competition is minimized," said Bernard Grofman, a political scientist at the University of California at Irvine.

Redistricting increases the possibility of turnover because most states must redraw their districts to accommodate population shifts within the state as well as accommodating the gain or loss of any house seats. Typically, some House members choose to retire rather than stand for election in redesigned districts.

See also: House of Representatives.

Green Party (1996–)

A political party, organized in the United States in 1996. With consumer activist Ralph Nader heading its ticket, the Green Party made an impressive debut in U.S. presidential politics in 1996. Nader received 685,040 votes, or 0.7 percent of the popular vote, finishing fourth. Four years later in the disputed 2000 election, he made an even more impressive showing, winning 2.9 million votes, or 2.7 percent of the total vote, and finished third— well ahead of other third party candidates. His strong showing probably tipped the

Green Party Registration, by State

State/Territory	Registered Greens	Percentage of Each States' Total Registration	State/Territory	Registered Greens	Percentage of Each States' Total Registration
Alabama			Montana		
Alaska	4,285	0.88	Nebraska	398	
Arizona	4,832	0.18	Nevada	3356	0.32
Arkansas	No Registration by Party in State		New Hampshire	Can Register Green	
California	157,565	0.95	New Jersey	632	
Colorado	4,666	0.16	New Mexico	9,509	0.87
Connecticut	2,045	0.11	New York	37,874	0.35
Delaware	626	0.11	North Carolina	Can Register Green	
District of Columbia	4,875	1.33	North Dakota	No Registration by Party in State	
Florida	6,646	0.06	Ohio	No Registration by Party in State	
Georgia	No Registration by Party in State		Oklahoma	Can Register Green	
Hawaii	No Registration by Party in State		Oregon	13,561	0.64
Idaho	No Registration by Party in State		Pennsylvania	15,788	0.19
Illinois	No Registration by Party in State		Rhode Island	No Registration by Party in State until on Ballot	
Indiana	No Registration by Party in State		South Carolina	No Registration by Party in State	
Iowa			South Dakota	Can Register Green	
Kansas	Almost Impossible to Register Green		Tennessee	No Registration by Party in State	
Kentucky	Can Register Green		Texas	No Registration by Party in State	
Louisiana	847	1.98	Utah	812	0.18
Maine	19,006	0.24	Vermont	No Registration by Party in State	
Maryland	7,549	0.23	Virginia	No Registration by Party in State	
Massachusetts	9,509		Washington	No Registration by Party in State	
Michigan	No Registration by Party in State		West Virginia	329	
Minnesota	No Registration by Party in State		Wisconsin	No Registration by Party in State	
Mississippi	No Registration by Party in State		Wyoming	Can Register Green	
Missouri	No Registration by Party in State				

The number of registered Green Party members varies greatly by state. Some states' laws make it difficult for third parties, such as the Greens, to register their party affiliations.

F-G

A – Z

outcome to the Republican Party in one or two states.

Nader received votes in every state except three—South Dakota, North Carolina, and Oklahoma—a significant increase from four years earlier when he was on the ballot in twenty-two states. As before, he ran best in Western states, but also drew a strong following in a few Northeastern states. His running mate was Winona LaDuke of the White Earth reservation in Minnesota. A Harvard graduate, LaDuke was active as an advocate and writer on human rights and Native American environmental causes.

Although new to the United States, the Green Party was part of a decentralized worldwide movement for peace, social justice, and the environment. Until the collapse of international communism and the fall of the Berlin Wall, the Greens were best known for their political inroads in Germany.

In 2000, unlike four years earlier, Nader and LaDuke ran an aggressive and active campaign. He took his populist, anticorporate campaign to the people in a variety of ways, ranging from TV studios to union meetings, trying to put together what he described as a "blue-green" coalition of disaffected voters. Nationwide polls in the summer of 2000 showed Nader drawing roughly 5 percent of the vote, and even more than that in several battleground states, including California. In the end, however, he received far fewer votes nationwide than expected.

Nader was on the ballot in a number of closely contested states, but the Democratic nominee, Al Gore, won most of these states. Gore was seen by analysts as the candidate most likely to be hurt by Nader's presence in the contest. Of these states, none was more important than Florida. In that state Nader took more than 97,400 votes in a contest decided by a few hundred in favor of Republican George W. Bush. That win put Bush over the top in electoral votes and gave the White House to the Republicans. Some political observers believed that, had Nader not been on the ticket, Gore would have won Florida and the White House.

In the 2004 presidential election, David K.

Cobb and Patricia LaMarche led the Green Party ticket, winning slightly more than 100,000 votes nationwide. Ralph Nader ran as an independent candidate.

See also: Election of 2000; Election of 2004; Third Parties.

Greenback Party (1874–1884)

A political party that opposed the **gold standard** and supported the use of paper money. The National Independent or Greenback-Labor Party, commonly known as the Greenback Party, was launched in Indianapolis in November 1874 at a meeting organized by the Indiana **Grange,** a farmers' association. The party emerged after the Panic of 1873, a post-Civil War economic depression, which hit farmers and industrial workers especially hard. Currency was the basic issue of the new party, which opposed a return to the gold standard and favored retention of the inflationary paper money—known as greenbacks—which were first introduced as an emergency measure during the Civil War (1861–1865).

In the 1876 presidential election, the party ran Peter Cooper, a New York philanthropist, and drafted a platform that focused entirely on the currency issue. Cooper received 75,973 votes, or 0.9 percent of the popular vote, mainly from farm voters. In 1878, with the depression continuing, a Greenback national convention effected the merger of the party with various labor reform groups and adopted a platform that addressed labor and currency issues. Showing voting strength in the industrial East as well as in the agrarian South and Midwest, the Greenbacks polled more than one million votes in the 1878 congressional elections and won fourteen seats in the U.S. House of Representatives. This marked the highpoint of the party's strength.

Returning prosperity and a split between the party's farm and labor leadership weakened the Greenback Party. In the 1880 election, the party elected only eight representatives and its presidential candidate, Representative James B. Weaver of Iowa, received 305,997 votes, or 3.3 percent of the popular vote, far less than party leaders expected.

The party slipped further four years later when the Greenbacks' candidate for president, former Massachusetts governor Benjamin F. But-ler, received 175,096 votes, or 1.7 percent of the popular vote. With the end of the Green-backs, most of the party's followers moved to the Populist Party, the farming reform movement that swept the South and Midwest in the 1890s.

See also: Third Parties.

H-J

A – Z

Hernandez, Joseph Marion

See Hispanics in Congress.

Hispanic Voters

Hispanics make up the fastest growing voting bloc in the United States. Hispanic voters, however, do not owe solid allegiance to either of the major parties. Instead they tend to support the candidates that best fill their communities' unique needs.

In key races across the nation, Hispanic voters have helped elect both Republicans and Democrats. For example, Florida tends to be populated by Cuban Americans who are strongly anticommunist and anti-Castro, and tend to vote Republican. Mexican Americans in Texas have tended to vote Democratic, but strongly supported George W. Bush in 2000 and 2004 because of his stand on immigration. In California, however, the state's Republicans, who have called for "English only" legislation and stricter immigration policies, have angered Hispanic vot-ers. Mexican American voters in California thus have overwhelmingly supported Democratic candidates. Similarly, Mexican Americans in the Southwest and Puerto Rican Americans in New York have tended to support Democrats.

See also: Hispanics in Congress; Voters, Voting Behavior, and Voter Turnout.

Further Reading

Chavez, Linda. *Out of the Barrio: Toward a New Politics of Hispanic Assimilation.* Jackson, TN: Basic Books, 1992.

Ramos, Jorge. *The Latin Wave: How Hispanics are Transforming Politics in America.* New York: Harper Paperbacks, 2005.

Sanchez, Leslie. *Los Republicanos: Why Hispan-ics and Republicans Need Each Other.* New York: Palgrave Macmillan, 2007.

Hispanics in Congress

The rapidly expanding Hispanic American population was expected to become a powerful voting bloc in Congress, but by 2007, the group remained significantly underrepresented. At the start of the 110th Congress that year, twenty-seven members and one nonvoting delegate from Puerto Rico identified themselves as

Hispanics—people of Spanish ancestry. The 2000 census, however, showed the nation's Hispanic population continuing to grow rapidly, to more than 12.5 percent of the population.

If Hispanics were represented proportionally in Congress, they would hold fifty-four seats. Hispanic voter turnouts traditionally have fallen well below the national average which group activists say is due to poverty, lack of education, language barriers, alienation resulting from discrimination, large numbers of young people, immigration status, and often a continuing attachment to their homelands.

The growth of Hispanic representation in the House was in large part the result of judicial interpretations of the Voting Rights Act requiring that minorities be given maximum opportunity to elect members of their own group to Congress. After the 1990 census, congressional district maps in states with significant Hispanic populations were redrawn with the aim of sending more Hispanics to Congress.

Representative Romualdo Pacheco, a Republican from California, was the only Hispanic to serve in Congress during the nineteenth century. Mexican-born, with an English stepfather and an English education, Pacheco helped to bridge the cultural gap between the Spanish-speaking settlers of California and the newly arrived Americans. After California was taken from Mexico and given statehood, Pacheco moved up in a series of political offices to the governorship in 1875, filling out the term of his predecessor who resigned to become a U.S. senator.

The next year Pacheco ran for Congress and was certified the victor in a disputed election and took his seat early in 1877. The House subsequently decided that his opponent was the rightful winner. Pacheco returned home and ran again—successfully—twice more. Upon leaving Congress, he became ambassador to Honduras and then Guatemala. No other Hispanic American was elected to Congress until 1912. After that, only in 1927–1931 and 1941–1943 was Congress without any Hispanic American members. By 2007, Hispanic members had been elected from Texas, California, New Mexico, New York, Louisiana, Florida, Arizona, Illinois, Colorado, and New Jersey.

Several notable Hispanics have had long congressional careers. Among them were Representative E. "Kika" de la Garza, a Democrat from Texas, a former chair and ranking member of the House Agriculture Committee, who served thirty-two years in the House; Representative Manuel Lujan, Jr., a Republican from New Mexico, who served ten House terms before becoming President George Bush's (1989–1993) secretary of the interior in 1989; and Bill Richardson, a Democrat from New Mexico, who left the House in 1993 after ten years to be-

Hispanic Americans in the 110th Congress

State	House	Senate
Arizona	Raul M. Grijalva (D) Ed Pastor (D)	
California	Joe Baca (D) Xavier Becerra (D) Grace F. Napolitano (D) Lucille Roybal-Allard (D) Linda Sanchez (D) Loretta Sanchez (D) Hilda Solis (D)	
Colorado	John Salazar (D)	Ken L. Salazar (D)
Florida	Lincoln Diaz-Balart (R) Mario Diaz-Balart (R) Ileana Ros-Lehtinen(R)	Mel R. Martinez (R)
Illinois	Luis V. Gutierrez (D)	
New Jersey	Robert Menendez (D)	
New York	Jose E. Serrano (D) Nydia M. Velázquez (D)	
Texas	Henry Bonilla (R) Charles Gonzalez (D) Rubén Hinojosa (D) Solomon P. Ortiz (D) Silvestre Reyes (D) Henry Cuellar (D)	

Despite increasing electoral gains, Hispanic Americans remain underrepresented in Congress.

JUSTICE FOR ALL

Joseph Marion Hernandez

Joseph Marion Hernandez holds the distinction of being the first person of Hispanic heritage to serve in the United States Congress. After the Florida Territory was organized, Hernandez was elected as a territorial delegate to the Seventeenth Congress, serving from September 30, 1822, until March 3, 1823.

After his service in Congress he joined the army, fighting against the Seminole in Florida and helping capture Chief Osceola. He retired with the rank of Brigadier General. In 1845, he unsuccessfully ran for the Florida Senate as a member of the Whig Party. He later moved to his family's estate in Cuba, where he died in 1857.

come U.S. Representative to the United Nations and then energy secretary in the Clinton administration. Richardson was elected governor of New Mexico in 2002 and later sought the 2008 Democratic presidential nomination.

See also: Hispanic Voters; Voting Rights Act of 1965; 📖 Voting Rights Act of 1965 in the **Primary Source Library.**

Further Reading

Vigil, Maurilio E. *Hispanics in Congress.* Lanham, MD: University Press of America, 1996.

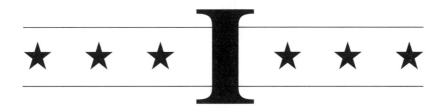

Impeachment and Removal, Gubernatorial

Term limits ensure a steady turnover of governors in most states. Elections every four years also enable the voters to replace an unpopular governor. In addition, governors guilty of unethical conduct or crimes and misdemeanors may be removed from office in the midst of their term through impeachment or recall.

The recall of a governor, which requires the holding of a special election if enough voters petition for removal, is an option in roughly one-third of the states. Nevertheless, it has been used only once against a governor. In 1921, North Dakota voters ousted Lynn J. Frazier of the Republican and National Prohibition Party, who had been forced into a special election with Reginald A. Nestos, an Independent Republican, which Nestos won. Frazier was in his third two-year term when he was removed, along with two cabinet members. The following year Frazier was elected to the U.S. Senate where he served until 1941.

Impeachment by the state legislature, similar to the federal system in which the House impeaches (charges) and the Senate acquits or convicts, was used five times in the twentieth century to remove governors. The most recent case was that of Arizona governor Evan Mecham, a Republican, who was impeached and convicted in January 1988. He was found guilty of obstructing an investigation and improperly using official funds. Mecham's removal through impeachment ended a recall movement against him.

Other governors have resigned after being convicted in the judicial system. Among such cases is that of Maryland governor Marvin Mandel, a Democrat, who served time in prison while

Evan Mecham, the twenty-first governor of Arizona took office in January 1987. He was of accused of perjury, fraud, and failure to report a campaign contribution and impeached in early 1988, although he was later acquitted of any criminal charges. Mecham died in February 2008. (AP Photo/Jeff Robbins)

Impeached Governors

Date	Accused	Office	Result
1862	Charles L. Robinson	Governor of Kansas	Acquitted
1871	William Woods Holden	Governor of North Carolina	Removed
1871	David Butler	Governor of Nebraska	Removed
1872	Henry C. Warmoth	Governor of Louisiana	Suspended from office
1876	Adelbert Ames	Governor of Mississippi	Resigned
1913	William Sulzer	Governor of New York	Removed
1917	James E. Ferguson	Governor of Texas	Resigned, but declared ineligible to hold office
1923	John C. Walton	Governor of Oklahoma	Removed
1929	Henry S. Johnston	Governor of Oklahoma	Removed
1929	Huey P. Long	Governor of Louisiana	Acquitted
1988	Evan Mecham	Governor of Arizona	Removed

To date, 11 governors have been impeached; of these, two were acquitted and remained in office. Other governors, such as California's Gray Davis, have been removed through state recall elections.

suspended from office after his 1977 conviction on federal mail fraud charges. After his conviction was reversed, Mandel served the remaining few hours of his term.

Alabama governor Guy Hunt, a Republican, was removed from office in 1993 after he was convicted of diverting inaugural funds to personal use. Jim Guy Tucker, as governor of Arkansas, resigned in 1996 after being convicted of bank fraud conspiracy in connection with the Whitewater real estate scandal. In September 1997, Arizona governor Fife Symington, a Republican, resigned after being convicted of making false statements to obtain loans for his real estate business.

See also: Impeachment, Presidential.

Impeachment, Presidential

Within the American constitutional system, impeachment is an extraordinary legislative check on both executive and judicial power. As such, it is one of the most potent, yet least exercised, powers of Congress.

Since 1789, impeachment proceedings have been initiated in the House of Representatives just sixty times. Only seventeen of these proceedings led the House, by simple majority vote, to lodge impeachment charges of "Treason, Bribery, or other high Crimes and Misdemeanors." Impeached were thirteen federal judges, two presidents, one senator, and one cabinet member. Three of these individuals resigned from office before a Senate trial could be held. The remaining fourteen were tried in the Senate, resulting in seven convictions and seven acquittals. (Convictions require a two-thirds vote of the senators present.) The three most significant impeachment cases, each of which ended in an acquittal, involved Supreme Court justice Samuel P. Chase in 1805, President Andrew Johnson in 1867–1868, and President Bill Clinton in 1998–1999. In all three instances, the proceedings were animated largely by political conflicts between the political parties. In 1974, the House Judiciary Committee voted to recommend impeachment charges against President Richard Nixon to the full House, but Nixon's resignation ended the process, which almost certainly would have led to his impeachment and removal.

Although impeachment is a political act whose penalty is removal from office and possible barring from later office holding, not criminal conviction or the obligation of civil damages, it often is discussed in legal-sounding terms. The House of Representatives acts first as a kind of grand jury by considering and adopting impeachment charges, and then as prosecutor by appointing a group of its members (called managers) to present the charges to the Senate. The Senate chamber becomes the courtroom, with the Senate acting as jury. Although the chief justice of the United States presides when the Senate tries a president, the Senate also acts as judge in many ways, because it decides procedural issues by majority vote. Since 1935, the Senate has routinely authorized a twelve-member Senate committee to try judicial impeachments. Such committees report, without recommenda-

tion, to the Senate, and the senators vote whether to convict.

Origins and Purposes of Impeachment

The Constitution stipulates that impeachment proceedings may be brought against "the President, Vice President and all Civil Officers of the United States." It is not specific, however, about who is and is not a civil officer. In practice, most impeachment efforts have been directed at federal judges who hold lifetime appointments "during good Behaviour" and thus cannot otherwise be removed from office. One early impeachment case raised the possibility that members of Congress could be impeached, but this idea was rejected by the Senate in favor of its less formal equivalent, expulsion. In other instances impeachment has been sought against executive officials such as cabinet members, diplomats, customs collectors, and a United States attorney. Of all these, only one cabinet member ever was impeached. The reason that removal of executive officials almost never requires full impeachment proceedings is that they can be dismissed from office by the president.

Constitutional Convention

American colonial governments adopted the English process of impeachment under which charges are brought by the lower house of the legislature and the upper house sits in judgment. Although the early state constitutions preserved this process, the Constitutional Convention debated whether the Senate was the appropriate body to conduct impeachment trials. No one questioned that the House of Representatives should be responsible for bringing impeachment charges. Framers James Madison and Charles Pinckney opposed assigning that role to the Senate, arguing that it would make presidents too dependent on the legislative branch. Suggested alternatives included the Supreme Court and a meeting of the chief justices of the state supreme courts. In the end, however, tradition was followed and the Senate was selected to conduct impeachment trials.

The convention also debated the definition of an impeachable offense. Initially, it was proposed

H-J

A-Z

In 1868, the House of Representatives impeached President Andrew Johnson. This sketch shows Johnson's trial in the Senate, where he was acquitted by one vote. Thus, he was allowed to remain in office. (Library of Congress)

that the president be subject to impeachment for "malpractice or neglect of duty." Later, this definition was changed to "treason, bribery, or corruption," then simply to "treason or bribery." George Mason argued that the latter grounds were "too narrow" and proposed adding "maladministration," which Madison in turn opposed as being too broad. In the end, impeachable offenses were defined in the Constitution as "Treason, Bribery, or other high Crimes and Misdemeanors."

The constitutional provisions related to impeachment are scattered among the first two articles of the Constitution. In Article I, the House is given "sole Power of Impeachment" and the Senate is accorded "the sole Power to try all Impeachments," with the chief justice of the United States presiding at presidential impeachment trials. Article II subjects "The President, Vice President and all Civil Officers of the United States" to impeachment for "Treason, Bribery, or other high Crimes and Misdemeanors." It also states that the consequences of a conviction by the Senate shall extend no further "than to removal from Office, and disqualification to hold and enjoy any Office of honor, Trust or Profit under the United States."

Impeachment Proceedings

The impeachment process has been used so seldom that no standard practice for initiating impeachment has been established. Instead, impeachment proceedings have been initiated in several ways: by the introduction of a resolution by a member of the House, by a letter or message from the president, by a grand jury action forwarded to the House from a territorial legislature, by a resolution authorizing a general investigation, and by a resolution reported by the House Judiciary Committee. In the cases that have reached the Senate since 1900, the latter method of initiating impeachment proceedings has been preferred.

After a resolution to impeach has made its way to the House floor, the House decides whether to adopt the resolution by majority vote. In making this decision, the House may choose to amend, delete, or add to the articles that make up the resolution.

If the House adopts the resolution, its next task is to select managers to serve as prosecutors at the Senate trial. The managers—usually an odd number ranging from five to eleven—have been selected in various ways: by adopting a resolution that fixes the number of managers and empowers the Speaker to appoint them, by adopting a resolution that fixes both the number and names of the managers, or by adopting a resolution that fixes the number but empowers the House to elect the managers later. Once selected, the House managers deliver the articles of impeachment to the Senate and inform it of the need to hold a trial. Any House member may attend the trial, but only the managers may actively represent and speak for the House.

The Senate trial is similar to a criminal proceeding. Both sides may present evidence and witnesses, and the defendant is allowed counsel and has the right to testify and conduct cross-examinations. If the president is on trial, the chief justice presides. The Constitution is silent, however, about who is to preside in other impeachment trials. In the past either the vice president or the president pro tempore of the Senate has done so.

The chief justice (or other presiding officer) rules on all questions of evidence, but any ruling may be overturned by a majority vote of the Senate. Indeed, the chief justice may ask the Senate to make a ruling by majority vote rather than make the ruling himself. The chief justice also questions witnesses and asks questions submitted in writing by senators who are not permitted to question witnesses directly.

At the conclusion of the testimony, the Senate goes into closed session to debate the question of guilt or innocence. During this session, each senator may speak no longer than fifteen minutes. The articles of impeachment are voted on separately. If any article receives two-thirds approval from the senators present, the impeached official is convicted. The Senate then votes to remove the now-convicted official from office and, later, may also vote to disqualify the convicted official from ever holding another federal office.

Controversial Questions

The constitutional grounds for and the character of impeachment have long been debated. Clearly, treason and bribery are grounds for impeachment, and their definitions have been well established. Treason and the requirements for its proof are defined in the Constitution, and bribery is defined in statutory laws that bar the giving, offering, or accepting of rewards in return for official favors. The meaning of the remaining grounds for impeachment—"other high Crimes and Misdemeanors"—however, is anything but clear and has been the subject of much contention. Most interpreters of the Constitution have advocated a definition of the phrase that includes not only criminal offenses, but also actions that constitute a serious abuse of office.

Perhaps the most extreme example of this construction can be found in a statement made by House Republican leader Gerald Ford when he was attempting to impeach Supreme Court justice William O. Douglas in 1970. Ford declared,

> An impeachable offense is whatever a majority of the House of Representatives considers it to be at a given moment in history; conviction results from whatever offense or offenses two-thirds of the other body considers to be sufficiently serious to require removal of the accused from office.

H-J

A – Z

H-J

A – Z

Conversely, narrow constructionists contend that "other high Crimes and Misdemeanors" refers only to indictable criminal offenses. As the lawyers for Richard Nixon argued in 1974, for example,

> Impeachment of a president should be resorted to only for causes of the gravest kind—the commission of a crime named in the Constitution or a criminal offense against the laws of the United States.

The debates at the Constitutional Convention seem to indicate that impeachable offenses were not meant to be limited to indictable crimes, but also included serious abuses of office. Conversely, the criminal code defines as crimes many actions of insufficient gravity to warrant impeachment. Thus, neither the broad nor the narrow construction of "other high Crimes and Misdemeanors" is fully acceptable. Not all indictable crimes constitute valid grounds for impeachment, yet indictable crimes are not the only valid grounds for impeachment either.

See also: Constitution, The U.S.; Constitutional Convention; Impeachment and Removal, Gubernatorial.

Further Reading

Benedict, Michael Les. *The Impeachment and Trial of Andrew Johnson*. New York: W.W. Norton & Company, 1999.

Cohen, Daniel. *The Impeachment of William J. Clinton*. Minneapolis, MN: Lerner Books, 1999.

Posner, Richard A. *An Affair of State: The Investigation, Impeachment, and Trial of Bill Clinton*. Cambridge, MA: Harvard University Press, 2000.

Income and Voter Turnout

See Voters, Voting Behavior, and Voter Turnout.

Incumbency

A term that describes an office-holder running for reelection. Incumbent presidents, senators, and representatives generally have huge advantages in their reelection campaigns. They are almost always well known, have the support of various interest groups and PACS, and have the power of their office behind them.

The record of twentieth-century U.S. presidential elections shows that a smooth path to renomination is essential for incumbents seeking reelection. Every president who actively sought renomination this century was successful. Those who were virtually unopposed within their own party won another term. All the presidents who faced significant opposition for renomination, however, ended up losing in the general election.

Incumbent Presidents Who Lost Their Reelection Bids, Since 1900	
William H. Taft	(1912)
Herbert Hoover	(1932)
Gerald R. Ford	(1976)
Jimmy Carter	(1980)
George Bush	(1992)

Incumbent presidents who faced serious opponents in their bid for renomination lost the general election.

Interest Groups

Also known as advocacy groups, special-interest groups, pressure groups, and lobbying groups, interest groups advocate, or attempt to influence, public policy. Interest groups are groups of citizens with a common concern. They may be loosely organized or they may work under a strictly controlled structure. Interest groups exist that support or oppose almost every issue that is a matter of public policy.

A major function of interest groups is to provide information. For example, an interest group's lobbyist may give members of Congress data and other information related to a bill under consideration. It is likely that the information will be biased to favor the group's concern. To make an informed decision, however, the members and their staffs often review materials from opposing interest groups.

Interest groups also report to their members on which members of Congress supported the group's position. This information may be influential in determining whether the member of Congress is reelected.

See also: Campaign Finance.

Further Reading

Ciglar, Allan J., and Burdett A. Loomis. *Interest Group Politics.* Washington, DC: CQ Press, 2006.

Rozell, Mark J., Clyde Wilcox, and David Madland. *Interest Groups in American Campaigns: The New Face of Electioneering.* Washington, DC: CQ Press, 2005.

Wright, John R. *Interest Groups and Congress: Lobbying, Contributions and Influence.* New York: Longman Press, 2002.

Independent Voters

See Voters, Voting Behavior, and Voter Turnout.

Internet Voting

See Voting Systems.

★ ★ ★ J-K ★ ★ ★

Jordan, Barbara

See Election of 1972.

Know Nothing (American) Party (1856)

Organized in the mid-1850s, a political party that opposed immigrants, especially Catholic immigrants. The Know Nothing Party of the 1850s was the most powerful nativist political organization in American history. For two years in

mid-decade, it was the nation's second-largest party. Nativism involved the fear of aliens and opposition to any minority believed to be un-American. Members of the American Party would be called Know Nothings because when asked about their organization they were instructed to say, "I know nothing." For them, fear and hatred of Catholics created this need for secrecy.

The Know Nothings emerged from the many nativist secret societies of the pre-Civil War period. The migration of millions of Catholics from Ireland and Germany created an intense anti-alien activism in the United States. Like nativists of earlier decades, leaders of the Know Nothing Party accused Catholics of undermining the public school system and of being responsible for a host of social problems that developed

could cement broken institutions and warring people.

The political divisions of the day meant that Know Nothing membership varied from section to section. In New York, where the party was born and had its strongest support, the leadership was composed of conservative Whigs—men who opposed the free soil and antislavery elements in their former party. In New England, the antislavery wing of the former Whig Party, "Conscience Whigs," made up much of the party's membership. Also swelling the party rolls in New England were abolitionists from the other major party, anti-Nebraska Act Democrats.

In the West, where Know Nothings struggled to find support, nativists sought to join with free soil activists. In the South, which contained a small immigrant population, nativism appealed to those who viewed aliens living in the Northeast and West as a threat to the Southern way of life. It was assumed that newcomers would be opposed to slavery.

Despite some political success at the state level in 1854 and 1855, the national Know Nothing Party could not survive the slavery controversy. At the party gathering in Philadelphia in June 1855, a proslavery resolution led to wild debate. Led by Massachusetts nativists, representatives from several states left the meeting in protest. Further divisions in the party, including personal rivalries among party leaders, created more problems.

In 1856, the party nominated former president Millard Fillmore (1850–1853) as its presidential candidate. However, Fillmore—who had joined a Know Nothing lodge as a political maneuver and had never been a real nativist—failed at the polls. He trailed in a three-way race with only 22 percent of the popular vote and won only Maryland's eight electoral college votes. The Know Nothings never recovered and quickly lost members. In 1857, the party held its last national council.

See also: Election of 1856; Third Parties.

Former president Millard Fillmore (1850-1853) was the Know Nothing Party presidential nominee in the Election of 1856. Fillmore won Maryland's eight electoral votes. (Library of Congress)

after the arrival of so many poverty-stricken newcomers into the great port cities.

The party emerged at a unique moment in American political history. The slavery controversy was ripping apart the Whig Party and the Democratic Party was splitting in different states and sections. At this time of political confusion, thousands of people turned to the new nativist movement. For many people, a party organized around nativist themes—one that advanced "American" interests and stood for stability and union—offered a way out of the conflict between northerner and southerner, abolitionist and slaveholder. A common crusade against foreigners, they thought,

Latinos in Congress

See Hispanics in Congress.

League of Women Voters

Founded in 1920, a strictly non-partisan organization created to improve government and inform the public. It grew out of the National American Women's Suffrage Association (NAWSA). The League strives to make democracy work for all citizens. Membership is open to both women and men. A decentralized group, the League operates in all 50 states, the District of Columbia, and Puerto Rico. The group's 900 state and local leagues make it one of the country's largest grass-roots organizations.

The League neither supports nor endorses candidates. It works to influence policy by informing citizens about various issues. The issues advocated by the League have changed with time. Among the issues supported by the League are health-care reform; campaign-finance reform; global climate change; and votes for D.C. residents. The League of Women Voters mission statement is:

> The League of Women Voters, a non-partisan political organization, encourages informed and active participation in government, works to increase understanding of major public policy issues, and influences public policy through education and advocacy.

Major Issues Supported by the League of Women Voters

Representative Government
Promote an open governmental system that is representative, accountable, and responsive

International Relations
Promote peace in an interdependent world by working cooperatively with other nations and strengthening international organizations

Natural Resources
Promote an environment beneficial to life through the protection and wise management of natural resources in the public interest

Social Policy
Secure equal rights and equal opportunity for all; Promote social and economic justice and the health and safety of all Americans.

In addition to educating voters, the non-partisan League of Women voters focuses its efforts on four broad areas—representative government, international relations, natural resources, and social policy.

Liberal Party (1944–)

Based in New York State, the Liberal Party was founded in 1944 by anticommunist trade unionists and other politically liberal individuals who left communist-dominated political parties. In 2000, the party described itself as providing an "alternative to a state Democratic Party dominated by local party machines rife with corruption and a Republican Party controlled by special interests." Many of the

A–Z

K-M

JUSTICE FOR ALL

Susan B. Anthony Arrested for Voting

On November 1, 1872, Susan B. Anthony and her three sisters tried to register to vote in Rochester, New York. The four women were a part of a group of 50 that Anthony had organized. Anthony based her demand to register on the recently ratified Fourteenth Amendment (1868) which stated, in part, "that all persons born and naturalized in the United States . . . are citizens of the United States . . . No State shall make or enforce any law which shall abridge the privileges . . . of citizens of the United States . . ." Anthony believed that one of these "privileges" was the right to vote. Anthony and some her group successfully registered to vote and then cast ballots on November 5, 1872. On November 14, Anthony was arrested, charged with violating the 1870 Enforcement Act. Her trial was to be held several months later.

During this time, Anthony worked to educate the people of Rochester and the surrounding areas. She gave a stirring speech, "Is it a Crime for Citizen of the United States to Vote?" In her speech, she quoted the Declaration of Independence, the U.S. Constitution, Thomas Paine, and James Madison. She ended her lecture, directly appealing to the potential jurors of her upcoming trial, "We appeal to the women everywhere to exercise their too long neglected 'citizen's right to vote.' . . . We ask the juries to fail to return verdicts of 'guilty' against honest, law-abiding, tax-paying United States citizens for offering their votes at our elections. Or against intelligent, worthy young men, inspectors of elections, for receiving and counting such citizens votes."

She was found guilty on June 17, 1873, and ordered to pay a $100 fine. After the trial, one New York paper observed, "If it is a mere question of who got the best of it, Miss Anthony is still ahead. She has voted and the American constitution has survived the shock. Fining her one hundred dollars does not rule out the fact that . . . women voted, and went home, and the world jogged on as before."

state's labor and educational leaders were involved in creating the party, which calls itself the nation's "longest existing third party."

The Liberal Party has played a major role in several elections. It provided crucial support for Franklin D. Roosevelt in 1944 and John F. Kennedy in 1960. Some political historians believe Roosevelt and Kennedy owed their national victories to the Liberal Party vote that carried New York State for them. John Lindsay, nominally a Republican, won reelection in New York City's 1969 mayoral race as the Liberal Party candidate. In 2000, Democrat Hillary Rodham Clinton won the Liberal vote in her campaign for the U.S. Senate.

The party nominates candidates based on "merit, independence, and progressive viewpoints." Many of the state's most prominent liberal politicians have sought and won the party's nomination for New York City mayor, governor, and U.S. senator, regardless of their major party affiliation. When the party has not run candidates of its own, it has usually been supportive of Democrats. Sometimes, however, the party's role has been that of a spoiler, particularly in close races, where its support represents the balance of power. In modern Senate races, for example, political analysts say Liberal Party endorsement of moderate or liberal candidates has sometimes drawn enough votes away from Democratic candidates to throw the election to conservative Republicans.

The party is active in pushing its political agenda, which is pro-choice, pro-universal healthcare, and pro-public education. Its successful Supreme Court suit for congressional reapportionment contributed to the 1968 election of New York's Shirley Chisholm, the first female African American congressional representative.

Through the latter part of the twentieth century, the Liberal Party served as a counterweight in New York politics to the state's Conservative Party. In 1966, for instance, each party's gubernatorial candidate drew over a half million votes.

Both parties have lost ground at the polls since then, the Liberals a bit more than have the Conservatives. In 1998, for instance, the Liberal Party's gubernatorial nominee drew fewer than 80,000 votes, while the Conservative Party provided Republican incumbent George E. Pataki with nearly 350,000 votes.

See also: Conservative Party; Election of 1944; Election of 1960; Third Parties.

Libertarian Party (1971–)

A political party whose members believe in as little government interference as possible. In the brief period of four years, 1972 to 1976,

the Libertarian Party leaped from a new political organization on the presidential ballot in only two states to the nation's largest third party. Formed in Colorado in 1971, the party nominated John Hospers of California for president in 1972. On the ballot only in Colorado and Washington, Hospers garnered 3,673 votes—including write-in votes from other states. However he received national attention when a Republican presidential elector from Virginia, Roger MacBride, cast his electoral vote for the Libertarian presidential nominee.

MacBride's action made him a hero among Libertarians, and the party chose him as its 1976 presidential candidate at its August 1975 convention in New York City. MacBride had served in the Vermont legislature in the 1960s, but was defeated for the Republican gubernatorial nomination in that state in 1964.

Making a major effort in 1976, the Libertarians got on the ballot in thirty-two states, more than Eugene J. McCarthy—who ran independent of any political party—or any other third-party candidate. The party won 173,011 votes, more than any other minor party candidate, but far below McCarthy's total of 740,460 votes and only 0.2 percent of the national vote. MacBride's strength was centered in the West; he received 5.5 percent of the vote in Alaska and 1.0 percent or more in Arizona, Hawaii, and Idaho. He also ran well ahead of his national average in California—0.7 percent—and Nevada–0.8 percent. His running mate was David P. Bergland, a California lawyer.

In 1980, the Libertarian Party appeared on the ballot in all fifty states and the District of Columbia for the first time. The party also fielded about 550 candidates for other offices, a number that dwarfed other third-party efforts. The party nominees, Edward E. Clark of California for president and David Koch of New York for vice president, garnered 921,299 votes, or 1.1 percent of the vote nationwide. As in previous elections, the major support for the Libertarians came from Western states.

Of all minor-party presidential candidates running in 1984, the Libertarians appeared on

A – Z

K-M

A – Z

K-M

the greatest number of ballots: thirty-eight states and the District of Columbia. David Bergland, who had run in 1976 for the second slot, was the party's presidential candidate, and Jim Lewis, a Connecticut business executive, was his running mate. In 1988, the Libertarian nominees—Ron Paul and Andre V. Marrou—were on the ballot in all forty-seven jurisdictions and received 432,179 votes.

In 1992, Nevada real estate broker Marrou was the presidential nominee with running mate Nancy Lord, a lawyer from Georgia. The pair was on the ballot in all states and the District of Columbia and had a campaign budget of $1 million. Marrou received 291,627 votes in a fourth-place finish behind Ross Perot, the most prominent third party candidate that year. The Libertarians maintained their strong base in the West, especially in California, Nevada, and Hawaii, where they also ran candidates in 1992 for most House seats.

In 1996, the Libertarians regained voting strength, but dropped to fifth place in the presidential race behind Ross Perot and Ralph Nader of the newly formed Green Party. The Libertarian candidates, financial analyst Harry Browne of Tennessee and running mate Jo Anne Jorgensen of South Carolina, drew 485,798 votes, or 0.50 percent of the total. It was the party's best showing since 1980.

The story in the 2000 presidential race was similar. The party won votes in forty-nine states, but its candidates, again Browne and running mate Art Olivier of California, won just 386,024 votes, or 0.37 percent of all votes, down 20 percent from four years earlier.

In 2004, Libertarian hopefuls Michael Badnarik and Richard Campagna were on the ballot in forty-eight states and the District of Columbia and raised about $1 million in campaign funds. Badnarik won 397,027 votes or 0.34 percent of the popular vote, placing fourth behind Republican George W. Bush, Democrat John H. Kerry, and independent Ralph Nader.

Individual responsibility and minimal government interference are the hallmarks of the Libertarian philosophy. The party has favored repeal of laws against so-called victimless crimes—such as pornography, drug use, and homosexual activity—the abolition of all federal police agencies, and the elimination of all government subsidies to private enterprise. In foreign and military affairs, the Libertarians have advocated the removal of U.S. troops from abroad, a cut in the defense budget, and the emergence of the United States as a "giant Switzerland" with no international treaty obligations. Libertarians also have favored repeal of legislation that they believe hinders individual or corporate action. They have opposed gun control, civil rights laws, price controls on oil and gas, labor protection laws, federal welfare and poverty programs, forced busing, compulsory education, Social Security, national medical care, and federal land-use restrictions.

See also: Third Parties.

Liberty Party (1828–1836)

A third party organized to oppose slavery. The Liberty Party came about because of a split in the anti-slavery movement. One faction, led by William Lloyd Garrison, favored action outside the political process; the second faction, led by James G. Birney, proposed action within the political system through the establishment of an independent antislavery party. The Birney faction launched the Liberty Party in November 1839. The following April a national convention with delegates from six states nominated Birney for the presidency.

Although the Liberty Party was the first political party to take an antislavery position, and the only one at the time to do so, most abolitionist voters in the 1840 election supported the Democratic or Whig presidential candidates. Birney received only 6,797 votes—0.3 percent of the popular vote.

Aided by the controversy over the annexa-

A staunch abolitionist, James G. Birney, was the presidential nominee of the Liberty Party in the Election of 1840. He won no electoral votes in that election, but the party again chose him as their nominee in 1844. (Library of Congress)

tion of slaveholding Texas, the Liberty Party's popularity increased in 1844. Birney, again the party's presidential nominee, received 62,103 votes—2.3 percent of the popular vote—but again, as in 1840, carried no states. The peak strength of the party was reached two years later in 1846, when in various state elections Liberty Party candidates received 74,017 votes.

In October 1847, the party nominated New Hampshire senator John P. Hale for the presidency, but his candidacy was withdrawn the following year when the Liberty Party joined the broader-based Free Soil Party.

Limited Government

See Constitution of the United States; Constitutional Convention.

Literacy Tests

A method used to limit the Southern franchise to whites. Voters were once required to read and/or write correctly—usually a section of the state or federal Constitution. Sometimes voters who could not pass the test could have the materials read to them, to see if they could "understand" or "interpret" it correctly. This provision allowed local voting officials, inevitably whites, to judge whether voters passed the tests; it usually resulted in whites passing and blacks failing.

By the 1970s, most formal bars to voting in the South, and many informal ones, had been lifted, either by constitutional amendment, federal laws, state action, or protest movements.

See Also: African American Voters; Poll Tax.

VIEWPOINTS

...EVERY AMERICAN CITIZEN MUST HAVE AN EQUAL RIGHT TO VOTE. THERE IS NO REASON WHICH CAN EXCUSE THE DENIAL OF THAT RIGHT...

HERBLOCK

LITERACY TEST

3/17/65

A 1965 political cartoon ridicules potential white voters who are not able to read and understand an excerpt from President Lyndon B. Johnson's American Promise speech, which led to the Voting Rights Act of 1965. (Herb Block Foundation)

A – Z

K-M

Majority Rule

A principle of government in which the view of the majority of those involved, more than half, is decisive. The principle of majority rule and the protection of minority rights may seem contradictory. Both principles, however, are essential to democratic government. Majority rule is a means for organizing government and deciding public issues; it is not a means to oppress others. A key concept behind majority rule is that no majority, even in a democracy, can take away the basic rights and freedoms of a minority group.

In a democracy, minorities—whether grouped on the basis of ethnic background, religious belief, geographic location, income level, or losers in elections—enjoy basic human rights that no government, and no majority, elected or not, should remove. Minorities need to trust that the government will protect their rights. Once this trust is established, such groups can participate in and contribute to the country's democratic institutions.

In the United States, basic human rights are spelled out in the Bill of Rights or other constitutional amendments. Among these rights are freedom of speech and expression; freedom of religion and belief; due process and equal protection under the law; and freedom to organize, speak out, disagree, and participate fully in the public life of society.

There is no one manner in which the minority rights can be protected. The knowledge that the democratic processes of tolerance, debate, and willingness to compromise allows free societies to reach agreements on various issues, providing for both majority rule and minority rights.

Minority Rights

See Majority Rule.

Media Coverage of Campaigns and Elections

See Campaign Finance.

Motor-Voter Registration

In most Western nations, government agencies sign up voters, but the United States places the burden for qualifying for electoral participation on the citizen. Signed into law by President Bill Clinton (1993–2001) on May 20, 1993, the motor-voter act required states to provide all eligible citizens the opportunity to register when they applied for or renewed a driver's license.

Motor-Voter also required states to allow mail-in registration and to provide voter registration forms at agencies that supplied public assistance, such as welfare checks or help for the disabled. Compliance with the federally mandated program was required by 1995. Costs were to be borne by the states.

Partly as a result of the legislation, a record number of new voters, some ten million, signed up in the first three years following implementation of the act. The Federal Election Commission (FEC) reported that motor voter registration accounted for a quarter of voter registration applications in the 1997–1998 election period. However the 140 million registered voters in 1998, or 70.8 percent of the voting-age population, was a drop from 1996 when it reached the highest level since 1960, when national registration figures first became available.

Congressional Republicans had opposed the legislation on political grounds, namely that it would allow citizens of traditionally Democratic constituencies—the urban poor and minorities, among others—easier access to the voting booth. Opponents also argued that easier registration could lead to election fraud. The motor-voter law had neither the negative results that critics feared nor the positive impact that supporters hoped. One year after the law was enacted, Republicans won control of both houses of Congress, which they retained through the 2000 elections. In spite of the increased number of registered voters, election turnout continued to decline slightly in the

---

POINT / COUNTERPOINT

Two Views on the Motor-Voter Law

On May 20, 1993, President Bill Clinton signed into law the National Voter Registration Act of 1993, often called the Motor-Voter Act, because it allows citizens to register to vote when they receive or renew their driver's licenses. President Clinton strongly supported the law. However, the National Review, a conservative publication, believed the law would increase voter fraud.

President Bill Clinton

The victory we celebrate today [the signing of the motor-voter act] is but the most recent chapter in the overlapping struggles of our Nation's history to enfranchise women and minorities, the disabled, and the young with the power to affect their own destiny and our common destiny by participating fully in our democracy . . .

Let us remember this in closing: Voting is an empty promise unless people vote. Now there is no longer the excuse of the difficulty of registration. It is the right of every American to vote. It is also the responsibility of every American to vote. We have taken an important step this morning to protect that right . . .

When we leave here today, we ought to say: This voting rights bill and the others will not be in vain. Every year from now on, we're going to have more registered voters and more people voting. We're going to make the system work. The law empowers us to do it. It's now up to us to assume the responsibility to see that it gets done.

Thank you very much.

(continued on next page)

A – Z

K-M

late 1990s, although there was an increase in the elections of 2000 and 2004.

The MotorVoter Act is also credited with helping to keep the voting rolls up to date. Voters who fail to respond to election board mailings can be placed on an inactive list and removed from the rolls if they do not vote during a specified period. The requirements for keeping accurate and current voting lists indi-

rectly affect political candidates as well. The registration indicates whether a candidate meets the residency requirements for the office being sought, and there have been numerous instances of candidates being kept off the ballot for being registered in the wrong area.

See also: Voters, Voting Behavior, and Voter Turnout.

The National Review

The debates in Congress [concerning the Motor-Voter bill] led the public to believe that Motor-Voter would simply allow people to register to vote at government agencies while conducting other business, such as renewing a driver's license or applying for unemployment or welfare. What could be more benign? After all, the proponents argued, these agencies all require some form of ID from people applying to them. Unfortunately, Motor-Voter went well beyond its original concept.

This law has taken all common-sense security measures out of the election process. NVRA [National Voter Registration Act] mandates that every state allow registration by mail and that "no formal authentication of ID may be required." Furthermore, the act requires every state actively to promote the registration of voters by "independent groups." For years, California's election code has allowed independent groups to conduct voter registration, and has waived ID requirements. As a result, there has been a tremendous amount of fraud in registration and voting here. The National Voter Registration Act will create similar problems, but on a national scale.

The goal of The National Voter Registration Act of 1993 is full registration of every eligible person, and the Fair Elections Group agrees with the concept. Unfortunately, Motor-Voter contains no provision for effectively stopping illegal registration and voting. We must wonder if the true wishes of the American people will be reflected in the results of the November election. And while we would like to give the benefit of the doubt to the authors of this law, we must question the motives of those who have made voting the only government-sponsored activity that does not require ID.

DOCUMENT-BASED QUESTION
What is the major concern of the National Review concerning the Motor Voter Law?

Nader, Ralph

See Election of 1996; Election of 2000; Election of 2004; Election of 2008: Campaigns; Green Party; Reform Party.

National Unity Party (1980–1988)

A short-lived third party organized by Republican representative John B. Anderson of Illinois. Anderson formed the National Unity Campaign as the vehicle for his independent presidential campaign in 1980. Anderson began his quest for the presidency by trying to win the Republican Party nomination. As a liberal in a party coming under conservative control, however, he won no primaries and could claim only fifty-seven convention delegates by April 1980. Anderson withdrew from the Republican race and declared his independent candidacy.

Anderson focused his campaign on the need to establish a viable third party as an alternative to domination of the political scene by the Republican and Democratic parties. The National Unity Campaign platform touted the Anderson program as a "new public philosophy"—more innovative than that of the Democrats, who "cling to the policies of the New Deal," and more enlightened than that of the Republicans, who talk "incessantly about freedom, but hardly ever about justice."

In general, the party took positions that were fiscally conservative and socially liberal. Anderson and his running mate, former Democratic governor Patrick J. Lucey of Wisconsin, tried to appeal to Republican and Democratic voters disenchanted with their parties and to the growing bloc of voters who classified themselves as independents.

The National Unity Campaign ticket was on the ballot in all fifty states in 1980, although Anderson had to wage costly legal battles in some states to ensure that result. In the end, the party won 6.6 percent of the presidential vote, well over the 5 percent necessary to qualify for retroactive federal campaign funding.

In April 1984, Anderson announced that he would not seek the presidency in that year. He said that instead he would focus his energies on building the National Unity Party, which he established officially in December 1983. He planned to concentrate initially on running candidates at the local level. In August, Anderson endorsed Walter F. Mondale, the Democratic nominee for president, and his running mate, Geraldine A. Ferraro.

The National Unity Party did not run a presidential candidate in the 1988 race. By 1992, it was no longer a political party.

Natural Law Party (1992–2004)

A short-lived third party committed to issues concerning the environment, education, economic growth, job creation, and lower taxes. The Natural Law Party ran three presidential campaigns—1992, 1996, and 2000—with John Hagelin as its nominee each time. The party won 39,179 popular votes in 1992, 113,688 in 1986, and 83,520 in 2000. Hagelin and the party advocated prevention-oriented government and meditative, tension-relieving programs "designed to bring national life into harmony with natural law."

Hagelin, a Harvard-trained quantum physicist, was born in Pittsburgh in 1954 and grew up in Connecticut. He became associated with Maharishi International University in Iowa in 1983. His running mate was fellow Maharishi scientist Mike Tompkins, a Harvard graduate and specialist in crime prevention programs.

In April 2004, the party announced it was closing its national headquarters and focusing its efforts on a new organization, the U.S. Peace Government, dedicated to creating peace in the United States and the world.

Suffragists picket in front of President Woodrow Wilson's White House during World War I (1917-1918) to protest his lack of support for a constitutional amendment granting women the right to vote. Wilson later supported what became the Nineteenth Amendment, which was ratified in 1920. (Library of Congress)

New Alliance Party (1988–1992)

A third party formed in the late 1980s to promote a variety of minority interests. The party described itself as "black-led, multiracial, pro-gay and pro-socialist." The party aggressively filed lawsuits to attain ballot access. In 1988, presidential candidate Lenora B. Fulani, a New York psychologist, drew 217,219 votes nationwide for a fourth-place finish. Her best showing was in the District of Columbia where she received more than 1 percent of the vote.

In 1992, with the party qualifying for $1.8 million in federal matching funds, Fulani ran again, this time with California teacher Maria Munoz as a running mate. The New Alliance ticket appeared on the ballot in thirty-nine states and the District of Columbia and received 73,714 votes, slightly less than 0.1 percent nationwide.

Nineteenth Amendment (1920)

Amendment to the Constitution that gave women the right to vote in all federal, state, and local elections. The women's suffrage movement was born in 1848 at the Women's Rights Convention held in Seneca Falls, New York. Suffragists encouraged women to assert their right to

vote after the passage of the Fourteenth Amendment in 1868, claiming this right under the equal protection clause. These attempts failed.

The suffrage forces had some success in the Western states. As a territory, Wyoming extended full suffrage to women in 1869 and retained it on becoming a state in 1890. Colorado, Utah, and Idaho granted women voting rights before the turn of the century. However, after that, suffragists encountered stronger opposition, and it was not until the height of the Progressive era that other states, mostly in the West, gave women full voting rights. Washington granted equal suffrage in 1910; California in 1911; Arizona, Kansas, and Oregon in 1912; Montana and Nevada in 1914; and New York in 1917.

Constitutional Amendment
On the eve of World War I (1917–1918), the advocates of militant tactics took the lead in a national campaign for women's rights. President Woodrow Wilson's (1913–1921) opposition to a constitutional amendment caused a series of demonstrations by the suffragettes around the White House after the United States had entered World War I. The protesters insisted that it was wrong for this country to be denying its own female citizens a right to participate in government, while at the same time it was fighting a war on the premise of "making the world safe for democracy."

Finally, President Wilson changed his mind, announcing on January 9, 1918, his support for the proposed suffrage amendment. The House of Representatives approved it the next day by a 274–136 vote, one vote more than the necessary two-thirds majority. The Senate, however, fell short of the two-thirds majority in October 1918 and again in February 1919. Nevertheless, when the Congress elected in November 1918 met for the first time on May 19, 1919, it took little more than two weeks to gain the required majorities in both chambers.

On August 18, 1920, Tennessee became the thirty-sixth state to approve the amendment, enough for ratification. On August 26, Secretary of State Bainbridge Colby (1920–1921) signed a proclamation formally adding the Nineteenth Amendment to the Constitution.

See also: League of Women Voters; Nineteenth Amendment in the **Primary Source Library;** Susan B. Anthony's Speech in the **Primary Source Library;** Women Voters.

Nominating Conventions

The means by which the Democrats, Republicans, and most third-party candidates select their presidential nominee every four years. Although the presidential nominating convention has often been a target of criticism, it has become a traditional fixture of American politics. The convention owes its long life and acceptance to the many functions the convention combines.

Nominating conventions have been used since the early 1830s to choose their candidates for president and vice president. The convention also produces a **platform** containing the party's positions on issues of the campaign. Convention delegates form the supreme governing body of the party and as such they make major decisions on party affairs. Between conventions, such decisions are made by the national committee with the guidance of the party chair.

The convention allows for compromise among the diverse elements within a party, allowing the discussion and often the satisfactory solution of differing points of view. As the ultimate campaign rally, the convention also gathers together thousands of party leaders and rank-and-file members from across the country in an atmosphere that varies widely, sometimes encouraging sober discussion, but often resembling a carnival.

The convention is an outgrowth of the American political experience. Nowhere is it mentioned in the Constitution nor has the authority of the convention ever been a subject of congressional legislation. Rather, the convention has evolved along with the presidential selection process. The convention has been the accepted nominating method of the major political parties since the election of 1832, but changes within the convention system have been massive since the early, formative years.

Locating and Financing Conventions

Before the Civil War, conventions frequently were held in small buildings, even churches, and attracted only several hundred delegates and a minimum of spectators. Transportation and communications were slow, so most conventions were held in the late spring in a city with a central geographical location. (See chart.)

Since 1976, presidential elections have been publicly funded. Early on, the Federal Election Commission (FEC) ruled that host-city contributions to conventions are allowable, enabling the parties to far exceed the technical limit on convention spending. In 1988, for example, the FEC allotted the two major parties $9.2 million each in public funds for their conventions. The money came from an optional check-off for publicly financing presidential campaigns on federal income tax forms. (Congress raised the original $1 check-off to $3 per taxpayer, beginning in 1993.)

In 1992, the Democrats spent a record $38.6 million on their New York City meeting. For the 1996 conventions, the FEC allotted the two major parties $12.4 million each in public funds, but the total spending for both parties, according to experts, was at least twice that amount. In 2004, the federal money given each of the two major parties for their conventions reached more than $14.5 million.

A-Z

N-O

Sites of Major Party Conventions, 1832–2008

	Total	Democratic conventions	Last hosted	Republican conventions	Last hosted
Chicago, Ill.	25	11	1996	14	1960
Baltimore, Md.	10	9	1912	1	1864
Philadelphia, Pa.	8	2	1948	6	2000
St. Louis, Mo.	5	4	1916	1	1896
New York, N.Y.	6	5	1992	1	2004
San Francisco, Calif.	4	2	1984	2	1964
Cincinnati, Ohio	3	2	1880	1	1876
Kansas City, Mo.	3	1	1900	2	1976
Miami Beach, Fla.	3	1	1972	2	1972
Cleveland, Ohio	2	0	–	2	1936
Houston, Texas	2	1	1928	1	1992
Los Angeles, Calif.	2	2	2000	0	–
Atlanta, Ga.	1	1	1988	0	–
Atlantic City, N.J.	1	1	1964	0	–
Charleston, S.C.	1	1	1860	0	–
Dallas, Texas	1	0	–	1	1984
Denver, Colo.	2	2	2008	0	–
Detroit, Mich.	1	0	–	1	1980
Minneapolis, Minn.	2	0	–	2	2008
New Orleans, La.	1	0	–	1	1988
San Diego, Calif.	1	0	–	1	1996
Boston, Ma.	1	1	2004	0	–

The chart above lists the twenty-two cities selected as the sites of major party conventions and the number of conventions they have hosted from the first national gathering for the Democrats (1832) and the Republicans (1856) through the 2008 conventions.

The national committees of the two parties select the sites about one year before the conventions are to take place.

Calling the Convention

The second major step in the convention process follows several months after the site selection with the announcement of the convention call; the establishment of the three major convention committees: credentials, rules, and platform (resolutions); the appointment of convention officers; and, finally, the holding of the convention itself. While these basic steps have changed little since the 1830s, there have been major modifications within the convention system.

The call to the convention sets the date and site of the meeting. It is issued early in each election year, if not before. The call to the first Democratic convention, held in 1832, was issued by the New Hampshire Legislature. Early Whig conventions were called by party members in Congress. With the establishment of national committees later in the nineteenth century, the function of issuing the convention call fell to these new party organizations. Each national committee has the responsibility for determining the number of delegates from each state.

Delegate Selection

Both parties have modified the method of allocating delegates to the individual states and territories. From the beginning of the convention system in the nineteenth century, both the Democrats and Republicans distributed votes to the states based on their Electoral College strength.

The Republicans made the first major change from this procedure after their divisive 1912 convention, in which President William Howard Taft won renomination over former President Theodore Roosevelt. Taft's nomination was due largely to almost solid support from the South—a region vastly overrepresented in relation to its number of Republican voters. Before their 1916 convention the Republicans reduced the allocation of votes to the Southern states.

At their 1924 convention the Republicans applied the first bonus system, by which states were awarded extra votes for supporting the Republican presidential candidate in the previous election. The concept of bonus votes, applied as a reward to the states for supporting the party ticket, has been used and expanded by both parties since that time.

The Democrats first used a bonus system in 1944, completing a compromise arrangement with Southern states for abolishing the party's controversial two-thirds nominating rule. Since then both parties have used various delegate-allocation formulas.

Only 116 delegates from thirteen states attended the initial national nominating convention held by the Anti-Masons in 1831, but with the addition of more states and the adoption of increasingly complex voting-allocation formulas by the major parties, the size of conventions spiraled. The 1976 Republican convention had 2,259 delegates, while the Democrats in the same year had 3,075 delegates casting 3,008 votes. (The number of delegate votes was smaller than the number of delegates because Democratic Party rules provide for fractional voting.)

The expanded size of modern conventions in part reflected their democratization, with less command by a few party leaders and dramatic growth among youth, women, and minority delegations. Increased representation for such groups was one of the major reasons given by the Republicans for the huge increase in delegate strength authorized by the 1972 convention (and effective for the 1976 gathering).

The Democrats adopted new rules in June 1978, expanding the number of delegates by 10 percent to provide extra representation for state and local officials. The new Democratic rules also required that women account for at least 50 percent of the delegates beginning with the 1980 convention. That party's national convention continued to grow throughout the next decade—from 3,331 delegate votes in 1980 to 4,353 in 2004. In contrast, 2,509 delegates attended the 2004 Republican convention in New York City.

Two basic methods of delegate selection were employed in the nineteenth century and continued to be used into the twentieth: the caucus method, by which delegates were chosen by meetings at the local or state level, and the appointment method, by which delegates were appointed by the governor or a powerful state leader.

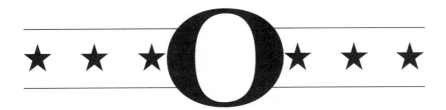

O'Connor, Sandra Day

See Bush v. Gore (2000).

One Person, One Vote

A Supreme Court standard noting that all persons' votes within a district or state should be equal in weight. The one person, one vote rule was first set out by the Court in *Gray v. Sanders* (1963). The Court found, 8–1, that Georgia's county-unit primary system for electing state officials—a system that weighted votes to give advantage to rural districts in statewide primary elections—denied voters the equal protection of the laws. All votes in a statewide election must have equal weight, held the Court:

> **H**ow then can one person be given twice or 10 times the voting power of another person in a statewide election merely because he lives in a rural area or because he lives in the smallest rural county? Once the geographical unit for which a representative is to be chosen is designated, all who par-

ticipate in the election are to have an equal vote—whatever their race, whatever their sex, whatever their occupation, whatever their income, and wherever their home may be in that geographical unit. This is required by the Equal Protection Clause of the Fourteenth Amendment. The concept of "we the people" under the Constitution visualizes no preferred class of voters but equality among those who meet the basic qualification. The idea that every voter is equal to every other voter in his State, when he casts his ballot in favor of one of several competing candidates, underlies many of our decisions. . . . The conception of political equality from the Declaration of Independence to Lincoln's Gettysburg Address, to the Fifteenth, Seventeenth, and Nineteenth Amendments can mean only one thing—one person, one vote.

Wesberry v. Sanders (1964): Congressional Districts

The Court's rulings in *Baker v. Carr* (1962), which held that the reapportionment of congressional districts was not a political question, and *Gray* concerned the equal weighting and counting of votes cast in state elections. In deciding *Wesberry v. Sanders* (1964), the Court applied the one person, one vote principle to congressional districts and set equality, not rationality, as the standard for congressional redistricting. Voters in Georgia's Fifth Congressional District—which includes Atlanta—complained that the population of their congressional district was more than twice the ideal state average of 394,312 persons per district and that the state's failure to redistrict denied them equal protection of the laws. They also challenged Georgia's apportionment scheme as a violation of Article I, Section 2, of the Constitution that declares that members of the House of Representatives are to be elected "by the people." In the majority opinion, Justice Black considered the historical context of the requirement in Article I, Section

2, that representatives be chosen "by the People of the several States." This means, he wrote,

. . .that as nearly as is practicable, one man's vote in a congressional election is to be worth as much as another's. . . .

To say that a vote is worth more in one district than in another would not only run counter to our fundamental ideas of democratic government, it would cast aside the principle of a House of Representatives elected "by the People.

While it may not be possible to draw congressional districts with mathematical precision, that is no excuse for ignoring our Constitution's plain objective of making equal representation for equal numbers the fundamental goal of the House of Representatives.

Justice Black did not invoke the equal protection clause in the case. Speculation as to why Black based this ruling on historical grounds rather than on the Fourteenth Amendment suggests that his approach was a compromise among members of the Court. Four months later, eight members would agree on the requirements of the Fourteenth Amendment for state reapportionment.

Reynolds v. Sims (1964): State Legislative Districts

By a vote of 8–1, the Supreme Court ruled in *Reynolds v. Sims* (1964) that the Fourteenth Amendment required equally populated electoral districts for both houses of bicameral state legislatures. The case, which concerned Alabama, was accompanied to the Supreme Court by a number of others involving other state legislatures. Therefore, the Court's decision immediately affected reapportionment not only in Alabama but also in Colorado, Delaware, New York, Maryland, and Virginia. Ultimately, however, every state legislature would feel the impact of *Reynolds v. Sims*. Chief Justice Earl Warren, writing what he would often describe as the most significant opinion of his judicial career, stated that the "controlling criterion" for any reapportionment plan must be equal population.

Chief Justice Warren set forth the reasoning behind the one person, one vote rule with clarity and firmness:

> The right to vote freely for the candidate of one's choice is of the essence of a democratic society, and any restrictions on that right strike at the heart of representative government. And the right of suffrage can be denied by a debasement of suffrage or dilution of the weight of a citizen's vote just as effectively as by wholly prohibiting the free exercise of the franchise. . . .
>
> Legislators represent people, not trees or acres. Legislators are elected by voters, not farms or cities or economic interests. As long as ours is a representative form of government, and our legislatures are those instruments of government elected directly by and directly representative of the people, the right to elect legislators in a free and unimpaired fashion is a bedrock of our political system. . . .
>
> The Equal Protection Clause demands no less than substantially equal state legislative representation for all citizens, of all places as well as of all races.

The effect of the Court's rulings was felt in every state. By the end of the 1960s, thirty-nine of the forty-five states that elect more than one member of the House had redrawn their district lines. Because the new districts were based on 1960 census figures, however, population shifts during the decade left the new districts far from equal. The redistricting following the 1970 census resulted in substantial progress toward population equality among each state's congressional districts. Three hundred eighty-five of the four hundred thirty-five members of the House of Representatives elected in 1972 were chosen from districts that varied less than 1 percent from their state's average congressional district population.

See also: Baker v. Carr; 📖 *Baker v. Carr* in the **Primary Source Library;** Census; Constitutional Convention; Reapportionment and Redistricting.

PACs: Political Action Committees

Political Action Committees, or PACs, have been around for decades. The Congress of Industrial Organizations (CIO) founded the first modern PAC in 1944 after labor unions were barred from contributing directly. However, their significance increased dramatically in the 1970s and 1980s. The number of registered PACs was 608 at the end of 1974, when the FEC first began its PAC count. It reached a high of 4,268 at the end of 1988 but had dropped to 3,907 by the end of 2007. Registration, however, does not necessarily imply that the PAC actually made contributions during an election cycle.

POINT / COUNTERPOINT

Two Views of PAC Reform

Running for political office is growing increasingly expensive. How to fund campaigns is an ongoing issue, especially the role of Political Action Committees (PACs). The nonpartisan Reform Institute favors further reform of PACs, but Professor Larry Sabato of the University of Virginia opposes further campaign limits.

The Reform Institute

There is great need for increased competition and voter participation in elections. In the 2002 election, which was anticipated to be competitive because of redistricting, less than five congressional races were deemed competitive. The decline of competitive political races mirrors a national trend in voter registration and political party participation. Voters are disengaged and potential candidates are weary of politics because of the high cost of campaigns. It is time to increase voter participation and competition in elections through state-level public financing reform proposal commonly called "Clean Elections laws."

The movement for public campaign funding began in the early 1990s and provides optional public funding for candidates seeking elected offices. The purpose of publicly financed elections is to break down the financial barriers of elections, enabling more qualified candidates to seek public elected office; reduce the dependence of candidates on political donations from powerful special interest groups; and encourage average Americans to participate in the electoral process by making low-level financial contributions to candidate campaigns . . .

At a time when success at the federal level has been achieved through the passage of McCain-Feingold, state-based campaign finance reform is under attack. These reform measures are in their infancy and it is important for reform to continue.

Direct Contributions

The more telling statistics on PAC growth are those on PAC giving. In the 1979–1980 election cycle, PACs contributed $55 million to congressional candidates; in the 1989–1990 election cycle, they reported contributions of nearly $150 million. According to the Federal Election Commission (FEC), in 2003–2004, PACs raised $629.3 million, spent $514.9 million, and contributed $205.1 million to federal candidates.

Why the explosive growth in PAC numbers and dollars? The answer can be found in part in the reform legislation of the 1970s. In 1971, Congress sanctioned the use of regular corporate and union funds to pay the overhead costs of PACs. Legislation in 1974 placed more stringent limits on individual contributions than on those

Professor Larry Sabato

Foremost among the currently popular proposals for campaign finance reform is limiting the amount of PAC money any member of Congress may accept. A number of legislative proposals have been made to restrict a congressional candidate's PAC total to a fixed amount. Like many reforms, it has a certain superficial appeal, but the hidden costs and consequences of the proposal are enormous and destructive.

The effects of a limitation on PAC gifts make it undesirable. First of all, limits could aid incumbents. While it is true that incumbents as a group raise far more PAC money than do challengers, in competitive races (where there is a good chance for the incumbent to lose) challengers sometimes raise substantial amounts from PACs, and that money is usually much more useful to a little-known incumbent. A low cap on PAC gifts would reassure incumbents that, should they find themselves in electoral difficulty, their challengers will have less chance to raise enough money to defeat them. The "PAC cap" may in reality be a "challenger cap."

Limitations on PAC gifts would also help wealthy candidates. Currently, any candidate can spend unrestricted personal funds on his own election; any reduction of an opponent's assets would thus obviously add to the power of the wealthy candidate. It is ironic, in light of the support for PAC limits by labor-oriented Democrats, that a PAC cap is likely to hurt labor and Democratic candidates more than the business interests and Republicans.

The most disturbing consequence of further limits on PAC contributions would be an inevitable increase in independent expenditures, which constitute the least accountable form of political spending. In addition, these contributions are often viciously negative in tone and should hardly be encouraged by the system of campaign finance.

DOCUMENT-BASED QUESTION
Why does the Reform Institute support campaign-funding reform? Why does Professor Sabato oppose further limits?

A – Z

P-R

of PACs. Most PACs, in fact, could give five times more than an individual contributor to a candidate—$5,000 versus $1,000. That same year Congress also lifted restrictions on the formation of PACs by government contractors.

Further PAC growth came in 1975 when the FEC ruled that the Sun Oil Co. could establish a PAC and solicit contributions to SunPAC from stockholders and employees; the ruling eliminated the last barrier that had prevented corporations from forming PACs. FEC figures show that the number of corporate PACs jumped from 139 at the time of the SunPAC ruling in November 1975 to 433 by the end of 1976. PACs also reaped benefits from the Supreme Court's 1976 decision striking down restrictions on independent spending. Reaction to the rapid growth of PAC numbers and influence varied dramatically. Some saw it as a manifestation of democracy at work in a pluralist society, while others perceived it as a threat by special interests to the integrity of the electoral system and governmental process.

Certain facts about PACs have been beyond dispute. For one thing, PACs have been overwhelmingly oriented toward incumbents. FEC figures showed that, of the $245.4 million that congressional candidates in the 1999–2000 election cycle reported receiving from PACs, $184 million went to incumbents, while only about $27 million went to challengers and about $34.3 million to open-seat candidates.

While some critics contended that PACs were out to buy votes with their contributions, many observers believed that their aim was to buy access to members in positions to help—or hinder—their cause. An example of this could be seen in the jump in contributions business PACs made to Democratic incumbents in the House during the 1980s. This increase was attributed to the persuasive powers of California Representative Tony Coelho, chairman of the Democratic Congressional Campaign Committee in the early 1980s, who was said to have convinced traditionally conservative PACs of the logic of having access to a sitting member of the House instead of wasting money on a challenger who was likely to lose.

Thus, pragmatism won out over ideology, as corporate PAC contributions to Democrats edged up to more than 50 percent. With the Republican takeover of Congress in the mid-1990s, corporate PACs returned to old loyalties.

In 1999–2000, corporate PACs gave more than twice as much to the Republicans as to the Democrats in both chambers—nearly $57 million to the GOP and about $27 million to the Democrats. Labor PACs, however, showed none of the corporate PACs' practicality. They were in the Democratic camp when the Democrats controlled Congress and they were in the Democratic camp when the GOP was in control. Of the $50.2 million labor PACs gave to congressional candidates in that same period, about $46 million went to Democrats.

Independent Expenditures

In addition to direct contributions to candidates, PACs also can make independent expenditures. According to a Library of Congress report, PACs made independent expenditures of $14.7 million for or against congressional candidates in the 2000 races. The amount was small when compared to overall PAC spending, but the potential for larger expenditures did exist because there were no limits on them. One often-cited example of the potency of carefully targeted independent expenditures occurred in 1980 when the National Conservative Political Action Committee (NCPAC) spent more than $1 million against six liberal Senate incumbents, four of whom were defeated. Independent spending did not become a major PAC tactic, however, because these expenditures can earn more hostility than gratitude from candidates. They also do not produce the close political relationship with candidates that PACs are seeking.

Leadership PACs

Although PACs are usually associated with interest groups outside Congress, a small but influential group of PACs called "leadership PACs"— also known as "personal PACs," "member PACs," or "politicians' PACs"—exists within Congress. These are separate PACs formed by members of Congress or other political leaders independent of their own campaign committees. They often are the PACs of presidential hopefuls, congressional leaders, or would-be leaders.

Leadership PACs offer several other advantages. If they qualify as multicandidate committees, the PACs can accept $5,000 from individual donors. Because these PACs are considered to be separate from a candidate's campaign committee, the candidate can accept contributions from the same source twice—once for the campaign committee and once for the leadership PAC. These PACs also are increasingly being used as a source of funding for a member's travel or other political expenses. By the late 1990s, several dozen leadership PACs had set up soft money nonfederal accounts to assist state candidates and to cover certain operating expenses.

See also: Buckley v. Valeo (1976); Campaign Finance.

Further Reading

Ainsworth, Scott H. *Analyzing Interest Groups: Group Influence on People and Politics.* New York: W.W. Norton and Company, 2002.

Ciglar, Allan, J., and Burdett A. Loomis. *Interest Groups Politics.* Washington, DC: CQ Press, 2006.

Rozell, Mark J., Clyde Wilcox, and David Madland. *Interest Groups in American Campaigns: The New Face of Electioneering.* Washington, DC: CQ Press, 2005.

Party Platforms

Statements of principles put forth at presidential nominating conventions, designed to represent the political party's policies and goals. The adoption of a party platform is one of the main functions of a convention. The platform committee is charged with the duty of writing a party platform, which is then presented to the convention for its approval.

The main challenge before the platform committee has traditionally been to write a platform all party candidates can use in their campaigns. For this reason platforms often fit the description given them by Wendell L. Willkie, Republican presidential candidate in 1940: "fusions of ambiguity."

Despite the best efforts of platform-builders to resolve their differences, they sometimes encounter a subject so controversial that it cannot be compromised. Under these conditions, dissenting committee members often submit a minority report to the convention floor. Open floor fights are not unusual and often reflect the strength of the various candidates.

When the party has an incumbent president, the platform often is drafted in the White House, or at least has the approval of the president. Rarely does a party adopt a platform that is critical of an incumbent president of the same party. At their 1896 convention, Democratic delegates—inspired by William Jennings Bryan's "Cross of Gold" speech—repudiated President Grover Cleveland and his support for a gold standard for hard currency. They went on to nominate Bryan for president on a "free silver" platform, thus breaking new ground in American politics. A similar change took place in 1948 when Democratic delegates, led by Minneapolis Mayor Hubert Humphrey, overturned a platform committee proposal by adopting a strong civil rights plank. This caused southern delegates to walk out of the convention. President Harry S. Truman accepted the Humphrey plank—and won with it.

The first platform was adopted by the Democrats in 1840. It was a short document, fewer than 1,000 words. Since then the platforms with few exceptions have grown longer and longer, covering more issues and appealing to more and more interest groups. One of the exceptions to the growth trend was the 4,500-word Democratic platform of 1988—about one-tenth the length of the 1984 platform. By 2004, however, the Democrats' platform had grown again, to more than 19,500 words, compared with about 48,000 words in its Republican counterpart.

Third Parties: Radical Ideas

Throughout American history, many daring and controversial political platforms adopted by third parties have been rejected as too radical by the major parties. Yet many of these proposals later have won popular acceptance and have made their way into the major party platforms—and into law. Ideas such as the abolition of slavery, prohibition, the graduated income tax, the popular election of senators, women's suffrage, minimum wages, Social Security, and the eighteen-year-old vote were advocated by Populists, Progressives, and other third parties long before they were finally accepted by the nation as a whole.

The radical third parties and their platforms are typically viewed with scorn by the major parties. Third-party platforms have been denounced as impractical, dangerous, destructive of moral virtues, and even traitorous. They have been antiestablishment and more far-reaching in their proposed solutions to problems than the major parties have dared to be.

Major Parties: Broader Appeal

In contrast with the third parties, Democrats and Republicans traditionally have been much

POINT / COUNTERPOINT

The 2004 Democratic and Republican Platforms

At their respective 2004 National Conventions, the Democratic Party and the Republican Party each explained to the American people how they would confront terrorism. Below are excerpts from each platform.

The 2004 Democratic Platform

A STRONG, RESPECTED AMERICA   Alone among nations, America was born in pursuit of an idea—that a free people with diverse beliefs could govern themselves in peace. For more than a century, America has spared no effort to defend and promote that idea around the world. And over and over, that effort has been marked by the exercise of American leadership to forge powerful alliances based on mutual respect with longtime allies and reluctant friends; with nations already living in the light of democracy and with peoples struggling to join them.

The might of our alliances, coupled with the strength of our democratic ideals, has been a driving force in the survival and success of freedom—in two World Wars, in the Korean War, in the Cold War, in the Gulf War and in Kosovo. America led instead of going it alone. We extended a hand, not a fist. We respected the world—and the world respected us. As Americans, we respect and honor our veterans. We are indebted to all those courageous men and women who have answered our country's call to duty. Their service and sacrifice, their dedication and love of country advance our cause of freedom and uphold our finest traditions as a nation.

That is the America we believe in. That is the America we are fighting for. And that is the America we can be.

John Kerry, John Edwards and the Democratic Party believe in a better, stronger America—an America that is respected, not just feared, and an America that listens and leads. Our vision has deep roots in our Declaration of Independence and Franklin Delano Roosevelt's Four Freedoms, and in the tough-minded tradition of engagement and leadership—a tradition forged by Wilson and Roosevelt in two world wars, then championed by Truman and Kennedy during the Cold War. We believe in an America that people around the world admire, because they know we cherish not just our freedom, but theirs. Not just our democracy, but their hope for it. Not just our peace and security, but the world's. We believe in an America that cherishes freedom, safeguards our people, forges alliances, and commands respect. That is the America we are going to build.

The 2004 Republican Platform

A Comprehensive Strategy to Win the War on Terror, Promote Peace, and Build a Better World   The world changed on September 11,

2001, and since that day, under the strong, steady, and visionary leadership of President George W. Bush, Americans have helped make the world not only safer, but better. The President continues to lead a steady, confident, systematic campaign to defend America against the dangers of our time. We are going after terrorists wherever they plot and plan and hide, changing the old course of pinprick strikes that did little to get at the root of terrorism. We eliminated many of al Qaeda's key leaders and put the world on notice that nations that train, harbor, or finance terrorists are just as guilty as the terrorists themselves. We will not allow the world's most dangerous regimes to possess the world's most dangerous weapons. Our message is getting through, as indicated by Libya's leader, who decided to turn over his weapons of mass destruction and cooperate with the international community. Today, because America has acted, and because America has led, the forces of terror and tyranny have suffered defeat after defeat, and America and the world are safer.

On September 11, 2001, we saw the cruelty of the terrorists, and we glimpsed the future they intend for us. They intend to strike the United States to the limits of their power. They seek weapons of mass destruction to kill Americans on an even greater scale. This danger is increased when outlaw regimes build or acquire weapons of mass destruction and maintain ties to terrorist groups. . . .

The President's most solemn duty is to protect our country. George W. Bush has kept that charge. . . .

We affirm the three commitments of the President's strategy for peace:

- Terrorists long ago declared war on America, and now America has declared war against terrorists. We are defending the peace by taking the fight to the enemy. We are confronting terrorists overseas so we do not have to confront them here at home. We are destroying the leadership of terrorist networks in sudden raids, disrupting their planning and financing, and keeping them on the run. Month by month, we are shrinking the space in which they can freely operate, by denying them territory and the support of governments.

- Nations that support terrorism are just as dangerous, and just as guilty, as the perpetrators of terrorism. Every nation must make a choice to support terror or to support America and our coalition to defeat terror . . .

- There is no negotiation with terrorists. No form of therapy or coercion will turn them from their murderous ways. Only total and complete destruction of terrorism will allow freedom to flourish . . .

DOCUMENT-BASED QUESTION
What common ground do the platforms share?

A – Z

P-R

more cautious about adopting radical platform planks. Trying to appeal to a broad range of voters, the two major parties have tended to compromise differences or to reject controversial platform planks.

The Democratic Party has been more ready than the Republican Party to adopt once-radical ideas. However, usually here is a considerable time lag between an idea's origin in a third party and its eventual adoption in a Democratic platform. For example, while the Democrats by 1912 had adopted many of the Populist planks of the 1890s, the Bull Moose Progressives of that year were already way ahead of them in proposals for social legislation. Not until 1932 were many of the 1912 Progressive planks adopted by the Democrats. Similarly, it was not until the 1960s that Democratic platforms incorporated many of the more far-reaching proposals originally put forward by the 1948 Progressive Party in that year.

See also: Anti-Masonic Party; Election of 1896; Election of 1912; Election of 1948; Nominating Conventions; Populist Party; Progressive Party.

Peace and Freedom Party (1967–)

A leftist third party that opposed the Vietnam War and favored black nationalism. Although founded in Michigan, the radical Peace and Freedom Party has been active largely in California—the only state where it appeared on the ballot in 1996. From the outset, the party worked with the California Black Panther Party. The first Peace and Freedom nominee for president, in 1968, was Black Panther leader Eldridge Cleaver (1935–1998). Running with various vice-presidential candidates, Cleaver received 36,563 votes.

Cleaver's autobiographical *Soul on Ice,* was published in 1968. After the election Cleaver, a paroled convict awaiting trial for murder, went into exile. On his return years later, he became a born-again Christian.

Before the 1968 election, African American activist-comedian Dick Gregory broke with the Peace and Freedom Party and set up the similarly named Freedom and Peace Party with

himself as the presidential nominee. He received 47,133 votes.

After 1968, no Peace and Freedom candidate attracted significant numbers of presidential votes until 1980 when Maureen Smith and Elizabeth Barron received 18,116. In 1972, however, noted pacifist and pediatrician Benjamin Spock, the People's Party nominee, ran under the Peace and Freedom banner in California. He received 55,167 votes there and 23,589 votes in other states.

In 1974, the California Peace and Freedom Party declared itself to be socialist. In recent elections, its presidential ticket has received at least 10,000 votes: 1988, Herbert Lewin and Vikki Murdock, 10,370; 1992, Ron Daniels and Asiba Tupahache, 27,961; and 1996, Marsha Feinland and Kate McClatchy, 25,332. In 2000, the party ran no presidential candidates. In 2004, however, the party ran Leonard Peltier and Janice Jordan, who received 27,607 votes.

Pelosi, Nancy

See Women in Congress.

People's Party (1891–1908)

See Populist Party (1891–1908).

People's Party (1971–)

A third party formed in 1971 in Dallas, Texas, by various activist and peace groups. The initial cochairmen were pediatrician Benjamin Spock and author Gore Vidal. The People's Party first ran a presidential candidate in 1972. They chose Dr. Spock for president and black activist Julius Hobson of Washington, D.C., for vice president. Despite hopes for widespread backing from the poor and social activists, the ticket received only 78,756 votes, 0.1 percent of the national total.

A total of 55,167 of those votes came from California alone.

At its next convention, held in St. Louis, Missouri, on August 31, 1975, the People's Party chose civil rights activist Margaret Wright of California for president and Maggie Kuhn of Pennsylvania, a leader in the Gray Panthers movement for rights for the elderly, for vice president. Kuhn, however, declined the nomination and was replaced on the ticket by Spock.

The party platform focused on cutting the defense budget, closing tax loopholes, and making that money available for social programs. Other planks included redistribution of land and wealth, unconditional amnesty for war objectors, and free health care. In her campaign, Wright stressed the necessity for active participation by citizens in the governmental process, so that institutions and programs could be run from the grass roots up rather than from the top down.

As in 1972, the party's main backing came in California, where it was supported by the state Peace and Freedom Party. Wright's total national vote in 1976 was 49,024, and 85.1 percent (41,731 votes) of those votes came from California. The party has not fielded presidential candidates since 1976.

See also: Peace and Freedom Party.

Political Parties, Development and Role of

Organizations whose leaders seek to gain control of government to further their social, economic, or ideological goals. The United States usually has had a two-party system, dominated since 1860 by the Democratic and Republican Parties. Yet more than eighty political parties have formed since the 1790s, and "third parties" have occasionally had a decisive impact on presidential elections. For example, in 1912 the Bull Moose Party of former president Theodore Roosevelt took enough Republican votes from the incumbent, William H. Taft, al-

lowing the Democrat, Woodrow Wilson, to win the election.

Development of Political Parties

The United States did not start out with a two-party system—or any parties at all. Initially there were no formal parties, and in the early 1820s, the nation had only one party. The Founders did not anticipate parties—which they scornfully called factions. This central aspect of American politics was unplanned and had no formal constitutional or legal status. Indeed, having seen the ill effects of overzealous parties in England and, beginning in 1789, in revolutionary France, the Founders hoped to avoid similar pitfalls in the young nation. Thus, in *Federalist Number 10*—one of a series of essays that supported the ratification of the Constitution—James Madison bragged that one of the Constitution's great virtues was that it would head off "the mischiefs of faction." In his 1796 farewell address George Washington warned that, in elective popular governments, the dangers of excess in the "spirit of party" demanded "a uniform vigilance to prevent its bursting into a flame."

By the time Washington issued his warning, however, he was viewed as the leader of the Federalist Party, which faded after 1800 and disappeared by 1821. Meanwhile, since 1794 Madison and Jefferson had been the leaders of another party, sometimes called the Democratic-Republicans, the Jeffersonian Democrats, or the Jeffersonian Republicans. The party of Jefferson and Madison is the source of today's Democratic Party.

Political Issues and the Emergence of Parties

The debate over ratification of the Constitution led to the organization of factions, but not political parties. Future Democratic-Republicans and Federalists—Madison and Alexander Hamilton, for example—worked together for ratification, just as future Democratic-Republicans and Federalists—James Monroe and Samuel Chase—worked against ratification of the Constitution.

Ratification brought about a new national government, but political parties did not yet exist. Presidential electors unanimously elected Washington as the first president, and nearly

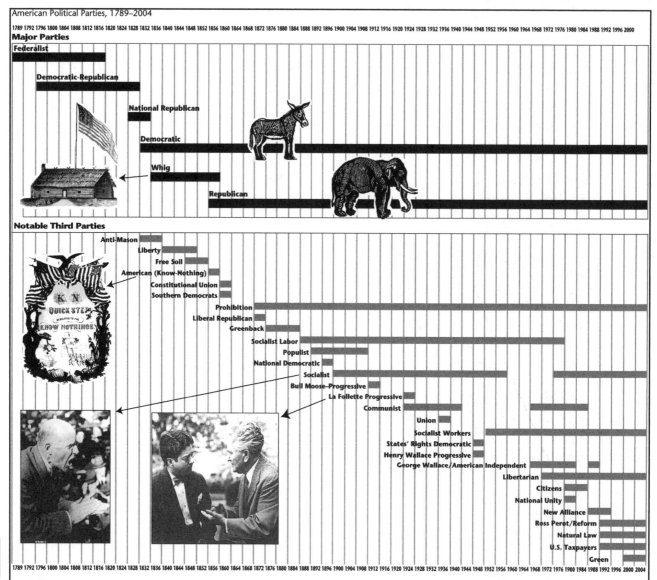

American Political Parties, 1789–2004

Although numerous "third parties" have developed over the years, the Democratic Party and the Republican Party have dominated U.S. politics since the mid-nineteenth century.

half of them supported Adams who was easily elected vice president. Washington's cabinet included future leaders of the nation's first two parties: the future Federalist leader Alexander Hamilton and the future leader of the Democratic-Republicans, Thomas Jefferson.

By the end of Washington's administration, two parties were fully engaged in politics. The parties differed over the nature of public policy and the interpretation of the Constitution. The Federalists, led by Hamilton, John Adams, and John Jay, favored a national government deeply involved in economic development. Key to the Federalist program was the establishment of a

national bank, federal funding at face value of all state and national bonds issued during the Revolution, and a flexible interpretation of the Constitution. The Federalists also wanted to strengthen diplomatic and commercial ties with Great Britain.

Jefferson's followers, called Democratic-Republicans at the time, opposed funding the war debts at face value because many of the original bondholders had sold their bonds at depreciated values to speculators. Their opposition to commerce and business also led them to fight the establishment of a national bank. Jefferson and his followers wanted a strict interpretation of the Constitution, favored states' rights over national power, and, in foreign policy, supported France in its wars with Britain.

On issues involving race, slavery, and foreign policy, the parties also differed. For example, the Federalists favored full diplomatic recognition for Haiti, an African American republic in the Caribbean, and refused to seek the return of slaves who had escaped with the British at the end of the Revolution. Jefferson, in contrast, unsuccessfully demanded the return of the slaves, but was successful as president in blocking any diplomatic ties to Haiti.

Presidents, Parties, and Policies, 1800–1860

By the time of Jefferson's election in 1800, political parties were well established in U.S. politics. Jefferson's election by the House of Representatives, after a tie electoral vote between him and Aaron Burr, led to adoption of the Twelfth Amendment to the Constitution in 1804. That amendment, which required electors to vote separately for president and vice president, further buried the likelihood of "partyless" U.S. elections.

Early Years

Federalists nearly won the presidency in 1800 and 1812, but the party quickly withered after the War of 1812 when many party leaders opposed the war and flirted with secession, most notably at the **Hartford Convention** of 1814–1815. By 1820, when James Monroe ran unopposed for reelection, the Federalist Party was gone.

A political system with only one party was less stable than a system with two or more parties. In 1824, four candidates competed for the presidency, with no one getting a majority of the popular or the electoral vote. The House chose John Quincy Adams who ran second in both categories. Andrew Jackson, who had led in popular and electoral votes, immediately began his campaign for the presidency, and he won in 1828. In 1832, the Anti-Masonic Party made its brief appearance, winning seven electoral votes, while Jackson was easily reelected.

Jackson was viewed as the successor to Jefferson and his party, while his political and personal opponents, including Daniel Webster, Henry Clay, and John Quincy Adams, switched in the 1830s to the newly formed Whig Party. In 1836, four Whigs, representing different regions of the country, competed for the presidency against Jackson's handpicked successor, Martin Van Buren.

Jacksonian Democrats vs. Whigs

The Whigs won the presidency in 1840 and 1848; Democrats won in 1836, 1844, 1852, and 1856. The Whigs favored a national bank, federal support for internal improvements, national bankruptcy laws, protective tariffs, and a relatively humane policy toward American Indians. The Democrats disagreed with all these positions. Whigs opposed territorial acquisition, especially by force, whereas Democrats annexed Texas and eventually pushed the United States into a war with Mexico to gain new territory in the Southwest, believing that it was the "manifest destiny" of the United States to control the continent. The Jacksonian Democrats pushed to give the vote to all adult white men, but at the same time worked to take the vote away from free African Americans and to strengthen slavery. Jackson's presidency is often remembered for his veto of the rechartering of the Second Bank of the United States, his successful opposition to internal improvements, and his policy of Indian removal, which pushed almost all Native Americans in the East into the Indian Territory, present-day Oklahoma.

Although the nation had two major parties in the 1840s, third parties influenced some elections. In 1844, the antislavery Liberty Party won enough votes in New York to cost the Whigs the state and the presidential election, assuming all the Liberty voters would have supported the Whigs. In 1848, however, the Free Soil candidate, former president Martin Van Buren, won more than 290,000 votes, many of which would have otherwise gone to the Democratic candidate, Lewis Cass of Michigan. As a result, the Whig candidate, General Zachary Taylor, won the election.

Yet the victorious Whigs of 1848 managed to carry only four states in 1852, and the party disappeared two years later. The 1856 election saw two new parties emerge: the Know Nothing, or American, Party and the Republican Party.

A–Z

P-R

The Republican Party

The Know Nothing Party was a single-issue party, opposed to immigration in general and Catholic immigration in particular. The Republican Party adopted many Whig policies but opposed the extension of slavery into the Western territories. Many Republican leaders were former Whigs, including Abraham Lincoln and William H. Seward. Others came from the antislavery wing of the Democratic Party, among them Hannibal Hamlin and Salmon P. Chase. By 1858, many Know Nothings had also joined the Republicans. In 1856 the Republican candidate, John C. Fremont, and the Know Nothing candidate, Millard Fillmore, together won about 400,000 more popular votes than did James Buchanan, but Buchanan had the plurality of popular votes and, more important, carried nineteen states to win the election. Buchanan was the first sectional president since 1824, as fourteen of the states he carried were in the South. The 1856 election clearly pointed out that the Democrats had become the party of slavery and of the South.

The proslavery Southerners who controlled the Democratic Party insisted on their program to expand slavery into the territories. This arrangement unraveled in 1860, as the Democrats split into two parties: regular Democrats nominating Stephen A. Douglas of Illinois and southern Democrats nominating John C. Breckinridge of Kentucky. The Republican candidate, Abraham Lincoln, carried every Northern state. Moderates in the North and the South supported the Constitutional Union Party, which hoped to hold the Union together by not discussing any of the key issues. The two Democratic parties and the Constitutional Unionists combined for more popular votes than Lincoln—who was not even on the ballot in many Southern states—but Lincoln carried eighteen states and easily won a majority of the electoral college.

Political Parties since 1860

Lincoln's 1860 victory set the stage for Republican dominance in national politics for the next half-century. During this period, the Republicans stood at various times for preservation of the Union, homestead laws to facilitate Western settlement, federal support for a transcontinental railroad, protective tariffs, abolition of slavery, guarantees of African American civil rights, and the suppression of Mormon polygamists in the West. Democrats favored lower tariffs; opposed emancipation and civil rights; and championed white immigrants (but not immigrants from Asia), labor unions, and, at the end of the century, small farmers in the South and West. In foreign affairs, the late-nineteenth-century Republicans favored expansion, ultimately leading to war with Spain and the acquisition of an overseas empire, while Democrats opposed these trends. Grover Cleveland—the only Democratic president in this period—refused to annex Hawaii.

From 1868 to 1908, various third parties—including the Liberal Republican, Greenback, Prohibitionist, Equal Rights, Anti-Monopoly, Workers, Socialist Labor, Socialist, United Christian, and Populist Parties—ran candidates. With the exception of the Populists in 1892, however, none ever won any electoral votes.

In 1912, a third party determined the outcome of the presidential race. The Republicans split as former president Theodore Roosevelt tried, and failed, to gain renomination after a term out of the White House. Roosevelt thought that his successor, William Howard Taft, had abandoned the progressive goals of the party. Running on the Progressive, or Bull Moose, ticket, Roosevelt carried six states and won about half a million more popular votes than did Taft. Together they outpolled Wilson, but Wilson carried forty states and won the election.

Between the 1910s and the 1940s, Democrats became increasingly internationalist, while Republicans opposed American entrance into the League of Nations after World War I and were isolationist in the 1930s as the world moved toward war. Democratic support came from labor, white Southerners, and most Northern urban immigrant groups. By the 1930s, African Americans began to leave the Republican Party, forced out by Southern white Republicans and welcomed into the emerging Democratic New Deal coalition. By this time, the Republicans had become the party of conservative business interests, white Protestants (outside the South), small town and rural Northerners, and owners of small businesses.

Several third parties ran presidential candidates in the 1920s and 1930s, but only Robert M. La Follette, running as the Progressive Party candidate in 1924, won any electoral votes. In 1948, though, Southern "Dixiecrats," who abandoned the Democratic Party to protest President Harry S. Truman's support for civil rights and racial equality, took four Deep South states. Some other Democrats supported former vice president Henry A. Wallace, running on the Progressive ticket that year. Despite these defections, Truman won.

By the 1960s, Republicans and Democrats had changed places on the issue of African American civil rights since a hundred years earlier. In 1964, large numbers of white Southerners left the Democratic Party over President Lyndon Johnson's support for civil rights. Since then, Democratic Party supporters have generally comprised urban, Northern, and far Western liberals; Catholics and Jews; African Americans, Hispanics, Asian-Americans, and ethnic minorities; blue-collar workers; and the underprivileged. Republicans are viewed as conservatives, Southerners, white Protestants, and the affluent.

In 1968, George C. Wallace, running as the presidential candidate of the segregationist American Independent Party, captured five states in the South. In 1980, former U.S. representative John Anderson ran on the National Unity Party ticket and won more than 5 million popular votes, but he did not affect the election of Ronald Reagan. In 1992, H. Ross Perot ran as an independent and won almost 20 million votes, and he may have cost the incumbent, George Herbert Walker Bush, a few states. When he ran again in 1996, however, he had no effect on the election. In 2000, Ralph Nader, running on the Green Party ticket, won enough votes in several states to give their electoral college votes to Republican George W. Bush instead of Vice President Al Gore.

See also: Democratic Party; Election of 1800; Election of 1824; Election of 1860; Election of 1948; Federalist Party; Progressive Party; Republican Party; Third Parties; The Twelfth Amendment; 📖 The Twelfth Amendment in the **Primary Source Library;** Whig Party.

Further Reading

Aldrich, John H. *Why Parties? The Origin and Transformation of Political Parties in America.* Chicago: University of Chicago Press, 1995.

Blevins, David. *American Political Parties in the 21st Century.* Jefferson, NC: McFarland & Company, 2006.

Scarrow, Susan E., ed. *Perspectives on Political Parties: Classic Readings.* New York: Palgrave Macmillan Press, 2002.

A – Z

P-R

JUSTICE FOR ALL

Virginia Foster Durr

Born in 1903, Virginia Foster Durr was a lifelong civil rights activist and lobbyist. In 1933, she and her husband moved to Washington, D.C. While living in Washington, Virginia Durr helped found the Southern Conference for Human Welfare, an interracial organization committed to easing segregation in the South. Working with First Lady Eleanor Roosevelt, Durr lobbied for laws to end the poll tax.

In 1951, she and her husband moved back to Montgomery, Alabama, where they became involved in the civil rights movement. Later, in 1955, Durr posted bail for Rosa Parks after Parks was arrested for refusing to give up her bus seat to a white person. Durr was a strong supporter of the civil rights movement for the rest of her life. She died in 1999.

Poll Tax

A device used in limiting both African American and white voters. The poll tax required the payment of a fee before voting. The amount of the poll tax ranged from one to two dollars, but in Alabama, Mississippi, Virginia, and Georgia before 1945, the tax was cumulative. Thus a new voter in Georgia could face up to $47 in fees. Various regulations as to the time and manner of payment of the tax also substantially reduced the number of voters. In Mississippi, for example, a person wanting to vote in the Democratic primary (usually held in August) had to pay the poll tax on or before the first day of the two preceding Februarys—long before most voters had even begun to think about the election.

The poll tax was barred in federal elections by ratification of the Twenty-fourth Amendment in January 1964. The amendment simply stated that the

> . . . **r**ight of citizens of the United States to vote in any primary or other election . . . shall not be denied or abridged by the United States or any other State by reason of failure to pay any poll tax or other tax.

See also: Twenty-fourth Amendment.

Popular Sovereignty

See Majority Rule.

Populist Party (1891–1908)

Founded in May 1891, in Cincinnati, Ohio, a third party that grew out of the era's agrarian unrest and remained politically active until 1908. Following the Civil War (1861–1865), farmers battled falling commodity prices, high railroad rates, and heavy mortgage debt. The Patrons of Husbandry, a farmers' group better known as the **Grange,** was organized in 1867 by Oliver Kelley. Its original purpose was to improve educational and social opportunities for farm men and women, but it soon adopted economic and political initiatives, such as the cooperative movement of the 1870s.

The inability of the Grange to give farmers an effective political voice led many Grangers, in the 1880s, to join the Farmers' Alliance. More aggressive and politically oriented, the Farmers' Alliance considered all agricultural problems to be economic problems. Existing racial prejudices led to the separate creation of a Colored Farmers' National Alliance in 1888.

In June 1890, Kansas farmers founded the People's Party based on the Southern Alliance platform. The platform called for government ownership of railroads and free and unlimited coinage of silver. It also favored a subtreasury, a

Populist Party presidential nominee James B. Weaver won a total of twenty-two electoral votes: three from Nevada, four from Colorado, ten from Kansas, three from Idaho, one from Oregon, and one from North Dakota. Weaver was the first third-party candidate to win any electoral votes since the election of 1860. (The Granger Collection, New York)

system in which farmers could turn over a staple crop to a government warehouse and receive a loan for 80 percent of its value at 2 percent interest per month. As a national third party in 1891, the Populists sought a farmer-laborer political coalition that championed the belief, expressed by Minnesota Populist Ignatius Donnelly, that the "public good is paramount to private interests."

For a time the party attempted to bridge the racial gulf and recruited African American as well as white farmers. Populism in the South, however, became mired in the race issue. The Populist Party was more concerned with achieving economic reforms and a humane industrial society than it was with attacking cultural issues. The party's greatest support came from white land-owning cotton farmers in the South and wheat farmers in the West. The Populists rallied behind a policy of monetary inflation, hoping it would increase the amount of currency in circulation, boost prices of farm products, and ease farmers' indebtedness. In 1892, when the People's Party nominated James B. Weaver of Iowa as its presidential candidate, its demands included a graduated income tax, antitrust regulations, public ownership of railroads, and unlimited coinage of silver and gold at a ratio of sixteen to one. Democrat Grover Cleveland was elected to a second term, with electoral strength for Weaver coming from the West. In 1896, the Populists nominated William Jennings Bryan, a free-silver candidate from Ne-

braska who was also the Democratic nominee, but the Republicans won with William McKinley.

Having lost on the silver issue and having lost their identity by aligning with the Democrats, the Populists declined in strength and influence, particularly as new discoveries of gold eased the monetary crisis and agricultural conditions improved. Although the People's Party declined, some of the reforms it championed, including a graduated income tax, were later instituted during the **Progressive era**. The Populists' significance was their visionary use of politics to turn a spotlight on the conditions facing farm families, thereby seeking more democratic reform measures.

Presidential Debates

Debates between presidential candidates are a relatively recent occurrence. Until the second half of the twentieth century, White House nominees

The Election of 1960 marked the beginning of televised debates between presidential candidates. Republican Vice President Richard M. Nixon (standing, far right) makes a point while Democratic Senator John F. Kennedy (seated, far left) takes notes. Many political experts believe that the debates persuaded many viewers to vote for Kennedy in the November election. (Bettmann/Corbis)

did not debate. Richard Nixon and John F. Kennedy began the debate tradition on September 26, 1960, with the first of four televised meetings. When Abraham Lincoln and Stephen Douglas held their famed debates in 1858, they were Senate candidates; they did not debate as presidential candidates two years later.

There were no debates from 1960 until 1976, when President Gerald R. Ford

POINT / COUNTERPOINT

Two Views on Presidential Debates

In 1960, the first televised presidential debates were held between Vice President Richard Nixon and Massachusetts Senator John F. Kennedy. At the time, most voters felt that Kennedy "won" the debates and they helped him with his close election victory. Presidential debates have been held prior to every election since 1976. Voters and experts disagree on the value of the debates. Professors William Benoit of the University of Missouri and Glenn Hansen of the University of Oklahoma believe the debates are useful. Many voters, however, seem to disagree.

The Debates are Valuable to Voters

There are several reasons political debates are important campaign events. First, debates present the leading candidates together discussing the same topics. This facilitates comparison of candidates by voters. A second reason debates matter is their length: ninety minutes for general election debates (after the four sixty-minute debates of 1960). This provides voters with an extended opportunity to hear the candidates. Although there are more television spots than debates, each debate is far longer than any individual ad (which are mostly thirty seconds in recent campaigns). Third, although the number who watch debates varies, millions of voters watch general debates . . . The size of the audience for presidential debates means they have a capacity for influence. Furthermore, the face-to-face nature of debates provides candidates a chance to reply to opponents (refuting allegedly

(1974–1977), running behind in the polls, agreed to debate the Democratic nominee, former Georgia governor Jimmy Carter. The relatively unknown Carter gained stature in the exchange when Ford made a gaffe by saying he did not believe East European nations were under Soviet Union control. Since 1976, all major party nominees have debated on live television. Independent candidate Perot was included in the presidential debates in 1992, but he was excluded as the Reform Party nominee in 1996. In 2000, Republican George W. Bush and Democrat Al Gore debated three times. In 2004, incumbent George W. Bush (2001–2009) and Democratic challenger John Kerry held three debates.

Unlike formal, academic debates, the presidential confrontations have been loosely structured,

at first with a panel of journalists or audience members asking the questions. Beginning in 1992 debate sponsors began having a journalist moderator question the candidates, with the audience sometimes allowed to participate. Throughout there have been no judges to award points and therefore no way to determine who "won" or "lost" except by public opinion polling. Media commentators make immediate assessments of winners and losers, however, and their judgments undoubtedly influence the public's opinion about which candidate "won" the debate.

With one exception, vice-presidential nominees have debated since 1976 when Ford's running mate Robert Dole faced Democrat Walter F. Mondale. There was no debate in 1980 between Vice President Mondale and the Republican nominee, George Bush. The nominees in

false attacks, puncturing unreasonable claims); such clash could be beneficial for voters. Finally, although candidates prepare extensively for debates, questions or statements from opponents that have not been anticipated can offer voters a more spontaneous (and possibly less contrived) impression of the candidates than they can obtain from other messages . . .

The Debates Do Not Influence Voters

Fifteen percent (15%) of American adults say that Presidential debates are exciting. The latest Rasmussen Reports national telephone survey found that 58% say they are boring. Sixty-three percent (63%) of men and 54% of women find the debates boring.

Thirty percent (30%) say that the debates are informative while 50% say they are useless. Older Americans are more likely to find the debates useless than younger adults.

Ratings show that the most recent debate attracted 2.6 million viewers, a very small percentage of the electorate. A Rasmussen Reports analysis suggested that the debates may have little impact and that "only a major gaffe or startling policy pronouncement will break through the news clutter and impact the general public's view of the race."

DOCUMENT-BASED QUESTION
Compare the two views on presidential debates.

A–Z

P-R

2000, Republican Richard Cheney and Democrat Joseph I. Lieberman, debated once. In the 2004 contest, Republican Richard Cheney and Democrat John Edwards also debated once.

Early in the presidential debate era, the television networks or the League of Women Voters sponsored the debates. Since 1988, they have been sponsored by the bipartisan Commission on Presidential Debates.

See also: Elections, Presidential; Election of 1960; League of Women Voters.

Presidential Disability

See Twenty-fifth Amendment.

Pressure Groups

See Interest Groups; PACs.

Primary Elections, Presidential

A revolutionary new mechanism for delegate selection emerged during the early 1900s: the presidential primary election in which the voters directly elected convention delegates. Initiated in Florida at the turn of the twentieth century, by 1912 the presidential primary was used by thirteen states. In his first annual message to Congress the following year, President Woodrow Wilson advocated the establishment of a national primary to select presidential candidates:

> I feel confident that I do not misinterpret the wishes or the expectations of the country when I urge the prompt enactment of legislation which will provide for primary elections throughout the country at which the voters of several parties may choose their nominees for the presidency without the intervention of nominating conventions.

Wilson went on to suggest the retention of conventions for the purpose of declaring the results of the primaries and formulating the parties' platforms.

Before any action was taken on Wilson's proposal, the progressive spirit that prompted the growth of presidential primaries died out. Not until the late 1960s and early 1970s, when widespread pressures for change touched both parties, but especially the Democratic, was there a rapid growth in presidential primaries. In the mid-1980s, some states reverted to the caucus method of delegate selection, but their revival quickly ended. A record 34 states held primaries in 2008, plus the District of Columbia and Puerto Rico.

In many states, participation in the presidential primary is restricted to voters belonging to the party holding the primary. In some states, however, participation by voters outside the party is allowed by state-mandated open primaries, usually with the caveat, though, that the party in which they cast a primary ballot is publicly recorded.

Rules in the 1980s and 1990s

In June 1982, the Democratic National Committee (DNC) adopted several changes in the presidential nominating process recommended by the party's Commission on Presidential Nominations, chaired by Governor James B. Hunt, Jr., of North Carolina. The Hunt Commission, as it came to be known, suggested

revisions to increase the power of party regulars and give the convention more freedom to act on its own. It was the fourth time in twelve years that the Democrats, struggling to repair their nominating process without repudiating earlier reforms, had rewritten their party rules.

One major change in the Democrats' rules was the creation of a new group of "superdelegates," party and elected officials who would go to the 1984 convention uncommitted and would cast about 14 percent of the ballots. The DNC also adopted a Hunt Commission proposal to weaken the rule binding delegates to vote for their original presidential preference on the first convention ballot. The new rule also allowed a presidential candidate to replace any disloyal delegate with a more faithful one.

One of the most significant revisions was the Democrats' decision to relax proportional representation at the convention and end the ban on the "loophole"—primary-winner-take-all by district. Proportional representation is the distribution of delegates among candidates to reflect their share of the primary or caucus vote, both statewide and in congressional districts. Mandated by party rules in 1980, it was blamed by some Democrats for the protracted primary fight between President Jimmy Carter and Senator Edward M. Kennedy of Massachusetts. Because candidates needed only about 20 percent of the vote in most places to qualify for a share of the delegates, Kennedy was able to remain in contention. While the system kept the Kennedy campaign going, it did nothing to help his chances of winning the nomination.

Although the Democrats' 1984 rules permitted states to retain proportional representation, they also allowed states to take advantage of two options that could help a front-running candidate build the momentum to wrap up the nomination early in the year.

One was a winner-take-more system. States could elect to keep proportional representation but adopt a winner bonus plan that would award the top vote-getter in each district one extra delegate.

The other option was a return to the **loophole primary,** which party rules outlawed in 1980—with exceptions allowing Illinois and West Virginia to retain their loophole voting systems. In the loophole states, voters balloted directly for delegates, with each delegate candidate identified by presidential preference. Sometimes several presidential contenders would win at least a fraction of the delegates in a given district, but the most common result is a sweep by the presidential front-runner, even if he or she has less than an absolute majority. Loophole primaries aid the building of a consensus behind the front-runner, while still giving other candidates a chance to inject themselves back into the race by winning a major loophole state decisively.

The DNC retained the delegate-selection season adopted in 1978, a three-month period stretching from the second Tuesday in March to the second Tuesday in June. In an effort to reduce the growing influence of early states in the nominating process, however, the Democrats required Iowa and New Hampshire to move their highly publicized elections to late winter. Party rules maintained the privileged status of Iowa and New Hampshire before other states, but mandated that their initial nominating rounds be held only eight days apart in 1984. Five weeks had intervened between the Iowa caucuses and New Hampshire primary in 1980.

The DNC also retained rules requiring primary states to set candidate filing deadlines thirty to ninety days before the election and limiting participation in the delegate selection process to Democrats only. This last rule eliminated cross over primaries where voters could participate in the Democratic primary without designating their party affiliation. African Americans and Hispanics won continued endorsement of affirmative action in the new party rules. Women gained renewed support for the equal division rule, which required state delegations at the national convention to be divided equally between men and women.

The Democratic Party's 1988 presidential nominating process remained basically the same as that used in 1984. The rules adopted by the national committee included only minor modifications suggested by the party's rules review panel, the Fairness Commission.

The bloc of uncommitted party and elected officials, or superdelegates, was expanded slightly to 16 percent and rearranged to reserve more convention seats for members of Congress, governors, and the DNC. The rules, restricting participation in Democratic primaries and caucuses to Democrats only, were relaxed so the open primaries in Wisconsin and Montana could be conducted with the approval of the national party. In addition, the share of the vote a candidate needed to win in a primary or caucus to qualify for delegates was lowered from the 20 percent level, used in most places in 1984, to 15 percent.

Only the rule regarding the 15 percent "threshold" spawned much debate during the rules-writing process, and though the discussion of the issue seldom was harsh, it did reveal a gap in the party on what the proper role of the national convention should be.

Most party leaders, including DNC Chairman Paul G. Kirk Jr. wanted a threshold of at least 15 percent because they thought it would help steadily shrink the field of presidential candidates during the primary and caucus season and ensure that the convention would be a "ratifying" body that confirmed the choice of the party's voters.

Civil rights leader and presidential candidate Jesse L. Jackson, however, saw it differently, as did several other liberal activists. They wanted a convention that was more "deliberative," and they complained that getting one was virtually impossible under the system as it existed because it discriminated against long-shot candidates and produced an artificial consensus behind one candidate.

Most Democratic leaders were satisfied with the way the nominating process operated in 1984, and they felt it would be a disaster for the party to go through a free-wheeling, multiballot convention. Not since 1952—at the beginning of the television age—has a national party taken more than one ballot to nominate its presidential candidate.

A – Z

P-R

At the DNC meeting where the new rules were approved, some African-American committee members joined with a few white liberal activists in proposing to eliminate the 15 percent threshold altogether. The proposal was rejected by voice vote. A second proposal to lower the threshold to 10 percent was defeated 92 to 178.

The Democrats required all states, beginning in 1992, to divide their publicly elected delegates proportionally among candidates who drew at least 15 percent of the primary or caucus vote. The Democratic Party also continued to steadily increase the number of superdelegates, expanding their number to 1,260 for the 2004 convention.

During the 1972–1996 period the Republican Party followed an entirely different approach and made few changes in its nominating rules. While the Democratic party rules were revised somewhat for each presidential cycle, the GOP rules remained stable. For the year 2000, however, the Republicans changed their minds on the desirability of deciding the nomination contest by March or April; they provided a bonus for those states that choose their delegates to the 2000 GOP convention after March 15th.

Before the 2000 convention was even held, though, Republicans were considering even more controversial solutions to spread out the primary calendar which had become congested with events in February and March. The so-called "Delaware Plan" would have put the smallest states at the beginning of the nominating season in 2004, the largest states at the end. Nevertheless, after winning the approval of the Republican National Committee (RNC) at its preconvention meeting, the proposal was killed by the convention rules committee at the behest of the party standard-bearer, Governor George W. Bush of Texas, who wanted to remove any semblance of controversy.

Republicans, though, did make several changes in delegate-selection rules for 2004, including elimination of the bonus delegates and creation of automatic superdelegate seats for members of the RNC.

Credentials Disputes

Before the opening of a convention, the national committee compiles a temporary roll of delegates. The roll is referred to the convention's credentials committee which holds hearings on the challenges and makes recommendations to the convention, the final arbiter of all disputes.

Some of the most bitter convention battles have concerned the seating of contested delegations. In the twentieth century, most of the heated credentials fights have concerned delegations from the South. In the Republican Party the challenges focused on the power of the Republican state organizations to dictate the selection of delegates.

The issue was hottest in 1912 and 1952, when the party throughout most of the South was a skeletal structure whose power was restricted largely to selection of convention delegates. Within the Democratic Party the question of southern credentials emerged after World War II on the volatile issues of civil rights and party loyalty. Important credentials challenges on these issues occurred at the 1948, 1952, 1964, and 1968 Democratic conventions.

There were numerous credentials challenges at the 1972 Democratic convention, but, unlike those at its predecessors, the challenges involved delegations from across the nation and focused on violations of the party's new guidelines.

After their 1952 credentials battle, the Republicans established a contest committee within the national committee to review credentials challenges before the convention. After their divisive 1968 convention, the Democrats also created a formal credentials procedure to review all challenges before the opening of the convention.

Convention Rules

Equally important to the settlement of credentials challenges are the rules under which the convention operates. The Republican Party adopts a completely new set of rules at every convention. Although large portions of the existing rules are enacted each time, general revision is always possible.

After its 1968 convention the Democratic Party set out to reform itself and the convention system. The Commission on Rules and the Commission on Party Structure and Delegate Selection, both created by the 1968 convention, proposed many changes that were accepted by the national committee. As a result, a formal set of rules was adopted for the first time at the party's 1972 convention.

Controversial Rules

Although it did not have a formal set of rules before 1972, the Democratic Party had long operated with two controversial rules never used by the Republicans: the unit rule and the two-thirds nominating rule. The unit rule enabled the majority of a delegation, if authorized by its state party, to cast the entire vote of the delegation for one candidate or position. In use since the earliest Democratic conventions, the unit rule was abolished by the 1968 convention.

From their first convention in 1832 until the 1936 convention, the Democrats employed the two-thirds nominating rule which required any candidate for president or vice president to win not just a simple majority, but also a two-thirds majority. Viewed as a boon to the South since it allowed that region a virtual veto power over any possible nominee, the rule was abolished with the stipulation that the South would receive an increased vote allocation at later conventions.

In its century of use, the two-thirds rule frequently produced protracted, multiballot conventions, often giving the Democrats a degree of turbulence the Republicans, who required only a simple majority, did not have. Between 1832 and 1932, seven Democratic conventions took more than ten ballots to select a presidential candidate. In contrast, in their entire convention history, the Republicans have had just one convention that required more than ten ballots to select a presidential candidate.

One controversy that surfaced during the 1980 Democratic Party convention concerned a rule that bound delegates to vote on the first ballot for the candidates under whose banner they had been elected. Supporters of Senator Kennedy had devoted their energy to prying the nomination from incumbent President Carter by defeating that rule. Nevertheless, the final tally showed 1,936.42 delegates favoring the binding rule and 1,390.58 opposing it. Passage of the binding rule ensured Carter's renomination, and shortly after the vote Kennedy announced that his name would not be placed in nomination.

Convention Officers

Credentials, rules, and platform are three of the major convention committees. Within the Republican Party, though, the committee on permanent organization ratifies the slate of convention officials. In the Democratic Party, this function is performed by the rules committee.

In both the Democratic and Republican parties, the presiding officer during the bulk of the convention is the permanent chairman. Oftentimes, since the end of World War II, the position of chairman went to the party's leader in the House of Representatives, particularly at the GOP convention. However, this loose precedent was broken in the Democratic Party by a rule adopted at the 1972 convention requiring that the presiding officer position alternate every four years between the sexes.

See also: Democratic Party; Republican Party; Super Tuesday.

Further Reading

Cook, Rhodes. *United States Presidential Primary Elections 2000–2004: A Handbook of Election Statistics.* Washington, DC: CQ Press, 2006.

Goff, Michael. *The Money Primary: The New Politics of the Early Presidential Nomination Process.* Lanham, MD: Rowman & Littlefield, 2007.

Scala, Dante J. *Stormy Weather: The New Hampshire Primary and Presidential Politics.* New York: Palgrave Macmillan, 2003.

Principles of U.S. Government

See Elections; Electoral College.

Progressive (Bull Moose) Party (1912)

A third party formed in 1912 because of a split in the Republican Party. A bitter personal and ideological dispute between president William Howard Taft (1909–1913) and former President Theodore Roosevelt (1901–1909) resulted in the withdrawal of the Roosevelt forces from the Republican Party after the June 1912 convention. The split further resulted in the creation of the Progressive Party two months later.

The new party was known popularly as the Bull Moose Party, a name resulting from Roosevelt's assertion early in the campaign that he felt as fit as a bull moose. While the Taft-Roosevelt split was the immediate reason for the new party, the Bull Moosers were an outgrowth of the Progressive movement that had been a powerful force in both major parties in the early years of the twentieth century.

In 1908, Roosevelt had handpicked Taft as his successor. Roosevelt soon grew disappointed with Taft's conservative philosophy, and with the support of progressive Republicans, Roosevelt challenged the incumbent for the 1912 Republican presidential nomination. Roosevelt outpolled Taft in the presidential primary states. Taft nevertheless won the nomination with nearly solid support in the South and among party conservatives.

Although few Republican politicians followed Roosevelt in his bolt, the new party demonstrated a popular base at its convention in Chicago in August 1912. Thousands of delegates, mostly middle- and upper-class reformers from small towns and cities, attended the convention that launched the party and nominated Roosevelt for president. California governor Hiram Johnson was chosen as his running mate. Roosevelt appeared in person to deliver his "Confession of Faith," a speech detailing his nationalistic philosophy and progressive reform ideas. The Bull Moose platform reflected key beliefs of the Progressive movement, calling for more extensive

VIEWPOINTS

A 1912 political cartoon shows incumbent President Taft (1909–1913) on the Republican elephant riding beside Democratic presidential nominee Woodrow Wilson(1913–1921) on the Democratic donkey. Progressive candidate Theodore Roosevelt (1901–1909) is riding on a bull moose, nipping at the elephant's hide. (The Granger Collection, New York)

government antitrust action and for labor, social, government, and electoral reform.

Roosevelt was wounded in an assassination attempt while campaigning in Milwaukee, Wisconsin, in October, but he finished the campaign. In the general election, Roosevelt received more than 4 million votes (27.4 percent of the popular vote) and carried six states. His percentage of the vote was the highest ever received by a third-party candidate in American history, but his candidacy split the Republican vote and enabled the Democrats' nominee, Woodrow Wilson, to win the election. The Progressive Party had minimal success at the state and local levels, winning thirteen House seats but electing no senators or governors.

Roosevelt declined the Progressive nomination in 1916 and endorsed the Republican candidate, Charles Evans Hughes. With the defection of its leader, the decline of the Progressive movement, and the lack of an effective party organization, the Bull Moose Party ceased to exist.

See also: Election of 1912; Election of 1916; Republican Party.

Further Reading

Chace, James. *1912: Wilson, Roosevelt, Taft & Debs—The Election that Changed the Country.* New York: Simon and Schuster, 2004.

Progressive Party (La Follette) (1924)

A short-lived reform party that emerged in the mid-1920s. Like the Bull Moose Party (1912–1916) of Theodore Roosevelt (1858–1919), the Progressive Party was led by a Republican. Wisconsin senator Robert M. La Follette Sr. led the new Progressive Party, a separate entity from the Bull Moosers, which, unlike the middle- and upper-class Roosevelt party of the previous decade, had its greatest appeal among farmers and organized labor.

The La Follette Progressive Party grew out of the Conference for Progressive Political Action (CPPA), a coalition formed in 1922 by railway union leaders and some Bull Moosers. The Socialist Party joined the coalition the following year. Throughout 1923, the Socialists and labor unions argued over whether their coalition should form a third party, with the Socialists in favor and the labor unions against it. Finally, they decided to run an independent presidential candidate, La Follette, in the 1924 election, but not to field any state or local candidates. La Follette was given the power to choose his running mate and selected Montana senator Burton K. Wheeler, a Democrat.

Known as "Fighting Bob" La Follette, Robert M. La Follette, Sr., was a reform governor and senator from Wisconsin before he ran as the 1924 Progressive Party presidential nominee. (Library of Congress)

Opposition to corporate monopolies was the major issue of the La Follette campaign, although the party advocated various other reforms, particularly aimed at farmers and workers, which were proposed earlier by either the Populists or Bull Moosers. The Progressive Party itself, however, became a major issue in the 1924 campaign, as the Republicans attacked the alleged radicalism of the party.

Although La Follette had its endorsement, the American Federation of Labor (AFL) provided minimal support. The basic strength of the Progressives, like that of the Populists in the 1890s, came from rural voters west of the Mississippi River. La Follette received 4,832,532 votes—16.6 percent of the popular vote—but carried just one state, his native Wisconsin. When La Follette died in 1925, the party collapsed as a national force. It was revived by La Follette's sons on a statewide level in Wisconsin in the mid-1930s.

See also: Election of 1924.

Progressive Party (Wallace) (1948)

A reform party that emerged in the late 1940s from dissatisfied liberal elements in the Democratic Party. In particular, these liberal Democrats disagreed with the leadership of President Harry S. Truman (1945–1953), especially in the area of foreign policy. The Progressive Party was one of two bolting groups from the Democratic Party in 1948; conservative southern elements withdrew to form the States' Rights Party, or Dixiecrats.

Henry Wallace, the founder of the Progressive Party, was secretary of agriculture, vice president, and finally secretary of commerce under President Franklin Roosevelt. He carried the reputation of one of the most liberal idealists in the Roosevelt administration. Fired from the Truman cabinet in 1946 after breaking with administration policy and publicly advocating peaceful coexistence with the Soviet Union, Wallace began to consider the idea of a liberal third-party candidacy. Supported by the American Labor Party, by the Progressive Citizens of America, and by other progressive organizations in California and Illinois, Wallace announced his third-party candidacy in December 1947.

The Progressive Party was launched formally the following July at a convention in Philadelphia, which ratified the selection of Wallace for president and Idaho Senator Glen H. Taylor, a Democrat, as his running mate. The party adopted a platform that emphasized foreign policy—opposing the cold war anticommunism of the Truman administration and specifically urging abandonment of the Truman Doctrine and the Marshall Plan. These measures were designed to contain the spread of communism and bolster noncommunist nations. On domestic issues, the Progressives stressed humanitarian concerns and equal rights for both sexes and all races.

Minority groups—women, youth, African Americans, Jews, and Hispanic Americans—were active in the new party, but the openness of the Progressives brought Wallace a damaging endorsement from the Communist Party. Believing the two parties could work together, Wallace accepted the endorsement while characterizing his philosophy as "progressive capitalism."

In 1948, the Progressives appeared on the presidential ballot in forty-five states, but the Communist endorsement helped keep the party on the defensive during the entire campaign. In the November election Wallace received only 1,157,326 votes (2.4 percent of the national popular vote), with nearly half of the votes from the state of New York. Not only were the Progressives unable to carry a single state, but in spite of their defection from the Democratic Party, President Truman won reelection. The Progressives had poor results in the congressional races, failing to elect one representative or senator.

The Progressive Party's opposition to the Korean War in 1950 drove many moderate elements out of the party, including Henry Wallace. The party ran a national ticket in 1952, but received only 140,023 votes nationwide or 0.2 percent of the national popular vote. The party crumbled completely after the election.

See also: Dixiecrats; Election of 1948.

R

Race and Voter Turnout

See Voters, Voting Behavior, and Voter Turnout.

Rankin, Jeanette

See Election of 1916.

Reapportionment and Redistricting

Reapportionment, the redistribution of the 435 seats in the House of Representatives among the states to reflect shifts in population, and *redistricting*, the redrawing of congressional district boundaries for the House within the states, are among the most important and controversial processes in the U.S. political system. These two procedures help to determine whether Democrats or Republicans, or liberals or conservatives will dominate the House, and whether districts will be drawn to favor the election of candidates from particular racial or ethnic groups.

Frequency and Process

Reapportionment and redistricting occur every ten years based on the census. States where populations grew quickly during the previous ten years typically gain congressional seats, while those that lost population or grew much more slowly tend to lose seats. The number of House members for the rest of the states remains the same.

The states that gain or lose seats usually must make extensive changes in their congres-

sional maps. Even those states that keep the same number of representatives must make adjustments to take into account population shifts within their boundaries, in accordance with Supreme Court "one-person, one-vote" rulings.

In most states, the state legislatures are responsible for drafting and enacting the new congressional district map. Thus, the majority party in each state legislature is often in a position to draw a district map that enhances the fortunes of its incumbents and candidates at the expense of the opposing party.

The Framers' Intentions

What did the Framers of the Constitution have in mind about who would be represented in the House of Representatives and how? The Constitution declares only that each state is to be allotted a certain number of representatives. It does not state specifically that congressional districts must be equal or nearly equal in population. Nor does it explicitly require that a state create districts at all. However, it seems clear that the first clause of Article I, Section 2, providing that House members should be chosen "by the People of the several States," indicates that the House of Representatives, in contrast to the Senate, was to represent people rather than states. The third clause of Article I, Section 2, provided that congressional apportionment among the states must be according to population.

Reapportionment: The Number of Seats

The Constitution made the first apportionment, which was to remain in effect until the first census was taken. No reliable figures on the population were available at the time. The Constitution's apportionment yielded a sixty-five member House. The seats were allotted among the thirteen states as follows: New Hampshire,

HOUSE SEATS, 2000 REAPPORTIONMENT

Gainers
Arizona 2
California 1
Colorado 1
Florida 2
Georgia 2
Nevada 1
North Carolina 1
Texas 2

Losers
Connecticut 1
Illinois 1
Indiana 1
Michigan 1
Mississippi 1
New York 2
Ohio 1
Oklahoma 1
Pennsylvania 2
Wisconsin 1

Loser

No Change

Gainer

Because the population of states in the south and west increased between 1990 and 2000, the number of members of the House of Representatives from those states increased. Conversely, states that lost population lost seats in the House.

three; Massachusetts, eight; Rhode Island and Providence Plantations, one; Connecticut, five; New York, six; New Jersey, four; Pennsylvania, eight; Delaware, one; Maryland, six; Virginia, ten; North Carolina, five; South Carolina, five; and Georgia, three. This apportionment remained in effect during the First and Second Congresses (1789–1793).

Apportionment by Congress

Congress enacted apportionment legislation after the first census was taken in 1790. The first apportionment bill was sent to President George Washington (1789–1797) in March 1792. The bill had incorporated the constitutional minimum of 30,000 as the size of each district. The population of each state was not a simple multiple of 30,000; significant fractions were left over. For example, Vermont was found to be entitled to 2.85 representatives, New Jersey to 5.98, and Virginia to 21.02.

The president sent the bill back to Congress without his signature—the first presidential **veto.** Washington's veto was based on the belief that eight states would receive more than one representative for each 30,000 people under this plan.

A motion to override the veto was unsuccessful. A new bill, meeting the president's objections, approved in April 1792, provided for a ratio of one member for every 33,000 inhabitants and fixed the exact number of representatives to which each state was entitled. The total membership of the House was to be 105. In dividing the population of the various states by 33,000, all remainders were to be disregarded. President Thomas Jefferson (1801–1809) devised this solution, known as the method of rejected fractions.

Jefferson's Method

Jefferson's method of reapportionment resulted in great inequalities among districts. A Vermont district would contain 42,766 inhabitants, a New Jersey district 35,911, and a Virginia district only 33,187. Jefferson's method emphasized what was considered to be the ideal size of a congressional district rather than what the size of the House ought to be.

The reapportionment act based on the census of 1800 continued the ratio of 33,000, which provided a House of 141 members. The third apportionment bill, enacted in 1811, fixed the ratio at 35,000, yielding a House of 181 members. Following the 1820 census Congress set the ratio at 40,000 inhabitants per district, which produced a House of 213 members. The act of May 22, 1832, fixed the ratio at 47,700, resulting in a House of 240 members.

Dissatisfaction with inequalities produced by the method of rejected fractions grew. Launching a vigorous attack against it, Daniel Webster urged adoption of a method that would assign an additional representative to each state with a large fraction. Webster outlined his reasoning in a report he submitted to Congress in 1832:

> The Constitution, therefore, must be understood not as enjoining an absolute relative equality—because that would be demanding an impossibility—but as requiring of Congress to make the apportionment of Representatives among the several states according to their respective numbers, *as near as may be.* That which cannot be done perfectly must be done in a manner as near perfection as can be. . . . In such a case approximation becomes a rule.

Following the 1840 census Congress adopted a reapportionment method similar to that advocated by Webster. The method fixed a ratio of one representative for every 70,680 people. This figure was reached by deciding on a fixed size of the House in advance (223), dividing that figure into the total national "representative population," and using the result (70,680) as the fixed ratio. The population of each state was then divided by this ratio to find the number of its representatives and the states were assigned an additional representative for each fraction more than one-half. Under this method the actual size of the House dropped.

The modified reapportionment formula adopted by Congress in 1842 was more satisfactory than the previous method, but another change was made following the census of 1850. Proposed by Representative Samuel F. Vinton of Ohio, the new system became known as the Vinton method.

Vinton Formula

Under the Vinton formula, Congress first fixed the size of the House and then distributed the seats. The total qualifying population of the country was divided by the desired number of representatives, and the resulting number became the ratio of population to each representative. The population of each state was divided by this ratio, and each state received the number of representatives equal to the whole number in the quotient for that state. Then, to reach the required size of the House, additional representatives were assigned based on the remaining fractions, beginning with the state having the largest fraction. This procedure differed from the 1842 method only in the last step, which assigned one representative to every state having a fraction larger than one-half.

Proponents of the Vinton method pointed out that it had the distinct advantage of fixing the size of the House in advance and taking

A–Z

P-R

into account at least the largest fractions. The concern of the House turned from the ideal size of a congressional district to the ideal size of the House itself.

Six reapportionments were carried out under the Vinton method—1850, 1860, 1870, 1880, 1890, and 1900. The 1850 census act contained three provisions not included in any previous law. First, it required reapportionment not only after the census of 1850 but also after all the subsequent censuses; second, it fixed the size of the House permanently at 233 members; and third, it provided in advance for an automatic apportionment by the secretary of the interior under the method prescribed in the act. Later reapportionment acts increased the size of the House—241 members in 1862, 283 in 1872, 325 in 1882, 356 in 1892, and 386 in 1902.

Maximum Membership of House

In 1911, the membership of the House was fixed at 433. Provision was made for the addition of one representative each from Arizona and New Mexico, which were expected to become states in the near future. Thus, the size of the House reached 435, where it has remained with the exception of a brief period, 1959–1963, when the admission of Alaska and Hawaii raised the total temporarily to 437.

Limiting the size of the House amounted to recognition that the body soon would expand to unmanageable proportions if Congress continued the practice of adding new seats every ten years to match population gains without depriving any state of its existing representation. Agreement on a fixed number made the task of reapportionment even more difficult when the population not only increased but also became much more mobile. Population shifts brought Congress up hard against the politically painful necessity of taking seats away from slow-growing states to give the fast-growing states adequate representation.

A new mathematical calculation was adopted for the reapportionment following the 1910 census. This new system established a priority list that assigned seats progressively, beginning with the first seat above the constitutional mini-

mum of at least one seat for each state. When there were forty-eight states, this method was used to assign the forty-ninth member, the fiftieth member, and so on, until the agreed upon size of the House was reached. The method was called "major fractions" and was used after the censuses of 1910, 1930, and 1940. There was no reapportionment after the 1920 census.

The results of the 1920 census were announced in December, just after the short session of the Sixty-sixth Congress convened. The 1920 census showed that for the first time in history most Americans were urban residents. During the early 1920s, Congress considered several reapportionment bills, but these were blocked in committees by rural representatives who believed that rural residents were undercounted.

Because two decades had passed between reapportionments, a greater shift than usual took place following the 1930 census. California's House delegation was almost doubled, rising from eleven to twenty. Michigan gained four seats; Texas three; and New Jersey, New York, and Ohio two each. Twenty-one states lost a total of twenty-seven seats; Missouri lost three; and Georgia, Iowa, Kentucky, and Pennsylvania each lost two.

Method of Equal Proportions

Congress adopted a new "equal proportions" method to be used in reapportionment calculations after the 1950 and subsequent censuses. The method of equal proportions involves complicated mathematical calculations. It is designed to make the proportional difference in the average district size in any two states as small as possible. After the 2000 reapportionment, for example, average population per district increased to 647,000. Montana's single district was the most populous with 902,195 people; Wyoming's single district was the least populous with 493,782 residents.

Redistricting: Drawing the Lines

Although the Constitution contained provisions for the apportionment of U.S. House seats among the states, it was silent about how the members should be elected. From the beginning, most states divided their territory into geographic districts, permitting only one member of Congress to be elected from each district.

Some states allowed would-be House members to run at large, with voters able to cast as many votes as there were seats to be filled. Still other states created what were known as multi-member districts, in which a single geographic unit would elect two or more members of the House. At various times, some states used combinations of these methods. For example, a state might elect ten representatives from ten individual districts and two at large.

Those states that used congressional districts quickly developed what came to be known as the **gerrymander**. The term refers to the practice of drawing district lines so as to maximize the advantage of a political party or interest group. The name originated from a salamander-shaped congressional district created by the Massachusetts legislature in 1812 when Elbridge Gerry was governor.

Constant efforts were made during the early 1800s to lay down national rules by means of a constitutional amendment for congressional districting. In Congress, Senator Mahlon Dickerson proposed such an amendment regularly almost every year from 1817 to 1826. It was adopted by the Senate three times—in 1819, 1820, and 1822—but each time it failed to reach a vote in the House. Although the constitutional amendment was unsuccessful, a law passed in 1842 required contiguous single-member congressional districts. That law required representatives to be

> . . .elected by districts composed of contiguous territory equal in number to the representatives to which said state may be entitled, no one district electing more than one Representative.

Several unsuccessful attempts were made to enforce redistricting provisions. Despite the districting requirements enacted in 1842, New Hampshire, Georgia, Mississippi, and Missouri elected their representatives at large that autumn. When the new House convened for its first session, on December 4, 1843, objection was made to seating the representatives of the four states.

The House debated the matter in February 1844. With the Democratic Party holding a majority of more than sixty, and with eighteen of the twenty-one challenged members being Democrats, the House decided to seat the members. However, by 1848 all four states had come around to electing their representatives by districts.

Court Action on Redistricting

After the deadlock over reapportionment in the 1920s, those who were unhappy over the inaction of Congress and the state legislatures began taking their cases to court. At first, the protesters had no luck. But as the population disparities grew in both federal and state legislative districts and the Supreme Court began to show a tendency to intervene, the objectors were more successful.

Finally, in a series of decisions beginning in 1962 with *Baker v. Carr,* the Court exerted great influence over the redistricting process, ordering that congressional districts as well as state and local legislative districts be drawn so that their populations would be as nearly equal as possible.

Congress and Redistricting

Congress considered several proposals in the post–World War II period to enact new legislation on redistricting. Only one of these efforts was successful—enactment of a measure barring at-large elections in states with more than one House seat.

In January 1951, President Harry S. Truman asked for a ban on gerrymandering, an end to at-large seats in states having more than one representative, and a sharp reduction in the huge differences in size among congressional districts within most states. On behalf of the administration, Emanuel Celler, chairman of the House Judiciary Committee, introduced a bill reflecting these requests, but the committee took no action.

Celler regularly introduced his bill throughout the 1950s and early 1960s, but it made no headway until the Supreme Court handed down the

A–Z

P-R

Wesberry v. Sanders decision in 1964. The House passed a version of the Celler bill in 1965, largely to discourage the Supreme Court from imposing even more rigid criteria. The Senate, however, took no action and the measure died.

In 1967, after defeating a conference report that would have prevented the courts from ordering a state to redistrict or to hold at-large elections until after the 1970 census, Congress approved a measure to ban at-large elections in all states entitled to more than one representative. Exceptions were made for New Mexico and Hawaii, which had a tradition of electing their representatives at large. Both states, however, soon passed districting laws, New Mexico for the 1968 elections and Hawaii for 1970.

Bills to increase the size of the House to prevent states from losing seats as a result of population shifts have been introduced after most recent censuses. Congress, however, has given little consideration to any of them.

See also: Baker v. Carr; Elections, House of Representatives; Gerrymandering; One Person, One Vote; *Wesbury v. Sanders.*

Further Reading

Canon, David T. *Race, Redistricting, and Representation: The Unintended Consequences of Black Majority Districts.* Chicago: The University of Chicago Press, 1999.

Cox, Gary W., and Jonathan N. Katz. *Elbridge Gerry's Salamander: The Electoral Consequences of the Reapportionment Revolution.* New York: Cambridge University Press, 2002.

Jacobson, Gary C. *The Politics of Congressional Elections.* New York: Longman, 2003.

Reform Party (1992–)

A reform-based party that emerged in 1992 under the leadership of Texas billionaire H. Ross Perot. That year Perot drew the highest vote share of any independent or third party candidate in eighty years. Relying heavily on his own wealth and on grassroots volunteer efforts to get his name on the ballot in all fifty states and the District of Columbia, Perot received 19,741,657 votes, or 18.9 percent of the nationwide vote. He did not win any sizable constituency or receive any electoral votes, but he drew a respectable 10 percent to 30 percent in popular voting across the nation.

Perot, who announced the possibility of his candidacy in February 1992, ran his early unofficial campaign mainly on one issue—eliminating the federal deficit. He had the luxury of funding his entire campaign, which included buying huge amounts of television time. Drawing on the disenchantment of voters, Perot and his folksy, no-nonsense approach to government reform struck a populist chord. He also demonstrated his quirkiness, however, by abruptly withdrawing from the presidential race in mid-July and then reversing himself and reentering in October. He chose as his running mate retired Admiral James B. Stockdale, who as a navy flier had been a prisoner during much of the Vietnam War.

United We Stand America (UWSA), formed from the ashes of Perot's candidacy, did not bill itself as an official political party. Promoting itself instead as a nonpartisan educational organization, UWSA called for a balanced budget, government reform, and health care reform. The group's leaders did not endorse candidates or offer them financial assistance.

In 1993, Perot, rather than UWSA, commanded considerable attention in the nation's capital marshaling grassroots support on congressional reform and unsuccessfully opposing the North American Free Trade Agreement (NAFTA). Democrats and Republicans were unable to co-opt his following as they had those of major third-party movements in the past. Perot continued to use his supporters' anger with government and the political process to sustain himself as an independent political force. In the fall of 1995, Perot created a full-fledged political party, the Reform Party, and ran as its nominee in a campaign financed with federal funds.

The Reform Party effort of 1996 qualified for federal funding and went along with the limitations that acceptance of the money entailed. By winning more than 5 percent of the 1992 presidential vote, Perot's party qualified in 1996 for some $30 million, less than half the amount he spent from his own pocket four years earlier.

Perot was challenged for the Reform Party nomination by Richard D. Lamm, a former Democratic governor of Colorado who had shown a willingness to risk voter displeasure. Lamm had called, for example, for deep cuts in Medicare, the popular health care program for the elderly.

Perot defeated Lamm in an unusual two-stage procedure, with a preliminary vote after nominating speeches at a convention in Long Beach, California, followed by a mail and electronic vote with the winner announced a week later in Valley Forge, Pennsylvania. Ballots had been sent to 1.3 million voters who were registered party members or signers of its ballot access petitions. Less than 50,000 votes, though, were actually cast, with Perot a winner by a margin of nearly 2 to 1.

Perot again was on the general election ballot in all states. He chose as his running mate Pat Choate, a native Texan and economist who had coached Perot in his unsuccessful fight against NAFTA. The Reform Party also had congressional candidates in ten states.

Locked out of the presidential debates, Perot spent much of his campaign money on television "infomercials" explaining the party's principles. Besides a balanced budget, these included higher ethical standards for the White House and Congress, campaign and election reforms, a new tax system, and lobbying restrictions.

Even with the restricted budget, Perot again placed third in the national election after the two major party candidates. However, his 8,085,402 votes, 8.4 percent of the total, came to less than half of his 1992 achievement of 18.9 percent, a third-party figure surpassed in the twentieth century only by former president Theodore Roosevelt and his Bull Moose candidacy of 1912. Perot had his best showing in Maine, where he received 14.2 percent of the vote. He won no electoral votes.

In 1998, the Reform Party scored a high-profile victory when former professional wrestler Jesse Ventura was elected governor of Minnesota running on the party label. After Ventura's victory, several well-known personalities publicly considered running for the party's presidential nomination in 2000, including former Connecticut governor Lowell P. Weicker, Jr., and financier Donald Trump. Ultimately, they did not run, although Patrick J. Buchanan did, bolting the Republican Party in October 1999.

Highly public party infighting followed, with Perot loyalists arrayed against Buchanan supporters. The latter claimed they offered the party energy and new blood; the former contended Buchanan was intent on a hostile takeover designed to make the Reform Party socially conservative.

Calling the party "dysfunctional," Ventura announced in February 2000 that he was leaving to become an independent. In June, Perot publicly distanced himself from his party by declining to run against Buchanan in the party's mail-in primary in July. Nevertheless, John Hagelin, the candidate of the Natural Law Party in 1992 and 1996, did enter.

The Reform Party's convention in Long Beach, California, in August, disintegrated into two competing meetings: one favorable to Buchanan; the other, dominated by Perot loyalists, favorable to Hagelin. After Buchanan wrested control of the party and nomination, the Hagelin forces set up a splinter Reform Party. Hagelin chose Nat Goldhaber of California for the vice-presidential spot on his ticket. In September, the splinter group joined in coalition with the Natural Law Party, Hagelin's old party.

Nevertheless, Buchanan retained control of the base party's apparatus, and a federal court awarded him full use of the $12.6 million in federal funds that Perot's 1996 showing had qualified the party's 2000 nominee to receive. Buchanan chose for his running mate Ezola Foster, a California teacher. The bipartisan Commission on Presidential Debates, however, denied Buchanan participation in the three presidential debates held in October. Buchanan support in the polls was under the 15 percent required to enter the debates.

The 2000 election results were a major disappointment to Reform Party supporters.

A – Z

P-R

Although commentators thought Buchanan's message would attract many social conservatives, the party garnered only 448,868 votes, just 0.43 percent of the total presidential vote. Some commentators, however, noted that Buchanan was on the ballot in four competitive states that were won by Democratic candidate Al Gore. They argued that the Reform vote in those states may have drawn off enough support from Republican George W. Bush to swing the states' thirty electoral votes into the Democratic column. In 2004, the Reform Party did not run a presidential candidate and endorsed the independent candidacy of Ralph Nader.

See also: Election of 1992; Election of 1996; Election of 2000; Nader, Ralph; Natural Law Party; Perot, H. Ross.

Further Reading

Bibby, John F., and L. Sandy Maisal. *Two Parties–Or More?: The American Party System.* Jackson, TN: Westview Press, 2002.

Rosenstone, Steven J., Roy L. Behr, and Edward H. Lazarus. *Third Parties in America.* Princeton, NJ: Princeton University Press, 1996.

Sifry, Micah L. *Spoiling For a Fight: Third Party Politics in America.* London: Routledge, 2003.

Reid, Henry

See Elections, Senate.

Republican Party (1854–)

One of the two major American political parties, founded in 1854. The Republican Party dominated national politics from 1860 to the New Deal (1933–1938) era and again from 1968 to the present.

The party emerged in 1854–1856 out of a political conflict revolving around the expansion of slavery into the western territories. The new party was so named because "republicanism" was the core value of American politics, and it seemed to be threatened by the expanding "slave power." The enemy was not so much the institution of slavery or the mistreatment of the slaves. Rather, it was that the political-economic system that controlled the South exerted disproportionate control over the national government and threatened to seize power in the new territories.

Origins

The party came into being in reaction to federal legislation–the Kansas-Nebraska Act–allowing the settlers of the Kansas Territory to decide for themselves whether to adopt slavery. This law **nullified** the Compromise of 1820 which explicitly forbade slavery there. The new party lost on this issue, but in addition to bringing in most northern Whigs, it gained support from "Free Soil" northern Democrats who opposed the expansion of slavery. Only a handful of abolitionists joined. The Republicans adopted most of the modernization programs of the Whigs, favoring banks, tariffs, and internal improvements and adding, as well, a demand for a homestead law that would provide free farms to western settlers.

The 1856 campaign was a crusade for "Free Soil, Free Labor, Free Men, and Fremont!" John C. Fremont was defeated by the Democratic candidate James Buchanan. By the late 1850s, the new Republican party dominated every northern state. It controlled enough electoral votes to win the presidency, despite its almost complete lack of support in the South. In 1860, Abraham Lincoln, with only 40 percent of the popular vote, swept the North and easily carried the electoral college. Interpreting the Republican victory as a signal of intense, permanent Northern hostility, seven states of the Deep South immediately seceded and formed the Confederate States of America. Four additional Southern states joined the Confederacy after Lincoln's inauguration.

Lincoln proved brilliantly successful in uniting all the factions of his party to fight for the

Union. Most northern Democrats were likewise supportive until fall 1862, when Lincoln added the abolition of slavery as a war goal. In Congress, the party passed major legislation to promote rapid modernization, including measures for a national banking system, high tariffs, homestead laws, and aid to education and agriculture.

Ulysses S. Grant was elected president in 1868 with strong support from radical Republicans and the new Republican state governments in the South. He in turn vigorously supported radical Reconstruction programs in the South, the Fourteenth Amendment, and equal civil and voting rights for the freedmen. Most of all, he was the hero of the war veterans, who gave him strong support.

Late Nineteenth Century

The Compromise of 1877 resolved the disputed election of 1876 by giving the White House to the Republicans and all of the Southern states to the Democrats. The Grand Old Party (GOP), as it was now nicknamed, split into "Stalwart" and "Half-Breed" factions. In 1884, "Mugwump" reformers split off and helped elect Democrat Grover Cleveland.

In the 1888 election, and for the first time since 1872, the Republicans gained control of the White House and both houses of Congress. The Republicans, relying on the loyal supporters that had always dominated the party's voting base, were badly defeated in the 1890 off-year election and the 1892 presidential contest, won by Cleveland. A severe economic depression struck both rural and urban America in 1893—on Cleveland's watch. The depression, combined with violent nationwide coal and railway strikes and factionalism inside the Democratic Party, led to a sweeping victory for the GOP in 1894.

The Republican Party seemed invincible in 1896, until the Democrats unexpectedly selected William Jennings Bryan as their presidential candidate. Bryan's hugely popular crusade against the gold standard, financiers, railroads, and industrialists—indeed, against the cities—created a crisis for Republican candidate William McKinley and his campaign manager,

Marc Hanna. Because of civil service reforms, parties could no longer finance themselves internally. Hanna solved that problem by directly obtaining $3.5 million from large corporations threatened by Bryan.

McKinley promised prosperity for everyone and every group, with no governmental attacks on property or ethnic groups. The business community, factory workers, white-collar workers, and commercial farmers responded enthusiastically, becoming major components of the new Republican majority.

Early Twentieth Century

Rejuvenated by their triumphs in 1894 and 1896 and by the glamour of a highly popular short war in 1898—against Spain over Cuba, the Philippines, and other Spanish possessions—the Republicans rolled to victory after victory. However, the party had again grown too large, and factionalism increasingly tore it apart.

The break within the party came in 1912 over the issue of progressivism. President William Howard Taft favored conservative reform controlled by the courts; former president Theodore Roosevelt went to the grass roots, attacking Taft, bosses, courts, big business, and the "malefactors of great wealth." Defeated at the convention, Roosevelt bolted and formed a third party, the Progressive, or Bull Moose Party. The vast majority of progressive politicians refused to follow Roosevelt's action, allowing conservatives to seize control of the GOP. Roosevelt's split of the party also allowed Democrat Woodrow Wilson to gain the White House with only 40 percent of the vote. After Wilson's fragile coalition collapsed in 1920, the GOP won three consecutive presidential contests.

Herbert Hoover, elected president in 1928, represented the epitome of the modernizing engineer, bringing efficiency to government and the economy. His weak political skill hardly seemed to matter when the economy boomed in the 1920s and Democrats were in disarray. However, when the Great Depression hit in the 1930s, his political ineffectiveness compounded the party's weaknesses.

A - Z

P-R

New Deal and Democratic Dominance

The Great Depression sidelined the GOP for decades as their conservative formulas for prosperity had failed. The Democrats, by contrast, built up majorities that depended on labor unions, big city machines, federal relief funds, and the mobilization of Catholics, Jews, and African Americans. However, middle-class hostility to new taxes, and fears about a repeat of the First World War, eventually led to a Republican rebound.

In 1952, the issues of the war in Korea, communism, and corruption gave World War II hero Dwight D. Eisenhower a victory for Republicans, along with narrow control of Congress. However, the GOP remained a minority party and was factionalized, with a northeastern liberal element favorable to the New Deal and the policy of containing Communist expansion, versus midwestern conservatives who bitterly opposed New Deal taxes, regulation, labor unions, and internationalism.

Both conservative and liberal factions exploited the issue of anticommunism and attacked the Democrats for harboring spies and allegedly allowing Communist gains in China and Korea. New York governors Thomas E. Dewey, who also ran for the presidency in 1948, and Nelson Rockefeller, who governed from 1958 to 1973, led the liberal wing, while Senators Robert Taft of Ohio and Barry Gol water of Arizona spoke for the conservatives.

Richard Nixon, who was Eisenhower's vice president, was nominated in 1960 to succeed Eisenhower. Nixon lost. The defeat of yet another candidate sponsored by the eastern "establishment" opened the way for Goldwater's 1964 crusade against the New Deal and then-president Lyndon Johnson's Great Society programs. Goldwater permanently weakened the eastern liberals. Goldwater in 1964 and former Arkansas governor George Wallace in 1968 took southern whites and many northern Catholics away from their Democratic roots; however, at the same time, the Democratic commitment to civil rights won more than nine-tenths of all African American voters.

Republican Revival

President Johnson, who was Kennedy's vice president, succeeded him on Kennedy's assassination in 1963. Johnson won an overwhelming victory in 1964 and brought with him a large Democratic majority in Congress that enacted sweeping social programs that Johnson called the Great Society, although support for some of these programs later collapsed.

Nixon seized the moment and ran again, winning narrowly in 1968. Nixon was not to serve out his second term, however. The Watergate scandal, which revealed White House and presidential involvement in criminal activities, forced him to resign from office in the face of certain congressional impeachment and removal from office. Nixon's criminal activities and subsequent resignation wreaked havoc in the 1974 election, in which Democrats swept to a massive victory in off-year contests, and set the stage for the 1976 Carter victory.

Georgia governor Jimmy Carter won the White House for the Democrats, but foreign affairs issues plagued his presidency. Public opinion saw failure in his policies toward the Soviet Union, Middle Eastern nations that forced an energy crisis by withholding oil supplies, and Iranian revolutionaries who held Americans hostage for months. "Stagflation" in the economy meant a combination of high unemployment and high inflation. Most of all there was a sense of drift or, worse, of malaise. The country craved leadership.

Ronald Reagan answered that need. A former movie actor and Republican governor of California, Reagan had been a supporter of Goldwater and an articulate spokesman for the conservative views that the 1964 presidential candidate set in motion. Reagan led a political revolution in 1980, capitalizing on grievances and mobilizing an entirely new voting bloc, the religious right.

A – Z

In 1854, the Republican Party was founded at a meeting held in this schoolhouse in Ripon, Wisconsin. The U.S. Department of the Interior declared the Little White Schoolhouse a national historic landmark in 1974. (Ripon Chamber of Commerce)

P-R

By the time of the 1984 election, even though the national debt had skyrocketed, inflation had declined significantly, unemployment had eased, profits were soaring, some changes had been made in the Social Security system, and Reagan carried forty-nine states in winning reelection. Reagan engaged in an aggressive pursuit of cold war policy which, with other factors, ultimately led to the collapse of the Soviet Union and the end of international communism in most nations. For the first time since 1932, the GOP pulled abreast of the Democrats in terms of party identification on the part of voters.

George Herbert Walker Bush, Reagan's vice president, rode to the White House in 1988 on Reagan's popularity and could himself claim important victories in the cold war and in the

Middle East, where the Persian Gulf War liberated Kuwait in 1991 after an invasion by neighboring Iraq. Yet Bush—knowledgeable on international affairs—seemed indifferent about taxes, deficits, and other domestic issues that bothered Americans far more. Most importantly, Bush was plagued by the remains of a recession in 1990–1991 just as he was running for reelection in 1992, allowing Arkansas governor Bill Clinton to take back the White House for the Democrats.

The 1990s was not a good decade for the Republican Party. It lost the 1992 and 1996 presidential elections to Clinton, the first time the GOP had lost successive White House elections since 1960 and 1964. Clinton proved a popular president, raising the possibility that the generally Republican trend of recent decades had finally been broken. However, the GOP came back in 1994, gaining control of Congress—both the House and Senate—for the first time since 1952, as well as control of governors' mansions in nearly all the major states.

The bitter leadership of Speaker of the House Newt Gingrich soured politics in Washington, D.C. Thus, he was unable to deliver on most of his conservative program called the "Contract with America." The Republican image worsened when the party attempted to impeach and remove Clinton from office over a scandal that had its roots in an affair between Clinton and a young female intern in the White House. The public, although appalled at the scandal, never showed enthusiasm for removing Clinton and the Senate refused to convict the president after the House impeached him.

Nevertheless, in the 2000 elections the Republican Party achieved success. In a hotly contested election, former president Bush's son, George W. Bush, defeated Democrat Al Gore. Although Gore won the popular vote, this victory revived the GOP dominance of national level politics that began with Richard Nixon in 1968. Equally important, the GOP retained control of Congress, giving it complete control of the federal government for the first time since 1953. In 2004, George W. Bush was reelected with more than 50 percent of the popular vote, but the Republican Party lost control of both houses of Congress for the first time since 1993.

See also: Democratic Party; Impeachment; Watergate; Whig Party; 📖 Contract With America in the **Primary Source Library**.

Further Reading

Engs, Robert F., and Randall M. Miller (eds.). *The Birth of the Grand Old Party: The Republicans' First Generation.* Philadelphia: University of Pennsylvania Press, 2002.

Gould, Lewis L. *Grand Old Party: A History of the Republicans.* New York: Random House, 2003.

Lutz, Norma Jean, and Arthur M. Schlesinger. *History of the Republican Party.* New York: Chelsea House, 2000.

Rock the Vote

See: Twenty-Sixth Amendment.

Separation of Powers

The concept that a government be divided into three separate branches with distinct or shared powers. Many of the delegates to the Constitutional Convention (1787) believed that in order to preserve liberty, government should be designed to incorporate the principle of separation of powers. Various political philosophers of the seventeenth- and eighteenth-century period known as the Enlightenment, including John Locke (1632–1704), had articulated this idea, but no version was more familiar to the delegates than that of the French author, Baron de

Montesquieu (1689–1755). As the author of *L'Esprit des Lois* (The Spirit of the Laws) in 1748, Montesquieu was "the oracle who is always consulted and cited" on the subject of separation of powers, wrote James Madison (1809–1817) in *Federalist* No. 47. According to a passage from Montesquieu's book, which the delegates knew well and which was quoted in *Federalist* No. 47, the philosopher had written:

> **W**hen the legislative and executive powers are united in the same person, or in the same body of magistracy, there can be no liberty; because apprehensions may arise lest the same monarch or senate should enact tyrannical laws, to execute them in a tyrannical manner. . . . Were the power of judging joined with the legislative, the life and liberty of the subject would be exposed to arbitrary control, for the judge would then be the legislator.

As applied in the Constitution, the separation of powers principle did not require a strict division of labor, in which each branch of the government was assigned exclusive power to perform certain functions. Indeed, the Constitution assigns few powers to the federal government that are not shared by two or more branches. Separation of powers actually meant something more like "separated institutions sharing powers" to the delegates, a separation in which the membership of one branch does not overlap and cannot persecute the membership of the other.

From the beginning, the convention imposed two prohibitions to preserve institutional separation within the government. The first prohibition was against alterations in the incumbent executive's salary. The other was against simultaneous membership in the legislative and executive branches. Both prohibitions were stated in the Virginia Plan and remained substantially unaltered in the final Constitution.

See also: Constitution, The U.S.; Constitutional Convention.

Seventeenth Amendment (1913)

Ratified in 1913, the Seventeenth Amendment to the Constitution provided for direct popular election of United States senators. Under the terms of Article 1, Section 3, of the Constitution, senators were elected by state legislatures:

> **T**he Senate of the United States shall be composed of two Senators from each state, chosen by the legislature thereof, for six years; and each Senator shall have one vote.

The main criticism of legislative elections was that they distorted—or even blocked—the will of the people. Five times around the turn of the twentieth century, the House of Representatives passed constitutional amendments to provide for Senate elections by popular vote: in the Fifty-second Congress on January 16, 1893; in the Fifty-third Congress on July 21, 1894; in the Fifty-fifth Congress on May 11, 1898; in the Fifty-sixth Congress on April 13, 1900; in the Fifty-seventh Congress on February 13, 1902. Each time the Senate refused to act.

Pressures continued to mount for a switch to popular elections. Reformers began calling for a convention to propose this and perhaps other amendments to the Constitution. At about this same time, progressives of both the Democratic and Republican parties made strong gains in the 1910 midterm elections. Finally, the Senate debated and passed the amendment on June 12, 1911, by a vote of 64–24. The House concurred with the Senate version on May 13, 1912, by a vote of 238–39. Ratification of the Seventeenth Amendment was completed on April 8, 1913, and was proclaimed a part of the Constitution by Secretary of State William Jennings Bryan (1913–1915) on May 31, 1913.

The first popularly elected senator was chosen in a special election in November 1913. He

A–Z

S–T

was Senator Blair Lee, Democrat of Maryland (1914–1917), elected for the remaining three years of the unexpired term of Democratic Senator Isidor Rayner (1905–1912), who had died in office.

See also: Senate Elections; 📖 Seventeenth Amendment in the **Primary Source Library.**

Socialist Party (1901–)

A leftist political party founded in 1901 by New York attorney Morris Hillquit and railroad worker and labor leader Eugene Debs. The start of the Socialist Party marked a unique, brief era of leftist organizational unity.

The Socialist Party brought together the Social Democratic Party; Social Laborites; Christian Socialists; a wing of the Socialist Labor Party; and followers of Henry George, Edward Bellamy, and assorted populist sympathizers. Rapid growth and early success continued through the 1912 presidential election, when Debs earned 6 percent of the votes cast and some 1,200 Socialist Party candidates won state and local elections.

Despite the party's continued strong showing in the 1916 and 1920 elections, World War I (1914–1918) took a toll on the Socialist Party. Although party members were already persecuted for their opposition to the war, the Sedition Act of 1918 resulted in additional arrests and prevented the Socialist Party from using the mail to communicate with branches beyond its East Coast and Midwest bases. While many, including Debs, were being sent to prison for either their pacifist views or Sedition Act violations, the 1917 Bolshevik Revolution in Russia led by Vladimir Lenin further hastened the party's demise.

By 1919, Leninist sympathizers threatened the Socialist Party leadership. A schism ensued, resulting in the expulsion of radical party elements and the invalidation of the national executive committee elections. Thereafter, the Socialist Party and the Communist Party became two distinct organizations with decidedly different agendas.

One of the founders of the Socialist Party, Eugene V. Debs was the party's presidential nominee five times—1900, 1904, 1908, 1912, and 1920. (Library of Congress)

By breaking with its labor roots, the Socialist Party lost its legitimacy as an agent of radical social action.

Debs' death in 1926 signaled the end of the worker-oriented party and the start of a more urban-middle-class-centered party under Norman Thomas' leadership. The Socialist Party, which had 9,500 members in 1929, experienced a revival between 1929 and 1934: membership increased during the Great Depression to almost 17,000 in 1932, when Thomas polled almost 900,000 votes in the presidential race, and to 20,000 in 1934.

Many new members were young militants who increasingly disagreed with the party's old guard. Until Hillquit died in 1933, the old guard held their own, but they lost their grip thereafter. At the 1934 party convention in Detroit, the young militant wing, joined by Thomas and the Milwaukee mayor, Daniel W. Hoan, passed a new Socialist Party declaration of principles that the old guard believed encouraged too forcefully the nonelectoral seizure of power and sympathized too greatly with Soviet Russia. The old guard formally broke away in 1936 and formed the Social Democratic Federation (SDF). Party membership fell to 12,000 in 1936 and shrank to 6,500 the following year. More important, Thomas garnered only 187,000 votes during the 1936 presidential election and less than 100,000 in 1940.

From 1933 to 1940, the Socialist Party experienced further internal strains by criticizing President Franklin D. Roosevelt and the New Deal. Party members viewed New Deal programs as more sympathetic to corporate interests than to organized labor's concerns. Remaining party members split over wartime policy, with Thomas leading a pacifist faction. The party lost any influence it had as it was effectively co-opted by Roosevelt. Only in the cities of Bridgeport, Connecticut, and Milwaukee, Wisconsin, did the old Socialist Party maintain a real presence. However, Thomas continued to run as the Socialist presidential candidate through the 1948 election.

In the post–World War II era, all radicalism was suspect. Although the Socialists made inroads into the Congress of Industrial Organizations (CIO) and helped organize Detroit autoworkers and southern sharecroppers, the party disintegrated as an organization. The party continued to field a presidential candidate until the 1960 election, when it failed to run a candidate. Radicals shifted their emphasis from organized labor to civil rights and, later, worked against the war in Vietnam.

In the early 1960s, the Democratic Socialist Organizing Committee (DSOC), the New American Movement (NAM), and the Students for a Democratic Society (SDS) became the main organizational vehicles for the New Left. The SDS faded after Martin Luther King's assassination in 1968 and the Paris Peace Accords in 1973. Meanwhile NAM devoted its energies to feminism, gay rights, and local community organizing in the early 1980s.

The DSOC continued to operate in the old socialist manner as the left wing of the New Deal coalition—not as a separate political party as much as a socialist force within the Democratic Party. The DSOC was successful in attracting activists such as machinist union leader William Winpisinger, feminist and author Gloria Steinem, and gay rights activist Harry Britt. Bernard Sanders, member of Congress from Vermont who was elected in 1991, was the first self-avowed socialist elected to Congress in decades.

NAM and DSOC completed a formal merger in 1983 and emerged as the Democratic Socialists of America (DSA). The DSA brought together for the first time since World War I the disparate segments of leftist opinion, including the SDF and former socialists and communists. Although the American left was in disarray in the late 1960s and the administrations of Richard M. Nixon, Ronald Reagan, George H.W. Bush, Bill Clinton, and George W. Bush were by and large conservative, a kind of socialist revival occurred at the end of the twentieth century. Membership has remained low, but Socialist Party influences such as government-supported health care, minimum wage, and human rights were more apparent in the national political debate than at any time since the

A – Z

S-T

1960s. In addition, more than one socialist faction has fielded a candidate in every presidential election since 1976.

See also: Communist Party; Democratic Party; Socialist Workers Party (1938).

Socialist Workers Party (1938–)

A leftist party formed in 1938 by followers of the Russian revolutionary Leon Trotsky. Originally a faction within the U.S. Communist Party, the Trotskyites, as the faction was known, were expelled in 1936 on instructions from Soviet leader Joseph Stalin. A brief Trotskyite coalition with the Socialist Party ended in 1938 when the dissidents organized independently as the Socialist Workers Party. Through its youth arm, the Young Socialist Alliance, members of the Socialist Workers Party were active in the anti–Vietnam War movement and participated in civil rights protests.

Since 1948, the party has run a presidential candidate, but its entries have never received more than 0.1 percent of the popular vote. In 1992 presidential candidate James Warren was on the ballot in thirteen states and the District of Columbia and drew 23,096 votes nationwide. The party's 2000 candidate, James E. Harris, Jr., of Georgia, received 7,378 votes. In 2004, the party ran two presidential candidates— James E. Harris, Jr., who received 7,102 votes, and Róger Colero, who received 3,689 votes.

Special Elections, House of Representatives

When a vacancy occurs in the House, the usual procedure is for the governor of the affected state to call a special election. Such elections may be held at any time throughout the year, and there are usually several during each two-year Congress.

At times, there are delays in the calling of special elections. One of the longest periods in modern times when a congressional district went unrepresented occurred after the death of Representative James G. Polk, a Democrat from Ohio (1931–1941, 1949–1959), on April 28, 1959. An election to replace him did not take place until November 1960, when it was held simultaneously with the general election. Because different candidates were nominated for the two congressional races, the winner of the special election, Republican Ward M. Miller, had only two months remaining in his term.

In the days of the lame-duck sessions of Congress, elections for the remainder of a term quite often were held simultaneously with the general election, because the session following the election was an important working meeting that lasted until March 4. However, since the passage of the Twentieth Amendment in 1933 and the ending of most lame-duck sessions, elections for the remaining two months of a term have become less common. Miller, for example, never was sworn in because Congress was not in session during the period when he was waiting to serve as a representative.

Usually states are more prompt in holding special House elections than was Ohio in 1959–1960. One of the most rapid instances of succession occurred in Texas' Tenth District in 1963. Democratic representative Homer Thornberry (1949–1963) submitted his resignation on September 26, 1963, to take effect December 20. Based on Thornberry's postdated resignation, a special election was held in his district— the first election was held November 9 and the runoff on December 17. The winner, Democrat J. J. Pickle, was ready to take his seat as soon as Thornberry stepped down. He was sworn in the next day, December 21, 1963.

See also: House of Representatives; Special Elections, Senate.

Special Elections, Senate

An election called for the special purpose of filling a vacant Senate seat. In the United States Constitution, governors were given specific authority to make temporary appointments to the Senate. Article I, Section 3, Paragraph 2, states:

> If vacancies happen by resignation, or otherwise, during the recess of the legislature of any state, the executive thereof may make temporary appointments until the next meeting of the legislature, which shall then fill such vacancies.

Before the Seventeenth Amendment

As early as 1794, however, the principle was established that a vacancy created solely because a state legislature had failed to elect a new senator could not be filled by appointment, because the vacancy had not occurred "during the recess of the legislature." For example, the term of Senator Matthew Quay, a Pennsylvania Republican, (1887–1899, 1901–1904) expired March 3, 1899. The legislature was in session, but had not reelected him. Nor did it elect anyone before adjourning that April 20. Thereupon, the governor appointed Quay to the vacancy; but the Senate did not allow Quay to take the seat, because the vacancy had occurred during the meeting of the legislature. In 1901, the legislature elected Quay for the remainder of the term.

On the other hand, if a senator's term expired and the legislature was *not* in session, a governor was able to make an appointment—but only until the legislature either elected a successor or adjourned without electing one. For example, on March 3, 1809, the term of Senator Samuel Smith, Democratic-Republican from Maryland, (1803–1815, 1822–1833) expired. The legislature was not then in session and had not

elected a successor. Therefore, the governor appointed Smith to fill the vacancy until the next meeting of the legislature, which was scheduled for June 5, 1809. The Senate ruled that he was entitled to the seat. During the subsequent meeting of the state legislature that year, Smith was elected to a full term.

Whatever the condition under which an appointment had been made, it was to last only through the next state legislative session. Even if a legislature failed to elect a new senator, the appointed senator's service was to expire with the adjournment of the state legislature.

This principle was confirmed in the case of Senator Samuel Phelps, a Vermont Whig, (1839–1851, 1853–1854). Phelps was appointed in January 1853 to a vacancy caused by the death of Senator William Upham, another Vermont Whig, (1843–1853), whose term was to run through March 3, 1855. As the legislature was in recess, Phelps continued to serve until the expiration of the Thirty-second Congress on March 3, 1853, and also during a special session of the Thirty-third Congress in March and April 1853. The Vermont legislature met during October and December without electing a senator to fill the unexpired term. Phelps then showed up for the regular session of the Thirty-third Congress in December, but the Senate in March 1854 decided he was not entitled to retain his seat, because the legislature had met and adjourned without electing a new senator.

The Seventeenth Amendment and Special Elections

The adoption of the Seventeenth Amendment in 1913, providing for popular election of senators, altered the provision for gubernatorial appointment of senators to fill vacancies. The amendment provided that, in case of a vacancy,

> ...the executive authority of such state shall issue writs of election to fill such vacancies: *Provided,* that the legislature of any state may empower the executive thereof to make temporary

appointments until the people fill the vacancies by election as the legislature may direct.

Under this provision, state legislatures allowed governors to make temporary appointments until the vacancy could be filled by a special election. Special elections—elections held to fill unexpired terms—were usually held in November of an even-numbered year. Some states, however, provided for special elections to be held within just a few months after the vacancy occurred.

Before ratification of the Seventeenth Amendment, the term of an appointee generally ended when a successor was elected to fill the unexpired term or at the end of the six-year term, whichever occurred first. After the ratification of the Seventeenth Amendment, but before ratification of the Twentieth Amendment in 1933, senators who were elected to fill lengthy unexpired terms usually could take office immediately, displacing an appointee. If an appointee was serving near the close of a six-year term, most states would hold simultaneous elections to fill both the six-year term and the four-month "lame-duck" term. Sometimes different persons would be elected to each term.

To eliminate the lame-duck sessions that ran from December of an even-numbered year through March 3 of the next year, the Twentieth Amendment changed the March 3 beginning date of the terms for Congress to January 3. After the so-called lame-duck amendment took effect, senators elected to fill vacancies in terms that had several years to run would take office immediately, as before. If a vacancy occurred near the end of a six-year term, however, an appointee would often serve until the January 3 expiration date, eliminating the necessity for a special election.

Some states, however, have held elections in November for the remaining two months of a term. In 1972, for example, Georgia voters found on the ballot two Senate elections, one for a six-year term and one for a two-month term to fill the unexpired term of Democratic Senator Richard B. Russell (1933–1971), who died in office.

See also: Special Elections, House of Representatives.

Further Reading

Gould, Lewis L. *The Most Exclusive Club: A History of the Modern United States Senate.* Jackson, TN: Basic Books, 2006.

Lee, Frances E., and Bruce I. Oppenheimer. *Sizing Up the Senate: Unequal Consequences of Equal Representation.* Chicago: University of Chicago Press, 1999.

Mayhew, David R. *Congress: The Electoral Connection.* New Haven, CT: Yale University Press, 2004.

Suffrage

See Fifteenth Amendment; Nineteenth Amendment; Twenty-sixth Amendment.

Suffragists

See Women Voters.

Super Tuesday and Regional Primaries

Critics have often cited the length of the primary season (nearly twice as long as the general election campaign), the expense, the physical strain on the candidates, and the complexities of state laws as problems of presidential primaries. To deal with these problems, several states in 1974 and 1975 discussed the possibility of creating regional primaries in which individual states within a geographical region would hold their primaries on the same day. Supporters of the idea believed it would reduce candidate expenses and strain and would permit concentration on regional issues.

The idea achieved limited success in 1976 when three western states (Idaho, Nevada, and

Oregon) and three southern states (Arkansas, Kentucky, and Tennessee) decided to hold regional primaries. However, both groups chose May 25 to hold their primaries, thus defeating one of the main purposes of the plan by forcing candidates to shuttle across the country to cover both areas.

Attempts also were made in New England to construct a regional primary. New Hampshire, however, would not participate because its law required the state to hold its primary at least one week before any other state. Hesitancy by the other New England state legislatures defeated the idea. Only Vermont joined Massachusetts, on March 2, in holding a simultaneous presidential primary, although New Hampshire voted only one week earlier.

In 1980 and 1984, limited regional primaries were held again in several areas of the country. Probably the most noteworthy was the trio of southern states (Alabama, Florida, and Georgia) that voted on the second Tuesday in March—first in 1980, then again in 1984. It became the basis for "Super Tuesday," which became a full-blown southern-oriented regional primary in 1988.

The biggest change was that more and more states, hoping to increase their impact on the presidential campaign, decided to hold their primaries early. When South Dakota announced that it would hold its presidential primary in 1988 on February 23, New Hampshire moved its date to February 16.

Sixteen states—a dozen from the South—held primaries on Super Tuesday, March 8, 1988. The long-held goal of many southern political leaders to hold an early regional primary was finally realized. Most of the Republican primaries were winner-take-all, and when Vice President George Bush swept every Republican primary on Super Tuesday, he effectively locked up the GOP nomination. His major opponent, Senator Robert Dole of Kansas, withdrew by the end of the month. For the Democrats, Massachusetts Governor Michael S. Dukakis also fared well on Super Tuesday. Nevertheless, the Reverend Jesse Jackson—the first serious black candidate for a major-party presidential nomination—kept the contest going into June.

March Madness

In 1992, Super Tuesday had become part of a general rush among states to hold their primaries as early as possible. Dubbed "March Madness," the early clustering of primaries—seventeen states held primaries in February or March—was viewed with dismay by some political analysts. They said it could lead to nominees being locked in before most voters knew what was happening, resulting in less informed and deliberative voting in the general election.

As winner in the eight Super Tuesday primaries, (six of which were again in the South) on March 10, 1992, President Bush was well on his way to renomination on the GOP side. Although he lost the two New England primaries (Massachusetts and Rhode Island) that day, Bill Clinton, by winning all six southern primaries (Florida, Louisiana, Mississippi, Oklahoma, Tennessee, and Texas), established himself as the Democratic front-runner. Most of his competitors had dropped out of the race by the end of the following week. Former Governor Jerry Brown of California held out until the Democratic convention, but Brown was never able to establish any sort of momentum to overtake Clinton.

In 1996, the process was even more heavily weighted in favor of early primaries, as more than two-thirds of them were held before the end of March. The idea of regional primaries also came the closest to realization in 1996. "Junior Tuesday Week" (March 2–7) featured primary voting in ten states (five of which were in New England); Super Tuesday (March 12) had seven primaries (six of which were in the South); and "Big Ten" Tuesday (March 19) had four primaries in important midwestern states. By the time California (which had moved its primary forward in the hope of increasing its sway on the nominating process) had its primary on March 26 (along with two other western states—Nevada and Washington), Senator Robert Dole had all but clinched the Republican nomination.

2000 Outcome

In 2000, there were not only a glut of early primaries, but a large number on a single day, the first Tuesday in March (March 7). The cluster-

A – Z

S-T

Point / Counterpoint

Two Views on Super Tuesday

Since 1984, the term Super Tuesday has been used to refer to groups of presidential primary elections held on the same day in early March in the year before the November election. In 1988, several southern states decided to hold their primaries on the same day, hoping to give the region more weight in the nomination process. For the 2008 election, about 20 states moved their primaries up to February hoping to make a big impact on the nomination process. Views differ on the effectiveness of Super Tuesday. *The Christian Science Monitor* sees positives in Super Tuesday, but Professor Andrew C. Busch of the University of Denver looks at the negatives of the 2004 Super Tuesday.

Super Tuesday's Primaries are a Positive

The "Super Tuesday" primary next February [2008] includes so many states, it's dubbed "Tsunami Tuesday." Much media and political commentary is voicing alarm, mostly about money and timing. The concerns aren't baseless, but perhaps the best course is to ride this wave, not beat against it.

The issue of the primary schedule has been years in cresting. States that vote midway through or at the end of the primary process complain of less influence—or none at all—compared to those at the beginning, notably Iowa, New Hampshire, and South Carolina.

The remedy has been to bunch up and move up on the election primary calendar . . .

This development actually has some significant benefits.

First, and most important, states are on a more equal footing, which is what a democracy should strive for in voting.

Second, more states voting early means that a more diverse group of Americans can be heard sooner. One of the big beefs about the Hawkeye State [Iowa] and the Granite State [New Hampshire] going first is they aren't sufficiently representative of the nation.

Hispanics and African-Americans, for instance, will be more heavily represented in states such as Nevada, which will hold a caucus on January 19 (five days after Iowa), in the political bellwether state of Florida, which has advanced its primary to January 29, and in the Tsunami Tuesday states, which include several large states, such as California . . .

ing on this date was not coincidental. It was the earliest date allowed by Democratic rules for states other than Iowa and New Hampshire to hold their primary or caucus. Eleven states

scheduled primaries on March 7, 2000, creating a de facto national primary that became variously known as "Titanic Tuesday" or the new "Super Tuesday," although the large southern-

More equal-opportunity voting, more diversity earlier in the process, and the potential for more competition—that's not a long list of advantages, but a weighty one.

Super Tuesday's Primaries are a Negative

With John Kerry's near-sweep of the March 2 [2004] "Super Tuesday" primaries and caucuses, and John Edwards' altogether prudent decision to end his candidacy, the Democratic presidential race has come to a close eight months before election day and before 21 states have even voted. There are two ways of thinking about the newly-clarified picture.

First, substantively, a Kerry nomination means that Democrats have opted for a candidate who. . was broadly acceptable to most Democrats, because he was in the best position to benefit from the Dean-Gephardt meltdown [caucus losses] in Iowa, and because he offered a promise of "electability" due to his military service in Vietnam, which Democrats hope will inoculate him against the charge of softness on defense . . .

Second, in a more procedural vein, the outcome of Super Tuesday—ultimately, the end of the Democratic nominating race—shows in sharp relief the flaws of the current nominating system. The nominee is now determined when 21 states have yet to vote, including large states like Texas, Florida, Illinois, Pennsylvania, and New Jersey . . . A nominee was determined only six weeks after Iowa, giving precious little time for voters in later states to assess or reassess the candidates and giving little time for candidates who lost early to regain their footing and make it a race. For all practical purposes, it has not been a really competitive contest since February 10, when Kerry's momentum carried him to wins in Tennessee and Virginia and it became obvious that neither [Democratic hopefuls] Howard Dean nor John Edwards had the strength to stop him . . . Finally, a nominee was determined eight months before election day and five to six months before the party conventions, leaving an awkward and absurdly long "interregnum" between the moment of effective nomination and the moment of formal nomination. It may be impossible to predict the winner of the Bush-Kerry contest with certainty, but it is not at all difficult to predict that Americans will be sick to death of presidential politics by November.

DOCUMENT-BASED QUESTION:
Do "Super Tuesday Primaries" add to or detract from the democratic process?

oriented vote of the same name remained on the second Tuesday in March.

Political analysts predicted the huge volume of early primaries would result in both parties'

nominations being decided by the ides of March (March 15). They were right. George W. Bush and John McCain battled almost evenly through the seven states that held Republican primaries in February—Bush winning four, McCain, three. Once the calendar turned to March, however, Bush's superior organization and financial resources proved decisive as he dominated the vote on March 7 and drove McCain from the race.

With Democratic rules preventing a wholesale movement of states into February, the early Democratic calendar was quite different from the Republican one. After the early February voting in New Hampshire, the Democrats held a huge number of primaries March 7. The result, however, was the same on the Democratic side as it was on the Republican, an early knockout by the front-runner. Vice President Al Gore was closely contested by his major challenger, former Senator Bill Bradley of New Jersey, in raising funds and drawing media attention during the long stretch before the primaries. Once the balloting began, Bradley proved no match for Gore. The vice president won the late January caucuses in Iowa decisively, the New Hampshire primary narrowly, and swept all the Democratic primaries and caucuses March 7, driving Bradley to the sidelines. Only half the states had voted by then, but the Democratic and Republican races were over.

2004 Primaries

In 2004, incumbent President George W. Bush faced virtually no opposition. He won every Re-

publican nomination contest and swept the primaries on Super Tuesday. On the other hand, ten candidates vied for the 2004 Democratic presidential nomination. Among them were former Vermont Governor Howard Dean, retired general Wesley Clarke, North Carolina Senator John Edwards, and Massachusetts Senator John Kerry. Early in the campaign, Dean appeared to be the front-runner, doing well in most polls and leading in fund-raising. Kerry, however, scored well in the Iowa caucuses. He then proceeded to dominate in the primaries, winning all but four states' and the District of Columbia's primaries. John Kerry had secured the nomination well before the Democratic Convention in July 2004.

See also: Democratic Party; Election of 2008: Campaigns; Nominating Conventions; Republican Party.

Further Reading

Cook, Rhodes. *United States Presidential Primary Elections 2000–2004: A Handbook of Election Statistics.* Washington, DC: CQ Press, 2006.

Goff, Michael. *The Money Primary: The New Politics of the Early Presidential Nomination Process.* Lanham, MD: Rowman & Littlefield, 2007.

Scala, Dante J. *Stormy Weather: The New Hampshire Primary and Presidential Politics.* New York: Palgrave Macmillan, 2003.

Term Limits

The concept that elected officials should be limited by law to a specific number of terms in office. The term limits movement began in 1990

when Colorado became the first state to try to limit the number of terms that members of Congress could serve. A referendum approved by more than two-thirds of Colorado voters limited House members to six two-year terms and senators to two six-year terms. The measure also set term limits on state legislators and statewide elected offices. Prior to the 1994 congressional elections, the Republicans submitted the "Contract With America," a policy statement that also called for term limits.

By 1995, backers of term limits had won ballot initiatives or laws in at least twenty-three states. In 1995, the Supreme Court ruled in *U.S. Term Limits v. Thornton* and *Bryant v. Hill* that states could not impose limits on congressional terms. These rulings left term limits supporters only one solution: a constitutional amendment. However, constitutional amendments are difficult to pass. They must receive a two-thirds majority vote from both houses of Congress and then be ratified by three-fourths of the states.

Term limits supporters argued that mandatory retirement after twelve years was necessary to bring new people and fresh viewpoints into Congress, to reduce the constant pressure to be reelected, and to control federal spending, which they said resulted from career politicians getting too close to special interest groups seeking federal funds. Opponents countered that term limits would strip Congress of experienced legislators, diminish the political power of less-populated states that were helped by their members gaining seniority, and would merely speed up, not solve, the problem of legislators getting too close to special interest groups. Depriving voters of the right to vote for an incumbent would be undemocratic, opponents added.

In the House, the term limits constitutional amendment immediately ran into trouble. The House Judiciary Committee agreed on February 28, 1995, to send its version of the measure to the floor without recommendation. Committee Chairman Henry J. Hyde, an Illinois Republican, staunchly opposed term limits, calling the concept "a terrible mistake, a kick in the stomach of democracy." He even filed a brief outlining his opposition when the Supreme Court took up the issue in its 1994–1995 term.

On March 29, the House rejected a term limits constitutional amendment that proposed a twelve-year lifetime limit on members of each chamber. The 227–204 vote fell 61 votes short of a two-thirds majority. Forty Republicans voted against the measure, and thirty of the

forty who opposed it chaired a committee or subcommittee.

In the Senate, a term limits amendment limiting senators to two six-year terms and representatives to six two-year terms stalled on the Senate floor in April 1996. A vote to shut off debate on the measure failed, 58–42, two short of the 60 votes needed. All fifty-three Senate Republicans voted for cloture, even though some opposed limiting congressional terms, leaving the Democrats to take the heat for blocking the Senate from moving to an up-or-down vote.

Term limits supporters again tried to pass a constitutional amendment through the House in 1997. In February, members voted on eleven versions of the term limits amendment. The broad underlying measure—restricting House members to six years and senators to twelve—received a simple majority of 217–211. The tally was 69 votes short of the necessary two-thirds majority needed for passage. The House then considered ten alternative proposals. Some would have made the limits retroactive, given the states the authority to adopt stricter limits, or restricted House members to six or eight years. All were soundly defeated. The momentum for term limits seems to have stalled and the future for term limits looks uncertain.

See also: Contract with America in the **Primary Source Library;** Twenty-second Amendment.

Further Reading

Carey, John M. *Term Limits and Legislative Representation.* London: Cambridge University Press, 1998.

Farmer, Rick. *The Test of Time: Coping with Legislative Term Limits.* Lanham MD: Lexington Books, 2003.

Third Parties

In the United States, a political party other than either of the two major parties, namely, the Democrats and the Republicans. Although the United States has always had a two-party

POINT / COUNTERPOINT

Two Views on Term Limits

The discussion about term limits is as old as the Constitution—the delegates discussed it at the Constitutional Convention in 1787. In the mid-1990s, the U.S. Supreme Court ruled that states cannot limit the number of terms for their Congressional representatives. However, the organization of New York Third Parties cites reasons in favor of term limits. Another group, the People's Legal Front, opposes term limits.

Term Limits Are a Good idea

One of the biggest debates that goes on among people who watch and discuss politics is whether or not there should be term limits for politicians. Some states have enacted term limits on both a state and federal level. Those who argue against these limits usually cite the arguments that they take away choice from the voter, as well as limit the career of an effective politician. They also argue that if voters really wanted a change, they could always vote the incumbents out. Unfortunately, these arguments hold true only if we live in a perfect world, which we obviously do not. The truth is that the powers of the incumbency are all too real and they overshadow any arguments one can muster against term limits.

One of the problems of unlimited terms is that in order to stay in office, politicians must acquire vast sums of money to wage a re-election campaign. This means that they are prone to pleasing special interest groups that provide the PAC money that finances their campaign. The problem is that this money easily corrupts an incumbent's vote in order to keep that money flowing. Secondly, politicians' need to keep pleasing the voters, since they need their re-election vote. Since the incumbent must now pander to a fickle electorate, they are prone to pork barrel spending and ill conceived projects to make them look good back home. Too much of the electorate seems to be fooled and have a disconnect between the taxes that they pay and the pork barrel spending that goes on. Many of our elected representatives know this and seem all too happy to go on fooling them. The result of PAC money, and the problem of pandering to the wants of the electorate so as not to alienate them, is that urgent problems that need attention are going unattended and unresolved. This will come back to haunt us later on . . .

Now, do term limits really limit the careers of effective politicians? Well, that depends on how you define "effective". I've seen many new politicians

system, third parties have frequently played a vital role in the politics. No third-party candidate has ever been elected to the presidency, but many have been elected to other federal, state, and local offices. The votes third parties have garnered have also been a crucial factor in the outcome of elections. Moreover, the issues spotlighted by minor parties have often ended up being co-opted into the platforms of the major parties.

get elected with a "change the system" attitude. After several terms in office, they end up being no better than the people that they originally replaced. They effectively learned the system, and that's how they became "effective". Essentially, the system corrupted them. A democracy demands that new people with new ideas be continually incorporated into the system. This prevents stagnation and corruption from flourishing, as the incumbent's number one concern of staying in power is negated. The system we have now actually stifles new ideas since the same people hold the same offices year after year.

Term Limits Are a Bad Idea

Term limits is and always has been a bad idea. The reason it's a bad idea is because it limits the choices of people the public has to vote for. If you have a really good public servant and you want to keep him, you can't. You have to get rid of the good candidate and replace him with someone who's inexperienced. By having term limits, we are eliminating the people who have wisdom and experience from political life. Like any job, it takes years to be good at what you do. About the time our elected officials have become good public servants, we're required to throw them out.

And what is the advantage of that? Well, for the lazy stupid voters it creates change for people who don't care enough to find out what the issues are or have the self control to not vote for the incumbent. Term limit laws are an acknowledgement by the voters that they are too dumb to make an informed decision at the ballot box.

It doesn't matter how much money someone spends, when you go in to vote, there's no one holding a gun to your head making you vote for the guy who spent the most money or who is already in office. Believe it or not, you have free will. You can vote these people out. If you think the incumbent has an unfair advantage, you're right. That's why we need to reform the system and prohibit politicians from taking certain kinds of bribes (campaign contributions, we know what they really are). But if Americans are too damn lazy to figure out who to vote for they deserve the politicians who get elected.

DOCUMENT-BASED QUESTION:
What are the pros and cons of term limits?

Nineteenth-Century Third Parties

As the original party system of Hamiltonian Federalists and Jeffersonian Democratic-Republicans broke down, the National Republican Party developed into the Whig Party. The Anti-Masonic Party also arose in the 1830s. In 1832, the Anti-Masons ran William Wirt for president earning almost 8 percent of the popular vote. Nonetheless, they achieved some state and local offices, particularly in New York State where the party originated.

In 1844 the Liberty Party, which opposed slavery, won 2.3 percent of the popular vote, and it may have affected the outcome of the election. In 1848, however, the less radical Free Soil Party, which was dedicated to stopping the spread of slavery in the territories, played the role of spoiler. Running former president Martin Van Buren, the party won enough votes, mostly from Democrats, to enable the Whig candidate, Zachary Taylor, to defeat the Democrat, Lewis Cass. It ran John P. Hale for president in 1852, obtaining 5 percent of the popular vote. The end of the Free Soil Party was hastened by the rise of the Republican Party, which took up its stance in opposition to slavery in the territories.

In the 1850s, the Know Nothing Party, or the American Party, won large votes in Pennsylvania and New York and even briefly gained control of the Massachusetts government. The party's main goals were excluding Catholics from public office, enacting restrictive immigration laws, and establishing literacy tests for voting.

Parties such as the Greenback Party (1874–1884) and the Prohibition Party, which started in 1869 and has continued to this day, never attracted many votes on the national level, but their success rested on convincing one of the major parties to take up their cause. Eventually the Republican Party embraced Prohibition, while the Democratic Party favored the expansion of the money supply.

The Populist (or People's) Party, which represented the interests of farmers and labor, arose in the South Third West in the 1880s. The Populist platform would eventually be adopted by the Democratic Party under its 1896 presidential candidate, William Jennings Bryan.

The Socialist Party came to prominence in the **Progressive era**, with members winning state and local offices and serving in Congress. In 1904, it ran Eugene V. Debs for president, winning 3 percent of the vote against the Republican incumbent Theodore Roosevelt and Alton B. Parker, the Democrat. Debs would run again in 1908, 1912, and 1920, and in this last election (campaigning from a federal penitentiary, where he was imprisoned for opposition to World War I) he tallied 915,490 votes (3.4 percent). Later, Norman Thomas would serve as the Socialist Party candidate in several elections, with his largest vote in 1932 when he won 884,649 votes (2.2 percent).

Some minor parties have served as vehicles for the candidacies of certain individuals. The Progressive, or Bull Moose, Party became a vehicle for Theodore Roosevelt's attempt to recapture the White House in 1912, running against Democrat Woodrow Wilson and Republican William Howard Taft. In that race, all three candidates were Progressives to an extent. When Taft's people prevented Roosevelt delegates from some states from being seated at the Republican convention, Roosevelt bolted the party and ran as a Progressive. The result was a split of the Republican vote and a victory for Wilson.

In 1924, the Progressive Party ran Robert M. La Follette for president, capturing 16.6 percent of the vote. In 1948, using the Progressive Party label, Henry A. Wallace, Franklin D. Roosevelt's former vice president and secretary of agriculture, scored 2.4 percent of the vote in a

Consumer advocate Ralph Nader ran for the presidency five times–1992, 1996, 2000, 2004, and 2008. In 1992 and 1996, he ran as a write-in candidate, but in 2000, he was the nominee of the Green Party. In 2004, he ran as an independent but was endorsed by the Reform Party; in 2008, he again ran as an independent. (votenader.org)

Top Vote-Winning Third Parties, 1832–1996

Party	Election year	Candidate	Popular vote (percent)	No. electoral votes
Anti-Masonic	1832	William Wirt	7.8	7
Free Soil	1848	Martin Van Buren	10.1	0
American ("Know-Nothing")	1856	Millard Fillmore	21.5	8
Southern Democrats	1860	John C. Breckinridge	18.1	72
Constitutional Union	1860	John Bell	12.6	39
Populist	1892	James B. Weaver	8.5	22
Socialist	1912	Eugene V. Debs	6.0	0
Progressive (Bull Moose)	1912	Theodore Roosevelt	27.4	88
Progressive	1924	Robert M. La Follette	16.6	13
American Independent	1968	George C. Wallace	13.5	46
Independent	1980	John B. Anderson	6.6	0
Independent	1992	H. Ross Perot	18.9	0
Reform	1996	H. Ross Perot	8.5	0

The parties (or independents) shown in the above table received more than 5.6 percent of the popular vote, which is the average third party vote historically cast for president.

A–Z

S–T

four-way race that saw Truman reelected. The 1948 election also saw the emergence of another third party, the States' Rights, or Dixiecrat, Party. The Dixiecrats ran J. Strom Thurmond, the governor of South Carolina, for president, opposing the Democratic Party's adoption of a civil rights plank in its 1948 platform. Thurmond won 2.4 percent of the vote.

Third parties continued to run presidential candidates, and in some places candidates for Congress and state and local offices. In the 1960s John Lindsay, a former Republican congressman, was elected mayor of New York City on the Liberal Party ticket, and in 1970 James L. Buckley won a U.S. Senate seat from New York, running as a member of the Conservative Party. Nevertheless, third-party candidates have also been spoilers, as in 1980 when incumbent Republican senator Jacob Javits of New York lost his party's nomination and ran as a Liberal Party candidate, dividing the votes of moderates, liberals, and Democrats, and thus allowing the election of conservative Republican Alfonse D'Amato.

In the close 1968 presidential race between Richard M. Nixon and Hubert H. Humphrey, George C. Wallace, the governor of Alabama, captured 13.5 percent of the popular vote and forty-six electoral votes. He ran on the American Independent ticket, pushing a conservative and somewhat racist agenda. In 1980, John B. Anderson ran as an independent against Ronald Reagan and Jimmy Carter and received 6.6 percent of the popular vote, but no electoral votes. In 1992 H. Ross Perot ran for president as an Independent, receiving 18.9 percent of the vote, but no electoral votes. In 1996, he ran again under the Reform Party banner. This party has run candidates for state and local office across the country, and in 1998, Jesse Ventura was elected governor of Minnesota as the Reform Party candidate. In 2000, the Reform Party was in disarray as it split over the contested nomination of Patrick J. Buchanan for president.

Today the Libertarian Party and the Green Party offer consistent ideologies through their third-party movements. Because they are primarily ideologically based, however, they are the more likely to be absorbed eventually by a major party that has co-opted their ideas and raided their constituencies.

See also: American Independent Party; Anti-Masonic Party; Free Soil Party; Green Party; Greenback Party; Know-Nothing Party; Liberty Party; Libertarian Party; Populist Party; Progressive Party; Reform Party; Socialist Labor Party; Socialist Workers Party.

Further Reading

Lutz, Norma Jean, and Arthur M. Schlesinger. *The History of the Third Parties.* New York: Chelsea House Publications, 2000.

Richardson, Darcy G. *Others: Third Parties During the Populist Period.* Lincoln, NE: iUniverse, Inc., 2007.

Sifry, Micah L. *Spoiling for a Fight: Third-Party Politics in America.* London: Routledge, 2003.

Third Term

See Election of 1940; Twenty-second Amendment.

Twelfth Amendment (1804)

Amendment to the Constitution that changed the system by which electors voted for president. Under the Constitution, electors cast two votes for president, with the candidate receiving the largest majority elected as president and the second-place finisher elected as vice president. Under the Twelfth Amendment, the electors vote separately for president and vice president, with a majority of electoral votes required to win each office.

Also under the Twelfth Amendment, the number of candidates from which the House would select the president—if no candidate received a majority of electoral votes for president—was reduced from five to the three highest electoral vote winners. Authority to select a vice president if the electoral college failed to do so was placed solely in the Senate. The amendment authorizes the Senate to choose from the two highest electoral vote getters for vice president, with a majority vote of the entire membership of the Senate required for election. The Constitution's age, residency, and citizenship requirements for president were extended to the vice president. Finally, the amendment stated that if a vice president, but no president, is chosen by the March 4 following the election, "the Vice President shall act as President as in the case of the death or other constitutional disability of the President."

The Old System Breaks Down

The original electoral college designed by the Constitutional Convention assumed that political parties would not arise and dominate the presidential election process. Instead, the delegates had believed that states and **ad hoc groups** would nominate candidates for president. The most popular and, presumably, the best-qualified candidate would be elected as president and the second most popular as vice president.

Despite the Framers' intentions, two political parties—the Federalists and the Democratic-Republicans—were formed during George Washington's first term (1789–1793) as president. Within a few years, the parties began nominating complete national tickets: Federalist and Democratic-Republican candidates for president and for vice president. In 1800, all seventy-three Democratic-Republican electors (a majority of the electoral college) cast one of their votes for president for Thomas Jefferson and the other for Aaron Burr, the Democratic-Republican candidates. Although these electors wanted Jefferson to be elected as president and Burr as vice president, the vote was constitutionally recorded as a tie between Jefferson and Burr for the office of president. Under Article II, Section 1, Clause 3, the House of Representatives was then forced to choose between them.

Dominated by a lame-duck Federalist majority, the House, through thirty-five ballots, denied Jefferson the majority of state delegations that was required for election. On the thirty-sixth ballot, urged by Federalist leader Alexander Hamilton, the House finally elected Thomas Jefferson (1801–1809) as president and Aaron Burr (1801–1805) as vice president.

Proposal and Ratification

Aware both of the problems of the Constitution's presidential election process and the new reality of party politics, the Democratic-Republican controlled Congress proposed the Twelfth Amendment in December 1803. All but the most fervent Federalist states quickly ratified the amendment, and it became part of the Constitution in June 1804, in time for the presidential election later that year.

Separate Balloting for President and Vice President

The Twelfth Amendment's requirement that electors vote separately for president and vice president completely solved the problem that had occasioned the amendment's enactment. Not since 1800 has there been any confusion about who was running for president and who for vice president.

One issue of electoral college voting that emerged after the ratification of the Twelfth Amendment was that of the faithless elector. In practice, electors have always been chosen to vote for the candidate supported by their state, not to exercise independent judgment in deciding whom to support. No constitutional requirement binds electors to do so, however. Twenty-four states and the District of Columbia currently have laws that require electors to support the candidates whom they are pledged to represent.

See also: Democratic-Republican Party; Election of 1800; Election of 1804; Faithless Electors; Federalist Party; 📖 Twelfth Amendment in the **Primary Source Library**.

Further Reading

Koruda, Tadahisa. *The Origins of the Twelfth Amendment in the Early Republic, 1787–1804.* Westport, CT: Greenwood Press, 1994.

Twentieth Amendment (1933)

Ratified in 1933, the Twentieth Amendment, also known as the "lame-duck" amendment, was written to shorten the time between the election of the president, vice president, and members of Congress and their entry into office. The gap for newly elected representatives and senators (unless the president called Congress into special session) had been thirteen months—from the first Tuesday after the first Monday in November (election day) until the first Monday in December of the following year, the date established by Article I, Section 4, Clause 2, of the Constitution.

The delay for presidents and vice presidents had been about four months, from election day until the following March 4. The source of this date for presidential inauguration was a decision by the Congress of the Articles of Confederation. After the Constitution was ratified, Congress had declared March 4, 1789, the date "for commencing proceedings under the said Constitution." A 1792 law confirmed March 4 as the starting date for future presidential terms.

Senator George W. Norris (1913–1943), a Republican from Nebraska, was the main author of the Twentieth Amendment. He sought to remedy three major flaws in the traditional arrangement, which he regarded as better suited to an age when travel was difficult and time-consuming and the business of the government was relatively minor. The first flaw was the biennial lame-duck session of Congress, which typically lasted from the December after the election until the following March and which included many outgoing members of the defeated party. Second, by not having Congress begin its term before the president, the procedures then in place empowered the lame-duck

A–Z

S–T

Congress, not the most recently elected one, to choose the president and vice president in the event of an electoral college deadlock. This had happened in 1801 and 1825. Finally, Norris regarded four months as too long for the nation to have, in effect, two presidents—an outgoing incumbent and an incoming president-elect.

Section 1 of the Amendment

To remedy the lame-duck and two-presidents problems, Section 1 of the Twentieth Amendment established noon on January 20 as the beginning of the president's and vice president's four-year terms. Noon on January 3 was set as the start of the term for members of Congress.

Section 3 of the Amendment

Norris also used the Twentieth Amendment to address two other potential problems in the presidential and vice-presidential selection process. Thus, Section 3 provides that if the president-elect dies before the start of the term, the vice president–elect would be inaugurated as president. Under Section 2 of the Twenty-fifth Amendment, which became part of the Constitution in 1967, the vice president–elect who thus succeeds to the presidency then would appoint a new vice president, pending congressional approval.

In addition to death, Section 3 also specifies that if, by inauguration day, no presidential candidate has received the electoral vote majority or, failing that, the majority of state delegations in the House of Representatives that is required for election, the vice president–elect becomes acting president until a president is chosen. The amendment also allowed Congress to legislate for the possibility that a vice president–elect might not be chosen either, whether through failure to secure an electoral vote majority or inability to win a Senate election. Congress passed such a law in 1947, the Presidential Succession Act. The act stated that the Speaker of the House would serve as the acting president until a president or vice president is elected.

Section 4 of the Amendment

The possibility that either a winning presidential or vice-presidential candidate might die before officially receiving "elect" status when Congress counts the electoral votes on January

Order of Presidential Succession

Vice President
Speaker of the House of Representatives
President Pro Tempore of the Senate
Secretary of State
Secretary of the Treasury
Secretary of Defense
Attorney General
Secretary of the Interior
Secretary of Agriculture
Secretary of Commerce
Secretary of Labor
Secretary of Health and Human Services
Secretary of Housing and Urban Development
Secretary of Transportation
Secretary of Energy
Secretary of Education
Secretary of Veterans Affairs

The Presidential Succession Act of 1947 estimated the current order or succession to the presidency. The cabinet officers are ordered in the line of succession according to the date their offices were established.

6 is addressed in Section 4. It simply calls on Congress to legislate in these instances.

Congress never has done so, however, which means that if such a death were to occur, it would have to improvise. One of Congress' options would be to declare the dead candidate elected, thus, if the presidential candidate had died, triggering Section 1 of the amendment, under which the vice president–elect would become president. Or, if the winning vice-presidential candidate had died, Section 2 of the Twenty-fifth Amendment would go into effect, under which the vice-president-elect-turned-president would nominate a new vice president after being sworn in as president. Congress's other choice—less absurd than electing a dead person but politically more problematic—would be to allow the House of Representatives to elect one of the defeated presidential candidates as president.

Proposal and Ratification

The Twentieth Amendment passed easily through Congress on March 2, 1932, and was ratified without controversy on February 6, 1933. The wisdom of the amendment seemed confirmed when, nine days later, an assassin shot at President-elect Franklin D. Roosevelt in Miami, Florida.

See also: Election of 1800; Election of 1824; Election of 1932.

Twenty-fifth Amendment (1967)

Amendment to the United States Constitution concerning presidential disability and succession, which took effect in 1967. The amendment provided for continuity in carrying out the functions of the presidency in the event of presidential disability and for filling a vacancy in the vice presidency. The amendment was approved by the Senate and House in 1965 and took effect February 10, 1967, after ratification by thirty-eight states.

Congressional consideration of presidential disability had been prompted by President Dwight D. Eisenhower's heart attack in 1955. The ambiguity of the language of the disability clause (Article II, Section 1, Clause 5) of the Constitution had caused debate ever since the Constitutional Convention of 1787. However, it never had been decided how far the term *disability* extended or who would be the judge of it.

Clause 5 provided that Congress should decide who was to succeed to the presidency if both the president and the vice president died, resigned, or became disabled. Congress enacted succession laws three times. By the Act of March 1, 1792, it provided for succession—after the vice president—of the president pro tempore of the Senate, then of the House Speaker, and then, if those offices were vacant, states were to send electors to Washington to choose a new president.

That law stood until passage of the Presidential Succession Act of January 19, 1886, which changed the line of succession to run from the vice president to the secretary of state, secre-

tary of the Treasury, and so on through the cabinet in order of rank. Sixty-one years later the Presidential Succession Act of July 18, 1947, which is still in force, placed the Speaker of the House and the president pro tempore of the Senate ahead of cabinet officers in succession after the vice president.

Before ratification of the Twenty-fifth Amendment, no procedures were in place to cover presidential incapacity or of a vacancy in the office of vice president. Two presidents had had serious disabilities—James A. Garfield, shot in 1881 and confined to his bed until he died two and a half months later, and Woodrow Wilson, who suffered a stroke in 1919. In each case, the vice president did not assume any duties of the presidency for fear he would appear to be taking over the powers of that office.

Ratification of the Twenty-fifth Amendment established procedures that clarified these areas of uncertainty in the Constitution. The amendment provided that the vice president should become acting president under either one of two circumstances: (1) if the president informed Congress of inability to perform duties, the vice president would become acting president until the president could resume normal responsibilities; or (2) if the vice president and a majority of the cabinet, or another body designated by Congress, found the president to be incapacitated, the vice president would become acting president until the president informed Congress that the disability had ended. Congress was given twenty-one days to resolve any dispute over the president's disability; a two-thirds vote of both chambers was required to overrule the president's declaration of being no longer incapacitated.

Vacancy in the Vice Presidency

The Twenty-fifth Amendment also specified what to do when a vacancy occurred in the office of the vice president, by death, succession to the presidency, or resignation. Under the amendment, the president nominates a replacement vice president, with the nomination subject to confirmation by a majority vote of both chambers of Congress. Within only eight years after ratification, two

The provisions of the Twenty-fifth Amendment were first used in 1973 when President Richard M. Nixon nominated Gerald R. Ford (left) to the vice presidency upon the resignation of Spiro T. Agnew. The following year, Ford assumed the presidency after Nixon resigned. In turn, Ford nominated Nelson A. Rockefeller (right) as vice president. (Library of Congress)

presidents used the power to appoint a new vice president.

In October 1973 when Vice President Agnew resigned, President Nixon nominated Gerald Ford as the new vice president. Ford was confirmed by both houses of Congress and sworn in December 6, 1973. On Nixon's resignation August 9, 1974, Ford succeeded to the presidency, becoming the first president in American history who was elected neither to the presidency nor to the vice presidency. President Ford chose as his new vice president Nelson A. Rockefeller, former governor of New York, who was sworn in December 19, 1974.

With both the president and vice president holding office through appointment rather than election, some members of Congress and the public expressed concern about the power of a president to appoint, in effect, his own succes-

sor. Accordingly, Senator John O. Pastore, a Rhode Island Democrat, introduced a proposed constitutional amendment February 3, 1975. This proposed amendment would provide for a special national election for president when more than one year remained in a presidential term. Hearings were held before the Senate Judiciary Subcommittee on Constitutional Amendments, but no action was taken.

The Reagan Shooting and Disability

In the aftermath of the attempted assassination of President Ronald Reagan in March 1981, there was no need to invoke the presidential disability provisions of the Twenty-fifth Amendment. Soon after news of the shooting became known, the members of the Reagan cabinet gathered in the White House, ready to invoke the amendment's procedures, if necessary. Vice President George Bush was on an Air Force jet returning to Washington, D.C., from Texas.

Criticism of the administration's failure to act after Reagan was shot shaped its response to the second instance of presidential disability, Reagan's cancer surgery on July 13, 1985. This time Reagan did relinquish his powers and duties to Bush before undergoing anesthesia. However, he did not explicitly invoke the Twenty-fifth Amendment, saying instead that he was not convinced that the amendment was meant to apply to "such brief and temporary periods of incapacity."

Still, a precedent was established that the Twenty-fifth Amendment would work as intended in future administrations. This precedent was followed in May 1991 when President Bush said he would turn power over to Vice President Dan Quayle if his irregular heartbeat required electroshock therapy. It did not. In 2002, just before undergoing a medical procedure requiring sedation, President George W. Bush briefly transferred his presidential powers to Vice President Richard B. Cheney.

See also: 📖 Twenty-fifth Amendment the **Primary Source Library.**

Further Reading

Feerick, John. *The Twenty-fifth Amendment: Its Complete History and Application.* New York: Fordham University Press, 1992.

Thompson, Kenneth W. *Papers on Presidential Disability and the Twenty-fifth Amendment, Volume IV.* Lanham, MD: University Press of America, 1997.

Twenty-fourth Amendment (1964)

Amendment to the Constitution that outlawed poll taxes in federal elections. After the Civil War (1861–1865), the states of the former Confederacy implemented the poll tax—a fee to be paid by the voter to be allowed to vote. The purpose of the poll tax was to keep African

Americans and poor whites from voting. By the 1930s, however, most states had dropped the poll tax, and by 1960, only four states required payment from voters.

In August 1962, the House of Representatives approved a constitutional amendment—already accepted by the Senate—that outlawed poll taxes in federal elections. The Twenty-fourth amendment was ratified in January 1964. In 1966, the Supreme Court held that the poll tax was an unconstitutional requirement for voting in state and local elections as well. Justice William O. Douglas (1939–1975) wrote for the majority in *Harper v. Virginia Board of Elections:*

> **V**oter qualifications have no relation to wealth nor to paying or not paying this or any other tax. Wealth, like race, creed, or color, is not germane to one's ability to participate intelligently in the electoral process.

See also: Poll Tax.

Twenty-second Amendment (1951)

Amendment to the Constitution that limits the president to two terms in office. The Twenty-second Amendment, ratified on February 27, 1951, prohibits any person from being elected president more than two times. It also prevents successor presidents from being elected more than once if they have served more than two years of a departed president's four-year term. If they serve two years or less of an unexpired term, they may be elected two times on their own, for a maximum tenure of ten years. The amendment was written in such a way as to exempt Harry S. Truman (1945–1953), who was president at the time Congress was considering the matter, from its coverage.

The Two-Term "Tradition"

Thomas Jefferson (1801–1809) was the first president to argue that no president should serve more than two terms. In response to a letter from the Vermont state legislature urging him to run for a third term (six other states had sent similar letters), Jefferson cited George Washington's two-term precedent (1789–1797) as wise and sound. Jefferson's defense of a two-term limit took root quickly in presidential politics. Indeed, the Whig Party and many Democrats soon argued for a one-term limit. Andrew Jackson (1829–1837) was the last president until Abraham Lincoln (1861–1865) to be elected to two terms, and even Jackson said he would prefer a constitutional amendment barring more than one presidential term (although Jackson favored a six-year term).

In the late nineteenth and early twentieth centuries, the issue of a third term arose only occasionally. Ulysses S. Grant (1869–1877) and Woodrow Wilson (1913–1921) probably would have liked to serve another four years. Both presidents, however, were too unpopular at the end of their second terms even to be renominated by their parties.

Theodore Roosevelt's (1901–1909) situation was more complicated. He was elected president only once, in 1904, but, as vice president, he had served all but six months of the term of his assassinated predecessor, William McKinley (1897–1901). In 1908, Roosevelt declined a certain renomination and, considering his great popularity, a probable reelection, calling the two-term limit a "wise custom." Four years later, however, he ran for president again, first as a Republican, then as a third party candidate.

Franklin D. Roosevelt

In 1940, the two-term tradition was broken by President Franklin Roosevelt (1933–1945). In 1937, Roosevelt, although not flatly ruling out a third term, had declared that his "great ambition on January 20, 1941" (the day his second term would expire) was to "turn over this desk and chair in the White House" to a successor. As Roosevelt's second term wore on, however, Congress' resistance to his policies and programs increasingly frustrated him. In 1939, World War II broke out in Europe in response to German, Italian, and Soviet aggression, with little prospect that the United States

would be able to remain at peace. Waiting until the Democratic convention in July 1940, Roosevelt finally signaled his willingness to be renominated. The delegates overwhelmingly approved.

Public opinion polls had shown that the voters were deeply divided about the propriety of Roosevelt's candidacy. Republicans took up the cry "No third term!" on behalf of their nominee, business leader Wendell Willkie. Roosevelt won the election, but by a much narrower popular vote margin than in 1936—five million votes, compared with eleven million. In 1944, with the United States and its allies nearing victory in World War II, Roosevelt won another term, by three million votes. Ill at the time of his fourth election, he died on April 12, 1945, less than three months after his fourth inauguration.

Proposing the Amendment

In the midterm elections of 1946, the Republicans regained a majority of both houses of Congress. On February 6, 1947, less than five weeks after the opening of the Eightieth Congress, the House passed a strict two-term amendment to the Constitution by a vote of 285–121. The House bill provided that any president who had served one full term and even one day of another would be barred from seeking reelection. Republicans supported the amendment unanimously (238–0); Democrats opposed it by a 47–121 vote, with most of the Democratic yea votes coming from southerners. Five weeks later, on March 12, the Senate passed a slightly different version of the amendment (it allowed a president who had served one full term and less than half of another to seek an additional term) by a vote of 59–23. Republican senators, like their House colleagues, were unanimous in their support (46–0); Democrats opposed the amendment by a vote of 23–13. The differences between the two versions of the amendment were ironed out quickly in favor of the Senate's version and final congressional action took place on March 24, 1947.

Ratification

Once proposed, the Twenty-second Amendment received a mixed response from the states. Only one other amendment to the Constitution has taken longer to ratify than the three years, eleven months, required for the two-term limit—the Twenty-seventh Amendment, which took more than 200 years. Eighteen state legislatures—exactly half the needed number—approved the amendment in 1947, all of them in predominantly Republican states. Afterward, ratification proceeded slowly, with most victories coming in the South. The adoption of the Twenty-second Amendment was certified on February 27, 1951.

See also: Election of 1912; Election of 1940; Election of 1944; Term Limits.

Twenty-sixth Amendment (1971)

Amendment to the United States Constitution that lowered the voting age to eighteen for federal, state, and local elections. Twenty-one was the minimum voting age in every state until 1943, when Georgia lowered it to eighteen—the age at which young men were being drafted to fight in World War II (1941–1945). The slogan, "Old enough to fight, old enough to vote," certainly seemed logical. However, no other state followed Georgia's lead until after the war. In 1946, South Carolina Democrats authorized eighteen-year-olds to vote in party primaries, but later withdrew that privilege. In 1955, Kentucky voters lowered the voting age to eighteen. Upon entering the Union in 1959, Alaska adopted a minimum voting age of nineteen and Hawaii adopted a voting age of twenty.

Meanwhile, in 1954, President Dwight D. Eisenhower had proposed a constitutional amendment granting eighteen-year-olds the right to vote nationwide, but the proposal was rejected by the Senate. Three reasons probably influenced a change in Congress: (1) America's growing youth population, which during the 1960s had begun to capture the nation's

DECISION MAKERS

Rock the Vote

Founded in 1990, Rock the Vote is a non-profit organization dedicated to bringing young people into the political process. Members of the recording industry who were concerned about the increasing amount of censorship in the music business founded the group. Rock the Vote's first campaign was "Censorship is UnAmerican." Today, Rock the Vote attempts to bring young voters and the entertainment community together to show that political participation is "cool." Athletes, actors, musicians, and comedians have all worked with Rock the Vote in an attempt to reach out and engage young voters.

Although its major goal is to increase youth voter turnout, Rock the Vote also works with young people to help them improve their communities and get involved in issues they care about. Rock the Vote also partners with civil-rights groups to produce public service ads encouraging young people to be active citizens—all the time, not just at election time.

attention; (2) the hopes of Republicans and Democrats to win new voters; and (3) the Vietnam War, in which the young were called on to fight again. Thus, in the Voting Rights Act of 1970, Congress added a provision to lower the voting age to eighteen in all federal, state, and local elections, effective January 1, 1971.

President Richard Nixon signed the bill into law, but restated his belief that the provision was unconstitutional because Congress had no power to extend suffrage by law. He directed Attorney General John N. Mitchell to ask for a court test of the law's validity. The Supreme Court, ruling in *Oregon v. Mitchell* only weeks before the law was due to take effect, held that it was applicable to federal elections, but held it unconstitutional in regard to state and local elections.

After the Court ruled, Congress quickly approved and sent to the states a proposed Twenty-sixth Amendment to the Constitution, stating:

Тhe right of citizens of the United States, who are eighteen years of age or older, to vote shall not be denied or abridged by the United States or by any State on account of age.

The Congress shall have power to enforce this article by appropriate legislation.

The proposal received final congressional approval on March 23, 1971, and was ratified by the necessary three-fourths of the states by July 1, record time for a constitutional amendment.

More than twenty-five million Americans became eligible to vote for the first time in the 1972 presidential election. It was the biggest influx of potential voters since women won the right to vote in 1920. Yet the younger age group has never fulfilled its potential power at the polls; in election after election, younger voters had the lowest turnout rate of any age category.

See also: Twenty-sixth Amendment in the **Primary Source Library.**

U.S. Labor Party (1973–)

Group formed in 1973 as the political arm of the National Caucus of Labor Committees (NCLC). The U.S. Labor Party made its debut in national politics in 1976. The NCLC, a Marxist group, was organized in 1968 by splinters of the radical political and social movements of the 1960s. New Yorker Lyndon LaRouche, the party's chairman and a self-taught economist who worked in the management and computer

fields, became the party's 1976 presidential nominee and Wayne Evans, a Detroit steelworker, his running mate.

The party directed much of its fire at the powerful and wealthy Rockefeller family. It charged that banks controlled by the Rockefellers were strangling the U.S. and world economies. In an apocalyptic vein, the party predicted a world monetary collapse by election day and the destruction of the country by thermonuclear war by the summer of 1977.

LaRouche's party developed a reputation for harassment because of its shouted interruptions and demonstrations against its political foes, including the Communist Party and the United Auto Workers. Members accused some left-wing organizations and individuals, such as linguist Noam Chomsky and Marcus Raskin and his Institute for Policy Studies, of conspiring with the Rockefellers and the Central Intelligence Agency (CIA).

During the 1976 campaign, LaRouche was more critical of challenger Jimmy Carter than President Gerald R. Ford. He depicted Ford as a well-meaning man out of his depth in the presidency, but Carter as a pawn of nuclear war advocates and a disgracefully unqualified presidential candidate. LaRouche captured only 40,043 votes, less than 0.1 percent of the national vote. He was on the ballot in twenty-three states and the District of Columbia.

Although the U.S. Labor Party did not run a presidential candidate in the 1980 election, LaRouche ran a strident campaign—as a Democrat. By this time, LaRouche's politics had shifted to the right, and his speeches were fraught with warnings of conspiracy. He continued his crusade in 1984 but as an "independent Democrat," dismissing Democratic presidential nominee Walter F. Mondale as an "agent of Soviet influence." LaRouche received 78,807 votes, or 0.1 percent of the vote, in the fall election.

In 1988, LaRouche again attempted to run as a Democrat but, failing the nomination, gar-

nered 25,562 votes under the banner of the National Economic Recovery Party. On December 16, 1988, LaRouche and six of his associates were convicted on forty-seven counts of mail fraud and conspiracy to commit mail fraud. LaRouche was sentenced to fifteen years in prison.

In 1992, the untiring LaRouche ran again for president from his jail cell. As a convicted felon, he no longer had the right to vote himself. LaRouche ran as an independent although his name appeared on several state ballots under various party names, including Economic Recovery. His supporters, experienced in winning ballot access, placed him on the ballot in seventeen states and the District of Columbia. He received 26,333 votes nationwide.

In 1996, LaRouche's name disappeared from the general election ballot, although he entered the Democratic primaries. LaRouche ran in the party's primaries in every election from 1980 through 2000, with his best showing in 1996 when President Bill Clinton had no major opposition for renomination. That year, LaRouche drew nearly 600,000 Democratic primary votes—5.4 percent of the party's total primary ballots. In 2000, LaRouche received only 3,743 votes in the Democratic primaries. In 2004, LaRouche again entered the Democratic primaries, but the Democratic Party did not consider him a legitimate candidate and he received very little support.

Voter Registration

The process by which qualified voters are recognized. To prevent election fraud states use several methods to restrict voting within their jurisdictions to those persons legally entitled to

do so. Chief among these protections is the voter registration process. The need for such a system is a reflection of America's growth in population and diversity.

When the United States was primarily a rural nation, its communities were small and most people knew each other. Voting was a relatively simple matter: a voter simply had to show up at

Voter Registration Requirements by State

State	Age Requirement	Minimum Residency Requirement*	State	Age Requirement	Minimum Residency Requirement*
Alabama	Be 18 before the next election	none	Missouri	Be at least 17½ to register, but 18 to vote	none
Alaska	Be 18 within 90 days of registration	none	Montana	Be 18 by the next election	live in your county for at least 30 days
Arizona	Be 18 before the next general election	live in Arizona 29 days before registration	Nebraska	Be 18 by the next election	none
Arkansas	Be 18 before the next election	none	Nevada	Be 18 by the next election	live your county for at least 30 days and in your precinct for 10 days before the election
California	Be 18 before the next election	none
Colorado	Be 18 on or before election day	live in Colorado 30 days before the election	New Hampshire	Be at least 18	none
Connecticut	Be 18 on or before election day	none	New Jersey	Be at least 18	live in New Jersey at the same address for at least 30 days
Delaware	Be 18 on the date of the next general election	none	New Mexico	Be at least 18	none
District of Columbia	Be 18 on the date of the next general election	live in DC 30 days before the election	New York	Be 18 by the date of the election or the primary in which you want to vote	be a resident of the country or the City of New York for at least 30 days
Florida	Be 18 years old, but may pre-register at 17	none
Georgia	Be 18 within 6 months of registration and be 18 by election day	none	North Carolina	Be 18 by election day	live in your county for at least 30 days
Hawaii	Be at least 16 years old to register, but be 18 to vote	none	North Dakota	No voter registration requirements	
			Ohio	Be 18 by election day	live in Ohio for at 30 days before the election
Idaho	Be at least 18 years old	live 30 days in the county	Oklahoma	Be 18 by election day	none
Illinois	Be 18 on or before the next election day	live in your election precinct at least 30 days before the next election	Oregon	Be 18 by election day	none
			Pennsylvania	Be 18 by election day	live in Pennsylvania and your district for at 30 days before the election
Indiana	Be 18 on or before the next election day	live in your election precinct at least 30 days before the next election	Rhode Island	Be 18 by election day	live in Rhode Island for at 30 days before the election
Iowa	Be at least 17½ to register, but 18 or vote	none
			South Carolina	Be 18 years by election day	none
Kansas	Be 18 on or before the next election day	none	South Dakota	Be 18 by election day	none
			Tennessee	Be 18 by election day	none
Kentucky	Be 18 on or before the next election day	live 28 days in the county	Texas	Be 17 years and 10 months old to register, but 18 to vote	be a resident of the county in which you register
Louisiana	Be 18 within 6 months of registration and be 18 by election day	none	Utah	Be 18 by election day	live in Utah for at least 30 days before the election
Maine	Be at least 17 to register, but 18 to vote	live in the municipality in which you vote	Vermont	Be 18 by election day	none
Maryland	Be at least 18	none	Virginia	Be 18 by election day	live in the precinct in which you register
Massachusetts	Be at least 18	none	Washington	Be 18 on or before the next election day	live in your county for at least 30 days before the next election
Michigan	Be at least 18 by the next election	be a resident of your city or township for at least 30 days
			West Virginia	Be 18 by election day	none
Minnesota	Be 18 years by election day	live in Minnesota for at days before the election	Wisconsin	Be 18 by election day	live in Wisconsin for at least 10 days
Mississippi	Be 18 years by the next election	live in your county or city for at least 30 days	Wyoming	Be 18 by election day	none

All states, except North Dakota, require voters to be state residents before they can register to vote. The Twenty-sixth Amendment lowered the voting age to 18, but each state determines its own requirements for registering.

the polls, be recognized by the election judges, and cast his ballot. If he were challenged, he could either sign or mark an affidavit that swore to his qualifications or produce other voters who were recognized from the area to attest to his standing. (At that time, women's suffrage had not come into existence, so all voters were men.)

However, toward the end of the nineteenth century, the country was becoming less rural in nature. The growth of cities and their concentrations of people made the simple system of voter recognition and approval, while still workable in some places, impractical and highly subject to fraudulent voting practices.

In urban areas, practices such as "repeating" (casting ballots at multiple polling places), and "voting the graveyard" (using the names of dead people to cast ballots), became commonplace. As more groups of people won the right to vote, the sheer numbers of voters outweighed the ability of election judges to know who was eligible to vote and who was not. States began to turn to systems of registering voters, and, by the beginning of the twentieth century, all the states had a type of registration in place. When women gained the right to vote, more names were added to the mushrooming rolls.

Registration Forms

Registration forms common in most states are simple and straightforward. An applicant is asked to check off whether the registration is a new one or represents a change of address or name. The applicant then fills in his or her name, address, date of birth, mailing address (if different from residence), a home telephone (optional), and information about the previous voter registration, including the county name, if it is in a different voting area.

The potential voter is also asked to "swear or affirm" that he or she is a U.S. citizen, that

Rock the Vote works to get younger voters involved in the political process. (rockthevote.org)

the address provided is correct, that he or she will be eighteen years of age on or before the next election, and is not on parole, probation, or serving a sentence for any indictable offense under federal or state law. This affidavit form also asks if the signer understands that making a false or fraudulent registration may subject him or her to a fine and/or imprisonment.

Once the form is completed, signed, and received by election officials, the new voter is registered on the election rolls of the appropriate voting precinct. The registration office may, if the voter is reregistering at a new address, inform the voter's previous voting district that his or her name should be removed.

The closing date for registration before an election varies from state to state. Some allow registration up to election day, but on average registration must take place twenty-eight days prior to the election.

Voter registration lists are a public record and copies are available to candidates and others, usually for a fee. Some states, however, have passed legislation creating secret voting lists to protect women from abusive partners. Such laws allow the abuse victims to be put on the secret list and vote by mail if they receive a court restraining order against the partner trying to locate them. Civil libertarians have opposed the laws, however, arguing that voter registrations are "the quintessential public record" and should be kept that way.

Fraud Protection

The overriding purpose of all registration systems is to ensure that votes are cast only by eligible voters. To foil the election day schemes of the dishonest, all the systems provide a register, prepared in advance, of all voters in a given district eligible to vote in that election. This roster offers some assurance that, in almost

A – Z

U-V

every situation, eligibility questions have been answered and that a voter listed on the rolls can vote when he or she reaches the polls.

Types of System

The states employ a variety of registration systems, but all follow one of two basic approaches. The first is the *periodic* system, in which the existing voting rolls are cast aside at certain stipulated periods and new lists are drawn up, requiring voters to reregister. The second is the *permanent* system, under which the same list of voters is used indefinitely, with legally specified types of updates regarding additions and deletions of voters' names. Because the permanent system offers states some savings in time and money, and because it appears to be safer from fraudulent practices, it is the preferred choice.

In the United States, the burden of registering to vote rests primarily with the individual voter. Except in North Dakota, which has no formal registration system, registration is a prerequisite to voting, and the citizen of voting age must take the initiative of getting on the rolls. This policy is in contrast to that in most other Western democracies, where registration is virtually automatic. As a rule, American voters must go to a designated office to register or to obtain a registration form that can be mailed in.

Motor-Voter: Making Registration Easier

In most Western nations, government agencies sign up voters, but the United States places the burden for qualifying for voting on the citizen. Signed into law by President Bill Clinton on May 20, 1993, "motor-voter" required states to provide all eligible citizens the opportunity to register when they applied for or renewed a driver's license. It also required states to allow mail-in registration and to provide voter registration forms at agencies that supplied public assistance, such as welfare checks or help for the disabled. Compliance with the federally mandated program was required by 1995. Costs were to be borne by the states.

Partly because of the legislation, a record number of new voters—about ten million—signed up in the first three years following implementation of the act. The Federal Election Commission reported that motor-voter registration accounted for a quarter of voter registration applications in the 1997–1998 election period. The Motor Voter Act is also credited with helping to keep the voting rolls up to date.

Keeping accurate and current voting lists also helps ensure that political candidates meet the residency requirements for the office being sought. There have been numerous instances of candidates being kept off the ballot for being registered in the wrong area.

Removing Obstacles to Voting

In the late twentieth century, the federal government and the states experimented with various other measures designed to increase citizen participation in the electoral process. The Voting Rights Act of 1970 helped pave the way in removing residency restrictions which had previously required new voters to reside in their state for longer than ninety days. Other measures to increase voter turnout came at the state level, with a number of states experimenting with new voting methods, such as election-day voter registration, easier absentee balloting, and mail-in ballots.

See also: Absentee Voting; Voting Rights Act of 1965; 📖 Voting Rights Act of 1965 in the **Primary Source Library**.

Further Reading

Lane, Janet B. *Voter Registration*. Hauppauge, NY: Nova Science Publishers, 2002.

Voters, Voting Behavior, and Voter Turnout

The American political system has changed significantly over the years, as has the electorate. Since the early days of the nation, when the voting privilege was limited to the upper economic classes, one voting barrier after another has fallen to pressures for wider **suffrage**. First, men who did not own property, then women, then African Americans, and finally young people obtained the franchise. By the early 1970s, virtually every adult citizen eighteen and older had won the right to vote.

By the elections of 2004, just more than half of those eligible to vote were exercising that right in high-profile presidential elections and barely one-third of those eligible were bothering to vote in midterm congressional elections.

Broadening the Franchise

During the nation's first decades, all thirteen of the original states limited voting to adult male property holders and taxpayers. The Framers of the Constitution apparently were content to continue this practice. The Constitutional Convention (1787) adopted without dissent the advice of its Committee of Detail that qualifications for the electors of the House of Representatives "shall be the same . . . as those of the electors in the several states of the most numerous branch of their own legislatures."

Under this provision, fewer than half of the adult white men in the United States were eligible to vote in federal elections. With most women and indentured servants disqualified, fewer than one of every four white adults could cast a ballot. Slaves also were ineligible to vote, although freed slaves could vote in some states if they met whatever other qualifications the state placed on its voters.

Those practices actually represented a lifting of voting restrictions that had prevailed in the colonial period. Roman Catholics had been **disenfranchised** in almost every colony; Jews in most colonies; Quakers and Baptists in some. Not until 1842 did Rhode Island permit Jews to vote.

Voting for president and U.S. senators was even more restricted. The Founders who wrote the Constitution were wary of direct election by the masses. As a result, they provided for indirect election of the president by what would later be known as the electoral college. Electors in the states would vote for president but the method of selecting the electors was left to the states. In the early elections, most electors were chosen by state legislatures, but after the first

three elections (1789, 1792, and 1796), popular vote increasingly became the preferred method. By 1824, only six of the twenty-four states still used legislative appointment. Senators were chosen by state legislatures for a much longer time, until 1913 when the Seventeenth Amendment required their selection by popular vote.

For half a century before the Civil War (1861–1865), the electorate was steadily broadened. The new western settlements usually allowed all men to vote, and Jacksonian democracy—named for President Andrew Jackson (1829–1837) who became associated with enlarging the number of voters—encouraged this practice. Gradually, seven states that had limited voting strictly to men who owned property substituted a taxpaying qualification, and by the middle of the nineteenth century, most states had removed even that requirement.

The Fourteenth Amendment, **ratified** in 1868, made everyone born or naturalized in the United States a citizen and directed Congress to reduce the number of representatives from any state that disenfranchised adult male citizens for any reason other than commission of a crime. Although no such reduction was ever made, that amendment—together with the Fifteenth Amendment (1870), which said that the right to vote could not be denied on the basis of "race, color, or previous condition of servitude"—legally opened the polling booths to black men.

Former slaves did vote in the years immediately following the Civil War (1861–1865), but by the turn of the twentieth century, most southern states had in place laws and election practices that effectively barred African Americans from voting. Not until passage of the Voting Rights Act of 1965 would the promise held out by the Fifteenth Amendment begin to be fulfilled.

Women fought for nearly ninety years to win their right to vote; success came with ratification of the Nineteenth Amendment in 1920. Residents of the District of Columbia were given the right to vote in presidential elections with ratification of the Twenty-third Amendment in 1961. In 1970, Congress authorized residents of the nation's capital to elect a nonvoting delegate to the House of Representatives.

A – Z

U-V

In 1971, the Twenty-sixth Amendment lowered the voting age to eighteen for federal, state, and local elections. A Supreme Court ruling in 1972 effectively required states to reduce the time citizens had to be a resident to be eligible to vote; no state now requires more than a thirty-day residency. By the end of the twentieth century, only insanity, a felony conviction, or failure to meet a residency requirement barred voting-age citizens from going to the polls.

Turnout Trends

Most significant changes of election law have resulted in a sharp increase in voting. From 1824 to 1856, a period of gradual relaxation in the states' property and taxpaying qualifications for voting, voter participation in presidential elections increased from 3.8 percent to 16.7 percent of the population. In 1920, when the Nineteenth Amendment gave women the franchise, it rose to 25.1 percent.

Between 1932 and 1976, both the voting-age population and the number of voters in presidential elections roughly doubled. Except for the 1948 presidential election, when barely half the people of voting age went to the polls, the turnout in the postwar years through 1968 was approximately 60 percent. This relatively high figure was likely due to a high sense of civic duty that filled American society in the years after World War II (1941–1945), a stable population, and new civil rights laws encouraging African Americans to vote.

Despite larger numbers of people voting, the rate of voter participation slumped after 1968. In that year's presidential election, 61 percent of the voting-age population went to the polls. That mark fell to 60 percent in 2000, but rose to 64 percent with the 2004 presidential election.

The number of registered voters nationwide at any given time is impossible to calculate. States have different registration deadlines; people who move may be registered in more than one state at the same time, or temporarily may not be recorded in any state; and some states do not require preregistration before voting, while others do not require towns and municipalities to keep registration records.

The postwar baby boom, together with a lower voting age, had produced by the early 1970s a large number of young voters—voters who are the least likely to vote. In the 1972 presidential election, the first in which eighteen-year-olds could vote nationwide, about eleven million young voters entered the electorate. The actual number of voting participants, however, was only 4.4 million greater than in 1968, resulting in a five-point drop in the ratio of eligible to actual voters.

Growth of Independents

Although more people identify themselves as Democrats than Republicans, there has been a steady rise over the last half century in voters who do not identify with either party. Yet when it comes to the act of voter registration, most voters still sign up with one of the two major parties. That is the case in the twenty-seven states (and the District of Columbia) where such a choice can be made. According to the political newsletter *Ballot Access News* in late 2000, Democrats had the registration advantage in thirteen states plus the District of Columbia (a total that included the four most populous states where voters can register by party—California, Florida, New York, and Pennsylvania). Republicans led in seven states (all in the Plains or Rocky Mountain region), and independents had the edge in seven states, five of them in the Northeast (Connecticut, Maine, Massachusetts, New Hampshire, and New Jersey). Overall, Democrats led in registration with 43.8 percent of the total. Republicans had 32.8 percent and independents and miscellaneous categories accounted for 21.6 percent. None of the operating third parties in 2000 had more than 0.4 percent.

See also: Democratic Party; Electoral College; Fifteenth Amendment; Nineteenth Amendment; Republican Party; Seventeenth Amendment; Third Parties.

Further Reading

Flanigan, William H., and Nancy H. Zingale. *Political Behavior of the American Electorate.* Washington, DC: CQ Press, 2005.

Voting Rights Act of 1965, The

Major legislation that enforced the guarantees of African Americans' right to vote. The Voting Rights Act of 1965 closed several loopholes in earlier laws designed to prevent discrimination at the polls. Congress has extended the provisions of the law several times, most recently in 2006. These provisions have extended voting protections to Hispanic Americans, Native Americans, Asian Americans, and Alaskan natives, as well as to citizens who are not fluent in English.

As the Civil Rights movement began to gather force in the 1950s, the Eisenhower administration urged Congress to use federal power to ensure the voting rights of African American citizens. Congress' first action was passage of the Civil Rights Act of 1957, intended to enforce the pledge set out in the Fifteenth Amendment, guaranteeing African American men the right to vote.

The 1957 act authorized the attorney general to bring lawsuits to stop any interference with the right of African American people to vote. The law also created the Civil Rights Commission to investigate and publicly disclose problems of racial discrimination, including problems, such as being denied the right to vote. Responding to reports that progress in securing voting rights for African Americans remained slow, Congress in 1960 passed a measure that permitted the U.S. attorney general to sue a state for refusing to let citizens vote. In addition, the 1960 law authorized the appointment of special federal "voting referees" to oversee voter registration in counties where a federal court detected a pattern of voter discrimination.

Congress passed the Civil Rights Act of 1964, mandating state adoption of standard procedures and requirements for all persons seeking to register to vote. The law also required local officials to justify rejecting an applicant who had completed the sixth grade. Other provisions of the 1964 law sped up the movement of voting rights cases to the Supreme Court.

In two cases brought under the 1964 act, *United States v. Louisiana* and *United States v. Mississippi*, the Supreme Court in 1965 approved the government's efforts to break the pattern of case-by-case proceedings of voting rights violations. The Court upheld federal power to challenge a state's entire constitutional legal framework

After signing the Voting Rights Act of 1965, president Lyndon B. Johnson (left) shakes hands with civil rights leader Martin Luther King, Jr. (center). The Voting Rights Act greatly increased the number of registered African American voters. (LBJ Photo Library, Yoichi R. Okamoto.)

A - Z

U-V

POINT / COUNTERPOINT

Extending the Voting Rights Act of 1965

President Lyndon B. Johnson signed the Voting Rights Act of 1965 on August 6. The 1965 Act ended poll taxes, literacy tests, and other voter tests and authorized federal supervision of voter registration in states and individual voting districts where such tests were being used. The law has been renewed or extended several times, most recently in 2006. President George W. Bush supported the extension of the Voting Rights Act, but Georgia Congressman Lynn A. Westmoreland opposed certain provisions of the new law.

President George W. Bush

Thank you. Good morning. Welcome. Thanks for being here on this special day. Please be seated. America began with a Declaration that all men are created equal. This Declaration marked a tremendous advance in the story of freedom, yet it also contained a contradiction: Some of the same men who signed their names to this self-evident truth owned other men as property. By reauthorizing this act, Congress has reaffirmed its belief that all men are created equal; its belief that the new founding started by the signing of the bill by President Johnson is worthy of our great nation to continue.

The right of ordinary men and women to determine their own political future lies at the heart of the American experiment, and it is a right that has been won by the sacrifice of patriots. The Declaration of Independence was born on the stand for liberty taken at Lexington and Concord. The amendments to our Constitution that outlawed slavery and guaranteed the right to vote came at the price of a terrible civil war.

The Voting Rights Act that broke the segregationist lock on the ballot box rose from the courage shown on a Selma bridge one Sunday afternoon in March of 1965. On that day, African Americans, including a member of the United States Congress, John Lewis, marched across the Edmund Pettus Bridge in a protest intended to highlight the unfair practices that kept them off the voter rolls.

One week after Selma, President Lyndon Johnson took to the airwaves to announce that he planned to submit legislation that would bring African Americans into the civic life of our nation. Five months after Selma, he signed the Voting Rights Act into law in the Rotunda of our nation's capitol. In a little more than a year after Selma, a newly enfranchised black community used their power at the ballot box to help defeat the sheriff who had sent men with whips and clubs to the Edmund Pettus Bridge on that bloody Sunday.

In four decades since the Voting Rights Act was first passed, we've made progress toward equality, yet the work for a more perfect union is never ending. We'll continue to build on the legal equality won by the civil rights movement to help ensure that every person enjoys the opportunity that this great land of liberty offers . . . .

Congressman Lynn A. Westmoreland

"The Voting Rights Act has a proud and important legacy in my home state of Georgia and across the United States. With minor changes that would modernize the Voting Rights Act and better reflect the reality of what's happening in the 21st century, I would be joining many of my colleagues and voting "yes" today.

But the bill we have before us is fatally flawed, Mr. Chairman. This rewrite is outdated, unfair and unconstitutional. I cannot support it in its current form.

This renewal treats Georgia as if nothing's changed in the past 41 years. In other words, this rewrite seems based on the assumption that the Voting Rights Act hasn't worked.

As a Georgian who's proud of our tremendous progress and proud of our current record of equality, I'm here to report to my colleagues in the House that the Voting Rights Act HAS worked in my state and now it's time to modernize the law to deal with the problems of today, not yesteryear.

Mr. Chairman, it's true that when the Voting Rights Act was first passed in 1965, Georgia needed federal intervention to correct decades of discrimination.

Now, 41 years later, Georgia's record on voter equality can stand up against any other state in the union. Today, black Georgians are registered to vote at higher percentages than white Georgians and black Georgians go to the polls in higher percentages than white Georgians. One-third of our statewide elected officials are African-Americans, including our attorney general and the chief justice of the state Supreme Court. Plus, African-Americans' representation in the state Legislature closely mirrors their representation in Georgia's population.

. . . Though it defies common sense, this renewal of the Voting Rights Act gives NO CONSIDERATION to any changes that may have occurred since the first law was passed in 1965. . . .

We have repented and we have reformed, and now, as Fannie Lou Hamer famously said, 'I'm sick and tired of being sick and tired.'

Instead, this bill states EXPLICITLY that my constituents can't be trusted to act in good faith without federal supervision. That assertion is as ignorant as it is insulting.

I cannot and will not support a bill that is outdated, unfair and unconstitutional."

DOCUMENT-BASED QUESTION:
How are the perspectives of President Bush and Congressman Westmoreland different? Also, on what issues, if any, do they agree?

A - Z

U-V

for voter registration and the conduct of elections.

Yet progress remained slow. For example, in Dallas County, Alabama, three new federal laws and four years of litigation had led to the registration of only 383 African American voters out of a potential pool of fifteen thousand. On March 8, 1965, the Rev. Martin Luther King, Jr., led a "Walk for Freedom" to dramatize the need for additional efforts on behalf of registering African American voters in Selma, the county seat, and elsewhere in the South. The violent reaction of local white law enforcement officers and white bystanders to the peaceful demonstration drew nationwide attention to the problem.

A week later, President Lyndon B. Johnson addressed a joint session of Congress to ask for passage of a new voting rights measure to close loopholes that allowed local officials to stall African American voter registration. Johnson explained that "no law that we now have on the books . . . can ensure the right to vote when local officials are determined to deny it." Within five months, Congress had approved the sweeping Voting Rights Act of 1965.

The law suspended literacy tests and provided for the appointment of federal supervisors of voter registration in all states and counties where literacy tests or similar qualifying devices were in effect on November 1, 1964, and where fewer than 50 percent of the voting-age residents had registered to vote or voted in the 1964 presidential election.

The law also established criminal penalties for persons found guilty of interfering with the voting rights of others. State or county governments in areas of low voter registration were required to obtain federal approval of any new voting laws, standards, practices, or procedures before implementing them. A state or county covered by the act could become exempt from the law's provisions if it could persuade a three-judge federal court in the District of Columbia that no racial discrimination in registration or voting had occurred in the previous five years. The act placed federal registration officials in six southern states—Alabama, Georgia, Mississippi, South Carolina, Louisiana, and Virginia—

as well as Alaska, twenty-eight counties in North Carolina, three counties in Arizona, and one in Idaho.

Passage of the voting rights act brought a significant increase in the number of African Americans registered to vote. Within four years, almost one million African Americans had registered to vote under its provisions. The Civil Rights Commission reported in 1968 that registration of blacks had climbed to more than 50 percent of the black voting-age population in every southern state. Before the act, black registration had exceeded 50 percent in only three—Florida, Tennessee, and Texas. The most dramatic increase occurred in Mississippi, where black registration rose from 6.7 percent to 59.8 percent of the voting-age population.

Voting Law Extended

In renewing the Voting Rights Act in 1970 for an additional five years, supporters turned back the efforts of southern senators who wished to weaken key provisions. State and local governments were forbidden to use literacy tests or other voter-qualifying devices.

Under the 1970 law, the requirement that the U.S. Department of Justice had to approve any changes to voting requirements was applied to those areas affected by the 1965 law and ten more: three Alaska districts; Apache County, Arizona; Imperial County, California; Elmore County, Idaho; the Bronx, Kings (Brooklyn), and New York (Manhattan) counties, New York; and Wheeler County, Oregon.

By the time the act was due for its second extension in 1975, an estimated two million African Americans had been added to the voting rolls in the South, more than doubling the previous total. The number of African Americans holding elective office also increased. The Joint Center for Political Studies reported that the number of African American elected officials in the seven southern states covered by the Voting Rights Act had gone up from fewer than one hundred in 1964 to 963 in just ten years. The total count included one member of the House of Representatives, thirty-six state legislators, and 927 county and municipal officials.

The Voting Rights Act was renewed for seven years and substantially expanded in 1975. The law was amended to extend minority voter protections to any state or county that was using a literacy test in 1972 and where less than 50 percent of the residents eligible to vote had registered as of November 1, 1972. Two additional provisions gave greater protection to certain language minorities, defined as persons of Hispanic heritage, Native Americans, Asian Americans, and Alaskan natives.

The requirement of federal approval to any changes to voting laws was expanded to apply to any jurisdiction where:

- The Census Bureau determined that more than 5 percent of the voting-age citizens were of a single language minority.
- Election materials had been printed only in English for the 1972 presidential election.
- Fewer than 50 percent of the voting-age citizens had registered for or voted in the 1972 presidential election.

These amendments significantly expanded coverage of the Voting Rights Act, bringing in all of Alaska, Texas, and Arizona, and selected counties in several other states, including California and Florida. In addition, provisions were added requiring certain parts of the country to provide bilingual voting materials.

Congress approved a third extension of the act on June 23, 1982, two months before the law was due to expire. The 1982 legislation represented a major victory for civil rights groups that included African American, Hispanic, labor, religious, and civic organizations. The bill received widespread bipartisan support and strong backing from members of both chambers of Congress, including southerners. More than twice as many southern Democrats in both the Senate and House voted for passage in 1982 than in 1965 when the law was first approved. The steady upward trend in southern support for the act reflected changing social and political mores as well as a great increase in African American voting in the South.

The 1982 law had four main elements. First, it extended for twenty-five years provisions that required nine states and portions of thirteen others to obtain Justice Department approval for any changes in their election laws and procedures. Second, starting in 1984, a state or county could be released from the restrictions by showing a clean voting rights record for the previous ten years. Third, it overturned a 1980 Supreme Court ruling that "intent to discriminate" must be shown to prove a violation. Fourth, it extended the bilingual election provisions through 1992.

In July 2006, President George W. Bush signed a twenty-five year extension of the Voting Rights Act. The act extends prohibition against the use of tests or devices to deny the right to vote in any federal, state, or local election. It also extends the requirement for certain states and local governments to provide voting materials in multiple languages. During the signing ceremony, Bush noted,

My administration will vigorously enforce the provisions of this law, and we will defend it in court. This legislation is named in honor of three heroes of American history who devoted their lives to the struggle of civil rights: Fannie Lou Hamer, Rosa Parks, and Coretta Scott King. And in honor of their memory and their contributions to the cause of freedom, I am proud to sign the Voting Rights Act Reauthorization and Amendments Act of 2006.

There is little doubt that the Voting Rights Act has had a positive effect on the numbers of African Americans winning elective office. Nationwide in January 2001, according to a study by the Joint Center for Political Studies, the number of African American elected officials included thirty-nine members of Congress; 597 state legislators; 454 mayors; and 4,023 other municipal officials; more than 970 judges or magistrates; and more than seventy police chiefs, sheriffs, and local marshals. (These to-

A-Z

U-V

JUSTICE FOR ALL

Fannie Lou Hamer

Known as the woman who was "sick and tired of being sick and tired," Fannie Lou Hamer was born October 6, 1917, in Montgomery County, Mississippi. The granddaughter of slaves, she and her family were sharecroppers.

In 1962, when Hamer was 44 years old, volunteers from the Student Nonviolent Coordinating Committee (SNCC) held a voter registration meeting in her town. She was surprised to learn that African Americans had a constitutional right to vote. When the SNCC members asked volunteers to go to the courthouse to register to vote, Hamer was the first to raise her hand. When Hamer and others went to the courthouse, they were jailed and beaten by the police. Because of Hamer's courageous act, she was thrown off the plantation where she labored as a sharecropper. She received death threats and was shot at. Still, Hamer would not be discouraged. She worked with the SNCC and traveled around the country speaking and registering people to vote.

In 1967, Hamer published *To Praise Our Bridges: An Autobiography*. She served as a member of the Democratic National Committee for Mississippi from 1968 to 1971 and the Policy Council of the National Women's Political Caucus from 1971 to 1977. She was an outspoken critic of the Vietnam War and worked to improve economic conditions in Mississippi. She died on March 14, 1977, at the age of 59.

tals were from the fifty states, the District of Columbia, and the Virgin Islands.)

Judicial Support

Not surprisingly, the use of federal power over electoral and voting matters included in the Voting Rights Act was immediately challenged as exceeding the constitutional authority of Congress and infringing on states' rights. Primarily, these challenges came from the South. In 1966, however, the Supreme Court firmly backed the power of Congress to pass such a law.

The Supreme Court rejected all constitutional challenges to the act. "Congress," wrote Chief Justice Earl Warren for the decision's 8–1 majority, "has full remedial powers [under the Fifteenth Amendment] to effectuate the constitutional prohibition against racial discrimination in voting." The federal approval requirement for new voting rules in the states covered by the act, Warren observed, "may have been an uncommon exercise of congressional power . . . but the Court has recognized that exceptional conditions can justify legislative measures not otherwise appropriate."

Although the constitutionality of the Voting Rights Act was settled, a steady stream of voting rights cases came to the Court in the late 1960s and the 1970s, testing the scope and application of the law. However, the Court continued to back and broadly interpret the act. In the 1969 case of *Gaston County v. United*

States, for example, the Court refused to let a North Carolina county reinstate a literacy test.

See also: Fifteenth Amendment; Literacy Tests; Twenty-fourth Amendment; Voting Rights Act of 1965 in the **Primary Source Library.**

Further Reading

American Government at Work, Volume 1: The Federal Legislative Branch. Danbury, CT: Grolier/Scholastic Library, 2001.

Landsberg, Brian K. *Free at Last: The Alabama Origins of the 1965 Voting Rights Act.* Lawrence, KS: University Press of Kansas, 2007.

Laney, Garrine P. *The Voting Rights Act of 1965: Historical Background and Current Issues.* Hauppauge, NY: Novinka Books, 2004.

McPherson, James M. *To the Best of My Ability: The American Presidents.* New York: Dorling Kindersley Publishing Inc., 2000.

Voting Systems

A variety of voting systems are used throughout the United States. Despite the many debates surrounding the 2000 presidential election, some of which continued in the 2004 elections, the nation's voters still use systems that are sometimes unreliable.

Punch Cards

Among all the voting systems, the one that seemed the most likely to be phased out was the old-fashioned punch card system widely used in Florida and in much of the nation. The technology, introduced in the 1960s, features the infamous *chad,* the tiny bit of paper that the voter punches out with a stylus to indicate his or her candidate choice. Failure to dislodge the chad fully (leaving it "hanging" or "dimpled") can lead to the vote not being counted by the electronic reader.

The lack of standards for discerning the voter's intent by visual inspection of punch-card ballots was at the heart of Florida's re-

count problem and the U.S. Supreme Court's action in *Bush v. Gore,* which halted the spectacle of election officials holding ballots up to the light, looking for dented or incompletely detached chads. Florida counties using punch cards reported about 4 percent of six million ballots cast (240,000 ballots) were void, four times the rate of counties using optical scanning systems.

Two basically similar punch-card systems, the Votomatic and the Datavote, were still in widespread use in 2000, 2002, 2004, and 2006. According to the Federal Election Commission (FEC), 37 percent of registered voters used punch-card systems, including 3.8 million in Los Angeles County, the largest U.S. voting jurisdiction.

Optical Scans

The next most common voting system was the increasingly popular optical scanning device being used by 25 percent of voters. In these systems, the voter uses a marker to fill in an incomplete arrow or other empty block to indicate candidate choice on a ballot card. The card is then fed into a device that "reads" the card and tabulates the votes.

An advantage of optical scan over punch cards is that the cards leave a "paper trail" that can be inspected in a manual recount. Ballots spoiled by overvotes or marks outside the designated areas are rejected by the machine and deposited by precinct officials in a locked box. The voter is then given a new ballot which the machine reads and stores if the new card is properly filled out. In case of a manual recount, the voted ballot cards can be tabulated with little or no guesswork as to the voter's intent.

Mechanical Lever Machines

Other than paper ballots, lever machines are the oldest type of voting system. One invented by Jacob H. Myers, a safemaker, was first officially used at Lockport, New York, in 1892, twenty-three years after Thomas A. Edison patented a similar machine. By the 1930s, voting machines were being used in almost all major U.S. cities.

The machine booths typically featured a large lever that closed a privacy curtain as the voter entered. The voter pressed small levers to indicate candidate choices, or a larger lever to vote a straight party ticket. The lever that closed the curtain also opened it, returned the levers to their unvoted position, and rotated counters to record the vote. When the polls closed, the machines were sealed to prevent tampering in case of a recount.

At the beginning of the twenty-first century, about 21 percent of voters were still using mechanical voting machines. However, they were no longer being made and computer-based systems were rapidly taking their place.

Paper Ballots

Before voting machines came into widespread use, most states adopted a type of government-printed ballot introduced in Australia in 1876. It gave voters more privacy by sparing them the need to ask for a party-printed ballot. In the age of computers, 2 percent of U.S. voters still were using paper ballots, primarily in small communities. Absentee voting was also largely by paper ballot. And one state, Oregon, began conducting all elections by mail.

Direct Recording Electronic

Called DRE for short, these are the newest voting systems. They display choices that the voter enters by touch-screen, button, or rotation device. A keyboard may be provided for write-in votes. The voter's choices are directly recorded in electronic memory and added to the totals for each candidate. Usage of DREs in 2000 was certain to surpass the 1996 figure of 8 percent of registered voters.

Support for Reform

Polls taken after the 2000 election showed broad public support for a stronger federal role in election administration. Many voters indicated they were unaware that states set most of the voting rules, even for presidential and congressional elections. A *Washington Post*–ABC News poll showed most Americans favored moving toward a national voting system, including a standard ballot design, a uniform poll-closing time, and consistent rules for manual recounts.

Many reform bills proposed funding for studies or modernization of equipment. Florida officials estimated it would cost $25 million to replace punch-card systems in twenty-four counties. In states where election officials were elected, as in Florida, reformers called for switching to bipartisan or nonpartisan appointed boards.

Although computer voting raised privacy and security concerns, prospects were bright for increased use of Internet voting systems. Arizona pioneered in this area in its 2000 Democratic primary, which gave voters a choice of using paper ballots, computer terminals, or mail-in ballots. The innovation produced a record turnout.

Three technology giants—Unisys, Dell Computer, and Microsoft—announced that they were teaming up to produce an integrated voting, registration, and reporting system. Other election equipment makers were optimistic that the 2000 and 2004 election difficulties had improved the market for their products.

See also: Bush v. Gore (2000); Election of 2000; Election of 2004; 🔲 E-voting Failures in the 2006 Elections in the **Primary Source Library.**

Further Reading

Amy, Douglas J. *Behind the Ballot Box: A Citizen's Guide to Voting Systems*. Westport, CT: Praeger Publishers, 2000.

Haulley, Fletcher. *The Help America Vote Act of 2002: Legislation to Modernize America's Voting Systems*. New York: Rosen Central, 2005.

★ ★ ★ W ★ ★ ★

Washington, Martha

See Election of 1789.

Watergate

The Watergate affair was perhaps the greatest political scandal in United States history. For the first time, a president was forced to leave office before his term expired. President Richard Nixon resigned on August 9, 1974, when it became apparent that the House of Representatives would impeach him for "high crimes and misdemeanors" and the Senate would convict him. In addition, a number of Nixon's aides, including his first attorney general and campaign manager, John Mitchell, would spend time in jail because of the scandal.

At its simplest, the Watergate scandal was "a third-rate burglary," followed by a cover-up by President Nixon and his aides. In the summer of 1972, several employees of the Committee to Re-elect the President (dubbed "CREEP") were arrested after they were discovered breaking into and bugging the Democratic National Committee's offices at the Watergate Hotel and office complex in Washington, D.C. Although the break-in itself was not a major issue in the 1972 election, the next year a Senate committee began an investigation of the entire affair. In the course of investigating the burglary at the Watergate complex, the special prosecutors and the Senate Select Committee uncovered a wide range of other illegal activities run by the Nixon White House.

During the investigation, a presidential aide revealed that Nixon had secretly and illegally taped Oval Office conversations with aides. When the Watergate special prosecutor, Archibald Cox, ordered Nixon to surrender the tapes in October 1973, Nixon ordered Cox fired.

VIEWPOINTS

Drawn during the 1973 Watergate scandal, this political cartoon observes that President Richard M. Nixon is much like the fictional character Pinocchio, whose nose grew longer whenever he told a lie. (The Granger Collection, New York)

Because Nixon's attorney general, Elliot Richardson, and assistant attorney general, William D. Ruckelshaus, refused to fire Cox, the task was carried out by Solicitor General Robert Bork, igniting a constitutional crisis dubbed the "Saturday night massacre."

Nixon soon handed over the tapes Cox had sought. In the summer of 1974, the Supreme Court ruled that Nixon had to surrender even more tapes, which indicated that he had played an active role in covering up the Watergate scandal. Nixon resigned the presidency when his impeachment and conviction appeared certain. The impeachment articles charged him with obstruction of justice, abuse of presidential powers, and contempt of Congress.

See also: Election of 1972; Election of 1976.

Whig Party (1834–1856)

A political party organized to oppose the Jacksonian Democrats. Whigs were nineteenth-century modernizers who saw President Andrew Jackson (1829–1837) as a dangerous man with a reactionary opposition to the forces of social, economic, and moral change. As Jackson purged his opponents, vetoed internal improvements, and killed the **Bank of the United States**, alarmed local and influential leaders fought back.

The Whigs, led by Henry Clay, endorsed Clay's vision of the "American System." They demanded government support for a more modern, market-oriented economy, in which skill, expertise, and bank credit would count for more than physical strength or land ownership. They also sought to promote industrialization through high tariffs, a business-oriented money supply based on a national bank, and a vigorous program of government-funded "internal improvements," especially expansion of the road and canal systems. To help modernize Americans, the Whigs helped create public schools, private colleges, charities, and cultural institutions.

The Democrats, by contrast, harkened to the Jeffersonian ideal of an egalitarian agricultural society, insisting that traditional farm life bred republican simplicity, whereas modernization threatened to create a politically powerful caste of rich aristocrats who might subvert democracy. In general, the Democrats enacted their policies at the national level; the Whigs succeeded in passing modernization projects in most states.

Although the Whigs won votes in every socioeconomic class, including the poorest, they appealed especially to more prosperous Americans. The Democrats likewise won support from all groups, but they often sharpened their appeals to the lower half by ridiculing the aristocratic airs of the Whigs. Most bankers, storekeepers, factory owners, master mechanics, clerks, and professionals favored the Whigs. Moreover, commercially oriented farmers in the

Henry Clay of Kentucky was the presidential nominee of the Whig Party twice—1832 and 1844 (Library of Congress).

North voted Whig, as did most large-scale planters in the South.

In general, the commercial and manufacturing towns and cities were heavily Whig, except for Democratic wards filled with recent Irish Catholic and German immigrants. Waves of Protestant religious revivals in the 1830s injected a moralistic element into the Whig ranks. Nonreligious individuals who found themselves the targets of moral reform, such as calls for prohibition, denounced the Whigs as Puritans and sought refuge in the Democratic Party. Rejecting the automatic party loyalty that was the hallmark of the tight Democratic Party organization, the Whigs suffered from **factionalism**. Yet the party's superb network of newspapers provided an internal information system.

Whigs clashed with Democrats throughout what historians term the "Second American Party System." When they controlled the Senate, Whigs passed a censure motion in 1834 denouncing Jackson's arrogant assumption of executive power in the face of the true will of the people as represented by Congress. Backing Henry Clay in 1832 and then several candidates in 1836, the Whigs finally rallied in 1840 behind a popular general, William Henry Harrison, proving that the national Whig Party could win. Moreover, in the 1840s Whigs won 49 percent of gubernatorial elections, with strong bases in the manufacturing Northeast and in the border states.

Yet the party revealed limited staying power. Whigs were ready to enact their programs in 1841, but Harrison died and was succeeded by John Tyler, an old-line Democrat who never believed in Whiggery and was, in fact, disowned by the party while he was president. Factionalism ruined the party's program and helped defeat Henry Clay, the Whig presidential candidate, in 1844. In 1848, opportunity beckoned as the Democrats split. By ignoring Clay and nominating a famous war hero, General Zachary Taylor, the Whigs papered over their deepening splits on slavery, and they won. The trend, however, was for the Democratic vote to grow faster and for the Whigs to lose more and more marginal states and districts. After the close 1844 contest, the Democratic advantage widened and the Whigs could win the White House only if the Democrats split.

The Whigs were unable to deal with the slavery issue after 1850. Almost all of their southern leaders owned slaves. The northeastern Whigs, led by Daniel Webster, represented business leaders who loved the nation and the national market, but cared little about slavery. Many Whig voters in the North, however, felt slavery was incompatible with a free labor–free market economy, and no one discovered a compromise that would keep the party united. Furthermore, the growing economy made full-time careers in business or law much more attractive than politics for ambitious young Whigs. For example, the party leader in Illinois, Abraham Lincoln, simply abandoned politics for several years after 1849. When new issues of nativism, prohibition, and antislavery burst on the scene in the mid-1850s, no one looked to the fast-disintegrating Whig Party for answers. In the North, most ex-Whigs joined the new Republican Party, and in the South they flocked to a new, short-lived "American" (Know Nothing) Party. During the Lincoln administration (1861–1865), ex-Whigs enacted much of the "American System"; in the long run, America adopted Whig economic policies coupled with a Democratic strong presidency.

See also: American (Know-nothing) Party; Democratic Party; Republican Party.

Women in Congress

By January 2007, a total of 242 women had been elected or appointed to Congress, starting with Representative Jeannette Rankin, a Republican from Montana, elected in 1916. Her state gave women the right to vote before the Nineteenth Amendment to the Constitution **enfranchising** women was ratified in 1920.

Certainly, the most prominent woman to be elected to the Senate was First Lady Hillary Rodham Clinton, who won election in 2000 as her husband was completing his second term as

A – Z

W-Z

DECISION MAKERS

Nancy Pelosi

Nancy Pelosi has represented the 8th District of California—the San Francisco area—since 1987. Pelosi was House Minority Leader from 2002 until 2006. In January 2007, she became the first woman Speaker of the House after the Democrats won control of Congress in the November 2006 elections. As Speaker, Pelosi is second in line to the presidency after Vice President Dick Cheney. Thus, she is the highest-ranking woman in the history of American government.

president. Elected from New York, she was the first first lady ever to serve in the Senate.

Several women served out unexpired terms of less than one year. Rebecca L. Felton, the first woman to serve in the Senate, did so for only one day. Felton, a Georgia Democrat, was appointed October 1, 1922, to fill the Senate vacancy created by the death of Thomas E. Watson. She was not sworn in until November 21, and the next day yielded her seat to Walter F. George, who had meanwhile been elected to fill the vacancy.

Gladys Pyle, a South Dakota Republican, was elected November 9, 1938, to fill the unexpired term of Representative Peter Norbeck, who died in office. His term ended the following January 3, however, before Congress convened and thus Pyle never took the oath of office.

In 1996, Kansas Lieutenant Governor Sheila Frahm was appointed by Governor Bill Graves to fill the Senate seat of Majority Leader Bob Dole, who had resigned from the Senate to run full time for president. Frahm held the seat less than five months. A special primary was held in August to fill Dole's seat, and Frahm lost it to a more conservative Republican, Sam Brownback, who went on to win the November general election.

The Widow's Mandate

In many states and districts, it became customary for the officeholder's party to run his widow for the seat, in the hope of tapping a sympathy vote. Sometimes she filled the office by brief appointment until the governor or party leaders could agree on a candidate.

The "widow's mandate," as such, marked the beginning of political careers for some women. Edith Nourse Rogers, a Massachusetts Republican, entered the House after her husband died in 1925 and remained there until her death in 1960. Margaret Chase Smith filled her late husband's House seat in 1940 and went on to serve four terms in the Senate (1949–1973). Hattie W. Caraway, an Arkansas Democrat, who was appointed to the Senate seat of her late husband in 1931, was returned to Congress by Arkansas voters in 1932 and 1938.

Representative Charlotte T. Reid, a Republican from Illinois, and Representative Marilyn Lloyd, a Democrat from Tennessee, became their parties' nominees when their husbands died between the primary and general elections (in 1962 and 1974, respectively). As women became more active in politics at all levels, the congressional tradition of the widow's mandate has weakened.

Marriages have also linked members of Congress. Representative Emily Taft Douglas, a Democrat from Illinois, was elected to Congress in 1944, four years before her husband, Senator Paul H. Douglas, also a Democrat from Illinois. Representative Martha Keys, a

Democrat from Kansas, married Representative Andrew Jacobs, a Democrat from Indiana, in 1976. This marriage between colleagues was the first of its kind in congressional history. In 1994, Representative Susan Molinari wed her New York state colleague, Representative Bill Paxon, joining together two House Republican leaders. In the 105th Congress (1997–1999), Molinari served as Republican conference vice chair and Paxon served as chair of the National Republican Congressional Committee. In 1996, Molinari gave birth to the couple's daughter.

Molinari earned another distinction as one of the few women in Congress who were daughters of representatives. She won the Staten Island seat of her father, Representative Guy Molinari, who left the House to become Staten Island (New York) borough president. California Democrat Lucille Roybal-Allard also shared that distinction by winning the House seat of her father, Edward R. Roybal, whose congressional career lasted thirty years. California Democrat Nancy Pelosi, who entered the House in 1987 and became Speaker of the House in 2007, was the daughter of Thomas J. D'Alesandro Jr., a House member from 1939 to 1947 and later mayor of Baltimore.

A Slow Gain

It has been a long, slow climb in women's membership since Rankin's election to Congress in 1916. Her seating was not followed by a surge of women members, even after women received the vote in 1920. The first notable increase came in 1928, when nine women were elected to the House. The number had scarcely more than doubled by 1961, when twenty women (two senators, eighteen representatives) served in Congress. After that, women's membership declined slightly and did not regain the 1961 level until 1977. Another slippage followed until 1981, when the membership reached twenty-one for the first time.

The thirty women sworn in as members of the 102nd Congress in January 1991 represented a record number to be elected in a single election. Thirty women also served in the 101st Congress, but only twenty-seven of them were elected in the 1988 general elections. Three

others—Ileana Ros-Lehtinen, a Republican from Florida, Jill L. Long, a Democrat from Indiana, and Susan Molinari—came to the House through special elections in 1989 and 1990.

The elections of 1992 found record numbers of women running for and being elected to Congress. The 103rd Congress, which opened in 1993, included forty-eight women in the House, an increase of nineteen, and seven in the Senate, an increase of four.

Several factors contributed to the success of women candidates in 1992. Many capitalized on the large number of retirements to run in open seats. They also benefited from reapportionment, which created dozens of opportunities for newcomers in the South and West. Another factor was public dissatisfaction with Congress, which allowed women to portray themselves positively as outsiders. The Senate's questioning of law professor Anita F. Hill's accusations of sexual harassment in the 1991 confirmation hearings of Supreme Court Justice Clarence Thomas also had an impact. The televised image of an all-male Senate Judiciary panel sharply questioning Hill brought home dramatically to many women their lack of representation in Congress. By the 100th Congress in 2007, there was an all-time high of eighty-nine women—seventy-three in the House and sixteen in the Senate—on Capitol Hill. (The House total does not include two nonvoting delegates.)

The number of women elected to full Senate terms increased dramatically in the 1990s. By 2001, twelve of the thirteen women serving in the Senate were elected to full terms and the thirteenth (Jean Carnahan) was appointed to fill the seat won by her husband after he died during the fall campaign. In the 100th Congress, three states—California, Maine, and Washington—were represented in the Senate solely by women: Democrats Barbara Boxer and Dianne Feinstein from California; Republicans Olympia J. Snowe and Susan Collins from Maine; and Democrats Patty Murray and Maria Cantwell from Washington.

In 1992, the first African American woman was elected to the Senate, Democrat Carol Moseley-Braun of Illinois. The daughter of a police officer and a medical technician, Moseley-Braun grew up in Chicago. She served in the state legislature from 1979–1988, where she rose to become the first woman assistant majority leader. She also served as the Cook County recorder of deeds (1988–1992). The outrage over the Senate's handling of the Thomas confirmation hearings propelled Moseley-Braun into the 1992 Illinois Senate race. She won that election with 53 percent of the vote, but lost in 1998 in her bid for reelection.

Before 1987, only four women ever won election to full Senate terms. They were Maurine B. Neuberger, Democrat from Oregon (1960); Nancy Landon Kassebaum, Republican from Kansas (1978, 1984, 1990); Paula Hawkins, Republican from Florida (1980); and Barbara A. Mikulski, Democrat from Maryland (1986). Kassebaum was the first woman ever elected to the Senate without being preceded in Congress by her husband.

Leadership Positions

Although women have been entering Congress in record numbers, at the end of the twentieth century they still were finding it difficult to move to the top of the committee and party leadership ladders. In 1995, Kassebaum became the first woman to chair a major Senate committee, Labor and Human Resources. She was joined in the House by fellow Kansas Republican, Jan Meyers, who chaired the Small Business Committee. Before Meyers, no woman had chaired a full House committee since 1977, when Merchant Marine Committee Chair Leonor K. Sullivan, a Democrat from Missouri, left Congress. Mae Ella Nolan, a California Republican who served from 1923 to 1925, was the first woman to chair a congressional committee; she headed the House Committee on Expenditures in the Post Office Department.

In 1989, Barbara Mikulski became the first woman to chair a Senate Appropriations subcommittee—the VA, HUD and Related Agencies panel. She became its ranking minority member when the Republican Party took control of the Senate in 1995. When the Senate unexpectedly switched to Democratic control in June 2001, Mikulski became the chair again. Three other Democratic women were also ele-

vated to chairs of Senate Appropriations subcommittees after the 2001 changeover: Dianne Feinstein of California, Mary Landrieu of Louisiana, and Patty Murray of Washington.

On the House Appropriations Committee, Barbara Vucanovich, a Republican from Nevada, chaired the Military Construction Subcommittee in the 104th Congress. In the 107th Congress, Ohio's Marcy Kaptur served as the ranking member of the Appropriations Agriculture subcommittee and California's Nancy Pelosi was the ranking member of that panel's Foreign Operations subcommittee.

In the wake of the 1998 elections, two women—Jennifer Dunn, a Republican from Washington, and Rosa DeLauro, a Democrat from Connecticut—challenged their party's leaders for a larger role in running the House. Each one was rejected. When the Republicans held leadership races for the 106th Congress, Dunn challenged Majority Leader Dick Armey of Texas for his job. Early in the 105th Congress, she had been elevated to an official leadership position, winning election as conference secretary. In July 1997, she moved further up in the leadership by winning the position of conference vice chair. Her effort to move Armey out of the second highest party slot failed. Had she won, she would have been the first woman majority leader.

During the Democrats' November 1998 organizational meetings, DeLauro challenged Martin Frost of Texas for the position of chairman of the House Democratic Caucus. Ten Democrats made nominating speeches on behalf of DeLauro, the caucus' outspoken chief deputy whip, but she still did not prevail. Finally, with the beginning of the 110th Congress in January 2007, a woman was elevated to the highest office of the House of Representatives. Nancy Pelosi, a Democrat from California, became the first woman Speaker of the House.

Congress has been an important starting point for women seeking national office, however. Shirley Chisholm, a Democratic representative from New York, ran for president in 1972, and Geraldine Ferraro, another New York Democrat who served in the House, was her party's vice-presidential nominee in 1984. In 2006, Senator Hillary Clinton, a Democrat from New York, declared her candidacy for the 2008 presidential nomination.

See also: Elections, Congress; Elections, House of Representatives; Elections, Senate; Nineteenth Amendment.

Further Reading

Dodson, Debra L. *The Impact of Women in Congress.* New York: Oxford University Press USA, 2006.

Palmer, Barbara, and Dennis Simon. *Breaking the Political Glass Ceiling: Women and Congressional Elections.* London: Routledge, 2006.

Rosenthal, Cindy Simon (ed.). *Women Transforming Congress.* Norman, OK: University of Oklahoma Press, 2003.

Zeinert, Karen. *Women in Politics.* Minneapolis, MN: Twenty-first Century Books, 2002.

Women Voters

Women's suffrage, which began in the late 1830s, was closely related in the beginning to the movement for abolition of slavery. Women, because of their extensive legal disadvantages under the law, often compared their lot to that of slaves and directed much of their political activity against proposals for extending slavery.

Women were disenfranchised at every level of government. Only in New Jersey did they have a theoretical right to vote. That right had been included unintentionally in the state constitutions of 1776 and 1797, but the state legislature repealed the provision at the outset of the nineteenth century when some women actually attempted to vote.

A-Z

W-Z

The number of women who vote in presidential elections has increased significantly since 1920, the first election after the ratification of the Nineteenth Amendment (AP Photo/Shealah Craighead).

A – Z

Early victories for the women's suffrage movement came mostly in connection with school elections. Kentucky in 1838 gave the right to vote in such elections to widows and unmarried women with property that was subject to taxation for school purposes. Kansas in 1861 gave women the vote on all school questions, and by 1880 Michigan, Minnesota, Colorado, New Hampshire, and Massachusetts had followed suit.

The Woman's Rights Convention at Seneca Falls, New York, in July 1848, is generally cited as the beginning of the women's suffrage movement in the United States. Nevertheless, the Declaration of Principles that Elizabeth Cady Stanton (1815–1902) read at that meeting was a much broader and more revolutionary document than a simple claim for the vote.

Carrie Chapman Catt, a leader of the women's suffrage movement, helped organize the League of Women Voters after the passage of the Nineteenth Amendment (Library of Congress).

W-Z

Steps toward the Vote

Direct-action tactics first were applied by suffragists shortly after the Civil War, when women's rights leader Susan B. Anthony (1820–1906) urged women to go to the polls and claim the right to vote under terms of the newly adopted Fourteenth Amendment.

In the national elections of 1872, Anthony voted in her home city of Rochester, New York; she subsequently was tried and convicted of the crime of "voting without having a lawful right to vote." For almost a quarter of a century, Anthony

and her followers pressed Congress for a constitutional amendment granting women's suffrage. On January 25, 1887, the Senate finally considered the proposal but rejected it by a 16–34 vote.

The suffrage forces had more success in some western states. As a territory, Wyoming extended full suffrage to women in 1869 and retained it upon becoming a state in 1890. Colorado, Utah, and Idaho granted women voting rights before 1901. After that time, however, the advocates of suffrage for women encountered stronger opposition, and it was not until the height of the Progressive movement that other states, mostly in the West, gave women full voting rights. Washington granted equal suffrage in 1910; California in 1911; Arizona, Kansas, and Oregon in 1912; Montana and Nevada in 1914; and New York in 1917.

Opponents argued that women were the "weaker sex," that their nature was unsuited to make the kinds of decisions necessary in casting a ballot, and that suffrage might alter the relationship between the sexes.

In the two decades preceding women's enfranchisement, extravagant claims were made by extremists on both sides. Radical feminists often insisted that women voters would be able to cleanse American politics of its corruption and usher in a golden age of politics. Anti-franchise forces were as far-reaching in their claims. Dur-

JUSTICE FOR ALL

Suffragists

Women and men who worked for women's right to vote were known as *suffragists.* Beginning with the 1848 Seneca Falls Declaration, men and women struggled to gain equality at the ballot box.

During World War I (1917–1918), a shortage of men pushed many women into non-traditional jobs. At about the same time, American women began an organized protest of President Woodrow Wilson's (1913–1921) White House, demanding that he support women's right to vote. One group, known as the Silent Sentinels, protested in front of the White House for 18 months. Finally, on January 9, 1918, the president announced his support of the proposed Nineteenth Amendment, guaranteeing women the right to vote. On May 21, 1919, the House of Representatives passed the amendment, followed by the Senate on June 4. The Nineteenth Amendment was ratified on August 26, 1920, after Tennessee, the thirty-sixth state to do so, approved it.

A – Z

ing World War I, Henry A. Wise Wood, president of the Aero Club of America, told the House Committee on Woman Suffrage that giving women the vote would mean "the dilution with the qualities of the cow of the qualities of the bull upon which all the herd's safety must depend." The January 1917 issue of *Remonstrance,* an antisuffrage journal, cautioned that women's suffrage would lead to free love and communism.

Constitutional Amendment

On the eve of World War I (1914–1918), the advocates of aggressive strategies took the lead in a national campaign for women's rights. In the congressional elections of 1914, they set out to defeat all Democratic candidates in the states where women had the right to vote. They held the majority Democrats in Congress responsible for not submitting a constitutional amendment to the states for their approval of women's voting rights. Only twenty of the forty-three challenged candidates were elected. However, this showing of electoral strength did not move President Woodrow Wilson (1913–1921) to take up their cause.

Wilson's opposition to a constitutional amendment prompted a series of stormy demonstrations by the suffragettes around the White House and other sites in Washington after the United States had entered World War I. The demonstrators insisted that it was unconscionable for this country to be denying its own female citizens a right to participate in government while at the same time it was fighting a war on the premise of "making the world safe for democracy."

At the direction of the administration, thousands of the women demonstrators were arrested and brought to trial. Some were beaten by hostile crowds—often made up of soldiers and sailors who viewed the demonstrations as unpatriotic. At their trials, many of the women stood mute or made speeches advocating suffrage and attacking President Wilson for his refusal to endorse the constitutional amendment.

The jailing of many of these women caused a severe housing problem for District of Columbia penal authorities and created a wave of sympathy for the suffragettes. Public support for

W-Z

their position was heightened by the prisoners' claims that they had been treated inhumanely and had been subjected to unsanitary conditions in prison. To protest these conditions, some of the prisoners went on a hunger strike, and the authorities resorted to forced feeding, an action that aroused even greater public sympathy.

President Wilson yielded, announcing on January 9, 1918, his support for the proposed suffrage amendment. The House of Representatives approved it the next day by a 274–136 vote, one vote more than the necessary two-thirds majority. The Senate, however, fell short of the two-thirds majority in October 1918 and again in February 1919. However, when the Congress elected in November 1918 met for the first time on May 19, 1919, it took little more than two weeks to gain the required majorities in both chambers.

On August 18, 1920, Tennessee became the thirty-sixth state to approve the amendment, enough for ratification. On August 26, Secretary of State Bainbridge Colby (1920–1921) signed a proclamation formally adding the Nineteenth Amendment to the Constitution. It stated simply that

The right of citizens of the United States to vote shall not be denied or abridged by the United States or by any state on account of sex.

In the 1920 presidential election, the first in which women could vote, it was estimated that only about 30 percent of those who were eligible actually voted. Analyses of the 1924 election indicated that scarcely one-third of all eligible women voted while more than two-thirds of the eligible men had done so. Women's voter turnout came as a bitter blow to the suffragists. In recent national elections, however, surveys have found that voting participation by women is about the same as that of men.

See also: League of Women Voters; Nineteenth Amendment; Nineteenth Amendment in the **Primary Source Library;** Susan B. Anthony's 1873 speech in the **Primary Source Library.**

Further Reading
Henneburger, Melinda. *If Only They Listened to Us: What Women Voters Want Politicians to Hear.* New York: Simon & Schuster, 2007.

ZZZ

Facebook. MySpace. YouTube. Countless other Internet sites catering to interests from puppies to quantum physics. Cable and satellite television, now available in high definition. Digital cameras. Cell phones that fit in the palm of your hand—and contain digital cameras. Personal digital assistants. High-powered video game systems. Tiny music players that store massive digital libraries.

These are just a few of the diversions that have, in recent years, captured the American public's attention to a degree far greater than politics and government. To many Americans, politics is one big snore—or *ZZZ*, the cartoon symbol of sleep. Veteran political reporters Jack Germond and Jules Witcover even titled their account of the 1992 presidential election *Wake Me When It's Over.*

Further, many voters feel that their vote does not count, despite the sharp evidence that a few votes' difference could have changed the outcomes of scores of close U.S. elections, notably the 1976 race between Gerald R. Ford and Jimmy Carter and the 2000 contest between George W. Bush and Al Gore, the national popular vote winner. A few thousand votes in certain states could have changed the result of the 1976 race, and the 2000 race hinged on the outcome of the tally in Florida, where Bush was certified as the winner by just 537 votes.

A stronger sense of civic duty once drove a stronger interest in politics—and was briefly invigorated a few generations ago by President John F. Kennedy's call to public service,

> Let every nation know, whether it wishes us well or ill, that we shall pay any price, bear any burden, meet any hardship, support any friend, oppose any foe, in order to assure the survival and the success of liberty . . . And so, my fellow Americans: ask not what your country can do for you—ask what you can do for your country.
> —President John F. Kennedy, inaugural address, January 20, 1961

Surely the concept of civic duty has not disappeared from American society. After all, more than 122 million people voted in the 2004 presidential election, the largest number in U.S. history.

The days in which Americans viewed politics as a form of entertainment are long gone. Before there was pervasive mass communication, torchlight parades, stem-winder speeches, and whistle-stop train tours brought color to citizens' lives in tightly packed cities as well as isolated rural towns. Such events do not belong only to the distant past. The ability of a visiting president to draw throngs of the curious and the persuaded President Kennedy to visit Dallas on November 22, 1963, and travel a well publicized motorcade route in an open convertible.

The gruesome murder of Kennedy that day is said by some historians and sociologists to have ended the age of American innocence. Then there were the subsequent assassinations of the president's brother, Senator Robert F.

Kennedy, and civil rights leader Reverend Martin Luther King Jr.; the menacing of President Gerald R. Ford and the shooting of presidential contender George Wallace and President Ronald Reagan by would-be assassins; the dangers inferred by the bombing in Oklahoma City in 1995 and the attacks on September 11, 2001. All of these events forced the nation's political leaders into tighter and tighter security bubbles, creating ever more distance between them and the citizens they govern.

Some commentators argue that the pervasive national sense of optimism, present for much of U.S. history, has been eroded by the events noted above as well as costly and controversial wars in Vietnam and Iraq. Others contend that the vibrancy of the nation's political interest is not waning, but flourishing. There is some evidence that they may be right.

Recent statistical analysis shows that voting among the youngest Americans, while still lagging behind the general population, has seen an uptick over recent elections, spurred by response to international terrorism, the war in Iraq, and concerns about the nation's energy supply and the environment. Politically oriented sites have flourished on the World Wide Web. The "mainstream media" and alternative sources offer news sites, while hosts of Web blogs, better known as blogs, offer town-hall style bipartisan discussion groups, rallying centers for political partisans, highly partisan perspectives that sometimes are intended mainly to irritate and outrage readers. Politicians have proven nimble in utilizing this still fairly new technology, using their own sites, blogs, and even social networking sites such as Facebook to grow and energize their support bases and raise money.

It appears there is reason for hope that the "ZZZ" represents more of a nap than a coma in the nation's political life. Technological improvements might allow political parties and candidates for office to campaign in ways that capture greater public interest. At the beginning of the twenty-first century, the nation was grappling with substantial issues that demanded greater public participation in politics and elections: the war in Iraq, global climate change, large federal budget deficits, illegal immigration, and a looming crisis in financing Social Security and Medicare benefits for future generations. The close 2000 and 2004 presidential elections, which revealed sharp differences between the nominees of the two major political parties, fully demonstrated that elections do indeed have consequences.

See also: Election of 1960; 📖 John F. Kennedy's Inaugural Address, 1961, in the **Primary Source Library.**

A – Z

W-Z

PART THREE

Primary Source Library

United States Constitution, Article I, Section 4, 1789

Article 1, Section 4, of the United States Constitution sets up the basic electoral procedures that are still used in the United States. Over time, various laws and amendments have modified the process.

United States Constitution, Article I, Section 4, 1789

The Times, Places and Manner of holding Elections for Senators and Representatives, shall be prescribed in each State by the Legislature thereof; but the Congress may at any time by Law make or alter such Regulations, except as to the Places of chusing Senators.

The Congress shall assemble at least once in every Year, and such Meeting shall be on the first Monday in December, unless they shall by Law appoint a different Day.

United States Constitution, Article II, Section 1, 1789

Article II, Section 1, established the office and term of the president and and vice president. It also establishes the electoral college system, rather than setting up a direct presidential election.

United States Constitution, Article II, Section 1, 1789

The executive Power shall be vested in a President of the United States of America. He shall hold his Office during the Term of four Years, and, together with the Vice President, chosen for the same Term, be elected, as follows:

Each State shall appoint, in such Manner as the Legislature thereof may direct, a Number of Electors, equal to the whole Number of Senators and Representatives to which the State may be entitled in the Congress: but no Senator or Representative, or Person holding an Office of Trust or Profit under the United States, shall be appointed an Elector.

The Electors shall meet in their respective States, and vote by Ballot for two Persons, of whom one at least shall not be an Inhabitant of the same State with themselves. And they shall make a List of all the Persons voted for, and of the Number of Votes for each; which List they shall sign and certify, and transmit sealed to the Seat of the Government of the United States, directed to the President of the Senate. The President of the Senate shall, in the Presence of the Senate and House of Representatives, open all the Certificates, and the Votes shall then be counted. The Person having the greatest Number of Votes shall be the President, if such Number be a Majority of the whole Number of Electors appointed; and if there be more than one who have such Majority, and have an equal Number of Votes, then the House of Representatives shall immediately chuse by Ballot one of them for President; and if no Person have a Majority, then from the five highest on the List the said House shall in like Manner chuse the President. But in chusing the President, the Votes shall be taken by States, the Representation from each State having one Vote; A quorum for this purpose shall consist of a Member or Members from two thirds of the States, and a Majority of all the States shall be necessary to a Choice. In every Case, after the Choice of the President, the Person having the greatest Number of Votes of the Electors shall be the Vice President. But if there should remain two or more who have equal Votes, the Senate shall chuse from them by Ballot the Vice President.

The Congress may determine the Time of chusing the Electors, and the Day on which they shall give their Votes; which Day shall be the same throughout the United States.

No Person except a natural born Citizen, or a Citizen of the United States, at the time of the Adoption of this Constitution, shall be eligible to the Office of President; neither shall any Person be eligible to that Office who shall not have attained to the Age of thirty five Years, and been fourteen Years a Resident within the United States.

In Case of the Removal of the President from Office, or of his Death, Resignation, or Inability to discharge the Powers and Duties of the said Office, the Same shall devolve on the Vice President, and the Congress may by Law provide for the Case of Removal, Death, Resignation or Inability, both of the President and Vice President, declaring what Officer shall then act as President, and such Officer shall act accordingly, until the Disability be removed, or a President shall be elected.

The President shall, at stated Times, receive for his Services, a Compensation, which shall neither be increased nor diminished during the Period for which he shall have been elected, and he shall not receive within that Period any other Emolument from the United States, or any of them.

Before he enter on the Execution of his Office, he shall take the following Oath or Affirmation:—"I do solemnly swear (or affirm) that I will faithfully execute the Office of President of the United States, and will to the best of my Ability, preserve, protect and defend the Constitution of the United States."

United States Constitution, Article II, Section 3, 1789

Article II, Section 3 establishes many key presidential responsibilities. It also sets forth the basic relationship between the president and Congress.

United States Constitution, Article II, Section 3, 1789

He shall from time to time give to the Congress Information of the State of the Union, and recommend to their Consideration such Measures as he shall judge necessary and expedient; he may, on extraordinary Occasions, convene both Houses, or either of them, and in Case of Disagreement between them, with Respect to the Time of Adjournment, he may adjourn them to such Time as he shall think proper; he shall receive Ambassadors and other public Ministers; he shall take Care that the Laws be faithfully executed, and shall Commission all the Officers of the United States.

George Washington's Farewell Address, 1796

President George Washington wrote what has become known as his Farewell Address in 1796. The president never read his address; instead, it was published in the American Daily Advertiser, *a Philadelphia newspaper. In the excerpt below, the president warns of the dangers of political parties, or factions.*

George Washington's Farewell Address, 1796

I have already intimated to you the danger of parties in the state, with particular reference to the founding of them on geographical discriminations. Let me now take a more comprehensive view, and warn you in the most solemn manner against the baneful effects of the spirit of party, generally.

This spirit, unfortunately, is inseparable from our nature, having its root in the strongest passions of the human mind. It exists under different shapes in all governments, more or less stifled, controlled, or repressed; but in those of the popular form, it is seen in its greatest rankness, and is truly their worst enemy.

The alternate domination of one faction over another, sharpened by the spirit of revenge, natural to party dissention, which in different ages and countries has perpetrated the most horrid enormities, is itself a frightful despotism. But this leads at length to a more formal and permanent despotism. The disorders and miseries which result gradually incline the minds of men to seek security and repose in the absolute power of an individual, and sooner or later the chief of some prevailing faction, more able or more fortunate than his competitors, turns this disposition to the purposes of his own elevation, on the ruins of public liberty.

Twelfth Amendment, 1804

The Twelfth Amendment was proposed in response to the contested Election of 1800, in which Thomas Jefferson and Aaron Burr each won the same number of electoral votes. Because of the tied vote, the House of Representatives selected the president, although clearly the electors intended Jefferson to be President and Burr to be Vice President.

Twelfth Amendment, 1804

The Electors shall meet in their respective states, and vote by ballot for President and Vice-President, one of whom, at least, shall not be an inhabitant of the same state with themselves; they shall name in their ballots the person voted for as President and in distinct ballots the person voted for as Vice-President, and they shall make distinct lists of all persons voted for as President, and of all persons voted for as Vice-President, and of the number of votes for each, which lists they shall sign and certify, and transmit sealed to the seat of the government of the United States, directed to the President of the Senate;—The President of the Senate shall, in the presence of the Senate and House of Representatives, open all the certificates and the votes shall then be counted;—The person having the greatest number of votes for President, shall be the President, if such number be a majority of the whole number of Electors appointed; and if no person have such majority, then from the persons having the highest numbers not exceeding three on the list of those voted for as President, the House of Representatives shall choose immediately, by ballot, the President, the votes shall be taken by states, the representation from each state having one vote; a quorum for this purpose shall consist of a member or members from two-thirds of the states, and a majority of all the states shall be necessary to a choice. And if the House of Representatives shall not choose a President whenever the right of choice shall devolve upon them, before the fourth day of March next following, then the Vice-President shall act as President, as in the case of the death or other constitutional disability of the President.—The person having the greatest number of votes as Vice-President, shall be the Vice-President, if such number be a majority of the whole number of Electors appointed, and if no person have a majority, then from the two highest numbers on the list, the Senate shall choose the Vice-President; a quorum for the purpose shall consist of two-thirds of the whole number of Senators, and a majority of the whole number shall be necessary to a choice. But no person constitutionally ineligible to the office of President shall be eligible to that of Vice-President of the United States.

First Use of the Democratic Donkey, 1828

The first use of the donkey as a Democratic symbol is usually traced back to 1828, when a presidential candidate's opponents tried to portray him as a jackass for his policies and his slogan "Let the people rule." In turn, Jackson's supporters used the donkey to symbolize General Andrew Jackson's stubborn opposition to the Bank of the United States.

Later, in the 1870s, cartoonist Thomas Nast popularized the donkey as the party's symbol. Nast first used the donkey in an 1870 cartoon to symbolize the "Copperhead Press," made up of northern Democrats opposed to the Civil War. The donkey is shown kicking a dead lion, symbolizing Lincoln's secretary of war, Edwin Stanton, who had recently died. The symbol caught on and Nast continued to use it in his cartoons.

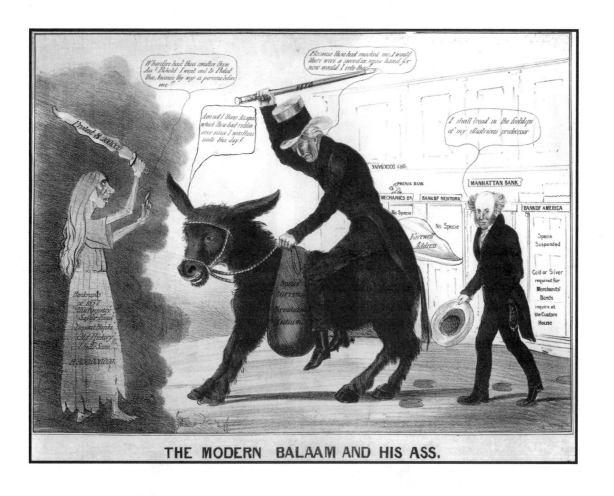

THE MODERN BALAAM AND HIS ASS.

Presidential Campaign Banner, 1872

In the 1872 election, the Republican Party appealed to workers with the humble origins of its candidates—incumbent President Ulysses S. Grant and vice-presidential nominee Henry Wilson. Early in his career, Grant was an unsuccessful tanner, and Wilson, who grew up impoverished, established a successful shoemaker shop. The Republican ticket scored an impressive victory in the electoral college—286 electoral votes.

First Use of the Republican Elephant, 1874

Cartoonist Thomas Nast first used the elephant as the symbol of the Republicans on November 7, 1874–to illustrate "Caesarism"–the possibility that President Ulysses S. Grant, who served from 1869–1877, might run for a third term. In the cartoon, the elephant is running away from Caesarism.

Speech After Being Convicted for Voting in the 1872 Presidential Election, 1873

When Susan B. Anthony, a tireless campaigner for women's rights, voted in the 1872 presidential election, she was arrested. In the excerpt below, Anthony justifies her belief that she did not break the law and that women have the same rights as men.

Susan B. Anthony's Speech, 1873

Friends and fellow citizens: I stand before you tonight under indictment for the alleged crime of having voted at the last presidential election, without having a lawful right to vote. It shall be my work this evening to prove to you that in thus doing, I not only committed no crime, but, instead, simply exercised my citizen's rights, guaranteed to me and all United States citizens by the National Constitution, beyond the power of any State to deny.

Our democratic-republican government is based on the idea of the natural right of every individual member thereof to a voice and a vote in making and executing the laws. We assert the province of government to be to secure the people in the enjoyment of their inalienable right. We throw to the winds the old dogma that government can give rights. No one denies that before governments were organized each individual possessed the right to protect his own life, liberty and property. When 100 to 1,000,000 people enter into a free government, they do not barter away their natural rights; they simply pledge themselves to protect each other in the enjoyment of them through prescribed judicial and legislative tribunals. They agree to abandon the methods of brute force in the adjustment of their differences and adopt those of civilization . . . The Declaration of Independence, the United States Constitution, the constitutions of the several States and the organic laws of the Territories, all alike propose to *protect* the people in the exercise of their God-given rights. Not one of them pretends to bestow rights.

All men are created equal, and endowed by their Creator with certain inalienable rights. Among these are life, liberty and the pursuit of happiness. To secure these, governments are instituted among men, deriving their just powers from the consent of the governed . . .

The preamble of the Federal Constitution says:

We, the people of the United States, in order to form a more perfect union, establish justice, insure domestic tranquility, provide for the common defense, promote the general welfare, and secure the blessings of liberty to ourselves and our posterity, do ordain and establish this Constitution for the United States of America.

It was we, the people; not we, the white male citizens; nor we, the male citizens; but we, the whole people, who formed the Union. And we formed it, not to give the blessings of liberty, but to secure them; not to the half of ourselves and the half of our posterity, but to the whole people—women as well as men. And it is a downright mockery to talk to women of their enjoyment of the blessings of liberty while they are denied the use of the only means of securing them provided by this democratic-republican government - the ballot . . .

Though the words persons, people, inhabitants, electors, citizens, are all used indiscriminately in the national and State constitutions, there was always a conflict of opinion, prior to the war, as to whether they were synonymous terms, but whatever room there was for doubt, under the old regime, the adoption of the Fourteenth amendment settled that question forever in its first sentence:

All persons born or naturalized in the United States, and subject to the jurisdiction thereof, are citizens of the United States, and of the State wherein they reside.

The second settles the equal status of all citizens:

No State shall make or enforce any law which shall abridge the privileges or immunities of citizens of the United States; nor shall any State deprive any person of life, liberty or property without due process of law, or deny to any person within its jurisdiction the equal protection of the laws.

For any state to make sex a qualification that must ever result in the disfranchisement of one entire half of the people, is to pass a bill of attainder, or, an ex post facto law, and is therefore a violation of the supreme law of the land. By it the blessings of liberty are forever withheld from women and their female posterity.

The only question left to be settled now is: Are women persons? I scarcely believe any of our opponents will have the hardihood to say they are not. Being persons, then, women are citizens, and no State has a right to make any new law, or to enforce any old law, which shall abridge their privileges or immunities. Hence, every discrimination against women in the constitutions and laws of the several States is to-day null and void, precisely as is every one against negroes.

Samuel Tilden's Speech, 1877

After losing the disputed presidential election of 1876 by one electoral vote, Samuel Tilden of New York made these comments to members of the Manhattan Club in New York City. Tilden made this speech on June 13, 1877, almost three months after Republican Rutherford B. Hayes was inaugurated as president.

Samuel Tilden's Speech, 1877

Mr. President and Gentlemen of the Manhattan Club:—I accepted your invitation under the idea that this was to be a merely social meeting, the special occasion of which was the presence in this city of Mr. Hendricks and of Governor Robinson and

Lieutenant Governor Dorsheimer. One of your guests, Mr. Hendricks, embarks tomorrow on a foreign excursion for rest and recreation. He will carry with him our best wishes for a prosperous voyage, pleasant visit and a safe return, and for the health and happiness of himself and family.

I have been availing myself, for similiar (sic) purposes, of a brief interval, and find myself now, with some reluctance, drawn away from those private pursuits. But the occasion and the apparent general expectation seem to require that I should say a word in respect to public affairs, and especially that I should allude to the transaction which, in my judgment, is the most portentous in our political history.

Everybody knows that, after the recent election, the men who were elected by the people President and Vice President of the United States were "counted out," and men who were not elected were "counted in" and seated.

I disclaim any thought of the personal wrong involved in this transaction. Not by any act or word of mine shall that be dwarfed or degraded into a personal grievance, which is, in truth, the greatest wrong that has stained our national annals. To every man of the four and a quarter millions who were defrauded of the fruits of their elective franchise it is as great a wrong as it is to me. And no less to every man of the minority will the ultimate consequences extend. Evils in government grow by success and by impunity. They do not arrest their own progress. They can never be limited except by external forces.

If the men in possession of the government can, in one instance, maintain themselves in power against an adverse decision at the elections, such an example will be imitated. Temptation exists always. Devices to give the color of law, and false pretences on which to found fraudulent decisions, will not be wanting. The wrong will grow into a practice, if condoned—if once condoned.

In the world's history changes in the succession of governments have usually been the result of fraud or force. It has been our faith and our pride that we had established a mode of peaceful change to be worked out by the agency of the ballot box. The question now is whether our elective system, in its substance as well as its form, is to be maintained.

This is the question of questions. Until it is finally settled there can be no politics founded on interior questions of administrative policy. It involves the fundamental right of the people. It involves the elective principle. It involves the whole system of popular government. The people must signally condemn the great wrong which has been done to them. They must strip the example of everything that can attract imitators. They must refuse a prosperous immunity to crime. This is not all. The people will not be able to trust the authors or beneficiaries of the wrong to devise remedies. But when those who condemn the wrong shall have the power they must devise the measure which shall render a repetition of the wrong forever impossible.

If my voice could reach throughout our country and be heard in its remotest hamlet I would say. "Be of good cheer. The Republic will live. The institutions of our fathers are not to expire in shame. The sovereignty of the people shall be rescued from this peril and be re-established."

Successful wrong never appears so triumphant as on the very eve of its fall. Seven years ago a corrupt dynasty [The Tweed Ring] culminated in its power over the million of people who live in the city of New York. It has conquered or bribed, or flattered and won almost everybody into acquiescence. It appeared to be invincible. A year or two later its members were in the penitentiaries or in exile. History abounds in similiar (sic) examples. We must believe in the right and in the future. A great and noble nation will not sever its political from its moral life. (Applause.)

Populist Party Platform, 1892

The People's Party, better known as the Populist Party, held its first presidential nominating convention in Omaha, Nebraska. The party stated that it represented the "common folk," especially farmers, rather than wealthy business interests. In July, the convention nominated James B. Weaver as its presidential candidate. Weaver ran on the platform excerpted below.

Populist Party Platform, 1892

We declare, therefore—

First.—That the union of the labor forces of the United States this day consummated shall be permanent and perpetual; may its spirit enter into all hearts for the salvation of the republic and the uplifting of mankind.

Second.—Wealth belongs to him who creates it, and every dollar taken from industry without an equivalent is robbery. "If any will not work, neither shall he eat." The interests of rural and civil labor are the same; their enemies are identical.

Third.—We believe that the time has come when the railroad corporations will either own the people or the people must own the railroads; and should the government enter upon the work of owning and managing all railroads, we should favor an amendment to the constitution by which all persons engaged in the government service shall be placed under a civil-service regulation of the most rigid character, so as to prevent the increase of the power of the national administration by the use of such additional government employees.

FINANCE.—We demand a national currency, safe, sound, and flexible issued by the general government only, a full legal tender for all debts, public and private, and that without the use of banking corporations; a just, equitable, and efficient means of distribution direct to the people, at a tax not to exceed 2 per cent, per annum, to be provided as set forth in the sub-treasury plan of the Farmers' Alliance, or a better system; also by payments in discharge of its obligations for public improvements.

1. We demand free and unlimited coinage of silver and gold at the present legal ratio of 16 to 1.
2. We demand that the amount of circulating medium be speedily increased to not less than $50 per capita.

3. We demand a graduated income tax.

4. We believe that the money of the country should be kept as much as possible in the hands of the people, and hence we demand that all State and national revenues shall be limited to the necessary expenses of the government, economically and honestly administered. We demand that postal savings banks be established by the government for the safe deposit of the earnings of the people and to facilitate exchange.

TRANSPORTATION.—Transportation being a means of exchange and a public necessity, the government should own and operate the railroads in the interest of the people. The telegraph and telephone, like the post-office system, being a necessity for the transmission of news, should be owned and operated by the government in the interest of the people.

LAND.—The land, including all the natural sources of wealth, is the heritage of the people, and should not be monopolized for speculative purposes, and alien ownership of land should be prohibited. All land now held by railroads and other corporations in excess of their actual needs, and all lands now owned by aliens should be reclaimed by the government and held for actual settlers only.

Cross of Gold Speech, 1896

Among the most famous political speeches in American history, the Cross of Gold speech was delivered by William Jennings Bryan on July 9, 1896, at the Democratic National Convention in Chicago. At the time, Bryan and the Democrats called for coinage of silver at a ratio of silver to gold, 16 to 1. This inflationary measure would have increased the amount of money in circulation, aiding debt-burdened farmers. (This idea was strongly opposed by the Republican Party, led by William McKinley.) Several U.S. Senators spoke on the subject. Then the thirty-six-year-old Bryan rose to speak. The former congressman from Nebraska wanted to be the Democratic nominee for president, and he had been quietly building support among the delegates. His spectacular speaking style stirred the delegates to a frenzy. The next day, on the fifth ballot, the convention nominated Bryan for president.

Cross of Gold Speech, 1896

. . . There are two ideas of government. There are those who believe that if you just legislate to make the well-to-do prosperous, that their prosperity will leak through on those below. The Democratic idea has been that if you legislate to make the masses prosperous their prosperity will find its way up and through every class that rests upon it.

You come to us and tell us that the great cities are in favor of the gold standard. I tell you that the great cities rest upon these broad and fertile prairies. Burn down your cities and leave our farms, and your cities will spring up again as if by magic. But destroy our farms and the grass will grow in the streets of every city in the country . . .

If they dare to come out in the open field and defend the gold standard as a good thing, we shall fight them to the uttermost, having behind us the producing masses of the nation and the world. Having behind us the commercial interests and the laboring interests and all the toiling masses, we shall answer their demands for a gold standard by saying to them, you shall not press down upon the brow of labor this crown of thorns. You shall not crucify mankind upon a cross of gold.

Seventeenth Amendment, 1913

The Seventeenth Amendment provides for the direct election of United States senators. Under the U.S. Constitution, senators were originally selected by the state legislatures. This process grew increasingly unpopular, especially as more people won the right to vote.

Another problem was that partisan disputes within state legislatures often left vacancies unfilled. In the 1850s, for example, conflict between Democrats and Republicans in Indiana prevented an election from being held for four years. The amendment was approved by Congress on May 13, 1912, and ratified on April 8, 1913.

Seventeenth Amendment, 1913

Clause 1. The Senate of the United States shall be composed of two Senators from each State, elected by the people thereof, for six years; and each Senator shall have one vote. The electors in each State shall have the qualifications requisite for electors of the most numerous branch of the State legislatures.

Clause 2. When vacancies happen in the representation of any State in the Senate, the executive authority of each State shall issue writs of election to fill such vacancies: Provided That the legislature of any State may empower the executive thereof to make temporary appointments until the people fill the vacancies by election as the legislature may direct.

Clause 3. This amendment shall not be so construed as to affect the election or term of any Senator chosen before it becomes valid as part of the Constitution

Nineteenth Amendment, 1920

Ratified in 1920, the Nineteenth Amendment gave women the right to vote. In 1878, a proposed amendment giving women the right to vote was introduced in Congress, but failed to win the two-thirds majority needed for passage. The same amendment was put before Congress for the next 41 years. In May 1919, Congress finally approved the amendment and sent it to the states for ratification. The amendment was ratified on August 18, 1920, after Tennessee became the thirty-sixth state to approve it.

Primary Source Library

*Nineteenth
Amendment, 1920*

Section 1. The right of the citizens of the United States to vote shall not be denied or abridged by the United States or by any State on account of sex.

Section 2. Congress shall have power to enforce this article by appropriate legislation.

Commemorative Presidential Campaign Stamp, 1924

The 1924 Republican slogan "Keep Cool with Coolidge" was used on political buttons, campaign banners, posters, and commemorative stamps, such as this one from Wisconsin. Incumbent President Calvin Coolidge and vice-presidential nominee Charles G. Dawes swept to victory with 382 electoral votes.

Franklin D. Roosevelt's First Inaugural Address, March 20, 1933

In November 1932, during the bleak depths of the Great Depression, Democrat Franklin D. Roosevelt was elected the thirty-third President of the United States. In his inaugural address, Roosevelt outlined his plans for economic recovery but, perhaps more importantly, he boosted the confidence of the downtrodden American people. His speech includes one of the most famous lines of American history: "The only thing we have to fear is fear itself."

Franklin D. Roosevelt's First Inaugural Address, March 20, 1933

President Hoover, Mr. Chief Justice, my friends: This is a day of national consecration, and I am certain that my fellow Americans expect that on my induction into the Presidency I will address them with a candor and a decision which the present situation of our nation impels.

This is pre-eminently the time to speak the truth, the whole truth, frankly and boldly. Nor need we shrink from honestly facing conditions in our country today. This great nation will endure as it has endured, will revive and will prosper.

So first of all let me assert my firm belief that the only thing we have to fear . . . is fear itself . . . nameless, unreasoning, unjustified terror which paralyzes needed efforts to convert retreat into advance.

In every dark hour of our national life a leadership of frankness and vigor has met with that understanding and support of the people themselves which is essential to victory. I am convinced that you will again give that support to leadership in these critical days. In such a spirit on my part and on yours we face our common difficulties. They concern, thank God, only material things. Values have shrunken to fantastic levels: taxes have risen, our ability to pay has fallen, government of all kinds is faced by serious curtailment of income, the means of exchange are frozen in the currents of trade, the withered leaves of industrial enterprise lie on every side, farmers find no markets for their produce, the savings of many years in thousands of families are gone.

More important, a host of unemployed citizens face the grim problem of existence, and an equally great number toil with little return. Only a foolish optimist can deny the dark realities of the moment.

Yet our distress comes from no failure of substance. We are stricken by no plague of locusts. Compared with the perils which our forefathers conquered because they believed and were not afraid, we have still much to be thankful for. Nature still offers her bounty and human efforts have multiplied it. Plenty is at our doorstep, but a generous use of it languishes in the very sight of the supply . . .

Our greatest primary task is to put people to work. This is no unsolvable problem if we face it wisely and courageously.

It can be accompanied in part by direct recruiting by the government itself, treating the task as we would treat the emergency of a war, but at the same time, through this employment, accomplishing greatly needed projects to stimulate and reorganize the use of our national resources . . .

There are many ways in which it can be helped, but it can never be helped merely by talking about it. We must act, and act quickly.

Finally, in our progress toward a resumption of work we require two safeguards against a return of the evils of the old order: there must be a strict supervision of all banking and credits and investments; there must be an end to speculation with other people's money, and there must be provision for an adequate but sound currency.

These are the lines of attack. I shall presently urge upon a new Congress in special session detailed measures for their fulfillment, and I shall seek the immediate assistance of the several States . . .

It is the way to recovery. It is the immediate way. It is the strongest assurance that the recovery will endure . . .

Our Constitution is so simple and practical that it is possible always to meet extraordinary needs by changes in emphasis and arrangement without loss of essential form.

That is why our constitutional system has proved itself the most superbly enduring political mechanism the modern world has produced. It has met every stress of vast expansion of territory, of foreign wars, of bitter internal strife, of world relations.

It is to be hoped that the normal balance of executive and legislative authority may be wholly adequate to meet the unprecedented task before us. But it may be that an unprecedented demand and need for undelayed action may call for temporary departure from that normal balance of public procedure.

I am prepared under my constitutional duty to recommend the measures that a stricken nation in the midst of a stricken world may require.

But in the event that the Congress shall fail to take one of these courses, and in the event that the national emergency is still critical, I shall not evade the clear course of duty that will then confront me.

I shall ask the Congress for the one remaining instrument to meet the crisis . . . broad executive power to wage a war against the emergency as great as the power that would be given to me if we were in fact invaded by a foreign foe.

For the trust reposed in me I will return the courage and the devotion that befit the time. I can do no less.

We face the arduous days that lie before us in the warm courage of national unity, with the clear consciousness of seeking old and precious moral values, with the clean satisfaction that comes from the stern performance of duty by old and young alike.

We aim at the assurance of a rounded and permanent national life.

We do not distrust the future of essential democracy. The people of the United States have not failed. In their need they have registered a mandate that they want direct, vigorous action . . .

In this dedication of a nation we humbly ask the blessing of God. May He protect each and every one of us! May He guide me in the days to come!

See also: Election of 1932.

Twentieth Amendment, 1933

Sometimes called the "Lame-Duck Amendment," the Twentieth Amendment was proposed on March 2, 1932, and ratified on January 23, 1933. By moving the presidential inauguration day from March 4 to January 20 of the year after the election, the amendment eliminated the long period when an out-going president—often with little power—remained in office.

The amendment also moved the opening of Congress from March 4 to January 3. The original March date reflected the travel time required to reach Washington, D.C. in the early years of the Republic. Sessions beginning in December of even years lasted only three months. Congressional representatives elected in those years did not take office for thirteen months, and those whom they had defeated continued service during the so-called "lame-duck" session. The sessions were generally unproductive, and in light of changes in travel and communications, they became obsolete.

Twentieth Amendment, 1933

Section 1. The terms of the President and Vice President shall end at noon on the 20th day of January, and the terms of Senators and Representatives at noon on the 3d day of January, of the years in which such terms would have ended if this article had not been ratified; and the terms of their successors shall then begin.

Section 2. The Congress shall assemble at least once in every year, and such meeting shall begin at noon on the 3d day of January, unless they shall by law appoint a different day.

Section 3. If, at the time fixed for the beginning of the term of the President, the President elect shall have died, the Vice President elect shall become President. If a President shall not have been chosen before the time fixed for the beginning of his term, or if the President elect shall have failed to qualify, then the Vice President elect shall act as President until a President shall have qualified; and the Congress may by law provide for the case wherein neither a President elect nor a Vice President elect shall have qualified, declaring who shall then act as President, or the manner in which one who is to act shall be selected, and such person shall act accordingly until a President or Vice President shall have qualified.

Section 4. The Congress may by law provide for the case of the death of any of the persons from whom the House of Representatives may choose a President whenever the right of choice shall have devolved upon them, and for the case of the death of any of the persons from whom the Senate may choose a Vice President whenever the right of choice shall have devolved upon them.

Section 5. Sections 1 and 2 shall take effect on the 15th day of October following the ratification of this article.

Section 6. This article shall be inoperative unless it shall have been ratified as an amendment to the Constitution by the legislatures of three-fourths of the several States within seven years from the date of its submission.

Chicago Daily Tribune Headline "Dewey Defeats Truman," 1948

Colonel Robert R. McCormick, the conservative publisher of the Chicago Daily Tribune *believed that Thomas E. Dewey, the Republican presidential candidate nominee, would win the election of 1948. Incumbent president Harry S. Truman won 303 electoral votes to Dewey's 189.*

Twenty-second Amendment, 1951

Ratified in 1951, the Twenty-second Amendment was a reaction to Franklin D. Roosevelt's four election victories. The amendment was written so that the president at the time of ratification, was exempted.

Twenty-second Amendment, 1951

Section 1. No person shall be elected to the office of the President more than twice, and no person who has held the office of President, or acted as President, for more than two years of a term to which some other person was elected President shall be elected to the office of President more than once. But this Article shall not apply to any person holding the office of President when this Article was proposed by Congress, and shall not prevent any person who may be holding the office of President, or acting as President, during the term within which this Article becomes operative from holding the office of President or acting as President during the remainder of such term.

Section 2. This article shall be inoperative unless it shall have been ratified as an amendment to the Constitution by the legislatures of three-fourths of the several States within seven years from the date of its submission to the States by the Congress.

Richard M. Nixon's "Checkers" Speech, 1952

At the 1952 Republican convention, Dwight D. Eisenhower selected California senator Richard M. Nixon as his vice-presidential nominee. During the campaign, Nixon was accused of enriching himself with a private "slush fund." Some Republicans believed that Eisenhower should drop Nixon from the ticket. Hoping to remain the vice-presidential nominee, Nixon went on national television to defend himself from the accusations.

Richard M. Nixon's "Checkers" Speech, 1952

My Fellow Americans,

I come before you tonight as a candidate for the Vice-presidency and as a man whose honesty and integrity has been questioned . . .

To me, the office of the Vice-presidency of the United States is a great office, and I feel that the people have got to have confidence in the integrity of the men who run for that office and who might attain them . . .

I am sure that you have read the charges, and you have heard it, that I, Senator Nixon, took $18,000 from a group of my supporters.

Now, was that wrong? And let me say that it was wrong. I am saying it, incidentally, that it was wrong, just not illegal, because it isn't a question of whether it was legal or illegal, that isn't enough. The question is, was it morally wrong? I say that it was morally wrong if any of that $18,000 went to Senator Nixon, for my personal use. I say that it was morally wrong if it was secretly given and secretly handled.

And I say that it was morally wrong if any of the contributors got special favors for the contributions that they made.

And to answer those questions let me say this—not a cent of the $18,000 or any other money of that type ever went to me for my personal use. Every penny of it was used to pay for political expenses that I did not think should be charged to the tax-payers of the United States.

It was not a secret fund . . .

Let me say, incidentally, that some of you may say, "Well, that is all right, Senator, that is your explanation, but have you got any proof?" And I would like to tell you this evening that just an hour ago we received an independent audit of this entire fund . . .

I am proud to report to you tonight that this audit and legal opinion is being forwarded to General Eisenhower and I would like to read to you the opinion that was prepared [by the auditors]: It is our conclusion that Senator Nixon did not obtain any financial gain from the collection and disbursement of the funds by Dana Smith [the fund's administrator]; that Senator Nixon did not violate any federal or state law by reason of the operation of the fund; and that neither the portion of the fund paid by Dana Smith directly to third persons, nor the portion paid to Senator Nixon, to reimburse him for office expenses, constituted income in a sense which was either reportable or taxable as income under income tax laws . . .

I should say this, that Pat doesn't have a mink coat. But she does have a respectable Republican cloth coat, and I always tell her she would look good in anything.

One other thing I probably should tell you, because if I don't they will probably be saying this about me, too. We did get something, a gift, after the election.

A man down in Texas heard Pat on the radio mention the fact that our two youngsters would like to have a dog, and, believe it or not, the day before we left on this campaign trip we got a message from Union Station in Baltimore, saying they had a package for us. We went down to get it. You know what it was?

It was a little cocker spaniel dog, in a crate that he had sent all the way from Texas, black and white, spotted, and our little girl Tricia, the six year old, named it Checkers.

And you know, the kids, like all kids, loved the dog, and I just want to say this, right now, that regardless of what they say about it, we are going to keep it . . .

And now, finally, I know that you wonder whether or not I am going to stay on the Republican ticket or resign. Let me say this: I don't believe that I ought to quit, because I am not a quitter. And, incidentally, Pat is not a quitter. After all, her name is Patricia Ryan and she was born on St. Patrick's day, and you know the Irish never quit.

But the decision, my friends, is not mine. I would do nothing that would harm the possibilities of Dwight Eisenhower to become President of the United States. And for that reason I am submitting to the Republican National Committee tonight through this television broadcast the decision which it is theirs to make. Let them decide whether my position on the ticket will help or hurt. And I am going to ask you to help them decide. Wire and write the Republican National Committee whether you think I should stay on or whether I should get off. And whatever their decision, I will abide by it.

But let me just say this last word. Regardless of what happens, I am going to continue this fight. I am going to campaign up and down America until we drive the crooks and the Communists and those that defend them out of Washington, and remember folks, Eisenhower is a great man. Folks, he is a great man, and a vote for Eisenhower is a vote for what is good for America.

1950s Commemorative G.O.P. Handkerchief

In the 1950s, the Republican Party gave away souvenir handkerchiefs to party loyalists. Republican presidents from Abraham Lincoln through Dwight D. Eisenhower are listed.

REPUBLICAN PARTY HISTORY

Intense opposition in nonslave states to further extension of the slavery system brought the Republican Party into being and it's first convention was held at Jackson, Michigan, July 6, 1854.

The first National Convention assembled in Philadelphia, Pa., June 17, 1856, and Abraham Lincoln was it's first successful standard bearer, being elected President of the United States in 1860 with Hannibal Hamlin as Vice President.

Fourteen Republican Presidents have served the United States since the "Grand Old Party" was first organized.

REPUBLICAN PRESIDENTS

	BORN	BIRTHPLACE	ELECTED FROM	DIED	BURIAL PLACE
ABRAHAM LINCOLN	Feb. 12, 1809	Hardin Ca. Ky.	Illinois	April 15, 1865	Springfield, Ill
ANDREW JOHNSON	Dec. 29, 1808	Raleigh, N.C.	Tennessee	July 31, 1875	Greenville, Tenn
ULYSSES S. GRANT	Apr. 27, 1822	Point Pleasant, Ohio	Illinois	July 23, 1885	New York, N.Y.
RUTHERFORD B. HAYES	Oct. 4, 1822	Delaware, Ohio	Ohio	Jan. 17, 1893	Fremont, Ohio
JAMES A. GARFIELD	Nov. 19, 1831	Orange, Ohio	Ohio	Sept. 19, 1881	Cleveland, Ohio
CHESTER A. ARTHUR	Oct. 5, 1830	Fairfield, Vt.	New York	Nov. 18, 1886	Albany, N.Y.
BENJAMIN HARRISON	Aug. 20, 1833	North Bend, Ohio	Indiana	Mar. 13, 1901	Indianapolis, Ind.
WILLIAM McKINLEY	Jan. 29, 1843	Niles, Ohio	Ohio	Sept. 14, 1901	Canton, Ohio
THEODORE ROOSEVELT	Oct. 27, 1858	New York, N.Y.	New York	Jan. 6, 1919	Oyster Bay, N.Y.
WILLIAM H. TAFT	Sept. 15, 1857	Cincinnati, Ohio	Ohio	Mar. 8, 1930	Arlington, Va.
WARREN G. HARDING	Nov. 2, 1865	Corsica, Ohio	Ohio	Aug. 2, 1923	Marion, Ohio
CALVIN COOLIDGE	July 4, 1872	Plymouth, Vt.	Mass.	Jan. 5, 1933	Plymouth, Vt.
HERBERT C. HOOVER	Aug. 10, 1874	W. Branch, Iowa	Calif.		
DWIGHT D. EISENHOWER	Oct. 14, 1890	Denison, Texas	New York		

"Give Us the Ballot, We Will Transform the South," 1957

Years before his eloquent "I Have a Dream" speech, Dr. Martin Luther King, Jr. gave another address at the Lincoln Memorial in Washington, D.C. He recognized the importance of voting. King's wishes finally came be realized with the passage of the Voting Rights Act of 1965.

"Give Us the Ballot, We Will Transform the South," 1957

Three years ago the Supreme Court of this nation rendered in simple, eloquent and unequivocal language a decision which will long be stenciled on the mental sheets of succeeding generations. For all men of good will, this May 17 decision came as a joyous daybreak to end the long night of segregation. It came as a great beacon light of hope to millions of distinguished people throughout the world who had dared only to dream of freedom. It came as a legal and sociological deathblow to the old Plessy doctrine of "separate-but-equal." It came as a reaffirmation of the good old American doctrine of freedom and equality for all people.

Unfortunately, this noble and sublime decision has not gone without opposition. This opposition has often risen to ominous proportions. Many states have risen up in open defiance. The legislative halls of the South ring loud with such words as "interposition" and "nullification." Methods of defiance range from crippling economic reprisals to the tragic reign of violence and terror. All of these forces have conjoined to make for massive resistance.

But, even more, all types of conniving methods are still being used to prevent Negroes from becoming registered voters. The denial of this sacred right is a tragic betrayal of the highest mandates of our democratic traditions and it is democracy turned upside down.

So long as I do not firmly and irrevocably possess the right to vote I do not possess myself. I cannot make up my mind—it is made up for me. I cannot live as a democratic citizen, observing the laws I have helped to enact—I can only submit to the edict of others.

So our most urgent request to the president of the United States and every member of Congress is to give us the right to vote. Give us the ballot and we will no longer have to worry the federal government about our basic rights. Give us the ballot and we will no longer plead to the federal government for passage of an anti-lynching law; we will by the power of our vote write the law on the statute books of the southern states and bring an end to the dastardly acts of the hooded perpetrators of violence. Give us the ballot and we will transform the salient misdeeds of blood-thirsty mobs into calculated good deeds of orderly citizens. Give us the ballot and we will fill our legislative halls with men of good will, and send to the sacred halls of Congress men who will not sign a Southern Manifesto, because of their devotion to the manifesto of justice. Give us the ballot and we will place judges on the benches of the South who will "do justly and love mercy," and we will place at the head of the southern states governors who have felt not only the tang of the human, but the glow of the divine. Give us the ballot and we will quietly and nonviolently, without rancor or bitterness, implement the Supreme Court's decision of May 17, 1954.

Inaugural Address, John F. Kennedy, January 20, 1961

At age 43, President John F. Kennedy, the youngest man elected to the presidency, delivered an eloquent, yet brief, Inaugural Address—the president spoke for less than 15 minutes. As the first president born in the twentieth century, Kennedy respected the traditions of the nation's past, but he announced a new era of leadership. Many historians believe that Kennedy's Inaugural Address is among the most moving of all such speeches.

Inaugural Address,
John F. Kennedy,
January 20, 1961

Vice President Johnson, Mr. Speaker, Mr. Chief Justice, President Eisenhower, Vice President Nixon, President Truman, reverend clergy, fellow citizens:

We observe today not a victory of party, but a celebration of freedom—symbolizing an end, as well as a beginning—signifying renewal, as well as change. For I have sworn before you and Almighty God the same solemn oath our forebears prescribed nearly a century and three quarters ago.

The world is very different now. For man holds in his mortal hands the power to abolish all forms of human poverty and all forms of human life. And yet the same revolutionary beliefs for which our forebears fought are still at issue around the globe—the belief that the rights of man come not from the generosity of the state, but from the hand of God.

We dare not forget today that we are the heirs of that first revolution. Let the word go forth from this time and place, to friend and foe alike, that the torch has been passed to a new generation of Americans—born in this century, tempered by war, disciplined by a hard and bitter peace, proud of our ancient heritage—and unwilling to witness or permit the slow undoing of those human rights to which this Nation has always been committed, and to which we are committed today at home and around the world.

Let every nation know, whether it wishes us well or ill, that we shall pay any price, bear any burden, meet any hardship, support any friend, oppose any foe, in order to assure the survival and the success of liberty.

This much we pledge—and more . . .

Finally, to those nations who would make themselves our adversary, we offer not a pledge but a request: that both sides begin anew the quest for peace, before the dark powers of destruction unleashed by science engulf all humanity in planned or accidental self-destruction.

We dare not tempt them with weakness. For only when our arms are sufficient beyond doubt can we be certain beyond doubt that they will never be employed.

But neither can two great and powerful groups of nations take comfort from our present course—both sides overburdened by the cost of modern weapons, both rightly alarmed by the steady spread of the deadly atom, yet both racing to alter that uncertain balance of terror that stays the hand of mankind's final war.

So let us begin anew—remembering on both sides that civility is not a sign of weakness, and sincerity is always subject to proof. Let us never negotiate out of fear, but let us never fear to negotiate.

Let both sides explore what problems unite us instead of belaboring those problems which divide us.

Let both sides, for the first time, formulate serious and precise proposals for the inspection and control of arms, and bring the absolute power to destroy other nations under the absolute control of all nations.

Let both sides seek to invoke the wonders of science instead of its terrors. Together let us explore the stars, conquer the deserts, eradicate disease, tap the ocean depths, and encourage the arts and commerce.

Let both sides unite to heed, in all corners of the earth, the command of Isaiah—to "undo the heavy burdens, and [to] let the oppressed go free."

And so, my fellow Americans, ask not what your country can do for you; ask what you can do for your country.

My fellow citizens of the world, ask not what America will do for you, but what together we can do for the freedom of man . . .

See also: Election of 1960 in "Elections A to Z."

Baker v. Carr, 1962

This landmark case came to the Supreme Court on appeal from the Federal District Court of Tennessee. In the case, the appellants believed that a 1901 Tennessee law, by underrepresenting urban voters, violated the equal protection of the Fourteenth Amendment.

The district court ruled that it lacked jurisdiction in the case. However, The Supreme Court determined that the courts do have the right to determine the constitutionality of a state's voting districts. Therefore, the case was returned to the district court.

Baker v. Carr, 1962

Appellants are persons allegedly qualified to vote for members of the General Assembly of Tennessee representing the counties in which they reside. They brought suit in a Federal District Court in Tennessee . . . on behalf of themselves and others similarly situated, to redress the alleged deprivation of their federal constitutional rights by legislation classifying voters with respect to representation in the General Assembly. They alleged that, by means of a 1901 statute of Tennessee arbitrarily and capriciously apportioning the seats in the General Assembly among the State's 95 counties, and a failure to reapportion them subsequently notwithstanding substantial growth and redistribution of the State's population, they suffer a "debasement of their votes" and were thereby denied the equal protection of the laws guaranteed them by the Fourteenth Amendment. They sought, inter alia, a declaratory judgment that the 1901 statute is unconstitutional and an injunction restraining certain state officers from conducting any further elections under it. The District Court dismissed the complaint on the grounds that it lacked jurisdiction of the subject matter and that no claim was stated upon which relief could be granted. Held:

1. The District Court had jurisdiction of the subject matter of the federal constitutional claim asserted in the complaint.
2. Appellants had standing to maintain this suit.
3. The complaint's allegations of a denial of equal protection presented a justiciable constitutional cause of action upon which appellants are entitled to a trial and a decision . . .

This civil action was brought . . . to redress the alleged deprivation of federal constitutional rights. The complaint, alleging that by means of a 1901 statute of Tennessee apportioning the members of the General Assembly among the State's 95 counties, "these plaintiffs and others similarly situated, are denied the equal protection of the laws accorded them by the Fourteenth Amendment to the Constitution of the United States by virtue of the debasement of their votes," was dismissed by a three-judge court . . . in the Middle District of Tennessee. The court held that it lacked jurisdiction of the subject matter and also that no claim was stated upon which relief could be granted. We noted probable jurisdiction of the appeal. We hold that the dismissal was error, and remand the cause to the District Court for trial and further proceedings consistent with this opinion.

We conclude that the complaint's allegations of a denial of equal protection present a justiciable constitutional cause of action upon which appellants are entitled to a trial and a decision. The right asserted is within the reach of judicial protection under the Fourteenth Amendment.

The judgment of the District Court is reversed and the cause is remanded for further proceedings consistent with this opinion.

Twenty-fourth Amendment, 1964

Ratified in 1964, the Twenty-fourth Amendment prohibited the states from requiring potential voters to pay any type of tax in order to vote. After Reconstruction ended in 1877, eleven southern states enacted poll taxes to prevent poor African Americans and whites from voting. The amendment was proposed by Congress on August 29, 1962, and ratified on January 23, 1964, after South Dakota became the thirty-eighth state to approve it.

Twenty-fourth Amendment, 1964

Section 1. The right of citizens of the United States to vote in any primary or other election for President or Vice President, for electors for President or Vice President, or for Senator or Representative in Congress, shall not be denied or abridged by the United States or any State by reason of failure to pay any poll tax or other tax.

Section 2. Congress shall have power to enforce this article by appropriate legislation.

Twenty-fifth Amendment, 1967

The Twenty-fifth Amendment provided for the President to fill the office of Vice President, should it become vacant. The amendment also provided procedures in the event of presidential disability. Congress approved this amendment and sent it to the states for ratification on July 6, 1965, less than two years after the assassination of President John F. Kennedy.

Twenty-fifth Amendment, 1967

Section 1. In case of the removal of the President from office or of his death or resignation, the Vice President shall become President.

Section 2. Whenever there is a vacancy in the office of the Vice President, the President shall nominate a Vice President who shall take office upon confirmation by a majority vote of both Houses of Congress.

Section 3. Whenever the President transmits to the President pro tempore of the Senate and the Speaker of the House of Representatives his written declaration that he is unable to discharge the powers and duties of his office, and until he transmits to them a written declaration to the contrary, such powers and duties shall be discharged by the Vice President as Acting President.

Section 4. Whenever the Vice President and a majority of either the principal officers of the executive departments or of such other body as Congress may by law provide, transmit to the President pro tempore of the Senate and the Speaker of the House of Representatives their written declaration that the President is unable to discharge the powers and duties of his office, the Vice President shall immediately assume the powers and duties of the office as Acting President.

Thereafter, when the President transmits to the President pro tempore of the Senate and the Speaker of the House of Representatives his written declaration that no inability exists, he shall resume the powers and duties of his office unless the Vice President and a majority of either the principal officers of the executive department or of such other body as Congress may by law provide, transmit within four days to the President pro tempore of the Senate and the Speaker of the House of Representatives their written declaration that the President is unable to discharge the powers and duties of his office. Thereupon Congress shall decide the issue, assembling within forty-eight hours for that purpose if not in session. If the Congress within twenty-one days after receipt of the latter written declaration, or, if Congress is not in session within twenty-one days after Congress is required to assemble, determines by two-thirds vote of both Houses that the President is unable to discharge the powers and duties of his office, the Vice President shall continue to discharge the same as Acting President; otherwise, the President shall resume the powers and duties of his office.

See also: Twenty-fifth Amendment in Elections A to Z.

Lyndon B. Johnson's The American Promise, March 15, 1965

Throughout the 1950s and early 1960s, many southern African Americans remained disenfranchised. After the 1964 election, several civil-rights groups joined to work for African American voting rights. The Selma to Montgomery marches and the murder of civil-rights worker Viola Liuzzo were two pivotal events that finally led to federal intervention. President Lyndon Baines Johnson, in a dramatic joint-session address to Congress, called for a strong voting rights bill to enforce the Fourteenth and Fifteenth Amendments. The Voting Rights Act of 1965 eliminated legal methods designed to keep African Americans and other minorities from voting.

Lyndon B. Johnson's The American Promise, March 15, 1965

Mr. Speaker, Mr. President, Members of the Congress: I speak tonight for the dignity of man and the destiny of democracy.

I urge every member of both parties, Americans of all religions and of all colors, from every section of this country, to join me in that cause.

At times history and fate meet at a single time in a single place to shape a turning point in man's unending search for freedom. So it was at Lexington and Concord. So it was a century ago at Appomattox. So it was last week in Selma, Alabama.

There, long-suffering men and women peacefully protested the denial of their rights as Americans. Many were brutally assaulted. One good man, a man of God, was killed . . .

Rarely are we met with a challenge, not to our growth or abundance, our welfare or our security, but rather to the values and the purposes and the meaning of our beloved Nation.

The issue of equal rights for American Negroes is such an issue. And should we defeat every enemy, should we double our wealth and conquer the stars, and still be unequal to this issue, then we will have failed as a people and as a nation . . .

There is no Negro problem. There is no Southern problem. There is no Northern problem. There is only an American problem. And we are met here tonight as Americans—not as Democrats or Republicans—we are met here as Americans to solve that problem . . .

Many of the issues of civil rights are very complex and most difficult. But about this there can and should be no argument. Every American citizen must have an equal right to vote. There is no reason which can excuse the denial of that right. There is no duty which weighs more heavily on us than the duty we have to ensure that right. Yet the harsh fact is that in many places in this country men and women are kept from voting simply because they are Negroes.

Every device of which human ingenuity is capable has been used to deny this right. The Negro citizen may go to register only to be told that the day is wrong, or the hour is late, or the official in charge is absent. And if he persists, and if he manages to present himself to the registrar, he may be disqualified because he did not spell out his middle name or because he abbreviated a word on the application.

And if he manages to fill out an application he is given a test. The registrar is the sole judge of whether he passes this test. He may be asked to recite the entire Constitution, or explain the most complex provisions of State law. And even a college degree cannot be used to prove that he can read and write.

For the fact is that the only way to pass these barriers is to show a white skin . . .

In such a case our duty must be clear to all of us. The Constitution says that no person shall be kept from voting because of his race or his color. We have all sworn an oath before God to support and to defend that Constitution. We must now act in obedience to that oath.

There is no constitutional issue here. The command of the Constitution is plain.

There is no moral issue. It is wrong—deadly wrong—to deny any of your fellow Americans the right to vote in this country.

There is no issue of States rights or national rights. There is only the struggle for human rights . . .

As a man whose roots go deeply into Southern soil I know how agonizing racial feelings are. I know how difficult it is to reshape the attitudes and the structure of our society.

But a century has passed, more than a hundred years, since the Negro was freed. And he is not fully free tonight.

It was more than a hundred years ago that Abraham Lincoln, a great President of another party, signed the Emancipation Proclamation, but emancipation is a proclamation and not a fact.

A century has passed, more than a hundred years, since equality was promised. And yet the Negro is not equal.

A century has passed since the day of promise. And the promise is unkept.

The time of justice has now come . . .

Because all Americans just must have the right to vote. And we are going to give them that right.

All Americans must have the privileges of citizenship regardless of race. And they are going to have those privileges of citizenship regardless of race.

My first job after college was as a teacher in Cotulla, Texas, in a small Mexican-American school. Few of them could speak English, and I couldn't speak much Spanish. My students were poor and they often came to class without breakfast, hungry. They knew even in their youth the pain of prejudice. They never seemed to know why people disliked them. But they knew it was so, because I saw it in their eyes. I often walked home late in the afternoon, after the classes were finished, wishing there was more that I could do. But all I knew was to teach them the little that I knew, hoping that it might help them against the hardships that lay ahead.

Somehow you never forget what poverty and hatred can do when you see its scars on the hopeful face of a young child.

I never thought then, in 1928, that I would be standing here in 1965. It never even occurred to me in my fondest dreams that I might have the chance to help the sons and daughters of those students and to help people like them all over this country.

But now I do have that chance—and I'll let you in on a secret—I mean to use it. And I hope that you will use it with me . . .

I want to be the President who educated young children to the wonders of their world. I want to be the President who helped to feed the hungry and to prepare them to be taxpayers instead of taxeaters.

I want to be the President who helped the poor to find their own way and who protected the right of every citizen to vote in every election.

I want to be the President who helped to end hatred among his fellow men and who promoted love among the people of all races and all regions and all parties . . .

I want this to be the Congress, Republicans and Democrats alike, which did all these things for all these people . . .

See also: Voting Rights Act of 1965 in "Elections A to Z."

Voting Rights Act of 1965

President Lyndon B. Johnson signed the Voting Rights Act of 1965 into law on August 6, 1965. Passed at Johnson's urging, this landmark legislation outlawed discriminatory voting practices, including literacy tests, which prevented thousands of African Americans from voting. Over time, the provisions of the law have been expanded to eliminate other

unfair voting practices. Extensions to the law have also been passed several times, most recently in 2006.

Voting Rights Act of 1965

Be it enacted by the Senate and House of Representatives of the United States of America in Congress assembled, That this Act shall be known as the "Voting Rights Act of 1965."

Sec. 2.

No voting qualification or prerequisite to voting, or standard, practice, or procedure shall be imposed or applied by any State or political subdivision to deny or abridge the right of any citizen of the United States to vote on account of race or color . . .

Sec. 4.

(a) To assure that the right of citizens of the United States to vote is not denied or abridged on account of race or color, no citizen shall be denied the right to vote in any Federal, State, or local election because of his failure to comply with any test or device in any State . . .

Sec. 11.

(a) No person acting under color of law shall fail or refuse to permit any person to vote who is entitled to vote under any provision of this Act or is otherwise qualified to vote, or willfully fail or refuse to tabulate, count, and report such person's vote.

(b) No person, whether acting under color of law or otherwise, shall intimidate, threaten, or coerce, or attempt to intimidate, threaten, or coerce any person for voting or attempting to vote, or intimidate, threaten, or coerce, or attempt to intimidate, threaten, or coerce any person for urging or aiding any person to vote or attempt to vote, or intimidate, threaten, or coerce any person for exercising any powers or duties under section 3(a), 6, 8, 9, 10, or 12(e).

Sec. 12.

(a) Whoever shall deprive or attempt to deprive any person of any right secured by section 2, 3, 4, 5, 7, or 10 or shall violate section 11(a) or (b), shall be fined not more than $5,000, or imprisoned not more than five years, or both. (b) Whoever, within a year following an election in a political subdivision in which an examiner has been appointed (1) destroys, defaces, mutilates, or otherwise alters the marking of a paper ballot which has been cast in such election, or (2) alters any official record of voting in such election tabulated from a voting machine or otherwise, shall be fined not more than $5,000, or imprisoned not more than five years, or both . . .

See also: Voting Rights Act of 1965 in "Elections A to Z."

Lyndon B. Johnson Announces That He Is Not a Presidential Candidate, March 31, 1968

The war in Vietnam was a major issue in the 1968 presidential election campaign. Incumbent president Lyndon Johnson had planned to run for reelection, but early polls showed that, because of the war, he was losing the support of the American people. Thus, at the end of March 1968, Johnson sought new peace initiatives. He also startled the nation when he announced that he would not seek the Democratic presidential nomination.

Lyndon B. Johnson Announces That He Is Not a Presidential Candidate, March 31, 1968

Good evening, my fellow Americans: Tonight I want to speak to you of peace in Vietnam and Southeast Asia.

No other question so preoccupies our people. No other dream so absorbs the 250 million human beings who live in that part of the world. No other goal motivates American policy in Southeast Asia.

For years, representatives of our Government and others have traveled the world— seeking to find a basis for peace talks . . .

If they [the Communists] do mount another round of heavy attacks, they will not succeed in destroying the fighting power of South Vietnam and its allies.

But tragically, this is also clear: Many men—on both sides of the struggle—will be lost. A nation that has already suffered 20 years of warfare will suffer once again. Armies on both sides will take new casualties. And the war will go on.

There is no need for this to be so.

There is no need to delay the talks that could bring an end to this long and this bloody war.

Tonight, I renew the offer I made last August—to stop the bombardment of North Vietnam. We ask that talks begin promptly, that they be serious talks on the substance of peace. We assume that during those talks Hanoi will not take advantage of our restraint.

We are prepared to move immediately toward peace through negotiations.

So, tonight, in the hope that this action will lead to early talks, I am taking the first step to deescalate the conflict. We are reducing—substantially reducing—the present level of hostilities.

And we are doing so unilaterally, and at once . . .

It is to save the lives of brave men—and to save the lives of innocent women and children. It is to permit the contending forces to move closer to a political settlement.

I call upon President Ho Chi Minh [of North Vietnam] to respond positively, and favorably, to this new step toward peace . . .

Finally, my fellow Americans, let me say this:

Of those to whom much is given, much is asked. I cannot say and no man could say that no more will be asked of us.

Yet, I believe that now, no less than when the decade began, this generation of Americans is willing to "pay any price, bear any burden, meet any hardship, support any friend, oppose any foe to assure the survival and the success of liberty."

Since those words were spoken by John F. Kennedy, the people of America have kept that compact with mankind's noblest cause.

And we shall continue to keep it.

Yet, I believe that we must always be mindful of this one thing, whatever the trials and the tests ahead. The ultimate strength of our country and our cause will lie not in powerful weapons or infinite resources or boundless wealth, but will lie in the unity of our people.

This I believe very deeply.

Throughout my entire public career I have followed the personal philosophy that I am a free man, an American, a public servant, and a member of my party, in that order always and only.

For 37 years in the service of our Nation, first as a Congressman, as a Senator, and as Vice President, and now as your President, I have put the unity of the people first. I have put it ahead of any divisive partisanship.

And in these times as in times before, it is true that a house divided against itself by the spirit of faction, of party, of region, of religion, of race, is a house that cannot stand.

There is division in the American house now. There is divisiveness among us all tonight. And holding the trust that is mine, as President of all the people, I cannot disregard the peril to the progress of the American people and the hope and the prospect of peace for all peoples.

So, I would ask all Americans, whatever their personal interests or concern, to guard against divisiveness and all its ugly consequences . . .

Through all time to come, I think America will be a stronger nation, a more just society, and a land of greater opportunity and fulfillment because of what we have all done together in these years of unparalleled achievement.

Our reward will come in the life of freedom, peace, and hope that our children will enjoy through ages ahead.

What we won when all of our people united just must not now be lost in suspicion, distrust, selfishness, and politics among any of our people.

Believing this as I do, I have concluded that I should not permit the Presidency to become involved in the partisan divisions that are developing in this political year.

With America's sons in the fields far away, with America's future under challenge right here at home, with our hopes and the world's hopes for peace in the balance every day, I do not believe that I should devote an hour or a day of my time to any personal partisan causes or to any duties other than the awesome duties of this office—the Presidency of your country.

Accordingly, I shall not seek, and I will not accept, the nomination of my party for another term as your President.

But let men everywhere know, however, that a strong, a confident, and a vigilant America stands ready tonight to seek an honorable peace—and stands ready tonight to defend an honored cause—whatever the price, whatever the burden, whatever the sacrifice that duty may require.

Thank you for listening.

Good night and God bless all of you.

Twenty-sixth Amendment, 1971

Proposed on March 23, 1971, the Twenty-sixth Amendment was ratified by the states on July 1, 1971—the shortest ratification time in history. The Amendment lowered the voting age from 21 to 18 years of age. Pressure to lower the voting age came as a result of the Vietnam War. Supporters of the lower voting age argued that if a citizen was old enough to be drafted and sent into combat at age 18, that person was old enough to vote.

Twenty-sixth Amendment, 1971

Section 1. The right of citizens of the United States, who are eighteen years of age or older, to vote shall not be denied or abridged by the United States or by any State on account of age.

Section 2. The Congress shall have the power to enforce this article by appropriate legislation.

See also: Twenty-sixth Amendment in "Elections A to Z."

Buckley v. Valeo, 1976

This very complicated court case centered on two issues: whether or not the campaign-donation limits imposed on individuals by the Federal Election Campaign Act violated the First Amendment and whether or not limits can be placed on the use of a candidate's personal finances for a campaign. The Court came to two important conclusions.

First, it held that restrictions on individual contributions to political campaigns and candidates did not violate the First Amendment since the limitations of the Federal

Primary Source Library

Election Campaign Act enhance the "integrity of our system of representative democracy" by guarding against unscrupulous practices.

Second, the Court found that governmental restriction of independent expenditures in campaigns, the limitation on expenditures by candidates from their own personal resources, and the limitation on total campaign expenditures did violate the First Amendment. The Court determined that these practices do not necessarily enhance the potential for corruption; thus, the Court found that restricting them did not serve a government interest great enough to warrant a curtailment on free speech and association.

Buckley v. Valeo, 1976

The Federal Election Campaign Act of 1971 (Act), as amended in 1974, (a) limits political contributions to candidates for federal elective office by an individual or a group to $1,000 and by a political committee to $5,000 to any single candidate per election, with an overall annual limitation of $25,000 by an individual contributor; (b) limits expenditures by individuals or groups "relative to a clearly identified candidate" to $1,000 per candidate per election, and by a candidate from his personal or family funds to various specified annual amounts depending upon the federal office sought, and restricts overall general election and primary campaign expenditures by candidates to various specified amounts, again depending upon the federal office sought; (c) requires political committees to keep detailed records of contributions and expenditures, including the name and address of each individual contributing in excess of $10, and his occupation and principal place of business if his contribution exceeds $100, and to file quarterly reports with the Federal Election Commission disclosing the source of every contribution exceeding $100 and the recipient and purpose of every expenditure over $100, and also requires every individual or group, other than a candidate or political committee, making contributions or expenditures exceeding $100 "other than by contribution to a political committee or candidate" to file a statement with the Commission; and (d) creates the eight-member Commission as the administering agency with recordkeeping, disclosure, and investigatory functions and extensive rulemaking, adjudicatory, and enforcement powers, . . .

In summary, we sustain the individual contribution limits, the disclosure and reporting provisions, and the public financing scheme. We conclude, however, that the limitations on campaign expenditures, on independent expenditures by individuals and groups, and on expenditures by a candidate from his personal funds are constitutionally infirm. Finally, we hold that most of the powers conferred by the Act upon the Federal Election Commission can be exercised only by "Officers of the United States," appointed in conformity with Art. II, 2, cl. 2, of the Constitution, and therefore cannot be exercised by the Commission as presently constituted.

See also: Campaign Finance in "Elections A to Z."

Contract with America, 1994

Introduced six weeks before the 1994 Congressional elections, the Republican Contract with America detailed ten key actions the party would undertake, if they were to win control of the House. The Republicans did win control of the House—for the first time in forty years. Once in power, however, the Republicans achieved mixed results when attempting to implement the Contract. Some elements of the Contract did not pass the House, others died in the Senate, and President Bill Clinton vetoed others.

Contract with America, 1994

As Republican Members of the House of Representatives and as citizens seeking to join that body we propose not just to change its policies, but even more important, to restore the bonds of trust between the people and their elected representatives.

That is why in this era of official evasion and posturing, we offer instead a detailed agenda for national renewal, a written commitment with no fine print.

This year's election offers the chance, after four decades of one-party control, to bring to the House a new majority that will transform the way Congress works. That historic change would be the end of government that is too big, too intrusive, and too easy with the public's money. It can be the beginning of a Congress that respects the values and shares the faith of the American family.

Like Lincoln, our first Republican president, we intend to act "with firmness in the right, as God gives us to see the right." To restore accountability to Congress. To end its cycle of scandal and disgrace. To make us all proud again of the way free people govern themselves.

On the first day of the 104th Congress, the new Republican majority will immediately pass the following major reforms, aimed at restoring the faith and trust of the American people in their government:

FIRST, require all laws that apply to the rest of the country also apply equally to the Congress;

SECOND, select a major, independent auditing firm to conduct a comprehensive audit of Congress for waste, fraud or abuse;

THIRD, cut the number of House committees, and cut committee staff by one-third;

FOURTH, limit the terms of all committee chairs;

FIFTH, ban the casting of proxy votes in committee;

SIXTH, require committee meetings to be open to the public;

SEVENTH, require a three-fifths majority vote to pass a tax increase;

EIGHTH, guarantee an honest accounting of our Federal Budget by implementing zero base-line budgeting.

Thereafter, within the first 100 days of the 104th Congress, we shall bring to the House Floor the following bills, each to be given full and open debate, each to be given a clear and fair vote and each to be immediately available this day for public inspection and scrutiny.

THE FISCAL RESPONSIBILITY ACT

A balanced budget/tax limitation amendment and a legislative line-item veto to restore fiscal responsibility to an out-of-control Congress, requiring them to live under the same budget constraints as families and businesses.

THE TAKING BACK OUR STREETS ACT

An anti-crime package including stronger truth-in-sentencing, "good faith" exclusionary rule exemptions, effective death penalty provisions, and cuts in social spending for this summer's "crime" bill to fund prison construction and additional law enforcement to keep people secure in their neighborhoods and kids safe in their schools.

THE PERSONAL RESPONSIBILITY ACT

Discourage illegitimacy and teen pregnancy by prohibiting welfare to minor mothers and denying increased AFDC for additional children while on welfare, cut spending for welfare programs, and enact a tough two-years-and-out provision with work requirements to promote individual responsibility.

THE FAMILY REINFORCEMENT ACT

Child support enforcement, tax incentives for adoption, strengthening rights of parents in their children's education, stronger child pornography laws, and an elderly dependent care tax credit to reinforce the central role of families in American society.

THE AMERICAN DREAM RESTORATION ACT

A $500 per child tax credit, begin repeal of the marriage tax penalty, and creation of American Dream Savings Accounts to provide middle class tax relief.

THE NATIONAL SECURITY RESTORATION ACT

No U.S. troops under U.N. command and restoration of the essential parts of our national security funding to strengthen our national defense and maintain our credibility around the world.

THE SENIOR CITIZENS FAIRNESS ACT

Raise the Social Security earnings limit, which currently forces seniors out of the work force, repeal the 1993 tax hikes on Social Security benefits and provide tax incentives for private long-term care insurance to let Older Americans keep more of what they have earned over the years.

THE JOB CREATION AND WAGE ENHANCEMENT ACT

Small business incentives, capital gains cuts and indexation, neutral cost recovery, risk assessment/cost-benefit analysis, strengthening the Regulatory Flexibility Act and unfunded mandate reform to create jobs and raise worker wages.

THE COMMON SENSE LEGAL REFORM ACT

"Loser pays" laws, reasonable limits on punitive damages and reform of product liability laws to stem the endless tide of litigation.

THE CITIZEN LEGISLATURE ACT

A first-ever vote on term limits to replace career politicians with citizen legislators.

George W. Bush, et al., petitioners, v. Albert Gore, Jr., et al., 2000

The 2000 presidential election between George W. Bush and Al Gore was one of the closest—and most bitterly contested—in American history. Ultimately, the election's outcome hinged on Florida's 25 electoral votes. Because the margin of difference between the two candidates was so narrow, the ballots were subject to an automatic recount. This tally, too, was contested, and subjected to a partial manual recount. On December 12, 2000, the United States Supreme Court ruled that employing various means of recounting ballots violated the equal protection clause of the Constitution.

George W. Bush, et al., petitioners, v. Albert Gore, Jr., et al., 2000

. . . On November 8, 2000, the day following the Presidential election, the Florida Division of Elections reported that petitioner, Governor Bush, had received 2,909,135 votes, and respondent, Vice President Gore, had received 2,907,351 votes, a margin of 1,784 for Governor Bush. Because Governor Bush's margin of victory was less than "one-half of a percent . . . of the votes cast," an automatic machine recount was conducted under §102.141(4) of the election code, the results of which showed Governor Bush still winning the race but by a diminished margin. Vice President Gore then sought manual recounts in Volusia, Palm Beach, Broward, and Miami-Dade Counties, pursuant to Florida's election protest provisions. A dispute arose concerning the deadline for local county canvassing boards to submit their returns to the Secretary of State. The Secretary declined to waive the November 14 deadline imposed by statute. The Florida Supreme Court, however, set the deadline at November 26. We granted certiorari and vacated the Florida Supreme Court's decision, finding considerable uncertainty as to the grounds on which it was based (*Bush I*).

On November 26, the Florida Elections Canvassing Commission certified the results of the election and declared Governor Bush the winner of Florida's 25 electoral votes. On November 27, Vice President Gore, pursuant to Florida's contest provisions, filed a complaint in Leon County Circuit Court contesting the certification. He sought relief pursuant to §102.168(3)(c), which provides that "[r]eceipt of a number of illegal votes or rejection of a number of legal votes sufficient to change or place in doubt the result of the election" shall be grounds for a contest. The Circuit Court denied relief, stating that Vice President Gore failed to meet his burden of proof. He appealed to the First District Court of Appeal, which certified the matter to the Florida Supreme Court.

Accepting jurisdiction, the Florida Supreme Court affirmed in part and reversed in part. The court held that the Circuit Court had been correct to reject Vice President Gore's challenge to the results certified in Nassau County and his challenge to the Palm Beach County Canvassing Board's determination that 3,300 ballots cast in that county were not, in the statutory phrase, "legal votes."

The right to vote is protected in more than the initial allocation of the franchise. Equal protection applies as well to the manner of its exercise. Having once granted the right to vote on equal terms, the State may not, by later arbitrary and disparate treatment, value one person's vote over that of another . . .

There is no difference between the two sides of the present controversy on these basic propositions. Respondents say that the very purpose of vindicating the right to vote justifies the recount procedures now at issue. The question before us, however, is whether the recount procedures the Florida Supreme Court has adopted are consistent with its obligation to avoid arbitrary and disparate treatment of the members of its electorate.

Much of the controversy seems to revolve around ballot cards designed to be perforated by a stylus but which, either through error or deliberate omission, have not been perforated with sufficient precision for a machine to count them. In some cases a piece of the card—a chad—is hanging, say by two corners. In other cases there is no separation at all, just an indentation.

The record provides some examples. A monitor in Miami-Dade County testified at trial that he observed that three members of the county canvassing board applied different standards in defining a legal vote. And testimony at trial also revealed that at least one county changed its evaluative standards during the counting process. Palm Beach County, for example, began the process with a 1990 guideline which precluded counting completely attached chads, switched to a rule that considered a vote to be legal if any light could be seen through a chad, changed back to the 1990 rule, and then abandoned any pretense of a *per se* rule, only to have a court order that the county consider dimpled chads legal. This is not a process with sufficient guarantees of equal treatment . . .

The State Supreme Court ratified this uneven treatment. It mandated that the recount totals from two counties, Miami-Dade and Palm Beach, be included in the certified total. The court also appeared to hold *sub silentio* that the recount totals from Broward County, which were not completed until after the original November 14 certification by the Secretary of State, were to be considered part of the new certified vote totals even though the county certification was not contested by Vice President Gore. Yet each of the counties used varying standards to determine what was a legal vote. Broward County used a more forgiving standard than Palm Beach County, and uncovered almost three times as many new votes, a result markedly disproportionate to the difference in population between the counties . . .

That brings the analysis to yet a further equal protection problem. The votes certified by the court included a partial total from one county, Miami-Dade. The Florida Supreme Court's decision thus gives no assurance that the recounts included in a final certification must be complete. Indeed, it is respondent's submission that it would be consistent with the rules of the recount procedures to include whatever partial counts are done by the time of final certification, and we interpret the Florida Supreme Court's decision to permit this. This accommodation no doubt results from the truncated contest period established by the Florida Supreme Court in *Bush I,* at respondents' own urging. The press of time does not diminish the constitutional concern. A desire for speed is not a general excuse for ignoring equal protection guarantees.

In addition to these difficulties the actual process by which the votes were to be counted under the Florida Supreme Court's decision raises further concerns. That order did not specify who would recount the ballots. The county canvassing boards were forced to pull together ad hoc teams comprised of judges from various Circuits who had no previous training in handling and interpreting ballots. Furthermore, while others were permitted to observe, they were prohibited from objecting during the recount.

The recount process, in its features here described, is inconsistent with the minimum procedures necessary to protect the fundamental right of each voter in the special instance of a statewide recount under the authority of a single state judicial officer. Our consideration is limited to the present circumstances, for the problem of equal protection in election processes generally presents many complexities.

The question before the Court is not whether local entities, in the exercise of their expertise, may develop different systems for implementing elections. Instead, we are presented with a situation where a state court with the power to assure uniformity has ordered a statewide recount with minimal procedural safeguards. When a court orders a statewide remedy, there must be at least some assurance that the rudimentary requirements of equal treatment and fundamental fairness are satisfied . . .

Upon due consideration of the difficulties identified to this point, it is obvious that the recount cannot be conducted in compliance with the requirements of equal protection and due process without substantial additional work. It would require not only the adoption (after opportunity for argument) of adequate statewide standards for determining what is a legal vote, and practicable procedures to implement them, but also orderly judicial review of any disputed matters that might arise. In addition, the Secretary of State has advised that the recount of only a portion of the ballots requires that the vote tabulation equipment be used to screen out undervotes, a function for which the machines were not designed. If a recount of overvotes were also required, perhaps even a second screening would be necessary. Use of the equipment for this purpose, and any new software developed for it, would have to be evaluated for accuracy by the Secretary of State, as required by Fla. Stat. §101.015 (2000).

The Supreme Court of Florida has said that the legislature intended the State's electors to "participat[e] fully in the federal electoral process. . . ." That statute, in turn, requires that any controversy or contest that is designed to lead to a conclusive selection of electors be completed by December 12. That date is upon us, and there is no recount procedure in place under the State Supreme Court's order that comports with minimal constitutional standards. Because it is evident that any recount seeking to meet the December 12 date will be unconstitutional for the reasons we have discussed, we reverse the judgment of the Supreme Court of Florida ordering a recount to proceed . . .

The judgment of the Supreme Court of Florida is reversed, and the case is remanded for further proceedings not inconsistent with this opinion . . .

It is so ordered.

Vice President Al Gore's Concession Speech, December 13, 2000

The 2000 presidential election between George W. Bush and Albert Gore was one of the most closely contested in United States history. For 36 days, the election outcome hung in the balance, waiting for the final Florida popular vote count which would determine who received the state's 25 electoral votes—and the presidency. Eventually, the issue came before the United States Supreme Court, in the case **Bush v. Gore.** *The Court ruled in favor of Bush, noting that different counties used different methods for the popular vote recounts, thus violating the equal protection clause of the Fourteenth Amendment. On December 13, 2000, Vice President Gore conceded the election to Bush and called for national unity after the divisive election.*

Vice President Al Gore's Concession Speech, December 13, 2000

Good evening.

Just moments ago, I spoke with George W. Bush and congratulated him on becoming the 43rd president of the United States, and I promised him that I wouldn't call him back this time.

I offered to meet with him as soon as possible so that we can start to heal the divisions of the campaign and the contest through which we just passed.

Almost a century and a half ago, Senator Stephen Douglas told Abraham Lincoln, who had just defeated him for the presidency, "Partisan feeling must yield to patriotism. I'm with you, Mr. President, and God bless you."

Well, in that same spirit, I say to President-elect Bush that what remains of partisan rancor must now be put aside, and may God bless his stewardship of this country.

Neither he nor I anticipated this long and difficult road. Certainly neither of us wanted it to happen. Yet it came, and now it has ended, resolved, as it must be resolved, through the honored institutions of our democracy.

Over the library of one of our great law schools is inscribed the motto, "Not under man but under God and law." That's the ruling principle of American freedom, the source of our democratic liberties. I've tried to make it my guide throughout this contest as it has guided America's deliberations of all the complex issues of the past five weeks.

Now the U.S. Supreme Court has spoken. Let there be no doubt, while I strongly disagree with the court's decision, I accept it. I accept the finality of this outcome which will be ratified next Monday in the Electoral College. And tonight, for the sake of our unity of the people and the strength of our democracy, I offer my concession.

I also accept my responsibility, which I will discharge unconditionally, to honor the new president elect and do everything possible to help him bring Americans together in fulfillment of the great vision that our Declaration of Independence defines and that our Constitution affirms and defends.

Let me say how grateful I am to all those who supported me and supported the cause for which we have fought. Tipper and I feel a deep gratitude to Joe and Hadassah Lieberman who brought passion and high purpose to our partnership and opened new doors, not just for our campaign but for our country.

This has been an extraordinary election. But in one of God's unforeseen paths, this belatedly broken impasse can point us all to a new common ground, for its very closeness can serve to remind us that we are one people with a shared history and a shared destiny.

Indeed, that history gives us many examples of contests as hotly debated, as fiercely fought, with their own challenges to the popular will.

Other disputes have dragged on for weeks before reaching resolution. And each time, both the victor and the vanquished have accepted the result peacefully and in the spirit of reconciliation.

So let it be with us.

I know that many of my supporters are disappointed. I am too. But our disappointment must be overcome by our love of country.

And I say to our fellow members of the world community, let no one see this contest as a sign of American weakness. The strength of American democracy is shown most clearly through the difficulties it can overcome.

Some have expressed concern that the unusual nature of this election might hamper the next president in the conduct of his office. I do not believe it need be so.

President-elect Bush inherits a nation whose citizens will be ready to assist him in the conduct of his large responsibilities.

I personally will be at his disposal, and I call on all Americans—I particularly urge all who stood with us to unite behind our next president. This is America. Just as we fight hard when the stakes are high, we close ranks and come together when the contest is done.

And while there will be time enough to debate our continuing differences, now is the time to recognize that that which unites us is greater than that which divides us.

While we yet hold and do not yield our opposing beliefs, there is a higher duty than the one we owe to political party. This is America and we put country before party. We will stand together behind our new president.

As for what I'll do next, I don't know the answer to that one yet. Like many of you, I'm looking forward to spending the holidays with family and old friends. I know I'll spend time in Tennessee and mend some fences, literally and figuratively.

Some have asked whether I have any regrets and I do have one regret: that I didn't get the chance to stay and fight for the American people over the next four years, especially for those who need burdens lifted and barriers removed, especially for those who feel their voices have not been heard. I heard you and I will not forget.

I've seen America in this campaign and I like what I see. It's worth fighting for and that's a fight I'll never stop.

As for the battle that ends tonight, I do believe as my father once said, that no matter how hard the loss, defeat might serve as well as victory to shape the soul and let the glory out.

So for me this campaign ends as it began: with the love of Tipper and our family; with faith in God and in the country I have been so proud to serve, from Vietnam to the vice presidency; and with gratitude to our truly tireless campaign staff and volunteers, including all those who worked so hard in Florida for the last 36 days.

Now the political struggle is over and we turn again to the unending struggle for the common good of all Americans and for those multitudes around the world who look to us for leadership in the cause of freedom.

In the words of our great hymn, "America, America": "Let us crown thy good with brotherhood, from sea to shining sea."

And now, my friends, in a phrase I once addressed to others, it's time for me to go.

Thank you and good night, and God bless America.

George W. Bush's Acceptance Speech, 2000

In December 2000, after Vice President Al Gore conceded defeat, President-elect Bush addressed the American people. He called for unity and promised to work to heal, the country after the highly contested Election of 2000.

George W. Bush's Acceptance Speech, 2000

Thank you all.

Thank you very much. Thank you.

Thank you very much. Good evening, my fellow Americans. I appreciate so very much the opportunity to speak with you tonight.

Mr. Speaker, Lieutenant Governor, friends, distinguished guests, our country has been through a long and trying period, with the outcome of the presidential election not finalized for longer than any of us could ever imagine.

Vice President Gore and I put our hearts and hopes into our campaigns. We both gave it our all. We shared similar emotions, so I understand how difficult this moment must be for Vice President Gore and his family. He has a distinguished record of service to our country as a congressman, a senator and a vice president. This evening I received a gracious call from the vice president. We agreed to meet early next week in Washington and we agreed to do our best to heal our country after this hard-fought contest.

Tonight I want to thank all the thousands of volunteers and campaign workers who worked so hard on my behalf.

I also salute the vice president and his supporters for waging a spirited campaign. And I thank him for a call that I know was difficult to make. Laura and I wish the vice president and Senator Lieberman and their families the very best.

I have a lot to be thankful for tonight. I'm thankful for America and thankful that we were able to resolve our electoral differences in a peaceful way. I'm thankful to the American people for the great privilege of being able to serve as your next president. I want to thank my wife and our daughters for their love. Laura's active involvement as first lady has made Texas a better place, and she will be a wonderful first lady of America.

I am proud to have Dick Cheney by my side, and America will be proud to have him as our next vice president. Tonight I chose to speak from the chamber of the Texas House of Representatives because it has been a home to bipartisan cooperation. Here in a place where Democrats have the majority, Republicans and Democrats have worked together to do what is right for the people we represent.

We've had spirited disagreements. And in the end, we found constructive consensus. It is an experience I will always carry with me, an example I will always follow.

I want to thank my friend, House Speaker Pete Laney, a Democrat, who introduced me today. I want to thank the legislators from both political parties with whom I've worked.

Across the hall in our Texas capitol is the state Senate. And I cannot help but think of our mutual friend, the former Democrat lieutenant governor, Bob Bullock. His love for Texas and his ability to work in a bipartisan way continue to be a model for all of us.

The spirit of cooperation I have seen in this hall is what is needed in Washington, D.C. It is the challenge of our moment. After a difficult election, we must put politics behind us and work together to make the promise of America available for every one of our citizens.

I am optimistic that we can change the tone in Washington, D.C.

I believe things happen for a reason, and I hope the long wait of the last five weeks will heighten a desire to move beyond the bitterness and partisanship of the recent past.

Our nation must rise above a house divided. Americans share hopes and goals and values far more important than any political disagreements.

Republicans want the best for our nation, and so do Democrats. Our votes may differ, but not our hopes.

I know America wants reconciliation and unity. I know Americans want progress. And we must seize this moment and deliver.

Together, guided by a spirit of common sense, common courtesy and common goals, we can unite and inspire the American citizens.

Together, we will work to make all our public schools excellent, teaching every student of every background and every accent, so that no child is left behind.

Together we will save Social Security and renew its promise of a secure retirement for generations to come. Together we will strengthen Medicare and offer prescription drug coverage to all of our seniors.

Together we will give Americans the broad, fair and fiscally responsible tax relief they deserve.

Together we'll have a bipartisan foreign policy true to our values and true to our friends, and we will have a military equal to every challenge and superior to every adversary.

Together we will address some of society's deepest problems one person at a time, by encouraging and empowering the good hearts and good works of the American people.

This is the essence of compassionate conservatism and it will be a foundation of my administration.

These priorities are not merely Republican concerns or Democratic concerns; they are American responsibilities.

During the fall campaign, we differed about the details of these proposals, but there was remarkable consensus about the important issues before us: excellent schools, retirement and health security, tax relief, a strong military, a more civil society.

We have discussed our differences. Now it is time to find common ground and build consensus to make America a beacon of opportunity in the 21st century.

I'm optimistic this can happen. Our future demands it and our history proves it. Two hundred years ago, in the election of 1800, America faced another close presidential election. A tie in the Electoral College put the outcome into the hands of Congress.

After six days of voting and 36 ballots, the House of Representatives elected Thomas Jefferson the third president of the United States. That election brought the first transfer of power from one party to another in our new democracy.

Shortly after the election, Jefferson, in a letter titled "Reconciliation and Reform," wrote this. "The steady character of our countrymen is a rock to which we may safely moor; unequivocal in principle, reasonable in manner. We should be able to hope to do a great deal of good to the cause of freedom and harmony."

Two hundred years have only strengthened the steady character of America. And so as we begin the work of healing our nation, tonight I call upon that character: respect for each other, respect for our differences, generosity of spirit, and a willingness to work hard and work together to solve any problem.

I have something else to ask you, to ask every American. I ask for you to pray for this great nation. I ask for your prayers for leaders from both parties. I thank you for your prayers for me and my family, and I ask you to pray for Vice President Gore and his family.

I have faith that with God's help we as a nation will move forward together as one nation, indivisible. And together we will create an America that is open, so every citizen has access to the American dream; an America that is educated, so every child has the keys to realize that dream; and an America that is united in our diversity and our shared American values that are larger than race or party.

I was not elected to serve one party, but to serve one nation.

The president of the United States is the president of every single American, of every race and every background.

Whether you voted for me or not, I will do my best to serve your interests and I will work to earn your respect.

I will be guided by President Jefferson's sense of purpose, to stand for principle, to be reasonable in manner, and above all, to do great good for the cause of freedom and harmony.

The presidency is more than an honor. It is more than an office. It is a charge to keep, and I will give it my all.

Thank you very much and God bless America.

President George W. Bush, Press Conference After the Democratic Congressional Victories, 2006

The Republican Party lost control of both the House of Representatives and the Senate after the 2006 congressional elections. Many experts attributed the Democratic victory to the unpopularity of President George W. Bush, the Iraq War, and Republican leadership. The day after the election, President Bush addressed the Democratic leaders, vowing to work together.

President Bush's Comments on the 2006 Election

THE PRESIDENT: Thank you. I say, why all the glum faces?

Yesterday, the people went to the polls and they cast their vote for a new direction in the House of Representatives. And while the ballots are still being counted in the Senate, it is clear the Democrat Party had a good night last night, and I congratulate them on their victories.

This morning I spoke with Republican and Democrat leadership in the House and Senate. I spoke with Republican leaders, Senator Frist and Senator McConnell and Speaker Hastert, and John Boehner and Roy Blunt. I thanked them for their hard-fought contests. I appreciate the efforts they put in for our candidates.

I'm obviously disappointed with the outcome of the election, and as the head of the Republican Party, I share a large part of the responsibility. I told my party's leaders that it is now our duty to put the elections behind us and work together with the Democrats and independents on the great issues facing this country.

This morning I also spoke with the Democrats. I spoke with Senators Reid and Durbin. I congratulated them on running a strong campaign in the Senate, and I told them that, regardless of the final outcome, we can work together over the next two years. I also congratulated Congresswoman Pelosi and Congressman Hoyer. They ran a disciplined campaign. Their candidates were well-organized and did a superb job of turning out their votes.

I told Congresswoman Pelosi that I look forward to working with her and her colleagues to find common ground in the next two years. As the majority party in the House of Representatives, they recognize that in their new role they now have greater responsibilities. And in my first act of bipartisan outreach since the election, I shared with her the names of some Republican interior decorators who can help her pick out the new drapes in her new offices. (Laughter.)

I believe that the leaders of both political parties must try to work through our differences. And I believe we will be able to work through differences. I reassured the House and Senate leaders that I intend to work with the new Congress in a bipartisan way to address issues confronting this country. I invited them to come to the White House in the coming days to discuss the important work remaining this year and to begin conversations about the agenda for next year.

The message yesterday was clear: The American people want their leaders in Washington to set aside partisan differences, conduct ourselves in an ethical manner, and work together to address the challenges facing our nation.

Speaker-Elect Nancy Pelosi Addresses Democratic Colleagues, 2006

Following the 2006 Democratic congressional victories and shortly after receiving the nomination as speaker of the house from her Democratic colleagues in the House, Congresswoman Pelosi spoke to Democrats. Pelosi notes the Democrats' intention to work in a unified way for all Americans.

Speaker-Elect Nancy Pelosi Addresses Democratic Colleagues, 2006

What an honor it is to be nominated by my colleagues to be the Speaker of the House. Everyone is very excited about the thought that I am the first woman

Speaker—I'm just absolutely delighted that we have a Democratic Speaker and a Democratic majority in the House of Representatives.

We've had our differences in our party. We have now come together. I wish all of the American people could have heard the discussion of our Caucus this morning. They would have heard speeches of mutual respect regardless of who anyone was supporting for party office. They would have heard speeches of unity for a new direction for our country.

As you know our colleagues chose our distinguished Whip Steny Hoyer, to be the Democratic Leader of the House. I extend great congratulations to him and we will hear from him in a moment. I look forward to working with him in a unified way to bring our country to a new direction for all Americans, not just the privileged few.

I want to acknowledge the magnificent contribution of Mr. Murtha to this debate on the war on Iraq. I thank him for his courage for stepping forward one year ago to speak truth to power, to change the debate in this country in a way that gave us this majority this November. Mr. Murtha won the JFK Profile in Courage Award; he's a great Member of Congress, I was proud to support him for Majority Leader because I thought that would be the best way to bring an end to the war in Iraq. I know that he will continue to take the lead on that issue for our Caucus, for this Congress, for our country . . .

I said to my colleagues: 'As we say in church, let there be peace on earth, and let it begin with us.' Let the healing begin.

E-Voting Failures in the 2006 Mid-Term: A 2007 Report by VotersUnite!

Since the 2000 presidential election, increasing reports of voting-machine failures and other difficulties brought the validity of election results into question. VotersUnite!, an independent watchdog organization, and other vigilant groups have compiled a report citing major issues that affect American voters.

This account of the November 7, 2006, election draws on surveys from participants in Pollworkers for Democracy, reports from voters who called the Election Incident reporting System and Voter Action, and reports collected by VotersUnite.Org from the national and local media. In all, we looked at 1,022 reports of problems associated with electronic voting equipment from 314 counties in states.

Many reports depicted multiple problems experienced by a single voter or pollworker; thus the total number of problems discussed in this paper is greater than the number of reports reviewed. While some reports reference a single incident, others reference widespread incidents (such as the 800 e-voting machines that malfunctioned in Westmoreland County, Pennsylvania). The first section of our report shows the geographical extent of problems. The second, a set of case studies, explores the problems in four locales in greater depth.

The mid-term election revealed that the promise of easier voting, more accurate tallies, and faster results with electronic systems has not been fulfilled. Voters in some jurisdictions waited in line for hours to cast their ballots. Others cast their ballots accidentally before they were done because they pressed the wrong button or left without casting their ballots because they didn't press the right button. Many voters watched the machine highlight a candidate they didn't select or fail to indicate a vote for a candidate they did select and were then blamed for not being able to use a computer correctly.

Many polling places couldn't open on time because of machine failures, and complex procedures often left pollworkers frustrated and reluctant to serve again. Election directors were often forced to rely on voting equipment vendors to set up the election, administer it, and tally the votes because it was too complicated for their personnel to handle. Others blamed themselves for not following the poorly documented, non-intuitive procedures required to collect and tally the votes.

After the polls closed, poll workers and election officials struggled with a myriad of reporting problems. Many couldn't retrieve data from memory cards or couldn't get the tally software to combine totals from different computerized systems, while others couldn't figure out why the software was subtracting votes instead of adding them, or adding them two and three times instead of only once; couldn't determine for sure whether the first set of results was correct, or the second set, or the third; couldn't explain why one out of every six voters didn't have an electronic vote recorded for a hotly contested race; or why the machines recorded more ballots than the number of voters who signed in to vote.

Often hidden from public view, equipment malfunctions such as these have normally been exposed only when they are severe enough to attract media coverage. Reports from Pollworkers for Democracy and voters provided additional insight into the extent of these problems. The frequency of reports of difficulties retrieving results even casts doubt on the accuracy of the certified results in affected areas, particularly since it is reasonable to assume that many such retrieval problems were never reported.

An increasing number of voters, poll workers, and election officials are finding the election process to be more difficult, not easier, and confidence in the final tallies has been undermined. While our source material is neither a complete list of problems nor even a representative sampling, the number of incidents and the broad range of problems reported is indicative of the widespread failure of electronic voting systems across the country and how this failure affected the experience of voters on November 7, 2006.

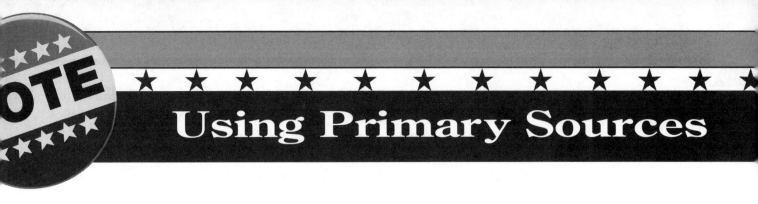

Using Primary Sources

Researching With Primary and Secondary Sources

A primary source is first-hand information or data. A primary source has not been subject to analysis by someone else. Typical primary sources—such as the Twelfth Amendment, William Jennings' Cross of Gold Speech, and excerpts from *Bush v. Gore* (2000)—are eyewitness accounts of an event, letters, diary entries, photographs, and documents. In the Primary Source Library in Part Three of this volume, there is a variety of primary sources, which are especially useful when researching how the U.S. government was formed and how it runs.

In contrast, a secondary source is information that has been reviewed and analyzed by someone else. For example, historian David McCullough's biography of the second U.S. president John Adams is a secondary source. The author (McCullough) has reviewed and analyzed a variety of primary and secondary sources to present a biography of his subject (Adams). Most magazine articles, books, and Internet sources are secondary sources.

Developing Research Questions

When you are assigned a report and select a topic for research, it is important to begin with a clear sense of direction. Ask yourself several questions that will help you limit your topic. For example, for a report on the importance of the presidential election of 1800, you will likely be able to find hundreds of primary and secondary sources. However, to help narrow the topic, ask yourself the following questions:

- Who were the candidates?
- To what political parties did they belong?
- What leaders supported the candidates?
- How did they campaign for office?
- What was the electoral vote? Why is the vote noteworthy?
- What was the issue that need to be resolved?
- How was the election finally settled?
- What was the impact of the election of 1800?

With answers to these questions, you will have the focus you need to begin further research.

Identifying Sources of Information

You likely will begin looking for information in your school or local library. You also can locate other sources of information within your community, such as local government sources, newspaper offices, historical societies, and museums. Although all of these sources can provide valuable information, you must determine if the information will be useful to your research topic. Therefore, you must evaluate and decide on the usefulness of each source. Useful sources should contain the following characteristics:

- **Pertinent and appropriate** Is the information related to you topic? Skim the content, and check the table of contents and the index.
- **Trustworthy and dependable** Is the source objective? Does it seem accurate? What sources did the author of the book or article use?
- **Current and recent** How old is the source? Is the information out-of-date? Keep in mind that historical documents such as the U.S. Constitution and topics such as the election of 1800 are researched and evaluated by political scientists and historians. Be sure that some of your sources are current analyses.
- **Typical and representative** Be certain to find balanced or unbiased sources. If you are writing about a controversial topic, such as the election of 2000, be sure to use sources that represent both sides of the issue.

Planning and Organizing

As you gather various primary and secondary sources, you will begin to develop a plan for your report. This might include a preliminary outline with headings and subheadings that will help you organize your resources and thereby structure your report. With this plan you can decide what information to include in your notes.

Thorough note-taking is essential; you will want to document all the information you have gathered for your report. Following are useful tips for taking notes:

- Use ruled index cards.
- Use a separate card for each item of information.
- Use a separate card for each source.

Use the following techniques to record information:

- **Quote** Copy the information exactly as it appears in the source. Use quotation marks to indicate a direct quote.
- **Paraphrase** Rewrite the information in your own words.
- **Summarize** Condense the information, noting essential material and key ideas.

Documenting Sources for the Bibliography

On index cards, keep a record of the books, newspaper or magazine articles, Internet sites, and other sources you have consulted. As you locate useful sources, record the publishing data on your index cards so that you can easily find the information later. This data will be essential for compiling the bibliography at the end of your report.

Citing Sources

All writers must identify the sources of the words, facts, and thoughts that they find in other works. Noting your sources allows your reader to check those sources and determine how reliable or important a particular piece of information is.

What You Should Document

- Someone's exact words
- A close paraphrase of another's ideas or several ideas
- Information on the topic which is not found in most books on the subject or which is not generally known

What You Do Not Have To Document

- Simple definitions, commonly used sayings, or famous quotations
- Information that is common knowledge or that is easily found in most sources

Author and Publication Information

Author information should always appear at the beginning of your citation, with the author's last name first.

- For books with two authors, reverse only the first author's name, followed by a comma and the second author's name.
- If no author is noted, list the editor; if no editor is identified, start with the title of the work.
- Should you use more than one work by the same author, you do not need to list the author information each time. Use three hyphens followed by a period to begin the line.
- The name of the work (underlined or in italics) appears next, followed by a period.

Publication information (place, publisher, and copyright date) follows the author and title of the work. You also may need to include the editor's name, volume or edition number, and a series name.

Citing On-line Sources

When citing on-line sources, you likely will not be able to include all the information in the list that follows. Many on-line sources do not provide all this information. Therefore, provide as much information as possible.

- Author or editor of the source
- Title of a book (underlined or in italics)
- Title of an article, short work, or poem (in quotation marks)
- Publication information for any print version of the source
- Title of the database, scholarly project, periodical, or professional site (underlined or in italics)
- Version number of the source or journal; volume number, issue number, or other identifier
- Date of the electronic version or last update.

Using the Primary Source Library in This Volume

In Part Three of this volume, you will find a wealth of primary sources useful for various research topics. In chronological order, important source documents appear that are related to or that affected the nation's electoral process. To help you find out about the election of 1800, for example, the following primary sources would likely be useful:

- U.S. Constitution, Article II, Section 1
- Washington's Farewell Address (1796)
- Twelfth Amendment (1804).

For more information about doing research with authoritative sources, consult your local librarian, teacher, or one of numerous available publications.

Glossary

abolition A social movement that emerged before the Civil War (1861–1865) which demanded an end to slavery; practiced by **abolitionists**

absentee ballot A ballot that allows a person to vote without going to the polls on election day

ad hoc groups Groups formed for or concerned with one specific purpose

Alien and Sedition Acts of 1798 Laws passed by the Federalist-controlled Congress that were designed to increase the time for foreigners to become American citizens and limit criticism of the federal government

aliens Those belonging or owing allegiance to another country or government

American dream An American social ideal that stresses egalitarianism and material prosperity

amnesty A group pardon to individuals for an offense against the government

anarchist One who believes in the doctrine that all forms of government are oppressive and should be abolished.

Bank of the United States One of two official national banks of the United States. The First Bank of the United States existed from 1791 to 1811; the Second Bank of the United States existed from 1816 until 1836, when its federal charter expired. President Andrew Jackson almost destroyed the bank when he ordered the Department of the Treasury to stop depositing the nation's money into the bank.

bicameral Consisting of a two-house legislature

biennial Lasting for two years

bill of attainder A law that establishes guilt and punishes people without a trial

bipartisan Involving members of two political parties

bloc A group united to promote a common interest

"bloody shirt" Something intended to stir up or revive partisan animosity

bosses Powerful political party leaders

caucus Organized group of legislators with a common background or goals; also, a closed meeting of party members within a legislative body to decide on questions of policy or leadership

census A periodic governmental count of the population

civil service reform The changing of the administrative service of the government exclusive of the armed forces

cloture The closing or limitation of debate in a legislative body

conservative Someone who believes that the role of the government should be very limited and that individuals should be responsible for their own well-being

dark-horse candidate An unexpected or unknown successful candidate

decennial Lasting for ten years

decennial reapportionment The act of allotting representatives among the states every ten years

demagogy Of or relating to the characteristics of a demagogue, one who makes impassioned pleas that manipulate audiences by appealing to their emotions and prejudices

disenfranchise To take away the right to vote

disenfranchisement The deprivation of the right to vote; being **disenfranchised** deprives one of the right to vote

Emancipation Proclamation The formal document delivered by President Abraham Lincoln which announced that slaves in rebel territory were free and became effective on January 1, 1863

embargo A country's banning the export and import of goods to and from another country

enfranchising Granting the right to vote

engrossed Prepared as the formal or official copy of a document or a bill

***ex post facto* laws** After the fact; making crimes of acts that were legal when they were committed

faction A group of people with a united interest

factionalism The existence of interest groups within a country's political parties

favorite sons Candidates with strong support from one state or region of the country

filibuster An attempt to extend debate upon a bill or a proposal to delay or prevent its passage

financial panic An economic situation in which business activity decreases, people lose their jobs, and banks fail

"floater" A person without fixed duties

franchise The right to vote

free enterprise The opportunity to make economic gains and to control one's economic decisions

free trade Trade based on the unrestricted international exchange of goods

front-runner The early leader in an election campaign

gold standard A monetary system that requires the paper money issued by a government to be supported by an equal amount of gold bullion in that nation's treasury

grandfather clauses Provisions that make exemptions in the law for a certain group based on previous conditions

grange A farmers' association

Hartford Convention A meeting of Federalist Party members opposed to the War of 1812. The convention called for a number of amendments that would weaken the federal government; it also raised the issue of secession

ideological Dealing with a particular set of beliefs about life, culture, government, or society

ideological PACs Political Action Committees organized on ideological or political grounds

illiterate Unable to read or write

impeachment The formal accusation of misconduct in office against a public official

imperialist Extending power and authority to gain control over the political and economic lives of others

incumbent Politician running for the office that she or he is currently holding

indentured servitude The condition in which people are forced to work for little or no pay for a set period of time in order for them to pay off debts

internationalist A person or group that believes that a country should be involved in world affairs

isolationism The avoidance of involvement in world affairs; an **isolationist** supports this type of foreign policy

laissez-faire The theory that government should not interfere in the economy

lame-duck A politician who, at the end of his or her current term, will be succeeded either due to choice or to term limits

leftist Individual who follows the supports or practices of the political Left

liberal In the modern era, someone who believes the national government should be active in helping individuals and communities promote health, education, justice, and equal opportunity

loophole primary A type of primary election in which voters express a preference for a presidential nominee, but also elect convention delegates who are then to support the winner of the presidential preference vote at the nominating convention

machine A highly organized political group under the leadership of a boss or small clique

majority-minority districts Legislative districts created specifically to include a majority of a minority group in order to increase the possibility that a member of that minority group will be elected from that district

malapportionment Inappropriate or unfair distribution of representatives within a legislative body

Manifest Destiny The belief that it was obvious, certain, and right for the United States to expand its territory to cover North America and spread republican democracy

nationalism A strong feeling of pride in one's nation, culture, or heritage

nativist One who supports a policy of favoring inhabitants as opposed to immigrants

new right A political movement primarily made up of Protestants, who were especially opposed to secular humanism and concerned with issues of the church and state, patriotism, laissez-faire economics, pornography, and abortion

nullification The process by which a law is declared null and void

nullified To have made something of no consequence or value

patronage The practice of granting favors to reward party loyalty

philanthropist One who practices goodwill to others

plaintiff The person who brings charges in a court of law

platform A political party's statement of principles, beliefs, and positions on important issues

plurality A simple majority; the largest share (as of votes)

political machine An organized and highly efficient group of politicians who work together as a well-oiled machine to achieve their political goals; in general, political machines operate by trading favors, especially government jobs, benefits, and contracts for votes and support

polygamist A person involved in a marriage arrangement in which a spouse has more than one mate; most often a man having multiple wives

popular sovereignty The concept that citizens in a region should vote to decide an issue, often used before the Civil War (1861–1865) to mean that the voters in the states should determine whether to allow slavery

Populist Era The late 1800s in the United States and the time when a third political party, known as the Populist Party, organized and claimed to represent the goals of the common people

precedent An established course of action in a given situation

primary election An election in which qualified voters nominate or express a preference for a particular candidate or group of candidates for political office

progressive Wanting social, economic, and governmental reforms, especially in the late 1800s and early 1900s

Progressive era The late 1800s and early 1900s when reformers sought social, economic, and governmental reforms

progressivism The principles, beliefs, or practices of the Progressives

prohibition Forbidding the sale of alcohol

quorum A specific number of an organization's members required to conduct business

Radical Republicans Members of the Republican Party who advocated extreme measures to bring about change in the South after the Civil War (1861–1865)

rank-and-file The individuals who constitute the body of an organization, society, or nation as distinguished from the organization's leaders

ratification A formal approval or confirmation (of an amendment or treaty)

ratified Approved

reapportion To reallocate, as in the allotment or representatives among the states

Reconstruction The period in United States history when the former Confederate States were brought back into the Union, lasting from about 1865 until 1877

registrars Official recorders or keepers of records

religious right Beginning in 1980, a term used to describe those groups of citizens who, because of their conservative religious beliefs, voted for conservative political candidates

secession The act of leaving or withdrawing from a nation or other political entity or organization

secessionist One who joins a secession or maintains that secession is a right

sectional divisions Differences in political opinions arising from differences in location

segregationist A person who believes in or practices segregation (especially of races)

soft money Political donations made to avoid federal campaign laws, such as a donation of money to a political organization rather than directly to a candidate

special interest groups Organized individuals seeking to influence legislative or government policy to further often narrowly defined interests

speculator Someone who takes on a business risk in the hopes of gaining large profits

spoils system A term that stemmed from the phrase "to the victors go the spoils of the enemy," credited to Andrew Jackson

standard bearer The leader of an organization, movement, or party

state machines Political machines organized at the state level, attempting to control the state government as well as local governments

states' rights The concept that the rights and laws of individual states override the powers of the federal government

suburbanization The process of making a smaller community adjacent to or within commuting distance of a city

suffrage The right to vote

suffragist A person who advocates the extension of suffrage

"swing states" The deciding states in an election

Tammany Hall Headquarters of the Tammany Society, a political organization in New York City associated with corruption and bossism

tariff Tax on imported goods

temperance laws Laws that restrict the sale, use, or consumption of alcoholic beverages

third party In a two-party political system, as in the United States, any political party other than the two main parties—Democratic and Republican

third-party candidate A candidate from any political party other than one of the two major parties

two-thirds nominating rule A nomination based on the approval by two-thirds of the whole

unicameral Consisting of a one-house legislature

veto Rejection of a bill

Virginia Dynasty The era spanning the presidencies of the first five presidents of the United States, four of whom were from Virginia; George Washington is often excluded from the list because of his political views; the Virginia Dynasty ended after James Monroe's second term

vote-by-mail A method of voting in which a person fills out a ballot and mails it

war hawks Political figures who favor engaging in military conflicts

"whip" Assistant to the party floor leader

Wilmot Proviso A part of an appropriation bill, introduced in 1846 into the House of Representatives by David Wilmot, which would have banned slavery in any territory that the United States obtained from Mexico after the Mexican-American War (1846–1848); the proviso did not become law

SELECTED BIBLIOGRAPHY

Abramowitz, Alan. *Voice of the People: Elections and Voting in the United States.* New York: The McGraw-Hill Companies, 2003.

Aldrich, John H. *Why Parties? The Origin and Transformation of Political Parties in America.* Chicago: University of Chicago Press, 1995.

American Government at Work, Volume 1: The Federal Legislative Branch. Danbury, Connecticut: Grolier/Scholastic Library, 2001.

Anthony, Carl Sferrazza. *The Kennedy White House: Family Life and Pictures, 1961–1963.* New York: Simon and Schuster, 2001.

Appleby, Joyce. *Thomas Jefferson.* New York: Times Books, Henry Holt and Company, 2003.

Auchincloss, Louis. *Theodore Roosevelt.* New York: Times Books, 2001.

Blevins, David. *American Political Parties in the 21st Century.* Jefferson, NC: McFarland & Company, 2006.

Brands, H.W. *Woodrow Wilson.* New York: Times Books, 2003.

Brinkley, Douglas. *Gerald R. Ford.* New York: Times Books, 2007.

Bunting, Josiah, III. *Ulysses S. Grant.* New York: Times Books, 2004.

Burns, James MacGregor, and Susan Dunn. *George Washington.* New York: Times Books, Henry Holt and Company, 2004.

Calhoun, Charles W. *Benjamin Harrison.* New York: Times Books, 2005.

Caro, Robert A. *The Years of Lyndon Johnson: The Path to Power.* New York: Alfred A. Knopf, Inc., 1982.

Caro, Robert A. *The Years of Lyndon Johnson: Means of Ascent.* New York: Alfred A. Knopf, Inc., 1990.

Caro, Robert A. *The Years of Lyndon Johnson: Master of the Senate.* New York: Alfred A. Knopf, Inc., 2002.

Carwardine, Richard. *Lincoln.* New York: Alfred A.Knopf, 2006.

Chace, James. *1912: Wilson, Roosevelt, Taft, and Debs–The Election That Changed the Country.* New York: Simon & Schuster, 2004.

Colacello, Bob. *Ronnie & Nancy: Their Path to the White House–1911–1980.* New York: Warner Books, 2004.

Crigler, Anne N. (ed.), *et al. Rethinking the Vote: The Politics and Prospects of American Election Reform.* New York: Oxford University Press, 2003.

Dallek, Robert. *An Unfinished Life: John F. Kennedy 1917–1963.* New York: Little Brown and Company, 2003.

Dean John W. *Warren G. Harding.* New York: Times Books, 2004.

Diggins, John Patrick. *John Adams.* New York: Times Books, Henry Holt and Company, 2003.

Diggins, John Patrick. *Ronald Reagan: Fate, Freedom, and the Making of History.* New York: W. W. Norton & Co., 2007.

Donald, Herbert David. *Lincoln.* New York: Simon & Schuster, 1995.

Drew, Elizabeth. *Richard M. Nixon.* New York: Times Books, 2007.

Dunn, Susan. *Jefferson's Second Revolution: The Election Crisis of 1800 and the Triumph of Republicanism.* Boston: Houghton Mifflin Company, 2004.

Ellis, Joseph J. *His Excellency: George Washington.* New York: Alfred A. Knopf, 2004.

Ferling, John. *Adams vs. Jefferson: The Tumultuous Election of 1800.* New York: Oxford University Press, 2004.

Frederickson, Kari. *The Dixiecrat Revolt and the End of the Solid South, 1932–1968.* Chapel Hill, NC: The University of North Carolina Press, 2000.

Ford, Gerald R. *A Time To Heal: The Autobiography of Gerald R. Ford.* New York: Harper & Row Publishers, 1979.

Fortier, John C. *Absentee and Early Voting.* Washington, D.C.: AEI Press, 2006.

Graff, Henry A. *Grover Cleveland.* New York: Times Books, 2002.

Grant, James. *John Adams: Party of One.* New York: Farrar, Straus and Giroux, 2005.

Grant, Ulysses S. *Personal Memoirs.* New York: Modern Library, 1999.

Greenberg, David. *Calvin Coolidge.* New York: Times Books, 2006.

Hannaford, Peter, ed. *The Quotable Calvin Coolidge.* Bennington, VT: Images of the Past, Inc., 2001.

Harris, William C. *Lincoln's Rise to the Presidency.* Lawrence, KS: University of Kansas Press, 2007.

Hart, Gary. *James Monroe.* New York: Times Books, Henry Holt and Company, 2005.

Harwood, Richard, and Haynes Johnson. *Lyndon.* New York: Praeger Publishers, 1973.

Jackson, Robert H. *That Man: An Insider's Portrait of Franklin D. Roosevelt.* New York: Oxford University Press, 2003.

Jenkins, Roy. *Franklin Delano Roosevelt.* New York: Times Books, 2003.

Karabell, Zachary. *Chester Alan Arthur.* New York: Times Books, 2004.

Koestler-Grack, Rachel A. *The House of Representatives.* New York: Chelsea House Publications, 2007.

Levine, Lawrence W., and Cornelia R. Levine. *The People and the President: America's Conversation with FDR.* Boston: Beacon Press, 2002.

Lutz, Norma Jean, and Arthur M. Schlesinger. *The History of the Third Parties.* New York: Chelsea House Publications, 2000.

McCullough, David. *John Adams.* New York: Simon & Schuster, 2001.

McPherson, James M. *To the Best of My Ability: The American Presidents.* New York: Dorling Kindersley Publishing, 2000.

Nixon, Richard. *The Memoirs of Richard Nixon.* New York: Grosset & Dunlap, 1978.

Phillips, Kevin. *William McKinley.* New York: Times Books, 2003.

Reagan, Ronald. *The Reagan Diaries.* Douglas Brinkley, ed. New York: Harper Collins Publishers, 2007.

Reagan, Ronald. *An American Life: The Autobiography.* New York: Simon & Schuster, 1990.

Reeves, Richard. *President Nixon: Alone in the White House.* New York: Simon & Schuster, 2001.

Reeves, Richard. *President Reagan: The Triumph of Imagination.* New York: Simon & Schuster, 2005.

Remini, Robert V. *John Quincy Adams.* New York: Times Books, Henry Holt and Company, 2002.

Remini, Robert V. *The House: The History of the House of Representatives.* New York: HarperCollins, 2006.

Richardson, Darcy G. *Others: Third Parties During the Populist Period.* Lincoln, NE: iUniverse, Inc., 2007.

Robbins, Charles. *Last of His Kind: An Informal Portrait of Harry S. Truman.* New York: William Morrow and Company, Inc., 1979.

Rutkow, Ira. *James A. Garfield.* New York: Times Books, 2006.

Salinger, Pierre. *John F. Kennedy: Commander in Chief.* New York: Gramercy Books, 1997.

Scarrow, Susan E., ed. *Perspectives on Political Parties: Classic Readings.* New York: Palgrave Macmillan Press, 2002.

Schlesinger, Arthur. M., Jr. *The Age of Jackson.* Old Saybrook, CT: Konecky and Konecky, 1971.

Schislinger, Galbraith. *Of the People: The 200 Year History of the Democratic Party.* North York, ON: Stoddart, 1992.

Seigenthaler, John. *James K. Polk.* New York: Times Books, Henry Holt and Company, 2004.

Sifry, Micah L. *Spoiling for a Fight: Third-Party Politics in America.* London: Routledge, 2003.

Trefousse, Hans L. *Rutherford B. Hayes.* New York: Times Books, 2002.

Wagner, Heather Lehr. *The History of the Democratic Party.* New York: Chelsea House Publications, 2007.

Wallison, Peter J. *Ronald Reagan: The Power of Conviction and the Success of His Presidency.* Boulder, CO: Westview Press, 2004.

Waugh, John C. *Reelecting Lincoln: The Battle for the 1864 Presidency.* Cambridge, MA: Da Capo Press, 1997.

Wicker, Tom. *One of Us: Richard Nixon and the American Dream.* New York: Random House, Inc., 2001.

Wicker, Tom. *Dwight D. Eisenhower.* New York: Times Books, 2002.

Widmer, Ted. *Martin Van Buren.* New York: Times Books, Henry Holt and Company, 2005.

Wilentz, Sean. *Andrew Jackson.* New York: Times Books, Henry Holt and Company, 2005.

Wills, Gary. *James Madison.* New York: Times Books, Henry Holt and Company, 2002.

Witcover, Jules. *Party of the People: A History of the Democrats.* New York: Random House, 2003.

INDEX

Note: Page numbers in ***bold italic*** type indicate main encyclopedia entries. Page numbers in *italic* type indicate illustrations, figures, tables, or maps. Page numbers in **bold** type refer to terms that are highlighted in **bold** in the text and also defined in the Glossary.